Managerial Accounting

Managerial Accounting

ARTHUR J. FRANCIA
University of Houston

ROBERT H. STRAWSER
University of Houston

1980

Dame Publications, Inc., Box 35556, Houston, Texas

ISBN 0-931920-20-5
Library of Congress Catalog Card No.80-67312
Printed in the United States of America

First edition   1977
Second edition 1978
Third edition   1980

Preface

THE THIRD EDITION of this text, like its predecessors, is intended to be an integrated work in management accounting. Emphasis is placed upon those aspects of internal accounting with which business majors should be familiar. If an overall theme were used to describe this text, it would focus on five key areas: cost accumulation and analysis; accounting aspects of planning; accounting aspects of control; accounting aspects of performance evaluation; and, relevant internal uses of managerial accounting information for many different management needs. These key areas were selected as the underlying theme for this text because we believe they best describe the "core" or "heart" of management accounting. We felt that if the core material were covered, the student would find the subject matter relevant in other business courses and, more importantly, in practice throughout his or her career.

This book may be used as a basic text for the student who has completed the first semester or quarter course in financial accounting at either the undergraduate or graduate level using its companion volume, *Financial Accounting* or any financial accounting text. The perspective is balanced and where optional treatments or approaches exist, these are identified and discussed.

The text employs a continuous example to maintain and illustrate the continuity of management information flows within an organization. This continuous example permits the student to consider each topic separately while recognizing that the topic is not a separate subject, but is interrelated and maintains its specific role in the information system available to management for decision making.

Selected problems adapted from both the Uniform CPA Examination and the Certificate in Management Accounting Examination have been added to allow a problem selection that ranges from relatively easy to follow illustrative problems to difficult thought provoking exercises that may be used for further class discussion.

Organization of the Text

Following each chapter are a number of questions, exercises, and two Problem Series A and B. Problem Series A and B were intended to permit alternative selections of problems that cover the same conceptual material. For example, if Problem 2A-1 were assigned, the student can go to Problem 2B-1 and review the same concepts in a slightly different problem format. The majority of the problems adapted from the Uniform CPA Examination and the Certificate in Management Accounting Examination have been placed at the end of Series B problems.

The text is designed to provide an integrated approach to managerial accounting by using a building block approach, however, various chapters may be omitted or assigned out of sequence. Chapters 1 and 2 provide the necessary background, overview and stimulus for the continued study of managerial accounting. After providing a foundation in managerial accounting the emphasis of the course may focus on either a strictly managerial orientation or a systems/cost/managerial accounting approach (or some combination of the two).

For example, an instructor who desired a strictly managerial orientation might assign Chapters 1 through 3 and 7 through 14, while a systems/cost/managerial accounting orientation would include the entire text with the option of completing the course at any point after Chapter 12 was covered. In both sequences, Chapters 4 through 6 and 13 and 14 can be covered in any order that is desired. Chapter 12, Performance Reporting for Profit Centers and Investment Centers, is an optional topic that many of the adopters of the prior editions chose to omit in the systems/cost/managerial accounting sequence.

Acknowledgments

We have received invaluable assistance, ideas, comments and constructive criticisms from both our students and our colleagues. A necessary ingredient in the writing of any textbook is the environment in which the effort took place. Our special thanks go to A. Benton Cocanougher of the University of Houston and John E. Pearson, formerly of Texas A&M University and now with 3D International, for their role in providing this environment.

Numerous professors and graduate students have provided invaluable help, ideas, comments, and constructive criticisms. We are especially indebted to the following professors for their advice and support in the preparation of this text: R. Mark Alford, Donald Anderson, James Bryant, Michael N. Cassell, Edward S. Goodhart, Paul A. Janell, Larry Klein, Michael R. Lane, Richard Lindhe, James E. Meddaugh, William G. Mister, Thomas H. Oxner, Richard Pitre, Mattie C. Porter, Richard A. Rivers, Gary L. Schugart, David E. Stout, Forrest Thompson, Daniel Verrault, and Robert B. Welker.

We appreciate the permissions received from the American Institute of Certified Public Accountants and the Institute of Management Accounting of the National Association of Accountants allowing us to use problem materials from past Uniform CPA Examinations and CMA Examinations, respectively. Of course, the authors are responsible for any shortcomings of this text.

May 1980

Arthur J. Francia
Robert H. Strawser

Contents

and *Performance Evaluation. Identification of Weak Areas of the Firm. Motivation for Management.* General Comprehensive Budgeting Relationships. Role of Standard Costs in Budgeting. Budgeting: A Comprehensive Example. *Management Policies and Forecasts Affecting the Operating Budget—1981 Management Policies and Forecasts Affecting the Financial Budget—1981.* Development of the Major Operating and Performance Budget. *Sales Budget (Budget #1). Finished Goods Inventory Budget and Production Budgets (Budgets #2 and #3). Direct Materials Requirements and Purchases Budgets (Budgets #4, #5 and #6). Direct Labor Budget (Budget #7). Manufacturing Overhead Budgets (Budgets #8 and #9). Non-Manufacturing Expense Budgets (Budgets #10 and #11).* Development of the Major Operating or Performance Budgeted Financial Statements. *Budgeted Cost of Goods Manufactured Statement (Budget #12). Budgeted Cost of Goods Sold Statement (Budget #13). Budgeted Income Statement (Budget #14).* Development of the Major Financial or Resource Budgets. *Accounts Receivable Budget (Budget #15). Inventory Budgets (Budgets #16 and #17). Fixed Asset Budgets (Budget #18). Accounts Payable and Wages Payable Budget (Budget #19). Long-Term Debt Budget (Budget #20).* Development of the Major Financial or Resource Budgeted Financial Statements. *Cash Budget (Budget #21). Budgeted Stockholders' Equity Statement (Budget #22). Budgeted or Pro Forma Balance Sheet (Budget #23).* Summary. Key Definitions. Questions. Exercises. Problems.

Evaluation of Investment Centers. Budgeted ROI Versus Actual ROI. Summary. Key Definitions. Questions. Exercises. Problems.

Learning Objectives

Chapter 1 introduces management and cost accounting systems. Studying this chapter should enable you to:

1. Understand the nature and purpose of both financial and management accounting.
2. Trace the information flows in a typical management accounting system.
3. Identify the basic uses of budgets and budgeting.
4. Discuss how cost accounting is related to both financial and management accounting.
5. Identify the different cost classifications.
6. Distinguish between product costs and period costs, and explain the importance of this distinction in determining income.
7. Distinguish between line and staff functions.
8. Determine the general role of the controller in an organization.

1

Management Accounting: An Introduction

ACCOUNTING MAY be thought of as consisting of two basic segments: financial accounting and managerial accounting. Although there is considerable overlap between these two segments, the primary difference lies in the basic orientation of each. Financial accounting is primarily concerned with users who are *external* to the firm and managerial accounting is concerned with *internal* users. Financial accounting attempts to provide external user groups (such as current or potential owners, creditors, government agencies, and other interested parties) with information concerning the status of the firm and the results of its operations. Managerial accounting, on the other hand, attempts to provide internal user groups with data and information which serve as a basis for internal decision making.

A further distinction in accounting is between managerial accounting and cost accounting. But in today's complex business environment the nature and purpose of the different accounting systems are difficult to distinguish. Management uses cost accounting and cost accumulating systems for gathering data and for making management decisions. In addition, cost accounting also serves the purposes of financial accounting by providing a system for accumulating cost information. This cost information is used as the basis for much of the financial information needed for financial reports to stockholders, compliance with government requirements for financial information, and many other users' needs. In a sense then, cost accounting may be regarded as a subdivision of both financial and managerial accounting.

1

BASIC DIFFERENCES BETWEEN FINANCIAL AND
MANAGEMENT ACCOUNTING—FURTHER COMMENTS

Financial and management acccounting methods were developed for different purposes and for different users of financial information. There are, however, numerous similarities and areas of overlap between financial and managerial accounting methods. It is difficult to classify a particular technique or approach as belonging exclusively to financial or managerial accounting.

Financial accounting is primarily intended to provide external user groups with information concerning the current status of the firm and the results of its operations. The accounting system of a company, therefore, accumulates and communicates financial information that is basically historical in nature. Of course, this information is usually presented in the form of financial statements, tax returns, and other formal reports distributed to various external users. The same information may also be used internally to provide a basis for financial analysis by management.

Financial accounting is required for many firms organized as corporations because of the regulations of the Securities and Exchange Commission (SEC). The SEC is an agency of the federal government which regulates companies whose stock is sold publicly and traded on organized stock exchanges. Most of the large corporations and many medium-sized corporations fall within the jurisdiction of the SEC.

The Internal Revenue Service also requires financial accounting information for compliance with the nation's tax laws. Many state governments require this data for compliance with the various state tax laws. Information based on accounting data is required for all firms without regard to their size.

Interested third parties without substantial influence over the firm, such as individual stockholders of a large corporation, must use the general purpose financial statements made available to them by management. Financial statements prepared for users (other than governmental regulatory agencies that are authorized to establish their own disclosure laws by legislation) must be prepared in accordance with what are known as generally accepted accounting principles. Generally accepted accounting principles serve as guidelines which are used by accountants in disclosing the financial information which is made available to the general public. Knowledgeable users of general financial information can then interpret the data presented in financial statements with some assurance as to consistency of methodology underlying the data. The auditors' report also adds to the reliability of general purpose financial statements.

Managerial accounting has developed over time to meet the need of management for quantitative information to be used internally for planning, control, performance evaluation and internal decision making. The emphasis of management accounting is then directed toward the internal user of information; therefore, the structure of the managerial accounting system is not nearly as rigid as that of the financial accounting system. The best data available are used as the basis for the information which management relies upon to make its decisions. It is important to note that management accounting is by no means separate and distinct from financial accounting. Financial accounting data are used in the managerial accounting system. Management decisions made today will affect the financial statements of future periods. Managerial accounting does not utilize generally accepted accounting principles per se, but there are general practices that should be followed to maximize the benefits of planning, control and performance evaluation. There is no requirement or legislation that mandates the format or use of managerial accounting. Rather, managerial accounting methods are tools that are available for use to management.

Financial accounting attempts to present some degree of precision in reporting historical information while at the same time emphasizing verifiability and freedom from bias in the information, relevance to the general user and some element of timeliness in reporting. The presentation of historical financial information which is precise, verifiable and free from bias is not as critical for managerial accounting. The timing of information and its relevance to the decision at hand has greater significance to the internal decision maker. If the information is useful in making a good internal decision, management is not *primarily* concerned with precision, verifiability or the bias which might be built into the data on hand. Obviously, management cannot wait until tomorrow for information that is required for today's decision.

Theoretically, a managerial accounting system could provide individualized or tailor-made information which is relevant for each user or for each decision. As a practical matter, however, this simply cannot be done because of the high cost involved. The accounting reports that are prepared should include relevant information for that user's segment of the organization.

The measuring base used in management accounting does not necessarily have to be restricted to dollars. Various bases may be appropriate to report managerial information. Examples include: (1) an economic measure such as dollars, (2) a physical measure such as pounds, gallons, tons, or units, and (3) a relationship measure such as ratios. If all of these and other measures are appropriate to management's needs, then this information should be presented in the same report. Relevance to the decision or to the user is a primary consideration when deciding which measurement technique to use.

THE MANAGEMENT ACCOUNTING CYCLE

Management accounting may be regarded as having a forward-looking emphasis. A decision is made; the plan is implemented; and the actual results are measured, recorded and communicated. Illustration 1–1 presents a logical format which is used in viewing the information flows in a typical managerial accounting system from an overall perspective.

The sequential nature of the steps included in this illustration may give an impression that a firm could complete the planning cycle at the beginning of an accounting period and then simply follow the steps indicated. This may not be possible, however, since the economic environment in which a firm operates is changing continuously and management wishes to utilize the best and most current information available in its decision-making process. If the economic climate changes for a segment of the firm, it may then be necessary or desirable to alter plans accordingly. Planning, control, performance evaluation and the related decision-making processes must, therefore, take place simultaneously and continuously as economic conditions change.

GATHERING DECISION-MAKING INFORMATION—STEP ONE

Two general categories of decisions in which accounting information is frequently helpful are: (1) routine or recurring decisions and (2) special or nonrecurring decisions. A business may develop its management accounting system to provide information useful in making routine decisions since the need for this type of information usually may be anticipated. Nonrecurring decisions, however, will frequently require input of specific information that must often be obtained by a special study. The planning for these special decisions is discussed in Chapter 13.

A management accounting system does not always provide all the information which is required for decision-making purposes. Management should, of course, utilize the best information currently available in making a particular decision at any point in time. In addition to the data obtained from the financial accounting system, management should also utilize any other information which may be available. This "other" information may include subjective estimates made by qualified personnel as well as information from other sources both internal and external, that is pertinent for evaluating the alternative courses of action under consideration.

EVALUATING THE FEASIBILITY OF ALTERNATIVES— STEP TWO

When sufficient information has been accumulated to evaluate the alternative courses of action, the data are analyzed and the course of action

Illustration 1-1
Information Flows in the
Management Accounting System

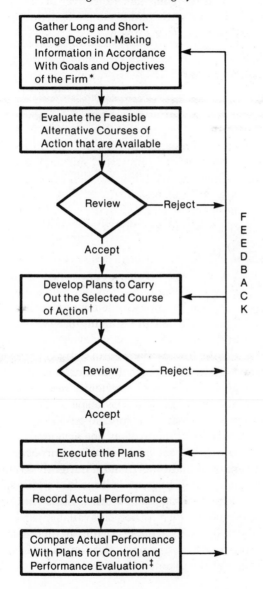

* Goals and Objectives are discussed in Chapter
10.
† Planning is discussed in Chapters 2, 9, 10, 13,
and 14.
‡ Control and Performance Evaluation are discussed
in Chapters 11 and 12.

is selected which is considered by management to be the best alternative available consistent with the goals and objectives of the organization. If the data are analyzed and no acceptable course of action is found, the information gathering process begins again.

DEVELOPING PLANS—STEP THREE

The formulation of plans, a process often referred to as budgeting, is necessary if all of the various segments of the firm are to work together efficiently and effectively. Comprehensive budgeting includes both long and short-term planning. From the perspective of top management, the budgeting process should produce projected financial statements as well as other necessary supplementary budgets, such as a cash budget. From the viewpoint of lower level management, budgets must be prepared in adequate detail to provide the manager with a realistic framework from which his or her segment of the firm can be operated on a current or day-to-day basis.

After the plans made for the various segments of the firm and for the firm as a whole have been reviewed, if management finds a segment budget or the total budget unacceptable, then the management accounting process must begin again with appropriate changes made in the budget. Short-range planning is discussed in Chapter 10, while long-range planning is considered in Chapter 14.

Budgeting may also be regarded as a process of communication, control, and motivation. Budgeting, as a communications process, reaches all relevant levels or segments of the organization—each with its own plan or target—and coordinates them with the plans of all other segments of the firm. Budgeting is necessary for control purposes because both the firm as a whole and individual segments of the firm must be able to assess their comparative positions at selected points in time. Moreover, budgets can show both meaningful and timely comparisons or variances of actual and planned performances. Budgets are also useful in providing a stimulus to assist in motivating managers and other employees of the firm. In certain instances, incentives such as bonuses may be used in this regard. If managers or other employees actively participate in the setting of goals, they are more likely to attempt to meet the challenge of attaining these goals and performing at the planned levels.

EXECUTION OF THE PLANS—STEP FOUR

Budgets are prepared by each segment of the organization, and all segments and department managers are responsible for carrying out the plans of the budget to the best of their ability. These managers need sufficient detail in their budgets to operate in accordance with the plans and to provide the basic data required for control and performance evaluations. Therefore, it is necessary to segment the firm by economic function for planning purposes. For example, budgets may be developed by: (1) organizational lines such as departments, divisions, branches, or legal entities; (2) business activity such as product lines, sales territories geographic markets, industries, domestic activities or foreign activities; and (3) elements of managerial responsibility such as costs, profits or a return-on-investment.

RECORDING PERFORMANCE—STEP FIVE

As plans are translated into performance, actual operating results are entered in the accounting system. The accounting records used for management accounting purposes include additional detailed information not generally required for financial accounting. For example, a management accounting system may include such information as data regarding the physical units of products purchased or shipped, regular and overtime hours worked, and accounts of key customers visited by salesmen.

COMPARING ACTUAL PERFORMANCE WITH PLANNED PERFORMANCE—STEP SIX

In addition to the budget's other uses, the budgeting process provides a means for delegating responsibility to managers of the various segments within the organization. If the firm's planning process is to be meaningful and if managers are expected to operate in an efficient responsible manner, then an effective system of control must be established.

Uses of Budgets and Budgeting Methods

Management accounting contributes to establishing a control system by providing what is usually referred to as financial control. Financial control is the formal process of measuring the performance of segments of the organization to determine if the plan which was adopted has been attained and to analyze any differences or variances between the planned and the actual results.

Financial control is established within the firm to provide management with the appropriate information regarding planned versus actual results for segments of the organization at defined points in time. Effective feedback in the reporting process is established to allow management to take effective action on a problem at the earliest possible time.

The procedure for reporting planned performance versus actual performance and the analysis of any differences or variances is referred to as performance evaluation and variance analysis. These topics are discussed in depth in Chapters 7, 8, 11, and 12.

THE ROLE OF COST ACCOUNTING IN FINANCIAL AND MANAGEMENT ACCOUNTING

The function of cost accounting is to serve both external financial reporting purposes and the internal needs for management information. For external financial reporting purposes, cost accounting provides a cost accumulation system. This is used, for example, in determining the cost of goods manufactured for the accounting period and, therefore, the inventory values and the cost of goods sold. From the standpoint of inventory costing, the cost accounting system accumulates all of the elements of manufacturing cost for a given accounting period and converts these costs into inventory production cost on a per unit, per pound, per gallon or some other basis of physical measurement. Cost accounting systems for product cost accumulation are discussed in Chapters 3 through 7.

Cost accounting is closely related to management accounting in that it provides a system of cost accumulation which is used in planning, control, performance evaluation and decision making. The cost accountant is involved in cost accumulation problems that management encounters during the normal course of operating the business.

COST CLASSIFICATIONS

The cost classifications which are used in accounting are generally determined by the purpose for which the cost information is intended. Four major cost classification categories defined by purpose are discussed in this text: [1]

1. Income determination
2. Planning
3. Control and performance evaluation
4. Special decisions requiring accounting information

For purposes of income determination, costs are normally classified on a functional basis, that is, according to the type of function, i.e., salaries, rent, depreciation etc. The general functional cost classifications which are used for income determination purposes are product costs and period costs.

---

[1] Cost classifications for income determination are discussed in this chapter; planning in Chapter 2; control and performance evaluation in Chapter 11; and special decisions requiring accounting information in Chapter 13.

PRODUCT COSTS: FOR INCOME DETERMINATION

Product costs are those costs that can be directly identified with the purchase or production of those goods made available for sale by the firm. These costs are recorded and inventoried as assets until the goods are sold. For example, the inventory purchased by a retailer is considered an asset until the time that it is sold. When the sale takes place, the cost of the asset (inventory) becomes an expense (cost of goods sold) and is reported as such on the income statement.

The cost flows of a manufacturing firm differ substantially from those of a retail business. In a manufacturing company, the process of producing a marketable product for sale causes the accounting process to be somewhat more complex than it is for the retailer. The manufacturer acquires raw materials and converts these materials into a finished product. During this production process, the manufacturer purchases labor and services, utilizes manufacturing facilities, and usually employs a unique process. Thus, value is added to the raw materials by the manufacturing process which ultimately results in a product that is marketable at a price in excess of its cost. The manufacturer must accumulate all of the production costs incurred, along with the cost of raw materials used during a period, in order to determine the cost of goods manufactured during that period.

PRODUCT COST FLOWS IN MANUFACTURING

The three basic elements of product cost incurred by a manufacturing company are: (1) direct materials, (2) direct labor, and (3) manufacturing overhead. *Direct materials* are those raw materials used in the production process which can be directly identified with the finished products. For example, lumber is a direct material used in the production of furniture. *Direct labor* includes the wages of production employees who work directly with a product and whose efforts may be directly traced to specific units or batches of production output. Thus, the wages of an employee who applied paint or varnish to furniture would be a direct labor cost in the production of that furniture. Manufacturing costs which are associated with the production process but which are not directly traceable to specific units of output either as direct materials or direct labor are classified as *manufacturing overhead*. Examples of manufacturing overhead include depreciation on plant, building, and equipment; maintenance costs; indirect labor costs; costs of factory supplies; salaries of production foremen; etc.

As a product is manufactured, the direct materials, direct labor and manufacturing overhead costs used in the process are accumulated and combined in a special inventory account called work-in-process. When the production process is completed, the costs associated with the resulting goods are transferred from the work-in-process inventory account to the finished goods inventory account. These costs remain as assets in this inventory account until the goods are sold. When the sale is made, the cost of the inventory is transferred to the cost of goods sold account for income determination purposes. Product cost accumulation is discussed in detail in Chapters 3 through 7.

PERIOD COSTS: FOR INCOME DETERMINATION

Those expenses incurred by the company which are associated with the passage of time are normally referred to and classified as period costs. In contrast to product costs, period costs are costs which generally cannot easily be traced to either the purchase or the manufacture of a particular product. Period costs are not considered to be assets because these expenses normally do not yield benefits to the firm beyond the current accounting period or because the possibility of such benefits is not readily measureable. For these reasons, period costs are treated as expenses of the period in which they are incurred. Examples of period costs include such costs as interest expense, salaries of administrative employees, depreciation on non-manufacturing facilities, salesmen's salaries, advertising expense, and insurance expense for non-manufacturing facilities.

IMPORTANCE OF THE DISTINCTION BETWEEN
PRODUCT AND PERIOD COST

The distinction between product costs and period costs is essential for purposes of income determination. A brief example may add insight to this important distinction.

Pete Rose and Joe Morgan are both employed by Redleg Manufacturing Company, and each earns an annual salary of $25,000. Rose works as a salesman while Morgan is employed as a department head in a manufacturing area. Last year, Redleg Manufacturing Company produced a single product. In all, 10,000 units of this product were manufactured and, of these, 8,000 units were sold. Under these circumstances, Rose's salary is considered a period cost and is classified as an expense on the income statement. Morgan's salary is considered to be a cost of manufacturing the product, since he is directly involved with producing the product. Only $20,000 of Morgan's earnings is considered a part of the cost of goods sold included on the income statement, since Morgan is involved in the manufacturing process and only 80 percent (8,000 of the 10,000 units produced) of the current period's production was sold. The remaining portion of Morgan's salary ($5,000 or 20 percent) is considered a part of the ending inventory asset value. Therefore, the importance of the distinction between product costing and period costing is obvious in that the classification of the costs directly impacts on the reported profitability of the firm.

AUTHORITY AND RESPONSIBILITY IN ORGANIZATIONS

Illustration 1–2 represents a partial organization chart of the Sax Company. Sax Company includes three production divisions: Yuke Chemical Division, Avalon Chemical Division and the Power Turbine Shaft Division. Only the Power Turbine Shaft Division is represented in the partial organization chart presented in Illustration 1–2. Each division employs its own salesmen because the products of each division are sold in different markets. Sax Company's corporate headquarters is responsible for coordinating the efforts of the three divisions.

An organization chart identifies the major decision-making centers of a firm, as well as the formal lines of authority and responsibility within an organization. These lines of authority can be followed in the organization chart in Illustration 1–2. For example, the Machining Department Manager reports to the Production Manager who reports to the General Manager. The General Manager reports to the Manufacturing Vice President who reports to the President. The President reports to the Board of Directors. The Board of Directors is chosen by the stockholders to represent their interests, and the Board's responsibility is to act according to the best interests of the stockholders. The directors discharge their responsibility by reviewing, approving, and/or disapproving the major activities of management.

The lines of authority and responsibility within an organization usually follow the same path as does the reporting function. Supervisors are usually responsible for the efficiency and effectiveness of the personnel who report to them.

LINE AND STAFF RELATIONSHIPS IN ORGANIZATIONS

Authority and responsibility within an organization is usually represented by the division of segments and/or individuals into line relationships and staff relationships. Line managers are those operating personnel who produce and sell goods or services. On the other hand, the function of a staff manager is to provide specialized assistance or knowledge to a line manager whenever the line manager needs it.

The distinction between line and staff determines the connecting lines in the partial organization chart presented in Illustration 1–2. The line functions may be traced through the Sax Company by following the vertical lines of authority in the organization chart. Note that a direct line of

Illustration 1-2
Partial Organizational Chart of Sax Company

command extends from the President downward. Operating responsibility also extends down through this line of authority. The respective operating managers are expected to meet their responsibilities in an efficient and effective manner.

In the Power Turbine Shaft Division of the Sax Company, the managers responsible for maintenance, engineering, quality control, and the division controller are all considered to be staff positions. These staff department managers do not have line authority (except over the personnel in their respective departments); no line of command for the staff departments exists outside of their own departments. A staff department manager never attempts to "manage" a line manager. The function of staff positions is limited to providing advice and support to other departments.

THE CONTROLLER

The corporate controller operates in a staff function, but this position is usually included in the top management of the firm. A major responsibility of the corporate controller is to accumulate and interpret accounting information for use in planning, controlling and evaluating both performance and any special decisions that management is required to make. The corporate controller is also responsible for governmental reporting for tax purposes, and for any other financially oriented reports required by federal and state governmental agencies. All accounting and most information processing functions fall under the sphere of responsibility of the corporate controller.

A division controller in a large organization has functions similar to those of the corporate controller; however, this accounting responsibility is limited to a segment of the organization. The division controller usually reports to the corporate controller. These duties and responsibilities are illustrated throughout the text.

THE CERTIFICATE IN MANAGEMENT ACCOUNTING

In the last few years management accounting has gained increased recognition as a professional area in accounting with its own individual core of required knowledge and its own program of certification. The Certificate in Management Accounting (CMA) examination is administered by the Institute of Management Accounting of the National Association of Accountants (NAA). The NAA is an international association which is comprised of individuals who are interested in any phase of accounting. The CMA Examination is divided into five parts:

1. Economics and Business Finance
2. Organization and Behavior, Including Ethical Considerations
3. Public Reporting Standards, Auditing and Taxes
4. Periodic Reporting for Internal and External Purposes
5. Decision Analysis, Including Modeling and Information Systems

The general purpose and objectives of the examination are discussed in the following excerpts from an Institute of Management Accounting brochure.

> More and more people—inside the business world and out—realize the significant changes which have been taking place for years in accounting and in the role of the accountant in business. The accountant is no longer simply a recorder of business history but now plays a dynamic role in making business decisions, in future planning and in almost every aspect of business operations. This new accountant, the Management Accountant, who sits with top management has key responsibilities for developing, producing and analyzing information to help management make sound decisions. Many management accountants earn their way into top management positions.
>
> The CMA program requires candidates to pass a series of uniform examinations and meet specific education and professional standards to qualify for and maintain the Certificate in Management Accounting. NAA has established the Institute of Management Accounting to administer the program, conduct the examinations and grant certificates to those who qualify.
>
> The objectives of the program are threefold:
>
> 1. To establish management accounting as a recognized profession by identifying the role of the management accountants and the underlying body of knowledge, and by outlining a course of study by which such knowledge can be acquired.
> 2. To foster higher educational standards in the field of management accounting; and
> 3. To assist employers, educators, and students by establishing an objective measure of an individual's knowledge and competence in the field of management accounting.

SUMMARY

Financial accounting is primarily concerned with accumulating historical data and communicating this data to interested external users that require the data. Management accounting, on the other hand, is primarily concerned with providing information for internal planning, control, performance evaluation, and decision making. Therefore, management accounting information is generally more future-oriented than is financial accounting information.

In a typical management accounting system, information is gathered, feasible alternatives are evaluated, a decision is made, plans are developed and executed, actual performance is recorded, and, finally, a comparison between planned and actual performance is made. The economic environment in which a firm operates provides a significant influence on this entire process. In fact, a given change in the economic environment may require substantial revisions in the plans and/or even the goals and objectives of the firm.

In developing plans to support the decisions of the firm, it is generally necessary for management to engage in both long and short-term budgeting to insure that all segments of the firm will operate together in an efficient and effective manner. Budgets are generally prepared by segments of the organization in sufficient detail to provide lower management with a framework within which to operate. Therefore, the budgeting process is a primary means of communicating the overall goals and corporate objectives to the various levels in the firm. In addition, by comparing actual performance to budgeted performance, the budget becomes a significant factor in the control system of the firm.

Cost accounting is a segment of accounting that accumulates cost information used in external financial reporting (usually as inventory costs) and in managerial decision making and control. The cost classifications which are used in accounting are determined by the purpose for which the cost information is to be used. Four major categories of cost classifications defined by purpose are those for: (1) income determination; (2) planning; (3) control and performance evaluation; and (4) special decisions requiring accounting information.

In a manufacturing firm, those costs used for determining income are further classified into product costs (direct material, direct labor, and manufacturing overhead costs which are directly identifiable with the production or purchase of goods made available for sale) and period costs (costs associated with the passage of time). Distinguishing between product and period costs is necessary for proper income determination. This is because period costs are considered expenses in the period incurred, but product costs are carried in inventory valuations and are charged to expense only as the associated products are sold.

The controller of an organization is the top accounting executive in the firm. The controller's job is a staff function under which all accounting functions and most information processing functions will fall.

The significance of the role of the management accountant has become increasingly apparent in recent years. The Certificate in Management Accounting (CMA) is one indication of this recognition.

This chapter serves as an overview to the various elements of management and cost accounting. The remaining chapters in the text provide detailed discussions of these elements.

KEY DEFINITIONS

Budgeting—a process of formulating short-term or long-term plans for the organization. A budget is particularly important for control purposes since the plan for each relevant level or segment can later be compared with actual performance. The budget also provides a means for delegating responsibility within the organization.

Certificate in Management Accounting—a certificate earned after passing a uniform examination and meeting specific education and professional standards as required by the National Association of Accountants. It is a certificate which recognizes professional competence and educational attainment in the field of management accounting.

Controller—a staff position included in the top management of the firm and is responsible for all accounting and information processing in the organization.

Cost accounting—a system of accumulating cost information for external financial reporting and internal management accounting.

Cost classifications—general classifications of accounting costs used for: (1) Income determination, (2) Planning, (3) Control and performance evaluation, and (4) Special decisions requiring accounting costs.

Direct labor—a product cost which includes the wages of production employees whose effort may be traced directly to specific units or batches of output.

Direct materials—a product cost which includes the cost of raw materials used in the production process and directly identified with the finished products.

Financial accounting—a method of accounting which provides external user groups with information concerning the status of the firm and the results of its operations.

Financial control—the formal process of measuring the performance of segments of the organization to: (1) Determine if the plan which was adopted has been followed, and (2) Analyze and explain differences between the planned and actual results.

Finished goods—a special inventory account where the production costs of goods already completed but not yet sold remain as assets until the point of sale.

Line manager—a manager who supervises operating personnel who produce and sell goods or services.

Management or managerial accounting—a type of accounting which is concerned with providing information for internal uses of management such as planning, control, performance evaluation and other decision-making activities. Management accounting utilizes financial accounting data as well as other internal and external information which may be available.

Management accounting cycle—a system of information flows including: (1) Gathering decision-making information, (2) Evaluating alternative courses of action, (3) Developing plans and budgets, (4) Executing plans, (5) Recording performance, and (6) Comparing actual results with budgeted results.

Manufacturing overhead—a product cost that includes manufacturing costs associated with the production process, but not directly traceable to specific units of output either as direct materials or direct labor.

Organization chart—identifies the major decision-making centers as well as the formal lines of authority and responsibility within an organization.

Period costs—costs that are associated with the passage of time and are usually not easily identified with either the purchase or the manufacturing of products. Period costs are recorded as expenses in the period incurred.

Product costs—all costs that can be directly identified with the purchase or production of goods made available for sale by the firm. These costs are inventoried and carried as assets and then expensed as cost of goods sold when the product is sold.

Staff manager—a staff manager's function is to provide specialized assistance or knowledge to a line manager when the line manager needs it.

Work-in-process—a special inventory account where the costs of direct materials, direct labor and manufacturing overhead are accumulated as the product is manufactured.

QUESTIONS

1. What differences exist between financial accounting and management accounting? Is management accounting separate and distinct from financial accounting?

2. How does management accounting serve both external financial reporting purposes and the internal needs for management information?

3. Define product cost. What three general elements make up a product cost? Define them.

4. How are the costs used in accounting classified for purposes of income determination and planning?

5. Define period cost. Give examples.

6. Why are period costs not inventoriable?

7. What are the two general categories of decisions in which accounting information may be helpful? Explain.

8. Of what importance is budgeting to the corporation—from the perspective of top management and lower management?

9. Define financial control. Distinguish financial control from accounting control.

10. What basic assumption underlies the thinking in management accounting with respect to analyzing costs?

11. Briefly explain the operation of a typical management accounting system.

12. Budgeting may be regarded as a process of communication, control, and motivation. Explain how each of these processes is served.

13. Why is management accounting information more "future-oriented" than financial accounting? (i.e. What purpose does this orientation serve?)

14. Which pieces of information do we take from cost accounting and use to determine cost of goods manufactured in an accounting period?

15. Define manufacturing overhead. Give examples.

16. What is the purpose of an organizational chart?

17. What is the difference between line and staff managers?
18. What function does the corporate controller serve?
19. What are the three objectives of the National Association of Accountants with regard to the Certificate in Management Accounting Examination?

EXERCISES

1-1 The following management accounting cycle steps are not in order. Place the appropriate number beside each to indicate the proper place of the step in the cycle.

_____ Developing Plans
_____ Gathering Decision-Making Information
_____ Comparing Actual Performance with Planned Performance
_____ Evaluating the Feasibility of Alternatives
_____ Recording Performance
_____ Executing Plans

1-2 Classify each of the following items as either a period cost (P) or a product cost (PR).

a. Direct materials
b. Depreciation on office building
c. Property taxes on office building
d. Direct labor
e. Salesmen's salaries
f. Indirect materials for manufacturing
g. Rent on administrative building
h. Power for manufacturing machines
i. Administrative salaries
j. Office building maintenance

1-3 The Small Manufacturing Company employs only six people. There are Max Small, President; Tony Brown, salesman; Bill Russel, foreman; and three people on the assembly line. The salaries for these people in 1979 were $28,000, $16,000, $17,000, and $10,000 each respectively. In 1979 the company produced 20,000 units of product and sold 18,000 units.

Required:

Determine whether each person's salary is a period cost or a product cost. If it is a product cost, determine how the salary should be allocated.

1-4 The manager of the Parts Division of the ABC Tool Company must make a decision regarding whether or not a specific part should be manufactured internally or purchased from the XYZ Company, an outside supplier. The manager has the following information:

1. The XYZ Company can sell the part to ABC Tool Company for $100.
2. If ABC manufactures the part, the following costs would be incurred:

Raw materials	$40
Direct labor	20
Overhead costs	10
Total cost	$70

Required:

Based upon the information given above, should the manager decide to purchase the part from the XYZ Company or manufacture it? Show your work.

1–5 Classify each of the following accounts of the Baker Manufacturing Company as to product costs or period costs:

a. Direct labor
b. Raw materials used in production
c. Depreciation on manufacturing machinery
d. Production manager's salary
e. Salesman's salary
f. Rent expense for administrative offices
g. Advertising expense
h. Maintenance on factory machines
i. Salary of company president

1–6 The following are employed by the Randolph Manufacturing Company in New York:

	Annual Salary
John Smith—President	$50,000
Lewis Clark—Vice President	30,000
David Jones—Manufacturing Department Head	20,000
Paul Frey—Manufacturing Department Head	20,000
Jerry Lawson—Sales Manager	15,000
James Ryan—Salesman	10,000
Joe Phillips—Production Foreman	10,000

Last year the Randolph Manufacturing Company produced a total of 100,000 units of their product of which 60,000 units were sold.

Required:

How would each of the above salaries be recorded on the income statement? In other words, which would be classified as cost of goods sold and which as salary expense.

1–7 Classify each of the following manufacturing costs incurred by the the Jones Desk Manufacturing Company as follows:

1. Direct Material (DM)
2. Direct Labor (DL)

3. Manufacturing Overhead (OH)
   a. Wood
   b. Sandpaper
   c. Paint
   d. Salary of manufacturing employee
   e. Salary of factory supervisor
   f. Heat, light and power
   g. Depreciation of machinery
   h. Maintenance
   i. Salary of manufacturing foreman
   j. Salary of employee who paints desk

1–8 Indicate which of the costs below are product costs and which are period costs for the Toy Manufacturing Company:

   a. Salaries of salesmen
   b. Christmas party for employees
   c. Entertainment expenses
   d. Depreciation of manufacturing equipment
   e. Toy materials
   f. Salaries of production employees
   g. Supplies for manufacturing department

1–9 Classify each of the following positions as either a line position (L) or a staff position (S).

   a. Controller
   b. Manufacturing Vice President
   c. Sales Manager
   d. Personnel Vice President
   e. Treasurer
   f. Production Manager
   g. Machining Department Manager
   h. Salesmen
   i. Finishing and Pressing Department Manager
   j. Marketing Vice President

PROBLEMS SERIES A

1A–1 The following information is available from the records of the Raleigh Paint Company:

Salesmen salaries	$50,000
Administrative costs	1,000
Maintenance costs	500
Paint & varnish	5,000
Production employees' salaries	10,000
Raw materials	4,000
Indirect labor	1,000
Supervisor's salary	1,000

Depreciation on equipment   500
Heat, light & power (manufacturing facilities)   500
Advertising costs (administrative)   200

Required:

Classify each of the above costs (if applicable) as direct materials, direct labor or manufacturing overhead. Give a total for each classification.

1A–2   Jeff Sims and Jim Ryan are employed by the Ace Manufacturing Company. Mr. Sims, the production manager, and Mr. Ryan, the sales manager, each earn an annual salary of $30,000. During the year, 10,000 units of the Company's product were produced of which 6,000 units were sold and 4,000 units remained in inventory as finished goods.

Required:

Using only the above data, calculate the following:

> BALANCE SHEET
> Finished Goods Inventory . . . . *(a)*
>
> INCOME STATEMENT
> Cost of Goods Sold . . . . *(b)*
>
> Expense . . . . *(c)*

1A–3   John and Frank Ryan are both salesmen for the Brown Manufacturing Corporation. They each make a salary of $20,000. Bill Snow, the production manager, has a salary of $22,000; John Adams, a production foreman, makes $10,000. During the year of 1979, the corporation produced 100,000 units of its product and sold 75,000 units.

Required:

Which of the salaries above would be classified as product costs and which as period costs? Give the total amount of product costs and the total period costs that would appear on the income statement.

PROBLEMS SERIES B

1B–1   During a study of the Hardwood Furniture Company's accounting system, the following information was taken from the records:

Delivery expense $21,000
Raw material costs   85,000
Depreciation on factory building   3,500
Depreciation on production equipment   2,700
Office salaries   24,000
Property taxes on manufacturing facilities   450
Production workers' wages   68,000
Production supervisors' salaries   30,000
Cleaning supplies used in production area   580
Sales commissions   16,000

Repair expenses on production equipment   5,600
Research and development expenditures   27,000

Required:

Classify each of the above costs as direct materials, direct labor, manufacturing overhead or general operating expenses. Give the total amount of each classification.

1B–2   During the year the Texas Plastics Company produced 20,000 units of the company's product. Of this amount, 12,000 units were sold with 8,000 units remaining in the finished goods inventory. The following information shows the components of major cost items for the company:

Salaries & Wages
    Executive salaries . . . . $ 50,000
    Sales salaries and commissions   30,000
    Office salaries   21,000
    Production employees wages   65,000
    Factory maintenance employee wages   15,000
                                              $181,000

Depreciation Expense
    On office building and equipment . . . . $ 15,800
    On factory building and equipment   9,500
                                          $ 25,300

Supplies Expense
    Supplies used in offices . . . . $ 2,200
    Supplies used in production   1,600
                                          $ 3,800

Required:

Using the above information only (ignoring direct materials), calculate the finished goods inventory, cost of goods sold and operating expenses for Texas Plastics.

1B–3   Nikki Antl, chief accountant for Fashion Girl Cosmetics, Inc. was in the process of determining Christmas bonuses to be paid to officers and employees. To do this she organized the following list of employees, job descriptions and annual salaries to help her in her work:

Name	Job Description	Annual Salary
Nick Russo	President	$ 40,000 per
Nikki Antl	Chief accountant	30,000 per
Jane Thomas	Production manager	20,000 i P
Larry Wilmer	Sales manager	20,000 per
Jim Wright	Production employee	16,000 DP
Jerry Stern	Production employee	16,000 DP
Chris Jones	Production foreman	19,000 i P
Dick Scott	Production maintenance	15,000 i P
Ann Garvey	Secretary	15,000 per
John Doe	Delivery truck driver	10,000 per
		$201,000

The company produced 90,000 units and sold 60,000 units during the year.

Required:

Which of the above salaries would be classified as product costs and which as period costs? Give the total amount of each that would appear on the income statement as the cost of goods sold or as period expense. Also, classify each of the product costs as direct or indirect costs.

Learning Objectives

Chapter 2 discusses the fundamental patterns of cost behavior and certain of the basic techniques which may be used to determine and analyze these patterns. Studying this chapter should enable you to:

1. Define a cost behavior pattern and discuss the relationship of cost behavior to a relevant range of activity.
2. Identify, discuss, and give examples of each of the primary and related cost behavior patterns.
3. Distinguish between the various categories of costs, such as committed fixed costs and managed fixed costs.
4. Identify and apply the common accounting and statistical techniques which may be used to determine and analyze cost behavior patterns.

2

Costs for Planning: Cost Behavior Patterns

PLANNING Is, by its very nature, essentially a future-oriented process. A basic objective of management is to employ the available resources of the firm in the most efficient and effective manner possible. In order to achieve this objective, management must utilize the best information available, irrespective of the source of the data, in making its plans for the future. Some of the most important information used in the planning process is concerned with the behavior of costs.

THE RELEVANT RANGE

In any analysis of cost information, management accounting makes the basic assumption that most cost behavior may be associated with measures of activity within a relevant range. For our purposes, the relevant range may be defined as that operating range or span over which a firm finds it practical to operate in a short-run time period. There is, of course, an upper limit of operating capacity when some short-run constraining factor prevents the firm from operating at a higher level. There is also a lower limit of operating capacity below which it would be impractical for the firm to operate.

Generally, the total cost function for a given range of output is not linear (See Illustration 2–1). The economic nature of costs suggests that at some point in time economies of scale occur. These economies occur when the firm is able to produce higher quantities of output without a

Illustration 2-1

proportionate increase in costs. In the relevant range of a firm's operating capacity, the curve representing total cost is approximately equal to a linear curve. Therefore, for planning convenience, managerial accounting frequently assumes linear cost functions within the relevant range of activity. Of course, the estimate of the linear cost function is not precise, but then neither is the planning process.

The activity base or quantity of output within the relevant range depends on the particular cost being measured. A few selected examples may help to illustrate and explain the concept of activity measures.

1. The total cost of raw materials in a manufacturing process is directly related to the number of units which are produced. The activity measure in this instance would be units produced.

2. The total cost of gasoline for a truck is directly related to the number of miles driven. The activity measure in this case would be miles driven.

3. The total cost of meals in a hospital is directly related to the number of beds occupied by patients. The activity measure in this circumstance would be the number of beds occupied.

4. If the firm uses a billing service to mail out its accounts receivable billings and the charge is twenty-five cents per billing, the total cost is related to the number of customers billed. The activity measure in this situation would be the number of customers billed.

In establishing an activity base, a firm attempts to identify those causal relationships that explain fluctuations in costs. In this regard, it is important to note that certain costs will not appear to change in relation to any particular activity measure. For example, rent or interest costs are normally related to the passage of time rather than to some level of activity.

VARIABLE COSTS

Variable costs are those costs which vary directly and proportionately with some measure of activity within the relevant range. If, for example, the base activity increases by five percent, the *total* variable cost will also increase by five percent. Total variable costs increase and decrease as the level of activity changes within the relevant range. Illustration 2–2 provides a graphic example of two different variable costs.

In Example 1 of Illustration 2–2, the indicated relevant range of production is from 75,000 to 150,000 units, and the variable cost of raw materials is $4 for each unit produced. If the production for the period was scheduled at a level of 100,000 units, the planned raw material cost would total $400,000 (100,000 × $4). At a production level of 120,000 units, the anticipated raw material cost would total $480,000 (120,000 × $4). At production levels of fewer than 75,000 units or more than 150,000 units, the total variable cost cannot be as readily estimated since these levels of output are outside the relevant range of activity.

The relevant range of miles driven in Example 2 of Illustration 2–2 is from 20,000 to 50,000 miles. The variable cost of gasoline is assumed to be $.10 per mile driven. If it were anticipated that the truck would be driven a total of 30,000 miles, the projected gasoline cost would be $3,000 (30,000 × $.10). At 40,000 miles, the planned gasoline cost would total $4,000 (40,000 × $.10).

Of course, the variable costs per unit could change over time due to such factors as inflation or evolving technology. Naturally, any changes which may be foreseen should be taken into consideration in formulating the budget plan.

FIXED COSTS

Fixed costs are those costs which are not related to activity within the relevant range. As the name implies, fixed costs are those expenditures which remain fixed or constant for a given period of time. Changes in fixed costs may be expected, however, and do occur either over long periods of time or outside the relevant range of activity. Fixed costs provide the capacity required to sustain a planned volume of activity within a

Illustration 2-2
Examples of Variable Costs

Example 1   Example 2

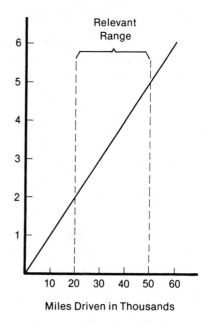

Production in Thousands of Units   Miles Driven in Thousands

Raw Materials Cost: $4 per   Gasoline Cost on a Truck:
unit produced $.10 Per Mile Driven

Relevant Range 75,000 to   Relevant Range: 20,000 to
150,000 units   50,000 Miles

given time period. Total fixed costs and their relationship to activity are presented graphically in Illustration 2–3.

The fixed costs identified in Illustration 2–3 will remain at $1,500,000 at production levels anywhere within the relevant range, which is assumed to be from 75,000 to 150,000 units. Below 75,000 units or above 150,000 units, the total fixed cost may change.

Illustration 2-3
Fixed Costs and Activity

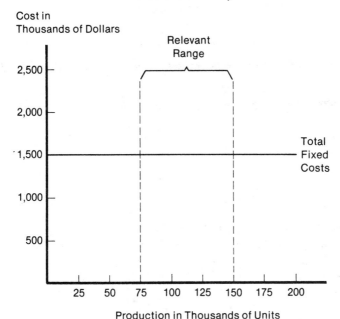

Total Planned Fixed Costs: $1,500,000
Planned Activity: Production of 100,000 units
Relevant Range: 75,000 to 150,000 units

Per Unit Fixed Cost

The fixed cost per unit of activity is an amount which must be considered and used with some degree of caution. In the previous discussions of variable cost included in this chapter, it was noted that the variable cost per unit was constant, and that the total variable cost within the relevant range increased and decreased according to the level of activity.

Total fixed costs, by definition, remain constant within the relevant range for a given time period, irrespective of the level of activity. At higher levels of activity, the fixed cost per unit will be lower than the fixed cost per unit at lower levels of activity simply because the identical amount of cost is being allocated or spread over additional units of activity. For example, in Illustration 2-3, at 75,000 units of production the fixed cost is $1,500,000 or $20 per unit ($1,500,000 ÷ 75,000). At 100,000 units of production, the total fixed cost remains at $1,500,000, but the fixed cost per unit is reduced to only $15 per unit ($1,500,000 ÷ $100,000).

Total Costs

Economics identifies the traditional cost function as being very similar to the one presented in Illustration 2–4. The component parts of total cost include fixed costs plus variable costs. Therefore the total cost equation is:

$$\text{Total Cost} = \text{Total Fixed Costs} + \text{Total Variable Costs}$$

Within the relevant range of production capacity, total cost and its component parts—fixed costs and variable costs—are assumed to be linear.

Illustration 2-4

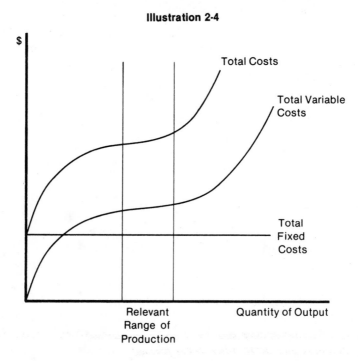

COMMITTED AND MANAGED FIXED COSTS

For purposes of planning, fixed costs may be conveniently classified into two distinctly different categories. These categories are committed fixed costs and managed fixed costs.

Committed Fixed Costs

Committed fixed costs represent those fixed costs which the firm will incur because of the past decisions or commitments made by management. This type of fixed cost relates to the capacity of the firm to engage in its operations at a planned volume or level of activity. Of the two classifications of fixed costs, committed fixed costs are less responsive than are managed costs to the short-term decision-making process.

Committed fixed costs essentially represent the long-term costs of maintaining a given capacity to produce. It is therefore expected that these costs will be associated with the ownership of an organization as well as the related long-term resources or assets that are required to operate the business. Committed fixed costs are those costs which are related to acquiring and maintaining the organization and its long-term assets. Costs such as depreciation on fixed assets, lease or rental costs of buildings, equipment or other assets, property taxes, salaries of key personnel, and insurance are all examples of committed fixed costs.

Managed Fixed Costs

Managed fixed costs (also referred to as discretionary, programmed or planned fixed costs) are those fixed costs incurred on a short-term basis in accordance with an established objective of management. This type of fixed cost does not necessarily relate to the anticipated level of activity. Rather, management will decide on the expenditures it considers necessary to attain a specific objective at some future date. The funds are then spent, unless the objective or economic climate varies and causes a change in management plans.

Examples of managed fixed costs include research and development costs, product improvement costs, public relations costs, advertising costs, sales promotion costs, major plant rearrangement costs, outlays for cost reduction programs, costs of employee training programs and charitable donations. Theoretically, managed fixed costs could be substantially reduced by management decisions in any given period and the profits for that period would be increased (since expenses would have been decreased without a corresponding reduction of revenues). Any adverse impact of reducing a managed fixed cost would probably not be realized until some future time period, assuming that the expenditure would, in fact, have ultimately yielded future benefits.

Illustration 2–5 identifies the two major fixed cost classifications and the relationship of each to production levels. Total fixed costs are projected in the amount of $1,500,000, consisting of a committed cost element of $1,000,000 and a managed cost element of $500,000. Assuming a level of production within the relevant range of 75,000 to 150,000 units, the total fixed cost could be any amount between $1,000,000 (committed costs only) and $1,500,000 (committed costs plus all managed costs), depending on which managed fixed costs management chooses to incur.

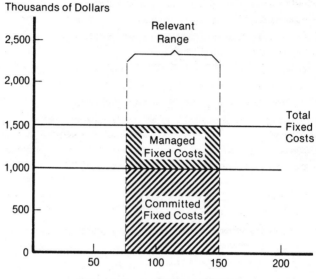

Illustration 2-5
Managed and Committed Fixed Costs

Total Planned Committed Fixed Costs:	$1,000,000
Total Planned Managed Fixed Costs:	500,000
Total Planned Fixed Costs:	$1,500,000

Planned Activity: Production of 100,000 units
Relevant Range: 75,000 to 150,000 units

SEMIVARIABLE COSTS

Semivariable costs, also referred to as mixed costs, are those costs which are comprised of both a fixed and a variable component. As the level of activity increases, the total cost will also increase, but the increase will be less than proportional in amount. A typical example of the variation which occurs with this type of cost is a rental car.

The cost for a short-term rental car has two components. There is a basic charge, usually a daily or weekly amount. The total rental charge can never fall below this fixed base even if the vehicle is not used. A charge on a per mile driven basis plus this basic per day or week charge are the components of the total charge. The total cost for the car for the time period used will therefore be a semivariable cost, a cost which is comprised of both a fixed (the basic per day or per week charge) and a variable (the charge on a per mile driven basis).

Illustration 2-6
Semivariable Cost
Hypothetical Car Rental Bill For A Given Day

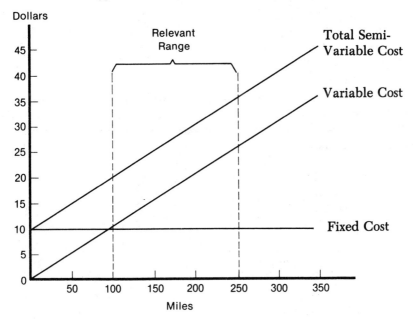

Total Fixed Cost:	$10.00 per day
Variable Cost Per Mile Driven:	$.10
Relevant Range:	100 to 250 Miles Daily

A hypothetical rental charge is presented graphically in Illustration 2–6. To simplify this illustration, assume that the basic charge for the car is $10.00 per day with an additional charge of $.10 per mile for every mile driven. In other words, the basic charge of $10.00 simply makes the use of the car available to the renter and does not entitle the renter to drive any miles (without paying the additional charge of $.10 per mile for each mile driven).

As indicated above, the rental charge for any given day can never be less than $10.00. If a hundred miles were driven in one day the total bill for that day would be $20.00 [$10.00 + (100 miles × $.10)]; and if 200 miles were driven in a day the bill would be $30.00 [$10.00 + (200 × $.10)]).

Graphically, the slope of the total semivariable cost line is identical to the slope of the variable cost line portion of the semivariable cost. These two lines are parallel because the slope of the lines is based entirely on the variable cost component of the total charge. Each mile driven would cause the variable cost component of the semivariable cost to increase in total by $.10. Consequently, the total semivariable cost would also increase by $.10 for every mile driven in a given day.

Other possible examples of semivariable costs include repair costs for most types of equipment (normally the greater the usage, the higher the cost), power costs, clerical costs, telephone costs, and delivery costs.

STEP COSTS

Step costs are those costs which must be incurred in a series of fixed amounts. Generally, a cost behaving as a step cost remains constant over a given range of activity and then increases or decreases in a fixed incremental amount. Although step costs are said to vary according to the level of activity, it should be noted that their relationship to activity is not necessarily a proportionate one.

The salary of a supervisor, such as a foreman, is a typical example of a step cost. The cost of supervisory personnel will remain fixed over a broad range of activity; but when a certain level of production is reached, it will be necessary to hire an additional supervisor and the total cost will increase to a new level. The cost will then remain fixed at this new level for another range of activity.

Illustration 2–7 presents an example of a step cost. In this illustration, the total cost of the salaries of production foremen, within the relevant range, will be $60,000 per year for production levels from 75,000 to 100,000 units, $70,000 per year for output between 100,001 to 125,000 units and $90,000 per year for levels of production from 125,001 to 150,000 units.

ANALYZING COST BEHAVIOR PATTERNS

Ideally, for both planning purposes and for making certain types of decisions, all costs would be classified as either fixed or variable, with semivariable costs being separated into their fixed and variable components. Although this optimal classification usually cannot be attained in practice, cost behavior patterns may be and are often approximated for use in planning and decision-making.

Two general approaches which may be used in studying or analyzing historical cost behavior patterns include the accounting approach and the statistical approach.[1] Neither of these approaches should be considered "the best method." They are complementary methods which are most effective if used in conjunction with one another.

---

[1] The statistical technique discussed in this text is the method of least squares. It should be noted that the accounting measures for cost estimation do not provide a measure of probable error in the cost analysis while statistical techniques can provide measures of probable error.

Illustration 2-7
Step Costs and Activity

Cost: Production Foremen
Planned Activity: Production of 100,000 units
Relevant Range: 75,000 to 150,000 units
Cost Structure: 75,000 to 100,000 units $60,000 per year
 100,001 to 125,000 units $70,000 per year
 125,001 to 150,000 units $90,000 per year

Certain basic assumptions are made in analyzing the behavior of costs. Three major assumptions often made are:

1. Costs will be linear within the relevant range.
2. There is a single factor that causes a variable cost, or the variable portion of a semivariable cost, to fluctuate in total.
3. Historical cost behavior patterns will continue to be valid in the future.

The final assumption requires further comment. Costs are analyzed in order to aid management in its future decision-making. Many of the cost analysis tools that assist management in its future planning and decision-making activities employ historical cost as a starting point. However, factors such as technological advances, inflation, changes in management policy, the addition of new product lines, or changes in the equipment used could—and often do—alter cost behavior patterns. At a minimum, any use of the analysis of past costs for future cost estimation should be viewed with caution and attention to the inherent limitations of the process.

ACCOUNTING TECHNIQUES FOR DETERMINING COST BEHAVIOR PATTERNS

The techniques which may be classified as accounting approaches used to measure cost behavior patterns include: (1) account analysis, (2) the high–low method, and (3) the semi–averages method. All three of these techniques are based on historical costs.

Account Analysis

Account analysis is accomplished by visually inspecting the details of specific accounts and identifying those amounts or costs which are clearly variable and those which are clearly fixed. The past experience of the firm with regard to those costs clearly variable and those clearly fixed may be tested by further analyzing the details of the appropriate ledger balances for a selected period of time. The semivariable costs, or any other costs, which cannot be clearly defined as to behavior pattern by inspection would, of course, require further analysis using other techniques.

The other accounting and statistical techniques presented in this chapter which are used for analyzing cost behavior patterns may be used to analyze either fixed or variable costs. These approaches are formulated so as to separate the fixed costs from the variable costs in the analysis of semivariable costs, but may also be used to analyze costs that are either solely fixed or variable.

High-Low Method

The high-low method uses accounting data selected from two extreme points for both the amount of cost and for the level of activity; it then assumes a linear behavior of costs between these two points. As the name of this technique implies, the points selected are the highest level of activity with the highest cost amount and the lowest level of activity with lowest cost amount. These figures are taken from the recent operating records of the firm. For purposes of illustrating this method of analysis, the cost of the power required to operate a machine has been accumulated for one year. The results of this analysis are presented in Illustration 2-8.

Illustration 2-8

Power Cost

Month	Hours Used	Power Cost
January	40	$14
February	60	18
March	60	18
April	50	16
May	30	12
June	90	24
July	80	20
August	80	19
September	60	18
October	80	20
November	80	19
December	70	18

The month of June shows the highest level of activity with 90 hours of machine running time and an associated total power cost of $24. May is the lowest activity month with 30 hours of running time and a total power cost of $12. When using the high-low technique, the formula for determining the variable cost component of the total cost to be analyzed may be expressed as follows:

$$\frac{\text{High Cost} - \text{Low Cost}}{\text{High Activity} - \text{Low Activity}} = \text{Variable Cost Per Unit of Activity}$$

Using the data from our example, the calculation would be as follows:

$$\frac{\$24 - \$12}{90 \text{ Hours} - 30 \text{ Hours}} = \frac{\$12}{60 \text{ Hours}}$$

$$= \$.20 \text{ Variable Cost Per Hour}$$

In order to identify the fixed component of the total cost, either the high or low point may be used to determine the total variable cost; any remaining amount is, of course, the fixed cost component.

	90 Hours High Point	30 Hours Low Point
Total Cost	$24	$12
Less: Variable Cost	18 (a)	6 (b)
Fixed Cost Component	$ 6	$ 6

(a) 90 X $.20 variable cost per hour = $18.
(b) 30 X $.20 variable cost per hour = $6.

The high-low formula determines the slope of a straight line which extends between the two points selected. The slope of this line represents the variable cost per unit of activity.

Method of Semi-Averages

The method of semi-averages is a slightly more sophisticated version of the high-low technique described above. A period of time is selected for historical cost analysis. The high activity periods are averaged for both levels of activity and related or corresponding costs, and the low activity periods are averaged for these same factors. The averages are then used in the high-low formulation. Illustration 2–9 was prepared using the same power cost data originally presented in Illustration 2–8 in order to demonstrate the difference between the method of semi-averages and the high-low technique.

Illustration 2-9
Method of Semi-Averages

Month	High Six Months Hours Used	Cost	Month	Low Six Months Hours Used	Cost
June............	90	$ 24	January.........	40	$14
July............	80	20	February........	60	18
August.........	80	19	March..........	60	18
October........	80	20	April..........	50	16
November.......	80	19	May............	30	12
December.......	70	18	September.......	60	18
	480	$120		300	96
Divided by	÷ 6	÷ 6	Divided by	÷ 6	÷ 6
Averages........	80	$ 20	Averages........	50	$16

Applying the high-low technique to the averages presented in Illustration 2-9, the average variable cost per hour may be determined as follows:

$$\frac{\$20 - \$16}{80 \text{ Hours} - 50 \text{ Hours}} = \frac{\$4}{30 \text{ Hours}}$$

$$= \$.133 \text{ Variable Cost Per Hour}$$

In order to identify the fixed cost component, again either the average high point or the average low point may be used to substitute the variable cost per unit in the formula for total variable cost; any remaining cost would be classified as fixed costs.

	80 Hours High Average	50 Hours Low Average
Total Average Cost.............	$20.00	$16.00
Less: Variable Cost.............	10.64 (a)	6.65 (b)
Fixed Cost Component.........	$ 9.36 (c)	$ 9.35 (c)

(a) 80 X $.133 variable cost per hour = $10.64.
(b) 50 X $.133 variable cost per hour = $6.65.
(c) Difference caused by rounding.

Recall that the comparable cost components which were determined using the high-low technique were $.20 for each variable cost per hour worked and $6 for the fixed cost component of the semi-variable cost.

BASIC STATISTICAL TOOLS FOR DETERMINING COST BEHAVIOR PATTERNS

There are numerous statistical tools available which may be used for analyzing cost behavior patterns. In general, these tools rely on historical accounting data but are more sophisticated than the accounting tools; they provide management information that may be used with a greater degree of reliability.

Two basic statistical techniques often used for the analysis of cost data are the scattergraph method and the method of least squares. As was the case with the accounting approaches described previously, these two techniques assume: (1) costs are linear within the relevant range; (2) a single causal factor is responsible for the variable cost component of a semivariable cost; and, (3) cost behavior patterns of the past are indicative of those of the future.

The Scattergraph

A scattergraph requires the plotting of both cost and activity observations on a graph. The vertical scale of the graph is normally used to represent dollars of cost, and the horizontal scale represents the activity measure that is causing a change in the total cost amount. This graphical illustration should provide insight into "how well" the cost observations are related (correlated) to the activity measure which has been identified on the horizontal scale.

The scattergraph technique may be used as an initial indicator of the behavior of a specific cost factor. Since all of the numerical techniques described previously will provide an answer in terms of fixed and variable costs, it may seem that a scattergraph is unnecessary. However, remember that the mathematics of these techniques "force" an answer even though the relationship between the cost and activity may be weak or, in some instances, nonexistent. Hence, the determination of an implied cost behavior pattern by means of a scattergraph adds strength to a numerical solution which defines the same cost behavior.

Illustration 2-10
Cost Behavior Patterns on a Scattergraph

| Activity: | Activity: | Activity: |
| Variable Cost | Fixed Costs | Semi-variable Cost |

The basic cost behavior patterns that would imply a specific cost categorization on a scattergraph are presented in Illustration 2–10. If the relationship between the activity and cost may be defined in some meaningful pattern, a trend line (or a regression line as it is referred to in statistics) can be fitted to the graph by inspection. (This trend line may also be calculated mathematically using the method of least squares which will be discussed in the next section of this chapter.)

The power cost data from Illustration 2–8 are plotted on a scattergraph in Illustration 2–11. The pattern of the observations in the graph implies that the power cost is a semivariable cost. The trend line depicted in Illustration 2–11 was drawn with a straight-edge. In drawing this line, an attempt was made to minimize the total deviations of the observations from the trend line. The line intersects the vertical axis at a level of $6. This $6 represents the fixed cost portion of the power cost as determined using the scattergraph approach. The total variable component of the semi-variable cost at a given level of activity may be determined by subtracting the fixed cost from the total cost at that level of activity. To determine the variable cost per unit of activity, the total variable cost would be divided by the level of activity.

At 35 hours of power usage, the total cost is $13. The fixed cost component is $6. Total variable cost is therefore $7 ($13 — $6) or $.20 per hour of power usage ($7 ÷ 35). To calculate the variable cost per hour, the total variable cost is divided by the activity, that is, $7 ÷ 35 hours.

Total Cost at 35 Hours......................	$13
Less: Fixed Cost Component..................	6
Total Variable Cost........................	$ 7
Variable Cost Per Hour $7 ÷ 35 hours =	$.20

The pattern of the observations in the graph implies that the power cost is a semivariable cost which consists of fixed cost of $6 and variable cost of $.20 per hour.

Method of Least Squares

The method of least squares may be used to mathematically calculate the trend line that was drawn by inspection with the scattergraph tech-

Illustration 2-11
Scattergraph Plot of Power Costs

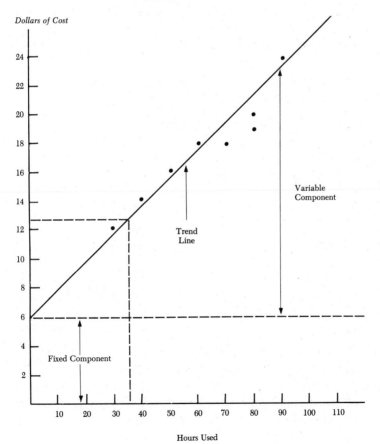

nique. It should be noted that this technique fits a trend line to cost data even if no relationship actually exists. Therefore, this method must be used with caution; in fact, the method of least squares should only be used if a relationship is believed to exist.

The scattergraph technique presented evidence that the data in Illustration 2–8 are representative of a semivariable cost. This data is used again to calculate the trend line using the method of least squares. If the scattergraph is studied and there are levels of activity for which the costs appear to be somewhat out of line, a statistician might wish to further investigate these observations to ascertain whether or not some event out of the ordinary occurred that might have caused the higher than normal cost experienced. If the cost was indeed caused by unusual circumstances, then the observation should be excluded from the calculations. For the purposes of the following discussion, it is assumed that there were no unusual circumstances so all of the observations are included in the analysis.

The method of least squares linear regression which minimizes the total deviations in the cost data is simply one technique used to estimate the equation of a line. As stated in the initial section of this chapter, total costs equal fixed costs plus variable costs. The least squares method estimates the values of 'a'—fixed costs (in mathematical terms, slope intercept) and 'b'—variable costs (slope of the line) per unit of activity (x) or:

$$Y = a + b(x)$$

Here 'Y' represents total costs. Illustration 2–12 shows the method and presents the equation used to estimate fixed and variable costs. Recall that the original data were presented in Illustration 2–8.

Therefore variable costs are $.14 per hour and fixed costs are $8.90, as indicated by the calculations made and presented in Illustration 2-12. At this point, the student may wish to work through this least squares method example carefully and then compare this method to those which were described previously and which were based upon the same data.

If it is considered desirable to simplify this method of estimating costs, then one should first estimate variable costs given the equation in Illustration 2–12. Then using the average level of activity as shown in Illustration 2-12 of 65 hours and the average total cost of $18, one can estimate fixed costs using the following method:

Total Average Cost at 65 Hours...............	$18.00
Less: Average Variable Cost (65 X $.14)........	9.10
Estimate of Fixed Cost.....................	$ 8.90

Illustration 2-12

Method of Least Squares

Activity (X)	Cost (Y)	Deviations from Average Activity (X-X̄)	Deviations from Average Cost (Y-Ȳ)	Deviations from Average Activity Squared (X-X̄)²	Deviations of X Multiplied by Deviations of Y (X-X̄)(Y-Ȳ)
40	$ 14	− 25	$ − 4	625	$100
60	18	− 5	0	25	0
60	18	− 5	0	25	0
50	16	− 15	− 2	225	30
30	12	− 35	− 6	1,225	210
90	24	+ 25	+ 6	625	150
80	20	+ 20	+ 2	400	40
80	19	+ 20	+ 1	400	20
60	18	− 5	0	25	0
80	20	+ 20	+ 2	400	40
80	19	+ 20	+ 1	400	20
70	18	+ 5	0	25	0
780	$216	0	$ 0	4,400	$610

Average: $\bar{X} = 780 \div 12 = 65$
$\bar{Y} = \$216 \div 12 = \$18$

$Y = a + b(X)$ $\hat{Y} = \hat{a} + \hat{b}(X)$ $\hat{a}$ and $\hat{b}$ are estimates of the cost parameters.

Estimated Variable Cost per unit of activity * $= \hat{b} = \dfrac{\Sigma(X-\bar{X})(Y-\bar{Y})}{\Sigma(X-\bar{X})^2} =$

$\dfrac{\$610}{\$4,400} = \$.14$ (rounded)

Estimated Fixed Costs ** $= \hat{a} = \bar{Y} - \hat{b}(\bar{X}) = \$18 - \$.14\ (65) = \$8.90$
Estimated Total Cost Equation: $\hat{Y} = \$8.90 + \$.14\ (X)$

* An alternative equation for estimating the variable cost $\hat{b}$ is:

$$\hat{b} = \frac{n(\Sigma XY) - (\Sigma X)(\Sigma Y)}{n(\Sigma X^2) - (\Sigma X)^2}$$

** An alternative equation for estimating the fixed cost $\hat{a}$ is:

$$\hat{a} = \frac{(\Sigma X^2)(\Sigma Y) - (\Sigma X)(\Sigma XY)}{n(\Sigma X^2) - (\Sigma X)^2}$$

SUMMARY

Effective planning for the future requires that a firm accumulate certain basic information regarding the behavior patterns of its costs. A cost behavior pattern is the typical manner in which a particular cost behaves in relation to a change in a given level of activity. Cost behavior is generally associated with activity within a relevant range; that is, the operating range over which the firm finds it practical to operate in the short-run. In establishing an activity base for a particular cost, the firm attempts to identify those causal relationships that explain the fluctuations in the cost under consideration.

For planning purposes, costs are commonly classified into two major categories according to behavior patterns. These classifications are fixed costs and variable costs. Variable costs are those costs that vary directly and proportionately with the associated activity measure. Fixed costs, on the other hand, generally do not vary according to activity, but instead remain fixed or constant within the relevant range over a given period of time. Fixed costs may be further classified into committed fixed costs (those costs that must be incurred because of past management decision) and managed fixed costs (those costs over which management has the short-run ability to change).

Although the variable and fixed dichotomies are the major categories used for cost classification according to cost behavior patterns, many costs simply cannot be identified as either entirely variable or entirely fixed. Therefore, other related cost categories are required to accurately describe all of the cost behavior patterns of a firm. Semivariable costs are those costs that include both a fixed and a variable component. A step cost is a cost that must be incurred in a series of fixed amounts.

In analyzing cost behavior patterns, it is generally assumed that costs are linear within the relevant range, that a single factor causes the variable portion of a cost to fluctuate, and that past cost behavior patterns will remain valid in the future. A number of techniques are commonly used for determining cost behavior patterns.

Accounting techniques for cost behavior determination generally use the historical data provided by the accounting information system. These techniques include account analysis, the high-low method and the method of semi-averages. Account analysis is simply a visual inspection of the accounts made to determine obvious behavior patterns. The high-low method assumes a linear relationship between the highest and lowest activity levels and the costs associated with those levels. The method of semi-averages employs the high-low technique, but uses an averaging process to obtain the relevant data points.

Two of the basic statistical techniques available for determining cost behavior patterns are the scattergraph and the method of least squares. The scattergraph method requires the graphical plotting of both cost and activity data, and the visual fitting of a trend or regression line to the resulting graph. The method of least squares goes a step further by mathematically calculating the trend line that was previously drawn by inspection.

This chapter has provided a detailed discussion of the primary classifications of costs used for planning purposes. An understanding of these classifications and how they are determined is essential to obtain a further insight into the planning process.

KEY DEFINITIONS

Account analysis—an accounting approach used to determine cost behavior patterns by visually inspecting the accounts and identifying those costs which are clearly variable or clearly fixed.

Committed fixed costs—fixed costs which the firm will incur because of the past decisions or commitments made by management, such as those costs related to acquiring and maintaining the organization and its long-term assets.

Fixed costs—costs which do not change in relationship to an activity within a relevant range and which are fixed or constant for a given period of time.

High-low method—accounting method of determining cost behavior which assumes a linear behavior of costs between the highest level of activity and its related cost and the lowest level of activity and its related cost. These figures are taken from the recent operating records of the firm for a selected period of time.

Managed fixed costs—discretionary, programmed, or planned fixed costs. These are fixed costs incurred on a short-term basis in accordance with an established management objective.

Method of least squares—statistical approach used to determine cost behavior patterns by mathematically calculating the variable and fixed components of the costs, and the trend line that best fits the cost observations.

Method of semi-averages—a more sophisticated version of the high-low method of determining cost behavior patterns. This method assumes a linear behavior of costs between the average of the high activity period and corresponding costs, and the average of the low activity period and corresponding costs over a selected period of time.

Relevant range—range of operating capacity where the firm finds it practical to operate in the short-run. Total fixed costs remain constant within this range.

Scattergraph—a statistical approach used to determine cost behavior patterns and which requires the plotting of both cost and activity observations on a graph.

Semi-variable costs—costs which have both a fixed and a variable component so that as the level of activity increases the total cost will increase, but in a less than proportional amount.

Step costs—costs which are constant over a given range of activity, but which increase or decrease in a fixed incremental amount as the level of activity changes.

Variable costs—costs which vary directly and proportionally with the level of activity.

QUESTIONS

1. Define relevant range.
2. List two examples which help to explain the concept of activity measures.
3. Define variable costs. Give examples.
4. (*a*) Define fixed costs. (*b*) Give two categories into which fixed costs may be classified. Define each and give examples.

5. Define semi-variable costs. Give examples.
6. Define step costs. Give examples.
7. What assumptions are made in analyzing cost behavior?
8. "Past cost behavior patterns will continue to be valid in the future." Why should this assumption be viewed with caution?
9. What are the accounting techniques that may be classified as accounting approaches for determining cost behavior patterns? On what are they based?
10. Discuss account analysis.
11. Describe the high-low method for determining cost behavior patterns.
12. Describe the method of semi-averages.
13. What are the two basic statistical techniques that are often used for the analysis of cost data? On what are they based?
14. Since the numerical techniques for calculating the fixed and variable components of a cost always provide some answer, why is a scattergraph necessary?
15. Why must the method of least squares be used with caution?

EXERCISES

√ 2–1   From the following scattergraphs, state the type of cost each represents.

Dollars

a.

Activity
VC

Dollars

b.

Activity
FC

Dollars

c.

Activity
Step cost

Dollars

d.

Activity
Semivariable

✓2-2   The Weinberg Company is in the process of developing and marketing a new product. From the list of fixed costs listed below, categorize
each cost according to whether it is a committed or managed fixed cost
as relates to this new product.

a.   Research and development costs M
b.   Building modifications M
c.   Depreciation on existing building C
d.   Market tests M
e.   Initial training expenses of salesmen M
f.   Salary of the vice president of the new product department C
g.   Product samples distributed by salesmen M

2-3   Angus, Inc. has found that the maintenance of its machine costs $300
per month plus $.19 per hour the machine is run. Within a relevant
range of 2,800 to 9,000 hours, compute the maintenance costs if the
machine is run 3,000, 3,600, 4,100 and 4,250 hours.

✓2-4   The power for the Evans Company costs $.02 for every unit used.
There is a minimum charge of $20 per month. Determine the bill for
each of the following months:

	Units Used
January	1,500
February	1,720
March	1,200
April	860
May	1,070
June	1,440

✓2-5   Given the following, you are to approximate the variable and fixed
cost behavior of the monthly repairs for the delivery truck using the
high-low method.

Miles Traveled	Monthly Maintenance Costs Incurred
1,000	$250
3,000	350
6,000	500

2-6   Using the method of semi-averages, determine the fixed and variable
components of the following costs for the past year.

Quarter	Hours Worked	Cost
1	20,000	$41,000
2	28,000	55,000
3	32,000	67,000
4	30,000	57,000

2-7   Given the following, determine the fixed and variable components of
the maintenance costs using the method of least squares.

Quarter	Hours Worked	Cost
1	19,500	$69,000
2	17,600	62,300
3	21,200	74,500
4	25,700	90,100

2–8 Given the data in Exercise 2–7, use the high-low method to determine the fixed and variable cost components.

2–9 Johnson Company would like to determine the variable rate per direct machine hour in order to estimate the electricity costs for the months of May and June. Below is listed relevant information.

Months	Machine Hours Worked	Electricity Cost
January	1,200	$50
February	1,300	53
March	1,400	56
April	1,500	60

Estimated units to be produced:

Months	Units
May	1,067
June	1,134

Each unit requires 1.5 machine hours.

Required:

a. Compute the variable and fixed electricity cost components of the total electricity cost using the high-low method.

b. Using the rates calculated above, estimate the electricity for the months of May and June.

2–10 The Simpson Company wants to estimate their gross profit for the first two quarters of next year. The price per unit is $50 and the historical costs are listed below.

	Units Produced	Cost
1	2,000	$ 84,000
2	2,500	102,500
3	2,800	112,000
4	3,400	129,200

It is estimated that 3,600 and 4,000 units will be produced and sold in the first and second quarters.

Required:

Using the method of semi-averages, calculate the fixed costs and variable cost per unit and the expected gross profit for each of the first two quarters.

2–11 Repeat Exercise 2–10 using the high-low method.

2–12   Using the method of semi-averages, determine the fixed and variable components of the following costs.

	Units Produced	Total Cost	Cost Per Unit
January	300	$800	$2.67
February	250	675	2.70
March	280	750	2.68
April	360	950	2.64
May	312	830	2.66
June	292	780	2.67

Why would it be wrong to use the total cost per unit as a basis for pricing the product (such as mark-up on cost), rather than using the variable and fixed components?

2–13   Moore Co. has one truck that it uses for delivery of goods within the local area. It costs the company $.15 per mile to use this truck each year, within the relevant range of 5,000 to 20,000 miles. For each of the following, compute the costs to the company.

a.   5,950 miles
b.   10,800 miles
c.   19,000 miles
d.   20,100 miles

PROBLEMS SERIES A

2A–1   Given below are the sales figures and several related expense figures for six years for the Deckett Company. You are to decide whether the costs are variable, fixed, semi-variable, or step costs by using a graphical analysis.

Year	1	2	3	4	5	6
Sales (in units)	6,000	8,000	8,500	10,000	10,100	10,250
Direct materials	$18,000	$24,000	$25,500	$30,000	$30,300	$30,750
Rent	1,000	1,000	1,000	1,000	1,000	1,000
Selling expense .	17,000	22,000	23,250	27,000	27,250	27,625
Electricity	15,000	19,000	20,000	23,000	23,200	23,500
Maintenance . .	2,000	2,500	2,500	3,000	3,000	3,000

2A–2   The Royal Corporation has just added a new product and wants to know what it should charge for the product. They will have $250,000 fixed costs and $5.25 per unit in variable costs. The marketing research department feels that Royal can expect the sales volume given below by using the suggested prices.

Expected sales (in units)	450,000	625,000	730,000	1,000,000
Unit sales price	$12.00	$10.30	$8.25	$5.50

Required:

Using the information given above, what should Royal use as its selling price? (Base your answer on the highest expected profit.)

2A–3   Terry Company has collected the following production cost data:

	0 Units Produced	100 Units Produced	200 Units Produced
Depreciation	$500	$700	$ 900
Supplies	0	950	1,900
Property Taxes	600	600	600
Labor	0	425	850

In addition, the company has found that maintenance expense exhibits the following "step" behavior:

For   0–75 units, maintenance costs = $ 800
For   76–150 units, maintenance costs =   1,600
For 151–225 units, maintenance costs =   2,400

Required:

What would you expect the total production costs to be if Terry Company produced 125 units?

2A–4   Using the high-low method, determine the fixed and variable components of the power for X Company using the following data.

Month	Hours Used	Power Cost
January	2,500	$1,000
February	4,200	1,340
March	4,600	1,420
April	4,000	1,300
May	3,800	1,260
June	4,200	1,340
July	4,700	1,450
August	5,000	1,500
September	4,700	1,440
October	3,900	1,280
November	4,300	1,350
December	4,700	1,440

2A–5   Given the data in Problem 2A–4, use the method of semi-averages to determine the fixed and variable components.

2A–6   Using the method of semi-averages, determine the fixed and variable components of the following costs:

Month	Hours Used	Cost
January	1,800	$ 990
February	2,000	1,090
March	2,500	1,175
April	2,400	1,170
May	2,600	1,256
June	3,000	1,290
July	2,900	1,320
August	2,500	1,200
September	2,800	1,374
October	2,200	1,110
November	1,900	1,000
December	2,300	1,140

2A-7   Using the method of least squares, determine the fixed and variable costs from the following data:

Month	Activity	Cost
January	4,000	$2,120
February	4,200	2,280
March	4,500	2,350
April	4,400	2,400
May	5,000	2,610
June	4,900	2,460
July	5,600	2,780
August	5,100	2,690
September	4,600	2,540
October	4,800	2,600
November	5,100	2,730
December	5,400	2,800

2A-8   The We-Haul-It Company gathered the following data on the miles driven per month and costs per month for gasoline and routine maintenance on its trucks. Using the method of semi-averages, determine the fixed and variable costs of gasoline and maintenance for these trucks.

Month	Miles Driven	Cost
January	8,200	$ 840
February	9,150	930
March	7,850	784
April	8,100	835
May	8,530	860
June	9,600	960
July	10,050	1,015
August	9,800	971
September	9,200	920
October	8,940	887
November	8,870	900
December	8,990	910

LOW - 851 C
8415 A

High 951 C
9465 A

2A-9   For the past six months the Duben Company has been collecting data on the cost of power to run its plant. You have been hired to determine the cost components of the power using the method of least squares.

Month	Hours	Costs
January	10,500	$4,800
February	11,200	4,970
March	11,600	5,060
April	10,900	4,900
May	10,700	4,870
June	11,100	4,920

2A-10   The Huff Company is trying to estimate its costs for the first three months of next year. It estimates production to be 30,000 units for January; 31,500 units for February; and 35,000 units for March. Given the following data, estimate the costs for these months.

```
Pounds of material per unit . . . . . . . . . . . . . . . . . . . . . .      2
Cost per pound of material . . . . . . . . . . . . . . . . . . . . . . $  1.50
Direct labor hours per unit . . . . . . . . . . . . . . . . . . . . .     1.5
Cost per direct labor hour . . . . . . . . . . . . . . . . . . . . . . $  4.25
Fixed maintenance within relevant range of
  0      units–25,000 units . . . . . . . . . . . . . . . . . . . . . . $140.00
  25,001 units–31,000 units . . . . . . . . . . . . . . . . . . . . . . $180.00
  31,001 units–50,000 units . . . . . . . . . . . . . . . . . . . . . . $220.00
Power costs—minimum . . . . . . . . . . . . . . . . . . . . . . . . . . $100.00
  Variable cost per direct labor hour . . . . . . . . . . . . . . . . $  .02
Heating cost—basic charge . . . . . . . . . . . . . . . . . . . . . . . $ 25.00
  Plus, charge per direct labor hour . . . . . . . . . . . . . . . . . $  .015
```

2A–11   Given below are the hours used and the maintenance costs incurred for the production machinery of the Lawrence Company. The company wants to know what the variable and fixed components are for the maintenance costs. Use (a) the high-low technique, (b) the method of semi-averages, and (c) the method of least squares to determine the cost components. Compare all three methods and give reasons for using the method you feel is best.

Month	Hours Used	Cost
January	3,200	$1,590
February	3,560	1,820
March	3,800	1,890
April	4,050	2,000
May	3,900	1,930
June	3,650	1,825
July	3,740	1,890
August	3,460	1,760
September	3,400	1,700
October	3,550	1,775
November	3,800	1,910
December	4,200	2,050

PROBLEMS SERIES B

2B–1   Using a graphical analysis, determine whether the following costs are variable, fixed, semi-variable, or step.

	Jan.	Feb.	March	April	May	June
Sales (in units) . . .	4,500	5,000	5,300	5,800	6,000	6,100
Direct materials . . .	$9,000	$10,000	$10,600	$11,600	$12,000	$12,200
Direct labor	5,400	6,000	6,360	6,960	7,200	7,320
Property taxes	150	150	150	150	150	150
Maintenance	300	300	350	350	400	400
Power	725	750	765	790	800	805
Sales expense	1,300	1,400	1,460	1,560	1,600	1,620

2B–2   King, Inc. is considering several selling prices for its newest product. Variable costs are $12.50 per unit, while fixed costs are $425,000. Based on a study by the marketing department, the following sales volumes can be achieved by using the suggested prices.

Unit sales price $20.00 $18.50 $17.00 $16.25
Projected sales (in units) 80,000   95,000   105,000   120,000

Required:

Using the given information, determine what the sales price should be, based on the highest profits.

2B–3   Given the following information, what would the total production costs be if the XYZ Company produced (*a*) 3,000 units (*b*) 4,500 units, and (*c*) 5,000 units.

	0 Units Produced	2000 Units Produced	4000 Units Produced	6000 Units Produced
Depreciation	$1,000	$1,100	$ 1,200	$ 1,300
Property taxes	500	500	500	500
Supplies	0	3,000	6,000	9,000
Labor	0	6,500	13,000	19,500
Power	200	1,700	3,200	4,700
Foreman's salary	900	900	900	900

2B–4   The Cutler Company has gathered the following labor cost data for a six month period. They know that there is a certain amount of fixed labor cost included in these figures. Your job is to determine the fixed and variable portions of the labor cost using the high-low method.

Month	Hours Worked	Labor Cost
January	3,200	$13,800 —
February	3,500	14,850
March	3,650	15,600 —
April	3,550	15,200
May	3,400	14,000
June	3,460	14,700

2B–5   Given the data in Problem 2B–4, use the method of semi-averages to determine the fixed and variable components. However, assume that only 2,800 hours were worked in January, rather than 3,200.

2B–6   The Topsi Company is unsure of the fixed and variable cost components of the materials used per unit in the production of their product. The fixed portion is caused by spoilage. They have collected the cost data for 12 months and have asked for you to determine the fixed and variable components using the method of semi-averages.

Month	Units Produced	Material Cost
January	5,000	$15,160
February	5,100	15,310
March	5,250	16,000
April	5,200	15,670
May	5,500	16,460
June	5,450	16,410
July	5,600	16,950
August	5,550	16,820
September	5,400	16,210
October	5,350	16,060
November	5,200	15,860
December	5,150	15,660

2B-7   Sam and Sons, Inc. would like to know what the fixed cost component is for the electricity used in their manufacturing plant. You are to use the method of least squares to determine the fixed cost.

Month	Hours	Cost
January	2,500	$680
February	3,250	860
March	3,500	900
April	3,600	910
May	3,550	860
June	3,400	840
July	3,000	750
August	3,100	780
September	2,700	700
October	2,850	720
November	3,150	790
December	3,200	810

2B-8   Using the method of least squares, determine the fixed and variable portions of the maintenance cost on the machinery.

Month	Hours Used	Cost
July	1,650	$630
August	1,500	580
September	1,550	615
October	1,600	625
November	1,700	655
December	1,750	675

2B-9   Using the method of semi-averages, determine the fixed and variable costs of gas used in the Chemco Manufacturing Company.

Month	Units Used	Cost
January	680	$404
February	630	360
March	640	382
April	625	373
May	660	395
June	675	402
July	685	405
August	695	410
September	690	407
October	670	398
November	705	415
December	715	419

2B-10   Bowen, Inc. is considering adding a new product to its line. Management feels that if 10,000, 12,000, and 13,000 units are produced in the first three months, it will be able to sell all of these units. They would like to have an estimate of the cost incurred in producing these units. Therefore, it is your job to estimate the total costs which will be incurred each month from the following data:

Pounds of material per unit   3
Direct labor hours per unit 75
Cost per pound of material . . . . $ 1.20
Cost per direct labor hour . . . . $ 4.60
Selling expense per unit . . . . $ .25
Maintenance cost within relevant range of:
    0   – 5,000 units $200
    5,001 –10,000 units $250
    10,001–15,000 units $300
Power cost–fixed charge $150
    Plus, charge per direct labor hour . . . . $ .02
Depreciation on machinery per unit produced . . . . . $ .05

2B–11   Using (a) the high-low technique, (b) the method of semi-averages, and (c) the method of least squares, determine the fixed and variable portions of the following costs. Compare all three methods and give reasons for using the method you feel is best.

Month	Hours Used	Cost
January	800	$1,240
February	950	1,430
March	1,000	1,540
April	980	1,500
May	930	1,370
June	900	1,350
July	850	1,290
August	880	1,330
September	860	1,300
October	840	1,270
November	870	1,310
December	910	1,360

Learning Objectives

Chapter 3 describes job order cost accounting and illustrates how job order costing systems are used to accumulate inventory costs. Studying this chapter should enable you to:

1. Discuss and give examples of each of the basic elements of product costs.
2. Describe a "full" product cost and explain its derivation.
3. Calculate a predetermined overhead rate.
4. Explain the basics of job order cost accounting and job order costing systems.
5. Identify and illustrate alternative methods of handling overapplied and underapplied manufacturing overhead.
6. Discuss the cost of goods manufactured statement.

3

Cost Accounting
for Inventories:
Job Order Costing

THIS CHAPTER and Chapters 4, 5, and 7 emphasize manufacturing cost accumulation systems used for inventory costing purposes. Inventory costing, on either a per unit or a per batch basis, is necessary to determine a valuation for inventory which is used for planning and control purposes. This inventory is also used as an input in preparing the balance sheet, and in determining the cost of goods sold for income statement purposes.

There are two fundamental systems of cost accumulation: job order costing and process costing. Each of these cost systems provides a product cost for inventory on a physical measure basis. Examples of physical measures used as bases for product costing purposes include units, pounds, gallons, and tons. Job order costing is considered in this chapter and process costing will be discussed in Chapter 4.

THE ELEMENTS OF PRODUCT COST

The basic elements of product cost for a manufacturing firm were identified in Chapter 1 as direct materials, direct labor, and manufacturing overhead. Accounting for product costs is based on the assumption that each of these basic elements of product cost attaches to, or can be matched or identified with, specific units or batches of production.

For income determination purposes, the product cost to be used will, of course, represent the full or total cost of manufacturing. The use of this full or total cost implies that the total manufacturing costs for a given accounting period are allocated or assigned to those units produced during that period. The full costing method requires that a portion of the manufacturing overhead costs incurred during the period, as well as the costs of direct labor and direct materials used in the production process, be allocated or assigned to each unit or batch of products produced.

Direct Materials Cost

As previously indicated, direct materials are those materials which are used in the production process and which can be directly traced to, or identified with, specific units of product or batches of production. In certain instances, direct materials may include certain materials acquired in a semi-finished state from a supplier as well as those materials normally regarded as raw materials. By definition, the total cost of the direct materials introduced and used in the production process will be proportional to the number of units produced, i.e., the amount of goods manufactured. Therefore, the cost of direct materials is, by its very nature, a variable cost of production.

In practice, certain raw materials may be traced directly to units of product or batches of production. However, the cost of doing so exceeds the additional benefits or accuracy which would be derived from this allocation process. The cost of the raw materials which fall into this category are usually classified as indirect materials simply as a matter of convenience. Examples of indirect materials include: lubricants, sandpaper, wiping rags, packing materials, etc. The costs of indirect materials are considered to be a part of manufacturing overhead costs and are allocated to production as such.

Direct Labor Cost

Direct labor costs include expenses incurred for, and related to, the activities of those employees who are involved in the production process and whose efforts may be directly traced to the manufacturing of specific units of product or batches of production. Direct labor cost is a variable manufacturing cost. As is the case for materials, it may not be efficient to trace certain types of labor costs related to production (such as the salaries of foremen, maintenance personnel, janitors, etc.) to units of product or batches of production. Therefore, such expenditures are normally classified as indirect labor costs. Consistent with the treatment suggested for indirect materials costs, indirect labor costs are considered to be a part of manufacturing overhead costs and are accounted for as such as a matter of convenience.

Manufacturing Overhead Cost

Manufacturing overhead includes all manufacturing costs *other* than direct materials and/or direct labor costs which are incurred in order to manufacture the product. Examples of cost items considered part of manufacturing overhead include: depreciation on plant and equipment; heat, light and power pertaining to the factory; factory supplies; insurance and property taxes on the plant; costs of service departments such as maintenance for the plant; and indirect materials and labor.

Any other costs incurred by the firm not related to the production process are considered to be period costs, not manufacturing overhead. Expenses such as depreciation on the administrative and sales facilities, salaries of salesmen, utilities expense for administrative and sales facilities, office supplies expense, rental expense for administrative or sales facilities, and property taxes on administrative buildings are all examples of expenditures classified as period costs. As such, they are included as expenses in the income statement in the time period in which they were incurred. Period costs are not included in computing the cost of manufacturing the product.

Manufacturing overhead includes both fixed and variable cost components. The fixed component of overhead normally includes such costs as insurance, property taxes, and depreciation on plant facilities. Variable cost components usually include costs such as indirect materials, indirect labor, and utilities.

FLOW OF MANUFACTURING COSTS

Manufacturing costs are accumulated for purposes of inventory costing on what is referred to as a full cost basis. The use of "full costing" indicates that the cost of the products produced during a period should include the costs of all direct materials and direct labor used as well as a *normal* share of both variable and fixed manufacturing overhead incurred. The overhead that should be included as a portion of the cost of the products manufactured is that overhead which is incurred under normal operating conditions. (The treatment of "abnormal" or excess costs are considered in Chapters 7 and 8).

The product cost flows generally experienced by a manufacturing firm may be traced in the following diagram:

Product Cost Flows

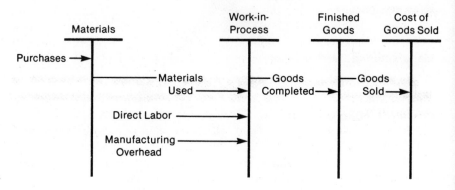

These cost flows may also be summarized in the form of a statement referred to as the cost of goods manufactured and sold statement, as follows:

Cost of Goods Manufactured and Sold Statement

Raw Materials

Beginning Inventory	$ xx
Add: Purchases	x
Raw Material Available for Use	$xxx
Less: Ending Inventory	(xx)
Cost of Raw Materials Used	$xxx
Direct Labor	xx
Manufacturing Overhead	xx
Total Manufacturing Costs	$xxx
Add: Beginning Work-in-Process Inventory	xx
Total Cost of Work-in-Process During Period	$xxx
Less: Ending Work-in-Process Inventory	(xx)
Total Cost of Goods Manufactured, Completed and Transferred during the Period	$xxx
Add: Beginning Finished Goods Inventory	xx
Goods Available for Sale	$xxx
Less: Ending Finished Goods Inventory	(xx)
Cost of Goods Sold During the Period	$xxx

The cost of the direct materials, direct labor, and manufacturing overhead incurred are combined and accumulated in a work-in-process inventory account. As goods are completed, the production costs of these goods are determined and transferred to a finished goods inventory account. It is important to note that the raw materials, work-in-process, and finished goods accounts are *all* inventory accounts. The raw materials inventory account reflects the cost of all direct materials on hand which are available for use in the manufacturing process, but which have not yet been used in production during the period. The work-in-process inventory represents the cost of partially completed products on hand at the close of the period and, as such, is composed of transfers from the direct materials, direct labor, and manufacturing overhead accounts. The finished goods inventory indicates the cost of the inventory which has been completed, but which is unsold and remains on hand at the end of the period. These three inventory accounts are all classified as current assets on the balance sheet. As sales are made from the finished goods inventory, the related cost of the products sold is transferred from the asset account to the cost of goods sold expense account.

PREDETERMINED OVERHEAD RATES

As previously indicated, overhead cost includes both variable and fixed cost components. The benefits which may be derived from a precise or exact accounting for certain of the variable components of overhead are usually not justified in terms of the cost of doing so. The fixed cost component of overhead represents, in general, the long-range commitment that management has made to both obtain and retain the firm's ability to produce. These fixed costs are incurred whether production is at the lower or at the upper end of the relevant range.

For example, if the actual fixed overhead costs of $1,000 incurred during January were assigned by a firm to the production of that month when a total of 200 units of product were manufactured, then the fixed overhead per unit would be $5 ($1,000 divided by 200 units). If the production during June increased to 500 units while the fixed overhead remained constant at $1,000, then fixed overhead per unit would be only $2 ($1,000 divided by 500 units). Under these circumstances, this firm would experience fluctuating monthly production costs per unit (product costs) because a constant amount of fixed overhead ($1,000 per month) is allocated to a different number of units produced each month. The variable cost per unit is normally relatively constant within the relevant range since variable costs, by definition, are incurred in proportion to activity.

To eliminate certain problems which might be encountered in the direct allocation of fixed overhead over a short time span, a *predetermined overhead rate* may be established and used. The use of this rate is implemented under the concept of *normal costs*. The overhead rate used for product costing purposes is determined before the production process is completed, thus the rate is identified as predetermined. This rate is based on the total normal overhead cost expected to be incurred for the time period under consideration assuming usual operating conditions.

The time period chosen for "normalizing" overhead should be sufficiently long to eliminate the effects of any seasonal aspects of production. Even if no seasonal fluctuations exist, the time period chosen must be long enough to eliminate any unusual events which might occur during a given period. For purposes of illustration in this text, a year will normally be considered a sufficient period for use in establishing an overhead rate. One should note that both the fixed and the variable overhead cost components are included in the predetermined rate. For example, assume that a firm anticipates the production of 40,000 units for 1981 and that total overhead costs (i.e., both fixed and variable overhead) of $100,000 are expected for the year. The predetermined overhead per unit is calculated as follows:

$$\frac{\text{Planned Total Overhead Costs}}{\text{Planned Production}} = \frac{\$100,000}{40,000 \text{ units}} =$$
$$\$2.50 \text{ of overhead per unit produced}$$

Each unit produced during 1981 includes the actual costs of the direct materials and direct labor used and, in addition, an allocation of $2.50 per unit produced for manufacturing overhead. This $2.50 allocation for overhead is considered the normal overhead cost applied to each unit without regard to the actual level of production that may take place within any given period—for example, a week or month during the year.

It should be noted that units of production are not always the best measure or denominator for calculating a predetermined overhead rate. In fact, the use of units as a base frequently poses certain problems, as in the case of a firm which produces a number of different products. If the production process for each product differs in such a firm, then the firm might wish to use different overhead rates for each of its products or product groups.

APPLICATION BASES FOR OVERHEAD RATES

There are many bases that may be used for *allocating, absorbing* or *applying* overhead costs to the production of a period. The criteria for selecting a base should emphasize ease of measurability and a causal relationship to the incurrence of variable overhead.

Planned production was used as the application base in calculating the predetermined overhead rate in the previous illustration. Direct labor hours could also have been used. If the firm were a multiple product company, and if the incurrence of variable overhead were related to the number of direct labor hours worked, then the rate could have been established on the basis of planned direct labor hours. Under these circumstances, the product costs for each unit or batch of units produced would absorb an amount of predetermined overhead based on the actual number of direct labor hours worked. Thus, in order to calculate the predetermined overhead rate, the direct labor hours per unit must be computed.

The predetermined rate could also have been based on other factors which have a causal relationship to overhead. If direct labor cost is closely related to the incurrence of overhead, it is not uncommon to use a percentage of this labor cost as a basis for the application of overhead, rather than using an overhead rate based on labor hours. In a firm where there is limited use of labor and extensive use of equipment, machine hours used might be an appropriate base for applying or allocating overhead costs to products. Whatever basis is used for applying overhead, the concept is to have each unit of product produced absorb into its cost its proportional share of the predetermined manufacturing overhead cost.

INVENTORY COST ACCUMULATION: JOB ORDER COSTING USING NORMAL COSTS

As the title "job order costing" implies, costs are accumulated by individual jobs or job lots under a job order costing system. A job is defined as either a single unit or as a batch of units. The costs of direct materials and direct labor traced to the specific job become a part or component of the cost of that job. Normal overhead is assigned to the job using a predetermined overhead rate.

The application of normal overhead is the basis for the term normal costs. Actual costs of direct labor and direct materials are charged to each job, but a normal or a "fair share" of overhead costs is also allocated to the individual jobs. If the causal basis of variable overhead is also the application base for product costing, then normalization is related to the fixed portion of overhead. The projected portion of overhead which is fixed is usually allocated over the projected activity base to develop a cost per unit of activity. Through the use of a predetermined overhead rate, the allocated cost is charged to individual jobs as if it were a variable cost. The total or full cost overhead application rate will be comprised of both the fixed and variable components of overhead.

INVENTORY LEDGERS

The inventory records used in a job order costing system include both the control and the underlying subsidiary ledger accounts. The control accounts used include the following general ledger accounts: raw materials inventory, work-in-process inventory, and finished goods inventory. The subsidiary accounts include the detail which underlies or supports the control account balances. Illustration 3–1 presents the inventory account relationships in "T" account format. Illustration 3–2 is a typical example of the format of the subsidiary ledger inventory accounts.

Illustration 3-1
Inventory Control and Subsidiary Ledger Balances
for Manufacturing Inventories

The relationships of the subsidiary and control accounts in the manufacturing inventory accounting system do not differ either in purpose or in use from those used in a retailing concern. In both cases, subsidiary accounts are updated on a periodic basis and the balances of the subsidiary accounts are posted to the control accounts at appropriate intervals.

JOB COST SHEET

The basis of a job order cost system is the job cost sheet. This subsidiary ledger is the cost accumulation device for each job. In other words, each job has its own job cost sheet which serves as the subsidiary ledger account on which costs are accumulated for that specific job. Direct material and direct labor costs are traced to the individual job, and overhead costs are applied or allocated to that job. Per unit costs are calculated directly from the job cost sheet.

Illustration 3-2
Sax Company
Subsidiary Ledger Accounts for Manufacturing Inventories
Raw Materials Inventory Card in Subsidiary Ledger

Material	101 1″ Copper Bushing			Reorder Point	2,000	
Location	Aisle 29			Maximum Order	7,000	

| Date | Issue Requisition Number | Quantity | | Unit Cost | Balance | |
		Received	Issued		Quantity	Total Cost
1/1 Bal.				.25	2,000	500
2/10		7,000		.25	9,000	2,250
2/16	1704		1,000	.25	8,000	2,000

JOB COST SHEET

Manufactured For		Job No.	1001	
Customer	John Doe	Due Date	2/26	
Stock	✓	Date Started	2/16	
Product	E	Date Finished	2/26	
Quantity in Job	500 units			

| Direct Material | | | | Direct Labor | | | Overhead Rate 100% of Direct Labor Cost |
| Date | Requisition Number | Amount | | Date | Hours | Cost | |
		Q	$				
2/16	1704	1,000	250	2/16	10	40	40
Totals							

Cost Summary			
Direct Material	$250	Total Cost	$330
Direct Labor	40	Units	500
Overhead	40	Cost Per Unit	$.66
Total	$330		

Finished Goods Inventory Card in Subsidiary Ledger

Product	A		Restock Point	3,000
Location	Aisle 51		Production Run	6,000

| Date | Order Number | Job Cost Number | Quantity | | Unit Cost | Balance | |
			Received	Shipped		Quantity	Total Cost
1/1 Bal.					3.00	6,000	18,000
1/15	1055			4,000	3.00	2,000	6,000
1/25		760	6,000		3.00	8,000	24,000
1/28	2,010			4,000	3.00	4,000	12,000

If you have had your automobile repaired, you have no doubt dealt with a job cost sheet, perhaps without realizing it. The garage prepares a cost sheet which also serves as your bill. Generally, this cost sheet includes the cost of both parts and labor. In the case of a garage, the overhead charge is usually included in the labor charge for billing purposes. The profit earned by the garage is added to the cost of the parts and the combined labor and overhead rate. In this case, the job cost sheet also serves as a pricing mechanism and invoice for the customer.

MANUFACTURING OVERHEAD CONTROL ACCOUNT

The predetermined overhead rate is assigned to jobs as they are completed or as the accounts are closed. In order to achieve a full cost valuation of work-in-process inventory accounts for reporting purposes, it is necessary to maintain the overhead on the job cost sheets on a current basis.

The amount of overhead applied to a particular job is recorded by a debit to the work-in-process control account and a credit to the manufacturing overhead control account. This entry is normally made when the control accounts are updated.

The actual overhead costs for the period are recorded in the accounts by debits to the manufacturing overhead control account and credits to the other appropriate accounts. For example, if the depreciation expense related to the manufacturing equipment is $1,000 for a particular month, then the manufacturing overhead control account is debited $1,000, and accumulated depreciation—manufacturing equipment is credited $1,000. If actual factory supplies of $200 are used during the month, then the manufacturing overhead control account is debited $200, and factory supplies inventory is credited $200.

The inflows and outflows associated with the manufacturing overhead control account are presented in Illustration 3-3. Any balance remaining in the manufacturing overhead control account at the end of an accounting period represents either an *over* or an *under application* of predetermined overhead. If the overhead applied to the production for the period is greater than the actual overhead incurred, the firm will have overapplied its overhead and the manufacturing overhead control account will have a credit balance at the end of the period. If the overhead applied to production is less than the actual overhead incurred, then the firm will have underapplied overhead and the manufacturing overhead control account will have a debit balance at the end of the period.

Theoretically, the amount of actual overhead incurred during a period should be equal to the overhead applied during that period. In practice, this perfect matching will rarely, if ever, be the case and will only occur

Illustration 3-3
Product Cost Flows

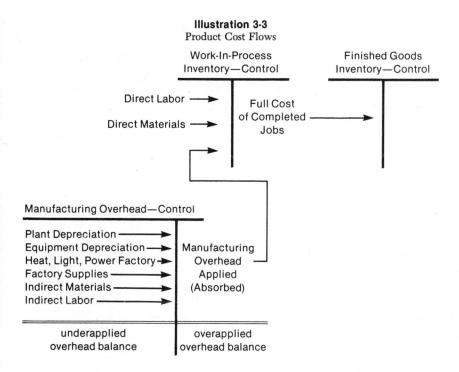

if the predetermined overhead rate is exactly equal to the actual overhead rate for the period and if actual production is exactly equal to planned production. Of course, this equality is extremely unlikely. If the over or underapplied overhead is an immaterial amount, then an adjustment is made to cost of goods sold in order to close out the overhead account and adjust the cost of goods sold amount. A debit balance in the manufacturing overhead control account (actual overhead costs exceed the overhead applied to the jobs) indicates an increase (debit) in the cost of goods sold, because the manufacturing overhead account must be credited in order to close the account. Alternatively, a credit balance in the manufacturing overhead control account represents overapplied overhead and therefore a decrease in cost of goods sold for the period.

If the balance of over or underapplied overhead for the period is considered to be a significant amount, this balance should be allocated to or prorated among the cost of goods sold, finished goods, and work-in-process accounts. The pro rata allocation to these accounts is necessary to eliminate a distortion of the reported income for the period and the financial position of the company at the end of that period.

A COMPREHENSIVE EXAMPLE: BASIC DATA

The Sax Company uses a job order cost system. The company also uses a predetermined overhead rate for applying overhead costs to its manufactured products. Sax Company has found that there appears to be a cause and effect relationship between the direct labor hours worked during a period and the manufacturing overhead incurred for that same period. Last November, Sax's accountant prepared an estimate of the total manufacturing overhead costs anticipated for the current year. This analysis is presented in Illustration 3–4 which indicates that Sax will include an overhead allocation of $10 per direct labor hour worked as a part of the product cost of each job worked on this year.

Illustration 3-4
Sax Company
Projected Manufacturing Overhead Rate

Projected Activity: 60,000 Direct Labor Hours
Projected Total Manufacturing Overhead Costs: $600,000

	Variable Costs Per Direct Labor Hour	Fixed Costs	Total Costs
Indirect Material and Supplies	$3.10	$ 14,000	$200,000
Indirect Labor	1.00	40,000	100,000
Electricity	.10	34,000	40,000
Heat	0	8,000	8,000
Equipment Depreciation	0	48,000	48,000
Plant Depreciation	0	144,000	144,000
Factory Property Taxes	0	60,000	60,000
	$4.20	$348,000	$600,000

Predetermined Manufacturing Overhead Rate:

$$\frac{\text{Total Projected Manufacturing Overhead Cost}}{\text{Total Projected Activity}} = \frac{\$600,000}{60,000 \text{ hours}} = \$10 \text{ Per Direct Labor Hour}$$

January is an ideal time to follow a job through Sax's manufacturing process and accounting records since the firm closes for two weeks at the end of December for employee vacations. Each January, the firm begins its operations without any work-in-process inventory since all jobs are completed during December prior to the shut-down of the plant. The company uses a perpetual inventory system for all of its inventories. Indirect materials and factory supplies are accounted for in terms of dollars only, and not units.

Sax's production schedule for January consists of a single production run of metal shafts for power turbines, a standard inventory product for the company. Normally, Sax would also engage in other transactions during January, but for purposes of illustration we will focus on tracing Job Number 3032, a production run of 7,000 power turbine shafts, through the manufacturing process and the accounts. We will assume that the transactions which are identified and discussed in this example are the only transactions which occurred in January.

A summarized post-closing trial balance as of December 31, 1980 for Sax Company is presented in Illustration 3-5.

Illustration 3-5

Sax Company

Post-Closing Trial Balance

December 31, 1980

	Debit	Credit
Cash	$ 60,000	
Accounts receivable	20,000	
Indirect materials and factory supplies	30,000	
Raw materials inventory	40,000	
Work-in-process inventory	–0–	
Finished goods inventory	70,000	
Equipment	300,000	
Accumulated depreciation—equipment		$ 184,000
Plant	1,082,000	
Accumulated depreciation—plant		600,000
Accounts payable		34,000
Federal income taxes payable		–0–
Property taxes payable		–0–
Long-term debt		400,000
Common stock		250,000
Retained earnings		134,000
Total	$1,602,000	$1,602,000

The normal cost to produce a power turbine shaft is $19, calculated as follows:

One Direct Labor Hour	$ 5
One Round Steel Billet (Shaft)	4
Overhead Applied (One Hour @ $10.00)	10
Total Cost of One Shaft	$19

A summary of the manufacturing transactions that occurred during the month of January follows:

January 2 Materials with a cost of $49,000 were issued to production. Of this amount, $28,000 (representing the cost of 7,000 units of materials) was related to direct materials and was issued from raw materials and the balance, $21,000, was for indirect materials and factory supplies and was issued from that account. The raw materials requisition number was 1012, and the indirect materials and factory supplies requisition number was 1013.

January 15   Paid wages to manufacturing employees totaling $25,000. Of this amount, $20,000 (representing the cost of 4,000 hours of direct labor) was incurred for direct labor and the balance, $5,000 was for indirect labor.

January 31   Paid wages of $19,000 to manufacturing employees. Of this amount, $15,000 (for 3,000 hours of direct labor) was for the cost of direct labor incurred and the balance, $4,000, was incurred for indirect labor.

January 31   Manufacturing overhead of $70,000 (7,000 direct labor hours multiplied by the overhead rate of $10 per direct labor hour) was applied to the production of 7,000 power turbine shafts.

January 31   The units that were completed were transferred to finished goods.

January 31   The plant electricity bill of $3,700 for the month of January was paid.

January 31   The plant heating bill of $2,000 for the month of January was paid.

January 31   Sold 2,000 of the power turbine shafts which were produced during January at a sales price of $50 per shaft. The proceeds of the sale were received in cash. The entry for cost of goods sold was made.

January 31   The selling and administrative expenses for January totaled $28,000.

January 31   Depreciation expense for the month (from Illustration 3–4) is calculated as follows (assuming the straight-line method of depreciation is used):

$$\text{Equipment:} \quad \$\ 48,000 \times \frac{1}{12} = \$\ 4,000$$
$$\text{Plant:} \qquad\ \ \$144,000 \times \frac{1}{12} = \$12,000$$

Accrued property taxes on the factory for January (from Illustration 3–4) are as follows:

$$\$60,000 \times \frac{1}{12} = \$5,000$$

A COMPREHENSIVE EXAMPLE:
MANUFACTURING JOURNAL ENTRIES

The entries necessary to record the transactions described above are presented below in general journal form. An explanation follows each entry.

		Debit	Credit
January 2	Work-In-Process Inventory—Control	28,000	
	Manufacturing Overhead—Control	21,000	
	Raw Materials Inventory—Control		28,000
	Indirect Materials and Factory Supplies		21,000

The issue of direct materials to the production process was recorded by a debit of $28,000 to the work-in-process inventory—control account and a corresponding credit to the raw materials inventory—control account. The indirect materials and supplies represent *actual* overhead costs so the manufacturing overhead—control account is increased to reflect these costs. The normal costs of these indirect materials and supplies have been considered in determining the overhead rate, and are therefore components of the rate applied to Job Number 3032 when this job is completed. If a separate inventory account is not maintained for the inventory or indirect material and supplies, the raw materials account is also credited for the $21,000 cost of the indirect material and supplies which were transferred to the work-in-process inventory, thus making the total credit $49,000.

January 15	Work-In-Process Inventory—Control	20,000	
	Manufacturing Overhead—Control	5,000	
	Cash		25,000

All Sax Company employees are paid on the fifteenth and on the final day of each month. The direct labor cost for the first fifteen days of January was $20,000, while indirect labor costs for the same period totaled $5,000. The indirect labor cost represents an actual overhead cost and is recorded as a debit in the manufacturing overhead—control account, just as indirect materials and supplies were recorded in the entry made on January 2.

January 31	Work-In-Process Inventory—Control	15,000	
	Manufacturing Overhead—Control	4,000	
	Cash		19,000

This entry represents the cost of employee wages for the latter half of January. Again, the indirect labor costs are recorded by a debit to manufacturing overhead—control and not to work-in-process inventory—control, because these indirect costs are part of the predetermined manufacturing overhead rate which is applied to the job upon its completion.

January 31	Work-In-Process Inventory—Control	70,000	
	Manufacturing Overhead—Control		70,000

This journal entry recognizes the normal overhead for January using the predetermined overhead rate of $10 per direct labor hour for each

hour worked on Job Number 3032. The normal portions of all of the manufacturing overhead costs identified in Illustration 3–4 are included in
the overhead rate of $10 per direct labor hour.

January 31   Finished Goods Inventory—Control 133,000
                     Work-In-Process Inventory—Control . .   133,000

The full cost of the completed inventory includes the direct material
cost of $28,000 (January 2), direct labor cost of $35,000 (January 15 and
31), and the manufacturing overhead applied of $70,000 (January 31).
The preceding journal entry transferred the accumulated costs of Job
Number 3032 from the work-in-process—control account to the finished
goods inventory—control account.

January 31   Manufacturing Overhead—Control 3,700
                     Cash   3,700

This journal entry records the electricity expense incurred for the
month, at its actual cost, as a component of manufacturing overhead. The
anticipated cost of electricity had been used in establishing the predetermined manufacturing overhead rate just as the indirect labor and indirect
materials and supplies were considered. Therefore, the normal cost of
electricity had already been absorbed as a part of the cost of the job when
the overhead was applied.

January 31   Manufacturing Overhead—Control 2,000
                     Cash   2,000

This entry recognizes the actual factory heating cost for January. As
was the case with indirect materials and supplies, indirect labor costs,
and electricity costs, the normally expected costs of heating were considered in determining the predetermined overhead rate and were thus absorbed into the job. Consequently, the actual heating expense for January
is recorded by a debit to the manufacturing overhead—control account.

January 31   Cash 100,000
                     Sales Revenue   100,000

Sax sold 2,000 of the power turbine shafts produced during January at
a sales price of $50 per shaft for a total selling price of $100,000. The proceeds of the sale were received in cash.

January 31   Cost of Goods Sold 38,000
                     Finished Goods Inventory   38,000

Sax uses a perpetual inventory system. Therefore, the cost of goods
sold is recognized at the time the sale is made. Cost of goods sold, as
may be seen in the following calculation, is $19 per unit for 2,000 units

or a total of $38,000. A total of $133,000 was transferred to the finished goods—control account on January 31. This amount represented the full cost of the 7,000 units completed during January. The full cost per unit would be $19 ($133,000 divided by 7,000 units).

January 31   Selling and Administrative Expenses 28,000
             Cash   28,000

The total selling and administrative costs for January were $28,000, and we will assume that all of these amounts are paid in cash.

January 31   Manufacturing Overhead—Control 21,000
             Accumulated Depreciation—Equipment .   4,000
             Accumulated Depreciation—Plant   12,000
             Accrued Property Taxes Payable   5,000

Other actual overhead costs, which have not yet been recognized but which were included in the job as part of the overhead applied, include depreciation expense of $4,000 on equipment and $12,000 on plant. Accrued property taxes of $5,000 on the plant also have not previously been recognized in the accounts. The above adjusting journal entry brings the manufacturing overhead—control account up to date as of January 31.

The depreciation expense and accrued taxes are considered as a part of the overhead costs which were included in determining the predetermined overhead rate. Even if this entry were not made—and in most cases it is likely that it would not be made for purposes of the monthly management reports—the inventory values would reflect the normal cost of depreciation and property taxes. These costs are reflected in the inventory values because they are included as a part of the predetermined manufacturing overhead application rate which was used to apply overhead to production.

A COMPREHENSIVE EXAMPLE: GENERAL AND SUBSIDIARY LEDGERS

The general ledger accounts are presented in "T" account format in Illustration 3–6, and the related subsidiary ledger inventory accounts are presented in Illustration 3–7. All beginning balances were taken from the post-closing trial balance which was included in Illustration 3–5. To fully understand the concept of manufacturing cost flows, the reader should trace the general journal entries through both the general ledger and the subsidiary ledger accounts.

The manufacturing overhead—control account included in the general ledger and the job cost sheet in the subsidiary ledger deserve special attention. Manufacturing overhead—control serves as an account that is

Illustration 3-6
Sax Company
General Ledger Accounts

Cash

1/1	60,000	25,000	1/15
1/31	100,000	19,000	1/31
		3,700	1/31
		2,000	1/31
		28,000	1/31
1/31	82,300		

Indirect Materials and Factory Supplies

1/1	30,000	21,000	1/2
1/31	9,000		

Raw Materials Inventory—Control

1/1	40,000	28,000	1/2
1/31	12,000		

Work-In-Process Inventory—Control

1/1	–0–	133,000	1/31
1/2	28,000		
1/15	20,000		
1/31	15,000		
1/31	70,000		
1/31	–0–	–0–	

Finished Goods Inventory—Control

1/1	70,000	38,000	1/31
1/31	133,000		
1/31	165,000		

Manufacturing Overhead—Control

1/1	–0–	–0–	
1/2	21,000	70,000	1/31
1/15	5,000		
1/31	4,000		
1/31	3,700		
1/31	2,000		
1/31	21,000		
		13,300	1/31

Accumulated Depreciation— Equipment

		184,000	1/1
		4,000	1/31
		188,000	1/31

Accumulated Depreciation— Plant

		600,000	1/1
		12,000	1/31
		612,000	1/31

Property Taxes Payable

		–0–	1/1
		5,000	1/31
		5,000	1/31

Sales Revenue

		–0–	1/1
		100,000	1/31
		100,000	1/31

Cost of Goods Sold

1/31	38,000		
1/31	38,000		

Selling and Administrative Expenses

1/31	28,000		
1/31	28,000		

Illustration 3-7
Sax Company
Subsidiary Ledger Accounts for Manufacturing Inventories

Material __Round Steel Billet 2″ diameter__   Reorder Point _____500_____
Location __Aisle 84__   Maximum Order __9,000__

Date	Issue Requisition Number	Quantity Received	Quantity Issued	Unit Cost	Balance Quantity	Balance Total Cost
1/1 Bal.				4	8,000	32,000
1/2	1012		7,000	4	1,000	4,000

Material __Ind. Mat. & Fac. Supp.__   Reorder Point __Visual Inspection__
Location __Aisle 29: Bins 40-50__   Maximum Order __Marked in Bin__

Date	Issue Requisition Number	Received	Issued	Balance
1/1 Bal.				30,000
1/2	1013		21,000	9,000

Job Cost Sheet

Manufactured for
Customer _____John Doe_____   Job No. ____3032____
Stock _____✓_____   Due Date ____1/31____
Product _____   Date Started____1/2____
Quantity in Job ____7,000____   Date Finished ____1/31____

	Direct Material	Amount Q	Amount $		Direct Labor		Overhead Rate $10 Per Direct
Date	Requisition Number	Q	$	Date	Hours	Cost	Labor Hour
1/2	1012	7,000	28,000	1/15	4,000	20,000	7,000 hours
				1/31	3,000	15,000	X $10
							$70,000
Totals		7,000	28,000		7,000	35,000	70,000

Cost Summary
Direct Material __$28,000__
Direct Labor__35,000__   Total Cost__$133,000__
Overhead __70,000__   Units ____7,000____
Total __$133,000__   Cost Per Unit __$19__

Product __Power Turbine Shafts__   Restock Point ____500____
Location __Aisle 76__   Production Run __7,000__

Date	Order Number	Job Cost Number	Quantity Received	Quantity Shipped	Unit Cost	Balance Quantity	Balance Total Cost
1/1 Bal.					19	3,684	70,000
1/31		3032	7,000		19	10,684	203,000
1/31	2051			2,000	19	8,684	165,000

used to accumulate the actual overhead costs as a debit amount. When overhead is allocated or applied to jobs, the application of the overhead is recorded by a credit to the manufacturing overhead—control account. A credit balance in the manufacturing overhead account at the end of an accounting period represents overapplied overhead, while a debit balance represents underapplied overhead.

The job cost sheet, which is the subsidiary ledger account for the work-in-process—control account, deserves special consideration because of the important role it plays in accumulating costs by specific jobs. This cost sheet is the basic cost accumulation instrument used in the job order costing system.

COMPREHENSIVE EXAMPLE: THE MANUFACTURING OVERHEAD—CONTROL ACCOUNT

The manufacturing overhead—control account used in Illustration 3–6 reflects the overhead applied or absorbed into production (the credit entry of $70,000) and actual overhead costs for January (the debit entries totaling $56,700). In this example, manufacturing overhead for the month was *overapplied* by a total of $13,300. The $70,000 of manufacturing overhead costs accumulated for inventory valuation purposes using the pre-determined overhead rate exceeded the actual costs of $56,700 incurred during January by $13,300.

This overapplication of manufacturing overhead may have been caused by a change in the anticipated volume of activity during January when manufacturing overhead was applied to production. Alternatively, the actual costs of the various components of manufacturing overhead may have differed from the costs which were planned for by the Sax Company when it computed its predetermined overhead rate. The overapplication could also have been the result of a combination of these, as well as other factors. The analysis of this difference is discussed in Chapter 8.

Theoretically, assuming a reasonable prediction is made for the overhead rate, at the end of each year the difference between actual and applied overhead should be negligible. This is because overapplications in some months will be offset in other months when overhead is underapplied. In our example, Sax Company must now decide how to treat the overapplied manufacturing overhead of $13,300 in its January financial reports. Remember that the predetermined rate is based on normal overhead for an entire year, so that one would usually expect either an overapplied or underapplied amount in any given month.

COMPREHENSIVE EXAMPLE: TREATMENT OF
OVERAPPLIED OR UNDERAPPLIED OVERHEAD

When a periodic closing of the accounts occurs, the over or underapplied overhead is normally immaterial in amount if the costs and level of anticipated activity for the period have been reasonably forecasted. If indeed the amount is immaterial, the procedure usually accepted as most expedient in general practice is to adjust the amount of cost of goods sold by the amount necessary to close out any debit or credit balance in the manufacturing overhead—control account. If overhead were overapplied, using the 13,300 from the illustration of Sax's January operations, this adjusting entry would be made as follows:

Manufacturing Overhead—Control 13,300
    Cost of Goods Sold   13,300

The effect of this entry would be to close out the manufactured overhead—control account and to decrease the cost of goods sold for the period by the amount of the overapplied overhead.

Alternatively, if manufacturing overhead were underapplied, the following adjusting entry would be required:

Cost of Goods Sold XX
    Manufacturing Overhead—Control   XX

The effect of this entry would be to increase the cost of goods sold by the amount of the underapplied overhead and to close out the balance in the manufacturing overhead—control account.

The normal treatment of over or underapplied overhead used by the Sax Company at its year-end is to make a direct adjustment to cost of goods sold assuming that the amount is not significant. In view of this annual treatment, we will assume for purposes of illustration that management has provided for the use of a monthly worksheet closing that is equivalent to the annual closing process. In practice, this procedure may cause a distortion of income on a monthly basis, but we will assume that management uses the financial reports only for internal purposes and is aware of this potential distortion.

Sax's management has also provided for an optional treatment of over or underapplied manufacturing overhead which has theoretical appeal and which should be used when the difference between the actual manufacturing overhead and the applied manufacturing overhead is considered to be a significant amount. This optional treatment is to apportion the over or underapplied amount of overhead among the ending work-in-process inventory, finished goods inventory and cost of goods sold accounts. In the normal situation, the largest portion of the difference will usually be closed to the cost of goods sold account because of the magnitude of this amount in relation to the inventory accounts on an annual basis. This apportionment approach or procedure is illustrated as follows. The data are taken from Sax Company's general ledger accounts as of January 31. (Illustration 3–6).

	Account Balance	Percent of Total	Amount of Overapplied Overhead Apportioned
Ending Work-In-Process	$ –0–	–0–%	$ 0
Ending Finished Goods Inventory	165,000	81	10,773
Cost of Goods Sold	38,000	19	2,527
Total	$203,000	100%	$13,300

The amount of the overapplied manufacturing overhead for the period was determined to be $13,300 ($70,000 applied less $56,700 actual). Since there was no ending work-in-process inventory, none of this overapplied overhead would be closed to this account. The ending finished goods inventory represents 81 percent of the total amount ($165,000 divided by $203,000). Therefore, 81 percent, or $10,773, of the overapplied overhead (.81 × $13,300) is closed to the finished goods inventory account. Cost of goods sold is 19 percent of the total ($38,000 divided by $203,000). This 19 percent, or $2,527, of the overapplied overhead (.19 × $13,300) is closed out to the cost of goods sold account. The resulting entry which is necessary to dispose of the overapplied overhead for the period is as follows:

Manufacturing Overhead—Control	13,300	
Finished Goods Inventory		10,773
Cost of Goods Sold		2,527

The adjusting entry for overhead made for Sax Company for January is recorded only on the worksheet. Cost of goods sold is then adjusted to reflect the overapplied manufacturing overhead. In either case (the direct write-off to cost of goods sold or the apportionment of the over or underapplied overhead), the impact of closing the manufacturing overhead—control account is to reflect an allocation of the total actual overhead to the appropriate accounts. If the predetermined overhead rate had been totally accurate and the total actual cost had been applied to the production of the accounting period, no adjustment would have been necessary. A worksheet adjustment made on an interim basis is still necessary, however, because of seasonal fluctuations in production.

COMPREHENSIVE EXAMPLE: THE WORKSHEET FOR FINANCIAL STATEMENT PREPARATION

Illustration 3–8 presents the worksheet used by Sax Company at the end of January. The adjusted trial balance was developed from the post-

Illustration 3-8
Sax Company
Worksheet
For the Month Ended January 31, 1981

	Trial Balance Before Adjustments	Adjustments	Trial Balance After Adjustment	Income Statement	Statement of Capital	Balance Sheet
Cash	82,300		82,300			82,300
Accounts receivable	20,000		20,000			20,000
Indirect materials and factory supplies	9,000		9,000			9,000
Raw materials inventory	12,000		12,000			12,000
Work-in-process inventory	-0-		-0-			-0-
Finished goods inventory	165,000		165,000			165,000
Equipment	300,000		300,000			300,000
Accumulated depreciation—equipment •	188,000		188,000			188,000
Plant	1,082,000		1,082,000			1,082,000
Accumulated depreciation—plant •	612,000		612,000			612,000
Accounts payable	34,000		34,000			34,000
Federal income taxes payable	-0-	(b) 22,704	22,704			22,704
Property taxes payable •	5,000		5,000			5,000
Long-term debt	400,000		400,000			400,000
Common stock	250,000		250,000			250,000
Retained earnings 1/1	134,000		134,000		134,000	
Manufacturing Overhead	13,300	(a) 13,300	-0-			-0-
Sales revenue	100,000		100,000	100,000		
Cost of goods sold	38,000	(a) 13,300	24,700	24,700		
Selling and administrative expenses	28,000		28,000	28,000		
Federal income taxes (48%)		(b) 22,704	22,704	22,704		
	1,736,300 1,736,300	36,004 36,004	1,745,704 1,745,704	75,404 100,000		1,670,300
Net income after taxes				24,596	24,596	
				100,000 100,000	-0- 158,596	
Retained earnings 1/31					158,596	158,596
					158,596 158,596	1,670,300 1,670,300

Key to Adjustments:
• Adjustments were made in the example directly to facilitate discussing overapplied and underapplied manufacturing overhead.
(a) To adjust cost of goods sold for overapplied manufacturing overhead.
(b) To adjust for income taxes. The before tax income was 47,300. The income tax rate used by Sax's management is forty-eight percent.

closing trial balance at December 31 (Illustration 3–5), and from the general ledger accounts (Illustration 3–6). The general ledger accounts included in Illustration 3–6 reflect the January 31 balances for all accounts that were affected by the transactions for January. If an account is not found in Illustration 3–6, it is because the January 31 ledger account balance is unchanged from the December 31 balance presented in Illustration 3–5.

The only adjusting entry required on the worksheet at the end of January, besides the closing of the manufacturing overhead-control account, is the accrual of income taxes assuming a rate of 48 percent. The calculations for this accrual are presented in Illustration 3–10. The adjusting entry is as follows:

Federal Income Taxes 22,704
  Federal Income Taxes Payable   22,704

COST OF GOODS MANUFACTURED STATEMENT

Sax Company maintains its inventories on a perpetual system so that a Cost of Goods Manufactured Statement can be prepared for the month of January from these records. If this were year-end, a physical inventory of work-in-process and finished goods might also be taken in order to verify and, if necessary, adjust the inventory records to reflect the cost of the goods that are actually on hand.[1]

A cost of goods manufactured statement may be regarded as an analysis of the work-in-process—control account, or, alternatively, as a summary of the job cost sheets for the accounting period. The usual format employed in the cost of goods manufactured statement is a chronological analysis of the work-in-process—control account. Illustration 3–9 presents the cost of goods manufactured statement for the Sax Company for January.

OTHER FINANCIAL STATEMENTS

The cost of goods sold statement, the income statement, the statement of retained earnings for January and the balance sheet as of January 31 for Sax Company are also presented in Illustration 3-9. These statements were prepared directly from the worksheet in Illustration 3-8, except as noted on the statements.

SUMMARY

Job order costing is one of two fundamental systems of cost accumulation employed by manufacturing firms. Inventory values provided by the cost accounting system of a firm are used to determine inventory valua-

---

[1] Alternatively, physical inventories may be taken throughout the year and the accounts adjusted as considered necessary to reflect any differences detected.

tion on the balance sheet and the cost of goods sold on the income statement. They are, therefore, instrumental in determining the financial position and the profitability of the firm. It follows, then, that the total or full cost of manufacturing the product must be used as the product cost. This "full" cost includes the total costs of the direct materials and direct labor

Illustration 3-9
Sax Company
Cost of Goods Manufactured for the
Month Ended January 31, 1981

Work-in-process inventory, January 1		–0–
Raw materials used:		
Beginning raw materials inventory	$40,000	
Add: Purchases	–0–	
Raw materials available for use	$40,000	
Less: Ending raw materials inventory	12,000	
Raw materials used in production		$ 28,000
Direct labor used in production		35,000
Manufacturing overhead costs applied		70,000
Total manufacturing costs		$133,000
Work-in-process inventory, January 31		–0–
Cost of goods manufactured in January		$133,000

Sax Company
Cost of Goods Sold Statement
For the Month Ended January 31, 1981

Beginning finished goods inventory (from Illustration 3–5)	$ 70,000
Cost of goods manufactured (from Illustration 3–9)	133,000
Goods available for sale	$203,000
Ending finished goods inventory (from Illustration 3–6)	165,000
Cost of goods sold before over or underapplied manufacturing overhead	$ 38,000
Less: Overapplied manufacturing overhead (adjusting entry) . . .	13,300
Cost of goods sold for January	$ 24,700

Sax Company
Income Statement
For the Month Ended January 31, 1981

Sales Revenues	$100,000
Less: Cost of goods sold (from cost of goods sold statement) . . .	24,700
Gross margin	$ 75,300
Less: Selling and administrative expenses	28,000
Operating income before taxes	$ 47,300
Less: Federal Income Taxes (at 48%—adjusting entry)	22,704
Operating income after taxes	$ 24,596

Sax Company
Statement of Retained Earnings
For the Month Ended January 31, 1981

Retained earnings balance, January 1 . . . . $134,000
Add: Operating income after taxes   24,596
                                                                   $158,596
Less: Dividends . . . .   -0-
Retained earnings balance, January 31 . . . . $158,596

Sax Company
Balance Sheet
January 31, 1981

ASSETS
Current Assets:
Cash . . . . $ 82,300
Accounts receivable   20,000
Indirect materials and factory supplies   9,000
Raw materials inventory   12,000
Work-in-process inventory . . . .   -0-
Finished goods inventory 165,000

Total Current Assets $288,300

Long-Term Assets:
Equipment . . . . $ 300,000
Less: Accumulated depreciation—equipment . .   188,000 $112,000
Plant $1,082,000
Less: Accumulated depreciation—plant   612,000   470,000

Total Long-Term Assets $582,000

TOTAL ASSETS $870,300

LIABILITIES AND STOCKHOLDERS' EQUITY
Current Liabilities:
Accounts payable . . . . $ 34,000
Federal income taxes payable   22,704
Property taxes payable   5,000

Total Current Liabilities . . . . $ 61,704

Long-Term Liabilities:
Long-term Debt 400,000

Total Liabilities $461,704

STOCKHOLDERS' EQUITY
Common stock $250,000
Retained earnings 158,596

Total Stockholders' Equity $408,596

TOTAL LIABILITIES AND STOCKHOLDERS' EQUITY $870,300

used as well as an allocated share of manufacturing overhead including
indirect costs incurred in the period.

Overhead costs are allocated using a predetermined overhead rate. This rate is determined by relating the expected or planned normal overhead costs to a planned level of activity. In this "normalizing" process, a time period is selected which is sufficiently long to avoid the effect of seasonal fluctuations in activity or cost levels. There are many activity bases that may be used to allocate costs. The basis selected should be easily measurable and should be the primary factor related to the incurrence of variable overhead. Some of the common bases used include: units of production, direct labor hours used, and machine hours used.

Under a job order costing system employing normal costs, product costs are usually accumulated in the work-in-process inventory account and transferred to the finished goods inventory account upon completion of the job. The costs are expensed and included as cost of goods sold when the products are sold. The same product cost information contained in the work-in-process inventory account is generally reflected in a specialized subsidiary ledger known as the job cost sheet. Each job will have its individual job cost sheet, and unit costs for inventory costing are often calculated directly from this sheet.

Since manufacturing overhead under a normal cost system is applied using a predetermined rate, it is necessary to accumulate actual overhead costs in a manufacturing overhead control account. Unless the actual costs incurred during a period coincide exactly with the costs used in calculating the predetermined application rate for that period (assuming the planned level of activity is achieved), then the firm will have either over or underapplied overhead at the end of the period. If the over or underapplication is immaterial in amount, a direct adjustment can be made to the cost of goods sold on the income statement. However, if the amount is significant, then the balance in the control account should be prorated to the cost of goods sold, finished goods, and work in process accounts.

The cost of goods manufactured statement is a specialized financial statement prepared by manufacturing firms. This statement can be regarded as an analysis of the work-in-process control account for the reporting period. It is usually presented along with the firm's regular cost of goods sold statement, income statement, statement of retained earnings, and balance sheet.

This chapter has discussed the basic elements and procedures involved in a job order cost accumulation system. The next chapter discusses process costing, which is the other fundamental system of cost accumulation employed by manufacturing firms.

KEY DEFINITIONS

Cost of goods manufactured statement—a statement which summarizes total manufacturing costs for the period. As such, the statement is regarded as an analysis of the work-in-process control account or as a summary of the job cost sheets for the accounting period.

Full cost basis—full costing of the products produced during a period includes the costs of direct materials, direct labor, and a normal share of both variable and fixed overhead incurred.

Job cost sheet—the job cost sheet serves as the subsidiary ledger account for each job. All cost applicable to the job are accumulated on the job cost sheet.

Job order costing system—under this system, costs are accumulated by individual jobs or job lots. These costs include actual costs of direct materials and direct labor and a normal or fair share of overhead costs applied to each job.

Manufacturing overhead-control account—a subsidiary ledger asset account which accumulates actual overhead costs. When overhead is applied or allocated to a job, the application of the overhead is recorded by a credit to this account.

Overapplied overhead—occurs when more overhead costs are allocated to production during a period than were actually incurred. Overapplied overhead is indicated by a credit balance in the manufacturing overhead control account at the end of the period.

Predetermined overhead rate—an overhead burden rate used to apply overhead costs to production. The predetermined overhead rate is based on the total normal overhead cost that is expected to be incurred for the time period (normally a year) in which the rate is to be used. The base selected for calculating the rate should be easily measurable and should be the factor which causes or is related to the incurrence of variable overhead.

Underapplied overhead—occurs when more overhead costs are actually incurred by the firm than were allocated to production during the period. Underapplied overhead is indicated by a debit balance in the manufacturing overhead-control account at the end of the period.

QUESTIONS

1. Why is inventory costing necessary?
2. What is a product cost? Why is full or total cost of manufacturing for product costs used in explaining income?
3. Define the components of product cost.
4. Explain the difference between fixed and variable costs of manufacturing.
5. Give some examples of fixed and variable manufacturing overhead costs.
6. What is meant by "full costing"?
7. What are the three inventory accounts of a manufacturing firm? What functions do they serve?
8. Describe the flow of product costs for a manufacturing firm.
9. What is meant by "normalizing" overhead?
10. How are application bases for overhead selected? Name three bases.

11. What do the control and subsidiary ledger accounts include when accounting for the inventories in manufacturing?

12. What is the importance of a job cost sheet?

13. What is the effect on net income if overhead is underapplied and the balance in the manufacturing overhead account is closed out to cost of goods sold?

14. How is an unallocated balance in an overhead control account at the end of an accounting period accounted for?

EXERCISES

✓3-1   The work-in-process account for the Starnes Company has the following balances:

Beginning Balance, May 1 = $24,000
Ending Balance, May 31 = $28,000

During May, the Starnes Company added $134,000 of labor, $64,000 of material and applied $60,000 of overhead to the production process.

Required:

What is the cost of goods manufactured for May?

3-2   The Johnson Company incurred the following costs in producing 40,000 units during April:

1. Raw materials purchased on account $50,000
2. Raw materials used $40,000
3. Direct labor $30,000
4. Indirect labor $10,000
5. Supplies purchased on account . . . . $ 3,000
6. Supplies used . . . . $ 2,400
7. Electricity purchased on account and
       consumed in production . . . . $ 3,600
   Units sold in April 32,000
8. Manufacturing overhead is applied on the basis of $.50 per unit produced.

Johnson Company has no beginning inventories in work-in-process or finished goods, and no ending inventory in work-in-process.

Required:

Set up the following "T" accounts and record the costs. Transfer the costs through the appropriate inventory accounts and into cost of goods sold.

Raw Material Inventory— Control	Work-In-Process Inventory—Control
Accrued Payroll	Electricity
Direct Labor	Finished Goods Inventory—Control
Indirect Labor	Accounts Payable
Cost of Goods Sold	Supplies Used
Supplies Inventory	Manufacturing Overhead—Control

3–3   The following "T" accounts are from the Martin Manufacturing Company on November 30:

Raw Materials Inventory—Control

11/1 Bal.	150	11/30 180	(b)
(a) 11/16	350		

Wages Payable

11/30	300	11/30 300 (c)

Manufacturing Overhead—Control

(c) 11/30	15	11/30 250	(d)
(f) 11/30	240		
	255		

actual overhead   *applied overhead*

Work-In-Process Inventory—Control

11/1 Bal.	50	11/30 675 (e)
(b) 11/30	180	
(c) 11/30	285	
(d) 11/30	250	
	765	

Finished Goods Inventory—Control

11/1 Bal.	80	11/30 700 (g)
(e) 11/30	675	

Required:

Prepare a cost of goods manufactured and a cost of goods sold statement for November.

3–4   The following items may be classified as either (a) direct materials, (b) direct labor, (c) factory overhead, or (d) selling and administrative expense. Place the appropriate letter in the blank before each item.

_____ 1. Depreciation on factory equipment
_____ 2. President's salary
_____ 3. Materials used in production
__b__ 4. Salaries of production workers
__c__ 5. Power bill for production plant
__d__ 6. Sales commissions
__c__ 7. Salary of factory foreman
__d__ 8. Boxes used for shipping product

3–5   Schneider, Inc. has budgeted overhead for next year of $5,640,000. They have 1,880,000 budgeted annual direct labor hours. What will their overhead rate be for next year?

3–6   You are presented with the inventory ledger accounts for one year of the ABC Company. You are called upon by the president of ABC Company to help determine what the various entries in the ledger accounts pertain to.

Materials & Supplies		Work-In-Process		Finished Goods	
30,000	35,000	50,000	76,000	40,000	90,000
40,000	4,000	(1) 35,000		(4) 76,000	
31,000		(2) 40,000		26,000	
		(3) 22,000			
		71,000			

Manufacturing Overhead

(5) 4,000	22,000
(6) 8,000	
(7) 6,000	
(8) 10,000	
6,000	

The president tells you that indirect labor during the year was 20% of direct labor and that factory supervision costs were 60% of other factory costs.

Required:

a. What do the entries (1)—(8) represent in the inventory ledger accounts?

b. What was the amount of cost of goods sold for the year?

3–7 Following are the ledger accounts of the Dull Manufacturing Company. Complete the posting of the manufacturing cost flow entries. The ending finished goods inventory is $8,500, work-in-process is $12,000, and raw materials is $4,500. The credit to factory wages payable represents direct labor costs.

Raw Materials	Work-In-Process	Finished Goods
Bal. 8,600	Bal. 15,500	Bal. 21,000
7,900		
10,000		

Factory Wages Payable	Cost of Goods Sold
23,000 | Bal. 1,000	80,000
24,000	

3–8 The Fixit Company has projected manufacturing overhead costs during June of $55,200. The basis for allocations to individual jobs is direct labor hours. The company is projecting 24,000 direct labor hours for June.

Required:

a. Compute the overhead application rate per direct labor hour for June.

b. 1,000 direct labor hours were used on Job #53, how much of the manufacturing cost should be allocated to this job?

c. Fixit Company has decided to change its allocation base from direct labor hours to direct labor costs. If the hourly wage rate is $1.50, how much manufacturing overhead should be applied to Job #53?

3–9 A job order cost system is used by the Poland Company. The company has no beginning or ending inventory in work-in-process or finished goods, and manufacturing overhead is applied at $4.50 per direct labor hour. Actual results for this year are:

Indirect labor	$ 120,000
Direct labor cost	600,000
Direct labor hours used	225,000
Raw materials used	300,000
Electricity used in factory	210,000
Indirect supplies used	37,500
Miscellaneous overhead	240,000
Cost of goods sold	$1,230,000

Required:

a. How much manufacturing overhead was applied to production during the year?

b. How much manufacturing overhead was actually incurred during the year?

c. Was manufacturing overhead under or overapplied during the year and by how much?

3–10 Below are the balances in selected accounts of the Mustang Company:

Direct labor used in production	$ 38,000
Finished goods inventory, January 1, 1979	10,200
Finished goods inventory, December 31, 1979	3,200
Manufacturing overhead used in production	41,000
Raw materials inventory, January 1, 1979	2,000
Raw materials inventory, December 31, 1979	4,000
Raw materials purchased	23,000
Sales	200,000
Selling expenses	60,000
Work-in-process inventory, January 1, 1979	4,800
Work-in-process inventory, December 31, 1979	8,800

Required:

Prepare: (a) a statement of cost of goods manufactured; and, (b) an income statement.

3–11 The Lowell Company uses an apportionment approach in allocating over or underapplied overhead among the ending work-in-process inventory, finished goods inventory, and cost of goods sold accounts. Below are the balances in selected accounts for the year.

Beginning work-in-process	$ 10,600
Ending work-in-process	10,654
Beginning finished goods inventory	195,000
Ending finished goods inventory	245,042
Cost of goods sold	809,704
Manufacturing overhead applied	345,000
Actual manufacturing overhead	467,000

Required:

a. What over or underapplied overhead was incurred for the year?

b. Journalize the allocation of the over or underapplied overhead among the appropriate accounts.

3–12   The following data pertain to the operations of the Misteak Corporation. You are required to prepare the necessary journal entries.

1. $30,000 of raw materials were placed into production.
2. $1,600 of supplies were used; $1,100 for production and $500 for general purposes.
3.   Depreciation for the month was $20,000 of which 70 percent was for production and 30 percent was on equipment used by the marketing department for selling goods to customers.

3–13   During its first month of operation, the Phoenix Company had the following transactions:

1.   Purchased raw materials for $20,000.
2. $15,000 of raw materials were transferred to production.
3.   Direct labor costs totaling $10,000 were paid in cash and total manufacturing overhead costs incurred and applied to work-in-process was $5,000.
4.   Total cost of goods completed was $25,000.
5.   Total cost of the goods sold was $17,000.

Required:

a.   Make journal entries for the above transactions.
b.   Determine the cost of the work-in-process inventory at the end of the month and the cost of the finished goods inventory at the end of the month.

3–14   The following information is available from the records of the Park Manufacturing Company for the month of December:

Work-in-process, December 31	$ 2,000
Raw materials, December 1	1,000
Labor	5,000
Purchases of raw material	10,000
Manufacturing overhead applied and actual	2,000
Raw materials, December 31	2,000
Work-in-process, December 1	1,000

Required:

Determine the cost of goods manufactured for December.

3–15   Determine the cost of goods sold during the period from the following information.

Raw materials, 1/1/80	$ 40,000
Raw materials, 12/31/80	43,000
Finished goods, 1/1/80	128,000
Finished goods, 12/31/80	105,000
Direct labor	48,500
Purchases of raw material	75,000
Work-in-process, 1/1/80	87,000
Work-in-process, 12/31/80	69,000
Manufacturing overhead applied and actual	72,500

PROBLEMS SERIES A

3A–1   The Vice President of Park Manufacturing Corporation has given you the following information:

1. Sales $130,000
2. Raw materials, Jan. 1   12,000
3. Raw materials, Dec. 31   20,000
4. Work-in-process, Jan. 1   18,000
5. Work-in-process, Dec. 31   14,000
6. Finished goods, Jan. 1   20,000
7. Finished goods, Dec. 31   28,000
8. Raw materials purchased   30,000
9. Direct labor   32,000
10. Manufacturing overhead applied and actual . .   26,000
11. Administrative expenses   16,000
12. Selling expenses   24,000

Required:

You have been asked to obtain the answers to the following questions for the December Board meeting.
What is:

a.   the cost of raw materials available?
b.   the cost of raw materials used?
c.   the cost of goods manufactured during the year?
d.   the cost of goods sold during the year?
e.   the net profit on sales?

3A–2   From the information below, prepare (a) a cost of goods manufactured statement, and (b) an income statement.

Drippy Pipe Company
Before Closing Trial Balance
December 31, 1980

Assets	$1,800	
Inventory—raw materials (Beginning)	100	
Inventory—Work-in-process (Beginning)	300	
Inventory—Finished goods (Beginning)	500	
Liabilities		$ 100
Capital stock		600
Retained earnings		550
Sales		3,000
Expenses	550	
Raw materials purchases	1,000	
	$4,250	$4,250

December 31, 1980
Ending inventories:
   Raw materials—$200
   Work-in-process—$400
   Finished goods—$600
Direct labor costs for 1980 was $800.
Manufacturing overhead actual and applied for 1980 was $400.

3A–3   You are given information concerning the production cost accounts of
Which Company for 1980.

> Raw materials purchased...................... $ 75,000
> Direct factory labor......................... 35,000
> Factory overhead applied..................... 28,000
> Raw materials inventory 12/31/80.............. 5,500
> Cost of goods sold........................... 143,000
> Finished goods inventory 1/1/80............... 21,000
> Finished goods inventory 12/31/80............. 19,600
> Work-in-process 1/1/80...................... 10,000
> Work-in-process 12/31/80.................... 11,500

(Hint: Construct a cost of goods sold statement before attempting to
answer the questions. Assume that there is not any over or under applied overhead.)

Required:

Compute the following:

a.   The maximum amount of finished goods that could have been sold
during 1980.

b.   The amount of goods manufactured during 1980.

c.   The total production costs incurred in 1980.

d.   Raw materials used during 1980.

e.   Raw materials inventory on 1/1/80.

3A–4   The Do-Little Company manufactures scratch pads using a job order
cost system. It assigns actual factory overhead to individual jobs at
the end of each month in proportion to the direct machine hours required of each job during the month.

The August 1 inventories consist of the following:

> Materials and supplies inventory $3,400
> Work-in-process inventory (Job #203) 200
> Finished goods inventory (Job #202) 4,500

Given below is information pertaining to the jobs worked on in August.

Job #	Materials Issued from Inventory	Labor	Machine Time (hrs.)
203	$ 200	$ 300	50
204	1,100	1,450	500
205	980	1,200	450
	$2,280	$2,950	1,000

Other costs incurred during the month were:

> Factory maintenance salaries $1,200
> Factory heat, light and power expense 2,300
> Factory supplies 850
> Depreciation of factory equipment 900
> $5,250

Job #202 was shipped to the customer. He was billed $5,260.
Job #203 and #204 were completed on August 28 and transferred to finished goods.

Required:

Fill in the following:

a.   The gross margin on Job #202 was $_____.
b.   The work-in-process inventory as of August 31 was $_____.
c.   The finished goods inventory as of August 31 was $_____.

/ 3A–5   Sneed, Inc., a construction company, uses a job order cost accounting system. The company's transactions for the month of July were as follows:

July 2   Company purchased materials for cash with an invoice cost of $2,000.
      5   Materials were issued to individual jobs as follows:
          #10–$800; #11–$600; #12–$200; #13–$150
      9   An analysis of the payroll indicated that direct labor charged to the jobs was as follows:
          #10–$200; #11–$300; #12–$100; #13–$50
      10 The overhead incurred during the month was $500.
      15 The application of overhead was made using the same rate as in June. The application rate is based on direct labor cost.
      25 Jobs #10 and #11 were completed and transferred to finished goods.
      30 Job #10 was sold for cash at a price which included a profit of 10%.

Additional data:

The June 30 inventory balances were as follows:

Finished goods	$1,600
Materials	840
Materials work-in-process	1,100
Labor work-in-process	400
Overhead work-in-process	240

Subsidiary records for work-in-process were as follows:

	Job #10	Job #11
Materials	$600	$500
Labor	280	120
Overhead	168	72

Required:

Prepare all the general journal entries for the month of July to record the above transactions.

3A–6   The factory of the Loser Company was completely destroyed by a tornado on December 31, 1980. You have been asked to assist in reconstructing the accounting records in order to prepare an insurance claim for the inventories lost. With the help of the company's bookkeeper, you were able to obtain the following information for the period December 1 to December 31.

Sales	$180,000
Purchases of materials	30,000
Direct labor	36,000
Indirect labor	10,000
Other overhead costs	20,000
Cost of goods manufactured	90,000

The inventory balances at November 30, 1980 were as follows:

Raw materials	$ 20,000
Work-in-process	30,000
Finished goods	40,000

The overhead rate used during December was $2.00 per dollar of direct materials used. The amount of underabsorbed overhead which was in the overhead control account at the date of the tornado was $2,000. Cost of goods sold was two-thirds of sales (before any adjustment for under or overabsorbed overhead was made).

Required:

Compute the cost of the raw materials, work-in-process and finished goods destroyed in the tornado.

3A–7   The following income summary "T" account was given to you by the bookkeeper of Backwards, Inc. for May.

Income Summary

Raw materials purchases	$15,000	Sales		$51,000
Direct labor	15,000	Gain on the sale of land		4,000
Manufacturing overhead	10,000	Closing inventories:		
Selling expenses	25,000	Raw materials (at cost)		3,000
Loss on fire	1,000	Work-in-process (at		
Opening inventories:		cost)		5,000
Raw materials (at cost)	4,000	Finished goods (at		
Work-in-process (at		selling price)		27,000
cost)	4,000	Net loss to balance for		
Finished goods (at		the year		2,000
selling price)	18,000			
	$92,000			$92,000

Required:

a.   Prepare a statement of cost of goods manufactured (in *proper* form).

b.   Prepare an income statement (in *proper* form).

Hint: Use the ratio of cost of goods manufactured at cost and at sales price in your calculations to arrive at the cost of goods sold.

3A–8   The Sorry Manufacturing Company manufactures a single commodity. A summary of its activities for the year is:

Sales	$245,000
Raw materials inventory 1/1	24,500
Work-in-process inventory 1/1	23,200
Finished goods inventory 1/1	38,000
Raw materials inventory 12/31	17,500
Work-in-process inventory 12/31	31,000
Finished goods inventory 12/31	35,400
Raw materials purchases	75,000
Direct labor	62,000
Manufacturing overhead actual and applied . .	48,000
Selling, general and administrative expenses . .	65,000

Required:

a.   Prepare a cost of goods manufactured statement for the year.
b.   Prepare an income statement for the year.

3A–9   The inventory accounts of the King Company at July 1 are as follows:

Raw materials inventory-control	$40,000
Work-in-process inventory-control	30,000
Finished goods inventory-control	25,000

The following transactions occurred during July:

1.   Raw materials were purchased on account in the amount of $20,000.
2.   Raw materials issued to production amounted to $30,000.
3.   Indirect materials amounting to $3,000 were issued.
4.   Wages amounting to $35,000 were paid. They were distributed as follows:

Direct labor	$25,000
Indirect labor	5,000
Selling	3,000
Administrative	2,000

5.   Manufacturing overhead is applied to production at 35% of direct labor cost.
6.   Units completed and transferred to the warehouse cost $75,000.
7.   Sales amounted to $100,000 and the units sold cost $70,000.

Required:

a.   Prepare journal entries for the above.
b.   Prepare all closing entries.

3A–10   For 1980, the Luker Manufacturing Company expected to produce 95,000 units. They also expected to incur $114,000 in overhead costs.

Actual production was 95,000 units. During the year they had the following expenses which were related to manufacturing overhead:

Indirect materials	$20,000
Indirect labor	25,000
Depreciation—plant	12,500
Depreciation—equipment	9,000
Property taxes	5,500
Electricity	27,000
Heating	18,000

Required:

a. Compute the predetermined overhead rate.
b. Prepare journal entries for manufacturing overhead.
c. Close any under or overapplied manufacturing overhead to cost of goods sold.

3A–11 Below is the post-closing trial balance for the Micro Company for the month ended July 31.

	Debits	Credits
Cash	$ 142,000	
Accounts receivable	11,000	
Raw materials inventory	8,000	
Work-in-process inventory	2,000	
Finished goods inventory	87,000	
Plant and equipment	1,000,000	
Accumulated depreciation		400,000
Accounts payable		17,000
Notes payable		10,000
Long-term debt		215,000
Common stock		225,000
Retained earnings		383,000
	$1,250,000	$1,250,000

The following transactions occurred during the month of August:

1. Raw materials of $17,000 were purchased for cash, and $13,000 of raw materials were purchased on account.
2. Raw materials costing $28,000 were issued to production.
3. Indirect materials worth $12,000 were purchased on account.
4. Direct labor of $90,000 and indirect labor of $19,000 were paid in cash.
5. Electricity bill was received but not paid. It totaled $1,500.
6. Indirect materials worth $10,500 were issued to production.
7. Depreciation amounts to 1 percent of the cost of plant and equipment per month.
8. The bill for heating was received but not paid and amounted to $3,400.
9. Manufacturing overhead is applied to production at a rate of 50 percent of direct labor cost.

10. Units completed and transferred to finished goods totaled $125,000.
11. Sales were $255,000 on account. The units sold cost $146,000. Fifty percent of this month's sales and 90 percent of accounts receivable as of July 31 were collected in August.
12. Selling and administrative expenses of $25,000 were paid in cash.
13. Federal income taxes amounting to $42,000 were accrued.

Required:

a. Journalize each of the above transactions.
b. Post the beginning balances and journal entries to "T"-accounts.
c. **Prepare a worksheet like that in Illustration 3-8 for the month ended August 31.**

3A–12 The Aye-Bea-Sea Corporation manufactures large wooden whales using a job order costing system. Job order number 2,468 is summarized below:

> Raw materials $4,960
> Labor 6,740
> Overhead . . . .   ?

Assuming that overhead is 50 percent of labor costs and that the job is now totally complete, show in ledger account format the effect of job order number 2,468 on the raw materials inventory, the work-in-process inventory, the manufacturing overhead control, and the finished goods inventory account.

3A–13 On January 1 the records of the Jones Manufacturing Company showed the following balances:

> Cash $65,000
> Raw materials inventory 5,000
> Work-in-process inventory 3,000
> Finished goods inventory 10,000

During the year the following transactions occurred:

1. Raw materials were purchased for $20,000 cash.
2. A total of $22,000 of raw materials was transferred to work-in-process.
3. A total of $30,000 direct labor costs was incurred during the year of which $25,000 was paid in cash by the end of the year.
4. Total manufacturing overhead costs incurred and applied to work-in-process were $10,000.
5. Cost of goods manufactured was $60,000.
6. Total costs of goods sold was $55,000.

Required:

Prepare journal entries for the above transactions and set up "T"-accounts for each account.

3A–14 Balances of selected accounts of the Baker Toy Company for the year ended December 31, 1979 are given below:

Factory Supervision	$12,000
Depreciation on production equipment	5,000
Direct labor	55,000
Heat, light and power	12,000
Finished goods, January 1, 1979	25,000
Finished goods, December 31, 1979	21,500
Raw materials, January 1, 1979	8,500
Raw materials, December 31, 1979	5,500
Purchases of raw materials	27,000
Work-in-process, January 1, 1979	14,000
Work-in-process, December 31, 1979	11,000
Other manufacturing overhead expenses	30,000

Required:

Using the information given above, calculate:

a. Cost of goods manufactured
b. Cost of goods sold

3A–15 Determine and fill in the missing amounts:

Raw materials, January 1	$ 4,000
Raw materials, December 31	*(a)*
Raw materials used	29,000
Raw materials available for use	34,000
Raw materials purchased	*(b)*
Manufacturing overhead	80,000
Direct labor used	*(c)*
Total manufacturing costs	159,000
Cost of goods manufactured	154,000
Work-in-process, January 1	*(d)*
Work-in-process, December 31	10,000
Cost of goods sold	151,000
Finished goods, December 31	6,000
Finished goods, January 1	*(e)*

3A–16 During August the Bryan Furniture Company recorded the following transactions:

1. Lumber was purchased for $5,000.
2. Lumber costing $4,000 was transferred from raw materials to other accounts. Of this transferred lumber, 80 percent was used to make the furniture while the remaining 20 percent of the lumber was used to make some signs for sales advertising.
3. 90 percent of the furniture in work-in-process was completed during August and was transferred to finished goods.
4. 75 percent of the completed furniture in finished goods was sold in August.

5. Assume that all inventory balances were zero at the beginning of the month.

Required:

Using the information given above, give the balances at August 31 for the following accounts:

a. Raw materials
b. Work-in-process
c. Finished goods
d. Cost of goods sold
e. Selling expenses

PROBLEMS SERIES B

3B–1   Use the following information to answer the questions below:

Finished goods on hand, January 1, 1980 . . .	$ 16,500
Work-in-process, January 1, 1980	9,250
Total production costs during the year	85,000
Cost of production completed during the year .	88,300
Cost of goods sold during the year	85,900
Sales	170,000
Selling expenses	30,700
General expenses	13,400
Retained earnings, January 1, 1980	42,000
Dividends	19,000
Allowance for uncollectible accounts	2,550

Required:

Determine the:

a. Work-in-process on hand, December 31, 1980.
b. Finished goods on hand, December 31, 1980.
c. Gross margin on sales.
d. Net operating income.
e. Retained earnings, December 31, 1980.

3B–2   Prepare a statement of cost of goods manufactured from the following information.

	Beginning Account Balance	Ending Account Balance
Finished goods inventory	$10,650	$ 9,530
Raw materials inventory	20,100	22,300
Accounts payable	11,500	10,450
Work-in-process	6,700	7,000
Sales		70,950
Purchases of raw materials (including transportation of $2,300)		15,600
Direct labor		23,200

	Beginning Account Balance	Ending Account Balance
All other non-manufacturing labor		6,000
Factory depreciation		3,500
All other depreciation (non-manufacturing)		5,200
All other manufacturing overhead costs		7,600
All other non-manufacturing expenses		1,250

3B-3 The beginning and ending inventories of Stapleton, Inc. for 1981 are:

Inventories	1/1/81	12/31/81
Raw materials	$38,600	$36,500
Work-in-process	9,800	10,600
Finished goods	18,000	23,400

The cost of goods sold for 1981 is $216,300. Direct labor for the year is $83,200 and factory overhead costs are $60,700.

Required:

Compute the following:

a. Cost of goods manufactured
b. Total manufacturing costs incurred this period
c. Cost of raw materials used this period
d. Cost of raw materials purchased this period

3B-4 The Swifty Manufacturing Company manufactures office machines to consumer's specifications using a job order cost system.

On August 31, 1980, their raw materials inventory was $27,600; work-in-process inventory was $7,300; and finished goods inventory for Job #1284 was $10,500. The work-in-process inventory consisted of Job #1285 which had the following accumulated costs:

Direct materials	$3,400
Direct labor	2,700
Manufacturing overhead	1,200
Total	$7,300

During the month of September, Jobs # 1286, 1287, and 1288 were begun. Direct materials used during September were:

Job #1285–$500; Job #1286–$4,250; Job #1287–$2,600; Job #1288–$5,700

Direct labor costs during September were:

Job #1285–$300; Job #1286–$3,200; Job #1287–$1,800; Job #1288–$3,500

Manufacturing overhead costs for September totaled $4,300; these were applied in proportion to the direct labor dollars used on each job. Jobs # 1285, 1286, and 1287 were completed and transferred to finished goods inventory. Jobs # 1284, 1285, and 1286 were shipped to the customers who were billed $11,200, $9,150, and $10,870, respectively.

Required:

a. Cost of Job #1285 $_____; #1286 $_____; #1287 $_____; and #1288 $_____.
b. Cost of goods sold, in September $_____.
c. Work-in-process inventory on September 30 $_____.
d. Gross margin on Job #1284 $_____; #1285 $_____; and #1286 $_____.

3B–5   Crash, Inc., a construction company, uses a job order cost accounting system. The company's transactions for the month of July were as follows:

July   2   Purchased materials—Invoice cost $1,000.
       5   Materials were issued to individual jobs as follows:
           #120–$400; #121–$540; #122–$180; #123–$220
       9   Analysis of payroll:
           #120–$180; #121–$200; #122–$90; #123–$30
      10   Actual overhead incurred was $35,000.
      15   Application of overhead—use the same rate as in June which was based on direct labor cost.
      25   Jobs #120 and #121 were finished and transferred to finished stock.
      30   Job #120 was sold for cash at a price which included a profit of 10%.

Additional data:

The June 30 inventory balances were as follows:

Finished goods	$800
Materials	420
Materials work-in-process	550
Labor work-in-process	200
Overhead work-in-process	120

Subsidiary records for work-in-process for June were as follows:

	#120	#121
Materials	$300	$250
Labor	140	60
Overhead	84	36

Required:

Prepare all general journal entries for the month of July.

3B–6   The factory of the Vollmer Company was completely destroyed by a fire on October 31, 1980. You have been asked to assist in reconstructing the accounting records in order to prepare an insurance claim for the inventories lost. With the help of the company's bookkeeper, you were able to obtain the following information for the period October 1 to October 31:

Sales	$18,000
Purchases of materials	7,000
Direct labor	3,600
Indirect labor	1,000
Other overhead costs	2,000
Cost of goods manufactured	9,000

The inventory balances at September 30, 1980 were as follows:

Raw materials	$2,000
Work-in-process	3,000
Finished goods	4,000

The overhead rate used during October was 50 cents per dollar of direct materials used. The amount of underabsorbed overhead which was in the overhead control account at the date of the fire was $200. Cost of goods sold was two-thirds of sales (before any adjustment for under or overabsorbed overhead was made).

Required:

Compute the cost of the raw materials, work-in-process and finished goods destroyed by the fire.

3B–7   The bookkeeper of Vernon, Inc., being somewhat inexperienced, is at a loss as to the preparation of the financial statements. From his college accounting courses, he remembers that certain accounts should be closed out to an "income summary" account at the end of each period. He has done this, but now seeks your help in preparing the financial statements. His "income summary" account is as follows:

INCOME SUMMARY

Cash	$ 100	Accounts payable	$ 250
Accounts receivable	400	Notes payable	400
Raw materials, 1/1/80	12	Capital stock	150
Work-in-process, 1/1/80	12	Retained income	200
Finished goods, 1/1/80	54 *	Sales	153 *
Fixed assets	200	Raw materials, 12/31/80	9
Raw materials purchased	45	Work-in-process, 12/31/80	15
Direct labor	45	Finished goods, 12/31/80	81 *
Overhead	30		
Selling expenses	50		
Administrative expenses	25		
"To balance"	285		
	$1,258		$1,258

* Sales and finished goods are included in the "income summary" at selling price; all other amounts are at cost.

Required:

Prepare a statement of cost of goods manufactured and an income statement for the year ended December 31, 1980.

3B–8   The data shown below appear on the books of the Anderson Corporation at December 31.

1.	Raw materials, Jan. 1	$ 1,200
2.	Raw materials, Dec. 31	200
3.	Work-in-process, Jan. 1	400
4.	Work-in-process, Dec. 31	80
5.	Finished goods, Jan. 1	1,600
6.	Finished goods, Dec. 31	480
7.	Direct labor	2,800
8.	Indirect labor	800–
9.	Factory supplies	240–
10.	Raw materials purchased	3,200
11.	Selling & administrative expenses	2,800
12.	Property tax on plant	40–
13.	Plant utilities	200–
14.	Depreciation on plant & equipment	360–
15.	Sales	14,500
16.	Miscellaneous manufacturing overhead . .	400–

Required:

Prepare an income statement supported by a cost of goods manufactured and sold statement.

3B–9   During the month of August, the following transactions occurred:

1. Raw materials costing $35,000 were purchased for cash.
2. Raw materials of $27,500 were issued to production.
3. Direct labor of $40,000 was paid.
4. Indirect materials amounting to $1,500 were issued.
5. The electricity bill was received. It amounted to $1,950.
6. Indirect labor of $4,000 was paid.
7. Plant depreciation of $2,000 was recorded.
8. Manufacturing overhead was applied to production at a rate of 20% of direct labor cost.
9. Product completed and transferred to finished goods amounted to $90,000.
10. Sales amounted to $150,000. The units sold cost $115,000.

Inventory accounts as of August 1 amounted to:

Raw materials inventory—control . . . . $ 1,000
Work-in-process inventory—control 30,000
Finished goods inventory—control 45,000

Required:

a. Prepare the journal entries for August.
b. Prepare all of the closing entries.

3B–10   During the year the Summo Company produced 87,250 units and incurred the following costs:

Indirect materials	$ 14,100
Direct materials	98,600
Property taxes on plant	6,300
Plant depreciation	36,000
Selling expense	18,600
Indirect labor	34,000
Electricity for plant	22,350
Office equipment depreciation	5,200
Manufacturing equipment depreciation	28,000
President's salary	80,000
Direct labor	275,000
Heating for plant	16,500

The company had predicted an overhead cost of $153,000 and the production of 90,000 units.

Required:

a.   Compute the predetermined overhead rate.
b.   Prepare the journal entries for manufacturing overhead.
c.   Determine the amount of any under or overapplied manufacturing overhead and close it out to cost of goods sold.

3B–11   Below is the post-closing trial balance for the Fairfield Company as of December 31, 1981:

	Debits	Credits
Cash	$ 160,000	
Accounts receivable	40,000	
Indirect materials	2,500	
Raw materials inventory	16,000	
Finished goods inventory	35,000	
Factory equipment	500,000	
Accumulated depreciation–equipment		25,000
Plant	800,000	
Accumulated depreciation–plant		400,000
Office equipment	40,000	
Accumulated depreciation–office equipment		36,000
Accounts payable		11,000
Federal income taxes payable		100,000
Long-term debt		400,000
Common stock		381,500
Retained earnings		240,000
	$1,593,500	$1,593,500

The following transactions occurred during the month of January, 1982:

1.   Raw materials worth $22,000 were purchased on account.
2.   Indirect materials costing $6,000 were purchased for cash.
3.   Direct labor amounting to $65,000 and indirect labor totaling $30,000 were paid.

4. Electricity and heat bills for the month, amounting to $4,500, were received but not paid.
5. Raw materials worth $26,000 and indirect materials worth $5,400 were issued to production.
6. $26,000 was paid on accounts payable.
7. Depreciation is calculated at 0.5 percent a month on plant and equipment and 1 percent a month on office equipment.
8. Manufacturing overhead is applied to production at a rate of 65 percent of direct labor cost.
9. Units completed and transferred to finished goods totaled $125,000.
10. Sales on account for the month totaled $360,000 and the cost of those sales amounted to $140,000.
11. $250,000 was received on accounts receivable.
12. Selling and administrative expenses totaled 3 percent of sales.
13. Federal income taxes of $100,000 were accrued.

Required:

a. Journalize the above transactions.
b. Post the beginning balances and journal entries to "T"-accounts.
c. Prepare a worksheet for the month of January like that in Illustration 3–8.

3B–12 The Lisa Corporation manufactures large flower pots using a job order costing system. Job order number 2,222 is summarized below:

> Raw materials $6,700
> Labor   3,900
> Overhead . . . .   ?

Assuming that overhead is 50 percent of labor cost and that the job is now totally complete, show in ledger account format the effect of job order number 2,222 on the raw materials inventory, the work-in-process inventory, the manufacturing overhead control, and the finished goods inventory accounts.

3B–13 On January 1, 1979 the Shipper Skateboard Manufacturing Company was formed to produce and sell skateboards. During 1979 the following transactions occurred:

1. The company issued capital stock for $550,000.
2. Raw materials were purchased on account for $75,000.
3. A total of $45,000 in raw materials was transferred to work-in-process during the year.
4. The company incurred $80,000 in direct labor costs and $25,000 in indirect labor costs. Only $100,000 of this amount was paid by the end of the year.
5. Supplies were purchased for $5,000 in cash. Of this amount, $2,000 was used in production during the year and $1,000 was used for general purposes.

6. Total depreciation expense on plant and equipment was $20,000. Of this amount, 75 percent was applicable to factory buildings and equipment. The other 25 percent was applicable to non-production plant and equipment.
7. All actual manufacturing overhead costs incurred were applied to work-in-process.
8. The cost of units completed and transferred to finished goods inventory was $90,000.
9. All sales for the period were made in cash. Sales for 1979 totaled $200,000. The cost of the units sold was $80,000.

Required:

a. Prepare journal entries for each of the above transactions.
b. Calculate the ending balances in raw materials, work-in-process and finished goods inventory accounts.

3B–14 Beginning balances on January 1 of selected accounts for the Goody Two Shoes Manufacturing Company are as follows:

Cash	$180,000
Raw materials	65,000
Work-in-process	32,000
Finished goods	18,000
Supplies	1,800

During the year the following transactions occurred:

1. Purchased for cash $25,000 of raw materials.
2. Paid direct labor costs of $89,000.
3. Paid total utility bills (gas, electricity, water, etc.) for production facilities of $12,000.
4. Supplies used in production were $950.
5. Raw materials costing $45,000 were used in production.
6. Depreciation on production equipment was $7,400.
7. All manufacturing overhead costs were applied to work-in-process.
8. Work-in-process on December 31 is $119,000.

Required:

a. Calculate the cost of goods manufactured for the year.
b. If the balance of finished goods inventory as of December 31 is $24,000, calculate the cost of goods sold for the year.

3B–15 Using the available information from the records of the Tipsy Bottling Company, fill in the missing amounts:

Raw materials, January 1, 1979	$ 3,250
Raw materials, December 31, 1979	5,000
Cost of raw materials used	(b)
Raw materials available for use	(a)
Raw materials purchased	12,000
Direct labor	22,000

```
Work-in-process, January 1, 1979 . . . . . . . .   17,200
Manufacturing overhead costs . . . . . . . . . .    (c)
Work-in-process, December 31, 1979 . . . . . .      950
Total manufacturing costs . . . . . . . . . . . .  39,750
Cost of goods manufactured . . . . . . . . . .     (d)
Cost of goods sold . . . . . . . . . . . . . . . .  51,000
Finished goods, January 1, 1979 . . . . . . . . .   (e)
Finished goods, December 31, 1979 . . . . . . .    14,500
```

3B–16   The following T-Accounts are shown for the Acme Bubble Gum Company during the month of January, 1979.

Cash		Raw Materials	
1/1/79 100,000	25,000 (b)	1/1/79 20,000	20,000 (c)
(j) 38,000	1,500 (d)	(a) 50,000	
	30,000 (e)		

Supplies		Manufacturing Overhead	
1/1/79 1,800	1,000 (f)	(f) 800	3,400 (h)
(d) 1,500		(g) 4,500	

Supplies Expense		Accounts Payable	
(f) 200		(e) 30,000	25,000 1/1/79
			50,000 (a)

Work-in-Process		Accumulated Depreciation	
1/1/79 69,000			22,500 1/1/79
(b) 30,000	34,000 (i)		7,500 (g)
(c) 20,000			
(h) 3,400			

Sales		Finished Goods	
	38,000 (j)	1/1/79 52,000	19,000 (j)
		(i) 34,000	

Depreciation Expense		Cost of Goods Sold	
(g) 3,000		(j) 19,000	

Wages Payable	
	5,000 (b) 1/1/79

Required:

Prepare brief explanations for each of the above transactions (a) through (j) which occurred during January.

Learning Objectives

Chapter 4 discusses process cost accounting and illustrates the use of a process costing system for accumulating costs. Studying this chapter should enable you to:

1. Discuss a process costing system and give examples of situations in which its use may be desirable.
2. Describe the format and purpose of the production cost report.
3. Explain and illustrate the concept of equivalent units and calculate equivalent units of production.
4. Derive unit costs in given situations.
5. Calculate inventory costs under both the weighted average and the first-in, first-out methods of inventory valuation.

4

Cost Accounting for Inventories: Process Costing

A PROCESS costing system is normally used for the accumulation of costs in those manufacturing situations characterized by the continuous production of a uniform product. Typical examples of industries where a process costing system may be appropriately used include petroleum refining, chemical manufacturing, paint manufacturing, flour milling and cement manufacturing.

Recall from Chapter 3 that in a job order costing system, manufacturing costs are accumulated by individual jobs or job lots. In a process cost accounting system, costs are accumulated by process rather than by individual job or job lots. At the conclusion of each reporting period, usually a month, a *production cost report* is prepared for each manufacturing department or process. The total output or production for the period is determined, and the costs of the direct materials and direct labor used as well as the overhead applied are accumulated and summarized. The unit cost of the production for the period is then calculated by dividing the total manufacturing costs (direct materials, direct labor and overhead applied) for the period by the number of units produced during that period.

At this point, it should be noted that a job order costing system could also be used under process costing conditions. In practice, however, the expense of maintaining a job order cost system under such circumstances would probably be prohibitive since job order costing requires numerous supporting source documents and extensive detail. These sources and details are normally considered unnecessary in a typical process costing situation. For example, accumulating costs by individual jobs or job lots requires maintaining detailed records of the direct labor applicable to each job; therefore, employee time tickets for each job are necessary. Also, materials must be requisitioned for a specific job and accounted for accordingly.

In a process cost system, however, direct labor cost is simply accumulated and assigned to the work in that particular process or department. Therefore, daily timecards for payroll are usually considered to be sufficient documentation for use in establishing and accumulating the cost of the direct labor incurred in that process. Since the production process is both continual and repetitive in a process costing situation, raw materials flow into the process continuously. Thus, the need for multiple purpose requisitions for materials, such as those required for job order costing, is substantially reduced. The resultant input-output relationships of raw materials to the finished product can usually be fairly well defined and documented in a process costing situation. A degree of control over materials is also available because of the well defined input-output production relationships.

All of these economies are directly related to the nature of the production process. Job order cost systems are established to account for the production of a number of different products with varying inputs of raw materials, direct labor, and overhead. Process costing is used in those circumstances where a limited number of products are produced in large volume by continuous production runs.

THE PRODUCTION COST REPORT

The production cost report serves as the basic document for inventory cost accumulation in a process costing system. A production cost report may be prepared and presented in the same general format as the Cost of Goods Manufactured Statement. The beginning work-in-process inventory plus the additions (materials, labor and overhead) made to work-in-process during the period, less the ending balance in the work-in-process inventory—is the cost of goods manufactured for the period. This relationship or flow is valid for the accountant working with either dollar amounts of cost or units of production. For purposes of process costing, this relationship must be defined in terms of units in order to derive the number of units which were produced during the period. The number of units produced is then divided into the total manufacturing costs for that period to arrive at a cost-per-unit figure. Of course, if there is neither a beginning nor an ending work-in-process inventory, the procedure is greatly simplified. All of the units started during the period would also have been completed. No partially completed units would exist to complicate the computation of number of units produced during the period.

In actual practice, however, the problem of accounting for beginning and ending work-in-process inventories exists in most, if not all, manufacturing situations. In order to deal with this problem, the accountant must calculate the production for the period in terms of the number of *equivalent units* produced. Thus both the beginning and the ending work-in-process inventories must be considered in order to determine the total production for the period.[1]

EQUIVALENT UNITS OF PRODUCTION

Equivalent units of production are measured in terms of the number of whole or completed units of product that could have been produced at the expended cost if every unit worked on had been started and completed during the period. The assumption is made that the effort and cost required to complete one unit, for example, is *equivalent* to having three units one-third complete, hence the term equivalent units. For example, assume that there was no work-in-process inventory at the beginning of a period, and that sufficient materials had been applied to those units included in the ending work-in-process inventory to manufacture exactly 100 complete units of a product. Also assume that if the labor and overhead which was applied to all 100 units included in the ending work-in-process inventory had been used to fully complete units at the normal cost for the period, 40 complete units could have been produced. Given these two assumptions, we can now calculate the number of equivalent units and the production cost per unit for this period.

To calculate these unit costs, we must first determine the equivalent number of units of production which were included in the ending work-in-process inventory. The number of equivalent units in the ending work-in-process inventory is then added to the number of fully-completed units of production for the period to arrive at the total production for the period stated in terms of equivalent whole units of production.

Therefore, in the example cited above, the equivalent units that would be used for the ending work-in-process inventory cost calculation for inventory valuation are 100 units for raw materials, 40 units for direct labor and 40 units for manufacturing overhead calculated as follows:

Manufacturing Cost Component	Number of Units that Could be Completed	Percent of Completion in terms of Cost Incurred at the End of the Period	Number of Equivalent Units
Raw Materials	100	100%	100 Units
Direct Labor	100	40	40
Manufacturing Overhead	100	40	40

[1] The beginning equivalent units do not need to be calculated when using the weighted average technique.

Remember, there are a total of 100 units in the ending work-in-process that could have been completed. To date, however, these units are fully complete only as far as materials are concerned. In terms of direct labor and manufacturing overhead, the 100 units are only 40% complete.

To illustrate the complete calculation of both the equivalent units of production and the cost per unit produced during the period, assume that the following costs were incurred during the current accounting period.

Cost Calculation

Total Direct Material Costs	$ 6,000
Total Direct Labor Costs	4,320
Manufacturing Overhead Applied	2,160
Total Costs of Production	$12,480

Data regarding the units produced are as follows:

Unit Calculation

	Equivalent Units
Beginning Work-In-Process	–0–
Units Completed During the Period	500
Ending Work-In-Process:	
Direct Material 100 Units, 100% Complete	100
Direct Labor 100 Units, 40% Complete	40
Manufacturing Overhead 100 Units, 40% Complete	40

The calculation of cost per unit is presented below:

Per Unit Cost Calculation

	Direct Materials	Direct Labor	Manufacturing Overhead
Total Cost	$6,000	$4,320	$2,160
Finished Units	500	500	500
Equivalent Units Included in Ending Work-In-Process . . .	100	40	40
Total Equivalent Units	600	540	540
Total Cost ÷ Total Equivalent Units	($6,000 ÷ 600) = $10	($4,320 ÷ 540) = $ 8	($2,160 ÷ 540) = $ 4

Cost Per Equivalent Unit . . . $10 (materials) + $8 (labor) + $4 (overhead) = 22

Cost of Goods Completed (500 Units @ $22)		$11,000
Cost of Ending Work-In-Process:		
Raw Materials (100 Units @ $10)	$1,000	
Direct Labor (40 Units @ $8)	320	
Manufacturing Overhead (40 Units @ $4)	160	1,480
Total Cost Accounted For		$12,480

The calculations which are made under a process costing system to compute the number of equivalent units included in the work-in-process inventory are usually not complex. Remember, the intent is to arrive at a unit cost for the production of an equivalent number of fully completed units.

In many firms, manufacturing overhead is applied using some predetermined base, such as direct labor hours or direct labor cost. In this situation, the costs associated with direct labor and manufacturing overhead are usually combined and referred to as *conversion costs*. Under these circumstances, the equivalent units for both direct labor and manufacturing overhead are identical.

A COMPREHENSIVE EXAMPLE: PROCESS COSTING

The production cost report serves as the basic document which is used in a process costing system for developing the inventory cost per equivalent unit. Several factors must be known in order to develop the cost per equivalent unit: (1) the cost and the number of equivalent units associated with the beginning work-in-process inventory; (2) the total manufacturing costs incurred during the period; (3) the number of equivalent units of product associated with the ending work-in-process inventory; and (4) the number of units which were produced during the period. The beginning equivalent units do not need to be calculated when using the weighted average technique because both the costs and units are averaged with the current period's units and costs. The formats which may be used for accumulating costs and calculating equivalent units are developed and presented in the example in the following paragraphs.

Beginning Work-in-Process Inventories

By definition, the beginning inventories of work-in-process under a process costing system consist of only partially completed units. The number of equivalent units and the related costs are identified at the end of the prior accounting period. It is, of course, possible that these costs may vary from one accounting period to the next.

Any inventory valuation method can be applied to the flow of costs under a process costing system. This chapter illustrates two basic methods: the weighted average method and the first-in, first-out (Fifo) method.[2]

---

[2] The Fifo method is illustrated assuming a clearly identifiable Fifo flow. In practice, the typical use of the Fifo method would include an averaging of the cost of goods transferred into a processing department. Cost of goods transferred out of a processing department would be on a Fifo basis.

More Than One Processing Department

If more than a single department is involved in the processing of products, those departments that work on products transferred from other departments must account for an additional input factor; that is, the costs accumulated in and transferred from a prior department or departments.

The initial department (i.e., the one that begins the manufacturing process) accounts for its inputs of raw materials, direct labor, and manufacturing overhead. Subsequent departments may also use additional raw materials, direct labor, and manufacturing overhead as they process the product further. However, all departments other than the one beginning the manufacturing process must consider an additional cost factor—the cost of the inventory which was transferred in from the preceding department. The flow of manufacturing costs is such that the last department that works on the product transfers the *total* cost of the completed products to the finished goods inventory. The cost transferred to the finished goods inventory, then, includes the total cost of the direct materials, direct labor, and manufacturing overhead incurred by all departments in the plant, less any costs associated with the ending work-in-process, plus any costs carried forward from the prior period in the beginning work-in-process. This flow of total costs is the same as was the case in job order systems.

COMPREHENSIVE EXAMPLE: THE BASIC DATA

The Yuke Chemical Division of Sax Company produces a number of chemicals which require similar general processing techniques. One of these chemicals is Floo. Floo is relatively simple to manufacture and store and, therefore, it is produced whenever it is expedient to do so in order to take up any slack in production. Floo is normally manufactured in production runs varying from 1,000 to 20,000 gallons, depending on the storage space available.

Floo is processed in two departments. The first department mixes the raw materials while the second department bleaches the mixed chemical transferred to it from the mixing department. The normal cost incurred to produce one gallon of Floo is presented in Illustration 4-1.

Illustration 4-1
Normal Cost to Make One Gallon of Floo

Mixing Department

Raw Materials (½ Pound @ $.50 Per Pound)	$ .25
Direct Labor (½ Hour @ $4.00 Per Hour)	2.00
Manufacturing Overhead (Applied on a Direct Labor Hour Basis. Predetermined Rate is $6.00 Per Hour)	3.00
Total Normal Cost of Mixing	$ 5.25

Bleaching Department

Raw Materials (½ Pound @ $1.00 Per Pound)............................. $ .50
Direct Labor (1 Hour @ $4.00 Per Hour).................................... 4.00
Manufacturing Overhead (Applied on a Direct Labor
    Hour Basis: Predetermined Rate is $6.00 Per Hour)........................ 6.00
Total Normal Cost of Bleaching.. 10.50
Total Normal Cost of Producing One Gallon of
    Floo ($5.25 + $10.50)... $15.75

All direct materials used in the mixing and bleaching departments are added at the beginning of each process. The actual quantity and cost data worksheets for both the mixing and the bleaching operations in January are presented in Illustration 4–2.

Reviewing the Data

The data included in Illustration 4–2 are used to calculate a unit cost for Floo using (1) the weighted average cost inventory technique and (2) the Fifo inventory technique. The most difficult aspect of these calculations is usually interpreting the available data so as to accurately compute the number of equivalent units, the total cost, and the cost per equivalent unit. The worksheets included in Illustration 4–2, therefore, require further explanation.

Quantity Data for Mixing

The quantity data worksheet summarizes, in terms of the number of units, the work-in-process inventory account. The beginning inventory of 500 gallons, plus the 2,000 gallons started during the period, less the 1,600 gallons completed and transferred to the mixing department gives the ending work-in-process inventory of 900 gallons (500 + 2,000 − 1,600 = 900). Note that the beginning work-in-process inventory of 500 gallons is 100 percent complete as to raw materials (since all materials are added at the beginning of the process), but that this inventory is only 50 percent complete as to direct labor and manufacturing overhead. This is because only half of the necessary labor and overhead costs to complete the units were incurred in the prior period. The same interpretation of percentage of completion may be applied to the ending work-in-process inventory using the information included on the worksheet. This inventory is also 100 percent complete as to materials, and 50 percent complete as to direct labor and manufacturing overhead.

Cost Data for Mixing

The cost data worksheet is used to summarize the costs of each of the three basic elements of manufacturing cost (materials, labor and over-

Illustration 4-2
Yuke Chemical Division Worksheets

Product: *Floo*   Month: *January*

Quantity (Gallons) Data for Mixing

	Gallons	Percentage of Direct Material	Percentage of Direct Labor	Percentage of Manufacturing Overhead Application
Beginning Work-In-Process	500	100%	50%	50%
Add: Gallons Started	2,000			
Total That Could Be Completed	2,500			
Less: Gallons Completed	1,600			
Ending Work-In-Process	900	100%	50%	50%

Cost Data For Mixing

	Direct Material	Direct Labor	Manufacturing Overhead Application	Total Costs
Beginning Work-In-Process	$125	$ 500	$ 750	$ 1,375
Cost Added This Month	500	3,600	5,400	9,500
Totals	$625	$4,100	$6,150	$10,875

Quantity (Gallons) Data for Bleaching

	Gallons—All Transferred from Mixing	Percentage of Direct Material	Percentage of Direct Labor	Percentage of Manufacturing Overhead Application
Beginning Work-In-Process	800	100%	25%	25%
Add: Gallons Transferred From Mixing This Month	1,600			
Total That Could Be Completed	2,400			
Less: Gallons Completed	1,800			
Ending Work-In-Process	600	100%	40%	40%

Cost Data for Bleaching

	Costs Transferred from Mixing	Direct Materials Added	Direct Labor Added	Manufacturing Overhead Applied	Total Costs
Beginning Work-In-Process . .	$4,800	$ 200 *	$ 800	$ 1,200	$7,000
Cost Added This Month . . .	?	800	7,040	10,560	?
Totals	?	$1,000	$7,840	$11,760	?

* Note that the 800 gallons included in the beginning work-in-process inventory in the Bleaching Department have an associated direct materials cost of only $200 although they are 100 percent complete as to materials. Normally, this cost is $400, but the company made a low cost purchase of its normal quality materials in the prior period. This bargain purchase accounts for the reduced cost of the beginning work-in-process inventories as to direct materials.

head) which are described in the quantity worksheet and which have been accumulated in the work-in-process inventory account. In our example, the costs accumulated for the 500 gallons of beginning inventory consist of $125 for direct materials, $500 for direct labor, and $750 for manufacturing overhead. The costs which were added by the mixing department in January included $500 for direct materials, $3,600 for direct labor, and $5,400 for manufacturing overhead (See Illustration 4–2). Direct labor and direct material are actual costs and manufacturing overhead is the normal (applied) cost.

Quantity Data for Bleaching

The bleaching operation takes place in the second department in the production process. Therefore, all of the bleaching department's inventory is initially obtained by transfer from the mixing department. The bleaching department receives the inventory transferred to it from the mixing department and adds additional raw materials, direct labor and manufacturing overhead to this inventory in its processing operations.

The 800 gallons of beginning work-in-process inventory in the bleaching department had been processed by the mixing department in a prior period. All of the raw materials that are to be added to this beginning work-in-process inventory in the bleaching process have already been added, so it is fully complete as to materials from both departments. However, the beginning work-in-process is only 25 percent complete as to the direct labor and manufacturing overhead input factors. The ending work-in-process inventory is 100 percent complete as to direct materials, but only 40 percent complete with regard to both direct labor and manufacturing overhead.

Cost Data for Bleaching

The 800 gallons of beginning work-in-process inventory in the bleaching department had accumulated costs totaling $7,000 as of January 1. The breakdown of this $7,000 cost into its components is given on the worksheet in Illustration 4–2. The $7,000 beginning inventory consists of $4,800 in costs transferred from the mixing department, and $2,200 in costs of direct materials, direct labor and manufacturing overhead applied by the bleaching department in the prior period.

The cost factors which were added to this inventory by the bleaching department during the current month should be carefully reviewed. Note that there is a question mark inserted in the Illustration for those costs which were transferred from the mixing department during the current month (January). The unit cost for the 1,600 gallons which were completed by the mixing department during January and transferred to the bleaching department cannot be entered on the worksheet until the cost calculations for the mixing department are completed. The direct material and direct labor costs added to the product as a result of the bleaching process are actual costs incurred by the bleaching department during January. The cost accumulations for the 1,600 gallons transferred from the mixing department must be completed to arrive at the unit cost per gallon for Floo.

MIXING PRODUCTION COST REPORT: USING THE WEIGHTED AVERAGE TECHNIQUE

The production cost report for the mixing department is prepared using the data included in the worksheets in Illustration 4–2. These data are necessary to prepare this report and could be incorporated as a part of the report. For management purposes, however, this detail is usually unnecessary. The production cost report for the mixing department is presented in Illustration 4–3.

Illustration 4-3
Production Cost Report—Mixing Department

Product: *Floo*   *Costs*   Month: *January*

	Direct Materials	Direct Labor	Manufacturing Overhead Applied	Total Costs
Totals	$625	$4,100	$6,150	$10,875

Equivalent Unit Calculation (Gallons)

	Direct Materials	Direct Labor	Manufacturing Overhead
Units Completed (Gallons)	1,600	1,600	1,600
Ending Work-in-process (900 Gallons):			
Direct Material 100% Complete	900		
Direct Labor 50% Complete . .		450	
Manufacturing Overhead 50% Complete			450
Equivalent Units	2,500	2,050	2,050

Cost Per Equivalent Units

Direct Material . . . . $\dfrac{\$\,625}{2,500} = \$.25$

Direct Labor . . . . $\dfrac{\$4,100}{2,050} = \$2.00$

Manufacturing Overhead . . . . $\dfrac{\$6,150}{2,050} = \$3.00$

Total Cost per Unit $\underline{\$5.25}$ ($.25 + $2.00 + $3.00)

For inventory costing purposes, each unit of inventory transferred from the mixing department to the bleaching department in January carries with it an associated inventory cost of $5.25. In total, the transfers to the bleaching department and the ending work-in-process inventory in the mixing department should equal a total production cost of $10,875. This amount represents the cost of the beginning work-in-process in the mixing department, plus those costs which were added to the production process during January.

Completed (1,600 Gallons @ $5.25)		$ 8,400
Ending Work-In-Process:		
Direct Material (900 Gallons @ $.25)	225	
Direct Labor (450 Gallons @ $2.00)	900	
Manufacturing Overhead (450 Gallons @ $3.00)	1,350	
Total		$10,875

The total costs for the bleaching department for January may now be computed. The cost data for the bleaching department from Illustration 4–2, with the costs transferred from mixing for January ($8,400), are presented in Illustration 4–4.

Illustration 4-4
Yuke Chemical Division Worksheets
Weighted Average Technique

Product: *Floo* Month: *January*

Cost Data For Bleaching

	Costs Transferred From Mixing	Direct Materials Added	Direct Labor Added	Manufacturing Overhead Applied	Total Costs
Work-in-Process— Beginning	$ 4,800	$ 200	$ 800	$ 1,200	$ 7,000
Costs Added This Month	8,400	800	7,040	10,560	26,800
Totals	$13,200	$1,000	$7,840	$11,760	$33,800

BLEACHING DEPARTMENT PRODUCTION COST REPORT: USING THE WEIGHTED AVERAGE TECHNIQUE

The production cost report for the bleaching department shown in Illustration 4–5 is prepared using the data included in the worksheets presented in Illustrations 4–2 and 4–4. Again, this data could be incorporated as a part of the report, but for management purposes, this detail is usually considered unnecessary.

Illustration 4-5
Production Cost Report—Bleaching Department
Weighted Average Technique

Product: *Floo*   Month: *January*

Costs

	Transferred From Mixing	*Direct Materials Added*	*Direct Labor Added*	*Manufacturing Overhead Applied*	*Total Cost*
Totals (Illustration 4–4)	$13,200	$1,000	$7,840	$11,760	$33,800

Equivalent Unit Calculations (Gallons)

	Gallons—All Transferred From Mixing	*Direct Materials*	*Direct Labor*	*Manufacturing Overhead*
Units Completed (Gallons)	1,800	1,800	1,800	1,800
Work-in-Process—Ending 600 Gallons				
Transferred In 100% Complete	600			
Direct Material 40% Complete		600		
Direct Labor 40% Complete			240	
Manufacturing Overhead 40% Complete				240
Equivalent Units	2,400	2,400	2,040	2,040

Cost Per Equivalent Unit

Transferred In Cost . . . . $\dfrac{\$13,200}{2,400} = \$5.50$

Direct Material . . . . $\dfrac{\$1,000}{2,400} = \$.42$ (Rounded)

Direct Labor . . . . $\dfrac{\$7,840}{2,040} = \$3.84$ (Rounded)

Manufacturing Overhead . . . . $\dfrac{\$11,760}{2,040} = \$5.76$ (Rounded)

Total Cost Per Unit $15.52 = ($5.50 + $.42 + $3.84 + $5.76)

The transfers to finished goods from the bleaching department plus the ending work-in-process in bleaching should equal the total production cost for the period of $33,800.

Completed	(1,800 Gallons @ $15.52)		$27,936.00
Work-In-Process—Ending:			
Transferred in	(600 Gallons @	5.50)	3,300,00
Direct Material	(600 ,, @	.42)	252.00
Direct Labor	(240 ,, @	3.84)	921.60
Manufacturing Overhead . .	(240 ,, @	5.76)	1,382.40
Total			$33,792.00 *

* Difference of $8.00 due to rounding.

As is implied by the title, the weighted average technique averages the costs of the beginning work-in-process inventory and the costs added to production during the accounting period on a weighted basis in order to arrive at a cost for the current period.

The costs which were transferred from the mixing department to the bleaching department will be used as an example to illustrate the averaging technique. The beginning work-in-process inventory in the bleaching department (Illustration 4–2) included 800 gallons of Floo that were transferred from the mixing department during a prior period. The cost of the Floo totaled $4,800 or $6.00 per gallon (slightly higher than the normal cost of $5.25). A total of 1,600 gallons was transferred to the bleaching department from the mixing department during January at a cost of $5.25 per gallon. The ending work-in-process inventory in the bleaching department consisted of 600 gallons. The average cost of the 600 gallons transferred to bleaching from the mixing department, which is included in the ending work-in-process on the Production Cost Report—Bleaching Department, is $5.50 per gallon. The calculations which were necessary to arrive at the weighted average figure of $5.50 per gallon are included on the production cost report for the bleaching department (Illustration 4–5).

PRODUCTION COST REPORTS: USING THE FIFO TECHNIQUE

The production cost reports using the Fifo technique of process costing are prepared using the same worksheets presented in Illustration 4–2. In applying the Fifo technique, a clearly identifiable first-in, first-out flow of costs is assumed, and the production costs and related production are accounted for in terms of specific batches of production. The Fifo concept in process costing is best illustrated in this manner. [3]

---

[3] The actual use of Fifo does not require the detailed records that one might initially expect because transfers to a department are averaged and only transfers out are made on a Fifo basis.

Illustration 4-6

Yuke Chemical Division
Production Cost Report—Mixing Department
First-In, First-Out Technique

Product: *Floo* Month: *January*

Costs

	Direct Materials	Direct Labor	Manufacturing Overhead	Total Costs
Costs Added *This Month*	$500	$3,600	$5,400	$9,500

Equivalent Units To Which Costs of This Month Apply

	Direct Materials	Direct Labor	Manufacturing Overhead
Units Completed (Gallons)	1,600	1,600	1,600
Add: Ending Work-in-Process (900 Gallons)			
Direct Material 100% Complete	900		
Direct Labor 50% Complete		450	
Manufacturing Overhead 50% Complete			450
Total Processed	2,500	2,050	2,050
Less: Beginning Work-in-Process (500 Gallons)			
Direct Material 100% Complete	500		
Direct Labor 50% Complete		250	
Manufacturing Overhead 50% Complete			250
Total Equivalent Units Processed *This Month*	2,000	1,800	1,800

Cost Added per Equivalent Unit *This Month*

Direct Material $\dfrac{\$\,500}{2,000} = \$.25$

Direct Labor $\dfrac{\$3,600}{1,800} = \$2.00$

Manufacturing Overhead $\dfrac{\$5,400}{1,800} = \$3.00$

Total Cost Added Per Equivalent Unit—Mixing $\underline{\$5.25} = (\$.25 + \$2.00 + \$3.00)$

Production Cost of Inventory

	Direct Materials	Direct Labor	Manufacturing Overhead	Total
Beginning Work-in-Process	$ 125	$ 500	$ 750	$1,375
Cost Added to Complete This Month				
Direct Materials	–0–			–0–
Direct Labor 250 Gallons @ $2		$ 500		$ 500
Manufacturing Overhead 250 Gallons @ $3			$ 750	$ 750
Total Cost Accumulation for Beginning 500 Gallons . . .				$2,625

Cost per Gallon $2,625 ÷ 500 = $5.25

Inventory Costs under Fifo				
Completed and Transferred (1,600 Gallons)				
First: 500 Gallons @ $5.25				$2,625
Second: 1,100 Gallons @ $5.25				5,775
Ending Work-in-Process—(900 Gallons)				
Direct Material 900 Gallons @ $ .25 . . .	$ 225			
Direct Labor 450 Gallons @ 2.00 . . .	900			
Manufacturing Overhead 450 Gallons @ 3.00 . . .	1,350			2,475
Total Cost Accounted for.				$10,875

Illustration 4-7
Yuke Chemical Division
Production Cost Report—Bleaching Department
First-In, First-Out Technique

Product: *Floo*   Month: *January*

	Direct Materials	Direct Labor	Manufacturing Overhead	Total Costs
Costs Added *This Month*	$800	$7,040	$10,560	$18,400

Equivalent Units to Which Costs of This Month Apply

	Direct Materials	Direct Labor	Manufacturing Overhead
Units Completed ((Gallons)) . . . . (600 Gallons)	1,800	1,800	1,800
Add: Ending Work-in-Process (600 Gallons)			
Direct Material 100% Complete	600		
Direct Labor 40% Complete		240	
Manufacturing Overhead 40% Complete			240
Total Processed	2,400	2,040	2,040
Less: Beginning Work-in-Process (800 Gallons)			
Direct Material 100% Complete	800		
Direct Labor 25% Complete		200	
Manufacturing Overhead 25% Complete			200
Total Equivalent Units Processed *This Month* . .	1,600	1,840	1,840

$$\text{Direct Material} \quad \frac{\$\ 800}{1,600} = \$.50$$

$$\text{Direct Labor} \quad \frac{\$7,040}{1,840} = \$3.83 \text{ (Rounded)}$$

$$\text{Manufacturing Overhead} \quad \frac{\$10,560}{1,840} = \$5.74 \\ \text{(Rounded)}$$

Total Cost Added per Equivalent Unit—Bleaching $10.07 = ($.50 + $3.83 + $5.74)

Production Cost of Inventory

	Transferred from Mixing	Direct Materials	Direct Labor	Total Maufacturing Overhead	Total
Beginning Work-in-Process	$4,800	$200	$ 800	$1,200	$ 7,000
Costs Added to Complete this Month	0				
Direct Materials					
Direct Labor 600 Gallons @ $3.83			$2,298		$ 2,298
Manufacturing Overhead 600 Gallons @ $5.74 . .				$3,444	$ 3,444
Total Cost Accumulation for Beginning 800 Gallons . .					$12,742

Cost Per Gallon $12,742 ÷ 800 = $15.93 (Rounded)
Inventory Costs Under Fifo
Completed and Transferred (1800 Gallons)

First: 800 Gallons @ $15.93					$12,742
Second: 500 Gallons					
Transferred from Mixing	$ 5.25				
Current Costs in Bleaching	10.07				
	$ 15.32 × 500 Gallons				7,660
Third: 500 Gallons					
Transferred from Mixing	$ 5.25				
Current Costs in Bleaching	10.07				
	$ 15.32 × 500 Gallons				7,660

Ending Work-in-Process (600 Gallons)

Transferred from Mixing 600 Gallons @ $5.25 . . .	$3,150.00				
Direct Material 600 Gallons @ $.50 . . .	300.00				
Direct Labor 240 Gallons @ $3.83 . . .	919.20				
Manufacturing Overhead 240 Gallons @ $5.74 . . .	1,377.60				5,746.80

Total Cost Accounted for . . . . $33,808.80 *

* Difference of $8.80 due to rounding.

The Production Cost Reports for the Mixing and Bleaching Departments using the Fifo method are presented in Illustrations 4–6 and 4–7. These reports are more complex than those required for the weighted average technique because the Fifo method requires that individual batches of inventory be accounted for separately. It is assumed that the first costs which were incurred during a period are those which are applicable to the beginning inventory. Any additional costs of the current period are attached to the units started or transferred during this period on a Fifo basis. Any ending work-in-process inventory consists of the units started or transferred in on a Fifo basis.

The key to these calculations lies in determining the cost which was incurred by a department during the current period and in determining the equivalent units to which these costs are attached. Consider the flow of information which is presented in Illustration 4–6.

1. The costs added in January are determined from the worksheet included in Illustration 4–2.
2. The number of equivalent units to which *January's costs* apply is then determined.
3. The production cost of the inventory is calculated. The order of the calculations should be noted. The beginning work-in-process inventory is considered first in terms of the current costs which were necessary to complete that specific batch of inventory.
4. Any inventory completed beyond the beginning work-in-process absorbs or carries the current period's cost per equivalent finished unit.
5. The cost of the ending work-in-process inventory is based on the number of finished equivalent units.
6. The total costs accounted for are calculated to ascertain that all costs incurred have, in fact, been absorbed into the inventory costs.

SUMMARY

Process costing systems are used to accumulate costs in those firms that manufacture uniform products in continuous production runs. Costs are normally accumulated for each process and a production cost report is then prepared at the end of the accounting period for each process. Unit costs are generally calculated using information from these reports.

The basic format of the production cost report resembles the cost of goods manufactured statement. Where no beginning or ending work-in-process inventories exist, the unit cost calculation simply involves dividing total costs by units completed. However, in most process manufacturing systems, beginning and ending inventories do exist and this fact complicates the unit cost calculation significantly.

In calculating the unit cost in a process costing system, it is normally necessary to determine the equivalent units of production. This represents the number of whole or completed units that could have been entirely processed with the materials, labor, and overhead that were actually expended or used up. This computation involves adding the equivalent units in the ending work-in-process to the equivalent units of completed production. The equivalent units of completed production are equal to the actual units completed less the equivalent units in the beginning work-in-process inventory.

Generally, it is necessary to calculate equivalent units for each element of product cost (i.e., direct material, direct labor, and manufacturing overhead). The total cost for each element is then divided by the number of equivalent units for that element to determine the unit element cost. The three unit element costs are then summed to yield a unit cost per equivalent unit of product.

Once the unit cost per equivalent is derived, the firm's normal inventory valuation method is employed to arrive at ending inventory values. The two primary inventory valuation methods used by process manufacturing firms are the weighted average method and the first-in, first-out method.

When more than one production department is involved in manufacturing a product, each department (except the initial processing department) must account for all costs previously incurred in the manufacture of the product. These costs from prior departments are generally referred to as "transferred" costs. The final department involved in the manufacture of the product will then transfer the total cost of the completed product to the finished goods inventory.

This chapter has discussed and illustrated the second of the fundamental cost accumulation systems used for product costing in manufacturing firms. At this point it may be beneficial to review and compare these two basic systems: job order costing and process costing.

KEY DEFINITIONS

Conversion costs—the costs of direct labor and manufacturing overhead incurred in a production process.

Cost data worksheet—summarizes the costs which are accumulated in the work-in-process account for each element of manufacturing cost described in the quantity data worksheet.

Equivalent units of production—a measure in terms of the number of whole or completed units of a product which could have been produced at the actual expended cost.

Process costing system—a cost accounting system in which costs are accumulated by the production process. This system is normally used in manufacturing situations characterized by continuous productions runs of a uniform product.

Production cost report—a report prepared at the end of an accounting period for each production process. It summarizes the amounts of production, total costs of direct materials, direct labor and applied overhead so that the unit cost of production may be calculated.

Quantity data worksheet—summarizes, in terms of units, the work-in-process account and the percentage of completion of each element of manufacturing cost for beginning and ending inventories.

QUESTIONS

1. When is is most appropriate to use a process costing system? May a job-order cost system be used under process costing conditions?

2. What is the purpose of a production cost report and what does it generally include?

3. In relation to requisitioning material, how does a job-order cost system differ from a process costing system?

4. How does the production cost report resemble the cost of goods manufactured statement? How do they differ?

5. Define equivalent units of production. Why are the costs associated with direct labor and manufacturing overhead usually combined when calculating equivalent units?

6. How does the process costing method handle the flow of costs if there is more than a single processing department?

7. What is the purpose of the cost data worksheet?

8. How does the weighted-average technique treat beginning work-in-process?

9. Transferred-in costs are costs which were incurred in a previous department and are now being transferred to another department. How may these transferred-in costs be treated in the latter department?

10. Which of the process costing techniques is the more difficult to apply, weighted-average or Fifo, and why?

11. How can one verify that the correct amount of production costs has been allocated to finished goods?

12. What three factors must be known in order to develop the cost per equivalent unit?

EXERCISES

4-1 Compute the equivalent units produced using the Fifo technique in each of the following independent situations.

		Units
a.	Beginning inventory—50% complete	15,000
	Ending inventory—50% complete	15,000
	Units started	120,000
b.	Beginning inventory—30% complete	72,000
	Ending inventory—75% complete	90,000
	Units transferred out	300,000
c.	Ending inventory—75% complete	42,000
	Units transferred out	78,000
	Units started	102,000
	Beginning inventory—80% complete	?
d.	Units transferred out	108,000
	Beginning inventory—75% complete	33,000
	Units started	90,000
	Ending inventory—45% complete	?

4-2 Compute the equivalent units of production for each element of cost (material, labor, and overhead) in each of the following UNRE-LATED instances: Assume Fifo cost flow.

a. Started into production–12,000 units (no beginning work-in-process); finished and transferred–10,500 units. Ending work-in-process 35%, complete as to direct labor and overhead, 100% complete as to materials.

b. Beginning work-in-process–9,000 units (fully complete as to materials, ⅓ complete as to labor and overhead); started into process–25,000 units; finished and transferred–23,000 units. (The ending work-in-process is ½ complete as to materials; ⅘ complete as to labor and overhead.)

c. Beginning work-in-process–6,000 units (¾ complete as to materials, ½ complete as to labor and overhead); started into production–60,000 units; finished and transferred–50,000 units. (Ending work-in-process is complete as to materials and ⅜ complete as to labor and overhead.)

4-3 The Keyso Company, a manufacturing firm, begins the month of March with 5,000 units in work-in-process. These units are 50% complete as to direct labor and 75% complete as to factory overhead. All raw materials are added at the beginning of the cycle. During the month, 15,500 units are started and 17,000 units are transferred to finished goods. Ending work-in-process is 30% complete as to direct labor and 60% complete as to factory overhead. Compute the equivalent units in ending work-in-process.

4-4   During 1979 the Ace Company completed and transferred to finished stock 100 wigets. The inventory of wigets in process at 1/1/79 totaled 40—they were 75% complete as to materials, 50% complete as to labor and overhead. The company began work on 80 new wigets in 1979; at the end of the year the wigets on hand were 80% complete as to materials; 50% complete as to labor and 40% complete as to overhead. Calculate the equivalent production of wigets (as to materials, labor and overhead) for 1979. Assume Fifo.

4-5   During 1980 the Diamond Company completed and transferred to finished goods a total of 100 wigets. The inventory of wigets-in-process on January 1, 1980 was 20 wigets; they were 60% complete as to conversion costs (all materials are added at the beginning of the process). The company began work on 130 new wigets in 1980. At the end of the year, the wigets on hand were 40% complete as to conversion costs. Assume Fifo cost flow.

Required:

Compute the equivalent units for 1980.

4-6   During April, the Brandon Manufacturing Company incurred the following costs:

$$\begin{array}{ll}
\text{Direct materials} \dots\dots\dots\dots & \$24{,}000 \\
\text{Direct Labor} \dots\dots\dots\dots\dots & 35{,}984 \\
\text{Manufacturing overhead} \dots\dots & 29{,}904
\end{array}$$

Production for April was as follows:
    Beginning work-in-process—0 units
    Units completed—4,000 units
    Ending work-in-process
        Direct materials—2,000 units, 100% complete
        Direct labor—2,000 units, 60% complete
        Manufacturing overhead—2,000 units, 40% complete

Required:

Compute the cost per equivalent unit.

4-7   Womsley Company has 400 units in beginning work-in-process for May. These units are 60% complete as to direct labor and factory overhead. All materials are added at the beginning of the process. During the month, 1,200 units are put into production for the first time. On May 31, there are 300 units still in work-in-process, 35% complete as to direct labor and overhead. Assuming the weighted average technique, compute the equivalent units of production for material, labor, and overhead for May.

4-8   Given the following information, compute the cost of finished goods manufactured.

	Direct Materials	Direct Labor	Manufacturing Overhead
Total cost	$126,000	$132,000	$99,000
Total equivalent units . .	12,600	8,250	8,250

Beginning finished goods inventory . . . . . 4,000 units
Number of units sold . . . . 10,200 units
Ending finished goods inventory . . . . 1,600 units

4–9 Simpson Company produces shoes. It takes two departments to produce these shoes, the Stitching and the Polishing departments. From the information listed below, calculate the total cost per pair of shoes for July (assume weighted average technique).

Polishing Department

Pairs of shoes transferred from Stitching Department 500
Beginning work-in-process (60% complete labor and overhead) . . . 100
Ending work-in-process (40% complete labor and overhead) 200
Material is added at the beginning of the process.

Costs

	Transferred from Stitching	Direct Materials	Direct Labor and Overhead
Total costs	$2,628	$1,350	$1,560

4–10 Assuming the Fifo technique, calculate the total equivalent units that relate to this period's cost under each of the following unrelated assumptions for each element of production cost:

a. Beginning work-in-process—1,500 units (materials are added at the *end* of the process; 60% of labor and 40% of overhead have been added); 8,000 units were put into production during the period. Ending work-in-process inventory consists of 3,500 units (70% complete as to both labor and overhead).

b. Beginning work-in-process—800 units (materials are added at the beginning of the process; 30% of labor and 50% of overhead have been added); 7,000 units were put into production during the period. There is no ending work-in-process inventory.

c. No beginning work-in-process inventory. 1,200 units were put into production during the period. 600 units are still in work-in-process inventory at the end of the period. (Material is added at the *end* of the period, 55% of both labor and overhead have been added.)

4–11 From the information listed below, calculate the total cost per equivalent unit.

	Direct Material	Direct Labor	Overhead Applied
Ending work-in-process:			
Direct material (100% complete)	650		
Direct labor (80% complete)		520	
Manufacturing overhead (80% complete)			520
Units completed	2,200	2,200	2,200
Cost incurred for each area	$1,425	$8,160	$12,240
There is no beginning work-in-process.			

4–12   Using the following division worksheet for the Stick-em Glue Corporation, prepare a production cost report using the weighted average
technique.

Quantity Data for Glue Processing

	Gallons	% of Direct Material	% of Direct Labor	% of Manufacturing Overhead Application
Beginning work-in-process . .	200	100%	60%	50%
Add: gallons started	3,500			
Total which could be completed	3,700			
Less: Gallons completed . . .	3,300			
Ending work-in-process	400	100%	30%	25%

Cost Data for Glue Processing

	Direct Material	Direct Labor	Manufacturing Overhead Applied	Total Costs
Beginning work-in-process . .	$ 40	$ 240	$ 300	$ 580
Actual costs added this month	700	6,600	9,900	17,200
Totals	$740	$6,840	$10,200	$17,780

PROBLEMS SERIES A

4A–1   Given the following information for Stacy, Inc., compute the
equivalent units and the cost per equivalent unit for the month of June
using the weighted average technique.

Production:
Beginning—work-in-process . . . . 20 units
   Direct materials . . . . 80% complete
   Direct labor . . . . 50% complete
   Manufacturing overhead . . . . 40% complete
Units completed . . . . 4,000 units
Ending—work-in-process . . . . 40 units
   Direct material . . . . 60% complete
   Direct labor . . . . 30% complete
   Manufacturing overhead . . . . 25% complete

Costs:
Beginning—work-in-process
   Direct material $96.00
   Direct labor 40.00
   Manufacturing overhead 24.00
Cost added this month:
   Direct material $24,048
   Direct labor 16,008
   Manufacturing overhead 12,006

4A-2 On December 31, 1980, Drippy Pipe, Inc., a manufacturer of plumbing supplies, had an ending work-in-process inventory in Department 1 of 60 faucets. These faucets are 100% complete as to materials, 80% complete as to labor, and 80% complete as to manufacturing overhead with costs of $150, $144, and $60 respectively. During the year, 1,500 faucets were completed and transferred to finished goods. On December 31, 1981, there were 70 units in work-in-process which were 40% complete as to materials, 20% complete as to labor, and 10% complete as to manufacturing overhead. During 1981, costs added to the production process were direct materials of $3,816.80, direct labor of $4,691.20, and manufacturing overhead of $1,896.70. Determine the cost of the inventory transferred to finished goods using the first-in, first-out method.

4A-3 The Frey Company uses a process cost system. At the beginning of the period they had 200 units in process. These units were 25 percent complete as to labor and overhead (all material is added at the beginning of the process). The costs associated with the beginning work-in-process are $180 for materials and $75 for labor and overhead. During the period 1,000 units were completed and transferred to finished goods. The current period costs were $720 for materials and $1,375 for labor and overhead. The ending work-in-process consisted of 400 units which were 75% complete as to labor and overhead.

Required:

Complete the following using Fifo.

a. The equivalent units produced during the period as to materials totaled . . . . _____.
b. The equivalent units produced during the period as to labor & overhead . . . . _____.
c. The total unit cost for the period was (per unit) . . . _____.
d. The total unit cost for the preceding period was (per unit) . . . . _____.
e. The unit cost of the units finished and transferred to finished goods during the period was (per unit) . . . . _____.
f. The number of units started during the period totaled _____.

4A-4 Joyce Company uses a process cost system. At January 1 it had 10 units in process. These units were 60% complete as to labor and overhead. (All material is added at the beginning of the process.) The costs associated with the beginning work-in-process are $90 for materials, $60 for labor and $30 for overhead. During the period 90 units were completed and transferred to finished goods. The current period costs were $1,010 for materials, $900 for labor and $450 for overhead. The ending work-in-process consisted of 20 units which were 30% complete as to labor and overhead.

Required:

Calculate the following, for both the average and the Fifo method:

		Fifo	Average
a.	The equivalent units produced during the period as to materials totaled	_____	_____
b.	The equivalent units produced during the period as to labor and overhead totaled . .	_____	_____
c.	The total unit cost for the period was (per unit)	_____	_____
d.	The total unit cost for the preceding period was (per unit)	_____	_____
e.	The unit cost of the units finished and transferred to finished goods during the period was (per unit)	_____	_____
f.	The number of units started during the period totaled	_____	_____

4A–5 Comfo, Inc., manufactures rocking chairs. These chairs are processed in two departments. In the first department the wood is cut and put together. In the second department the finishing work is done. Given the following information, compute the cost per equivalent unit using the weighted average inventory technique.

Production Data

	Number of Chairs	Percentage of Direct Materials	Percentage of Direct Labor	Percentage of Manufacturing Overhead Application
Cutting Department:				
Work-in-process— beginning	20	100%	50%	50%
Add: Chairs started	480			
Total that could be completed	500			
Less: Chairs completed . . .	490			
Work-in-process—ending . .	10	100	40	40
Finished Department:				
Work-in-process— beginning	30	100	10	10
Add: chairs transferred from cutting this month . .	490			
Total that could be completed	520			
Less: Chairs completed . . .	500			
Work-in-process—ending . .	20	50	25	25

Cost Data

	Cost Transferred from Cutting	Direct Materials	Direct Labor	Manufacturing Overhead
Cutting Department:				
Work-in-process—				
beginning		$ 680	$ 135	$ 80
Cost added this month		16,320	6,534	3,872
Totals		$17,000	$6,669	$3,952
Finishing Department:				
Work-in-process—				
beginning	$1,665	$ 195	$ 54	$ 33
Cost added this month	?	3,120	9,036	5,522
Totals	$?	$ 3,315	$9,090	$5,555

4A–6 Using the same information as given in Problem 4A–5, compute the cost per equivalent unit using Fifo.

4A–7 From the information listed below calculate the value of the ending work-in-process inventory for October using the Fifo method.

1. Beginning work-in-process—1,750—80% complete for material, 30% complete for labor and 40% complete for overhead. Costs were $3,248, $1,338.75, and $2,205, for material, labor, and overhead respectively.
2. Units started into production during October—9,245. Costs added were $21,480.88, $24,556.50, and $29,783.25, for material, labor, and overhead respectively.
3. Ending work-in-process—1,120 units—70% complete for material, and 25% complete for labor and overhead.

4A–8 The Hansen Company uses process cost accounting to determine their cost of goods manufactured. However, the company is undecided as to whether they should use the weighted average or the Fifo method. They prefer the method which gives them the highest cost of goods manufactured for income tax purposes, and they will use this method consistently in the future.

Below is production data for the year ended December 31.

Beginning work-in-process—3,500 units—100% complete for material and 70% complete for conversion costs (labor and overhead).

Finished and transferred to finished goods—32,000 units.

Ending work-in-process—2,100 units—100% complete for material and 60% complete for conversion costs.

Cost Summaries for the Year

Material:	Beginning work-in-process	$ 7,350.00	
	Current costs	68,160.00	$75,510.00
Conversion:	Beginning work-in-process	$ 5,414.50	
	Current costs	$73,280.00	$78,694.50

Required:

Compute the cost of goods manufactured under both the weighted average and the Fifo methods in order that the Hansen Company may choose that method which gives the highest value. Carry costs to the nearest cent.

4A–9 The Caldor Company would like you to calculate their gross profit for the year ended September 30, 1980. You are to use the weighted average method to calculate the company's cost of goods manufactured and the Fifo inventory method to determine their cost of goods sold. Cost and sales data for the year are listed below:

1. Sales for the year equals 4,500 units at $18 a unit.
2. Beginning finished goods inventory consisted of 500 units at $10.25 a piece.
3. Beginning work-in-process inventory contained 475 units, 100% complete as to material, and 52% complete as to labor and overhead. Costs were $1,591.25 for material and $1,712.16 for labor and overhead.
4. Units both *started* and *finished* during the year totaled 5,220 (not including those in beginning work-in-process). Costs added in 1980 were $18,505.40 for material and $37,431.36 for labor and overhead.
5. Ending work-in-process inventory consisted of 320 units, 95% complete for material and 85% complete for labor and overhead.

4A–10 Using the information in problem 4A–9, calculate the gross profit for the Caldor Company using the Fifo method to determine the cost of goods manufactured and the Lifo method to calculate cost of goods sold.

PROBLEMS SERIES B

4B–1 Using the first-in, first-out method of valuing inventories, determine the total equivalent units produced, the cost per unit of the beginning work-in-process and the total cost per unit produced this month from the following information.

Costs:
Beginning—work-in-process:
Direct materials . . . . $ 120.00
Direct labor . . . . $ 153.00
Manufacturing overhead . . . . $ 60.00
Costs added this month:
Direct materials $2,529.60
Direct labor $4,275.00
Manufacturing overhead $2,004.00

Production:
Beginning—work-in-process . . . . 30 units
Direct materials . . . . 80% complete
Direct labor . . . . 60% complete

```
Manufacturing overhead  . . . . . . . .  50% complete
Units completed  . . . . . . . . . . . . . .  500 units
Ending—work-in-process  . . . . . . . . . .  20 units
    Direct materials  . . . . . . . . . . . . . .  100% complete
    Direct labor . . . . . . . . . . . . . . . .  90% complete
    Manufacturing overhead . . . . . . . . . .  80% complete
```

4B–2   On December 31, 1980, Sudsy Floors, Inc., which manufactures commercial and home floor care products, took an inventory of its Wax Division. In particular, they were interested in the Mixing Department. They found that there were 400 gallons of wax in work-in-process. The wax was 100% complete as to materials, 60% complete as to labor, and 60% complete as to manufacturing overhead. Costs accumulated at that time were $200, $144, $72 respectively. During 1981, 21,000 gallons of wax were completed and transferred to the Bottling Department. Costs incurred during 1981 were $10,520 of direct materials, $12,588 of direct labor, and $6,294 of manufacturing overhead. At the end of the year, the 550 gallons in work-in-process were 80% complete as to direct materials and 40% complete as to direct labor and manufacturing overhead.

Required:

Your job is to determine the equivalent units produced in 1981, the cost per equivalent unit, and the total cost transferred to the Bottling Department using the weighted average method.

4B–3   The Ludwig Company uses a process costing system. At the beginning of the period it had 10 units in process which were 40% complete as to labor and overhead (all material is added at the beginning of the process). The costs associated with the beginning work-in-process were $10 as to materials, $6 as to labor and $10 as to overhead. During the period 100 units of product were completed and transferred to finished goods. The current period's costs were $110 for materials, $165 for labor and $275 for overhead. The ending work-in-process consisted of 20 units which were 70% complete as to labor and overhead.

Required:

Compute the following using the weighted average method.

a.   Equivalent units as to materials for the current period were . . . . _____.

b.   Equivalent units as to labor and overhead in the current period were . . . . _____.

c.   The unit cost (total) for the current period was . . . . _____.

d.   The unit cost (total) for the prior period was . . . . . _____.

e.   The unit cost of the units finished and transferred to finished goods during the period was . . . . _____.

f.   The number of units started during the period were . . _____.

4B–4   At January 1, 1980, Nancy Company had a work-in-process inventory of 1,000 units which was 60% complete as to materials and 25% complete as to labor and overhead. The costs associated with this inventory were $720 as to materials and $450 as to labor and overhead. During the period, a total of 8,000 units were completed and transferred to finished goods. The current period's production costs were $12,220 for materials and $16,830 for labor and overhead. The work-in-process inventory at December 31, 1980 consisted of 2,000 units which were 100% complete as to materials and 80% complete as to labor and overhead.

Required:

Calculate the following, for both the weighted average and the Fifo method:

	Fifo	*Average*
a. The equivalent units produced during the period as to materials totaled	_____	_____
b. The equivalent units produced during the period as to labor and overhead totaled . .	_____	_____
c. The total unit cost for the period was (per unit)	_____	_____
d. The total unit cost for the preceding period was (per unit)	_____	_____
e. The unit cost of the units finished and transferred to finished goods during the period was (per unit)	_____	_____
f. The number of units started during the period totaled	_____	_____

4B–5   Your job, as accountant for a blue jean manufacturer, is to determine the cost of one pair of blue jeans produced in April. The jeans go through three departments before they are sold to retail clothing stores in a five state area. In the first department, the jeans are cut out; in the second department, they are sewn; in the third department any labels are attached and the jeans are packaged for shipping since the jeans are sold in standard lots of one dozen jeans of the same size.

Required:

From the following information, compute the cost per equivalent unit using the weighted average inventory technique.

Production Data

	Number of Pairs of Blue Jeans	Percentage of Direct Materials	Percentage of Direct Labor	Percentage of Manufacturing Overhead Application
Cutting Department:				
Work-in-process—beginning	15	100%	80%	80%
Add: Jeans started	560			
Total that could be completed	575			
Less: Jeans completed	555			
Work-in-process—ending . . .	20	100	90	90
Sewing Department:				
Work-in-process—beginning	30	50	50	50
Add: Jeans transferred from cutting this month . . .	555			
Total that could be completed	585			
Less: Jeans completed	570			
Work-in-process—ending . . .	15	40	20	20
Packaging Department:				
Work-in-process—beginning	10	70	80	80
Add: Jeans transferred from sewing this month . . .	570			
Total that could be completed	580			
Less: Jeans completed	576			
Work-in-process—ending	4	25	50	50

Cost Data

	Transferred Costs	Direct Materials	Direct Labor	Manufacturing Overhead
Cutting Department:				
Work-in-process—beginning		$ 37.50	$ 24.00	$ 5.40
Costs added this month		1,400.00	1,122.00	252.45
Totals		$1,437.50	$1,146.00	$257.85
Sewing Department:				
Work-in-process—beginning	$148.50	$ 1.70	$ 63.00	$ 17.00
Costs added this month	?	55.90	2,400.90	556.00
Totals	?	$ 57.60	$2,463.90	$573.00
Packaging Department:				
Work-in-process—beginning	$103.50	$ .35	$ 9.20	$ 3.90
Costs added this month	?	28.50	626.60	285.10
Totals	?	$ 28.85	$ 635.80	$289.00

4B–6   Using the information given in Problem 4B–5, compute the cost per equivalent unit using Fifo.

4B–7   From the information listed below, calculate the value of the ending work-in-process inventory for July using the weighted average method.

Beginning work-in-process—250—25% complete for material, 25% complete for labor, and 90% complete for overhead. Costs were $1,575, $1,825, and $2,310, for material, labor, and overhead respectively.

Units finished and transferred to finished goods during October—765. Costs added were $5,052.80, $5,559.34, and $2,646.15, for material, labor, and overhead respectively.

Ending work-in-process—320—95% complete for material, 35% complete for labor and 40% complete for overhead.

4B–8   The Cooper Company uses the Fifo method to calculate their cost of goods manufactured. The company's cost of goods manufactured in 1980 totaled $269,067, and their net income before taxes using this method equaled $214,000.

Production Data

Work-in-process inventory, 1/1/80—12,000 units. Material is added at the end of the process. Inventory is 65% complete for labor and overhead.
Started during the period—35,000 units.
Work-in-process inventory, 12/31/80—7,500 units—65% complete for labor and 60% complete for overhead.

Cost Summaries for 1980

Material:	Work-in-process, 1/1/80	$ –0–
	Current costs	104,675
Labor:	Work-in-process, 1/1/80	4,704
	Current costs	46,771
Overhead:	Work-in-process, 1/1/80	12,600
	Current costs	121,600

Required:

Using the production data listed above, (a) compute the cost of goods manufactured using the weighted average method, and (b) determine net income using this method of process cost accounting.

4B–9   The Simpleton Company would like you to calculate their gross profit for December. You are to use the weighted average method to calculate the company's cost of goods manufactured and the Lifo method to determine their cost of goods sold. Cost and sales data for the year are listed below:

1.   Sales for December equal 4,500 units at $10.50 a unit.
2.   Finished goods inventory, 12/1. 25 units at $7.40 a piece.
3.   Work-in-process inventory, 12/1. 68 units, 75% complete for materials and 50% complete for conversion costs. Costs were $50.15 for material and $112.20 for conversion costs.
4.   Units finished during the month totaled 5,200 units. Costs added in

December were $16,080.45 for material and $17,711.10 for conversion costs.

5. Work-in-process inventory, 12/31. 268 units, 100% complete for material and 75% complete for conversion costs.

4B–10 Using the information in problem 4B–9, calculate the gross profit for the Simpleton Company using the Fifo method to determine the cost of goods manufactured and the average method to calculate cost of goods sold. Round numbers to the nearest cent.

4B–11 This problem is for the instructor that wants to introduce both normal and abnormal spoilage. Ranka Company manufactures high quality leather products. The company's profits have declined during the past nine months. Ranka has used unit cost data which were developed eighteen months ago in planning and controlling its operations. In an attempt to isolate the causes of poor profit performance, management is investigating the manufacturing operations of each of its products.

One of Ranka's main products is fine leather belts. The belts are produced in a single, continuous process in the Bluett Plant. During the process leather strips are sewn, punched, and dyed. Buckles are attached by rivets when the belts are 70 percent complete as to direct labor and overhead (conversion costs). The belts then enter a final finishing stage to conclude the process. Labor and overhead are applied continuously during the process.

The leather belts are inspected twice during the process: (1) right before the buckles are attached (70 percent point in the process) and (2) at the conclusion of the finishing stage (100 percent point in the process). Ranka uses the weighted average method to calculate its unit costs.

The leather belts produced at the Bluett Plant wholesale for $9.95 each. Management wants to compare the current manufacturing costs per unit with the prices which exist on the market for leather belts. Top management has asked the Bluett Plant to submit data on the cost of manufacturing the leather belts for the month of October. This cost data will be used to evaluate whether modifications in the production process should be initiated or whether an increase in the selling price of the belts is justified. The cost per equivalent unit which is being used for planning and controlling purposes is $5.35 per unit.

The work-in-process inventory consisted of 400 partially completed units on October 1. The belts were 25 percent complete as to conversion costs. The costs included in the inventory on October 1 were as follows:

Leather strips.......	$1,000
Conversion costs....	300
	$1,300

During October 7,600 leather strips were placed in production. A total of 6,800 good leather belts were completed. A total of 300 belts were identified as defective at the two inspection points—100 at the first inspection point (before buckle is attached) and 200 at the final inspection point (after finishing). This quantity of defective belts was considered normal. In addition, 200 belts were removed from the production line when the process was 40 percent complete as to conversion costs because they had been damaged as a result of a malfunction during the sewing operation. This malfunction was considered an unusual occurrence, and consequently, the spoilage was classified as abnormal. Defective (spoiled) units are not reprocessed and have zero salvage value. The work-in-process inventory on October 31 consisted of 700 belts which were 50 percent complete as to conversion costs.

The costs charged to production during October were as follows:

Leather strips.......	$20,600
Buckles............	4,550
Conversion costs....	20,700
	$45,850

Required:

a. In order to provide cost data regarding the manufacture of leather belts in the Bluett Plant to the top management of Ranka Company, determine for the month of October:
   1. The equivalent units for each factor of production.
   2. The cost per equivalent whole unit for each factor of production.
   3. The assignment of total production costs to the work-in-process inventory and to goods transferred out.
   4. The average unit cost of the 6,800 good leather belts completed and transferred to finished goods.
b. If Ranka Company decided to repair (rework) the 300 defective belts which were considered normal spoilage, explain how the company would account for the rework costs.

(CMA, adapted)

Learning Objectives

Chapter 5 examines the methods and procedures used in allocating joint product costs. Studying this chapter should enable you to:

1. Differentiate between joint products and by-products.
2. Discuss and apply the methods of allocating joint costs to products.
3. Identify and discuss the methods of accounting for the revenues from the sale of by-products under both certain and uncertain market conditions.

5

Cost Accounting for Inventories: Joint and By-Products

Due To the nature of a number of products and/or production processes involved, it is impossible to manufacture certain products without obtaining additional products from the production process. For example, when crude oil is processed the refiner obtains a combination of gasoline, kerosene, fuel oil, naptha, lubricating oil and numerous additional products. It is important to note that the refiner does not have a choice in deciding which of these products will be produced; they are all generated in the refining process. Under most circumstances, gasoline is the most profitable of these products, but in order to obtain gasoline, the other products must also be produced. However, the product mix or proportion of the products may be—and is—altered by the refiner within limitations.

When a packing house slaughters a steer, various cuts of meat with different sales values are obtained. These assorted cuts are basically different products. In addition, other products, such as hides, bone meal, glue, and grease, are also obtained from the steer.

The cost accumulation problem which results when more than a single major product is obtained from a manufacturing process is referred to as a joint or common cost problem. It is important to note that, of necessity, joint costs are assigned or allocated to products for inventory costing purposes by the use of an arbitrarily selected basis for the allocation. This allocation process is discussed in this chapter.

NATURE OF THE PRODUCTS OBTAINED FROM A JOINT PROCESS

Outputs of a joint cost manufacturing process, either in the form of joint raw materials, joint processing or both, are categorized for accounting purposes as either joint products or as by-products. Joint products are the *major* products which are obtained from a joint cost production process. It is anticipated that these products will make a significant contribution to the revenues of the firm. In general, joint products are those products usually considered to be the most desirable ones obtained from the production process. If it were possible, only joint products would be produced in most circumstances.

By-products represent those products obtained from the manufacturing process which are not usually of major importance or significance to the firm. Therefore, by definition, by-products are less important than joint products. The production of by-products is the natural result of the process undertaken to obtain the joint products. In comparison to the revenues generated by the sale of the joint products, by-product sales make a relatively minor contribution to revenues. This characteristic is helpful in classifying by-products. Such factors as small quantities of production, low per unit sales prices, or a combination of these and other factors are also measures considered in classifying a by-product. It is possible, however, in some circumstances that the total revenues which are realized from the sale of by-products of the production process may be substantial.

The exact point at which a distinction is made between a joint product and a by-product cannot always be identified or defined with precision. For inventory costing purposes, a manufacturing concern with substantial joint costs must make this distinction using the best judgment available, given the circumstances at hand.

JOINT PRODUCT COSTS

In every joint manufacturing process, there is some point where two or more co-products are physically identifiable as separate and distinct products. This point is usually referred to as the split-off point or the point of separation. In practice, there are numerous split-off points where various products become identifiable at different stages or points in the manufacturing process.

The costs incurred prior to the split-off point cannot be directly traced to any single product. Therefore, they are handled or accounted for as joint costs. Costs incurred after the split-off point which are attributable to the further processing of a physically identifiable product are not considered joint costs. Rather, these costs are treated as separate costs or further processing costs traceable to the specific product involved.

JOINT COST ALLOCATION TO JOINT PRODUCTS

The joint costs incurred in manufacturing products are *entirely* absorbed by those joint products produced in the manufacturing process. If all of the output produced from a joint cost process is sold in the period in which it is produced, no allocation of costs is necessary for inventory costing purposes. Because all of the products were sold in the period in which they were produced there are no finished goods inventories on hand at the end of the period. However, this is not usually the case.

The allocation techniques used for distributing joint costs fall into two major categories: (1) allocation based on physical measures and (2) allocation based on relative sales value measures. Remember that only joint costs are allocated; any separable costs that may be identified with the further processing of a specific product are absorbed into the cost of that particular product.

JOINT COST ALLOCATION BY PHYSICAL MEASURES

Joint costs are frequently allocated to joint products using a physical measure such as pounds, tons, or gallons. This method of allocation assumes that all units of the product, irrespective of the physical measure used, have identical manufacturing costs.

To illustrate the physical measure basis of joint cost allocation to joint products, assume that the Avalon Division of Sax Company has a manufacturing process from which a maximum of four chemicals may be obtained. Assume also that these chemicals are all considered to be joint products. Avalon has calculated the costs for this process for the month of February. These costs and the resultant outputs are presented and described in the diagram included in Illustration 5-1.

Avalon does not have a choice with regard to the production of either Chemical A or Chemical B. These two chemicals are the natural outputs of Process One, the initial production process. Chemical A is not processed further by Avalon. Chemical B may be further processed to yield Chemical C and Chemical D. Once Process Two is begun for Chemical B, Chemicals C and D are the natural outputs of this second production process.

In Illustration 5–1, the mathematical relationships between the inputs, outputs, costs and sales values remain proportionately the same irrespective of the quantity of inputs introduced into the production process (within the relevant range). Not all of Chemical B will always be processed further, although under most circumstances it is normally more profitable for the firm to undertake the additional processing. The sales value of Chemical B in the Illustration is $1,800. The combined

Illustration 5-1
Production Process of the Avalon Division

sales value of Chemicals C and D is $3,375. Therefore, for an additional expenditure of $1,350 made in Process Two, an additional $1,575 ($3,375 — $1,800) in revenue is obtained. A major reason Chemical B may not be processed further is the market demand for Chemicals C and D. If the demand for Chemicals C and D is considered insufficient, then Chemical B will be sold without further processing. (There is always a demand fo Chemical B.) An additional reason for not processing Chemical B further is that the extra profit made possible producing Chemicals C and D may not warrant sacrificing the processing time which could instead be used to produce additional units of Chemicals A and B.

Assume that during February only Chemical A, Chemical C and Chemical D were produced (i.e. All of Chemical B produced was processed into Chemicals C and D.) The joint costs assigned or allocated to Chemical A might be determined at the split-off point of Process One, based on the ratio of the number of gallons of A to the total number of gallons produced in Process One.

Chemical	Gallons Produced	Proportion to Total Gallons		Allocated Joint Cost	Cost per Gallon	
A........	600	($\frac{600}{2,400}$) or	25%	$ 600	($\frac{\$\ 600}{600}$) or	$1
B........	$\frac{1,800}{2,400}$	($\frac{1,800}{2,400}$) or	$\frac{75\%}{100\%}$	$\frac{1,800}{\$2,400}$	($\frac{\$1,800}{1,800}$) or	$1

Chemical A absorbs production costs in February totaling $600 or $1 for each gallon produced. Chemical A has a sales value of $5 per gallon. At this point, if it were not processed further, Chemical B would also have an assigned production cost of $1 per gallon. The sales value of Chemical B is only $1 per gallon. This allocation of joint production cost is, of course, arbitrary. Avalon cannot obtain Chemical A without also obtaining Chemical B. Chemical A is carried in the accounts at a cost of $1 for inventory costing purposes, an amount which is only 20 percent of its sales value. If Chemical B were not processed further, it would have an assigned production cost of $1 per gallon which is equal to its selling price. From an accounting standpoint, therefore, Avalon could not sell Chemical B at a profit. The failure to consider a per unit selling price is a major weakness of the physical measure basis of cost allocation in a joint cost situation.

Chemical C and Chemical D are assigned a cost based on February production and the costs which are subsequently incurred in Process Two. Thus, in total they are assigned a cost of $3,150; this cost is comprised of $1,800 (the cost of Chemical B determined from Process One) plus $1,350 (the costs of Process Two which are traceable to Chemicals C and D). From a production standpoint, Chemical B must be produced before Process Two can be initiated to obtain Chemicals C and D.

Chemical	Gallons Produced	Proportion to Total Gallons		Allocated* Joint Cost	Cost per Gallon	
C........	900	($\frac{900}{1,800}$) or	50%	$1,575	($\frac{\$1,575}{900}$) or	$1.75
D........	$\frac{900}{1,800}$	($\frac{900}{1,800}$) or	$\frac{50\%}{100\%}$	$\frac{1,575}{\$3,150}$	($\frac{\$1,575}{900}$) or	$1.75

*Total joint cost consists of $1,800 from Process One and $1,350 from Process Two or an aggregate amount of $3,150.

Under these conditions, Chemical C absorbs a production cost of $1.75 per gallon. This product has a sales price of $2.00 per gallon. Chemical D has both a production cost and a sales value of $1.75 per gallon.

The total production costs and sales values of Chemicals A, C, and D for February may be summarized in the following table.

Chem- ical	Gallons Pro- duced	Production Cost per Gallon	Total Production Cost	Sales Value per Gallon	Total Sales Value	Total Gross Profit
A	600	$1.00	$ 600	$5.00	$3,000	$2,400
C	900	1.75	1,575	2.00	1,800	225
D	900	1.75	1,575	1.75	1,575	0
	2,400		$3,750		$6,375	$2,625

Note that Chemical A has the highest profit margin (unit selling price of $5.00 less unit cost of $1.00 or a profit of $4.00 per unit). Chemical C, however, is only marginally profitable ($2.00 per unit selling price less $1.75 per unit cost for a profit of $.25 per unit), and Chemical D yields no accounting profit margin ($1.75 per unit selling price less $1.75 per unit cost for no profit). Remember that it was impossible to obtain any one product without obtaining the others, particularly Chemicals C and D which both result if Chemical B is processed further. Therefore, any managerial analysis of profitability which is made on the basis of cost accumulation data for inventory valuation is useless in a joint cost production process because of the arbitrary nature of the joint cost allocation process. However, it should be emphasized that the *total* gross profit amounting to $2,625 (total revenues minus total costs) would not change regardless of the cost allocation method used.

JOINT COST ALLOCATION BY RELATIVE SALES VALUES

The relative sales value approach to the allocation of joint costs assumes that each joint product absorbs a portion of the joint costs proportional to the ability of that product to generate revenues. The result of this approach is to assign to those products with higher sales values a proportionately higher amount of the joint costs. Note that this allocation process results in generating the same percentage of profit for each joint product.

As long as sales values are known at the split-off points and there are no separable processing costs, the relative sales value method or technique yields proportional profit percentages for joint products. If sales values are not obvious at the split-off points, the accountant, with the assistance of other members of the management team, must estimate a sales value for the joint products in order to make cost allocations using the relative sales value technique.

Allocation When Sales Values Are Known at Split-Off Points

As indicated in Illustration 5-1, the sales values of Chemicals A and B were known at the split-off point. Chemical A has a total sales value of $3,000 and Chemical B has a total sales value of $1,800. The joint cost of producing these two Chemicals is $2,400. The joint cost, using the relative sales value technique, may be allocated in two different ways. Both approaches will yield the same results.

1. *Percent of Relative Sales to Total Sales*

Chemical	Sales Value	Sales Value to Total Sales	Percent of Sales Value
A.............	$3,000	$3,000/$4,800	62.5%
B.............	1,800	$1,800/$4,800	37.5
	$4,800		100.0%

÷   *Joint Cost Allocation*

Chemical	Joint Cost Allocation	Gallons Produced	Cost per Gallon
A..............	$1,500	600	$2.50
B..............	900	1,800	.50
	$2,400	2,400	

2. *Percent of Joint Cost to Total Sales Value*

$$\frac{\text{Joint Cost}}{\text{Total Sales Value}} = \frac{\$2,400}{\$4,800} = 50\%$$

Chemical	Sales Value	Cost to Sales Value Percentage	Joint Cost Allocation	Gallons Produced	Cost per Gallon
A.........	$3,000	50%	$1,500	600	$2.50
B.........	1,800	50	900	1,800	.50
	$4,800	100%	$2,400	2,400	

If both Chemicals A and B were sold at this point, they would yield equally profitable gross margins on a percentage basis, as indicated previously. The following computations support this conclusion.

Chemical A				Chemical B		
	Amount	Percent			Amount	Percent
Sales Value..........	$3,000	100%		Sales Value..........	$1,800	100%
Cost of Goods Sold....	1,500	50		Cost of Goods Sold....	900	50
Gross Margin.........	$1,500	50%		Gross Margin.........	$ 900	50%

If Chemical B were processed further in order to obtain Chemicals C and D, the joint costs that Chemicals C and D would absorb would consist of $900 from Process One and $1,350 from Process Two. The allocation made to Chemicals C and D, using the relative sales value approach, would follow the same principles which are applied to Chemicals A and B in allocating the joint costs which were incurred in Process One.

Percent of Joint Cost to Total Sales
Chemical C and Chemical D
(assuming that Chemical B was processed further)

$$\frac{\text{Joint cost } \$900 + \$1,350}{\text{Total Sales Value*}} = \frac{\$2,250}{\$3,375} = 66.667\%$$

$$
\begin{array}{llll}
* \text{ C} & = 900 \text{ Gallons @ } \$2.00 & = & \$1,800 \\
 \text{ D} & = 900 \text{ Gallons @ } \$1.75 & = & \underline{1,575} \\
& & & \$3,375
\end{array}
$$

Chemical	Sales Value		Cost to Sales Value Percentage		Joint Cost Allocation		Gallons Produced		Cost per Gallon
C........	$1,800	✗	66.667%	=	$1,200	÷	900	=	$1.333
D........	1,575		66.667%		1,050		900		1.167
	$3,375				$2,250		1,800		

If Chemicals C and D were sold at this point, these products would
yield the same gross margin on a percentage basis, as demonstrated by
the calculations which follow.

Chemical C	Amount	Percent		Chemical D	Amount	Percent
Sales Value..........	$1,800	100.000		Sales Value..........	$1,575	100.000
Cost of Goods Sold....	1,200	66.667		Cost of Goods Sold....	1,050	66.667
Gross Margin.........	$ 600	33.333		Gross Margin.........	$ 525	33.333

Allocation When Sales Values are Unknown at Split-Off Point

The accountant must compute the approximate sales values at split-off
points when the joint products are not readily marketable at that point
in time. If the joint products are marketable, but management chooses to
process these products further rather than to sell them at the split-off
point, then the actual market (sales) value of the joint products at split-
off should be used in allocating the joint cost. This was the procedure
followed in the previous example.

Now, let us assume that all of the factors presented in Illustration 5–1
for the Avalon Division are identical, except that Chemical B does not
have a market value at the split-off point. The information in Illustration
5–1 is presented again in Illustration 5–2 for ease of this analysis. Illustration 5–2 has taken into consideration the fact that there is no current
market, and therefore no readily determinable sales value for Chemical B.

Since the relative sales value for Chemical B at the split-off point is
not known, the allocation process requires two steps.

1. Estimating the sales value for Chemical B.
2. Allocating the joint cost of $2,400 for Chemical A and Chemical B
    using the relative sales value technique for product costing.

For product costing purposes, the approximate sales value of Chemical B at the split-off point is determined by working backwards from the point at which Chemical B does become marketable due to additional processing. For the Avalon Division, this is the point at which Chemicals C and D become marketable as finished products. The calculations necessary to compute the approximate sales value for Chemical B are as follows:

Sales Value of Chemical C (900 Gallons @ $2.00)..............................	$1,800
Add: Sales Value of Chemical D (900 Gallons @ $1.75).........................	1,575
Total Sales Value..	$3,375
Deduct: Further Processing Costs Beyond Split-Off Point (Process Two)...........	1,350
Approximate Market Value of Chemical B at Split-Off Point....................	$2,025

The allocation of the joint costs incurred in Process One between Chemicals A and B follows.

Percent of Joint Cost to Total Sales

$$\frac{\text{Joint Costs}}{\text{Total Sales Value*}} = \frac{\$2,400}{\$5,025} = 47.76\% \text{ (rounded)}$$

$$
\begin{array}{rl}
* \ \text{Chemical A} = & \$3,000 \\
\text{Chemical B} = & \underline{2,025} \\
& \$5,025
\end{array}
$$

Chemical	Sales Value	Cost to Sales Value Percentage	Joint Cost Allocation	Gallons Produced	Cost per Gallon
A.........	$3,000	47.76%	$1,433	600	$2.388
B.........	2,025	47.76%	967	1,800	.537
	$5,025		$2,400	2,400	

In practice, the relative sales value technique is used more frequently than the physical measure methods. Possibly, this is due to a desire on the part of the accountants involved to value the inventory so as to represent the relative income-generating ability of the various items of inventory.

ACCOUNTING FOR BY-PRODUCTS

From an accounting standpoint, by-products which are not processed further should absorb no production costs. All production costs are allocated to and absorbed by the joint products. Thus, by-products do not have an associated accounting cost in the sense that joint products do. However, any revenue from by-product sales is recognized for accounting purposes.

There are numerous methods used in accounting for the revenues real-

Illustration 5-2
Production Process of the Avalon Division

ized from the sale of by-products. Two approaches based on the potential demand for the by-products are as follows:

1. Accounting treatment of by-product revenues when a known market price for the by-product exists.
2. Accounting treatment of by-product revenues when there is an uncertain market price for the by-products.

In either of the cases mentioned above, the net revenues to be received from the sale of by-products are treated as a reduction of the cost of goods sold or as other income for income statement purposes.

By-Products with a Ready Market

If by-products have a known market price, the cost of goods sold for a given accounting period may be reduced by the *expected* net revenues which will be obtained or realized from the sale of the by-products which were *manufactured* during that period. An alternative treatment is to recognize the net revenues to be realized from the sale of the by-products produced during the period as other income of that period.

To illustrate the accounting treatment of by-products with a ready market, assume that the Avalon Division decided to produce only Chemicals A and B during the month of February. The output of the production process includes 50 gallons of a marketable by-product, Chemical X, which may be sold at a price of $.80 per gallon. The costs of selling Chemical X are approximately $.10 per gallon. Avalon uses the relative sales value technique in order to allocate the joint costs to its joint products, Chemical A and Chemical B. There are no beginning inventories of either the joint products or the by-products. Three-fourths of February's production of Chemicals A, B, and X were sold during February. The data for the allocation of the $2,400 in joint costs which were incurred to produce the joint products, Chemicals A and B, was presented in Illustration 5-2.

The important points to note in Illustration 5-3 are the alternative income statement treatments and the related inventory values for balance sheet purposes at the end of February.

Illustration 5-3
Avalon Division
By-Products With a Ready Market

	Actual Production			Actual Sales		
	Gallons	Production Cost per Gallon	Production Cost in Total	Gallons Sold	Sales Price per Gallon	Total Sales
Chemical A......	600	$2.50	$1,500	450.0	$5.00	$2,250
Chemical B......	1,800	.50	900	1,350.0	1.00	1,350
Chemical X......	50	0	0	37.5	.80	30
	2,450		$2,400	1,837.5		$3,630

Anticipated Net Revenues *from By-Product Produced*

Anticipated Revenues...............	50 X	$.80 =	$40
Less: Selling Costs..................	50 X	.10 =	5
Net Revenues Anticipated...........	50 X	$.70 =	$35

Income Statement for February

	By-Product Net Revenues Treated as Reduction of Cost of Goods Sold	By-Product Net Revenues Treated as Other Income
Sales (Joint Products from *Actual Sales*).............	$3,600	$3,600
Income from the Sale of By-Products*..............	-0-	35
Total Sales and Other Income....................	$3,600	$3,635
Less: Cost of Goods Sold		
Chemical A $2.50 X 450 = $1,125		
Chemical B $ .50 X 1,350 = $ 675		
$1,800		1,800
Net Revenues From Chemical X Production (35) 1,765		
Gross Margin.....................................	$1,835	$1,835

*The income from the sale of by-products would normally appear after income from operations on a multiple step income statement.

Ending Inventory Values On the
February 28 Balance Sheet

	Gallons	Production Cost per Gallon	Valuation at Net Revenue	Total
Chemical A.......	150.0	$2.50		$375.00
Chemical B.......	450.0	.50		225.00
Chemical X.......	12.5	0	$.70	8.75
				$608.75

In arriving at the net revenues anticipated from by-product sales in Illustration 5–3, note that selling costs were deducted from the anticipated revenues. It is not uncommon for a firm to incur further processing costs, as well as handling, storage and delivery charges for its by-products, and any costs that can be specifically identified with the by-products are deducted from the anticipated revenues in order to arrive at net revenues.[1]

By-Products with an Uncertain Market

If by-products do not have a ready market, the cost of goods sold for a given accounting period is reduced by the *actual* net revenues obtained from the *sale* of the by-products during that period. Once again, an alternative treatment is to recognize the net revenues from the sale of by-products as other income in the period of sale. Any ending inventory of by-products has no associated cost, i.e. carrying value for balance sheet purposes. The uncertainty of marketability requires that the accountant wait until the by-product is actually sold before any formal recognition of revenue is made in the accounts. The alternate income statement treatments and the related inventory values for the February balance sheet (assuming that Chemical X is considered to be a by-product with an uncertain market) are presented in Illustration 5–4.

Illustration 5-4
Avalon Division
By-Products With an Uncertain Market

	Actual Production			Actual Sales		
	Gallons	Production Cost per Gallon	Production Cost in Total	Gallons Sold	Sales Price per Gallon	Total Sales
Chemical A......	600	$2.50	$1,500	450.0	$5.00	$2,250
Chemical B......	1,800	.50	900	1,350.0	1.00	1,350
Chemical X......	50	0	0	37.5	.80	30
	2,450		$2,400	1,837.5		$3,630

[1] The net revenues anticipated represent what is also referred to as the net realizable value.

Actual Revenues *from By-Product Sold*

Actual Revenues..............	(37.5 X $.80)	=	$30.00
Less: Selling Costs...........	(37.5 X .10)	=	3.75
Actual Net Revenues...........................			$26.25

Income Statement for February

	By-Product Net Revenues Treated as Reduction of Cost of Goods Sold	By-Product Net Revenues Treated as Other Income
Sales (Joint Products from *Actual Sales*)............ $3,600.00		$3,600.00
Income from the sale of By-Products................ -0-		26.25
Total Sales and Other Income.................... $3,600.00		$3,626.25
Less: Cost of Goods Sold		
Chemical A $2.50 X 450 = $1,125.00		
Chemical B $ .50 X 1,350 = 675.00		
$1,800.00		1,800.00
Net Revenues from Chemical X Sales (26.25) 1,773.75		
Gross Margin................................. $1,826.25		$1,826.25

Ending Inventory Values on the February 28 Balance Sheet

	Gallons	Production Cost per Gallon	Total
Chemical A.......	150.0	$2.50	$375.00
Chemical B.......	450.0	.50	$225.00
Chemical X.......	12.5	0	0
			$600.00

The difference in accounting for those by-products with a ready market and accounting for those by-products with an uncertain market is significant. With a ready market value for the by-products, revenue is recognized as the by-products are produced. Inventories of the by-products are carried in the accounts at their net realizable value. With an uncertain by-product market value, revenues are recognized only as the by-products are actually sold. In this latter case, the inventories of by-products do not absorb any costs of production and, therefore, have no accounting values for balance sheet purposes. These differences can be identified by comparing Illustration 5–3 with Illustration 5–4.

SUMMARY

Because of their very nature, certain manufacturing processes result in the production of more than a single product. When this occurs, it is necessary to allocate the common costs of production on some arbitrary basis in order to arrive at inventory costs for the various products. The manner in which these costs are allocated depends, in part, on the nature of the products produced.

The two basic types of products produced in a joint cost manufacturing process are joint products and by-products. Joint products are the main objectives of the production process and as such are the desirable products that normally make a significant contribution to the revenues of a firm. By-products, on the other hand, are inadvertent results of the production process. They are, therefore, generally of little importance to the firm and make only a nominal contribution to the firm's revenues.

The common costs that must be allocated are referred to as joint product costs and include all costs incurred prior to the split-off point or point of separation. In the case of joint products, joint costs are usually allocated on the basis of physical measures or relative sales value measures. When the physical measures allocation method is used, the costs are distributed uniformly according to some common physical unit, such as pounds, tons, or gallons. Alternatively, with the relative sales value approach, each product is assigned a cost proportionate to its ability to generate revenues.

When the relative sales value of each joint product is known at the split-off point, the allocation process is as follows: assign to each product the percentage of the total joint costs to the total sales value at split-off, times the relative sales value of the given product. Alternatively, each product can be assigned joint costs equal to the total joint costs multiplied by the ratio of relative sales value of each product to the total sales value of all products.

When the relative sales values at the split-off point are unknown, the accountant must work backwards from the point at which relative sales values are known in order to approximate the value at the split-off point. This is generally accomplished by subtracting further processing costs from the relative sales values at the latter point and then assuming that the result is equal to the relative sales values at the split-off point.

From an accounting standpoint, it is assumed that by-products do not absorb any joint product costs (all such costs are absorbed by the major or joint products). The accounting treatment of revenues from the sale of by-products differs according to whether or not a ready market exists for the product and whether the firm wishes to account for the revenues on the income statement as a reduction of the cost of goods sold for the accounting period or as other income for the period.

The primary difference in the treatments discussed lies in the timing of the recognition of the revenues. In the case of ready markets, the expected net revenues to be generated by the sale of the by-products are recognized as a reduction of the cost of goods sold or as other income as the products are produced. Where no ready market exists, net revenues are recognized as a reduction of the cost of goods sold or as other income only as the by-products are actually sold.

Finally, the various inventory cost accounting methods for joint products and by-products are of great significance to management. Since pricing policies are partially a function of cost, the cost accounting method used may significantly affect a firm's potential revenues and profits.

KEY DEFINITIONS

By-products—products produced by the production process as a natural result of obtaining the more desirable joint products. By products are not the main objectives of the production process and are not a major revenue source for the firm.

Joint costs—costs of the production process which are incurred prior to the split-off point and which cannot directly be traced to any single product.

Joint products—major products which are the output of a single production process and which are normally expected to make a significant contribution to revenues of the firm.

Net realizable value—revenue which is anticipated or estimated for the sale of a product less any expense associated with the sale.

Separable or further processing costs—costs incurred after the split-off point which are attributable to the further processing of a physically identifiable product. These costs are traceable to the specific product for which they were incurred.

Split-off point or point of separation—the point during a joint manufacturing process where two or more products are physically identifiable as separate and distinct products.

QUESTIONS

1. Define joint products and by-products.
2. Explain the split-off point.
3. How are costs treated before and after the split-off point?
4. What allocation techniques can be used for distributing joint costs?
5. Explain what is meant by allocating joint costs using a physical measure.
6. Explain what is meant by allocating joint costs using relative sales value.
7. What is required when the relative sales value for a product is not known at the split-off point?
8. Which technique, the relative sales value or the physical method, is more frequently used in practice to allocate joint costs? Why?
9. What two approaches are used in accounting for the revenues realized from the sale of by-products?
10. What is the effect on the income statement if by-products have a ready market?

11.   What is the effect on the income statement if by-products do not have a ready market?

EXERCISES

5-1   Stevenson Company produces three products; Alpha, Beta, and Gamma. All three products are initially put into process at the same time in Department A, and in this process, joint costs of $5,600 are incurred. Alpha is further processed in Department B, incurring $2,400 in additional costs. Beta and Gamma are further processed in Department C, incurring joint costs of $3,200. Beta and Gamma are then finished in separate departments (Departments D and E) where they incur additional costs of $300 and $500 respectively. In the month of April, 2,000 gallons of Alpha, 2,500 gallons of Beta, and 3,200 gallons of Gamma were produced. Alpha sells for $1.50 per gallon; Beta, $3.25 per gallon; and Gamma $2.75 per gallon.

Required:

Diagram the costs and outputs of this total process for the month of April.

5-2   ABC Company produces two joint products, Alpha and Beta, and a by-product Gamma. Alpha sells for $20,000, Beta sells for $30,000 and Gamma sells for $1,000. The production process costs $15,000.

Required:

Using the relative sales value, allocate the joint costs.

5-3   Samson Oil, Inc. uses a manufacturing process from which three products are obtained. The joint costs incurred to produce 24,000 gallons of Product One, 18,000 gallons of Product Two, and 18,000 gallons of Product Three are $141,000. The products sell for $2.80, $3.60, and $2.30, respectively.

Required:

Allocate the joint costs using the physical measures. Is this a good method of allocation? Why?

5-4   Gree-Dee, Inc. has two products, Gamma and Sigma which sell for $28 and $35, respectively. These two products are the natural result of one production process. The company incurs joint cost of $22,400 to produce 5,000 units of Gamma and 4,000 units of Sigma.

Required:

Allocate the joint cost using the relative sales value method.

5-5   Yason and Sons Chemical Company has two joint products, XYZ and JXL, and a by-product ABC. During 1980, 25,000 units of XYZ, 30,000 units of JXL and 400 units of ABC were produced. Allocated joint costs for XYZ were $3.30 per unit and $4.80 for JXL. Selling prices were $5.50,

$8.00, and $.75, respectively. Selling costs for ABC were $.12 per unit. During 1980, 18,900 units of XYZ, 26,200 units of JXL, and 400 units of ABC were sold.

Required:

Determine the gross margin by treating the net revenues from the by-product as (a) a reduction of cost of goods sold, and (b) other income.

5-6 The Starnes Chemical Company has two products, R and S, which are the natural output of their production process. This process, which costs $42,000, produces 10,000 gallons of R and 11,000 gallons of S. They sell for $35,000 and $49,000, respectively.

Required:

a. Allocate the production costs to R and S using the relative sales value.
b. If S can be further processed for $15,000 to produce T and U which sell for $40,000 and $70,000 respectively, use the relative sales value approach to allocate these costs.

5-7 The Cogwell Company produces two products in a joint process. Material, labor, and overhead for the month of October in this process were $2,025, $2,592, and $2,349 respectively. Product J sold for $4,500 and Product N sold for $3,600.

Required:

Allocate material, labor, and overhead joint costs to products J and N using the relative sales value method.

5-8 Consider the data listed below involving joint product costs.

1. Two products produced from the same process, Pro and Con.
2. Joint costs were $366,400.
3. 6,000 pecks of Pro and 8,800 bushels of Con were produced during the period.
4. Pro sells for $25 per peck and Con sells for $33 per bushel.
5. Beginning inventory included 200 pecks of Pro costing $18.00 per peck and 616 bushels of Con costing $23.00 per bushel.
6. There are no ending inventories.

Required:

Compute the gross margin for Pro and Con using the relative sales value method to allocate costs.

5-9 Jones Lumber Company produces plywood and lumber with shavings as a by-product. In May, 850 sheets of plywood and 4,125 board feet of lumber were produced at a total cost of $55,000. Joint costs included in this cost were $32,000. Separate costs to produce the plywood and lumber consisted of $13,000 and $10,000 respectively. The plywood sells for $50 a sheet and the lumber sells for $8 per board foot. There are 50 sheets of plywood in ending inventory. There were no beginning inventories. All of the lumber was sold. Two tons of shavings were the result of this process and they sold for $20 a ton. Costs incurred in selling the shavings included $3 per ton for transportation and $3.50 per ton for storage.

Required:

Using the relative sales value method, find the gross margin for the month of May, treating the revenue from the shavings as additional income from by-products.

5–10   As the accountant for the Beverly Company, you are to determine the price that should be charged next year for each of their joint products, Tic and Tac. During the year ending September 30, 3,000 units of Tic and 2,000 units of Tac were produced. Joint costs in the production of these items totaled $8,850. Allocate the joint costs using a physical measure basis.

Required:

If Beverly Company would like to have a 30% mark-up on costs as its selling price per unit, what would be that price for both Tic and Tac?

5–11   The Amsden Company allocates joint costs according to the number of liters of each of the joint products produced. Three products are produced and $36,000 worth of joint costs are incurred monthly. In the production process, 4,000 liters of product E are produced and 6,000 liters of products F and G are produced. E is sold for $3.00 per liter, F is sold for $2.50 per liter and G is sold for $2.25 per liter. Allocate the joint costs using a physical measure.

Required:

a.   What is the gross margin per product assuming all liters produced are sold?
b.   If the price of G goes down to $1.80 per liter due to market conditions, should the Amsden Company continue to produce product G assuming the joint costs would decrease by only $1,500 if production of G ceased (due to a savings in handling and separation costs)?

5–12   The Lectronics Company began operations in January. They produce two products, Timer and Tinkers, in a joint process, and allocate joint costs using the relative sales value method. However, they cannot decide whether to use Fifo or Lifo to cost their ending inventories and cost of goods sold. Below cost data are presented for the first two months of the year.

	January	February
Units of Timers produced	250	280
Units of Tinkers produced	230	290
Joint costs	$1,180.00	$2,000.00
Additional costs to produce Timers	$ 650.00	$ 655.00
Additional costs to produce Tinkers	$ 840.00	$ 825.00
Units of Timers sold	210	260
Units of Tinkers sold	180	270
Price of Timers per unit	$ 7.10	$ 7.15
Price of Tinkers per unit	$ 7.90	$ 8.10

Required:

Calculate the ending inventories for January and February under the Fifo and Lifo methods.

5–13 The Ames Company must make a decision concerning the further processing of a product produced in a joint process. The process produces three chemicals, AA, BB, and CC. AA and BB must be produced further in order to be salable. CC, however, may be produced further or may be sold after the joint process. From the information listed below, decide whether to produce CC further or to sell it in its initial form.

Joint costs per month	$12,000
Additional costs to produce AA	$10,000
Additional costs to produce BB	$16,000
Additional costs to produce CC	$14,000
Selling price of AA	$69
Selling price of BB	$85
Selling price of CC after joint process	$18
Selling price of CC after produced further . . .	$95
Tons of AA produced per month	250
Tons of BB produced per month	300
Tons of CC produced per month	200

The Ames Company uses relative sales values to allocate joint costs. Assume all units produced can be sold.

5–14 The Rite-cut Co. is a slaughter house which must allocate costs to the different cuts of beef.

Cuts	Amount Per Animal	Wholesale Selling Price
1. High quality steaks	180 lbs.	$1.65/lb.
2. Medium quality steaks	220 lbs.	1.40/lb.
3. Low quality steaks	240 lbs.	1.20/lb.
4. Hamburger	300 lbs.	.95/lb.
5. Roasts	200 lbs.	1.80/lb.
6. Liver	50 lbs.	.90/lb.
7. Other (by-products)	150 lbs.	1.00/lb.

It takes 3 union butchers 5 hours each to carve the animal at a cost of $16 per man per hour. (These are joint costs.)

Required:

Calculate the per pound cost for labor for each of the above cuts using (a) relative sales value method, and (b) physical units method (one pound = 1 unit). Which method is preferable? Why?

5–15   The Temper-Tone Steel Company produces two major products, a stainless steel sheet called Flextin and stainless steel silverware. Both products go through the same initial production process where the costs are inseparable. The total cost of this process last period was $550,000. The silverware goes through a second process for completion and the cost of this process is $10,000. The resulting volume is 500,000 pieces of silverware and 45,000 sheets of Flextin. The market value of the Flextin is $2,250,000 while the market value of the silverware is $250,000.

Required:

Using the relative sales value method, determine the unit cost of each product.

PROBLEMS SERIES A

5A–1   The King Chemical Company produces two chemicals, A and B. They use a joint process, but are unable to decide on the best allocation method. You have been asked to compare allocation methods and make your recommendations to the King Company. The necessary information follows:

Joint processing cost $60,000

At Split-off:	*Units made*	*Volume (Gal.)*	*Market Value*
Chemical A	15,000	30,000	$75,000
Chemical B	30,000	90,000	$15,000

Required:

a.   Allocate the joint costs to each chemical by the following methods:

  1. Units made
  2. Relative volume
  3. Market value

b.   Make your recommendations as to the best method.

5A–2   In February, the Berna Company spent $50,000 in production costs for three joint products, G, H, and I and a by-product Z up to the split-off point. There were 10,000 gallons of G produced, 15,000 gallons of H, 25,000 gallons of I, and 500 gallons of Z. G sells for $2.50 per gallon, H for $1.75 per gallon, I for $1.25 per gallon, and Z for $.70 per gallon. The company incurs selling costs of $.15 per gallon of Z sold. The company had no beginning or ending inventories in February.

Required:

a. Allocate the production costs using relative sales value.
b. Find the gross margin by treating the net revenues of the by-product as a reduction of cost of goods sold.
c. Find the gross margin by treating the net revenues of the by-product as other income.

5A-3 Jerry Company began operations on January 1. By processing raw material X, Jerry Company obtains two products: 1,000 gallons of A and 2,000 pounds of B. A may be sold at $3 per gallon and B's selling price is $1 per pound. The total processing cost for the year is $4,000.

Required:

a. If all of the production is sold, how should the processing cost be allocated to A & B?
b. If the ending inventory at December 31 consists of 500 gallons of A and 1,000 pounds of B, what would be the total cost of the inventories at year-end? (Use the relative sales value method.)
c. If the ending inventory is 100 gallons of A and 200 pounds of B, what would be the total carrying value of each inventory item at December 31 for balance sheet purposes? (Use the relative sales value method.)
d. If A is considered a major product and B is considered a by-product, what would be the total carrying value of 100 units of A at December 31 for balance sheet purposes? Is it logical to assume that B, is in fact, a by-product? Why or why not?

5A-4 The Blatz Chemical Company makes Chemicals A, B, and D in its production process with Chemical C as a by-product. It takes 600 gallons of raw material, X, at a cost of $800, to make 200 gallons of each of the chemicals (A, B, C, & D). 200 gallons of A sells at $800, 200 gallons of B sells at $200 and 200 gallons of D sells at $200. There is a market available for the 200 gallons of Chemical C which sells at $40.

Required:

What is the allocated cost of these joint products and by-products under the relative sales value method and the anticipated net revenues from the by-product if there is a selling cost of $.10 per gallon? (Assume no beginning or ending inventories.)

5A-5 The Stooges Chemical Company has three products (Larry, Moe and Joe) which are the natural outputs of their production. This process, which costs $12,000, produces 2,000 gallons of Larry, 1,500 gallons of Moe and 2,500 gallons of Joe.

Required:

a.   What would be the allocation of production costs to Larry, Moe and Joe under physical measures?

b.   If Larry retails at $7,000, Moe at $6,000 and Joe at $5,000, what would be the allocation by the relative sales value method?

5A–6   Dixie Chemical Corporation produces two products Y and X up to the split-off point; 7,500 gallons of each chemical are produced at a cost of $30,000. Y has a sales value at this point of $4.00 per gallon. The sales value of X is not known at this point.

X will be processed further to make chemicals M & N. The cost of this process is $22,500. In the process, 5,000 gallons of M and 2,500 gallons of N are produced. M has a sales value of $4.50 per gallon while N sells for $6.00 per gallon.

Required:

Using the relative sales value method, allocate the joint costs to Y and X and to M and N.

5A–7   The Sharon Company produces the three products listed below in a joint process:

	Ham	Cain	Abel
Units produced in May	2,125	1,500	2,000
Units sold in May	1,500	1,500	1,500
Price per unit	$12.00	$3.00	$9.50
Direct costs incurred in addition to joint costs	$8,000	$4,500	$19,000

Joint costs incurred up to split-off were $15,000. Each product is a natural output of this joint process.

Required:

Calculate the allocation of joint costs to Ham, Cain, and Abel using the relative sales value method. Cain and Abel are sold to provide a complete product line.

5A–8   The McMillon Company produces three products, Plain and Barbecued Potato Chips, and French Fries. 10,000 pounds of raw potatoes used in producing these products were put into production in May at a total cost of $7,000. These material and conversion costs are incurred in Department 1. In Department 2, 5,000 pounds of the potatoes were used to make 5,000 pounds of French Fries at a total cost of $700 for the month. The remaining 5,000 pounds of potatoes were cut up in a form in Department 3 which could be used to produce both Plain and Barbecued Potatoe Chips. In Department 3, total costs for May were $250. In Department 4, 2,500 pounds of the cut-up potatoes were used to make Barbecued Potato chips at an additional cost of $650; and in Department 4, the remaining 2,500 pounds were made into Plain Potato Chips at an additional cost of $550.

The French Fries sell for $.90 a pound, the Barbecued Potato Chips sell for $1.50 a pound, and the Plain Potato Chips sell for $1.40 a pound.

Required:

Calculate the total cost per pound of each product using the relative sales value method. It may be helpful to first draw a diagram of the flow of costs and outputs.

5A–9   The Robert Company uses the relative sales value method to allocate the joint costs of their two products, Chit and Chat. Costs incurred in this joint process for July were $12,000. From this cost, 2,000 units of Chit and 3,500 units of Chat were produced. Chit sells for $3.00 a unit and Chat sells for $3.25 a unit. Beginning and ending inventories for the month of July are as follows:

	Chit	Chat
Beginning inventory:		
Units	110	360.
Cost per unit	$1.90	$2.20
Ending inventory:		
Units	215	320
Cost per unit	?	?

Required:

Calculate the gross margin of each product using the average cost method to determine the cost of goods sold.

5A–10 The Smith Company is in its first year of business. The company produces four products in a joint process, H, I, J and K. The joint costs incurred for the first year ending December 31 were $87,500. Below is listed production and sales data for this year:

Product	Units Produced	Pounds Produced	Price per Unit	Total Sales Value
H	2,000	4,000	$5.00	$ 10,000
I	4,000	6,000	$5.50	22,000
J	6,000	8,000	$5.25	31,500
K	8,000	10,000	$5.75	46,000
	20,000	28,000		$109,500

Required:

a. Assuming 100 units of each product are in ending inventory, allocate costs for the Smith Company using allocation by units, pounds, and relative sales values.

b. Continuing from requirement a., find the gross margin under each method for product I, and select that method to be used for reporting purposes this year and consistently in the future which gives the highest gross margin for product I.

5A–11 In August, the Intac Co. incurred $196,000 of production costs for four joint products, S, T, U, V and one by-product Zap. There were

24,500 units of S, 49,000 units of T, 39,200 units of U, 98,000 units of V produced, and 12,000 units of Zap. (There was no beginning inventory.) In September, $187,000 of production costs were incurred. There were 22,000 units of S, 46,000 units of T, 35,000 units of U, 90,000 units of V produced, and 10,000 units of Zap. The selling price of S is $3.00 per unit, T is $1.90 per unit, U is $2.40 per unit, and V is $1.50 per unit. Zap has a ready market at $.15 per unit. Selling and transportation costs for Zap total $.08 per unit. August sales in units were: S = 19,500, T = 38,700, U = 36,080, V = 97,800, Zap = 11,300. September sales in units were: S = 21,500, T = 44,800, U = 31,100, V = 88,100, Zap = 8,500.

Required:

a. Allocate the production costs using relative sales values for each month.
b. Calculate the September ending inventory and cost of goods sold using Fifo and Lifo.

5A–12 Farmer Brown spends much of the winter indoors. He realizes that idle hands are the devil's workshop and therefore occupies his time by whittling. In one hour he can whittle down five 2 by 4's. Realizing that this would be a waste of time unless he could produce something worthwhile, he decided to carve out pencils, matches and toothpicks. He discovered that from each 2 by 4 he could produce 100 pencils, 500 matches and 1,000 toothpicks. Farmer Brown also obtains 1 pound of wood shavings from each 2 by 4 as a by-product. In the past month, he has whittled 200 hours and he considers an hour of his time worth $4. Other pertinent information is as follows:

Cost of a 2 by 4 . . . . $.80
Sales value of a pencil . . . . . $.02
Sales value of a match . . . . . $.005
Sales value of a toothpick . . . $.001
Sales value of 1 lb. of
shavings . . . . $.05

Required:

a. Calculate the joint costs incurred by Farmer Brown during the past month.
b. Allocate the joint costs using relative sales values.
c. Find the gross margin by treating the net revenues of the by-product as a reduction of cost of goods sold.

5A–13 The Howaya Perfume Company manufactures four types of perfume, W, X, Y and Z. Total joint processing costs were $195,200 in 1980. An activity report revealed the following information:

Product	Production (in ounces)	Price per Ounce	Sales	Additional Processing Costs
W	1,000,000	$ .2300	$230,000	$60,000
X	20,000	1.0000	20,000	12,000
Y	10,000	.8000	8,000	—
Z	18,000	3.3333	60,000 *	2,000

* Rounded

Required:

Calculate the gross margin for each product using the relative sales value method.

PROBLEMS SERIES B

5B-1   The Lawrence Chemical Company produces three chemicals, E, F, and G. They use a joint process, but are unable to decide on the best method of allocation. You have been asked to compare allocation methods and make recommendations to the company from the following information:

Joint processing cost = $180,000

at split-off:

Chemical	Units made	Volume (gallons)	Market value
E	110,000	22,000	$715,000
F	130,000	40,000	650,000
G	120,000	20,000	960,000

Required:

a.   Allocate the joint costs to each chemical by the following methods:

1.   Units made
2.   Relative volume
3.   Market value

b.   Make your recommendations as to the best method.

5B-2   In August, Samson, Inc. spent $80,000 in production costs up to the split-off point for three joint products, X, Y, and Z and a by-product A. There were 15,000 gallons of X, 25,000 gallons of Y, 30,000 gallons of Z, and 400 gallons of A produced. X sells for $3.50 per gallon, Y for $2.50 per gallon, Z for $4.50 per gallon, and A for $.65 per gallon. Selling costs of $.05 per gallon are incurred for each gallon of A sold. There were no beginning inventories in August. Ending inventories were as follows:

X = 2,000 gallons
Y = 3,500 gallons
Z = 3,000 gallons
A =   0 gallons

Required:

a. Allocate the production costs using the relative sales value method.
b. Find the gross margin by treating the net revenues of the by-product as a reduction of cost of goods sold.
c. Find the gross margin by treating the net revenues of the by-

5B-3   On April 1 the Richards Company began its operations. Richards Company obtains three products, A, B, and C, from one raw material. In April, 2,000 pounds of A, 1,500 pounds of B, and 3,000 pounds of C were obtained from the production process. A can be sold for $4.00, B for $2.00, and C for $3.00 per pound. Total processing costs for April were $6,000.

Required:

a. If all of the April production is sold, how should the processing cost be allocated?
b. If the ending inventory on April 30 consists of 500 pounds of A, 200 pounds of B, and 700 pounds of C, what would be the total cost in inventory on April 30? (Use the relative sales value method.)
c. If the ending inventory on April 30 is 300 pounds of A, 150 pounds of B, and 800 pounds of C, determine the gross margin using the relative sales value method.
d. Could B be considered a by-product? Why or why not? If it can, allocate the joint processing cost.

5B-4   The Stanga Chemical Company produces three chemicals, E, F, and G, in one process and a by-product Q. It takes 10,000 gallons of the raw material Z, at a cost of $30,000, to make 2,500 gallons of each of the chemicals (E, F, G, and Q). E sells for $7.00 per gallon, F sells for $8.00 per gallon, G sells for $5.00 per gallon, and Q sells for $.50 per gallon.

Required:

Allocate the joint costs using the relative sales value method and determine the anticipated net revenues from the by-product if there is a selling cost of $.12 per unit. (There were no beginning or ending inventories.)

5B-5   Split-leaf, Inc. has three products (Philo, Den, and Drum) which are the output of their joint production process. The joint cost for this process is $40,000. In May, 5,000 pounds of Philo, 7,000 pounds of Den, and 8,000 pounds of Drum were produced.

Required:

a. Allocate the production costs using physical measures.
b. If Philo sells for $2.50 per pound, Den for $3.50 per pound, and

Drum for $5.00 per pound, allocate the costs using the relative sales value method.

5B–6 Zev Manufacturing Company produces two products, S and B, up to the split-off point; 10,000 gallons of each product can be produced at a cost of $26,600. At this point, S has a sales value of $3.00 per gallon. The sales value of B is not known at this point.

B will be processed further to make M and L at a cost of $20,000. In the process, 3,000 gallons of M and 7,000 gallons of L are produced. M sells for $8.00 per gallon and L sells for $6.00 per gallon.

Required:

Using the relative sales value method, allocate the joint costs to S and B and to M and L.

5B–7 The Kicker Company produces the three products listed below in a joint process. Each product is a natural output of this joint process.

	Sun	*Moon*	*Stars*
Units produced in June	300,000	150,000	150,000
Units sold in June	200,000	100,000	75,000
Price per unit	$1.00	$ .80	$ .40
Direct costs incurred in addition to joint costs	$25,000	$120,000	$30,000

Joint costs incurred up to split-off were $60,000.

Required:

Calculate the allocation of joint costs to Sun, Moon, and Stars, using the relative sales value method.

5B–8 The Houston Company produces three products, facial soap, body soap, and hand soap (used for hard-to-remove grease and dirt). 50,000 gallons of liquid lye and various other indirect costs used in producing these products were put into production in 1980 at a total cost of $125,000. These material and conversion costs are incurred in Department 1. In Department 2, 12,500 gallons were used to make hand soap into its finished form at an additional cost of $6,500 for the year. The remaining 37,500 gallons were further processed in Department 3 in a manner which could be used to produce both facial soap and body soap. In Department 3, total costs for the year were $4,250. In Department 4, 18,750 gallons of processed lye soap were made into 300,000 bars of facial soap at a cost of $15,000. In Department 5, 18,750 gallons were processed into 300,000 bars of body soap at a cost of $9,000.

The hand soap sold for $10 a gallon, the facial soap sold for $.30 a bar, and the body soap sold for $.28 a bar.

Required:

Calculate the total cost per unit of each product using the relative sales value method. It may be helpful to first draw a diagram of the flow of costs and outputs.

5B–9   The Richards Company uses the relative sales value method to allocate the joint costs of their two products, A and B. Costs incurred in this joint process for the month of August were $132,000. From this cost, 12,000 units of A and 16,000 units of B were produced. A sells for $7.00 a unit and B sells for $6.50 a unit. Beginning and ending inventories for the month of July are as follows:

	A	B
Beginning inventory:		
Units	2,000	3,500
Cost per unit	$5.123	$4.876
Ending inventory:		
Units	1,500	1,200
Cost per unit	?	?

Required:

Calculate the gross margin of each product using the last-in, first-out method to determine cost of goods sold.

5B–10   The Johnson Company produces four products in a joint process, O, P, Q, and R. Being in their first year of business, they have decided to allocate these costs using that method which produces the highest gross margin for product Q. The joint costs incurred for this first year ended September 30 were $56,000. Below are listed production and sales data for this year:

Product	Units Produced	Gallons Produced	Price per Unit	Total Sales Value
O	3,000	4,500	$2.00	$ 6,000
P	5,000	5,800	$2.90	14,500
Q	7,000	6,900	$3.50	24,500
R	9,000	8,500	$1.40	12,600
	24,000	25,700		$57,600

2,500 units of each product were sold during the year.

Required:

Allocate costs for the Johnson Company using three different allocation methods, and select that method to be used for reporting purposes this year and in the future which gives the highest gross margin for product Q.

5B–11   The Oddball Company is a producer of a synthetic plastic. The initial mixing process yields two joint products, Plastex and Rubberoid as well as a residual or by-product, Glue-all. The production costs for Oddball for the month of May were $60,000. There were 12,000 gallons of Plastex and 8,000 gallons of Rubberoid produced in May as well as 700 gallons of Glue-all. Plastex has a market value of $4 per gallon, Rubberoid has a market value of $6 per gallon, and Glue-all is sold for $2 per gallon. Selling costs for Glue-all consist solely of salesmen's commissions of 10%.

Required:

a.   Allocate costs under the physical measure method.
b.   Allocate costs under the relative sales value method.
c.   How would you treat the by-product? Show figures.

5B–12   The Scalding Sport Company produces balls used in various athletic contests. The products of the manufacturing process are basketballs, soccerballs, and volleyballs. The manufacturing process costs total $50,000. Details concerning the output are as follows:

> 2,000 basketballs selling at $9.00 each
> 3,000 soccerballs selling at $8.00 each
> 5,000 volleyballs selling at $6.00 each

Required:

a.   Allocate the joint cost according to physical output.
b.   Allocate the joint cost according to relative sales value.

5B–13   The W. C. Redy Company manufactures lubricants. Total processing costs were $48,800 in 1980. An activity report revealed the following information:

Product	Production (in liters)	Sales Price per Liter	Sales	Additional Processing Costs
W	250,000	$ .2300	$57,500	$15,000
X	5,000	1.0000	5,000	3,000
Y	2,500	.8000	2,000	—
Z	4,500	3.3333	15,000	500

Required:

Calculate the gross margin for each product using the relative sales value method.

5B-14 Gosset Chemical Company uses comprehensive annual profit planning procedures to evaluate pricing policies, to finalize production decisions, and to estimate unit costs for its various products. One particular
product group involves two joint products and two by-products. This
product group is separately analyzed each year to establish appropriate
production and marketing policies.

The two joint products—ALCHEM-X and CHEM-P—emerge at the
end of processing in Department 20. Both chemicals can be sold at this
split-off point—ALCHEM-X for $2.50 per unit, and CHEM-P for
$3.00 per unit. By-product BY-D20 also emerges at the split-off point
in Department 20 and is salable without further processing for $0.50
per unit. Unit costs of preparing this by-product for market are $0.03
for freight and $0.12 for packaging.

CHEM-P is sold without further processing, but ALCHEM-X is
transferred to Department 22 for additional processing into a refined
chemical labelled as ALCHEM-XF. No additional raw materials are
added in Department 22. ALCHEM-XF is sold for $5.00 per unit. By-
product BY-D22 is created by the additional processing in Department
22, and it can be sold for $0.70 per unit. Unit marketing costs for BY-
D22 are $0.05 for freight and $0.15 for packaging.

Gosset Chemical Company accounts for by-product production by
crediting the net realizable value of by-products produced to production costs of the main products. The relative sales value method is used
to allocate net joint production costs for inventory valuation purposes.

A portion of next year's profit plan is presented below.

Shortly after this budget was compiled the company learned that a
chemical which would compete with ALCHEM-XF was to be introduced. The marketing department estimated that this would require a
permanent price reduction to $3.50 a unit for the ALCHEM-XF to be
sold in present quantities. Gossett must now reevaluate the decision to
process ALCHEM-X further.

The market for ALCHEM-X will not be affected by the introduction
of this new chemical. Consequently, the quantities of ALCHEM-X
which are usually processed into ALCHEM-XF can be sold at the
regular price of $2.50 per unit. The costs for marketing ALCHEM-X
are estimated to be $105,000. If the further processing is terminated,
Department 22 will be dismantled and all costs except equipment
depreciation, $18,400; supervisory salaries, $21,200; and general
overhead, $35,200; will be eliminated.

	Units of Production	
	CHEM-P	ALCHEM-XF
Estimated sales	400,000	210,000
Planned inventory change	8,000	6,000
Required production	392,000	204,000
Minimum production based upon joint output ratio	392,000	210,000
By-product output		
BY-D20		90,000
BY-D22		60,000

Costs

	Department 20	Department 22
Budgeted Production Costs		
Raw material	$160,000	-----
Costs transferred from 20*	-----	$225,000
Hourly direct labor	170,000	120,000
Variable overhead	180,000	140,800
Fixed overhead	247,500	188,000
	$757,500	$673,800

	CHEM-P	ALCHEM-XF
Budgeted Marketing Costs	$196,000	$105,000

*The cost transferred to Department 22 is calculated as follows:

Sales Value of Output

ALCHEM-X (210,000 x $2.50)	$ 525,000	31%
CHEM-P (392,000 x $3.00)	1,176,000	69
	$1,701,000	100%

Department 20 costs	$ 757,500	
Less: By-product (90,000 x $0.35)	31,500	
Net costs	$ 726,000	

ALCHEM-X	31%	$ 225,000	or $1.07 per unit
CHEM-P	69	501,000	or $1.28 per unit
Allocated net costs	100%	$ 726,000	

Required:

a.   Should Gossett sell ALCHEM-X at the split-off point or continue to process it further in Department 22? Prepare a schedule of relevant costs and revenues to support your answer.

b.   During discussions of the possible dropping of ALCHEM-XF one person noted that the manufacturing margin for ALCHEM-X would be 57.2 percent [($2.50 — $1.07)/$2.50] and 57.3 percent for CHEM-P. The normal mark-up for products sold in the market with ALCHEM-X is 72 percent. For the CHEM-P portion of the line the mark-up is 47 percent. He argues that the company's unit costs must be incorrect because the margins differ from the typical rates. Briefly explain why Gossett's rates for the two products are almost identical when "normal" rates are not.

(CMA, adapted)

Learning Objectives

Chapter 6 discusses the development of departmental manufacturing overhead rates. It illustrates the direct method of allocation and the step method of allocation of the costs of service or support departments to producing departments. Studying this chapter should enable you to:

1. Discuss the concept of a plant-wide manufacturing overhead application rate.
2. Discuss the concept of departmental manufacturing overhead application rates.
3. Discuss the development of a departmental overhead rate.
4. Explain the logic and use of the direct method of allocation.
5. Explain the logic and use of the step method of allocation.

6

Allocation of Service Department Costs to Producing Departments

In Chapters 3, 4, and 5, a plant-wide manufacturing overhead rate for the application of overhead to those products produced was used. The plant-wide rate is developed by projecting total overhead for the manufacturing plant, and dividing the *total* overhead by an application basis. This application basis might be machine hours, direct labor hours, direct labor cost, or any other basis that will provide an equitable application of overhead to the products produced.

$$\text{Plant-Wide Manufacturing Overhead Rate} = \frac{\text{Projected Total Factory Overhead Cost}}{\text{Projected Application Base}}$$

A plant-wide rate applies the same cost per unit of the application base to all products produced without regard to the unique production resource uses of the individual products.

For example, if the application basis was direct labor hours, all products would absorb the same overhead charge per direct labor hour worked in each department without regard to any differences in resource uses that would otherwise cause a different overhead rate to be applied to the production of each department. If direct labor hours were the basis for applying manufacturing overhead and one product used many direct labor hours but few machine hours to complete, this product would be absorbing a greater proportional cost of power to run equipment than a product that used many machine hours and few direct labor hours. The

labor intensive product should actually be absorbing a minimal allocation of power cost since it uses little power in the production process. If
a plant-wide rate is used, all of the projected overhead costs will be allocated to products produced without regard to the specific mix of overhead factors used to make the different products. Obviously, if products
follow similar production processes, little or no cost inequities would
occur in product costing with a plant-wide rate. The inequity occurs when
the nature and amount of overhead is different across the producing departments, and different products use the resources of the production departments in different ways.

Plant-Wide versus Departmental Manufacturing Overhead Rates

When a firm makes diverse products that pass through more than one
producing department and utilize the services of those departments differently, a departmental overhead rate is necessary if the different products are to absorb their equitable share of total factory overhead. A departmental overhead rate will permit the individual products to absorb
overhead costs of the department based on the product's utilization of
the resources of the department.

The departmental overhead rate is developed by projecting total overhead for that department and dividing the cost projection by the appropriate projected application basis.

$$\text{Departmental Manufacturing Overhead Rate} =$$
$$\frac{\text{Projected Total Departmental Overhead Cost}}{\text{Appropriate Projected Application Basis for that Department}}$$

Different departments will have different application bases. A labor intensive department would use direct labor hours or, possibly, direct labor
cost. A machine intensive department might use machine hours as the
basis. These different departments would have different manufacturing
overhead rates.

Even if the application base is the same, such as direct labor hours,
the rate per direct labor hour may be substantially different. If different
products spend varying amounts of time in different departments, an
equitable application of overhead may only be possible with different
overhead rates in each department.

Illustration 6-1 is an example of two producing departments with different projected manufacturing overhead application rates. Both departments will apply overhead on a direct labor hour basis with a plant-wide

rate because direct labor is the only common basis that both departments share.

Illustration 6-1
Plant-Wide Overhead Rate versus
Departmental Overhead Rate

	Plant-Wide Rate	
	Producing Department A	*Producing Department B*
Projected Annual Overhead	$10,000	$ 2,000
Projected Direct Labor Hours	1,000	2,000

Plant-Wide Overhead Rate:

$$\frac{\$10{,}000 + \$2{,}000}{1{,}000 \text{ Hours} + 2{,}000 \text{ Hours}} = \$4.00 \text{ Per Direct Labor Hour}$$

	Departmental Rate	
	Producing Department A	*Producing Department B*
Projected Annual Overhead	$10,000	$ 2,000
Projected Overhead Application Basis	5,000 Machine Hours	2,000 Direct Labor Hours

Departmental Overhead Rates:

$$\frac{\$10{,}000}{5{,}000 \text{ Machine Hours}} = \quad \$2 \text{ Per Machine Hour}$$

$$\frac{\$ 2{,}000}{2{,}000 \text{ Hours}} = \quad \$1 \text{ Per Direct Labor Hour}$$

Producing Department A is machine intensive and Producing Department B is labor intensive. If a plant-wide overhead rate is used, overhead will be applied at the rate of $4 per direct labor hour. Alternatively, if a departmental overhead rate is used, every job that passes through Department A will absorb $2 per machine hour used. If a departmental manufacturing overhead rate based on direct labor hours was used in Department A, the rate would be $10 per direct labor hour.

If a departmental overhead rate is used, every job that passes through Department B will absorb $1 per direct labor hour used. In the Illustration, if a plant-wide rate were used, overhead charges to the products produced would be shifted from the machine intensive department to the labor intensive department. The projected total overhead in Department B is $2,000, but the products passing through Department B would have absorbed $8,000 (2,000 hours × $4 per hour) if the projections were correct and the application of overhead was based on a plant-wide overhead rate.

The implications for product costing are substantial in Illustration 6–1. If two specific jobs, Jobs 101 and 102, were started and completed in a given time period and Job 101 was machine intensive and Job 102 was labor intensive, the amount of overhead charged to each job would be substantially different under the plant-wide overhead rate versus the departmental overhead rate. Assume that the following direct labor and machine hours were used on the two jobs:

		Department A		*Department B*	
Job		*Labor Hrs.*	*Machine Hrs.*	*Labor Hrs.*	*Machine Hrs.*
Machine Intensive . .	101	1	10	2	8
Labor Intensive	102	3	1	4	2

If a plant-wide overhead rate is used, the overhead charge to each job would be as follows:

	Job 101		*Job 102*	
	Department A	*Department B*	*Department A*	*Department B*
Direct Labor Hours	1	2	3	4
Manufacturing Over- Head Rate	× $4	× $4	× $4	× $4
Applied Manufacturing Overhead	$4	$8	$12	$16

Job 101 would absorb $12 and Job 102 would absorb $28 with a plant-wide rate. Job 102 is labor intensive and with direct labor hours as the basis for manufacturing overhead application to products, a greater absorption of overhead would be expected.

If the departmental overhead rates from Illustration 6–1 are used to apply overhead to each job, the overhead absorbed would be as follows:

	Job 101		*Job 102*	
	Department A	*Department B*	*Department A*	*Department B*
Machine Hours	10		1	
Direct Labor Hours		2		4
Manufacturing Over- Head Rate	× $2	× $1	× $2	× $1
Applied Manufacturing Overhead	$20	$2	$2	$4

Job 101 would absorb $22 and Job 102 would absorb $6 using a departmental overhead rate. Each job would absorb that overhead which reflects the use of the resource assumed to be the causal factor in incurring the overhead in each department. If the plant-wide and the departmental overhead applications were compared, the absorption by the two jobs is different.

	Job 101	Job 102	Total
Plant-Wide Rate	$12	$28	$40
Departmental Rate . . .	22	6	28

The difference in absorption of overhead by the jobs is caused by the difference in the basis for application under the two different approaches for applying overhead. The difference in the totals is not meant to imply that a departmental rate in some way reduces overhead. It just means that some other jobs will be absorbing more overhead by using the departmental rate than they would have by using the plant-wide rate.

Service Department Costs

All manufacturing overhead costs must be allocated to products produced under the full or absorption costing approach to product costing. For purposes of simplicity, the prior chapters assumed a plant-wide overhead rate and ignored service departments and the allocation of the costs of the service departments to the producing departments. The allocation of service department costs to producing departments is necessary if the departmental manufacturing overhead rate applied to products is to reflect the *full* or *total* manufacturing overhead costs. Some general examples of service departments in a manufacturing plant that would serve as support for production departments are as follows:

Cost Accounting	Maintenance
General Building Services	Power Plant
General Supervision	Production Planning
Plant Cafeteria	Purchasing
Plant Engineering	Toolroom

Allocating Service Department Costs—General Concepts

Any allocation of the costs of the service departments to producing departments in an equitable manner is complicated by the fact that some service departments will serve other service departments. The basis for the allocation of the costs of the service departments to the producing departments should be that basis which best reflects the services rendered to the producing departments. This basis will usually be different for different service departments. The interrelationship of the service departments in rendering service to each other would distort the allocation because some of the cost of service is caused by the needs of other service departments and not the producing departments.[1]

The concept of reciprocal services between service departments and

---

[1] This problem of reciprocal services can be solved using linear algebra or simultaneous equations. The step method of allocation, which is covered in this chapter, is an approximation of the linear algebra solution when reciprocal services are involved.

the allocation of the costs of the departments to the producing departments in establishing an overhead rate is presented in Illustration 6–2.

Illustration 6-2
Relationships of Service Departments and
Producing Departments

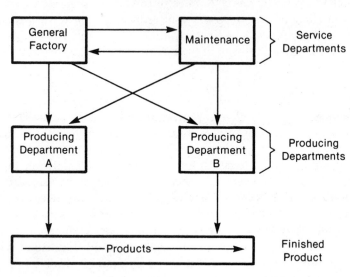

In Illustration 6–2, there are two service departments, Maintenance and General Factory. To keep the example simple, assume that the General Factory Department does everything associated with service except maintenance. General Factory and Maintenance provide service to each other and to the producing departments. In order to pass the total overhead cost on to the products which are produced, the service department costs will have to be allocated in total to the producing departments. The service department allocations will be added to the overhead costs in the producing departments to arrive at the total overhead projection for each producing department. These overhead projections and the basis for the allocations will serve to establish the predetermined overhead rate to be used in applying overhead costs to production. As the products pass through the producing departments, the manufacturing overhead will be applied using the predetermined overhead rate.

METHODS FOR ALLOCATING COSTS OF SERVICE DEPARTMENTS TO PRODUCING DEPARTMENTS

The two methods covered in this chapter for allocating the costs of the service departments to the producing departments are the direct method of allocation and the step method of allocation. The major difference between the two approaches is the recognition given to reciprocal services between service departments.

The basic data that will be used in illustrating both the direct method of allocation and the step method of allocation is presented in Illustration 6–3.

Illustration 6-3
Projected Overhead Costs for Service
Departments and Producing Departments

| | Service Departments | | Producing Departments | | |
	General Factory	Maintenance	Machining	Finishing and Pressing	Total
Departmental Identifiable (Traceable) Overhead Costs	$2,400	$4,000	$3,500	$2,500	$12,400
Services Furnished:					
1. General Factory Based on Square Feet	–0–	400	1,000	1,000	2,400
2. Maintenance Based on Projected Maintenance Hours Worked in Each Department	1,000	–0–	3,000	1,000	5,000
Basis For Allocation To Production:					
Projected Machine Hours			2,000		
Projected Direct Labor Hours				1,000	

In the example in Illustration 6–3, there are two service departments, General Factory and Maintenance, and two producing departments, Machining and Finishing and Pressing. The projected overhead costs for the General Factory Department are $2,400. This would be the total projected cost of this department for the period under consideration. The basis for the allocation of the $2,400 will be square feet of plant used in the other departments. This is the basis that is the most common denominator that can be used to measure the services provided by the General Factory Department to all other service departments and producing departments.

The projected cost of the Maintenance Department is $4,000. The basis of allocation of maintenance costs for the projected overhead rate will be projected maintenance hours to be worked in each service and production department. Maintenance hours are considered to be the common denominator in the other departments that provides a causal relationship with costs in the maintenance department.

The overhead directly identifiable with the producing departments is $3,500 for Machining and $2,500 for Finishing and Pressing. The basis that will be used to apply overhead to production in the Machining Department is machine hours. The basis in Finishing and Pressing will be direct labor hours. These bases for application are felt to be the most meaningful because of their relationship to overhead cost incurrence. The final predetermined manufacturing overhead rates will include the total $12,400 of projected costs when the rates for both producing departments are considered. That is, the combined application rates will attempt to pass the $12,400 of overhead to the products produced during the time period under consideration.

The Direct Method of Allocation

The direct method of allocation of service department costs allocates the projected costs of each service department directly to the producing departments. The interaction between service or support departments and the related costs that are incurred in one service department because of the needs of another service department is ignored.

The $2,400 of the costs of the General Factory Department will be allocated directly to the producing departments on a square foot basis. The $4,000 of projected costs of the Maintenance Department will be allocated to the producing departments on the basis of projected maintenance hours to be worked in each producing department. The $6,400 of the projected costs of all the service departments, therefore, will be allocated to the producing departments and included in the final predetermined overhead rate.

The direct method of allocation using those projected overhead costs for service departments and producing departments from Illustration 6–3, is presented in Illustration 6–4. Using the direct method of allocation, the order of the allocation of the costs of the service departments to the producing departments does not make any difference. Each of the producing departments uses 1,000 square feet of factory and the Maintenance Department uses 400 square feet. The Maintenance Department's use will be ignored in the allocation because the costs of the General Factory Department will be allocated directly to the producing department. The Machining Department and the Finishing and Pressing Department both use equal amounts of square feet of factory space; therefore, each will be allocated one-half of the cost of the General Factory Department or $1,200.

The costs of the Maintenance Department are allocated on the basis of

Illustration 6-4
Direct Method of Allocation of
Projected Service Department Costs

	Service Departments		Producing Departments		
	General Factory	Maintenance	Machining	Finishing and Pressing	Total
Overhead Costs Before Allocation	$2,400	$4,000	$3,500	$2,500	$12,400
Allocation:					
1. General Factory Based on Square Feet $\frac{1,000}{2,000}$ $\frac{1,000}{2,000}$ *	(2,400)		1,200	1,200	
2. Maintenance Based on Projected Maintenance Hours Worked in Each Department $\frac{3,000}{4,000}$ $\frac{1,000}{4,000}$ †		(4,000)	3,000	1,000	
Total Overhead to be Applied to Production			$7,700	$4,700	$12,400

Predetermined Departmental Overhead Rates:

Projected Overhead Costs in Machining	$7,700
Projected Machine Hours in Machining	$\overline{2,000}$ =
Overhead Application Rate Per Machine Hour	$3.85

Projected Overhead Costs in Finishing and Pressing	$4,700
Projected Direct Labor Hours in Finishing and Pressing	$\overline{1,000}$ =
Overhead Application Rate Per Direct Labor Hour	$4.70

* Each producing department uses 1,000 square feet (from Illustration 6–3).
† The projected maintenance hour usage is 3,000 hours for Machining and 1,000 hours for Finishing and Pressing (from Illustration 6–3).

projected maintenance hours to be worked in each department. Total projected maintenance hours are 3,000 hours for the Machining Department and 1,000 hours for the Finishing and Pressing Department. The appropriate allocation of the projected costs of the Maintenance Department are three-quarters (3,000 hours ÷ 4,000 hours) of the $4,000 projected costs to Machining and one-quarter (1,000 hours ÷ 4,000 hours) of the $4,000 projected costs to Finishing and Pressing. Therefore, $3,000 will be allocated to the Machining Department and $1,000 to the Finishing and Pressing Department. The projected manufacturing overhead rate that will be applied to products produced in the two production departments will include the allocated costs of the service departments and the manufacturing overhead costs of the production departments.

The predetermined manufacturing overhead rate for the Machining Department will include $3,500 of manufacturing overhead identified directly with the Machining Department, $1,200 allocated from the General Factory Department, and $3,000 allocated from the Maintenance Department, or $7,700 in manufacturing overhead in total. The manufacturing overhead application basis for the Machining Department in Illustration 6–4 is machine hours. Two thousand machine hours are projected; therefore, the predetermined overhead rate for the Machining Department will be $7,700 ÷ 2,000 hours or $3.85 per machine hour worked on a job. If a job uses 2 hours of machine time, the applied overhead on that job will be $3.85 × 2 hours or $7.70.

The Finishing and Pressing Department has $2,500 of manufacturing overhead identified directly with itself (Illustration 6–4). Twelve hundred dollars of manufacturing overhead is allocated from the General Factory Department. The Maintenance Department allocation is $1,000. In total, the projected manufacturing overhead that will be applied to products being worked on in the Finishing and Pressing Department is $4,700 ($2,500 + $1,200 + $1,000). The basis for the application of overhead in the Finishing and Pressing Department is direct labor hours. There are 1,000 direct labor hours projected. The predetermined manufacturing overhead rate will be $4.70 ($4,700 ÷ 1,000 direct labor hours) per direct labor hour worked. If a job uses two direct labor hours in Machining and Finishing, that job will absorb $4.70 × 2 hours or $9.40 in manufacturing overhead. If a job used 5 hours of machine time in the Machining Department and 3 hours of direct labor time in the Finishing and Pressing Department, the job would absorb ($3.85 × 5 hours) + ($4.70 × 3 hours) or $33.35 in manufacturing overhead.

The Step Method of Allocation

Direct allocation of the costs of the service department to the production departments is the most popular approach for service department cost allocations. Some accountants would argue that cost inequities result when using the direct method if there are reciprocal services between service departments. If some service departments serve other service departments, and if the use of service departments is different for different production departments, an unequitable allocation of service department costs, and thus overhead allocation to products, could result.

For example, a maintenance department would normally provide more service to a producing department that is machine intensive than to one that is labor intensive. If another service department is a large user of the Maintenance Department but provides a greater proportion of its resources to the labor intensive production department, that production department may be getting the benefits of maintenance expenditures without a proportional share of the maintenance costs if a direct method of allocation is used. The maintenance-using machine intensive department would be allocated a share of the maintenance cost based on its proportional use of the maintenance department. However, a large part of maintenance cost would be caused by the other service department that provides a greater share of its resources to the labor intensive production department.

To solve the allocation equitably, simultaneous equations would have to be used in making the allocation.[2] An approximation of an equitable solution using simultaneous equations can be achieved by using the step method of allocation. The step method of allocation is only an approximation to the extent that costs are allocated on a sequential basis starting with the service department that provided the most service to other service departments. The costs of this service department will be allocated to the remaining service departments and all production departments. Then, in turn, all costs of the service department that provided the next most service are allocated to the remaining service and production departments. The costs of the second service department would include an allocated portion of the costs of the first service department. This sequential system will continue until all service department costs are allocated to the production departments. Once a service department's costs are allocated, that service department will not be allocated any costs from the subsequent cost allocations of other service departments.

The Step Method of Allocation—An Illustration

Illustration 6–5 is an example of the step method of allocation using the data presented in Illustration 6–3. Assume that the costs of the General Factory Department will be allocated first because it provides more services to the Maintenance Department than the Maintenance Department provides to it. The General Factory Department costs will be allocated to the Maintenance Department, the Machining Department, and the Finishing and Pressing Department on the basis of square feet.

The Maintenance Department will be allocated $400 (400 square feet ÷ 2,400 square feet) × $2,400 of the General Factory Department's costs. Each of the producing departments will be allocated an equal amount of the remaining $2,000 of the General Factory Department's costs based on their proportional square feet of use (1,000 square feet ÷ 2,400 square feet) × $2,400, or $1,000.

---

[2] This approach will not be covered in this text. The practical application of service department allocations using simultaneous equations is not common and would probably be done using a computer.

Illustration 6-5
Step Method of Allocation of
Projected Service Department Costs

	Service Departments		Producing Departments		
	General Factory	Maintenance	Machining	Finishing and Pressing	Total
Overhead Costs Before Allocation	$2,400	$4,000	$3,500	$2,500	$12,400

Allocation:

1. General Factory
Based on Square Feet
$\frac{400}{2,400}$ $\frac{1,000}{2,400}$ $\frac{1,000}{2,400}$ *

	(2,400)		400	1,000	1,000

2. Maintenance
Based on Projected
Maintenance Hours
Worked in Each Department
$\frac{3,000}{4,000}$ $\frac{1,000}{4,000}$ †

		(4,400)	3,300	1,100	
Total Overhead to be Applied to Production			$7,800	$4,600	$12,400

Predetermined Departmental Overhead Rates:

Projected Overhead Costs in Machining	$7,800	
Projected Machine Hours in Machining	$\overline{2,000}$	=
Overhead Application Rate Per Machine Hour	$3.90	

Projected Overhead Costs in Finishing and Pressing	$4,600	
Projected Direct Labor Hours in Finishing and Pressing	$\overline{1,000}$	=
Overhead Application Rate Per Direct Labor Hour	$4.60	

* Maintenance uses 400 square feet, Machining 1,000 and Finishing and Pressing 1,000 (from Illustration 6–3).

† The projected maintenance hour usage is 3,000 hours for Machining and 1,000 hours for Finishing and Pressing (from Illustration 6–3).

The second step in the sequential allocation will be to allocate the Maintenance Department's costs to the producing departments. The Maintenance Department's costs to be allocated are $4,400 which is the cost of providing $4,000 of manufacturing overhead directly identifiable with the Maintenance Department in Illustration 6–5 plus the $400 of costs allocated from the General Factory Department. The Maintenance Department's costs of $4,400 will be allocated based on the projected usage of maintenance hours by the producing departments. No maintenance costs will be allocated back to the General Factory Department.

The projected usage of maintenance hours is 3,000 hours for the

Machining Department and 1,000 hours for the Finishing and Pressing Department. The allocation of the $4,400 will be three-fourths to the Machining Department (or $3,300) and one-fourth (or 1,100) to the Finishing and Pressing Department.

The total projected manufacturing overhead to be applied to production in the Machining Department is $7,800 of the $12,400 of manufacturing overhead for the entire plant. The basis for manufacturing overhead application for the Machining Department in Illustration 6–5 is 2,000 hours of projected machine usage. The appropriate application rate for applying manufacturing overhead to production will be $7,800 ÷ 2,000 projected machine hours, or $3.90 per machine hour worked on a job.

The total projected manufacturing overhead that will be applied to production in the Finishing and Pressing Department is $4,600. The basis for manufacturing overhead application for the Pressing and Finishing Department is the projected 1,000 hours of direct labor time usage. The manufacturing overhead rate per direct labor hour will be $4,600 ÷ 1,000 projected direct labor hours, or $4.60 per direct labor hour.

SUMMARY

A plant-wide manufacturing overhead rate provides one overhead rate to be used for applying manufacturing overhead to all of the products produced. If a plant-wide rate is used, all of the projected overhead costs will be allocated to the products produced without regard to the specific mix of overhead factors used to make the different products.

A departmental overhead rate is developed by projecting total overhead for each producing department and dividing the cost projection by the appropriate projected application base. Different production departments may have different manufacturing overhead rates and different overhead application bases.

The allocation of service department costs to producing departments is necessary if the departmental manufacturing overhead rate applied to products is to reflect the projected full or total manufacturing overhead costs. The two methods covered in this chapter for allocating the costs of the service departments to the producing departments are the direct method of allocation and the step method of allocation. The major difference between the two approaches is the recognition given to reciprocal services between service departments.

The direct method of allocation of the costs of service departments allocates each service department's projected costs directly to the producing departments. The interaction between service departments (reciprocal services) and the related costs incurred in one service department because of another service department's needs are ignored.

The step method of allocation of the costs of the service departments to the producing departments gives some recognition to reciprocal services between service departments. Costs of the service departments are allocated sequentially, starting with the service department that provided the most service to other service departments. That department's costs are allocated to the remaining service and production departments. Then the costs of the service department that provided the next most service are allocated to the remaining service and producing departments. This sequential system continues until the costs of all the service departments are allocated to the producing departments. Once a service department's costs are allocated, that service department is not assigned any costs in subsequent cost allocations. The final result of either the direct method or the step method of allocation is to include all projected manufacturing overhead costs of the plant in the departmental overhead rates so that full costs of manufacturing will be absorbed by the production of the time period under consideration.

APPENDIX: COST ACCOUNTING STANDARDS BOARD

On August 15, 1970 President Nixon signed Public Law 91-379 establishing the Cost Accounting Standards Board (CASB). The Board was funded and organized in 1971. The purpose of the CASB is to develop cost accounting standards that will achieve both *uniformity* and *consistency* in the accounting for costs by defense contractors and subcontractors who are awarded Federal Contracts. An indication of the importance of the CASB's effort is the fact that the Department of Defense spends annually in excess of one hundred billion dollars.

Jurisdiction of the CASB

All contractors or subcontractors awarded defense contracts exceeding ten million dollars during any fiscal year are required to file a lengthy disclosure statement regarding their cost accounting procedures. The initial contract exceeding five hundred thousand dollars during any fiscal year requires a contractor to follow the cost accounting standards issued by the CASB. After the initial five hundred thousand dollar contract, each subsequent one hundred thousand dollar contract also falls within the jurisdiction of the CASB. If a contractor fails to follow the prescribed cost accounting standards, the government can recover any increased costs plus interest.

If a Federal Contract is *negotiated*, all contracts of one hundred thousand dollars or more must follow the CASB's standards. A negotiated contract is one in which bids are not requested for the purchase. The purchasing agency negotiates the contract with the contractor and the final price is dependent on the cost of the goods or services.

The value of uniform and consistent cost accounting principles may be visualized in the context of a negotiated cost-plus contract. The final determination of the contract price will be the cost of the product or service. Since uniform and consistent cost accounting principles did not exist prior to the establishment of the CASB, the determination of those costs which were included as contract costs was dependent upon the output of the cost accounting system used by the company that held the contract. This, of course, led to many different interpretations of costs and cost allocations and, in effect, each contract had to be reviewed and analyzed on an individual basis.

Organization of the CASB

The CASB is comprised of five part-time members with the Comptroller General of the United States as the chairperson. Public Law 91-379 requires that the remainder of the Board represent various segments of the accounting profession; one member from a federal agency, one from industry and two from the accounting profession. With the exception of the chairperson, all four members are appointed for four-year terms. Approximately twenty-five professional staff are available to assist the Board members in their work. The Board reports directly to Congress.

Cost Accounting Standards

The primary objective of the Board is to promulgate the standards to be used by government contractors, not to negotiate or to assist in negotiation of contracts. In order to assure consistency and uniformity in the application of cost accounting standards. Congress gave the CASB the authority to carry out its day to day activities in a manner so as to assure that covered contractors follow the standards. When a standard is submitted to Congress by the CASB, it automatically becomes effective sixty days after the submitted date unless disappoved in both Houses of Congress.

The standards are numbered beginning with 400 in Title 4, Chapter III, Code of Federal Regulations. The initial standard, 400, is a general statement that is revised whenever a new standard is approved. This standard covers and defines any new technical terms that are used in the standards.

Discussing each standard would be beyond the scope of this text but listing the standards as of this writing will provide some indication of the problem areas in which the CASB found a lack of either or both consistency and uniformity and has taken action.

401   Consistency in Estimating, Accumulating and Reporting Costs
402   Consistency in Allocating Costs Incurred for the Same Purpose
403   Allocation of Home Office Expenses to Segments
404   Capitalization of Tangible Assets
405   Accounting for Unallowable Costs
406   Cost Accounting Period
407   Use of Standard Costs for Direct Material and Direct Labor
408   Accounting for Costs of Compensated Personal Absence
409   Depreciation of Capital Assets
410   Allocation of General and Administrative Expenses
411   Accounting for Acquisition Costs of Material
412   Composition and Measurement of Pension Costs
413   Adjustment and Allocation of Pension Costs
414   Cost of Money as an Element of the Cost of Facilities Capital
415   Accounting for the Cost of Deferred Compensation

The standards issued by the CASB do not represent *generally accepted accounting principles* and may not always represent the cost which is appropriate for use for external financial reporting purposes. Rather, the standards will be used by defense contractors and subcontractors holding Federal Contracts within the jurisdiction of the CASB for cost accounting on the contracts.

KEY DEFINITIONS

Allocation of service department costs—the process of assigning the costs of service departments to production departments so that the total manufacturing overhead of the plant will be reflected in the departmental overhead rates. The basis for the allocation of the costs of the service departments to the producing departments should be the basis which best reflects the services rendered to the producing departments.

Departmental manufacturing overhead rate—a rate is established for each department in a plant based on the unique overhead factors in that department. The overhead application basis will be the basis which is the causal factor for incurring manufacturing overhead in that department.

Direct method of allocation—the allocation of each service department's projected costs directly to the producing departments. The basis to be used for this allocation is the basis that best reflects the services used by the producing departments. Reciprocal services between service departments are ignored.

Plant-wide manufacturing overhead rate—one overhead rate that is established for the entire plant. Every department applies the same overhead rate on the same basis to its production as every other department. The same basis for overhead application would be used throughout the plant.

Reciprocal services—the services rendered by service departments to each other.

Service or support departments—the departments in a manufacturing plant that supply needed services to producing departments. The service departments do not produce products. The maintenance department and production planning would be examples of service departments.

Step method of allocation—the allocation of the projected costs of the service departments, on a sequential basis, starting with the service department that provided the most service to other service departments. This first department's costs are allocated to all the remaining service and producing departments. Then the costs of the service department that provided the next most service, in turn, is allocated to the remaining service and production departments. This process continues until all service department costs are allocated to the production departments.

QUESTIONS

1. Why might a departmental rather than a plant-wide manufacturing overhead rate be used?

2. Describe the development of a departmental overhead rate for a production department.

3. Why might different departments use different bases of application in developing their respective departmental overhead rates?

4. Why might the departmental overhead rates of two departments differ even though both departments use an identical basis for the application of overhead?

5. Why are the costs of service departments allocated to the producing departments in a manufacturing company?

6. Discuss the concept of reciprocal services. How may reciprocal services present a problem in the allocation of service department costs?

7. Identify and briefly describe two approaches for allocating the costs of several service departments to more than one producing department.

8. What does the step method of allocation specifically take into account that the direct method does not?

9. Which department has its costs allocated first in the step method of allocation? Which department is allocated next? Last?

EXERCISES

6–1 Production Departments A and B have the following budgeted amounts:

	Department A	Department B
Budgeted Overhead	$100,000	$100,000
Budgeted Direct Labor Hours	25,000	40,000
Budgeted Machine Hours	40,000	25,000

Department A is machine intensive and Department B is labor intensive. Determine the appropriate manufacturing overhead rates for these two departments.

6–2 Jobs 21 and 22 required the following input from Production Departments X, Y, and Z.

	Dept. X		Dept. Y		Dept. Z	
Job	Labor Hrs.	Mach. Hrs.	Labor Hrs.	Mach. Hrs.	Labor Hrs.	Mach. Hrs.
21 . .	½	1½	2	1	1	3
22 . .	1	½	1½	1	2	1¾

The wage rate is $3 per hour. Departments X, Y, and Z respectively apply overhead at the rates of $4.00 per machine hour, $6.00 per direct labor hour, and 70% of direct labor cost. Determine the amounts of overhead absorbed by Jobs 21 and 22 in production.

6–3 Service Department 1 provides maintenance to Production Departments 2 and 3. Service department costs are allocated according to projected usage of direct labor hours. Given the following information:

Department 1 projected costs $100,000
Department 2 projected usage is 2,500 hours of Department 1 labor
Department 3 projected usage is 3,500 hours of Department 1 labor

How much of the projected service department costs are to be allocated to each production department?

6–4 Ajax Company has two service departments, Maintenance and Power, and two production departments, Powders and Liquids. Budgeted costs for Maintenance and Power are $60,000 and $200,000 respectively. Service costs are allocated to production according to the number of labor hours of maintenance and the number of machine hours of power used. Powders and Liquids are expected to use the following:

	Expected Usage of Labor Hours of Maintenance	Expected Usage of Machine Hours of Power
Powders	500 Hours	2,500 Hours
Liquids	750 Hours	7,500 Hours

Allocate the service costs to the production departments.

6–5 Atlas Corporation has two service departments (A and B) providing services to three production departments (I, II, and III). All service department costs are allocated to the production department based on the projected amount of labor cost expected to be incurred by the respective service departments for each of the production departments. Expected service department costs are $10,000 for A and $20,000 for B. The wage rate for A is $5.00 per hour and for B is $4.00 per hour. The service departments are expected to be needed as follows:

Expected Departmental Requirements for Service Labor Hours

Dept.	A	B	I	II	III
A		10	20	30	40
B	50		60	70	80

By using a direct method of allocation, determine the amount of service costs allocated to each production department.

6–6   Redetermine the amount of service costs allocated to each production department in exercise number 5 by using a step method of allocation. Allocate A first.

6–7   The Accounting Department services two production departments, Food and Toys. The projected manufacturing overhead costs for Food and Toys are $5,000 and $10,000 respectively. The basis for application in each production department is machine hours. The projected number of machine hours for Food is 2,000 hours and for Toys is 2,500 hours. The Accounting Department, with expected costs of $1,500, allocates its costs according to the number of its labor hours used by the production departments. For the next period, it is expected that Accounting will spend 100 hours in Food and 200 hours in Toys. What are the appropriate predetermined departmental overhead rates for each of the production departments?

6–8   Given the following information:

	Service Departments		Production Departments	
	1	2	1	2
Application Basis	Sq. Footage Used	Direct Labor Hours Used	Machine Hours Used	Units Finished
Expected use of Service Dept. 1		100 Sq. Ft.	2,000 Sq. Ft.	1,200 Sq. Ft.
Expected use of Service Dept. 2	10 Hours		120 Hours	130 Hours
Expected Machine Hours	55 Hours	75 Hours	2,000 Hours	370 Hours
Expected Number of Units Finished				4,000 Units
Expected Service Costs	$15,000	$40,000		
Expected Manufacturing Overhead			$200,000	$350,000

Service Department 1 provides more service to Service Department 2 than Service Department 2 does to Service Department 1. Determine the amount of service cost allocated to each of the production departments from Service Department 2 if a direct allocation method is used.

6–9   Redetermine the amount of service cost allocated to each of the production departments from Service Department 2 in exercise number 8 if a step method of allocation is used.

6–10   If a step method of allocation is used in exercise number 8 to allocate the costs of the service departments to the production departments, what are the appropriate predetermined manufacturing overhead rates for Production Departments 1 and 2? Assume that Department 1 applies overhead on the basis of machine hours and Department 2 uses finished units.

PROBLEMS SERIES A

6A–1   The Dire Company has one service department which serves three production departments. The projected annual costs are $143,000 in the service department. The annual services provided are expected to be apportioned among the production departments according to one of the following bases:

Production Departments	Square Footage	Direct Labor Hours	Total Revenue of each Prod. Dept.
X	283,000	350,000	$150,000
Y	250,000	180,000	$300,000
Z	375,000	30,000	$250,000
Total	908,000	560,000	$700,000

Required:

Allocate the service departments expected annual costs to the production departments using the following allocation bases:

a.   Square footage
b.   Direct labor hours
c.   Total revenue

6A–2   The Abbott Co. has two service departments, maintenance and research and development, and two production departments, assembly and finishing. Projected overhead costs in the various departments are $500,000 in maintenance, $320,000 in research and development, $816,000 in assembly and $467,000 in finishing. Overhead in assembly is allocated in accordance with the number of machine hours used; the average annual amount is 37,000 hours. Finishing allocates overhead according to the number of direct labor hours worked; the average annual amount is 29,000 hours. Maintenance allocates overhead according to total projected labor hours which are 55,000, of which

13,000 are in research and development, 21,000 in assembly and 16,000 in finishing. Research and development allocates overhead in accordance with the number of projected direct labor hours worked for each department. These hours total 29,000, of which 7,000 are for maintenance, 19,000 for assembly, and 3,000 for finishing.

Required:

Using the direct method, allocate the projected service departments' overhead to the production departments and compute the predetermined overhead rate for each production department.

6A–3   The Clinton Company has two Production Departments, X and Y, and two Service Departments, I and II. Projected overhead amounted to $305,000 for X, $428,000 for Y, $298,000 for I and $367,000 for II. Overhead in Department X is allocated in accordance with the number of physical units of projected production, which is 350,000. Department Y allocates overhead based upon projected direct labor hours which totaled 293,000. Department I allocates its overhead based upon the projected number of machine hours used for other departments which amounted to 30,000 for X, 47,500 for Y and 20,450 for II. Department II allocates overhead based upon the projected units of direct materials that it handles for the various departments. These amounted to 29,000 units for X, 56,000 units for Y and 13,000 units for I.

Required:

Using the direct allocation method, allocate the overhead of the service departments to the production departments and compute the predetermined overhead rate for each production department.

6A–4   The Sched Manufacturing Company is made up of two production departments, A and B, and three service departments, I, II, and III. The projected fixed overhead of each department is: $578,000 for A; $479,000 for B; $323,000 for I; $289,000 for II; and $239,000 for III. The overhead allocation bases used by each department are direct labor hours for A, machine hours for B, pounds of materials handled for I, total labor hours for II, and units of finished product handled for III. The projected allocation bases are 48,000 direct labor hours for A and 67,000 machine hours for B. Department I handles 96,500 pounds of materials. Approximately 25% of the materials is handled for Department A, 46% for Department B, 15% for II and 14% for III. Department II has projected 60,000 total labor hours. The allocation of the labor hours is: 39% to A; 34% to B; 13% to I; and, 14% to III. Department III has projected handling 48,000 units of finished product. This amount is allocated 43% to A, 34% to B, 12% to I and 11% to II.

Required:

Using the direct method of allocation, redistribute the overhead of the service departments to the production departments and compute the predetermined overhead rates for each production department.

6A-5 The Trend Company manufactures calculators. It is made up of three production departments: the component, assembly and the testing departments. There are two service departments: engineering and materials handling. The overhead of the various departments amounted to $768,000 for component, $533,000 for assembly, $324,000 for testing, $993,000 for engineering, and $289,000 for materials handling. The component department's allocation base is units produced. The number of units projected is 239,000. The assembly department's allocation base is direct labor hours. The projected direct labor hours are 388,000. The testing department's projected allocation base is 387,000 direct labor hours. The engineering department's allocation base is total labor hours. The projected total labor hours of 248,500 have been allocated 34% to components, 37% to assembly, 21% to testing and 8% to materials handling. The materials handling department's allocation base is pounds of materials handled which is projected at 304,000 pounds: 42% for the component department; 21% for assembly; 18% for testing; and, 19% for engineering.

Required:

Using the direct method of allocation for service department costs, compute the predetermined overhead rates for each of the production departments.

6A-6 The Continental Company produces brass lamps, and is made up of two production and two service departments. The production departments are the electrical department and the finishing department, and the service departments are the maintenance department and the research department. The electrical department's overhead is $845,000 allocated on a direct labor hour basis. The finishing department's overhead is $920,000 allocated on the basis of units finished. The maintenance department's overhead is $803,000 allocated on the basis of labor hours worked. The research department's overhead is $700,000 allocated on the basis of labor hours. The projected annual direct labor hours of the electrical department are 190,000. The projected annual number of units finished by the finishing department are 109,000 units. The direct labor hours projected by the maintenance department are 172,000. Projected incurrence is: 30% by electrical; 40% by finishing; and 30% by research. The direct labor hours projected by the research department are 240,000 and are allocated 55% to electrical and 45% to finishing.

Required:

Using the direct method of allocation, assign service department costs to the production departments and compute a predetermined overhead rate for each department.

6A–7

	Service Departments		Production Departments		
	I	II	X	Y	Total
Overhead	$320,000	$510,000	$780,000	$405,000	
Number of Labor Hours of Dept I allocated to other Departments		38,000	60,000	70,000	168,000
Number of Pounds of Materials handled by Dept. II for the other Departments	87,000		285,000	190,000	562,000

The allocation based used by Department X is 250,000 projected labor hours. The allocation base for Department Y is projected production of 180,000 units.

Required:

Using the step method of allocation of service department costs, compute the predetermined overhead rate for each production department:

a. Assume Department I provides Department II with the greater amount of service.

b. Assume Department II provides Department I with the greater amount of service.

6A–8   The Zepher Company has two service departments and two production departments. The costs of operating the various departments are as follows:

	Service Departments		Production Departments		
	A	B	Y	Z	Total
Overhead	$30,000	$44,000	$75,000	$51,000	$200,000
Dept. A (allocation base is sq. ft. of area) Proportion allocable to each of the other Depts.		16%	39%	45%	100% of 350,000 sq. ft.
Dept. B (allocation base is direct labor hours) Proportion allocable to each of the other Depts.	20%		45%	35%	100% of 210,000 direct labor hours

Department Y's allocation base is labor cost. The projected labor cost is $390,000. Department Z's allocation base is direct labor hours. The projected direct labor hours are 130,000.

Required:

Assuming Department A provides the greater amount of services to B, compute the predetermined overhead rate for each department using the step method of allocation for service department overhead.

6A–9 The Clark Company has three service departments which provide services to two factory departments. The following annual costs have been budgeted for the various departments:

	Service			Production		
	I	II	III	Y	Z	Total
Overhead	$30,000	$50,000	$90,000	$25,000	$55,000	$250,000

The following amounts have been budgeted with regard to the services expected to be provided by the three service departments to the other departments:

Dept.	Allocation Base	Departments					
		I	II	III	Y	Z	Total
I	Machine Hrs.		70,000	80,000	100,000	100,000	350,000
II	Sq. Ft. of Space	40,000		60,000	80,000	120,000	300,000
III	Labor Cost	$100,000	$100,000		$250,000	$350,000	$800,000

Required:

Using the step method, allocate the budgeted costs of the service departments to the factory departments, assuming III renders the greatest service to the other service departments, followed by I and then II.

6A–10 The Birdsong Company manufactures cuckoo clocks. It has three service departments which serve three production departments. Annual fixed overhead of the various departments is budgeted as follows:

	Service			Production			
	I	II	III	X	Y	Z	Total
Overhead	$200,000	$300,000	$100,000	$500,000	$400,000	$600,000	$2,100,000

The following proportional breakdowns have been budgeted to the various departments:

Service Department	Allocation Base	Departments					
		I	II	III	X	Y	Z
I	Labor Hours		10%	5%	30%	25%	30%
II	Machine Hrs.	15%		15%	20%	30%	20%
III	Number of Orders	10%	12%		28%	25%	25%

Required:

Using the step method, allocate service department overhead to the various production departments assuming Department II provides services to the greatest number of other service departments, followed by I and then III.

PROBLEMS SERIES B

6B–1   The Gatler Company is made up of two production and two service departments. The production departments are the cylinder department and the finishing department, and the service departments are the maintenance department and the research department. The cylinder department's overhead is $130,000 allocated on a direct labor hour basis. The finishing department's overhead is $250,000 allocated on the basis of units finished. The maintenance department's overhead is $26,000 allocated on the basis of labor hours worked. The research department's overhead is $100,000 allocated on the basis of labor hours. The projected annual direct labor hours of the cylinder department are 10,000. The projected annual number of units finished by the finishing department are 20,000 units. The direct labor hours projected by the maintenance department are 3,000. Projected incurrence is: 30% by cylinder; 35% by finishing; and 35% by research. The direct labor hours projected by the research department are 4,000, and are allocated 70% to cylinder and 30% to finishing.

Required:

Using the direct method of allocation, assign service department costs to the production departments and compute a predetermined overhead rate for each department.

6B–2   The Light Company manufactures headlights. It is made up of three production departments: the wiring, hooking and the hitting departments. There are two service departments: engineering and materials handling. The overhead of the various departments amounted to $200,000 for wiring, $200,000 for hooking, $50,000 for hitting, $34,400 for engineering, and $48,000 for materials handling. The wiring department's allocation base is units produced. Forty thousand units are projected. The hooking department's allocation base is direct labor hours. The projected direct labor hours are 20,000. The hitting department's projected allocation base is 10,000 direct labor hours. The engineering department's allocation base is total labor hours. The projected total labor hours of 2,500 have been allocated 20% to wiring, 35% to hooking, 31% to hitting and 14% to materials handling. The materials handling department's allocation base is pounds of materials handled, which is projected at 15,000 pounds: 40% for the wiring department; 10% for hooking; 30% for hitting; and 20% for engineering.

Required:

Using the direct method of allocation for service department costs, compute the predetermined overhead rates for each of the production departments.

6B-3   The Overly Company is made up of two production departments, X and Y, and three service departments, M, N, and P. The projected fixed overhead of each department is: $100,000 for X; $150,000 for Y; $9,000 for M; $21,000 for N; and $32,000 for P. The overhead allocation bases used by each department are direct labor hours for X, machine hours for Y, pounds of materials handled for M, total labor hours for N, and units of finished product handled for P. The projected allocation bases are 5,000 direct labor hours for X and 8,000 machine hours for Y. Department M handles 20,000 pounds of materials. Approximately 35% of the material is handled for Department X, 55% for Department Y, 8% for N and 2% for P. Department N has projected 3,000 total labor hours. The allocation of the labor hours is 25% to X; 45% to Y; 15% to M; and 15% to P. Department P has projected handling 8,000 units of finished product. This amount is allocated 50% to X, 30% to Y, 7% to M and 13% to N.

Required:

Using the direct method of allocation, redistribute the overhead of the service departments to the production departments and compute the predetermined overhead rates for each production department.

6B-4   The Wyatt Company has two Production Departments, A and B, and two Service Departments, M and N. Projected overhead amounted to $20,000 for A, $30,000 for B, $8,000 for M, and $13,500 for N. Overhead in Department A is allocated in accordance with the number of physical units of projected production which is 4,000. Department B allocates overhead based upon projected direct labor hours which totaled 10,000 Department M allocates its overhead based upon the projected number of machine hours used for other departments, which amounted to 2,500 for A, 1,500 for B and 800 for N. Department N allocates overhead based upon the projected units of direct materials that it handles for the various departments, which amounted to 3,600 units for A, 5,400 units for B and 1,100 units for M.

Required:

Using the direct allocation method, allocate the overhead of the service departments to the production departments and compute the predetermined overhead rate for each production department.

6B-5   The Monday Co. has two service departments, design and maintenance, and two production departments, assembly and finishing. Projected overhead costs in the various departments are $3,000 in design, $4,800 in maintenance, $7,000 in assembly and $10,000 in finishing. Overhead in assembly is allocated in accordance with the number of machine hours used; the average annual amount is 1,000 hours. Finishing allocates overhead according to the number of direct labor hours worked; the average annual amount is 2,000 hours. Design allocates overhead according to total projected labor hours which are 5,500, of which 500 are in maintenance, 2,000 in assembly and 3,000 in finishing. Maintenance allocates overhead in accordance with the number of projected labor hours worked for each department which total 7,000, of which 1,000 are for design, 3,500 for assembly, and 2,500 for finishing.

Required:

Using the direct method, allocate the projected service departments' overhead to the production departments and compute the predetermined overhead rate for each production department.

6B–6   The Brasso Company has a maintenance department which serves three production departments. The projected annual costs are $250,000 in the maintenance department. The annual services provided are expected to be apportioned among the production departments according to one of the following bases:

Production Departments	Square Footage	Direct Labor Hours	Total Revenue of Each Prod. Dept.
A	40,000	52,500	$120,000
B	70,000	75,000	$160,000
C	90,000	22,500	$120,000
Total	200,000	150,000	$400,000

Required:

Allocate the service departments' expected annual costs to the production departments using the following allocation bases:

a. Square footage
b. Direct labor hours
c. Total revenue

6B–7   The Linen Company has three service departments which serve three production departments. Annual fixed overhead of the various departments is budgeted as follows:

	Service			Production			
	I	II	III	A	B	C	Total
Overhead	$170,000	$150,000	$100,000	$250,000	$200,000	$300,000	$1,170,000

The following proportional breakdowns have been budgeted to the various departments:

Service Department	Allocation Base	Departments					
		I	II	III	A	B	C
I	Labor Hours		20%	12%	20%	16%	32%
II	Machine Hrs.	20%		15%	40%	10%	15%
III	Number of Orders	7%	3%		27%	36%	27%

Required:

Using the step method, allocate service department overhead to the various production departments assuming Department II provides the greatest services to the other service departments, followed by I and then III.

6B–8   The Rosen Company has three service departments which provide services to two factory departments. The following annual costs have been budgeted for the various departments:

	Service			Production		
	M	N	P	X	Z	Total
Overhead	$50,000	$60,000	$100,000	$60,000	$80,000	$350,000

The following amounts have been budgeted with regard to the services expected to be provided by the three service departments to the other departments:

	Allocation	Departments					
Dept.	Base	M	N	P	X	Z	Total
I	Machine Hrs.		3,000	10,000	6,000	21,000	40,000
II	Sq. Ft. of Space	20,000		10,000	30,000	20,000	80,000
III	Labor Cost	$10,000	$10,000		$60,000	$120,000	$200,000

Required:

Using the step method, allocate the budgeted costs of the service departments to the factory departments assuming P renders the greatest service to the other service departments, followed by M and then N.

6B–9   The Sharon Company has two service departments and two production departments. The manufacturing overhead costs are as follows:

	Service Depts.		Production Depts.		
	1	2	Y	Z	Total
Overhead	$20,000	$10,000	$40,000	$50,000	$120,000
Dept. 1 (allocation base is sq. ft. of area) Proportion allocable to each of the other Depts.		15%	45%	40%	100% of 200,000 sq. ft.
Dept. 2 (allocation base is direct labor hours) Proportion allocable to each of the other Depts.	10%		45%	45%	100% of 2,000 direct labor hours

Department Y's allocation base is labor cost. The projected labor cost is $16,000. Department Z's allocation base is direct labor hours. The projected direct labor hours are 5,000.

Required:

Assuming Department 1 provides the greater amount of services to Department 2, compute the predetermined overhead rate for each department using the step method of allocation for service department overhead.

6B–10

	Service Depts.		Production Depts.		
	I	*II*	*A*	*B*	*Total*
Overhead	$20,000	$15,000	$40,000	$80,000	$155,000
Number of Labor Hours of Dept. I allocated to other Departments		1,500	5,500	3,000	10,000
Number of Pounds of Materials handled by Dept. II for the other Departments	4,000		12,000	4,000	20,000

The allocation base used by Department A is 8,000 projected labor hours. The allocation base for Department B is projected production of 2,500 units.

Required:

Using the step method of allocation of service department costs, compute the predetermined overhead rate for each production department:

a. Assume Department I provides Department II with the greater amount of service.

b. Assume Department II provides Department I with the greater amount of service.

Learning Objectives

Chapter 7 discusses and illustrates the use of a standard cost system. Studying this chapter should enable you to:

1. Distinguish between standard costs and normal costs.
2. Discuss the uses and advantages of a standard cost system.
3. Identify and explain the basic types of standards in general use.
4. Calculate the standard manufacturing overhead cost per unit.
5. Explain the sources of the direct materials and direct labor variances and how these variances are calculated.
6. Describe the alternative methods of treating variances that may be used at the end of the accounting period.

7

Cost Accounting for Inventories: Standard Costs

PRIOR To this chapter, the inventory costing systems used by manufacturing firms have been discussed and illustrated using actual historical costs for the accounting for both direct materials and direct labor. In these examples, manufacturing overhead was applied or absorbed into production using a predetermined overhead rate. Therefore, the inventory produced, absorbed or included a normal amount of overhead without regard to the actual level of production. These procedures are used in an attempt to smooth out the expected overhead costs over a sufficiently long time period in order to eliminate any distortions of cost. For example, distortions in per unit costs could be caused by fluctuations in the production schedule. These distortions are possible because the allocated fixed overhead remains relatively constant for each period, while the number of units produced varies according to production which is scheduled considering the anticipated demand for products.

It should be noted, however, that the inventory cost determined using the predetermined overhead rate introduced in Chapter 3 is not a standard cost. Rather, the overhead rate is a measure based upon the *expected* future costs that are allocated over the anticipated production and expressed per a selected unit of activity. The activity base chosen was used as the basis for applying or allocating the anticipated overhead costs to the production for the period. Standard costs, on the other hand, are based on the level of costs which *should* be incurred under efficient and effective operations. Thus standard costs do not necessarily reflect the costs which are expected to occur or actually do occur in a particular period. Standard costs are regarded as cost guidelines, or benchmarks, for the input factors of production and the related outputs resulting from the processing of these inputs.

When standard costs are used in accounting for the factors of production, the inventory cost system is referred to as a standard cost system. Standard costs may be used with either a job-order or a process cost system or with a combination and/or variation of these two basic methods for accumulating the costs of production.

PHYSICAL STANDARDS AND STANDARD COSTS

Physical standards for the production process relate to the standard requirements necessary to manufacture a product. These standards are stated or expressed in terms of quantities of raw materials, hours of direct labor, hours of processing time and similar measures. There is a general relationship between these input factors and the quantity or amount of output that may be expected or anticipated at standard levels of production. The standard costs of manufacturing are these physical standards expressed in terms of dollars of costs.

TYPES OF STANDARDS

The types of standards in general use in standard cost systems fall into three basic categories or classifications:

1. Standards based on historical or past performance.
2. Standards based on ideal performance.
3. Standards based on attainable performance.

Any standard based on historical or past performance will, by definition, include the efficiencies and inefficiencies of the period(s) of time used as the base in determining the standard. At best, this type of standard can be considered only a very rough benchmark or estimate of what may be anticipated or expected in the future. However, this does not indicate that historical performance should be ignored, but rather that it should not be used as the sole basis for establishing a standard cost for a specific cost factor for future periods.

Any standard based on ideal or engineering performance may not consider factors such as waste, downtime, fatigue, breakdowns, reworking, idle time or other similar inefficiencies. An "ideal" standard, therefore, represents perfection. All factors in the production process are assumed to interact perfectly. This type of standard cannot be ignored completely because it does represent what is possible under ideal or optimum conditions. In actual practice, an ideal standard is usually impossible to attain for all of the input factors of production for any sustained time period.

An attainable standard is an ideal or engineering standard which has been modified or adjusted for tolerable inefficiencies. Attainable standards represent a level of efficiency and effectiveness that can be attained over a sustained production period if all of the factors of production are operating and interacting at a satisfactory level. Theoretically, attainable standards are normally considered the proper standards to be applied to the many facets of management accounting.

AN IMPORTANT ADVANTAGE OF STANDARD COSTS FOR INVENTORY COSTING

For inventory costing purposes, a simple yet important advantage realized by using standard costs is clerical convenience. The raw materials inventory subsidiary ledgers can be maintained in terms of physical quantities, but without pricing these quantities at actual input prices. Material requisitions may be costed at their standard cost. When the manufacturing process is completed, the finished goods are costed and recorded at their standard cost. Historical costs are not traced to either specific units or to batches of product. Although it may seem to be somewhat unusual at first, these record keeping conveniences may make a standard cost system worthwhile even without considering the other advantages which the use of a standard cost system affords.

OTHER USES OF STANDARD COSTS

A standard cost system usually is not limited to a single primary use. Rather, standards have many and varied applications in any type of organization. Standards are useful aids to management in planning, control, performance evaluation, cost reduction programs, pricing studies, cost interpretation studies, and other types of special studies made to assist management in the decision-making process. Well designed and accepted standards enhance employee motivation, because practical guidelines or benchmarks for performance measurement are identified, communicated, and may be attained under efficient and effective operating conditions.

A COMPREHENSIVE EXAMPLE: USING STANDARD COSTS

In September 1980, the management of Sax Company decided that a standard cost system would assist the company in its planning, control, performance evaluation, and inventory costing activities. Prior to this time, the management of Sax Company had no experience in implementing a standard cost system. Therefore, it was decided that standard costs should first be introduced in the manufacturing area where the firm had the greatest production experience—the production of power turbine shafts. Power turbine shafts had become such a high volume item for Sax Company that the firm was scheduled to move into new production facilities for this product line during November. The company wished to have its standard cost job order inventory system on-line as of January 1, 1981.

Sax Company established a team for developing its standard cost system that included at least one representative from each of the basic areas involved: production management, engineering, personnel, purchasing and cost accounting. The task of this group was to develop physical standards for manufacturing from which the company's cost accounting department could determine standard costs for inventory costing and control purposes.

The team viewed its assignment as being comprised of four distinct steps:

1. Developing a standard operations routing sheet.
2. Developing a standard bill of materials.
3. Developing manufacturing overhead standards at a defined level of capacity.
4. Converting all of the manufacturing cost factors into a format that the cost accounting department could use in developing a standard cost sheet.

Operations Routing Sheet

The new facility has modern equipment and the capacity for manufacturing almost any type of turbine shaft. However, Sax's management anticipates a demand for only power turbine shafts which have been manufactured from a two-inch diameter steel shaft or billet. Sax Company also presses ball bearings onto the ends of the turbine shafts to conform to the orders of specific customers. Since the difference in size is minor, there is no difference in the cost of the bearings because of this added feature.

Two departments were established in the new facility. The machining department is charged with the responsibility for all of the initial machining work performed on the shafts. The finishing and pressing department does all of the finishing work and presses on the bearings as ordered by customers. Although many different turbines can be produced, separate operations are not necessary for the production of any of the versions currently manufactured.

The initial decision required of the standards team was to determine whether or not rework time, waiting time and setup time should be included in the operations routing sheet. After careful consideration and study, it was decided that these cost factors should be considered in determining the manufacturing overhead rate that is charged to specific jobs. There are simply too many uncontrollable variables to assume that these factors are associated with or caused by any one specific job. By including rework time, waiting time, and setup time in the manufacturing overhead charge, these costs would be allocated or spread over all of the production of any given time period instead of affecting just a few units or batches of production.

The final operations routing sheet developed by Sax's standards team is presented in Illustration 7-1.

The standard time required for processing a power turbine shaft in the machining department is 20 minutes. Sax Company wishes to use attainable standards; therefore, based on their prior experience, an 11 percent allowance for delays is built into the standard time. Remember, all rework time, waiting time, and setup time is included in the manufacturing overhead rate.

The standard time for the finishing and pressing operation is 10 minutes. Again, based on prior experience, an 11 percent allowance for delays is built into the standard time to arrive at an attainable standard.

Standard Bill of Materials

Sax Company employs two basic materials in manufacturing its power turbine shafts: a two-inch diameter steel billet and various sizes of ball bearings. As previously indicated, the ball bearings are fitted to order, but most of the production is accomplished using off-the-shelf items with standard size ball bearings. There is little or no cost differential for the materials. However, because of market conditions, Sax Company commands a higher selling price for its made-to-order power turbine shafts.

Certain indirect materials and supplies are also used in producing the power turbine shafts. The standards team felt that these items should be included in the manufacturing overhead standard, because the cost of accounting for these indirect materials and supplies probably exceed any benefits that might be derived from a separate accounting for these items as direct materials.

Illustration 7-2 presents the standard bill of materials that was prepared for the power turbine shaft production.

After preparing the standard bill of materials, the standards team had to decide on an appropriate capacity measure to be used for developing the standard manufacturing overhead rate. It was also necessary to select a base for applying the overhead to the products produced.

Illustration 7-1
Sax Company
Operations Routing Sheets

Operations Routing Sheet		
Department Machining		
Product Name Power Turbine Shafts		
Materials Round Steel Billet 2″ Diameter		
Operation	Minutes	Tools
Initial materials handling	2	
Put into lathe	3	Lathe
Machining	3	Lathe
Check machining	2	Micrometer
Machining	1	Lathe
Check machining	2	Micrometer
Final machining	3	Lathe
Materials handling	2	
Allowance for delays (11%)	2	
Standard Time	20	

Operations Routing Sheet		
Department Finishing and Pressing		
Product Name Power Turbine Shafts		
Materials Round Steel Billet from Machining		
Ball Bearings		
Operation	Minutes	Tools
Initial materials handling	2	
Finishing	3	Lathe and Polisher
Pressing	2	Hydraulic Press
Materials handling	2	
Allowance for delays (11%)	1	
Standard Time	10	

Manufacturing Overhead Costs

The standards team decided to use the practical capacity of the new facility in determining a standard for overhead. Practical capacity is that capacity that can be attained under efficient and effective operating conditions. The practical output that can be expected from the new production facility is 1,800 power turbine shafts per month. Standard direct

Illustration 7-2
Sax Company
Standard Bill of Materials

Standard Bill of Materials		
Product Power Turbine Shafts		
Location	Required Number	Description
Aisle 84	1	Round Steel Billet 2″ Diameter
Aisle 85	2	Ball Bearings — Size Varies by Order

labor hours were chosen as the base to be used for the application of overhead. Direct labor hours were considered the factor most closely related to the variable portion of manufacturing overhead in the past, and management anticipates that this relationship will hold in the new facilities. The standards team estimated that 900 direct labor hours are required to produce a total of 1,800 power turbine shafts.

The standards team made an analysis of the overhead factors and related costs that are anticipated in the new facility during 1981. The results of this study are presented in Illustration 7-3.

The standards team based its analysis of overhead costs on an output measure, the production of 1,800 units, which represents the practical capacity of the new facilities. Standard manufacturing overhead at this level of production is determined to be $3.40 per unit produced. As previously indicated, standard direct labor hours were the input measure chosen and used as the basis for applying manufacturing overhead to the products produced. The relationship between the input and output measures is known. Two power turbine shafts can be produced, at standard, for each direct labor hour worked. Overhead per direct labor hour is twice the overhead rate per unit produced since one direct labor hour is required to produce every two units of product. The standard variable overhead rate per standard direct labor hour is $2.80, and the standard fixed manufacturing overhead per standard direct labor hour totals $4.00.

The Standard Cost Sheet

After the standards team prepared a standard operations routing sheet, a standard bill of materials, and the manufacturing overhead cost standards, the entire study was forwarded to the cost accounting department. The cost accounting department made a further analysis of the data and

Illustration 7-3
Sax Company
Developing the Standard Manufacturing Overhead

Projected Practical Capacity: 1,800 Units
Standard Direct Labor Hours at Practical Capacity: 900 Hours

Standard Manufacturing Overhead Per Unit

	Variable per Unit Produced	Fixed	Total
Rework Time..........................	$ .10	0	$ 180
Waiting Time.........................	.06	0	108
Setup Time...........................	.08	0	144
Indirect Materials and Supplies...........	.60	$ 88	1,168
Indirect Labor.......................	.46	272	1,100
Electricity...........................	.10	240	420
Heat...............................	0	100	100
Equipment Depreciation................	0	600	600
Plant Depreciation....................	0	1,500	1,500
Factory Property Taxes.................	0	800	800
Totals...........................	$1.40	$3,600	$6,120

Standard Manufacturing Overhead per Unit:

Standard Variable Manufacturing Overhead per Unit................. $1.40

Standard Fixed Manufacturing Overhead per Unit........ $\dfrac{\$3,600}{1,800 \text{ units}}$ = 2.00

Standard Total Manufacturing Overhead per Unit................... $3.40

developed the standard cost sheet for power turbine shaft production that is presented in Illustration 7-4.

A COMPREHENSIVE EXAMPLE: ACCOUNTING FOR STANDARD COSTS

The actual process of record keeping for standard costs varies from company to company. To illustrate both the accounting for standard costs for purposes of inventory costing and the analysis of the related variances, assume that Sax Company wishes to integrate its standard costing system into its accounts as of January 1, 1981.

Sax Company decided that its standard cost system should be developed such that:

1. All inventories (raw materials, work-in-process, and finished goods) are accounted for at standard costs in preparing its internal monthly financial reports.

2. Any variances from standard costs are analyzed on a monthly basis, but the inventories will remain at standard costs. Variances are also analyzed and closed to the cost of goods sold account, **provided that**

Illustration 7-4
Sax Company
Standard Cost Sheet

Standard Cost Sheet
Product: Power Turbine Shafts
Basis for Cost Sheet: One Unit

Materials

Location	Standard Quantity	Standard Price per unit	Total
Aisle 84	1	$4.00	$4.00
Aisle 85	2	1.00	$2.00
			$6.00

Labor

Department	Standard Hours	Standard Hourly Rate	Total
Machining	1/3	$6.00	$2.00
Finishing and Pressing	1/6	6.00	$1.00
			$3.00

Manufacturing Overhead

Variable Overhead Per Unit	$1.40
Fixed Overhead Per Unit	2.00
Total Overhead Per Unit	$3.40

Cost Summary Per Unit

Materials @ Standard	1 Steel Billet @ $4.00	=	$ 4.00
	2 Ball Bearings @ 1.00	=	2.00
Direct Labor @ Standard	½ hour @ $6.00/hour	=	3.00
Variable Manufacturing Overhead @ Standard*		=	1.40
Fixed Manufacturing Overhead @ Standard*		=	2.00
Total Manufacturing Cost @ Standard			$12.40

*Basis of Application to Product is Standard Direct Labor Hours. Application Rate is $6.80 Per Standard Direct Labor Hour.

in so doing, the financial position and results of operations of Sax Company will not be materially distorted.

At this point, Sax Company feels that it lacks both the personnel and the expertise to make a thorough analysis of variances for control and cost reduction purposes. Sax does plan to introduce a more comprehensive system in the future.

Sax Company plans to test its standard cost system for at least a year before attempting to undertake any major modifications or refinements of the system. Recall that the company closes down for employee vacations during the last two weeks in December, so it will have sufficient time to modify the system if it appears necessary to do so.

During January, 1981, Sax Company entered into numerous transactions with regard to its power turbine shaft manufacturing operation. For purposes of this comprehensive example, these transactions are presented in summarized form along with the corresponding general journal entries. The related ledger accounts are also presented in "T" account format.

Recording Raw Material Purchases

Since Sax Company wishes to maintain all of its inventory balances at standard costs, any inventory increases or withdrawals that affect raw materials, work-in-process, or finished goods must be recorded in the accounts at standard costs. This procedure permits all of the subsidiary accounts to be maintained in terms of physical units without including the corresponding dollar amounts in these records.

As raw materials are purchased, an unfavorable price variance is recognized if the price actually paid for the materials exceeds the standard price. Alternatively, if the price paid is less than the standard price, a favorable price variance is recognized at the point of the purchase.[1]

Transaction 1. During the month, Sax Company purchased a total of 1,850 steel billets at an average price of $4.02 per billet. Assuming that all of these purchases were paid for in cash during the year, the summary journal and "T" account entries necessary to record the steel billet purchase transactions are as follows:

```
Raw Materials Inventory—Steel Billets ($4.00 X 1,850)....   7,400
Raw Materials Price Variance [($4.02-$4.00) X 1,850].....     37
    Cash ($4.02 X 1,850).............................               7,437
```

Cash		Raw Materials Inventory Steel Billets		Raw Materials Price Variance	
1/1 Bal. 20,000	7,437 (1)	(1) 7,400		(1) 37	

The raw materials price variances can also be calculated at this point using the following formula:

---

[1] In some instances, companies record their raw material inventories at actual cost. Under such a system, price variances are not recognized until the raw materials are introduced into the production process.

$$\begin{matrix} \text{Raw Materials} \\ \text{Purchase Price} \\ \text{Variance} \end{matrix} = \left(\begin{matrix} \text{Standard Price} \\ \text{per Unit} \end{matrix} - \begin{matrix} \text{Actual Price} \\ \text{per Unit} \end{matrix} \right) \times \begin{matrix} \text{Number of} \\ \text{Units} \\ \text{Purchased} \end{matrix}$$

$$= (\$4.00 - \$4.02) \times 1,850$$
$$= \$37 \text{ Unfavorable Price Variance}$$

Another method which may be used to calculate this variance is one which utilizes the total purchases of steel billets as follows:

Actual Purchases at Standard Prices (1,850 X $4.00)............ $7,400
Actual Purchases at Actual Prices (1,850 X $4.02)..............   7,437
Excess of Total Actual Prices over Standard Prices.............   ($ 37)

Both methods arrive at the identical answer.

Since all inventories are carried in the accounts at standard cost, the price variance is determined entirely within the accounting system. The debit to raw materials inventory or purchases will be at standard cost and the credit to accounts payable or cash will be at actual cost. The offsetting debit or credit will be the raw materials price variance. If the Sax Company had used actual costs in their accounting records, the formula approach could have been used for an analysis of the raw materials price variance. Both standard and actual costs must be analyzed in order to determine if the variance is favorable or unfavorable. In this case, an average price of $4.02 was actually paid for the steel billets. The standard price is $4.00. The price differential between the actual price ($4.02) and the standard price ($4.00) caused the price variance. If the standard price had been paid, any quantity could have been purchased and a price variance would not have been incurred. When standard costs are incorporated in an accounting system, an unfavorable variance is always recorded by a debit to a variance account while a favorable variance is indicated by a credit to a variance account. An unfavorable variance indicates that actual costs exceeded standard costs, while a favorable variance indicates that actual costs were less than standard costs.

Transaction 2. Sax Company purchased 4,000 ball bearings during the month and paid an average price of $.98 per ball bearing. These purchases of ball bearings caused a favorable material price variance since the price paid ($.98) was less than the standard price ($1.00).

Raw Materials Inventory—Ball Bearings ($1.00 X 4,000)...   4,000
    Raw Materials Price Variance [($1.00-$.98) X 4,000]......   80
    Cash ($.98 X 4,000)...............................   3,920

Cash		Raw Materials Inventory—Ball Bearings		Raw Materials Price Variance	
1/1 Bal. 20,000	7,437 (1) 3,920 (2)	(2) 4,000		(1) 37	80 (2)

Again, the raw materials price variance could have been calculated using the formula as follows:

$$\begin{array}{l}\text{Raw Materials} \\ \text{Purchase Price} \\ \text{Variance}\end{array} = \left(\begin{array}{l}\text{Standard Price} \\ \text{per Unit}\end{array} - \begin{array}{l}\text{Actual Price} \\ \text{per Unit}\end{array}\right) \times \begin{array}{l}\text{Actual} \\ \text{Number of} \\ \text{Units} \\ \text{Purchased}\end{array}$$

$$= (\$1.00 - \$.98) \times 4,000$$
$$= \$80 \text{ Favorable Price Variance}$$

If the total ball bearing purchases were used in the calculation, the variance would be computed as indicated below:

Actual Purchases at Standard Prices (4,000 X $1.00) $4,000
Actual Purchases at Actual Prices (4,000 X $.98) 3,920
Excess of Standard Prices over Actual Prices . . . . $ 80

Again, both of these methods will provide the same answer since the only difference is that the first calculation is made on a per unit basis while the second uses total figures.

When standard costs are incorporated into the accounting system, a favorable variance is reflected by a credit balance in a variance account. The term favorable when used in this regard indicates that the standard cost anticipated exceeded the actual cost incurred.

Recording Raw Material Transfers to Work-in-Process

Before a production run is initiated, a requisition is prepared for the standard amount of raw materials required to produce the goods. If the production run ultimately requires the use of additional raw materials, the foreman or other supervisory personnel in the production department must make a formal request for the additional raw materials needed. This request would, of course, ultimately cause an unfavorable raw materials quantity or usage variance. If less than the standard quantity of raw materials is used, then the excess materials are returned to the raw materials inventory. This return causes a favorable raw materials quantity or usage variance.

During January, Sax had formal production runs totaling 1,760 power turbine shafts. The materials requisitions, at standard quantities, were for 1,760 steel billets and 3,520 ball bearings. Additional requests for raw materials made by production foremen totaled 40 steel billets and 30 ball bearings. Therefore, the usage or quantity variances for both steel billets and ball bearings were unfavorable since the actual quantities used during the period exceeded the standard amounts.

Transaction 3. A total of 1,800 steel billets was transferred from the raw materials inventory to the work-in-process inventory. Of these billets, 1,760 were transferred by standard materials requisitions and 40 were transferred by excess materials requisitions. The summary journal entry necessary to record the transfer of all of the steel billets (both regular and excess) to work-in-process is as follows:

```
Work-in-process ($4.00 X 1,760)......................   7,040
Raw Materials Quantity Variance ($4.00 X 40)...........    160
   Raw Materials Inventory—Steel Billets ($4.00 X 1,800)..          7,200
```

Raw Materials Inventory Steel Billets		Work-in-Process	Raw Materials Quantity Variance
(1) 7,400	7,200 (3)	(3) 7,040	(3) 160

As was the case with raw materials, the work-in-process inventory account is recorded at standard costs. The raw materials quantity or usage variance can be calculated using the following formula:

$$\text{Raw Materials Quantity Variance} = (\text{Standard Quantity Allowed} - \text{Actual Quantity Used}) \times \text{Standard Price per Unit}$$

$$= (1{,}760 - 1{,}800) \times \$4.00$$
$$= \$160 \text{ Unfavorable Materials Quantity Variance}$$

Alternatively, if total amounts are used, the variance calculation is made as follows:

```
Standard Quantity Allowed at the Standard Price
   (1,760 X $4.00)..........................................   $7,040
Actual Quantity Used at the Standard Price (1,800 X $4.00).........    7,200
Excess of Quantity Used at the Standard Price....................   ($  160)
```

Again, both methods yield the identical result.

A quantity variance measures the deviation of actual from standard usage. The variance experienced by Sax Company in January was caused by the fact that an excess of 40 steel billets over the standard quantity was used during the year. The standard price is employed in calculating the variance for both the actual quantities used and the standard quantities that should have been used. Of course, a variance is introduced into the analysis only if the standard and actual quantities differ.

Transaction 4. A total of 3,550 ball bearings was transferred from raw materials inventory to the work-in-process inventory. Of these, 3,520 ball bearings were transferred by standard materials requisitions and 30 by excess materials requisitions. The summary transaction for the month would be recorded as follows:

Work-in-Process ($1.00 X 3,520)........................ 3,520
Raw Materials Quantity Variance ($1.00 X 30)...........   30
   Raw Materials Inventory—Ball Bearings ($1.00 X 3,550).   3,550

Raw Materials Inventory Ball Bearings		Work-in-Process		Raw Materials Quantity Variance	
(2) 4,000	3,550 (4)	(3) 7,040		(3) 160	
		(4) 3,520		(4) 30	

Again, both the raw materials account and the work-in-process account are maintained at standard cost. The transfer to work-in-process can be calculated at standard in either of two ways. Since 1,760 power turbine shafts were produced in January, the amount of the standard inventory transfer should have been $2.00 X 1,760 or $3,520. Alternatively, as was presented in the previous journal entry, 3,520 bearings should have been transferred at the standard price of $1.00.

The variance is calculated using the following formula:

$$\text{Raw Materials Quantity Variance} = \left(\begin{array}{c}\text{Standard Quantity Allowed}\end{array} - \begin{array}{c}\text{Actual Quantity Used}\end{array}\right) \times \begin{array}{c}\text{Standard Price per Unit}\end{array}$$

$$= (3{,}520 - 3{,}550) \times \$1.00$$
$$= \$30 \text{ Unfavorable Materials Quantity Variance}$$

If total amounts are used, the variance calculation is made as follows:

Standard Quantity Allowed at the Standard Price
(3,520 X $1.00).. $3,520
Actual Quantity Used at the Standard Price (3,550 X $1.00)......   3,550
Excess of Quantity Used at the Standard Price................. ($ 30)

This unfavorable material quantity variance was caused by the fact that 30 ball bearings in excess of the standard amount were used in the production process during the month.

Recording Direct Labor Costs

All direct labor costs are charged to jobs at the standard labor rate using the standard time established for performing a particular job or operation. However, employees are paid based on their actual pay rate and the actual amount of time that they work. Given these two statements, it is apparent that two types of direct labor variances are possible. A rate of pay either greater or lesser than the standard wage rate may be paid. This would cause Sax Company to recognize a rate variance for direct labor. In addition, the amount or quantity of direct labor worked may be more than or less than the standard amount. This would cause an efficiency or usage variance for direct labor.

Transaction 5. During January, a total of 890 direct labor hours was used by Sax Company to produce the 1,760 power turbine shafts. This amount, as per standard, *should* have been 880 hours. The actual payroll for this direct labor totaled $5,251. This amount represented an average cost of $5.90 for each direct labor hour worked. There were no wages payable at the end of the year.

When the standards team developed the standard for labor time (Illustration 7–1), it established the basis for recording the standard labor on the job cost sheets. As jobs progress through the factory, the actual time for each job is also recorded on the job cost sheets. The standard time at the standard rate is recorded by a debit to the work-in-process inventory account. Remember, all manufacturing inventory accounts are maintained at standard costs by Sax Company. Any difference between the standard time (recorded at the standard rate) and the actual time (recorded at the standard rate) is reflected in the labor efficiency or usage variance. The difference between the actual labor rates which were paid and the standard rates is multiplied by the actual hours worked to determine the labor rate variance.

The summary entry for January to record direct labor costs is as follows:

```
Work-in-Process ($6.00 X 880)............................   5,280
Direct Labor Efficiency Variance [$6.00 X (890-880)].........     60
    Cash.................................................           5,251
    Direct Labor Rate Variance [($6.00-$5.90) X 890]..........         89
```

Cash		Work-in-Process	
1/1 Bal. 20,000	7,437 (1)	(3) 7,040	
	3,920 (2)	(4) 3,520	
	5,251 (5)	(5) 5,280	

Direct Labor Efficiency Variance		Direct Labor Rate Variance	
(5) 60			89 (5)

The debit to the work-in-process account reflects the standard rate per hour ($6.00) multiplied by the standard number of hours (880) allowed to produce 1,760 power turbine shafts.

The debit to the direct labor efficiency variance account reflects the difference between the actual direct labor hours worked (890) and the standard hours that should have been worked (880) at the standard rate ($6.00). Since actual hours worked exceeded the standard established for hours worked, the direct labor efficiency variance is unfavorable. The credit to cash of $5,251 represents the actual direct labor wages paid to employees. The standard wage rate is $6.00 per hour, and employees were paid an average rate of $5.90 per hour for the 890 hours worked during January. Therefore, the direct labor rate variance was favorable and is recorded by a credit of $89 [($6.00 — $5.90) X 890] to the direct labor rate variance account.

Alternatively, the labor efficiency and rate variances could have been calculated using the following formulas:

$$
\begin{aligned}
\text{Direct Labor Efficiency Variance} &= \left(\begin{array}{c} \text{Standard Hours} \\ \text{Allowed} \end{array} - \begin{array}{c} \text{Actual Hours} \\ \text{Used} \end{array} \right) \times \\
&\qquad\qquad \begin{array}{c} \text{Standard Wage} \\ \text{Rate per Hour} \end{array} \\
&= (880 - 890) \times \$6.00 \\
&= \$60 \text{ Unfavorable Direct Labor Efficiency Variance}
\end{aligned}
$$

Or, if total amounts are used, the calculation is:

Standard Hours Allowed at the Standard Rate (880 X $6.00).......	$5,280
Actual Hours Used at the Standard Rate (890 X $6.00).............	5,340
Excess of Quantity Used at the Standard Price...................	($ 60)

$$
\begin{aligned}
\text{Direct Labor Rate Variance} &= (\text{Standard Rate} - \text{Actual Rate}) \times \\
&\qquad \text{Actual Quantity of Labor Used} \\
&= (\$6.00 - \$5.90) \times 890 \\
&= \$89 \text{ Favorable Direct Labor Rate Variance}
\end{aligned}
$$

Or, if total amounts are used:

Standard Rate at the Actual Hours Worked (890 X $6.00)..........	$5,340
Actual Rate at the Actual Hours Worked (890 X $5.90)............	5,251
Excess of Standard Rate at the Actual Hours Worked.............	$ 89

The above computations indicate that the method for calculating the labor efficiency or usage variance follows the same principles used to calculate the raw materials usage variance. The principles underlying the computation of the labor rate variance and the raw materials price variance are also identical.

Applying Manufacturing Overhead to Production

Sax Company has decided to use standard direct labor hours as a basis for applying manufacturing overhead to its products. At this point it should be noted that since all inventories are carried at standard costs, Sax Company uses standard direct labor hours rather than actual direct labor hours because to do otherwise would allow the efficiencies or inefficiencies of labor to affect the amount of overhead absorbed by a specific job. By using standard direct labor hours, the inventories are maintained at standard costs. The use of standard direct labor hours provides the same absorption of overhead by products as the output measure, units finished, would provide. Standard direct labor hours are relatively easy to calculate and are homogeneous in that one standard direct labor hour is identical to all other standard hours.

The manufacturing overhead applied at standard for Sax Company is determined by multiplying the total standard direct labor hours for January (880) by the manufacturing overhead rate at standard (obtained from the standard cost sheet presented in Illustration 7-4). The standard manufacturing overhead rate is $6.80 per standard direct labor hour.

Transaction 6. The manufacturing overhead applied to the 1,760 power turbine shafts produced in January totaled $5,984 ($6.80 X 880). The summary journal and "T" account entries required to record the overhead for January are as follows:

Work-in-Process ($6.80 X 880)............................ 5,984
    Manufacturing Overhead—Control ($6.80 X 880)........... 5,984

Work-in-Process		Manufacturing Overhead—Control	
(3) 7,040			5,984 (6)
(4) 3,520			
(5) 5,280			
(6) 5,984			

Recording Transfers from Work-in-Process

As goods are completed, they are transferred from the work-in-process inventory to the finished goods inventory at their standard cost.

Transaction 7. During January, a total of 1,760 power turbine shafts were completed and transferred to the finished goods inventory. The standard cost of one power turbine shaft is $12.40, according to Sax Company's standard cost sheet (Illustration 7-4). The total transferred to finished goods is therefore 1,760 X $12.40 or $21,824. The summary journal and "T" account entries required to recognize the transfers from work-in-process to finished goods are:

Finished Goods Inventory ($12.40 X 1,760)................... 21,824
    Work-in-Process ($12.40 X 1,760)....................... 21,824

Work-in-Process		Finished Goods	
(3) 7,040	21,824 (7)	(7) 21,824	
(4) 3,520			
(5) 5,280			
(6) 5,984			

For any goods sold during January, the cost of goods sold associated with these sales would also be recognized at standard cost. (Sales for the period will be recorded in Transaction 9.)

Recording Actual Manufacturing Overhead Costs

Sax Company's actual manufacturing overhead costs for January totaled $6,320. An analysis of the subsidiary records revealed the following components of the actual manufacturing overhead for January.

Rework Time..........................	$ 160
Waiting Time.........................	100
Setup Time...........................	140
Indirect Materials and Supplies...........	1,100
Indirect Labor.......................	1,160
Electricity............................	700
Heat	60
Equipment Depreciation...............	600
Plant Depreciation....................	1,500
Factory Property Taxes.................	800
	$6,320

The rework time, waiting time, setup time and indirect labor were all labor costs which were paid but which were not reflected in the direct labor payroll recorded in Transaction 5. The indirect materials and supplies were obtained from the materials and supplies inventory. The electricity, heat, and property taxes were all paid. The total cash outlay for the manufacturing overhead items for the period was $3,120.

Transaction 8. Actual manufacturing overhead costs incurred during the period are $6,320. The summary entry necessary to record the actual manufacturing overhead for January is as follows:

Manufacturing Overhead—Control.....................	6,320	
Cash...		3,120
Indirect Materials and Supplies Inventory.............		1,100
Accumulated Depreciation—Equipment...............		600
Accumulated Depreciation—Plant...................		1,500

Manufacturing Overhead—Control		Cash	
(8) 6,320	5,984 (6)	1/1 Bal. 20,000	7,437 (1)
			3,920 (2)
			5,251 (5)
			3,120 (8)

Indirect Materials and Supplies Inventory	
1/1 Bal. 2,000	1,100 (8)

Accumulated Depreciation—Equipment		Accumulated Depreciation—Plant	
	600 (8)		1,500 (8)

Manufacturing overhead of $5,984 at standard cost was applied to the products during the month in Transaction 6. As indicated in Transaction 8, however, the actual manufacturing overhead for the year was $6,320. Manufacturing overhead costs were, therefore, underapplied by a total of $336. This difference will be analyzed in Chapter 8.

Recording Cost of Goods Sold at Standard

The finished goods inventory is recorded and accounted for at standard cost. As the goods are sold, any cost of goods sold is also recognized at standard cost.

Transaction 9. A total of 1,600 power turbine shafts were sold during January at an average selling price of $50 per shaft. All but $2,000 of these sales had been collected by month-end.

The summary entry to record this transaction is as follows:

```
Cash [($50 X 1,600)—$2,000]........................     78,000
Accounts Receivable.................................      2,000
      Sales Revenue ($50 X 1,600)........................           80,000
```

Cash		Accounts Receivable	
1/1 Bal. 20,000	7,437 (1)	(9) 2,000	
(9) 78,000	3,920 (2)		
	5,251 (5)		
	3,120 (8)		

Sales Revenue	
	80,000 (9)

The cost of goods sold for January is recorded by the following entry:

```
Cost of Goods Sold ($12.40 X 1,600).....................     19,840
      Finished Goods Inventory ($12.40 X 1,600).............           19,840
```

Cost of Goods Sold		Finished Goods Inventory	
(9) 19,840		(7) 21,824	19,840 (9)

The cost of goods sold account represents the standard cost of the goods sold during the period. For income statement purposes, the management of Sax Company wishes to close out all of the variance accounts to the cost of goods sold account at the end of the month.

Closing the Variance Accounts

At the end of January, Sax Company decided to adjust the amount of cost of goods sold used for income statement purposes to include the net effect of all of the variances from standard costs which were experienced during the month. This means that the cost of goods sold account will absorb all of the differences between standard and actual costs that were recognized during the month. In effect, closing all the variance accounts to the cost of goods sold account will convert Sax's standard cost system to an actual cost system for income statement purposes.[2]

The balances in the cost of goods sold account and the individual variance accounts at the end of January are as follows:

Raw Materials Price Variance	
(1) 37	80 (2)
	43

Raw Materials Quantity Variance	
(3) 160	
(4) 30	
190	

Direct Labor Efficiency Variance	
(5) 60	
60	

Direct Labor Rate Variance	
	89 (5)
	89

Manufacturing Overhead—Control	
(8) 6,320	5,984 (6)
336	

Cost of Goods Sold	
(9) 19,840	
19,840	

Transaction 10. In order to close out the variance accounts to the cost of goods sold account, the following journal entry is necessary:

Cost of Goods Sold.........................	454	
Raw Materials Price Variance...............	43	
Direct Labor Rate Variance.................	89	
Raw Materials Quantity Variance.........		190
Direct Labor Efficiency Variance..........		60
Manufacturing Overhead—Control........		336

Raw Materials Price Variance	
(1) 37	80 (2)
(10) 43	43

Raw Materials Quantity Variance	
(3) 160	
(4) 30	
190	190 (10)

---

[2] As discussed in Chapter 3, the variances, if material in amount, should be apportioned on a weighted average basis among the ending inventories of work-in-process, finished goods and the cost of goods sold. All accounts would approximate actual costs via this apportionment.

Direct Labor Efficiency Variance	
(5) 60	
60	60 (10)

Direct Labor Rate Variance	
	89 (5)
(10) 89	89

Manufacturing Overhead— Control	
(8) 6,320	5,984 (6)
336	336 (10)

Cost of Goods Sold	
(9) 19,840	
(10) 454	
20,294	

By adopting this procedure, the management of Sax Company is assuming that the net variance of $454 is immaterial for purposes of financial reporting. This does not imply, however, that the individual variances are immaterial or insignificant for purposes of managerial analysis. Management will decide which variances to investigate in detail.

SUMMARY

A standard cost system is often used in conjunction with a job order or process costing system to facilitate the costing of inventory. In a standard cost system, products are costed at that cost which should have been incurred under efficient and effective operations. Any deviations from the standard cost are reflected as variances at the end of the period.

Standard costs differ from normal costs in that normal costs are a combination of actual and expected costs, whereas standard costs are entirely based on costs expected under a given set of conditions. In addition to the obvious clerical convenience resulting from their use, standard costs are useful aids in planning, control, performance evaluation, and other management activities. If well-designed, standard costs may also be an effective means of employee motivation.

Standard costs are based on the physical standards of production. Physical standards relate to the quantities of materials, labor, processing time, etc., that are required under standard conditions to produce the product. Several types of standard costs are in general use. These types include standards based on (1) historical or past performance, (2) ideal or engineering performance, and (3) attainable performance. Of these, standard costs based on attainable performance are preferred for management accounting purposes.

The variance in direct materials cost and in direct labor cost can usually be explained by two factors: (1) the actual price paid differing from the standard price (referred to as the price or rate variance) and (2) the actual quantity used differing from the standard quantity (referred to as the quantity or efficiency variance). When variance accounts are incorporated in the accounting system, the variance accounts will be closed at the end of the accounting period. If immaterial in amount, the variances are generally closed directly to the cost of goods sold for the period. However, if material in amount, the balances should be apportioned on a weighted average basis to the ending work-in-process, finished goods inventories, and to the cost of goods sold.

Following is a summary of the equations for your reference of the standard cost variances listed in this chapter.

1. Material Price Variance =
$$\left(\begin{array}{c} \text{Standard Price} \\ \text{per Unit} \end{array} - \begin{array}{c} \text{Actual Price} \\ \text{per Unit} \end{array} \right) \times \begin{array}{c} \text{Actual Number of} \\ \text{Units Purchased} \end{array}$$

2. Material Quantity Variance =
$$\left(\begin{array}{c} \text{Standard Quantity} \\ \text{Allowed} \end{array} - \begin{array}{c} \text{Actual Quantity} \\ \text{Used} \end{array} \right) \times \begin{array}{c} \text{Standard Price} \\ \text{per Unit} \end{array}$$

3. Direct Labor Rate Variance =
$$\left(\begin{array}{c} \text{Standard Rate} \\ \text{per Hour} \end{array} - \begin{array}{c} \text{Actual Rate} \\ \text{per Hour} \end{array} \right) \times \begin{array}{c} \text{Actual Number of Hours of} \\ \text{Direct Labor Used} \end{array}$$

4. Direct Labor Efficiency Variance =
$$\left(\begin{array}{c} \text{Standard Hours} \\ \text{Allowed} \end{array} - \begin{array}{c} \text{Actual Hours} \\ \text{Used} \end{array} \right) \times \begin{array}{c} \text{Standard Wage} \\ \text{Rate per Hour} \end{array}$$

KEY DEFINITIONS

Attainable standard—a satisfactory level of efficiency where the ideal standard has been modified to allow for normal tolerable inefficiencies.

Favorable variance—a variance which occurs in a standard cost accounting system when actual costs are less than standard costs. A favorable variance is recorded by a credit to a variance account.

Ideal standard—the highest level of efficiency attainable, based on all input factors interacting perfectly under ideal or optimum conditions.

Labor efficiency or usage variance—a variance occurring in a standard cost accounting system when the actual amount or quantity of direct labor used differs from the standard amount required.

Labor rate variance—a variance which occurs in a standard cost accounting system when the actual pay rate differs from the standard pay rate for direct labor.

Materials price variance—a variance which occurs in a standard cost accounting system when actual prices paid for raw materials differ from the standard prices.

Materials quantity or usage variance—a variance which occurs in a standard cost accounting system when the actual amounts of raw materials used to produce a good differ from the standard amounts required to produce that good.

Practical capacity—that level of production that can be attained under efficient and effective operating conditions.

Standard costs—costs which are assigned to the factors of production based on physical standards under efficient and effective operations required to manufacture the product, and not necessarily the costs which are expected to occur or actually do occur.

Standard cost system—an inventory cost system where standard costs are used in accounting for the factors of production.

Unfavorable variance—a variance which occurs in a standard cost accounting system when actual costs exceed standard costs. An unfavorable variance is recorded by a debit to a variance account.

QUESTIONS

1. What is the purpose of using standard costs?
2. How does allocating fixed overhead cause distortions in per unit costs from period to period?
3. What are the three basic classifications used to determine standard costs? Theoretically, which of these standards should be applied to a standard cost system?
4. Is there any one primary use of a standard cost system? If so, what is it?
5. What is the rationale behind including rework time, waiting time, and set up time in manufacturing overhead?
6. At what two times may a material price variance be recognized, and at which time do you feel it is the more correct for control reasons?
7. What are the two possible variances associated with direct labor costs and identify one reason why each could occur?
8. Which of the following variances are favorable (F)? Unfavorable (U)?

   a. Debit to direct labor efficiency variance.
   b. Credit to direct labor rate variance.
   c. Debit to raw material price variance.
   d. Credit to material quantity variance.

9. If end-of-the-period variances are material in amount, how should they be apportioned?
10. In conjunction with what type of cost systems may standard costs be used?

EXERCISES

7–1 The Walters Manufacturing Company has established the following standards for one unit of their product, Alpha.

Material . . . . 6 lb. @ $8.00/lb.
Labor . . . . 12 hr. @ $6.00/hr.

During August, the Walters Manufacturing Company purchased 7,000 pounds of material at $56,350 and incurred total labor costs of $71,248. 1,000 units of Alpha were produced. They used 6,220 pounds of material and 11,680 hours of labor.

Required:

a. Compute the material price and usage variances.
b. Compute the labor rate and efficiency variances.

7–2 The Goodness Company uses a standard cost system with the following standard costs:

Material, 5 pounds @ $6.00/pound $30.00
Labor, 3 hours @ $4.50/hour 13.50
Overhead, 3 hours @ $7.00/hour 21.00

Total standard cost per unit $64.50

During the year, 10,000 units were produced. Costs incurred for material and labor were $325,000 and $135,000 respectively.

Required:

Calculate the total material variance and labor variance from standard costs. It is not necessary to calculate price, rate, and efficiency variances.

7–3 You are given the following information about the King Company:

Standard cost of one whatisit:
1 pound of material @ $1 . . . . $1
2 hours of direct labor @ $2 per hour 4
$5

Required:

During the month of May, King produces 1 whatisit. Prepare journal entries to record the following transactions which occurred in May. You must use King's standard cost system.

a. Materials purchased and used in May—2 pounds at $2 per pound
b. Labor (Direct) for May—3 hours @ $1.50 per hour

Assume no beginning or ending material inventory.

7–4 You have been given the following information:

Actual labor hours used = 315 hours
Standard materials price = $2.50 per unit
Standard labor hours used = 300 hours
Standard quantity of materials used = 450 units
Actual labor rate per hour = $3.00
Actual quantity of materials purchased and used = 445 units
Standard labor rate per hour = $3.10
Actual materials price = $2.52 per unit

Required:

Prepare a schedule for the following variances:

a. Raw materials price variance
b. Raw materials quantity variance
c. Direct labor efficiency variance
d. Direct labor rate variance

7–5   The Simons Company manufactures bolts in standard batches of 5,000 units. The standard cost for a batch is as follows:

Raw materials 200 lbs. @ $.04 per lb.	$ 8.00
Direct labor 4 hrs. @ $5.15 per hour	20.60
Overhead (including variable overhead of $4.50)	10.00
Total standard cost	$38.60

Data for the month of March is as follows:

Planned production	240 batches
Actual production	250 batches
Cost of raw materials purchased (55,000 lbs.)	$2,310.00
Cost of raw materials used (51,250 lbs.)	$2,152.50
Direct labor cost (998 hours)	$5,189.60
Actual overhead cost	$2,560.00
Budgeted fixed overhead cost	$1,320.00

Required:

Compute the following variances indicating whether favorable or unfavorable.

a. Raw materials price variance
b. Raw materials quantity variance
c. Direct labor rate variance
d. Direct labor efficiency variance

7–6   Given the following information, what is the standard cost per finished unit?

Normal activity—10,000 units

Standard Costs:

Direct materials	$2 per lb.
Direct labor	$4.20 per hr.
Variable overhead	$2.75 per direct labor hr.
Fixed overhead	$30,000

Standard Quantity:

Direct materials	5 lbs. per unit
Direct labor	3 hrs. per unit

7–7   All of the items listed below are included in the budgeted manufacturing overhead costs of the Ames Company's only product. Projected production is 300,000 units. At standard, the overhead costs are:

	Fixed Costs	Total Costs
Rework time	$ –0–	$ 15,000
Set-up time	–0–	36,000
Indirect materials	10,200	250,200
Indirect supplies	2,000	8,000
Indirect labor	20,000	170,000
Electricity	1,075	1,075
Heat	1,900	1,900
Telephone	350	350
Equipment depreciation	15,000	15,000
Factory property taxes	9,475	9,475
	$60,000	$507,000

Required:

Calculate the standard variable manufacturing overhead per unit, the standard fixed manufacturing overhead per unit, and the total manufacturing overhead per unit.

7–8   The Taylor Company would like you to calculate for them the standard costs per unit for their product, widgets. Each unit must go through two departments, processing and finishing. The hourly employees in the processing department are paid $5.00 an hour and $6.15 an hour in finishing. Materials used in the processing department for making widgets include wids for $20 per kilogram and gets for $6 per kilogram. Practical capacity is expected to be 50,000 units per year. From the additional information listed below provided by various departments in the Taylor Company, calculate the standard cost per unit for material, labor, and overhead. Use the high-low method to calculate the fixed and variable cost components of manufacturing overhead.

Department	Processing	
Product Name	Widgets	
	Operation	Minutes per widget
	Materials handling	5
	Machining	6
	Check machining	2
	Final machining	4
	Materials handling	4
	Allowance for delays	3
		24

Department	Finishing	
Product Name	Widgets	
	Operation	Minutes per widget
	Materials handling	3
	Finishing	6
	Final inspection	2
	Materials handling	6
	Allowance for delays	3
		20

Standard Bill of Materials
Department   Processing
Product Name   Widgets

Material	Required number
Wids	1 Kilogram
Gets	3 Kilograms

Manufacturing Overhead Costs
Departments   Processing and Finishing
Product Name   Widgets

Year	Units Produced	Costs
1979	48,000	249,600
1980	45,000	240,000

7–9 The Loren Company produces one product with the following standard costs per unit:

Materials, 2 pounds at $3.25 . . . . $ 6.50
Labor, 5 hours at $2.05 . . . . 10.25
Manufacturing overhead:
  Variable $1.00 per hour × 5 hours = $5.00
  Fixed $120,000 = $.50 per hour × 5 hours = $2.50   7.50
      240,000 (hours practical yearly capacity)
                                                    _____
                                                    $24.25

Journalize the following transactions for the Loren Company for June. Units produced during the month totaled 3,000.

a. Purchased 6,400 pounds of material at a cost of $19,600 on account.

b. Issued 6,300 pounds of material to production to be used during June.

c. 21,500 labor hours were charged to production during June at a cost of $2.00 per hour.

d. Actual overhead incurred was $22,000 for variable overhead and $9,500 for fixed overhead. The variable overhead was paid for in cash and the fixed overhead was made up entirely of depreciation on plant and equipment.

e. Applied overhead was recorded based on standard direct labor hours.

f. Sales in June totaled 2,900 units at a mark-up of 40% on standard costs.

g. There were no beginning inventories on June 1. Variances are closed to the cost of goods sold at year end, on December 31.

7–10 Given the following balances in the variance accounts, journalize the closing entry.

Direct Materials Price Variance	
	9,750

Direct Materials Quantity Variance	
16,200	

Direct Labor Efficiency Variance		Direct Labor Rate Variance	
2,800			12,800

Manufacturing Overhead Control	
22,600	

7–11   During December the Strickem Co. produced 4,000 hunting knives which required 12,380 ounces of steel and 6,000 quarts of plastic (raw material plastic in liquid form). In order to do this, Strickem purchased 15,000 ounces of steel for $6,450 and 7,000 quarts of plastic for $2,100. The payroll for December amounted to $14,895. Total hours worked were 1,960 hours. The following are the per unit standards for material and labor established by Strickem.

Material
  Steel, 3 oz. @ $.40/oz.
  Plastic, 1.5 quarts @ $.30/quart
Labor
  ½ hour at $7.50/hr.

Required:

a.   Calculate the material price and quantity variances.
b.   Calculate the labor rate and efficiency variances.

7–12   The following summarizes the standard cost for producing one metal tennis racket frame for McMullian Corp. In addition, the variances for January's production are given. Note that all inventory accounts have zero balances at the beginning of January.

	Standard Costs/Unit	Standard Production Costs
Materials	$4.00	$ 8,400
Direct Labor, 2 hrs. @ $2.60	5.20	10,920
Manufacturing Overhead:		
Variable	1.80	3,780
Fixed	5.00	10,500
		$33,600

Variances

Material price	($222.50) *
Material quantity	(500.00)
Direct labor rate	(750.94)
Direct labor efficiency	(2,096.25)

Required:

Determine the following for a tennis racket frame:

a.   Actual direct labor hours.
b.   Actual direct labor rate.

c. Actual materials used.

d. Actual per unit price for materials.

° Brackets indicate unfavorable variances.

7–13 In July, fire destroyed the XYZ Company's manufacturing facilities and inventory. The company's accounting records were saved; however, all inventory accounts were kept at standard costs. As an insurance adjustor, you are required to use the available records to determine the actual materials and labor costs for the month of July. The materials price variance is as calculated at the point of transfer into work in process. (Note: Inventory accounts have zero balances at the end of June.)

	Per Unit Standard Costs
Materials, 5 lbs. @ $.50/lb.	$ 2.50
Labor, 2 hrs. @ $2.25/hr.	4.50
Variable manufacturing overhead, 4 hrs. @ $3.00/hr.	12.00
Total standard cost (variable)	$19.00
Standard production and actual production	900 units

Material Price Variance	Material Quantity Variance
$90	$50

Direct Labor Rate Variance	Direct Labor Efficiency Variance
$9.40	$177.50

7–14 Because of inflation and a new labor agreement, Miller Thunderbolt Co. is revising its standard costs of producing a toy race car. The new labor agreement increased direct labor rates $.15 per hour. In addition, Thunderbolt Co. is facing a 6 percent increase in the cost of materials. From the available information, calculate the new standard cost for material per unit produced and labor per hour. Raw materials used in production is the amount of raw materials purchased.

1. Normal production = 750 units
2. Actual material purchases = $2,195
3. Actual direct labor wages paid = $6,795
4. Actual production = 723 units
5. Materials price variance = $46.30 Favorable
6. Actual direct labor hours = 2,265
7. Direct labor rate variance = $135.90 Favorable

PROBLEMS SERIES A

7A–1 The Allen Production Company requires two materials, A and B, to manufacture their product, X. During January they produced 4,500,000 units of X. Allen Company purchased 310,000 gallons of material A at the cost of $24,180 and 25,000 pounds of material B for $3,250.

During January, Allen Company used 275,000 gallons of material A and 21,000 pounds of material B. The Allen Company has established the following material standards:

> For 1,000 units of X:
> Material A, 30 gallons @ $.08/gallon $2.40
> Material B, 2.5 pounds @ $.12/pound 30

Required:

Compute the material price and quantity variances for materials A and B.

7A-2   Dente Company has established the following standard costs for its materials and direct labor:

	Per Finished Unit
Materials, 20 gallons @ $4.00	$ 80
Direct labor, 10 hours @ $3.00	30
	$110

During the month, purchases amounted to 10,000 gallons of materials at a total cost of $50,000. The number of finished units budgeted for the period was 500; 480 were actually produced. The actual operating results were as follows:

> Materials, 9,500 gallons used
> Direct labor, 4,900 hours at a cost of $19,600

Required:

Show computations for all material and labor variances.

7A-3   Wilson Corporation makes one product, tennis rackets. During May, in preparation for the summer season, Wilson produced 500 tennis rackets. The established standard variable costs for one racket follow:

Materials, 10 pounds @ $ .45/pound	$ 4.50
Labor, 3 hours @ $2.15/hour	6.45
Variable manufacturing overhead, 3 hours @ $2.75/hour .	8.25
	$19.20

The Wilson Corporation purchased 5,500 pounds of material at a cost of $2,695. The production department used 5,150 pounds of material. The payroll for direct labor hours of 1,495 amounted to $3,289.

Required:

Calculate the material and labor variances for the Wilson Corporation.

7A-4   Krueger, Inc. uses a standard cost system. Given below is the standard cost information:

> For one unit of product: Materials—3 pounds @ $2 per pound
> Labor—4 hours @ $3.50 per hour

Additional information:

1. There was no beginning or ending work-in-process inventory. A total of 6,500 units of product were produced during the period.
2. A total of 19,580 pounds of materials which cost $38,181 were used during the period.
3. Direct labor costs totaling $93,528 were incurred during the period. Actual hours worked were 25,980.

Required:

Compute the variances from standard for materials and labor for the period. Label properly and indicate whether the variances are favorable or unfavorable. The quantity of materials purchased was the same as the quantity used in production.

7A–5 The Garner Manufacturing Company produces a single product. Its standard cost is as follows:

Materials, 2 pounds at $6.50 . . . . $ 13.00
Labor, 3 hours at $3.75 . . . . 11.25
Manufacturing expenses, 3 hours at $2.25
  (including $1.75 of variable overhead) 6.75
                                          $ 31.00

Standard manufacturing overhead expenses . . . $16,875
Standard labor hours . . . .   7,500 = $2.25 per hour

Production (2,500 units) started and completed for the month of June: Production capacity 2,500 units.

1. Purchases of materials, 6,000 pounds at $6.60
2. Materials requisitioned, 4,900 pounds
3. Payroll, 7,560 hours at $3.90 per hour
4. Manufacturing expenses incurred during June totaled $17,000 (including $4,000 fixed overhead)
5. Sales 2,000 units at $40

Required:

Journal entries to record the transactions for the month, using a standard cost system, and transferring variances to their proper accounts. (Do not distribute them to the ending inventory.) The Garner Manufacturing Company closes its books at the end of each month.

7A–6 A manufacturing firm produces three varieties of a basic product which are manufactured from *two* raw materials.

Finished Product	Standard Usage per Finished Unit Units of Raw Material		Standard Prices
	A	B	
R	1	2	Raw material A $4.00 per unit
S	2	2	Raw material B $3.00 per unit
T	2	3	

Purchases:

Material A 100,000 units $405,000
Material B 140,000 units $415,800

Usage:

Material A   75,600 units
Material B 115,000 units

Finished Units:	Variety	Amount
	R	15,000 items
	S	15,000 items
	T	15,000 items

Required:

Make the journal entries for materials: (*a*) purchases and (*b*) usage as they would appear under an actual cost system and as they would appear under a standard cost system. Assume no previous balances in any of the accounts.

7A–7   The Beaulieu Company uses a process cost system and standard costs. Below are the standard costs per unit for their only product, Bangles.

Material, 2 gallons @ $3.50/gallon $7.00
Labor, 0.2 hours @ $3.00/hour 60
Overhead: Variable @ $2.25/hour = .45
    Fixed ° @ $1.00/hour = .20 65
Total standard cost per Bangle $8.25

° Fixed overhead is based on a normal capacity of 10,100 Bangles.

Production statistics for January are as follows:

Bangles produced this month—8,000.
Ending work-in-process—3,000; 100 percent complete for material, 70 percent complete for labor, and 70 percent complete for overhead.
There was no beginning work-in-process inventory.
Costs incurred this month were $90,000, $6,900 and $6,600 for material, labor and overhead, respectively.
25,000 gallons of material and 3,000 labor hours were actually incurred.
The materials price variance is calculated at the time of transfer into work in process.

Required:

Using the weighted average method to determine the cost flow for January compute:

    a. The material price and usage variances.
    b. The labor rate and efficiency variances.

7A–8   The Scott Company would like to compare material costs in June to material costs in July. Below is relevant information for both months.

Month	Material Costs	Pounds of Material Used	Units Produced
June	$58,590	18,600	6,200
July	$63,488	19,840	6,400

Required:

Using June material prices and usage as a standard, calculate the material price and usage variances for July. Why can't you add these two variances together to arrive at the total material variance of $4,898 ($63,488 − $58,590)?

7A–9   *a.*   Which of the items listed below could *not* be considered a use of a standard cost system?

    1. Inventory costing.
    2. Bookkeeping convenience.
    3. Performance evaluation.
    4. Pricing studies.
    5. None of the above.

    b.   Which of the following is *not* a reason for a material price variance:

    1. Inadequate control over material requisitions.
    2. Seasonal purchases of material.
    3. Cheaper method of transportation.
    4. Volume purchasing of material.
    5. Less expensive sources for raw material.

    c.   At the end of the period, all variances in the individual variance accounts, theoretically should be

    1. closed to cost of goods sold.
    2. apportioned on a weighted average basis to the ending inventories of work-in-process, finished goods, and cost of goods sold.
    3. closed to the ending inventory of work-in-process.
    4. apportioned on a weighted average basis to the beginning inventories of work-in-process, finished goods, and cost of goods sold.
    5. closed to the ending inventory of finished goods.

7A–10   The Hanlon Co. manufactures a product called Pattimar which has the following Standard Cost Sheet:

Standard Cost Sheet

Product: Pattimar
Basis for Cost Sheet: One Unit

		Materials		
#	Location	Standard Quantity	Standard Price/Unit	Total
1	Bin 57	3	$2.00	$6.00
2	Bin 72	5	.60	3.00
				$9.00

	Labor		
Department	Standard Hours	Standard Hourly Rate	Total
Assembly	2	$4.50	$ 9.00
Finishing	1	5.00	5.00
			$14.00

Manufacturing Overhead

Variable overhead per unit	$ 7.00
Fixed overhead per unit	9.00
Total overhead per unit	$16.00

The company's records indicate the following production and cost figures:

```
Units produced . . . . . . . . .  18,000
Material used
     #1 . . . . . . . . . . . . . .  56,800 units
     #2 . . . . . . . . . . . . . .  91,200 units
Labor costs
Assembly (35,980 hours) . . . . .  $165,508
Finishing (18,200 hours) . . . . .  $ 88,270
Materials purchased:
     #1 . . . . . . . . . . . . . .  ( 60,000 units )for $129,000
     #2 . . . . . . . . . . . . . .  (100,000 units) for $ 55,000
```

Required:

Calculate materials price and quantity variances for each material and labor rate and efficiency variances for each department.

7A–11   You have been hired by Mama Verdi to discover why she is not making as large a profit as she had expected from her famous Italian sauce. The three main ingredients are Thats, Asum, and Asausa. Mama's secret formula calls for 2 parts Asum for every one part Thats for every

3 parts Asausa therefore yielding 6 parts of sauce. The following information was found in the records in Mama's kitchen:

1. 12,000 gallons of sauce made in August
2. 6,000 gallons of Thats purchased for $7,200
3. 7,000 gallons of Asum purchased for $13,800
4. 8,000 gallons of Asausa purchased for $12,400
5. Standard cost of Thats/gallon = $1.15
6. Standard cost of Asum/gallon = $2.00
7. Standard cost of Asausa/gallon = $1.50
8. 5,000 gallons of Asum used in August
9. 3,500 gallons of Thats used in August
10. 6,600 gallons of Asausa used in August

Required:

Calculate the material price and quantity variance for Thats, Asum, and Asausa for the month of August.

PROBLEMS SERIES B

7B–1   Three materials, Fe, Fi, and Fo, are required to produce one product, Fum. During August, the Giant Company produced 50,500 units of Fum. They purchased 60,800 pounds of Fe, 26,500 gallons of Fi, and 72,000 yards of Fo at a cost of $13,376, $3,577.50, and $23,040, respectively. Usage included 60,650 pounds of Fe, 25,200 gallons of Fi, and 70,745 yards of Fo. The following standards have been established for one unit of Fum by the Giant Company.

$$Fe = 1.2 \text{ pounds @ } \$.20 \text{ per pound}$$
$$Fi = .5 \text{ gallons @ } \$.14 \text{ per gallon}$$
$$Fo = 1.4 \text{ yards @ } \$.30 \text{ per yard}$$

Required:

Compute the material price and quantity variances for Fe, Fi, and Fo used in the production of Fum during August.

7B–2   Cooper, Inc. has established the following standards for direct materials and direct labor:

	Cost per Finished Unit
Materials, 5½ pounds @ $1.80	$ 9.90
Labor, 2 hours @ $6.00	12.00
	$21.90

During the month, 540 units were produced. Purchases and actual operating results were as follows:

Purchases—3,500 pounds at a cost of $6,475
Materials—3,000 pounds used
Direct labor—1,076 hours at a cost of $6,542.08

Required:

Show computations for all material and labor variances.

7B–3   Nancy Company produced 17,800 footballs during May. Material purchases amounted to 184,000 pounds at $2.10 per pound. Usage of the materials amounted to 92,200 pounds. The footballs required 53,000 hours of labor at $4.20 per hour. Nancy Company has established the following material and labor standards for one football:

> 5 lb. of material at $2.00 per lb. $10.00
> 3 hrs. of labor at $4.00 per hour 12.00

Required:

Compute the material and labor variances for May.

7B–4   Gentle Ben, Inc. uses a standard cost system. It manufactures a single product, teddy bears, and its standard costs are as follows:

> Materials, 4 pounds @ $.75 . . . . $ 3.00
> Direct labor, 2 hours @ $2.50 . . . . 5.00
> Variable overhead applied at $.90 per direct labor hour 1.80
> Fixed overhead, applied at $.60 per direct labor hour 1.20
> $11.00

The normal production per month is 1,200 bears. All material is introduced at the beginning of the operation. There were no beginning inventories. A total of 1,100 bears were completed during October. The 100 units in process at the end of the month were 30% complete as to labor and overhead.

Materials weighing 6,000 pounds were acquired during the month for $4,680. Material usage for October was 4,870 pounds. Direct labor incurred during October was 2,250 hours at $2.55 per hour.

Required:

Prepare a schedule showing your calculation of material and labor variances. Indicate whether the variances are favorable (F) or unfavorable (U).

7B–5   Babbic, Inc. produces a single product, socks. Its standard cost for a dozen pairs of socks is as follows:

> Materials, 1½ pound @ $.80 . . . . $1.20
> Labor, ½ hour @ $6.00 . . . . 3.00
> Manufacturing overhead, $8.00 per labor hour (including
> $5.00 per labor hour for variable overhead) 4.00
> $8.20

Additional information for January:

1. There were no beginning inventories.
2. Units started and completed = 6,400 dozen
3. Purchases = 10,000 pounds @ $.82
4. Materials requisitioned = 9,570 pounds
5. Payroll = 3,290 hours @ $6.12 per hour
6. Manufacturing overhead expenses incurred = $26,975 (including $9,500 for fixed overhead)
7. Sales = 6,000 dozen @ $10.00
8. Plant capacity = 6,400 dozen

Required:

Journal entries to record the transactions for January, using a standard cost system, and transferring the variances to the cost of goods sold account. The Babbic Company closes its books at the end of each month.

7B–6 A clothing company has just switched from an actual cost system to a standard cost system. The following information pertains to the new standard cost system they have just employed.

Material, 3½ yards @ $3.50 per yard.............	$12.25
Labor, 4 hours @ $3.00 per hour.................	12.00
Overhead, $1.50 per direct labor hour.............	6.00
	$30.25

The manager of the plant wants to see the difference between the actual cost system previously employed, and the newly initiated standard cost system.

Required:

Prepare the journal entries as they would appear under *each* system.

a. Purchased 40,000 yards of material—$150,000.
b. Production completed 10,000 units. There was no beginning or ending work-in-process inventory. 37,000 yards of material were used in production.
c. Direct labor hours used totaled 42,500 hours at a total cost of $131,750.

7B–7 The Monroe Company incorporates standard costs in their process costing system. The standard costs per unit for their only product, trinkets, are listed below:

Material, 2 pound @ 4.10/pound	$ 8.20
Labor, 0.6 hours @ $6.00/hour	3.60
Overhead, Variable @ $4.60/hour = $2.76	
Fixed * @ $2.00/hour = 1.20 ...	3.96
Total standard cost per trinket	$15.76

* Fixed overhead is based on a normal capacity of 132,000 trinkets.

Production statistics for this year are as follows:

Trinkets finished this year—110,000.

Costs incurred for this year were $1,037,850, $430,500, and $475,120 for material, labor, and overhead, respectively.

There was no beginning work-in-process inventory.

Ending work-in-process—15,000 trinkets; 100% complete for material, 80% complete for labor and overhead.

255,000 pounds of material and 70,000 labor hours were actually used. Monroe computes material price variances at the point of transfer to work in process.

Required:

Using the weighted average method of process cost accounting, compute (a) the material price and usage variances, and (b) the labor rate and efficiency variances.

7B–8   The Hinchey Company would like to compare labor costs in January to labor costs in February. Below is labor cost data for January and February:

Month	Labor Costs	Direct Labor Hours Incurred	Units Produced
January	$6,225	750	150
February	$6,435	780	150

Required:

Using January labor costs and usage as a standard, calculate the labor rate and efficiency variances for February.

7B–9   Simco has established the following standards for its product called Chewies.

Material
Caramel . . . . . 3 oz./bar @ $.02/oz.
Nuts . . . . ½ oz./bar @ $.02/oz.
Labor
Mixing   . . . . . 1/100 hr. @ $3.00/hr.

Caramel purchased . . . . . . 30,000 oz. for $1,050.00
Nuts purchased . . . . 7,500 oz. for $ 240.00
Labor for the period . . . . . 95 hours   for $ 280.25
Total bars produced 9,000
Total caramel used . . . . . . 28,125 oz.
Total nuts used . . . . 4,750 oz.

Required:

Calculate materials price and quantity variances for each material and labor rate and efficiency variances.

7B–10   The Organet Stamping Company manufactures a variety of products made of plastic and aluminum components. During the winter months substantially all of the production capacity is devoted to the production of lawn sprinklers for the following spring and summer season. Other products are manufactured during the remainder of the year. Because a variety of products are manufactured throughout the year, factory volume is measured by production labor hours rather than units of product.

Production and sales volume have grown steadily for the past several years as can be seen from the following schedule of standard production labor content of annual output:

```
1979....................32,000 hours
1978....................30,000 hours
1977....................27,000 hours
1976....................28,000 hours
1975....................26,000 hours
```

The company has developed standard costs for its several products. Standard costs for each year are set in the preceding October. The standard cost of a sprinkler for 1980 was $2.50, computed as follows:

Direct Materials
Aluminum   0.2 lbs. @ $0.40 per lb. $0.08
Plastic   1.0 lbs @ $0.38 per lb. 0.38
Production Labor 0.3 hrs @ $4.00 per hr. 1.20
Overhead (calculated using 30,000 production
               labor hours as normal capacity)
Variable   0.3 hrs. @ $1.60 per hr. 0.48
Fixed   0.3 hrs. @ $1.20 per hr. 0.36
                  Total $2.50

During February 1980, 8,500 good sprinklers were manufactured. The following materials and labor costs were incurred and charged to production:

Materials Requisitioned for Production
Aluminum   1900 lbs. @ $0.40 per lb. . . . . $ 760
Plastic—
Regular Grade   6000 lbs. @ $0.38 per lb. 2,280
Low Grade *   3500 lbs. @ $0.38 per lb. 1,330
Production Labor
Straight time   2300 hrs. @ $4.00 per hr. 9,200
Overtime   400 hrs. @ $6.00 per hr. 2,400

Material price variations are not charged to production but to a material price variation account at the time the invoice is entered. All materials are carried in inventory at standard prices. Material purchases for February were:

Aluminum   1800 lbs. @ $0.48 per lb. . . . . $ 864
Plastic—
Regular Grade   3000 lbs. @ $0.50 per lb. 1,500
Low Grade *   6000 lbs. @ $0.29 per lb. 1,740

* Due to plastic shortages, the company was forced to purchase lower grade plastic than called for in the standards. This increased the number of sprinklers rejected on inspection.

Every item below is related to the above facts and should be answered on the basis of those facts.

a. The standard material quantities already include an allowance for acceptable material scrap loss. In this situation the material use variations would most likely be caused by
1. defective aluminum.
2. improper processing by labor.
3. inadequate allowance for scrap loss.
4. substitute plastic.
5. none of the reasons enumerated above.

b. The labor efficiency (quantity) variation is the difference between standard labor hours of output and

1. 2,300 hours.
2. 2,700 hours.
3. 2,900 hours.
4. 2,500 hours.
5. some other amount not enumerated above.

c. The labor rate (price) variation is

1. $0.
2. $600 unfavorable.
3. $800 unfavorable.
4. $1,400 unfavorable.
5. $2,400 unfavorable.

d. The variations of material prices from standard would

1. best be reported as materials price variation—$36 favorable.
2. best be reported as materials price variations—aluminum, $144 unfavorable; plastic, $180 favorable.
3. best be reported as materials price variation—aluminum, $144 unfavorable; plastic, $360 unfavorable; material substitution, $540 favorable.
4. best be reported as materials price variation—aluminum, $144 unfavorable; plastic, $360 unfavorable; price difference due to plastic substitution not reported.
5. not be reported because material prices are uncontrollable.

(CMA Adapted)

7B–11 The Monkey Precinct Department Store has suffered a fire in its business office. Many of the records were destroyed and you have been called to piece things back together again. The store wants to know the amount and price of materials A, B, and C which were purchased and used during the past year. The following information was available from the records that were not destroyed.

1.   Cost of goods sold was $6,030 greater due to variances
2.   Total variance of A was $1,000 F
3.   Total variance of B was $4,000 U
4.   Actual price of A was $3 per unit
5.   Actual price of B was $.75 per unit
6.   Actual price of C was $2 per unit
7.   Standard price of B was $1 per unit
8.   Standard amount of A needed 5,000 units
9.   Standard amount of B needed 10,000 units
10. Standard amount of C needed 6,000 units
11. 4,000 units of A were purchased
12. 7,000 units of C were purchased
13. Material price variance of A = $1,000 U
14. Material price variance of B = $1,000 F
15. Material price variance of C = $2,030 U
16. Material quantity variance of C = $1,000 U

Required:

a.   Determine the standard price of A and C.
b.   Determine the actual number of B purchased.
c.   Determine the actual quantity of A, B, and C used.

Learning Objectives

Chapter 8 discusses the cost implications of manufacturing overhead and the analysis of any difference between actual manufacturing overhead costs incurred and standard manufacturing overhead costs applied to production. Studying this chapter should enable you to:

1. Understand the concept of the flexible budget.
2. Understand the underlying concepts of manufacturing overhead variance analysis.
3. Determine why the variances could occur.
4. Calculate the volume, budget, efficiency and spending variances for manufacturing overhead costs.

8

Analysis of Manufacturing Overhead Costs

THIS CHAPTER is an extension of Chapter 7 and focuses on variance analysis of manufacturing overhead costs. The basic data regarding manufacturing overhead developed in the standard cost illustrations from Chapter 7 will be presented in this chapter. The manufacturing overhead variances will be analyzed to review the cost implications of manufacturing overhead, and the differences between actual manufacturing overhead costs incurred and standard manufacturing overhead costs applied to production.

Controlling Manufacturing Overhead When
Compared to Other Product Costs

Manufacturing overhead is a major production cost. In fact, the total manufacturing overhead costs may be as large or larger than the direct material or direct labor costs. But the individual cost items in the total overhead cost may not justify the in-depth analysis and control techniques that can be justified for direct materials and direct labor. That is, the amount of cost at risk for the individual items may not be worth an item by item analysis on a continual basis. As a general statement, it can be said that direct material and direct labor costs and the effectiveness and efficiency of their use may be reviewed on a daily or hourly basis, but manufacturing overhead costs are reviewed and analyzed on a basis covering a longer time period such as a week or a month.

Direct materials and direct labor are considered to be variable costs within the relevant range of production. Total manufacturing overhead is a mixed cost (semi-variable) with both a fixed and variable component of cost within the relevant range of production. The directly variable relationship between the financial and physical aspects of both direct materials and direct labor make controlling and analyzing variances from these production costs easier and more meaningful than a similar analysis of manufacturing overhead. Standard costs can be used as a tool in controlling direct materials and direct labor costs on a daily basis. Standard costs in conjunction with departmental overhead budgets are used in controlling manufacturing overhead.

Concept of a Flexible Budget

A major underlying assumption of standard costs for manufacturing is that a known relationship exists between the production inputs and output. This relationship can be expressed in physical measures or in dollars when the physical inputs are multiplied by their respective costs. For example, the standard cost sheet for one power turbine shaft for Sax Company is presented in Illustration 8-1.

It takes one steel billet and two ball bearings to manufacture one power turbine shaft. The quantity of steel billets necessary to meet the January production of 1,760 power turbine shafts is 1,760 steel billets. The input to output relationship at standard is defined. The standard cost of a steel billet is $4.00. The standard cost of the steel billets needed to output 1,760 power turbine shafts is 1,760 billets X $4.00 or $7,040. The input to output relationship for ball bearings in Illustration 8-1 is a standard input of two ball bearings, at a standard cost of $1.00 per ball bearing, for every power turbine shaft produced.

Input to output relationships for labor and overhead from Illustration 8-1 could also be identified. The critical factor in identifying the relationships is a knowledge of the input to output factors and the cost per unit of the input factor. The knowledge of the cost behavior patterns and costs within the relevant range of production permits the use of the *flexible budget* in analyzing both the efficiency and effectiveness of the use of input factors in producing the required output at the required quality and cost. With a flexible budget, a budget can be established for any level of activity.

The Flexible Budget—An Example

If the production standards from Illustration 8-1 are used as the basis for a flexible standard cost budget for power turbine production, a

Illustration 8-1
Sax Company
Standard Cost Sheet

Standard Cost Sheet			
Product: <u>Power Turbine Shafts</u> Basis for Cost Sheet: <u>One Unit</u>			
Materials			
Location	Standard Quantity	Standard Price per unit	Total
Aisle 84 Aisle 85	1 2	$4.00 1.00	$4.00 $2.00 $6.00
Labor			
Department	Standard Hours	Standard Hourly Rate	Total
Machining Finishing and Pressing	1/3 1/6	$6.00 6.00	$2.00 $1.00 $3.00
Manufacturing Overhead			
Variable Overhead Per Unit Fixed Overhead Per Unit Total Overhead Per Unit		$1.40 2.00 $3.40	
Cost Summary Per Unit			

Materials @ Standard	1 Steel Billet @ $4.00	=	$ 4.00	
	2 Ball Bearings @ 1.00	=	2.00	
Direct Labor @ Standard	½ hour @ $6.00/hour	=	3.00	
Variable Manufacturing Overhead @ Standard*		=	1.40	
Fixed Manufacturing Overhead @ Standard*		=	2.00	
Total Manufacturing Cost @ Standard			$12.40	

*Basis of Application to Product is Standard Direct
Labor Hours. Application Rate is $6.80 Per Standard
Direct Labor Hour.

budget could be prepared for any level of activity. Illustration 8-2 has the flexible budget prepared at production levels of 1,700, 1,760, and 1,800 power turbine shafts. Once the output level of power turbine shafts is determined, the production input factors in Illustration 8-1 are used to develop the flexible budget.

Illustration 8-2
Sax Company
Flexible Budget for Power Turbine Shaft Production

Input Cost Factors	Budget Formula per Unit of Activity	Fixed Costs	Variable Costs Budgeted Activity Level		
			1,700 Units	1,760 Units	1,800 Units
Direct Material:					
Billets	$ 4.00 per Unit		$ 6,800	$ 7,040	$ 7,200
Bearings	2.00 per Unit		3,400	3,520	3,600
Direct Labor	3.00 per Unit		5,100	5,280	5,400
Manufacturing Overhead:					
Variable Costs	1.40 per Unit		2,380	2,464	2,520
Fixed Costs	-0-	$3,600			
	$10.40 per Unit	$3,600	$17,680	$18,304	$18,720

As can be seen from Illustration 8–2, the flexible portion of the flexible budget for production costs is caused by the variable cost components. The fixed cost component of the flexible budget is the *static* component of the budget. The flexible budget formula for total production cost is:

Total Production Costs = Std. or Budgeted Fixed Prod. Costs + Std. Variable Prod. Cost per Unit of Activity (Level of Activity)

This formula can provide the standard production cost in total for any projected activity level within the relevant range. For an after-the-fact analysis of what production costs should have been given the level of activity attained, the formula can be used by introducing the actual level of activity in the calculations. For example, using the data in Illustration 8-2, if 1,770 power turbine shafts were the projected or actual production, the total manufacturing costs should be or should have been, respectively:

Total Manufacturing Costs = $3,600 + ($10.40 X 1,770 Power Turbine Shafts)
= $3,600 + $18,408
= $22,008

Each of the individual cost items can also be calculated using the concept of the flexible budget. This concept was implicitly assumed in Chapter 7 when analyzing the variances from direct materials and direct labor. In this chapter, the flexible budget concept and its use must be explicitly used to perform the necessary calculations in analyzing manufacturing overhead costs.

A COMPREHENSIVE EXAMPLE: THE FLEXIBLE
MANUFACTURING OVERHEAD BUDGET

At the close of January, Sax Company knew the actual total overhead for the year was $6,320. The company also knew that the amount of manufacturing overhead that had been applied to production totaled $5,984. The difference between these two amounts, $336, represents the total overhead variance for the month. Sax's management is interested in an analysis of this variance and wishes to identify its underlying causes.

Recall that the standard costs used for the application of overhead were developed for a practical production level of 1,800 units, or 900 standard direct labor hours. Actual production in January totaled 1,760 units, or 880 standard direct labor hours. For any meaningful analysis of overhead, a concept not normally encountered in the accounting records must be introduced, that is, the concept of the flexible budget. With regard to manufacturing overhead, the flexible budget indicates the amount of overhead which should have been incurred at standard rates if Sax Company had known in advance that 1,760 rather than 1,800 units were going to be produced during January.

Illustration 8-3
Sax Company
Developing the Standard Manufacturing Overhead

Projected Practical Capacity: 1,800 Units
Standard Direct Labor Hours at Practical Capacity: 900 Hours

Standard Manufacturing Overhead

	Variable per Unit Produced	Fixed	Total
Rework Time	$ .10	0	$ 180
Waiting Time	.06	0	108
Setup Time	.08	0	144
Indirect Materials and Supplies	.60	$ 88	1,168
Indirect Labor	.46	272	1,100
Electricity	.10	240	420
Heat	0	100	100
Equipment Depreciation	0	600	600
Plant Depreciation	0	1,500	1,500
Factory Property Taxes	0	800	800
Totals	$1.40	$3,600	$6,120

Standard Manufacturing Overhead per Unit:
Standard Variable Manufacturing Overhead per Unit $1.40

Standard Fixed Manufacturing Overhead per Unit $\dfrac{\$3,600}{1,800 \text{ units}} = 2.00$

Standard Total Manufacturing Overhead per Unit $3.40

The total flexible budget for Sax Company may be developed after-the-fact from the information provided in Illustration 8-3. The standard variable manufacturing overhead cost was $1.40 per unit produced for a total of ($1.40 X 1,760 power turbine shafts) or $2,464 in January. Fixed manufacturing overhead *at standard* totaled $3,600. At 1,760 units, or 880 standard direct labor hours, the flexible budget is derived as follows:

$$\begin{matrix} \text{Flexible} \\ \text{Budget} \end{matrix} = \begin{bmatrix} \text{Standard Fixed} \\ \text{Manufacturing} \\ \text{Costs} \end{bmatrix} + \begin{bmatrix} \text{Actual Units} \\ \text{Produced} \end{bmatrix} \times \begin{bmatrix} \text{Standard Variable} \\ \text{Manufacturing Cost} \\ \text{per Unit} \end{bmatrix}$$

= $3,600 + [1,760 units X $1.40]
= $3,600 + $2,464
= $6,064

If the variable overhead costs are in fact variable and the fixed overhead costs are indeed fixed, at 1,760 units or 880 standard direct labor hours, Sax Company's planned total overhead cost would be $6,064. A flexible budget could have been prepared for each specific overhead cost and the total would have remained the same. Illustration 8-4 presents a flexible budget for manufacturing overhead costs at a production level of 1,760 units or 880 standard direct labor hours.

Illustration 8-4
Sax Company
The Flexible Budget

	Variable* per Unit Produced	Fixed*	Total Budgeted Cost at 1,760 Units or 880 Standard Hours
Rework Time.....................	$ .10	0	$ 176.00
Waiting Time.....................	.06	0	105.60
Setup Time......................	.08	0	140.80
Indirect Materials and Supplies.....	.60	$ 88	1,144.00
Indirect Labor..................	.46	272	1,081.60
Electricity.......................	.10	240	416.00
Heat...........................	0	100	100.00
Equipment Depreciation..........	0	600	600.00
Plant Depreciation...............	0	1,500	1,500.00
Factory Property Taxes...........	0	800	800.00
Total........................	$1.40	$3,600	$6,064.00

*From Illustration 8-3

A COMPREHENSIVE EXAMPLE: THE VOLUME VARIANCE FOR MANUFACTURING OVERHEAD

The total underapplied overhead of $336 for Sax Company is caused, in part, by a volume variance. Sax Company based its standard overhead rates for applying manufacturing overhead on an anticipated level of production of 1,800 units or 900 standard direct labor hours (Illustration 8-3). Since the actual production achieved was 1,760 units or 880 standard direct labor hours, a portion of the fixed manufacturing overhead incurred was not applied to production.

An analysis of the resultant volume variance can be made based either on the number of units produced or on the standard direct labor hours. Alternatively, the total flexible budget may be compared to the total overhead applied to production. Remember, the volume variance relates to the absorption of fixed manufacturing overhead—*not* variable manufacturing overhead—into the cost of production.

Volume Variance Based on Units Produced

Standard Fixed Overhead per Unit Produced...................	$ 2 *
Practical Capacity (units).....................................	1,800
Actual Production (units).....................................	1,760
	40
Unfavorable Volume Variance = 40 units X $2.00 =	$ 80

Volume Variance Based on Standard Direct Labor Hours Used

Standard Fixed Overhead per Standard Direct Labor Hour.......	$ 4 *
Practical Capacity (Standard Direct Labor Hours).............	900
Actual Production (Standard Direct Labor Hours).............	880
	20
Unfavorable Volume Variance = 20 Direct Labor Hours X $4.00 =	$ 80

Volume Variance Based on Applied Manufacturing Overhead and the Flexible Budget

Manufacturing Overhead Applied to Products.................	$5,984
Flexible Budget...	6,064
Unfavorable Volume Variance...........................	$ 80

*See Illustration 7-3 and Illustration 8-1.

Of course, each of these methods provides the identical answer because each examines the same variance. The volume variance for Sax Company is unfavorable because the company did not produce a sufficient number of units to apply all of the fixed manufacturing overhead at standard to its production. Thus, in effect, the company lost the opportunity to produce at a practical capacity level in January.

A COMPREHENSIVE EXAMPLE: THE BUDGET VARIANCE FOR MANUFACTURING OVERHEAD

The budget variance analysis determines the amount by which the total actual overhead deviated from the overhead determined by the flexible budget. For Sax Company, the budget variance represents an attempt to determine the portion of underapplied manufacturing overhead of $336 which was due to a deviation from the amount of manufacturing overhead costs that should have been incurred at standard costs and a production level of 1,760 units. Standard manufacturing overhead costs for this level of production can be determined by using the flexible budget. The actual amount of manufacturing overhead costs are obtained from the accounting records. For Sax Company, the actual manufacturing overhead costs for the year were recorded in Transaction 8 in Chapter Seven.

The budget variance plus the volume variance must equal the total overhead variance. In this case, the total overhead variance is $336 (unfavorable) and the volume variance is $80 (unfavorable); thus, the budget variance must be $256 (also unfavorable). Note that there is absolutely no reason why both components of the overhead variance should be either favorable or unfavorable. One of the variances may be favorable and the other unfavorable. The budget variance is calculated using either the actual units produced or standard direct labor hours, and then determining the difference between the total flexible budget costs and the actual costs incurred.

Budget Variance Based on Units Produced

Actual Manufacturing Overhead Costs......................	$6,320
Flexible Budget $3,600 + (1,760 units X $1.40)..............	6,064
Unfavorable Budget Variance...........................	($ 256)

Budget Variance Based on Standard Direct Labor Hours

Actual Manufacturing Overhead Costs......................	$6,320
Flexible Budget	
$3,600 + (880 Standard Direct Labor Hours X $2.80).......	6,064
Unfavorable Budget Variance...........................	($ 256)

In this example the budget variance is unfavorable because the actual manufacturing overhead costs were greater than anticipated at the actual level of 1,760 units of production, or 880 standard direct labor hours.

The cost items that caused the unfavorable variance can be identified. If the flexible budget for manufacturing overhead is calculated on an item-by-item basis and compared with the actual item costs, then the individual variances should total the budget variance. Illustration 8–5 presents an item-by-item analysis of the manufacturing overhead costs that caused the budget variance.

Illustration 8-5
Sax Company
Manufacturing Overhead Budget Variance

	Total Budgeted Cost * at 1,760 Units or 880 Standard Hours	Total Actual † Cost at 1,760 Units	Manufacturing ‡ Overhead Budget Variance
Rework Time..................	$ 176.00	$ 160.00	$ 16.00
Waiting Time.................	105.60	100.00	5.60
Setup Time...................	140.80	140.00	.80
Indirect Materials and Supplies...................	1,144.00	1,100.00	44.00
Indirect Labor...............	1,081.60	1,160.00	(78.40)
Electricity...................	416.00	700.00	(284.00)
Heat........................	100.00	60.00	40.00
Equipment Depreciation.......	600.00	600.00	0
Plant Depreciation............	1,500.00	1,500.00	0
Factory Property Taxes........	800.00	800.00	0
Totals..................	$6,064.00	$6,320.00	($256.00)

* From Illustration 8-4
† From information for Transaction 8 in Chapter Seven.
‡ ( )'s indicate an unfavorable variance.

Rework time, waiting time, setup time, indirect materials and supplies and heat caused favorable cost variances totaling $106.40. Indirect labor and electricity caused unfavorable cost variances totaling $362.40. The manufacturing overhead budget variance was the net unfavorable variance of the individual items, $256.

Dividing the under or overapplied overhead into two variances is referred to as two-way analysis of overhead variances. A two-way analysis of overhead variances is presented as follows:

Actual Manufacturing Overhead Costs......... $6,320

                                            Budget Variance   ($256)

Flexible Budget............................. $6,064   (Unfavorable)

                                            Volume Variance   ($ 80)

Applied Manufacturing Overhead Costs........ $5,984   (Unfavorable)

A COMPREHENSIVE EXAMPLE: THE EFFICIENCY AND SPENDING VARIANCES FOR MANUFACTURING OVERHEAD

The budget variance of $256 for the Sax Company may be separated into two additional factors or components that explain the cause of the budget variance. These two factors are: (1) the efficiency or inefficiency of the use of direct labor and (2) whether or not spending for overhead costs was appropriate considering the amount that should have been spent given the *actual* direct labor hours worked.

EFFICIENCY VARIANCE

The efficiency variance requires further explanation. If direct labor is a causal factor in incurring variable manufacturing overhead, the efficiency or inefficiency of direct labor will have an impact on the actual amount of the variable overhead incurred. If direct labor usage is less than standard, the variance will be favorable. If, as in the case of Sax Company, the actual use of direct labor exceeded the standard, the variance will be unfavorable.

The efficiency variance portion of the budget variance is calculated as follows:

Efficiency = (Actual Direct Labor Hours Used — Standard Direct
Variance   Labor Hours Allowed) X Variable Manufacturing
                 Overhead Rate per Standard Direct Labor Hour
         = (890 Hours — 880 Hours) X $2.80
         = $28 Unfavorable Efficiency Variance

For Sax Company, 10 direct labor hours in excess of the standard amount were used. If variable overhead is related to direct labor hours, this inefficiency would have caused an additional $28 of variable overhead to be incurred. An item-by-item analysis of the overhead efficiency variance is presented in Illustration 8-6.

Illustration 8-6
Sax Company
Manufacturing Overhead Efficiency Variance

	Variable * Per Direct Labor Hour	Total Budgeted Variable Cost at 880 Direct Labor Hours	Total Budgeted Variable Cost at 890 Direct Labor Hours	Efficiency † Variance
Rework Time............	$ .20	$ 176.00	$ 178.00	($ 2.00)
Waiting Time............	.12	105.60	106.80	(1.20)
Setup Time..............	.16	140.80	142.40	(1.60)
Indirect Materials and Supplies	1.20	1,056.00	1,068.00	(12.00)
Indirect Labor...........	.92	809.60	818.80	(9.20)
Electricity	.20	176.00	178.00	(2.00)
Heat	0	0	0	0
Equipment Depreciation...	0	0	0	0
Plant Depreciation........	0	0	0	0
Factory Property Taxes.....	0	0	0	0
Totals..............	$2.80	$2,464.00	$2,492.00	($28.00)

* From Illustration 8-3 or 8-4: Remember, the standard variable overhead per direct labor hour is twice the variable standard per unit.
† ( )'s indicate an unfavorable variance.

Note that every variance which is included in Illustration 8-6 is unfavorable. This is appropriate since only the variable manufacturing overhead hours are considered in relation to the standard labor hours. Because actual labor hours exceeded standard hours by 10 hours, each individual variable cost factor exceeds standard cost by its individual cost rate multiplied by this factor of 10 hours.

SPENDING VARIANCE

The spending variance is a measure of the overhead costs that were incurred at the actual level of activity (direct labor hours) as compared to the standard manufacturing overhead costs which should have been incurred at that level of activity. In the case of Sax Company, this variance is the difference between the total actual manufacturing overhead costs at 890 direct labor hours as compared to the standard manufacturing overhead costs at 890 direct labor hours. The spending variance portion of the budget variance is calculated as follows:

Spending   =[(Budgeted Total Fixed Manufacturing Overhead) + (Ac-
Variance   tual Direct Labor Hours Used X Standard Variable
                Manufacturing Overhead Rate)]   —   Actual Total
                Manufacturing Overhead Costs
        = [$3,600 + (890 X $2.80)] — $6,320
        = ($3,600 + $2,492) — $6,320
        = $228 Unfavorable Spending Variance

An item-by-item analysis of the overhead spending variance is presented in Illustration 8-7.

From the standpoint of spending for overhead costs at the actual level of activity, 890 direct labor hours, Sax Company performed favorably in the area of rework time, waiting time, setup time, indirect materials and supplies, and heat. Unfavorable spending variances were incurred for indirect labor and electricity.

The overhead spending variance can be further subdivided into a fixed overhead spending variance and a variable overhead spending variance, because additional expenditures could have been made for *both* fixed and variable manufacturing overhead over those that were anticipated in the flexible budget based on the actual level of activity for that period. This is not the case, however, with the efficiency and volume variances. The overhead efficiency variance is caused entirely by the efficiency or inefficiency of direct labor hours used; therefore the impact is on only the actual amount of *variable* overhead incurred. Alternatively, the volume

Illustration 8-7
Sax Company
Manufacturing Overhead Spending Variance

	Variable* per Direct Labor Hour	Fixed	Total Budgeted Manufacturing Overhead Costs at 890 Direct Labor Hours	Total † Actual Manufacturing Overhead Costs at 890 Direct Labor Hours	Spending ‡ Variance
Rework Time.....	$ .20	0	$ 178.00	$ 160.00	$ 18.00
Waiting Time.....	.12	0	106.80	100.00	6.80
Setup Time.......	.16	0	142.40	140.00	2.40
Indirect Materials and Supplies....	1.20	$ 88.00	1,156.00	1,100.00	56.00
Indirect Labor.....	.92	272.00	1,090.80	1,160.00	(69.20)
Electricity........	.20	240.00	418.00	700.00	(282.00)
Heat.............	0	100.00	100.00	60.00	40.00
Equipment Depreciation....	0	600.00	600.00	600.00	0
Plant Depreciation....	0	1,500.00	1,500.00	1,500.00	0
Factory Property Taxes..........	0	800.00	800.00	800.00	0
Totals........	$2.80	$3,600.00	$6,092.00	$6,320.00	($228.00)

* From Illustration 8-3 or 8-4: Remember, the standard variable overhead rate per direct labor hour is twice the variable standard per unit.
† From information for Transaction 8 in Chapter Seven.
‡ ( )'s indicate an unfavorable variance.

variance relates to the absorption of fixed manufacturing overhead into the cost of production and nothing else.

The variable overhead spending variance may be calculated as follows:

Variable Overhead Spending Variance = (Actual Direct Labor Hours Used × Standard Variable Manufacturing Overhead Rate) — Actual Variable Manufacturing Overhead Costs

The equation for the fixed overhead spending variance is shown below:

Fixed Overhead Spending Variance = Budgeted Fixed Manufacturing Overhead — Actual Fixed Manufacturing Overhead Costs

Since the actual manufacturing overhead incurred during January for the Sax Company is not separated into its fixed and variable components, it is not possible to calculate the company's fixed and variable overhead spending variances in this example.

When the budget variance is divided into its efficiency and spending components, the analysis of manufacturing overhead is referred to as a three-way analysis of manufacturing overhead variances. The three variances that are developed and analyzed are:

1. The impact of production volume (manufacturing overhead volume variance).
2. The impact of direct labor efficiency (manufacturing overhead efficiency variance).
3. The impact of spending for overhead costs (manufacturing overhead spending variance).

Below is a comparison showing the manufacturing overhead variances of the Sax Company in the form of both a two-way analysis and a three-way analysis. Notice that the efficiency and spending variances in the three-way analysis total the budget variance in the two-way analysis.

Two-Way Analysis of Overhead Variances

Budget Variance (Unfavorable)......................	($256)
Volume Variance (Unfavorable)......................	(80)
Unfavorable Manufacturing Overhead Variance........	($336)

(Unfavorable)

Three-Way Analysis of Overhead Variances

Efficiency Variance (Unfavorable)....................	($ 28)
Spending Variance (Unfavorable).....................	(228)
Volume Variance (Unfavorable)......................	(80)
Unfavorable Manufacturing Overhead Variance........	($336)

(Unfavorable)

The spending, efficiency and volume overhead variances may be isolated and accounted for when the journal entry is made to record the manufacturing overhead applied, rather than waiting until the end of the period when the closing entries are made. For example, instead of the journal entry which was made for Transaction 6 in Chapter Seven to record the manufacturing overhead applied without recording any overhead variances, the following journal entry could be made:

Work-in-Process ($6.80 X 880).........................	5,984	
Manufacturing Overhead Efficiency Variance..............	28	
Manufacturing Overhead Spending Variance..............	228	
Manufacturing Overhead Volume Variance................	80	
Manufacturing Overhead—Control....................		6,320

Notice that the credit to the manufacturing overhead control account represents the actual amount of overhead incurred during January. Thus, if this entry is made after the actual manufacturing overhead was journalized (Transaction· 8 in Chapter 7), then the manufacturing overhead control account is closed out, with any over or underapplied overhead already having been converted into the three overhead variances. At the end of the period, these three overhead variances—spending, efficiency and volume—are closed to cost of goods sold along with the material and labor variances.

SUMMARY

Total manufacturing overhead is a semi-variable cost with both a fixed and variable component. A flexible budget can be used to determine manufacturing overhead at standard costs at any level of production within the relevant range. The flexible portion of the flexible budget is caused by the variable cost components of manufacturing overhead. The fixed cost component of the flexible budget is the static component of the budget.

The analysis of overhead variances can be done using a two or three variance approach. In either case, the difference or total variance being analyzed is the difference between actual manufacturing overhead and manufacturing overhead applied to production. With a two-way analysis, this difference will be analyzed on the presumption that only two factors could have caused the variance: a volume deviation or a budget deviation. The volume variance occurs as the result of attaining a level of production other than the standard or practical capacity level, and over or under applying fixed manufacturing overhead to products produced. The budget variance is the difference between the flexible budget, based on actual activity, and the actual manufacturing overhead costs that were incurred.

A three-way analysis of variance also considers the volume variance, but divides the budget variance into the portion that was caused by the efficiency of the application base and the portion that was caused by spending for overhead costs. The manufacturing overhead efficiency variance and the manufacturing overhead spending variance must, therefore, sum to the budget variance.

Following is a summary of the equations for your reference of the standard cost variances listed in this chapter and Chapter 7.

1. Material Price Variance =
$$\left(\begin{array}{c}\text{Standard Price} \\ \text{per Unit}\end{array} - \begin{array}{c}\text{Actual Price} \\ \text{per Unit}\end{array}\right) \times \begin{array}{c}\text{Actual Number of} \\ \text{Units Purchased}\end{array}$$

2. Material Quantity Variance =
$$\left(\begin{array}{c}\text{Standard Quantity} \\ \text{Allowed}\end{array} - \begin{array}{c}\text{Actual Quantity} \\ \text{Used}\end{array}\right) \times \begin{array}{c}\text{Standard Price} \\ \text{per Unit}\end{array}$$

3. Direct Labor Rate Variance =
$$\left(\begin{array}{c}\text{Standard Rate} \\ \text{per Hour}\end{array} - \begin{array}{c}\text{Actual Rate} \\ \text{per Hour}\end{array}\right) \times \begin{array}{c}\text{Actual Number of Hours} \\ \text{of Direct Labor Used}\end{array}$$

Unfav Var — Dr   Fav Var — Cr

4. Direct Labor Efficiency Variance =
$$\left(\begin{array}{c} \text{Standard Hours} \\ \text{Allowed} \end{array} - \begin{array}{c} \text{Actual Hours} \\ \text{Used} \end{array} \right) \times \begin{array}{c} \text{Standard Wage} \\ \text{Rate per Hour} \end{array}$$

5. Volume Variance for Manufacturing Overhead =
$$\left(\begin{array}{c} \text{Standard} \\ \text{Production} \\ \text{Capacity} \\ \text{in units} \end{array} - \begin{array}{c} \text{Actual} \\ \text{Production} \\ \text{Capacity} \\ \text{in units} \end{array} \right) \times \begin{array}{c} \text{Standard Fixed} \\ \text{Overhead Rate} \\ \text{per Unit} \\ \text{Produced} \end{array}$$

(This equation may substitute direct labor hours if fixed overhead rate has also been calculated using direct labor hours.)

6. Fixed Overhead Rate $= \dfrac{\text{Total Fixed Overhead Costs at Standard}}{\text{Projected Practical Production Capacity}}$ (in units)

7. Budget Variance for Manufacturing Overhead =
Flexible Budget — Actual Manufacturing Overhead Costs

8. Flexible Budget for Manufacturing Overhead =
$$\left(\begin{array}{c} \text{Actual level} \\ \text{of Production} \\ \text{in units} \end{array} \times \begin{array}{c} \text{Variable per} \\ \text{Unit Costs} \\ \text{at Standard} \end{array} \right) + \begin{array}{c} \text{Fixed Costs at Standard} \\ \text{for Projected Practical} \\ \text{Capacity} \end{array}$$

(This equation may substitute standard direct labor hours allowed if variable costs are related to direct labor hours.)

9. Spending Variance = [(Budgeted Total Fixed Manufacturing Overhead) + (Actual Direct Labor Hours Used × Standard Variable Manufacturing Overhead Rate)] — Actual Total Manufacturing Overhead Costs

10. Efficiency Variance = (Actual Direct Labor Hours Used — Standard Direct Labor Hours Allowed) × Variable Manufacturing Overhead Rate per Standard Direct Labor Hour

KEY DEFINITIONS

Budget variance—an overhead variance which results when the actual total manufacturing overhead costs differ from the total manufacturing overhead costs budgeted for the actual level of production.

Flexible budget—a budget used to calculate a total budgeted manufacturing overhead cost for a given level of production.

Three-way analysis of overhead variances—a method which separates total overhead into volume, efficiency and spending variance components. The total of the manufacturing overhead efficiency and spending variances is equal to the budget variance.

Two-way analysis of overhead variances—a method which separates total overhead variance into volume and budget variance components.

Volume variance—an overhead variance which results when actual production differs from the practical capacity so that the total manufacturing overhead is under- or over-applied to the cost of production.

QUESTIONS

1. What is the purpose of the flexible manufacturing overhead cost budget?
2. Why is fixed cost considered the static component of the flexible budget?
3. What is the volume variance for manufacturing overhead cost analyzing?
4. What is the budget variance for manufacturing overhead cost analyzing?
5. When is a volume variance for manufacturing overhead cost favorable?
6. Why does the flexible budget have to be adjusted to the actual level of outputs or standard inputs to analyze manufacturing overhead cost variances?
7. When analyzing the volume variance or the budget variance, why must standard activity instead of actual activity be used when the basis for the flexible budget is an input factor such as direct labor hours?

EXERCISES

8-1   The Walters Manufacturing Company has established the following standards for one unit of their product, Alpha.

Material	6 lb. @ $8.00/lb. =	$ 48
Labor	12 hr. @ $6.00/hr. =	72
Variable M.O.H.	@ $18 =	18
F.M.O.H.	@ $25 =	25
Total Standard Cost		= $163

During August, the Walters Manufacturing Company purchased 7,000 pounds of material at $56,350 and incurred total labor costs of $71,248. 1,000 units of Alpha were produced. They required 6,220 pounds of material and 11,680 hours of labor. Normal capacity is 1,100 units. Actual manufacturing overhead was $45,000.

Required:

a. Compute the material price and usage variances.
b. Compute the labor rate and efficiency variances.
c. Compute the budget and volume variances for manufacturing overhead.

8-2   The Goodness Company uses a standard cost system with the following standard costs:

```
Material—5 pounds @ $6.00/pound . . . . . . $30.00
Labor—3 hours @ $4.50/hour . . . . . . . .  13.50
Overhead—3 hours @ $7.00/hour . . . . . . .  21.00
     Total standard cost per unit . . . . . . . . $64.50
```

During the year, 10,000 units were produced. Costs incurred for material, labor, and overhead were $325,000, $136,000, and $209,000 respectively. Normal capacity is 9,000 units. Variable overhead is $4 per standard direct labor hour.

Required:

a. Calculate the total variation from standard costs of the total costs incurred this year.
b. Calculate the total material variance, labor variance, and the overhead variance from standard costs. It is not necessary to calculate price, rate, and efficiency variances.
c. Calculate the budget and volume variances for manufacturing overhead.

8–3 Given the following balances in the variance accounts:

Direct Materials Price Variance		Direct Materials Quantity Variance	
	9,750	16,200	

Direct Labor Efficiency Variance		Direct Labor Rate Variance	
2,800			12,800

Manufacturing Overhead Control		Manufacturing Overhead Volume Variance	
22,600	21,000		1,500

Manufacturing Overhead Budget Variance	
3,100	

Required:

Prepare the entry that should have been made to close the manufacturing overhead control account when the overhead variances were recognized. Prepare the entry to close all variance accounts to the cost of goods sold account.

8–4 You have been given the following information:
Actual labor hours used = 315 hours
Actual variable overhead = $700
Standard materials price = $2.50
Standard labor hours used = 300 hours
Standard quantity of materials used = 450 units
Actual labor rate per hour = $3.00
Actual quantities of materials purchased and used = 445 units

Standard variable overhead per standard labor hour = $2.25
Standard labor rate per hour = $3.10
Actual materials price = $2.52 per unit

Required:

a. Variable overhead spending variance.
b. Variable overhead efficiency variance.
c. Total variable overhead variance.

8-5 Fremont, Inc. uses a standard absorption cost system. During June, 5,000 units were produced and sold. Given below are the standard costs for one unit:

Materials	A, 2 pounds @ $1.25	$ 2.50
Materials	B, 3½ pounds @ $.50	1.75
Materials	C, 1¼ pounds @ $2.00	2.50
Labor	3 hours @ $4.50	13.50
Variable overhead	$2.00 per labor hour	6.00
Fixed overhead	$1.25 per labor hour	3.75
Total Standard Costs		$30.00

Additional Data:

There are no beginning inventories. There is no ending work-in-process or finished goods.

Plant capacity 15,500 labor hours
Purchases   20,000 pounds of B @ $ .53
               11,000 pounds of A @ $1.23
                8,000 pounds of C @ $2.08
Actual material usage A, 10,200 pounds
                               B, 17,650 pounds
                               C, 6,000 pounds
Direct labor cost $70,610
Direct labor hours   15,350
Actual Variable Manufacturing Overhead $31,400
Actual Fixed Manufacturing Overhead $20,500
Selling price $45.00 per unit

Required:

a. Make the general journal entries for June.
b. Make the general journal entries to close out the variances.
     (Note: Separate the overhead variance into its spending, efficiency and volume variances.)

8-6 Sharon Corporation makes one product, tennis rackets. During May in preparation for the summer season, Sharon produced 500 tennis rackets. The established standard variable cost for one racket follows:

Materials	10 lbs. @ $.45/lb.	$ 4.50
Labor	3 hrs. @ $2.15/hr.	6.45
Variable manufacturing overhead	3 hrs. @ $2.75/hr.	8.25
Total standard cost		$19.20

The Sharon Corporation purchased 5,500 pounds of material at a cost of $2,695. The production department used 5,150 pounds of material. The payroll for direct labor hours of 1,495 amounted to $3,289 and actual variable manufacturing overhead was $4,186.

Required:

Calculate the variable manufacturing overhead variances for the Sharon Corporation.

8–7 Enter the transactions listed for the Kingston Company below into "T" accounts. Record all variances in separate accounts. Analyze any manufacturing overhead variance into its spending, efficiency, and volume variances.

a. Purchased 2,500 pounds of material at a cost of $5,875 on account. The standard cost per pound is $2.30.

b. During the period, 2,200 pounds of material were requisitioned. Assume all material was used efficiently. Each unit is made up of 2.2 pounds of material.

c. 4,500 hours were charged to production during the month at a cost of $16,875. Standard costs for labor were 4.2 hours per unit at a cost of $3.70 an hour.

d. Actual overhead incurred included $9,200 variable overhead expenses and $11,000 fixed overhead expenses. (The variable expenses are all included in accounts payable and the fixed are for depreciation on equipment.)

e. Overhead was applied at a rate of $5.00 per standard labor hour ($2.50 per hour which is variable). Normal production capacity is 1,000 units (or 4,200 hours).

f. Sales for the period were 900 units at $55 per unit, all sold on account.

g. Assume Kingston Company is in its first year of operations.

8–8 The Gibson Company would like you to calculate their spending, efficiency, and volume overhead variances for both the fixed and variable portion of their manufacturing overhead costs. Relevant data are listed below.

Normal capacity	8,000 units
Actual production	8,500 units
Standard variable overhead per hour	$2.00
Standard fixed overhead per hour	$1.00
Standard labor hours per unit	2 hours
Actual labor hours	16,500 hours
Actual variable overhead	$32,000
Actual fixed overhead	$16,900

8–9 The Loren Company produces one product with the following standard costs per unit:

Materials, 2 pounds at $3.25 . . . . $ 6.50
Labor, 5 hours at $2.05 . . . . 10.25
Manufacturing overhead:

Variable $1.00 per hour $\times$ 5 hours   = $5.00
Fixed $120,000 = $.50 per hour $\times$ 5 hours = $\underline{\ 2.50\ }$ 7.50
$\overline{240,000}$ (hours practical yearly capacity)

$\underline{\underline{\$24.25}}$

The company produced 3,000 units last month. A total of 21,500 direct labor hours were charged to production.

Actual overhead incurred was $22,000 for variable overhead and $9,500 for fixed overhead. The variable overhead was paid for in cash and the fixed overhead was made up entirely of depreciation on plant and equipment. Applied overhead was recorded based on standard direct labor hours.

Required:

a.   Calculate the volume variance, efficiency variance and spending variance for manufacturing overhead cost.

b.   Journalize the application of manufacturing overhead to work in process, the recognition of the actual overhead and the recognition of the variances.

PROBLEMS SERIES A

8A-1   Nancy Company produced 17,800 footballs during May. Material purchases amounted to 184,000 pounds at $2.10 per pound. Usage of the materials amounted to 92,200 pounds. The footballs required 53,000 hours of labor at $4.20 per hour while plant capacity is 60,000 labor hours. Manufacturing overhead actually incurred was $35,000 for fixed and $66,250 for variable. Nancy Company has established the following standards for one football:

5 lbs. of material at $2.00 per lb. $10.00
3 hrs. of labor at $4.00 per hour 12.00
Fixed manufacturing overhead
$1.00 per labor hour 3.00
Variable manufacturing overhead
$2.00 per labor hour . . . . $\underline{\ 6.00\ }$

$\underline{\underline{\$31.00}}$

Required:

Compute the material, labor, and manufacturing overhead budget and volume variances for May.

8A-2   The Monroe Company incorporates standard costs in their process costing system. The standard costs per unit for their only product, trinkets, are listed below:

```
Material: 2 pounds @ $4.10/pound  . . . . . . . . . . .  $ 8.20
Labor: 0.6 hours @ $6.00/hour  . . . . . . . . . . . .    3.60
Overhead:   Variable @ $4.60/hour = $2.76
          * Fixed @ $2.00/hour    =  1.20  . . . . . .    3.96
Total standard cost per trinket . . . . . . . . . . . . . $15.76
```

* Fixed overhead is based on a normal capacity of 132,000 trinkets.

Production statistics for this year are as follows:

Trinkets finished this year—110,000.

Costs incurred for this year were $1,037,850, $430,500, and $475,120 for material, labor, and overhead, respectively.

There was no beginning work-in-process inventory.

Ending work-in-process—15,000 trinkets; 100% complete for material, 80% complete for labor and overhead.

255,000 pounds of material and 70,000 labor hours were actually used. Monroe computes material price variances at the point of transfer to work in process.

Required:

Using the weighted average method of process cost accounting, compute:

a.   the material price and usage variances,
b.   the labor rate and efficiency variances, and
c.   the overhead budget and volume variances.

8A–3   Alpha Company produces electronic gadgets. The standard cost of one gadget is:

```
Direct Material—2 pounds @ $3.00/pound  . . .    6.00
Direct Labor—2 hours @ $4.00/hour . . . . . . .  $8.00
Manufacturing Overhead—Variable . . . . . . . .  $2.00
Manufacturing Overhead—Fixed  . . . . . . . . .  $1.50
Total Standard Cost per Gadget . . . . . . . . .  $17.50
```

Overhead is applied to products on a standard direct labor hour basis. Normal capacity for a month is 5,000 gadgets. Last month 4,800 gadgets were produced. The actual direct labor hours used were 9,800 hours. The actual manufacturing overhead costs were $17,500.

Required:

a.   Calculate the total manufacturing overhead variance.
b.   Calculate the volume variance, budget variance, spending variance and efficiency variance for manufacturing overhead costs.

8A–4   The Beaulieu Company uses a process cost system and standard costs. Below are the standard costs per unit for their only product, Bangles.

```
Material 2 gallons @ $3.50/gallon . . . . . . . . . $7.00
Labor 0.2 hours @ $3.00/hour . . . . . . . . . . .     .60
Overhead: Variable @ $2.25/hour = .45
              Fixed * @ $1.00/hour  = .20   . . . . .   .65
    Total standard cost per Bangle . . . . . . . . . $8.25
```

* Fixed overhead is based on a normal capacity of 10,100 Bangles.

Production statistics for January are as follows:

Bangles produced this month—8,000.
Ending work-in-process—3,000; 100 percent complete for material, 70 percent complete for labor, and 70 percent complete for overhead.
There was no beginning work-in-process inventory.
Costs incurred this month were $90,000, $6,900, and $6,600 for material, labor and overhead, respectively.
25,000 gallons of material and 3,000 labor hours were actually incurred.
The materials price variance is calculated at the time of transfer into work in process.

Required:

Using the weighted average method to determine the cost flow for January, compute:

a.   the material price and usage variances,
b.   the labor rate and efficiency variances, and
c.   the overhead budget and volume variances.

8A–5   The Barker Corporation has established the following manufacturing overhead standards for one unit of Beta Data:

```
Variable Manufacturing Overhead . . . . . . . . . $ 4.00
Fixed Manufacturing Overhead . . . . . . . . . . . $ 6.00
    Total Manufacturing Overhead per Unit . . . . $10.00
```

The normal capacity per month is 1,000 units of production. Last month, April, 950 equivalent units were produced at a cost of $20,200. The work in process control account and the manufacturing overhead control account contained the following entries:

Work in Process		Manufacturing Overhead Control	
Beg. Bal. 3,000	20,200	11,000	9,500
4,000			
4,700			
9,500			
End. Bal. 1,000			

Required:

a. Calculate the budgeted fixed cost for April.
b. Do a two-way analysis of overhead variance.

8A–6   Given the information in Problem 8A–5: assume that it takes 1.5 standard direct labor hours to make one unit of Beta Data and that 1,500 direct labor hours were actually worked. Calculate the volume variance, the budget variance, the spending variance and efficiency variance for manufacturing overhead cost.

8A–7   The Simons Company manufactures bolts in standard batches of 5,000 units. The standard cost for a batch is as follows:

Raw materials 200 lbs. @ $.04 per lb . . . . $ 8.00
Direct labor 4 hrs. @ $5.15 per hour 20.60
Overhead (including variable overhead of $4.50) 10.00

       Total standard cost $38.60

Data for March is as follows:

Planned production . . . . 240 batches
Actual production . . . . 250 batches
Cost of raw materials purchased (55,000 lbs.) . . $2,310.00
Cost of raw materials used (51,250 lbs.) $2,152.50
Direct labor cost (998 hours) $5,189.60
Actual overhead cost $2,560.00
Budgeted fixed overhead cost $1,320.00

Required:

Compute the following variances indicating whether favorable or unfavorable.

a. Raw materials price variance
b. Raw materials quantity variance
c. Direct labor rate variance
d. Direct labor efficiency variance
e. Overhead budget variance
f. Overhead volume variance.

8A–8   Given the information in Problem 8A–7: prepare a three-way analysis of variance for manufacturing overhead cost.

8A–9   The Holbrook Manufacturing Company produces paper boxes. The plant manager has requested an analysis of manufacturing overhead costs for the last month. The standards for manufacturing overhead costs are:

Standard Costs Per Batch

Variable Manufacturing Overhead $5.00
Fixed Manufacturing Overhead $2.00

    Total Manufacturing Overhead Per Batch $7.00

The flexible monthly manufacturing overhead cost budget on a direct labor hour basis is:

Standard Direct Labor Hours	Budgeted Overhead
1,000	$ 5,500
2,000	8,000
3,000 (Normal Capacity)	10,500
4,000	13,000
5,000	15,500

It takes two direct labor hours at standard to make one batch of boxes. Sixteen hundred batches of boxes were made last month. Actual total overhead was $12,000.

Required:

a. Calculate the flexible budget formula.
b. Do a two-way analysis of overhead variance.

8A–10   Given the information in Problem 8A–9: assume that 3,000 direct labor hours were worked. Prepare a three-way analysis of variance for manufacturing overhead costs.

PROBLEMS SERIES B

8B–1   The Green Thing Company produces green things. The standard cost of one green thing is:

Direct materials—1 pound at $2.00/pound	$2.00
Direct labor—1½ hours at $3.00/hour	4.50
Manufacturing Overhead—Variable	1.50
Manufacturing Overhead—Fixed	.60
Total Standard Cost per Thing	$8.60

Overhead is applied to things produced on a standard direct labor hour basis. Normal capacity per month is 10,000 things. Last month, 9,800 things were produced. Actual manufacturing overhead was $21,000, of which $15,000 was variable. Fourteen thousand direct labor hours at a total actual cost of $63,000 were used to produce the things. A total of 9,900 pounds of materials was used. Raw materials purchases of 10,000 pounds at $2.05 per pound were made last month.

Required:

Calculate the materials price and usage variances, the direct labor rate and efficiency variances, and the overhead budget and volume variances.

8B–2   The Baker Company makes cakes. The company uses a standard cost system for costing cakes. The following standards are currently in use for producing 100 cakes, a standard batch:

Raw materials 100 pounds @ $1.00/pound $100
Direct labor 15 hours @ $4.00/hour   60
Variable overhead $2 per standard direct labor hour . . .   30
Fixed overhead $3 per standard direct labor hour   45

Standard Cost per Batch $235

Normal capacity per month is 1,000 batches. Last month, 1,050 batches were produced. Purchases of raw materials amounted to 110,000 pounds at $1.05 per pound. Raw material usage totaled 106,000 pounds. Labor usage was 15,000 hours at an average cost of $4.10 per hour. Manufacturing overhead actually incurred was $31,000 variable and $50,000 fixed.

Required:

Compute the raw materials and direct labor variances and the budget and volume variances for manufacturing overhead costs.

8B-3   The Haywood Company is preparing to close their accounts. They have asked you to: (1) prepare the journal entry that would be made to close the manufacturing overhead control account; and (2) prepare the journal entry to close all variance accounts to the cost of goods sold account.

Direct Materials Price Variance		Direct Materials Quantity Variance	
4,000			2,000

Direct Labor Efficiency Variance		Direct Labor Rate Variance	
	2,200	400	

Manufacturing Overhead Control		Manufacturing Overhead Volume Variance	
27,000	30,000		1,000

Manufacturing Overhead Efficiency Variance		Manufacturing Overhead Spending Variance	
	4,000	2,000	

8B-4   Using the following information:

Actual labor hours used   14,000
Standard labor hours allowed   14,700
Actual total overhead $21,000
Actual variable overhead $15,000
Standard variable overhead per standard labor hour $1.00
Standard fixed overhead per standard labor hour . . . . $.40
Normal volume (direct labor hours)   15,000

Required:

Determine the volume variance and the budget variance for manufacturing overhead costs.

8B–5 Given the information in 8B–4: (1) prepare a three-way analysis of variance, and (2) calculate the variable overhead spending variance and the fixed overhead spending variance.

8B–6 Ceramic, Inc. had the following budget for three individual overhead cost items at a normal level of activity of 1,000 barrels for one month.

	Variable	Fixed	Total
Indirect Materials	$1,000	–0–	$1,000
Setup Time	200	300	500
Equipment Depreciation . . .	–0–	3,000	3,000
			$4,500

Actual production was 1,100 barrels. Direct labor hours, the overhead application basis, was two hours per barrel at standard, but actual hours averaged 1.75 hours per barrel. Actual overhead cost at 1,100 barrels was $1,150 for indirect materials, $500 for setup time and $3,000 for equipment depreciation. The actual cost incurrence for setup time was $150 of variable cost and $350 of fixed cost.

Required:

a. Calculate the manufacturing overhead applied to production for each of the items.

b. What was the total volume variance?
c. What was the volume variance per item?
d. What was the total budget variance?
e. What was the spending variance per item?
f. What was the efficiency variance per item?

8B–7 You have been given the following information:

Actual labor hours used = 315 hours
Standard materials price = $2.50
Standard labor hours allowed = 300 hours
Standard quantity of materials used = 450 units
Actual labor rate per hour = $3.00
Actual quantity of materials purchased and used = 445 units
Standard labor rate per hour = $3.10
Actual materials price = $2.52
Standard variable manufacturing overhead = $1.50 a unit
Actual variable manufacturing overhead in total = $925
Standard fixed manufacturing overhead = $3.50 a unit
Actual fixed manufacturing overhead = $1,900
Budgeted fixed manufacturing overhead = $1,750
Normal production = 500 units
Actual production = 600 units

Required:

Prepare a schedule for the following variances:

a. Raw materials price variance
b. Raw materials quantity variance
c. Direct labor efficiency variance
d. Direct labor rate variance
e. Volume variance for manufacturing overhead cost
f. Budget variance for manufacturing overhead cost

8B–8 Given the information in problem 8B–7, prepare a three-way analysis of variance for manufacturing overhead cost.

8B–9 Given the information in problem 8B–7, calculate the variable overhead spending variance and the fixed overhead spending variance.

8B–10 The Organet Stamping Company manufactures a variety of products made of plastic and aluminum components. During the winter months substantially all of the production capacity is devoted to the production of lawn sprinklers for the following spring and summer season. Other products are manufactured during the remainder of the year. Because a variety of products are manufactured throughout the year, factory volume is measured by production labor hours rather than units of product.

Production and sales volume have grown steadily for the past several years as can be seen from the following schedule of standard production labor content of annual output:

1979	32,000 hours
1978	30,000 hours
1977	27,000 hours
1976	28,000 hours
1975	26,000 hours

The company has developed standard costs for its several products. Standard costs for each year are set in the preceding October. The standard cost of a sprinkler for 1980 was $2.50, computed as follows:

Direct Materials
Aluminum . . . . 0.2 lbs. @ $0.40 per lb.	$0.08
Plastic . . . . 1.0 lbs. @ $0.38 per lb.	0.38
Production Labor . . . . 0.3 hrs. @ $4.00 per hr.	1.20
Overhead (calculated using 30,000 production	
labor hours as normal capacity)	
Variable . . . . 0.3 hrs. @ $1.60 per hr.	0.48
Fixed . . . . 0.3 hrs. @ $1.20 per hr.	0.36
Total . . . . :	$2.50

During February 1980, 8,500 good sprinklers were manufactured. The following costs were incurred and charged to production:

Materials Requisitioned for Production
Aluminum . . . . 1900 lbs. @ $0.40 per lb.	$ 760
Plastic—	
Regular Grade . . . . 6000 lbs. @ $0.38 per lb.	2,280
Low Grade . . . . 3500 lbs. @ $0.38 per lb.	1,330

Production Labor

Straight time	2300 hrs. @ $4.00 per hr.		9,200
Overtime	400 hrs. @ $6.00 per hr.		2,400
Overhead			
Variable			5,200
Fixed			3,100
	Costs Charged to Production		$24,270

Required:

Every item below is related to the above facts and should be answered on the basis of those facts.

a. The spending or budget variation for the fixed portion of the overhead costs is

   1. $100 unfavorable.
   2. $60 favorable.
   3. zero
   4. not calculable from the problem.
   5. not listed above.

b. The manufacturing overhead volume variation is

   1. the result of inadequate cost control effort.
   2. the result of sales volume exceeding production volume.
   3. the result of actual production hours exceeding standard production hours of output.
   4. the result of the over- or under-application of fixed costs to output.
   5. not the result of any of the reasons enumerated above.

c. The variable overhead budget variation would have been

   1. $1,120 unfavorable.
   2. $1,220 unfavorable.
   3. $1,160 unfavorable.
   4. $1,280 unfavorable.
   5. none of the above.

   (CMA adapted)

8B-11   The Carberg Corporation manufactures and sells a single product. The cost system used by the company is a standard cost system. The standard cost per unit of product is shown below:

Material—one pound plastic @ $2.00	$ 2.00
Direct Labor 1.6 @ $4.00	6.40
Variable overhead cost	3.00
Fixed overhead cost	1.45
	$12.85

The overhead cost per unit was calculated from the following annual overhead cost budget for a 60,000 unit volume.

Variable Overhead Cost	
Indirect labor 30,000 hours @ $4.00	$120,000
Supplies—Oil 60,000 gallons @ $.50	30,000
Allocated variable service department costs	30,000
Total Variable Overhead Cost	$180,000
Fixed Overhead Cost:	
Supervision	$ 27,000
Depreciation	45,000
Other fixed costs	15,000
Total Fixed Overhead Cost	$ 87,000
Total Budgeted Annual Overhead Cost at 60,000 Units	$267,000

The charges to the manufacturing department for November, when 5,000 units were produced, are given below:

Material	5,300 pounds	@	$2.00	$10,600
Direct labor	8,200 hours	@	$4.10	33,620
Indirect labor	2,400 hours	@	$4.10	9,840
Supplies—Oil	6,000 gallons	@	$0.55	3,300
Allocated variable service department costs				3,200
Supervision				2,475
Depreciation				3,750
Other				1,250
Total				$68,035

The purchasing department normally buys about the same quantity as is used in production during a month. In November, 5,200 pounds were purchased at a price of $2.10 per pound.

Required:

a. Calculate the following variances from standard costs for the data given:

1. materials purchase price
2. materials quantity
3. direct labor wage rate
4. direct labor efficiency
5. overhead budget

b. The company has divided its responsibilities such that the purchasing department is responsible for the price at which materials and supplies are purchased. The manufacturing department is responsible for the quantities of materials used. Does this division of responsibilities solve the conflict between price and quantity variances? Explain your answer.

c. Prepare a report which details the overhead budget variance. The report, which will be given to the manufacturing department manager, should display only that part of the variance that is the responsibility of the manager and should highlight the information in ways that would be useful to that manager in evaluating departmental performance and when considering corrective action.

d. Assume that the department manager performs the timekeeping function for this manufacturing department. From time to time analysis of overhead and direct labor variances have shown that the department manager has deliberately misclassified labor hours (e.g., listed direct labor hours as indirect labor hours and vice versa) so that only one of the two labor variances is unfavorable. It is not feasible economically to hire a separate timekeeper. What should the company do, if anything, to resolve this problem?

(CMA, adapted)

8B-12   The Justin Company has recently installed a standard cost system to simplify its factory bookkeeping and to aid in cost control. The company makes standard items for inventory, but because of the many products in its line, each is manufactured periodically under a production order. Prior to the installation of the system, job order cost sheets were maintained for each production order. Since the introduction of the standard costs system, however, they have not been kept.

The fabricating department is managed by a general supervisor who has overall responsibility for scheduling, performance and cost control. The department consists of four machine/work centers. Each work center is manned by a four-person work group or team and the centers are aided by a 12-person support group. Departmental practice is to assign a job to one team and expect the team to perform most of the work necessary to complete the job, including acquisition of materials and supplies from the stores department and machining and assembling. This has been practical and satisfactory in the past and is readily accepted by the employees.

Information regarding production cost standards, products produced, and actual costs for the fabricating department in March is presented below.

Unit Standard Costs

	Part		
	A7A	C6D	C7A
Material......................	$2.00	$ 3.00	$1.50
Direct labor..................	1.50	2.00	1.00
Overhead (per direct labor dollar)*:			
Variable..................	3.00	4.00	2.00
Fixed	.75	1.00	.50
	$7.25	$10.00	$5.00

*The departmental standard overhead rates are applied to the products as a percentage of direct labor dollars. The labor base was chosen because nearly all of the variable overhead costs are caused by labor activity. The departmental overhead rates were calculated at the beginning of the year as follows.

	Variable (Including Indirect Labor)	Fixed
Estimated annual cost...........	$360,000	$ 90,000
Estimated annual department direct labor dollars............	$180,000	$180,000
Overhead rate...................	200%	50%

Analysis of the Fabricating Department
Account for March

Charges
  Materials
Job No. 307-11	$ 5,200	
Job No. 307-12	2,900	
Job No. 307-14	9,400	$17,500

  Labor charges
Job No. 307-11	$ 4,000	
Job No. 307-12	2,100	
Job No. 307-14	6,200	
Indirect labor	12,200	24,500

  Variable overhead
    costs (e.g., supplies,
    electricity, etc.)   18,800

  Fixed overhead costs (e.g.,
    supervisor's salary, deprecia-
    tion, property tax
    and insurance, etc.)   7,000

  Total charges to department
    for March $67,800

Credits
  Completed Jobs
    Job No. 307-11
      2,000 units part
      A7A @ 7.25 $14,500
    Job No. 307-12
      1,000 units part
      C6D @ 10.00   10,000
    Job No. 307-14
      6,000 units part
      C7A @ 5.00   30,000 $54,500
  Variances transferred to the
    factory variance account
      Materials[1] $ 1,500
      Direct labor[2]   1,300
      Variable overhead   9,000
      Fixed overhead   1,500   13,300
  Total credits $67,800

---

[1] Material price variances are isolated at acquisition and charged to the Stores Department.
[2] All direct labor was paid at the standard wage rate during March.

Required:

a. Justin company assumes that its efforts to control costs in the fabricating department would be aided if variances were calculated by jobs. Management intends to add this analysis next month. Calculate all the variances by job that might contribute to cost control under this assumption.

b. Do you agree with the company's plan to initiate the calculation of job variances in addition to the currently calculated departmental variances? Explain your answer.

(CMA, adapted)

Learning Objectives

Chapter 9 discusses the variable costing format and the various approaches to cost-profit-volume analysis. Studying this chapter should enable you to:

1. Compare and contrast variable costing and absorption costing.
2. Understand the basic elements of short-range profit planning.
3. Distinguish between common and traceable cost factors.
4. Discuss and apply the general approaches to cost-profit-volume analysis.
5. Discuss and apply the basic methods of multiple product cost-profit-volume analysis.

9

Variable Costing and Cost-Profit-Volume Analysis

COST ACCUMULATION for inventory valuation using full inventory costs was discussed in Chapters 3, 4, 5 and 7. Full inventory costs include the costs of all direct materials, direct labor, variable manufacturing overhead used in the production process, and an allocated portion of the fixed manufacturing overhead based on normal or practical capacity. This approach stresses the accumulation of full costs in determining the cost of goods manufactured for a given accounting period. The determination of the cost of goods manufactured directly affects both the carrying value of the inventory reported on the balance sheet and the cost of goods sold included on the income statement.

Cost of goods sold is one of two broad cost categories normally included on a traditional full or absorption costing income statement. The amount which is reported as cost of goods sold represents a product cost. The other expenses included on the income statement are classified as period costs, and are normally classified and reported on a functional basis. The absorption costing income statement is generally accepted by the accounting profession for external reporting purposes.

For purposes of internal planning, control, performance evaluation, and decision-making by management, an alternative cost behavior format has been developed for the income statement which many accountants feel appears to be superior to the full or absorption costing format, at least for internal decision-making purposes. This alternative method is referred to as the variable costing or direct costing approach to income measurement.[1] The emphasis of this approach is focused on the separation of costs into their fixed and variable components on the income statement. From a managerial point of view, variable costing is considered an internal management tool. Normally a firm must prepare its external reports on an absorption costing basis for third party users. An income statement prepared under the variable costing concept includes separate classifications for variable and fixed costs. Variable costs include expenditures for such items as: raw materials, direct labor, variable manufacturing overhead, and variable selling and administrative expenses. Fixed costs include the fixed portion of manufacturing overhead and fixed selling and administrative expenses. A full absorption income statement summarizes the expenses for the period in traditional product cost and period expenditure form or format. Product costs, including both fixed and variable portions, are incorporated into cost of goods sold while period costs, also including both fixed and variable elements, are included in the expense section. These two income statement formats are shown in Illustration 9–1.

Illustration 9-1
Income Statement Formats

1. Using Variable Costing Methods

Sales Revenue		$xx
Variable Costs		
Production Costs	$xx	
Selling Expenses	xx	
Administrative Expenses	xx	xx
Contribution Margin		$xx
Fixed Costs:		
Manufacturing Overhead Costs	$xx	
Selling Expenses	xx	
Administrative Expenses	xx	xx
Net Income Before Taxes		$xx

2. Using Absorption Methods

Sales Revenue		$xx
Cost of Goods Sold:		
Direct Labor	$xx	
Direct Materials	xx	
Variable Manufacturing Overhead	xx	
Fixed Manufacturing Overhead	xx	xx
Gross Margin		$xx
Expenses:		
Selling Expenses	$xx	
Administrative Expenses	xx	xx
Net Income Before Taxes		$xx

---

[1] Since "variable costing" describes the approach more accurately than "direct costing" we will use the term "variable costing" in this chapter.

In summary, full or absorption costing includes fixed manufacturing overhead costs as a part of the cost of goods manufactured by applying a predetermined or standard rate for fixed manufacturing overhead. Variable costing treats fixed manufacturing overhead as a cost of the time period under consideration, i.e., a period cost. The cost of goods manufactured under absorption costing includes direct labor, direct materials, variable manufacturing overhead, and fixed manufacturing overhead. The cost of goods manufactured under variable costing will include only the variable elements of manufacturing costs: direct labor, direct materials, and variable manufacturing overhead. Fixed manufacturing overhead is a *product cost* under absorption costing, but a *period cost* under variable costing.

THE CONTRIBUTION MARGIN AND VARIABLE COSTING

The contribution margin is defined as the difference between revenues and all variable costs associated with those revenues. The contribution margin may be calculated on a total income statement basis, on a per unit basis, or as a percentage of sales. The contribution margin is a managerial decision-making tool. Moreover, variable costing may be regarded as a contribution margin approach to the measurement of income.

As indicated in Illustration 9–1, the format used in the variable costing income statement first deducts all variable manufacturing costs as well as all other variable costs (selling and administrative expenses) from total revenues in order to arrive at the contribution margin. The total fixed manufacturing costs and other fixed selling and administrative expenses are then deducted from the contribution margin to arrive at net income before taxes. Since total fixed manufacturing costs are expensed each period, there is no volume variance to consider at the end of each accounting period using variable costing.

EXTERNAL FINANCIAL REPORTING IMPLICATIONS

If inventory levels fluctuate during an accounting period (that is, if the beginning and ending inventory balances differ), then the variable costing and full or absorption costing techniques provide different income amounts for that period due to the different treatment of fixed costs.

The approach normally used to illustrate the different income statements is to prepare a comparative example that has no beginning or ending finished goods inventory. This permits an analysis which illustrates the fact that over the long-run, the two techniques will provide identical total income amounts when the income for all accounting periods is summed. The assumption made is that all other factors are equal. However, this is rarely, if ever, the case.

The three cases that must be considered in order to fully illustrate the impact of the two costing approaches on income are:

1. Production equals sales.
2. Production exceeds sales.
3. Sales exceed production.

AN ILLUSTRATION: ABSORPTION VERSUS VARIABLE COSTING

During January, 1981, the president of Sax Company decided that the power turbine shaft segment of the business should be established as a separate division with its own division manager, and that a planning, control and performance evaluation system should be added to its standard cost system. The standard cost system for manufacturing costs was discussed in Chapters 7 and 8. The planning, control and performance evaluation system is considered in Chapters 10 through 12.

A variable cost system for cost accumulation appears to be appropriate for internal use. The company uses absorption costing for external financial reporting purposes. The president requested that an analysis be made of the differences between variable costing and absorption costing in terms of the impact that each of these methods has on income. Implicit in his request was the fact that the president did not wish to maintain the accounts on both a variable costing basis for internal purposes and on an absorption costing basis for external financial reporting purposes.

Sax Company's president asked that the standard costs of manufacturing developed in Chapter 7 (Illustration 7-4) be used and, in addition, that a $20,000 budget for fixed selling and administrative costs be assumed. The variable selling costs are approximately $5 per unit sold. The production and sales levels which the president suggested for use in the analysis are rough estimates of the anticipated activity for the months of February, March, April and May and are presented in Illustration 9-2.

Factors other than volume are assumed to be constant for all months under consideration. Selling prices, standard costs of manufacturing, and selling and administrative costs should not change for any month of the time period under observation. For absorption costing purposes, the practical capacity of 1,800 power turbine shafts, or 900 direct labor hours, is used to allocate fixed overhead to production.

Illustration 9–2 summarizes the sales, production and cost data which the president of Sax Company wants used in the comparison of income calculations using absorption and variable costing.

Illustration 9-2
Sax Company
Power Turbine Shaft Division
Projected Cost, Sales and Production Data

Per Unit Sales and Production Costs:
Average Sales Price $50.00

Standard Production Cost:
Direct Material @ Standard 6.00
Direct Labor @ Standard 3.00
Variable Manufacturing Overhead @ Standard 1.40

Total Variable Production Cost $10.40
Fixed Manufacturing Overhead @ Standard * 2.00

                                                                           $12.40

Projected Selling and Administrative Expense:
Variable Selling Costs. . . . . $5 per unit
Fixed Selling and Administrative Expenses. $20,000

President's Estimate of Production and Sales Volumes in Units:

	February	March	April	May	Total
Beginning inventory.	0	0	550	150	—
Production	1,800	2,200	1,250	1,500	6,750
Sales.	1,800	1,650	1,650	1,650	6,750
Ending Inventory.	0	550	150	0	—

*Total fixed overhead is budgeted at $3,600 (Illustration 7-3) or $2.00 per unit.

The income statements prepared using absorption costing use the full cost of manufacturing, $12.40 per unit, which has been adjusted for any volume variance since Sax Company closes its variances to cost of goods sold at the end of each period. Remember, the basis for developing the fixed manufacturing overhead in Illustration 7-4 in Chapter 7 was 1,800 units of production or 900 standard direct labor hours. At any other level of production, a volume variance would appear in the accounts. The income statements prepared under both conventional absorption costing and variable costing for the four months are presented in Illustration 9-3.

To understand the computations included in Illustration 9-3, the absorption costing and the variable costing income statements should be reviewed for a month in which there is a volume variance. For example, in March projected sales are 1,650 units at $50 per unit or a total sales revenue of $82,500. Under absorption costing, cost of goods sold at standard would be 1,650 units at $12.40 per unit for a total of $20,460. Fixed overhead applied at standard is $2.00 per unit produced, and is based on a practical capacity of 1,800 units. Anticipated production in March is 2,200 units. The favorable volume variance is 400 units at $2.00 per unit or $800. If standard direct labor hours were used in the analysis, then the volume variance would still be projected at $800 (200 hours X $4 per

Illustration 9-3
Sax Company
Power Turbine Shaft Division

Comparison of Absorption and Variable Costing Income Statements (In Units)

	February	March	April	May	Total
Production (Budget)........	1,800	2,200	1,250	1,500	6,750
Sales (Budget)............	1,800	1,650	1,650	1,650	6,750
Projected Income Statements—Absorption Costing					
Sales.....................	$90,000	$82,500	$82,500	$82,500	$337,500
Less: Cost of Goods Sold After Adjustment*............	22,320	19,660	21,560	21,060	84,600
Gross Margin..............	$67,680	$62,840	$60,940	$61,440	$252,900
Less: Selling and Administrative Expenses................	29,000	28,250	28,250	28,250	113,750
Net Income Before Taxes............	$38,680	$34,590	$32,690	$33,190	$139,150

*Cost of Goods Sold After Adjustment for Volume Variance. Assume the entire variance is included in cost of goods sold.

February. No adjustment
March   —($12.40 X 1,650 units sold) + [(1,800 units — 2,200 units) x $2]
         $20,460 — $800 = $19,660
April   —$20,460 + [(1,800 units — 1,250 units) X $2]
         $20,460 + $1,100 = $21,560
May   —$20,460 + [(1,800 units — 1,500 units) X $2]
         $20,460 + $600 = $21,060

Sax Company
Power Turbine Shaft Division

Projected Income Statements—Variable Costing

	February	March	April	May	Total
Sales.....................	$90,000	$82,500	$82,500	$82,500	$337,500
Less: Variable Costs					
Product Costs	18,720	17,160	17,160	17,160	70,200
Selling Expenses	9,000	8,250	8,250	8,250	33,750
Contribution Margin.......	$62,280	$57,090	$57,090	$57,090	$233,550
Less: Fixed Costs					
Manufacturing Overhead..............	3,600	3,600	3,600	3,600	14,400
Selling and Administrative Expenses	20,000	20,000	20,000	20,000	80,000
Net Income Before Taxes............	$38,680	$33,490	$33,490	$33,490	$139,150

hour). The total selling and administrative expenses would consist of a fixed portion of.$20,000 and a variable portion of $5.00 per unit sold or $8,250.

The sales for March in the variable costing income statement would, of course, be identical to the amount of absorption costing sales—$82,500. Under variable costing, the cost of goods sold, however, would include only the variable manufacturing costs of $10.40 per unit (Illustration 9-2) for 1,650 units or a total of $17,160. The variable selling expenses would be $8,250 ($5.00 per unit sold). Total fixed manufacturing overhead is projected at $3,600 per month. The president projected fixed selling and administrative expenses of $20,000 per month. These fixed costs would be considered period, rather than product, costs under variable costing.

A number of observations concerning the two different income statement formats are appropriate:

1. Expense classifications under absorption costing are made on a functional cost basis while variable costing classifications are made on a cost behavior pattern basis (variable vs. fixed).
2. The gross margin obtained using the absorption costing format is not the same as the contribution margin under variable costing. Sales less all product costs equals the gross margin under absorption costing. Sales less all variable costs equals the contribution margin under variable costing.
3. Income under variable costing follows the level of sales. When sales increase, income increases; when sales fall, income declines; and when sales remain constant, income remains the same (March-May). Income under absorption costing is related to both the level of sales and to the level of production. Sales for the months of March through May are projected at the same level. By inspecting production levels shown in Illustration 9-3, we note that under the absorption method, income varies in those months in relationship to the levels of production.
4. When sales and production are identical, as in February, both costing methods yield the same net income before taxes. Under either approach, the total fixed manufacturing overhead is considered an expense on the income statement when sales and production are equal, since there is no change in the beginning or ending inventory balance. Classifications within the income statement differ, however. Cost of goods sold, including any volume variance, incorporates total fixed manufacturing overhead under absorption costing. Under variable costing, total fixed manufacturing overhead is reflected as a period cost.
5. When production exceeds sales (as is the case in March) absorption

costing yields a higher net income before taxes, because a portion of the fixed manufacturing overhead costs has been allocated to and included in the ending inventory, and thus, deferred to future periods. Under variable costing, all fixed manufacturing overhead costs are expensed during the period in which they are incurred.

6. When production is less than sales (April and May), variable costing yields a higher net income before taxes. Under absorption costing, the cost of goods sold, after taking volume variances into consideration, includes an amount of current and past applied fixed manufacturing overhead costs exceeding the total fixed manufacturing overhead costs incurred during the current period. The inventories are reduced to match decreased sales demands; therefore, the applied fixed manufacturing overhead in ending inventories is less than the applied fixed manufacturing overhead in the beginning inventories. Using variable costing methods, total fixed manufacturing overhead is considered to be an expense in each accounting period in which it is incurred; therefore, there is no deferral of fixed costs in the finished goods inventory accounts.

7. Over time, assuming that all factors except volume are equal, total income under the two income statement formats is the same. Furthermore, total production could not exceed total sales by a material amount in the long-run. If production did exceed sales over the long-run, the firm would have large quantities of finished goods inventories on hand.

AN ILLUSTRATION: RECONCILING ABSORPTION AND VARIABLE COSTING INCOME STATEMENTS

The differences between absorption costing and variable costing are explained by analyzing the beginning and the ending inventory amounts for each month. Alternatively, the difference in income can be calculated each month by considering the impact of fixed overhead on both production and sales levels.

The finished goods inventory levels under both absorption and variable costing from Illustration 9-2 are as follows:

Month	Beginning Inventory	Ending Inventory	Difference
February	0 units	0 units	0 units
March	0	550	550
April	550	150	(400)
May	150	0	(150)

The inventory values reported on the balance sheets at the end of each month are at the full standard manufacturing cost per unit ($12.40) under absorption costing, and at the variable manufacturing cost per unit ($10.40) under variable costing. The difference between these two values, $2.00, represents the allocated fixed manufacturing overhead cost per unit at standard cost.

In March, the president anticipates that inventory will increase by a total of 550 units. The costs accumulated for these 550 units under absorption costing are $6,820 (550 units X $12.40 per unit). The costs accumulated under variable costing are $5,720 (550 units X $10.40 per unit). The difference between the two inventory costs at the end of March is $1,100. Again, this difference of $1,100 represents the $2.00 per unit of fixed manufacturing overhead allocated to the 550 units which is deferred to future months under absorption costing. Since there is no beginning inventory, absorption costing shows a higher net income before taxes for March than does the variable costing method. As shown in Illustration 9-3, the net income under absorption costing is $34,590 and for variable costing income is $33,490; a difference of $1,100 (550 units @ $2.00 per unit).

If the inventory differences are calculated for April and May, then the same reconciliation can be made. It is not necessary to calculate the costs accumulated for both the beginning and the ending inventories; only the amount and direction of change need to be considered. In April, the president anticipates that the finished goods inventory will decrease by 400 units. The absorption costing income statement will include fixed overhead in cost of goods sold on the income statement in an amount larger than that which was incurred because production was less than sales by 400 units. The fixed overhead at standard included in these 400 units is $800; therefore, net income before taxes under absorption costing is $800 less than the comparable net income before taxes computed using variable costing. In May, the inventory decline is 150 units, and the absorption costing net income before taxes is $300 less than the variable costing net income before taxes.

The same analysis may be used to calculate the impact on inventories and net income before taxes by considering production and sales volumes in each month. As an example of these calculations, the projected April data from Illustration 9-3 are presented below.

April Sales.........1,650 units		
April Production.....1,250 units		
Net Income Before Taxes Under Variable Costing........		$33,490
Fixed Manufacturing Costs Included in Sales		
(1,650 X $2.00)...................................	$3,300	
Fixed Manufacturing Costs Included in		
Production (1,250 X $2.00).......................	2,500	
Inventory Level Impact.............................		(800)
Net Income Before Taxes Under Absorption Costing......		$32,690

Since finished goods inventory levels are projected to decrease during April, absorption costing includes fixed costs of manufacturing in cost of goods sold of $800 in excess of that incurred in April.

THE VARIABLE COSTING CONTROVERSY

For external reporting purposes, the concept of absorption costing is well entrenched and represents "generally accepted principles of accounting" as well as being the formally accepted method as required by the IRS for purposes of income tax determination. There have been many advocates of variable costing for external reporting, but the arguments for acceptance have met with very limited success to date. Generally accepted accounting principles and most, if not all, regulatory bodies require absorption costing income statements for external reporting purposes. For internal planning, control, performance evaluation, and decision-making, the variable costing approach has gained widespread managerial acceptance. For internal use, the concept of variable costing is usually adjusted to meet the particular information needs of the firm.

COST-PROFIT-VOLUME ANALYSIS

Cost-profit-volume analysis is a managerial technique which is used for analyzing profit planning information for short-range planning purposes. This technique is a modeling tool which may be used for estimating income or selecting between alternative short-run operating strategies. Cost-profit-volume analysis uses the variable costing concept of income determination, and provides a quick overview of a firm's profit structure which supplies management with estimates of limited accuracy. These estimates, however, are valuable for such purposes as analyzing potential changes in selling prices, sales mix, sales volume, variable costs, and fixed costs. These five elements represent managerial decisions which must be considered in short-range profit planning.

Cost-Profit-Volume Analysis: Common Versus Traceable Factors

Cost-profit-volume analysis may be applied to the entire firm or to one or more segments of the firm. When this technique is applied to the entire firm, all of the revenues and costs are directly traceable to the planning unit. Directly traceable costs and revenues are those costs and revenues that may be attributed to the segment under consideration on a non-arbitrary basis. Theoretically, if the segment were eliminated, the directly traceable costs or revenues would also be eliminated.

Cost-profit-volume analysis is also applied to individual segments of the firm such as product lines, divisions, or sales territories. The smaller the segment of the organization analyzed by this technique, the greater the problem of common cost allocation. Common costs are those costs which benefit more than one segment of the firm. If these costs are allocated, the allocation is usually made on an arbitrary basis. Fixed manufacturing overhead is an example of a common cost that is allocated to production. There are numerous other examples of common cost if one considers only a specific segment of the firm. The president's salary, costs of company production planning, research and development expenditures, market research costs, advertising campaign costs, and the costs incurred in the legal department are all examples of costs common to many segments of an organization.

By definition, a common cost problem does not exist in those circumstances when the unit being analyzed using cost-profit-volume analysis is the entire firm. The firm must generate revenues which are adequate to cover its total costs, but any segment cost-volume-profit analysis should use only those costs and revenues which are traceable to that segment. Furthermore, if all segments of a firm are engaged in cost-profit-volume analysis separately, certain common costs would not be considered in the analyses.

COST-PROFIT-VOLUME ANALYSIS: THE CALCULATIONS

After reviewing the absorption and variable costing income statements presented in Illustration 9-3, the president of Sax Company requested that a graph illustrating the cost-profit-volume relationships per month for the Power Turbine Shaft Division be prepared assuming changes in certain financial factors. These factors were: (1) a reduction in variable production costs to $10 per unit; (2) a reduction in fixed manufacturing overhead costs to $3,000 per month; and (3) a reduction to $18,000 per month in fixed selling and administrative expenses. The costs were reclassified into the following variable and fixed components:

		Amount	Percent
Sales Revenue Per Unit		$ 50	100 %
Variable Costs:			
Production Costs	$10		
Selling Expenses	5		
		15	30
Contribution Margin		$ 35	70 %
Fixed Costs:			
Fixed Manufacturing Overhead Costs		$ 3,000	
Fixed Selling and Administrative Expenses		18,000	
Total Fixed Costs		$21,000	

Illustration 9–4 presents the profit capabilities of the Power Turbine Shaft Division in a format which indicates areas of loss and profit and the break-even point for this division.

A break-even point is that point where total revenues are exactly equal to total costs. Revenues in excess of the break-even point produce a profit, while revenues in an amount less than that stipulated by break-even analysis indicate a loss. However, the break-even formula or relationship may also be used by the firm to determine the level of profit it wishes to obtain.

Break-Even Relationships:
Total Revenues = Total Costs
or Total Revenues = Variable Costs + Fixed Costs
or Total Revenues = Variable Costs + Fixed Costs + Desired Profit
Level

The president was especially pleased with the margin of safety indicated by the cost-profit-volume graph. The margin of safety is the amount that budgeted sales can decline before the break-even point is reached. In the near future, the president could not foresee a loss in the Power Turbine Shaft Division.

The next factor that the president wished to consider was the level of sales required to earn $56,000 in before-tax profits each month assuming a reduction in variable production costs to $10 per unit, and a reduction in total fixed costs to $21,000 with all other financial factors remaining constant. Four approaches may be used in cost-profit-volume analysis. Each of these approaches provides the same information, but in a different manner. The four approaches or techniques are:

1. Graphical
2. Equation
3. Contribution Margin
4. Contribution Percentage or Ratio

The graphical approach was presented in Illustration 9-4. The equation, contribution margin, and contribution ratio or percentage approaches may be used to respond to questions raised by management regarding changes in financial factors.

Equation Method

The equation method establishes the mathematical relationships between sales, variable costs, fixed costs, and desired net income before taxes. This approach provides a solution expressed in terms of units, which must be multiplied by the selling price per unit to obtain the solution in terms of sales dollars.

The general form of the equation, with X representing the number of units necessary to yield the desired net income before taxes is:

Illustration 9-4
Sax Company
Cost-Profit-Volume Graph for Power Turbine Shaft Division

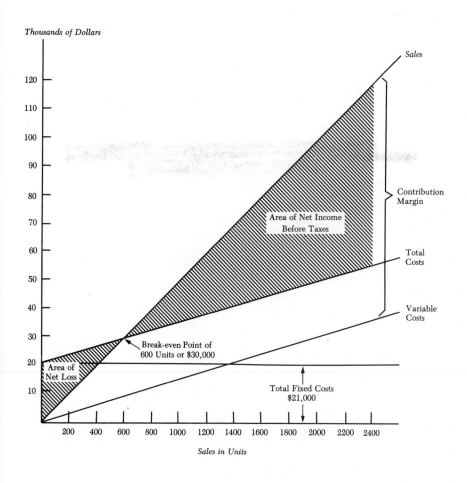

Unit Sales (X) Price	=	Variable Expenses (X) per Unit	+ Fixed Expenses +	Desired Net Income Before Taxes

1. To break-even

$$\$50\ (X) = \$15\ (X) + \$21,000 + \$0$$
$$\$35\ (X) = \$21,000$$
$$X = 600 \text{ units}$$
$$\text{Sales dollars} = 600 \times \$50 = \$30,000$$

2. To earn $56,000 net income before taxes

$$\$50 \ (X) \ = \ \$15 \ (X) \ + \ \$21,000 \ + \ \$56,000$$
$$\$35 \ (X) \ = \ \$77,000$$
$$X \ = \ 2,200 \ \text{units}$$
$$\text{Sales dollars} \ = \ 2,200 \ X \ \$50 \ = \ \$110,000$$

Contribution Margin Method

The contribution margin approach rearranges the equation, but also provides a solution in units. The general form of the contribution margin approach is as follows:

$$X = \frac{\text{Fixed Expenses} + \text{Desired Net Income Before Taxes}}{\text{Contribution Margin Per Unit}}$$

1. To break-even

$$X \ = \ \frac{\$21,000 \ + \ \$0}{\$50 \ - \ \$15}$$

$$= \ \frac{\$21,000}{\$35}$$

$$= \ 600 \ \text{units}$$

$$\text{Sales dollars} \ = \ 600 \ X \ \$50 \ = \ \$30,000$$

2. To earn $56,000 net income before taxes

$$X \ = \ \frac{\$21,000 \ + \ \$56,000}{\$50 \ - \ \$15}$$

$$= \ \frac{\$77,000}{\$35}$$

$$= \ 2,200 \ \text{units}$$

$$\text{Sales dollars} \ = \ 2,200 \ X \ \$50 \ = \ \$110,000$$

The results using the contribution margin approach are, of course, identical to those obtained under the equation approach. The contribution margin approach answers the question, "Given a $35 contribution margin, how many units must be sold in order to attain the desired profit?"

Contribution Percentage or Ratio Method

The contribution percentage or ratio approach provides an answer stated in terms of dollars of sales. If an answer in terms of units is desired, the dollars of sales must be divided by the selling price per unit. The contribution percentage approach uses the contribution margin approach and converts the contribution margin in the denominator to a percentage of contribution margin per sales dollar. The general formulation of the contribution percentage approach is:

Let Y = Necessary dollars of sales to yield the desired net income before taxes.

$$Y = \frac{\text{Fixed Costs} + \text{Desired Net Income Before Taxes}}{\left(\dfrac{\text{Contribution Margin Per Unit}}{\text{Sales Price Per Unit}}\right)}$$

1. To break-even

$$Y = \frac{\$21,000 + \$0}{\left(\dfrac{\$50 - \$15}{\$50}\right)}$$

$$= \frac{\$21,000}{\left(\dfrac{\$35}{\$50}\right)}$$

$$= \frac{\$21,000}{.70}$$

$$= \$30,000$$

$$\text{In units} = \$30,000 \div \$50 = 600$$

2. To earn $56,000 net income before taxes

$$Y = \frac{\$21,000 + \$56,000}{\left(\dfrac{\$50 - \$15}{\$50}\right)}$$

$$= \frac{\$77,000}{\left(\dfrac{\$35}{\$50}\right)}$$

$$= \frac{\$77,000}{.70}$$

$$Y = \$110,000$$

$$\text{In units} = \$110,000 \div \$50 = 2,200$$

The contribution margin percentage approach asks the question, "Given a contribution margin of $.70 for every $1 of sales, how many dollars of sales are necessary to cover fixed costs and attain the desired profit level?"

Summary of Methods

All of the above approaches provide identical answers because they are merely variations of the same equation and consider identical input factors. In choosing one approach as opposed to another, one must consider such factors as the purpose for which the information is intended, the form in which the information is desired, personal preference, and convenience.

COST-PROFIT-VOLUME ANALYSIS: MULTIPLE PRODUCTS

The analysis of cost-profit-volume relationships made by the Power Turbine Shaft Division was based on a single product. When two or more products are involved in cost-profit-volume analysis, the analysis becomes more complex and even less precise than the analysis of a single product. This is because different products normally have different selling prices, different variable costs, different contribution margins, and different sales forecasts that must be considered to arrive at the product mix.

The president of Sax Company is considering producing two different versions of an electric fan in a manufacturing plant that will become available in the near future. After reviewing the sales forecasts for electric fans, the marketing department feels that three small fans can be sold for every large fan. The manager that is responsible for the feasibility study wishes to calculate the level of sales that would be necessary to break-even each month and the sales level required to earn a net income of $5,200 before taxes each month.

It is anticipated that the small electric fan will sell for $10 per unit and the large electric fan will sell at a price of $20 per unit. The variable costs of production per unit is $4 and $12, respectively. The initial fixed costs per month are projected at $6,400 for manufacturing and $4,000 for selling and administrative expenses.

The Weighted Average Contribution Margin Percentage

There are certain obvious implications uncovered in an examination of the contribution margin percentages of the two products. In this case three small fans can be sold for every large fan.

	Small Electric Fans	Percent	Large Electric Fans	Percent
Selling Price..........................	$10	100	$20	100
Variable Costs.......................	4	40	12	60
Contribution Margin.................	$ 6	60	$ 8	40

The projected contribution margin percentage on small fans is 60 percent, and the large fans have a projected contribution margin percentage of 40 percent. The weighted average contribution margin percentage for the two products combined must fall somewhere between 40 and 60 percent.

The weighted average contribution margin percentage may be calculated in two ways. An obvious approach is to consider the two products as being sold in a package of three small fans and one large fan. The total contribution margin for this package is the weighted average contribution margin per package when expressed in dollars, and is the weighted average per dollar of projected sales when expressed on a percentage basis.

	Three Small Fans	One Large Fan	Total	Percent of Total
Selling Price.........................	$30	$20	$50	100
Variable Costs.......................	12	12	24	48
Contribution Margin.................	$18	$ 8	$26	52

The projected weighted average contribution margin is 52 percent for each package of three small fans and one large fan sold. Using the second method, the weighted average contribution margin is calculated by using the contribution margin percentages for each product, 60 percent for small fans and 40 percent for large fans, and weighting the contribution margins by their relative sales proportions.

Weighted Average Contributions:

$$\text{Small Electric Fans} = \frac{\text{Selling Price of Three Fans}}{\text{Total Selling Price for Both Fans}}$$

$$= \frac{\$30}{\$50} \times .60 \quad = .36$$

$$\text{Large Electric Fan} = \frac{\text{Selling Price of Large Fan}}{\text{Total Selling Price for Both Fans}}$$

$$= \frac{\$20}{\$50} \times .40 \quad = .16$$

Total Weighted Average Contribution Margin

$$= .36 + .16 \quad = .52$$

The above analysis indicates that, given the sales mix of three small fans and one large fan, $.36 is the contribution margin per dollar of sales from small fans, and $.16 is the contribution margin per dollar of sales from large fans. The total contribution margin per dollar of sales is $.52.

Multiple Product Cost-Profit-Volume Analysis: Package of Goods Approach

Any of the four general approaches to the cost-profit-volume analysis could be used to answer questions concerning the break-even point and the sales volume necessary to earn net income before taxes of $5,200. For purposes of illustration only, the equation and the weighted average contribution margin percentage approaches are utilized. The equation approach provides a basic solution in units, while the contribution margin percentage approach provides a basic solution in terms of sales dollars. Using the package of goods approach, the answer will be the number of packages of three small fans and one large fan that must be sold, and the total dollars of sales of the two products. The basic data developed for the electric fan analysis are presented in Illustration 9-5.

Illustration 9-5
Sax Company

Basic Data for Electric Fan Cost-Profit-Volume Analysis
Questions to be answered:
1. What is the break-even point?
2. What volume of sales is necessary to earn $5,200 net income before taxes?

Sales Mix (Projected):
Three small fans to one large fan.
Individual Product Contribution Margins (Projected):

	Small Electric Fans	Percent	Large Electric Fans	Percent
Selling Price........................	$10	100	$20	100
Variable Costs.......................	4	40	12	60
Contribution Margin.................	$ 6	60	$ 8	40

Weighted Average Contribution Margins (Projected):

	Three Small Fans	Percent	One Large Fan	Percent	Total	Percent of Total
Selling Price............	$30	100	$20	100	$50	100
Variable Costs..:........	12	40	12	60	24	48
Contribution Margin.....	$18	60	$ 8	40	$26	52

Fixed Costs (Projected):
Fixed Manufacturing Costs $6,400
Fixed Selling and Administrative Expenses $4,000

If the equation approach to cost-profit-volume analysis is used and sales are viewed as packages of three small fans and one large fan, the totals for the package may be used in the analysis as follows:

1. To break-even using the equation approach:

$$\$50 (X) = \$24 (X) + \$10,400 + \$0$$
$$\$26 (X) = \$10,400$$
$$X = 400 \text{ packages}$$

Since a package is comprised of three small fans and one large fan, the number of units of each fan that must be sold in order to break-even is as follows:

Small Fans = 400 packages X 3 units per package
= 1,200 units
Large Fan = 400 packages X 1 unit per package
= 400 units

2. To earn $5,200 net income before taxes using the equation approach:

$$\$50 \ (X) \ = \ \$24 \ (X) \ + \ \$10,400 \ + \ \$5,200$$
$$\$26 \ (X) \ = \ \$15,600$$
$$X \ = \ 600 \text{ packages}$$

The separation of the package would be made on the basis of the composition of the package: three small fans and one large fan per package.

$$\text{Small Fans} \ = \ 600 \text{ packages X 3 units per package}$$
$$= \ 1,800 \text{ units}$$
$$\text{Large Fan} \ = \ 600 \text{ packages X 1 unit per package}$$
$$= \ 600 \text{ units}$$

The contribution margin percentage approach, using the weighted average contribution margin percentage of .52, will yield the identical answers in sales dollars.

1. To break-even using the contribution margin percentage approach:

$$X \ = \ \frac{\$10,400 \ + \ \$0}{.52}$$

$$X \ = \ \$20,000$$

Using the equation approach, the break-even number of packages was 400. If this were multiplied by the selling price of a package, $50, the total sales necessary to break-even would have been $20,000.

The unit sales ratio is three small fans to one large fan, but the contribution margin percentage approach provides an answer in terms of sales dollars. The sales dollars ratio of one package is $30/$50 or 60% for small fans and $20/$50 or 40% for large fans.

$$\text{Small Fans}$$
$$\text{Sales Dollars} \ = \ \$20,000 \text{ X } 60\% \ = \ \$12,000$$
$$\text{Large Fan}$$
$$\text{Sales Dollars} \ = \ \$20,000 \text{ X } 40\% \ = \ \$ \ 8,000$$

2. To earn $5,200 net income before taxes using the contribution margin percentage approach:

$$X \ = \ \frac{\$10,400 \ + \ \$5,200}{.52}$$

$$X = \frac{\$15,600}{.52}$$

$$X = \$30,000$$

The equation approach solution in packages, when multiplied by the selling price of a package, would have provided the same answer. The sales ratios when multiplied by the total projected sales of $30,000 would provide the projected sales of each product.

Small Fans
Sales Dollars   = $30,000 X 60% = $18,000
Large Fan
Sales Dollars   = $30,000 X 40% = $12,000

Multiple Product Cost-Profit-Volume Analysis: Weighted Average Approach

The weighted average approach treats each product as a separate product instead of considering the unit as a package. The sales mix cannot be ignored, however. The sales mix is introduced into the calculations by weighting the individual financial factors included in the formulas. Again, any of the four approaches to cost-profit-volume analysis can be used. The equation approach and the contribution margin percentage approach will be illustrated here. The data presented in Illustration 9-5 are again used in these calculations.

When the cost-profit-volume equation is used, the solution is stated in terms of units. Therefore, the weighting factors are based on the unit sales mix of three small fans to one large fan. Seventy-five percent (3 of 4) of the units sold are small fans, and 25 percent (1 of 4) are large fans.

1. To break-even using the equation approach

$$.75 \ (\$10) \ X \ + \ .25 \ (\$20) \ X = .75 \ (\$4) \ X \ + \ .25 \ (\$12) \ X \ + \ \$10,400$$
$$\$7.50 \ X \ + \ \$5 \ X = \$3 \ X \ + \ \$3 \ X \ + \$10,400$$
$$\$12.50 \ X = \$6 \ X \ + \ \$10,400$$
$$\$6.50 \ X = \$10,400$$
$$X = 1,600 \ \text{units}$$

Both the selling prices and variable costs in this equation have been weighted by the projected sales mix. Of the break-even sales volume in units, 75 percent are small fans and 25 percent are large fans.

Small Fans = 1,600 X .75 = 1,200 units
Large Fan   = 1,600 X .25 =   400 units

21. To earn $5,200 net income before taxes using the equation approach

.75 ($10) X + .25 ($20) X = .75 ($4) X + .25 ($12) X
                                  + $10,400 +$5,200
$7.50 X + $5 X = $3 X + $3 X + $15,600
$12.50 X = $6 X + $15,600
$6.50 X = $15,600
X = 2,400 total units
Small Fans = 2,400 (.75) = 1,800 units
Large Fan = 2,400 (.25) = 600 units

When the contribution margin percentage approach is used, the solution is expressed in terms of sales dollars. The weighting factors must be based on the weighted average sales dollar which is $30/$50 or 60% for small fans and $20/$50 or 40% for large fans.

3. To compute break-even using the contribution margin percentage approach

$$X = \frac{\$10,400 + \$0}{[(.6) (.6) + (.4) (.4)]}$$

$$= \frac{\$10,400}{(.36 + .16)}$$

$$= \frac{\$10,400}{.52}$$

$$X = \$20,000$$

Small Fans Sales Dollars = $20,000 X .6 = $12,000

Large Fan Sales Dollars = $20,000 X .4 = $8,000

COST-PROFIT-VOLUME ANALYSIS: UNDERLYING ASSUMPTIONS

Conventional cost-profit-volume analysis is a static tool in that it assumes that all factors, with the exception of the single factor that is being analyzed, will remain constant over the relevant range. The equations are mathematical; therefore, any single factor may be computed given that all the other factors are known. The examples included in this chapter have all considered sales volume in units or dollars, which is the conventional approach.

Once the relationship of the following factors to volume are determined, this analysis assumes that the relationships with the following variables do not change over the relevant range of volume.

1. Variable costs
2. Fixed Costs
3. Selling prices
4. Sales mix
5. Efficiency
6. Productivity

Any projected change requires a new analysis. The linearity of the approach forces the user to consider all of the financial factors that affect profit and their relationships to volume. Note that this tool is not a precise planning tool, but it does provide an estimate of projected net income before taxes using the variable costing concept of income determination.

SUMMARY

For external reporting purposes, the use of full or absorption costing is required. However, for management accounting purposes, variable or direct costing is often more useful as a decision-making tool. Variable costing emphasizes the separation of manufacturing costs into their fixed and variable components.

From the standpoint of income determination, the primary difference between the two costing formats is in the treatment of fixed costs. Under the absorption costing format, fixed manufacturing overhead is allocated and inventoried as an element of product cost and is charged to expense only as the associated units of product are sold. In contrast, under the variable costing format, fixed manufacturing overhead is expensed as a period cost as it is incurred and the product cost includes only the variable cost elements.

This difference in the treatments of fixed manufacturing overhead means that net income under the two formats will vary whenever there is a difference between the sales and production for the period. When sales are equal to production, both formats will yield the identical net income figure.

The variable costing approach, although not acceptable for external financial accounting purposes, is instrumental in cost-profit-volume analysis for management purposes. Cost-profit-volume analysis is used as a tool for short-range profit planning purposes. The essential elements that must be considered in such planning include potential changes in selling prices, sales mix, sales volume, variable costs, and fixed costs. Usually such an analysis considers only those costs which are directly traceable to the unit under analysis, but in certain cases common costs are also considered.

Four general approaches to cost-profit-volume analysis include: (1) graphical, (2) equation, (3) contribution margin, and (4) contribution percentage or ratio. All four approaches yield approximately the same results, although in different formats, and all are based on the premise that sufficient sales revenue must be generated to cover both fixed and variable expenses as well as to produce the desired net income.

When more than a single product is involved in the cost-profit-volume analysis, the analysis process becomes more complex. The two primary approaches in multiple product cost-product-volume analysis are the package of goods approach (where the units sold are considered as a package) and the weighted average approach (where the units sold are considered as individual products). In either approach, the sales mix is a very important factor that must be taken into consideration.

This chapter has introduced short-range planning by discussing one of the tools of such planning, cost-profit-volume analysis. The next chapter continues the topic of short-range planning by illustrating the budgeting process.

KEY DEFINITIONS

Common costs—costs which benefit more than one segment of the firm. Any allocation of common costs will be arbitrary.

Contribution margin—the difference between revenues and all variable costs associated with those revenues.

Contribution margin approach—an approach to cost-profit-volume analysis which is similar to the equation approach but which bases its calculations on the contribution margin.

Contribution percentage approach—an approach to cost-profit-volume analysis which uses the contribution margin approach but bases its calculations on the percentage of contribution margin per dollar of sales.

Cost-profit-volume analysis—a technique using the variable costing concept of income determination in analyzing the impact of potential changes in selling prices, sales mix, sales volume, and variable and fixed costs on short-range profits.

Equation approach—the approach to cost-profit-volume analysis which establishes a basic mathematical relationship between sales, variable costs, fixed costs, and desired net income before taxes, and provides a solution in terms of units.

Full or absorption costing—the traditional type of costing generally used for external reporting puropses where fixed manufacturing overhead costs are included as a part of the cost of goods manufactured according to pre-determined rates of application.

Package of goods approach—a cost-profit-volume analysis for multiple products being sold in a given package or sales mix.

Traceable factors—those costs and revenues which may be directly traced on a non-arbitrary basis to a segment of the firm.

Variable or direct costing—a costing approach which includes only the variable portion of manufacturing overhead as a part of the cost of goods manu-factured, while treating the fixed portion of manufacturing overhead as a period cost. Variable costing is not generally used for external financial reporting but is an informative management tool.

Weighted average contribution margin—the contribution margin weighted by the product mix when two or more different products are sold.

QUESTIONS

1. What is the major use of a variable costing income statement? An absorp-tion costing income statement?
2. From an income determination standpoint, what is the only difference be-tween absorption and variable costing? Explain.
3. Explain the contribution margin approach to decision-making. In your ex-planation concentrate on the actual format of this type of income state-ment.
4. What causes income to vary under absorption costing? How does this dif-fer from variable costing? (That is, what causes income to vary under variable costing?)
5. When production is more than sales, which method produces the higher income, variable or absorption costing, and why?
6. How is cost-profit-volume analysis used? Give examples.
7. What is the difference between traceable and common costs?
8. Of the following which would you consider common costs?

    a. R & D expenditures
    b. Advertising costs
    c. Variable overhead costs
    d. Depreciation of executive office building
    e. Direct materials costs

9. What is the overall purpose of cost-profit-volume analysis?
10. Explain the equation approach to cost-profit-volume analysis. Does the answer it gives differ from that given under another approach?
11. Why is it difficult to use cost-profit-volume analysis when dealing with a firm which produces multiple products?

12. Name the underlying assumption in cost-profit-volume analysis.
13. Since the variable costing approach is not acceptable for external financial accounting purposes, why do firms bother with it?

EXERCISES

✓ 9–1   The Wax Company has the following operating information:

Production	14,000 units
Sales	11,200 units @ $5/unit
Variable costs	$35,000
Fixed costs	$14,000

Required:

Prepare an income statement using absorption costing and another using variable costing.

9–2   You are given the following information about the operations of the Queen Company:

Direct labor costs	$19,000
Direct materials purchases	7,000
Overhead (all variable except fixed rent of $1,000 and depreciation of $2,000)	14,000
General and administrative expense	2,000
Selling expenses	9,000
	$51,000

There were no beginning inventories. During the year 10,000 units were produced; 8,000 were sold. There were no inventories of materials or work-in-process at year-end—only finished goods. Prepare statements of cost of goods manufactured under each of the following assumptions:

a.   Full absorption
b.   Variable costing

✓ 9–3   Given below is cost information for the Sales Company for the month of June:

Sales	400 units
Variable manufacturing costs	$6 per unit
Total fixed manufacturing costs	$2,400
Total administrative expense (fixed)	$1,200
Finished goods beginning inventory	0 units
Finished goods ending inventory	200 units
Selling price	$25 per unit
Variable selling expense	$ 1 per unit

Required:

a. What is the net income under absorption costing?
b. What is the net income under variable costing?

✓9–4   Given the following break-even chart:

Identify the following items by numbers.

a. Total revenue line
b. Total cost line
c. Total fixed cost
d. Break-even volume
e. Break-even sales
f. Break-even point

✓9–5   The solid lines in the following break-even charts represent the present cost-profit-volume relationships in a firm. The dotted lines represent changes. Explain what financial factors changed the original relationships.

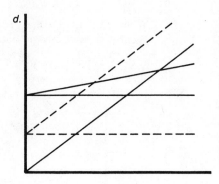

9-6　Given the following graph:

State the equation for total cost and for revenue in numerical terms. (Your answer will consist of 2 equations.)

9-7　Company Y has the following financial information regarding its sole product:

Revenue	$46,000
Net loss	($4,600)
Fixed expenses	$18,000
Selling price per unit	$5

What is the contribution margin per unit?

9-8　For the last year revenue was $400,000, total variable costs $180,000, total fixed costs $100,000, and net income $120,000. With no change in selling price, costs, or level of efficiency, what would the break-even point in sales be?

9-9　You are told the following about Jones Company's production costs:

```
Fixed costs . . . . . . . . . . .  $36,000
Variable costs:
    Materials  . . . . . . . . . .  $2.50 per unit
    Labor  . . . . . . . . . . . .  $1.70 per unit
    Other  processing . . . . . .  $ .80 per unit
                                     5.00
```

Required:

a. What is the *lowest price* at which you can sell the product and not lose money if you intend to produce and sell 60,000 units? (Use the equation method.)

b. At what price will you sell the product if you desire to have a 15% profit on sales?

9–10 The A&M Company has just been formed. In their first year of production, they have a plant capacity of 10,000 units which they feel they will be able to sell.

Their costs are:

Direct labor, $2.00 per unit
Direct materials, $1.00 per unit
Other variable costs, $.50 per unit
Fixed costs, $28,000

The company wants to make a profit of $25,000 in the first year. What should their selling price be? (Use the equation method.) What is the contribution margin?

9–11 A company produces a single product to sell for $5.00 per unit. The company incurs $18,000 in fixed costs, and variable costs run $3.00 per unit.

Required:

a. Compute the contribution margin per unit.
b. Compute the break-even point using the contribution margin approach.

9–12 The management of the Richards Company has developed the following estimates of costs and sales, assuming the company is able to operate at full capacity:

```
Total fixed expenses . . . . . . . . .  $ 80,000
Total variable costs . . . . . . . . .    30,000
Total sales revenues . . . . . . . . .   150,000
```

Fixed expenses are constant at all levels of business activity and variable expenses vary in direct proportion to sales.

Required:

a. Calculate the break-even point of the Richards Company using the contribution margin ratio approach.
b. Calculate the break-even point assuming the above *except* that

the total expenses at full capacity are composed of $60,000 fixed and $75,000 variable.

9–13   Calco Inc. has the following financial information:

Sales	$131,250
Units sold	25,000
Direct labor	$ 37,500
Direct material	$ 32,500
Fixed costs	$ 54,000
Other variable costs	$ 18,750

Required:

Calculate the break-even point and illustrate it graphically.

9–14   Soloco Inc.'s chief financial officer has given you the following infor- mation:

Fixed costs	$365,000.00
Selling price per unit	16.00
Direct labor per unit	2.20
Direct material per unit	4.00
Other variable costs	5.25

Required:

Calculate (a) the sales in dollars, and (b) the unit sales necessary to acquire a $55,000 profit.

PROBLEMS SERIES A

9A–1   The XYZ Company uses variable costing. At the beginning of the year, there were no beginning inventories. During the year, 15,000 units were started and completed and 12,500 units were sold at $8.50 per unit. Costs were:

Direct materials, $2.00 per unit
Direct labor, $1.50 per unit
Variable manufacturing expenses, $.75 per unit
Fixed costs, $20,000
Fixed selling and administrative expense, $10,000

Required:

Prepare a cost of goods manufactured statement and an income state- ment.

9A–2   Prepare a cost of goods manufactured statement and an income state- ment using: (a) variable and (b) absorption costing from the infor- mation given below:

Sales: Product A—3,500 units @ 27.50   *96250*
       Product B—4,000 units @ $32.00
Direct labor: Cutting: Product A—2 hours @ $2.00   *$4/unit*
                Product B—2½ hours @ $2.00   *$5/unit*

Finishing: Product A—2 hours @ $2.50
Product B—3 hours @ $2.50

Beginning finished goods inventory—0 units
Variable overhead: Cutting: Product A&B—$.50 per direct labor
hour
Finishing: Product A&B—$1.00 per direct labor
hour
Beginning work-in-process—0 units
Ending work-in-process—0 units
Direct materials: Product A—2 units @ $1.50
Product B—3 units @ $1.50
Fixed overhead: $18,000 (applied at a rate of $1.50 per unit of A and
$2.40 per unit of B)
Ending finished goods inventory: Product A—500 units
Product B—1,000 units
Beginning raw materials—4,000 units @ $1.50
Ending raw materials—3,000 units @ $1.50
Fixed selling and administrative expense—$20,000
Purchases of raw materials—22,000 units @ $1.50

9A–3 Whodunit, Inc. has given you the following information for 1980 concerning its products. They have hired you to:

a. Compute the selling price per unit.
b. Project an income statement for the year using variable costing.
c. Compute a break-even point expressed in dollars and in units assuming that $20,000 of overhead and the total administrative expenses are fixed but that all other costs are fully variable.

Estimated annual sales . . . . 25,000 units

	Amount	Per Unit
Estimated costs:		
Material	$ 93,750	$3.75
Direct labor	20,000	.80
Overhead	31,250	1.25
Administrative expense	50,000	2.00
Total	$195,000	$7.80

Selling expenses are expected to be 13% of sales and profit is to amount to $1.77 per unit.

9A–4 The JKL Company expects the following relationships between its products to exist in 1980:

	Product J	Product K	Product L
Sales	$3.50 per unit	$6.20 per unit	$8.40 per unit
Variable costs	$2.00 per unit	$3.80 per unit	$5.20 per unit
Volume	40,000 units	50,000 units	35,000 units
Fixed costs	$280,000		

Required:

The break-even point for the company in terms of J, K, and L.

9A-5   The Buffalo Company has just been formed and plans to produce a product which will sell for $12.00 per unit. A market survey showed that demand will be less than 15,000 units per year, but did not indicate how much less.

The company has found two machines suitable for its plant. Each of these machines has a capacity of 15,000 units per year. Machine 1 would have fixed costs of $30,000 per year and would yield a profit of $45,000 per year if sales were 15,000 units. Machine 2 has a fixed cost per year of $42,000 and would yield a profit of $48,000 per year at sales of 15,000 units. Variable costs behave linearly for both machines.

Required:

a.   Break-even sales in dollars and units for each machine.
b.   A second survey was taken which indicated that 11,500 units will probably be the company's average sales. Which machine should Buffalo buy?
c.   If average sales will be 14,500 units, which machine should Buffalo buy?

NOTE: Buffalo Company uses variable costing.

✓ 9A-6   The Rosen Company makes a single product which has the following costs:

Fixed costs—$400 (total)
Variable costs—$.10 (per unit)

The income tax rate is 40%. Rosen will make exactly 1,000 units this period.

Required:

a.   How much will Rosen have to charge per unit in order to break-even on the sale of the 1,000 units? (Use the equation method.)
b.   In order to make a profit of $120 (after taxes) on the sale of 1,000 units, how much will Rosen have to charge per unit?

9A-7   The Sales Company has just been formed to produce Z. The first year, the capacity of the plant will be 12,000 units which they feel they will be able to sell.

Their costs are: Direct labor, $2.50 per unit
Raw materials, $1.80 per unit
Other variable costs, $1.20 per unit
Fixed costs, $36,000

Required:

a. If the company wishes to make a profit of $30,000 the first year, what should their selling price be? What is the contribution margin?

b. At the end of the first year, they wish to increase their volume. An increase of $15,000 in annual fixed costs will increase their capacity to 30,000 units. They now want a profit of $70,000 and to achieve this end, they also invest $29,000 in advertising. No other costs change. Under these new conditions, how many units will they have to sell to realize this profit, if their new selling price will be $13.00 per unit? How many units will they have to sell to break-even?

9A–8 Company T has a relevant production range of 1,500 to 4,000 units. At 1,500 units, the total production cost is $2,500. At 4,000 units, the total production cost is $5,500. The selling price is $2.25 per unit.

Required:

a. What is the variable cost per unit?
b. What is the total fixed cost?
c. What is the break-even volume? (Use the contribution margin approach.)
d. What must variable cost per unit be if the break-even point is to be at 3,000 units.

9A–9 Given below is selected information concerning two products sold by the Kilmer Company.

	Rink	Dink
Selling price (per unit)	$10	$15
Variable cost (per unit)	7	5

The fixed costs associated with the manufacture of these two products are $48,000 per year.

Required:

Calculate the break-even point for the sale of Rink and Dink if the sales mix is 2 units of Rink and 1 unit of Dink.

9A–10 Following are data relative to the revenues and costs of the Montgomery Company for the calendar year 1980:

Sales		$300,000
Cost of goods manufactured and sold:		
Materials	$45,000	
Labor	50,000	
Variable manufacturing overhead	25,000	
Fixed manufacturing overhead	40,000	160,000
Gross margin		$140,000
Selling Expense:		
Variable	$20,000	
Fixed	18,000	38,000
		$102,000

Administrative expense:
Variable   25,000
Fixed   64,000   89,000

Net earnings . . . . $ 13,000

Required:

Find the dollar sales required for Montgomery Company to break-even, using the contribution ratio approach.

9A–11   The following is selected information from Melodies Co. which sells two products.

	Sing	Song
Selling price (per unit)	$5.50	$3.75
Direct materials (per unit)	1.20	.80
Direct labor (per unit)	2.00	1.85
Other variable costs	.60	.40

Total fixed costs associated with these two products are $68,530.

Required:

a.   Calculate the break-even point for the sale of Sing and Song if sales mix is 4 units of Sing and 3 units of Song.

b.   Assuming sales of $266,000, prepare a variable costing income statement. Assume no beginning or ending inventories and assume a 48% tax rate. Use the sales mix in part a.

9A–12   Farmer Green, your uncle, has decided that he is too old to continue to milk 100 cows each day and has decided, therefore, to purchase a milking machine. He has narrowed his choice down to the Super Milk and Easy Milk models. You have just returned from the big city and want to impress your uncle with some of your college learning. The following information is available concerning the two models.

	Super Milk	Easy Milk
Capacity	150 cows	200 cows
Fixed cost/year	$8,000	$10,000

Each cow can produce 8 gallons of milk a day which can be sold for $2.00 per gallon. Super Milk will produce a profit of $15,000 and Easy Milk can generate a profit of $19,000 when they are operated at full capacity.

Required:

Calculate sales in dollars and units per year for each machine needed to break even.

PROBLEMS SERIES B

9B-1   Fields, Inc. uses a variable costing system. On December 31, 1980 there were no ending inventories. During 1981, 48,000 units were produced and 45,654 units were sold for $5.50 per unit. Costs for 1981 were:

Direct materials, $.85 per unit
Direct labor, $2.00 per unit
Variable manufacturing expense, $.50 per unit
Fixed costs, $14,000
Variable selling expense, $.21 per unit
Selling and administrative expense, $25,000 (all fixed)

Required:

Prepare a cost of goods manufactured statement and an income statement.

✓ 9B-2   Crash Products has just perfected a rip-proof "rip-a-way" football jersey which it can sell to the Washington Deadskins LFN football team for $10 per jersey. Crash's economist forecasts that demand for this unique product (fiendishly designed to maim the fingers of enemy tacklers) will be 80 in 1981 and 110 in 1982. Production costs are estimated as follows:

	1981	1982
Fixed (in total)	$100	$100
Variable (per unit)	5	6

1060
1260
400   *660*

Because Crash's production facilities can accommodate only a single worker per shift, only 100 jerseys are turned out annually by the organization's skilled craftsman.

Required:

Prepare an income statement using variable costing and one using absorption costing for 1981 and 1982. Crash Products uses Fifo to cost their inventories.

9B-3   Whatisit, Inc. has given you the following information for 1981 concerning its product:

Estimated production . . . . 85,000 units
Estimated sales . . . . 80,000 units
Estimated costs:

	Amount	Per Unit
Material	$ 331,500	$ 3.90
Direct labor	527,000	6.20
Overhead	233,750	2.75
Administrative expense	340,000	4.00
Total	$1,432,250	$16.85

Selling expenses are expected to be 5% of sales and profit is to be $2.15 per unit.

They have hired you to:

a. Compute the selling price per unit.

b. Project an income statement for the year using variable costing, assuming that $63,750 of overhead and all administrative expenses are fixed but all other costs are fully variable.

c. Compute the break-even point expressed in units and in dollars.

9B–4 The Samson Company expects the following relationships to exist between its products in 1981:

	Product P	Product Q	Product R
Sales	$4.80 per unit	$6.30 per unit	$2.50 per unit
Variable costs	$3.00 per unit	$4.60 per unit	$1.50 per unit
Volume	63,000 units	45,000 units	72,000 units

Fixed costs are $300,000.

Required:

Compute the break-even point for the company in terms of P, Q, and R.

9B–5 The Southside Company has just been formed. The product will sell for $40.00 per unit. The company expects demand for their product to be less than 20,000 units for the first few years but to increase each year until it levels off at 20,000 units. However, they are not sure how much less than 20,000 units demand will be in the first year.

There are two machines available which suit the needs of the company. Each machine has a capacity of 20,000 units per year. If operated at full capacity; Machine 1 would have fixed costs of $60,000 and a profit of $80,000, Machine 2 would have fixed costs of $110,000 and a profit of $90,000.

Required:

a. Break-even sales in units and in dollars for each machine.

b. After more research, it was determined that 14,500 units could be sold in year 1. What would the net income be with each machine?

c. If 18,000 units are sold, what would the net income be?
NOTE: Southside uses variable costing.

9B–6 The Hall Company makes a single product which has the following costs:

Fixed costs—$200 (total)
Variable costs—$.20 (per unit)

The income tax rate is 40%. Hall will make exactly 500 units this period.

Required:

a. How much will Hall have to charge per unit in order to break even on the sale of the 500 units?

b. In order to make a profit of $240 (after taxes) on the sale of 500 units, how much will Hall have to charge per unit?

9B-7 Small, Inc. has just been formed to produce T. In the first year they expect to produce and sell 40,000 units. Their costs are:

Raw materials, $3.00 per unit
Direct labor, $4.50 per unit
Variable overhead, $2.00 per unit
Variable selling costs, $.50 per unit
Fixed costs, $60,000

Required:

a. Small, Inc. wants to make a profit of $20,000 the first year. In order to do this, what would their selling price have to be?
b. At the end of the second year the company wants to increase its volume by 25,000 units. This will increase fixed costs by $20,000 per year. In order to sell these extra units, the company will invest $25,000 in advertising. They plan to sell T for $12.50 per unit. Under these new conditions, what will net income be? What is the new break-even point? If only profit is considered, should the company make the investment?

✓ 9B-8 Sam's Pipe Company has a relevant production range of 2,500 to 7,000 units. Total production costs range from $10,500 to $24,900. The pipes sell for $4.00 per pipe.

Required:

a. What is the variable cost per unit?
b. What is the total fixed cost?
c. What is the break-even volume? (Use the contribution margin approach.)
d. If 5,652 pipes are sold, what is the net income under variable costing?
e. If the break-even point is 4,000 units, what must the contribution margin be?

9B-9 Given below is information concerning the three products sold by Cricket, Inc.

	A	B	C
Selling price (per unit)	$8	$12	$16
Variable cost (per unit)	4	9	11

The fixed costs associated with the manufacture of these three products are $84,000 per year.

Required:

a. Calculate the break-even point for the sale of A, B, and C if the sales mix is 4 units of A, 3 units of B, and 1 unit of C.

    b. Prepare an income statement using variable costing if 3,600 units of the mix are sold.

9B–10 Given below is an income statement for 1980 for Tropic, Inc.

Sales		$500,000
Cost of goods manufactured and sold:		
Materials	$62,500	
Labor	31,250	
Variable manufacturing overhead	18,750	
Fixed manufacturing overhead	50,000	162,500
Gross margin		$337,500
Selling expense:		
Variable	$ 7,500	
Fixed	20,000	27,500
Administrative expense:		
Variable	$15,000	
Fixed	55,000	70,000
Net earnings		$240,000

Required:

Find the dollar sales necessary for Tropic, Inc. to break even. Use the contribution ratio approach.

9B–11 Presented below is selected information from the records of Acto Co. concerning its two products, Ping and Pong.

	Ping	Pong
Selling price/unit	$220	$162
Variable cost/unit	$170	$124

The fixed costs associated with the manufacture of these products are $180,000.

Required:

    a. Calculate the break-even point for the sale of Ping and Pong assuming the sales mix is 1 Ping and 1 Pong. Assume Acto Co. wants to achieve a profit of $84,000. What sales volume is necessary?

    b. Present the income statement for the target profit of $84,000.

9B–12 You have just opened a business selling firewood. After a week of blisters you have decided to buy a chain saw. There are two models available and you need to decide between the Woodchuck and the Woodpecker. The Woodchuck can cut 10 cords of wood a day (the cords are selling for $25 each). The Woodpecker can cut 12 cords a day. (Assume 200 cutting days per year.) The fixed costs of operating the Woodchuck and Woodpecker are $10,000 and $15,000 respectively. The Woodchuck is guaranteed to give a profit of $12,000 while the Woodpecker will yield $15,000 per year.

Required:

Determine the break-even point in units and in dollars for both saws.

9B-13   Mr. Calderone started a pizza restaurant in 1978. For this purpose a building was rented for $400 per month. Two ladies were hired to work full time at the restaurant and six college boys were hired to work 30 hours per week delivering pizza. An outside accountant was hired for tax and bookkeeping purposes. For this service, Mr. Calderone pays $300 per month. The necessary restaurant equipment and delivery cars were purchased with cash. Mr. Calderone has noticed that expenses for utilities and supplies have been rather constant.

Mr. Calderone increased his business between 1978 and 1980. Profits have more than doubled since 1978. Mr. Calderone does not understand why his profits have increased faster than his volume.

A projected Income Statement for 1981 has been prepared by the accountant and is shown below:

Calderone Company
PROJECTED INCOME STATEMENT
For the Year Ended December 31, 1981

Sales		$ 95,000
Cost of Food Sold	$28,500	
Wages & Fringe Benefits of Restaurant Help	8,150	
Wages & Fringe Benefits of Delivery Boys	17,300	
Rent	4,800	
Accounting Services	3,600	
Depreciation of Delivery Equipment	5,000	
Depreciation of Restaurant Equipment	3,000	
Utilities	2,325	
Supplies (Soap, Floor Wax, etc.)	1,200	73,875
Net Income Before Taxes		$21,125
Income Taxes		6,338
Net Income		$14,787

Note: The average pizza sells for $2.50. Assume that Mr. Calderone pays out 30% of his income in income taxes.

Required:

a. What is the breakeven point in number of pizzas that must be sold?
b. What is the cash flow breakeven point in number of pizzas that must be sold?
c. If Mr. Calderone withdraws $4,800 for personal use, how much cash will be left from the 1981 income producing activities?
d. Mr. Calderone would like an after-tax net income of $20,000. What volume must be reached in number of pizzas in order to obtain the desired income?

e.   Briefly explain to Mr. Calderone why his profits have increased at a faster rate than his sales.

f.   Briefly explain to Mr. Calderone why his cash flow for 1981 will exceed his profits.

(CMA adapted)

9B-14   All-Day Candy Company is a wholesale distributor of candy. The company services grocery, convenience and drug stores in a large metropolitan area.

Small but steady growth in sales has been achieved by the All-Day Candy Company over the past few years while candy prices have been increasing. The company is formulating its plans for the coming fiscal year. Presented below are the data used to project the current year's after-tax net income of $110,400.

Average selling price...........	$4.00 per box
Average variable costs:	
Cost of candy...............	$2.00 per box
Selling expenses.............	.40 per box
Total	$2.40 per box
Annual fixed costs:	
Selling.....................	$160,000
Administrative..............	280,000
Total	$440,000

Expected annual sales volume (390,000 boxes) $1,560,000.

Tax rate 40%

Manufacturers of candy have announced that they will increase prices of their products an average of 15 percent in the coming year due to increases in raw material (sugar, cocoa, peanuts, etc.) and labor costs. All-Day Candy Company expects that all other costs will remain at the same rates or levels as the current year.

Required:

a.   What is All-Day Candy Company's breakeven point in boxes of candy for the current year?

b.   What selling price per box must All-Day Candy Company charge to cover the 15 percent increase in the cost of candy and still maintain the current contribution margin ratio?

c.   What volume of sales in dollars must the All-Day Candy Company achieve in the coming year to maintain the same net income after taxes as projected for the current year if the selling price of candy remains at $4.00 per box and the cost of candy increase 15 percent? (CMA adapted)

9B-15   Hewtex Electronics manufactures two products—tape recorders and electronic calculators—and sells them nationally to wholesalers and retailers. The Hewtex management is very pleased with the company's performance for the current fiscal year. Projected sales through December 31, 1980, indicate that 70,000 tape recorders and 140,000 electronic calculators will be sold this year. The projected earnings statement, which appears below, shows that Hewtex will exceed its earnings goal of 9 percent on sales after taxes.

The tape recorder business has been fairly stable the last few years, and the company does not intend to change the tape recorder price. However, the competition among manufacturers of electronic calculators has been increasing. Hewtex's calculators have been very popular with consumers. In order to sustain this interest in their calculators and to meet the price reductions expected from competitors, management has decided to reduce the wholesale price of its calculator from $22.50 to $20.00 per unit effective January 1, 1981. At the same time the company plans to spend an additional $57,000 on advertising during fiscal year 1981. As a consequence of these actions, management estimates that 80 percent of its total revenue will be derived from calculator sales as compared to 75 percent in 1980. As in prior years, the sales mix is assumed to be the same at all volume levels.

Hewtex Electronics
Projected Earning Statement
For the Year Ended December 31, 1980

	Tape Recorders		Electronic Calculators		
	Total Amount (000 omitted)	Per Unit	Total Amount (000 omitted)	Per Unit	Total (000 omitted)
Sales	$1,050	$15.00	$3,150	$22.50	$4,200.00
Production costs:					
Materials........	$ 280	$ 4.00	$ 630	$ 4.50	$ 910.00
Direct labor.....	140	2.00	420	3.00	560.00
Variable overhead	140	2.00	280	2.00	420.00
Fixed overhead...	70	1.00	210	1.50	280.00
Total production costs...........	$ 630	$ 9.00	$1,540	$11.00	$2,170.00
Gross Margin.......	$ 420	$ 6.00	$1,610	$11.50	$2,030.00
Fixed selling and administrative................................					1,040.00
Net income before income taxes......................................					$ 990.00
Income taxes (55%)......................................					544.50
Net income..					$ 445.50

The total fixed overhead costs will not change in 1981, nor will the variable overhead cost rates (applied on a direct labor hour basis). However, the cost of materials and direct labor is expected to change.

The cost of solid state electronic components will be cheaper in 1981. Hewtex estimates that material costs will drop 10 percent for the tape recorders and 20 percent for the calculators in 1981. However, direct labor costs for both products will increase 10 percent in the coming year.

Required:

a. How many tape recorder and electronic calculator units did Hewtex Electronics have to sell in 1980 to break even?
b. What volume of sales is required if Hewtex Electronics is to earn a profit in 1981 equal to 9 percent on sales after taxes?
c. How many tape recorder and electronic calculator units will Hewtex have to sell in 1981 to break even?

(CMA adapted)

9B-16   The S. T. Shire Company uses direct costing for internal management purposes and absorption costing for external reporting purposes. Thus, at the end of each year financial information must be converted from direct costing to absorption costing in order to satisfy external requirements.

At the end of 1980 it was anticipated that sales would rise 20 percent the next year. Therefore, production was increased from 20,000 units to 24,000 units to meet this expected demand. However, economic conditions kept the sales level at 20,000 units for both years.

The following data pertain to 1980 and 1981.

	1980	1981
Selling Price per Unit..........	$ 30	$ 30
Sales (units).................	20,000	20,000
Beginning Inventory (units).....	2,000	2,000
Production (units).............	20,000	24,000
Ending Inventory (units).......	2,000	6,000
Unfavorable Labor, Materials and Variable Overhead Variances (total)...........	$ 5,000	$ 4,000

Standard Variable Costs per Unit for 1980 and 1981:

Labor	$ 7.50
Materials....................	4.50
Variable Overhead...........	3.00
	$15.00

Annual fixed costs for 1980 and 1981
(Budgeted and Actual):

Production	$ 90,000
Selling and Administrative......	100,000
	$190,000

The overhead rate under absorption costing is based upon practical plant capacity which is 30,000 units per year. All variances and under or over absorbed overhead are taken to Cost of Goods Sold.

All taxes are to be ignored.

Required:

a. Present the income statement based on direct costing for 1981.
b. Present the income statement based on absorption costing for 1981.
c. Explain the difference, if any, in the net income figures. Give the entry necessary to adjust the book figures to the financial statement figure, if one is necessary.
d. The company finds it worthwhile to develop its internal financial data on a direct cost basis. What advantages and disadvantages are attributed to direct costing for internal purposes?
e. There are many who believe that direct costing is appropriate for external reporting and there are many who oppose its use for external reporting. What arguments for and against the use of direct costing are advanced for its use in external reporting?

(CMA adapted)

9B-17   The Sun Company, a wholly owned subsidiary of Guardian, Inc., produces and sells three main product lines. The company employs a standard cost accounting system for record keeping purposes.

At the beginning of 1981, the president of Sun Company presented the budget to the parent company and accepted a commitment to contribute $15,800 to Guardian's consolidated profit in 1981. The president has been confident that the year's profit would exceed the budget target, since the monthly sales reports that he has been receiving have shown that sales for the year will exceed budget by 10 percent. The president is both disturbed and confused when the controller presents an adjusted forecast as of November 30, 1981 indicating that profit will be 11 percent under budget. The two forecasts are presented below.

There have been no sales price changes or product mix shifts since the 1/1/81 forecast. The only cost variance on the income statement is the under absorbed manufacturing overhead. This arose because the company produced only 16,000 standard machine hours (budgeted machine hours were 20,000) during 1981 as a result of a shortage of raw materials while its principal supplier was closed by a strike. Fortunately Sun Company's finished goods inventory was large enough to fill all sales orders received.

Sun Company

Forecasts of Operating Results

	Forecasts as of 1/1/81	Forecasts as of 11/30/81
Sales	$268,000	$294,800
Cost of Sales at Standard	212,000*	233,200
Gross Margin at Standard	$ 56,000	$ 61,600
Over-(Under-)Absorbed Fixed Manufacturing Overhead	---	6,000
Actual Gross Margin	$ 56,000	$ 55,600
Selling Expenses	$ 13,400	$ 14,740
Administrative Expenses	26,800	26,800
Total Operating Expenses	$ 40,200	$ 41,540
Earnings before Tax	$ 15,800	$ 14,060

*Includes fixed manufacturing overhead of $30,000.

Required:

a. Analyze and explain why the profit has declined in spite of increased sales and good control over costs.
b. What plan, if any, could Sun Company adopt during December to improve their reported profit at year end? Explain your answer.
c. Illustrate and explain how Sun Company could adopt an alternative internal cost reporting procedure which would avoid the confusing effect of the present procedure.
d. Would the alternative procedure described in Part c be acceptable to Guardian, Inc. for financial reporting purposes? Explain.

(CMA, adapted)

Learning Objectives

Chapter 10 continues the introduction of short-range planning and provides a comprehensive example of the budgeting process. Studying this chapter should enable you to:

1. Describe the general budgeting process.
2. Identify and discuss the primary benefits of the budgeting process.
3. Prepare budgets and the associated schedules when given the necessary data.
4. Prepare the pro-forma financial statements that are the final products of the budgeting process.

10

Short-Range Planning

SHORT-RANGE planning, also referred to as budgeting or profit planning, is a measure of management's financial expectations for the near future, usually the coming year. Often, plans are made on a month-by-month basis. The short-range period is normally considered to be that period in which the firm faces constraining factors. Constraining factors are those factors which cannot be significantly altered in the short-run, such as capacity of equipment, number of employees, or demand for products.

All except perhaps the smallest of firms engage in some type of short-range planning. At a minimum, some analysis of projected cash flows must be considered in order to assure management that the firm will be able to meet its cash requirements during the coming period. If the plans are formalized, then these plans are usually referred to as budgets.

LONG-RANGE VERSUS SHORT-RANGE PLANNING

Long-range planning is also referred to as budgeting. The longer time period involved, however, means that plans developed for the distant future are less reliable and cannot be prepared in as much detail as plans developed for the near future. At the extreme, long-range plans can be considered goals that the firm would like to achieve or attain in the future. Goals are expressed in very general descriptive terms, such as the goal or objective to be the largest firm or the best quality producer in the industry. Intermediate-range plans are considered objectives the firm is striving to achieve in the next three to five years. Examples of intermediate objectives include increasing sales volume, increasing the asset base, and expanding product lines in the next five years.

Most short-range budgets must provide sufficient detail to allow day-to-day functioning at operational levels. Generally, the significant planning decisions are made and the formalized plans are prepared on a segment-by-segment basis for a firm. Examples of segments include divisions, product lines, and sales territories. Management participation is an integral part of the successful budgeting process. The management personnel in each segment should be involved in determining budget inputs, and, in return, these individuals should be held responsible for any variances that occur between actual and budgeted performances.

A NORMAL APPROACH TO BUDGET PREPARATION

In large firms, short-range budgeting normally begins with lower management and then progresses upward to the upper levels of management. The managers of the planning segments aid in the preparation of their segment's budget for the next operating period. If the budgeted operating period coincides with the calendar year, then a meeting is usually held late in the year, perhaps in October or November, to formalize the budgets for each segment in the organization and for the entire organization. The actual budget preparation, however, generally begins much earlier, normally in June or July. Top management of the firm, or a formal budget committee composed of selected top managers, receives the proposed budgets for the individual segments and for the total firm. Both the segment plans and the overall plans are reworked in order to provide a realistic and acceptable budget such that each segment of the company and the firm as a whole has operational plans on a month-by-month basis. The annual budget for the entire firm is then submitted to the board of directors for their approval or rejection.

The annual budget is not the end of the planning process. For budgeting purposes, the best information available must be used to constantly revise and update the annual budget. A new budget is prepared by each planning segment for the up-coming month before the current month is over. This revised monthly budget takes into account the additional information that has become available since the formulation of the annual budget.

BENEFITS OF SHORT-RANGE PLANNING

The general benefits of short-range planning in any firm include:

1. Communication and coordination.
2. Before-the-fact control.

3. A basis for after-the-fact control and performance evaluation.
4. Identification of weak areas in the firm.
5. Management motivation.

These are described in the sections which follow.

Communication and Coordination

Profit planning enables a manager to identify the overall short-range plans of the firm and how his or her managerial area fits into this plan. Profit planning also enables a manager to realize before-the-fact what is expected of him and his division.

The efforts of the functional areas of the business are coordinated by planning. For example, a sales forecast is an important consideration in planning production schedules. Advertising campaigns and salesmen's efforts must be coordinated to be fully effective. Raw material purchases must reflect production demand. Short-range financial plans are made in conjunction with projected cash flows.

If the managers of all areas of the business operated independently without a coordinated plan, then each manager would act according to his individual perceptions of the best interests of his department and the firm. The production manager might plan long production runs in order to minimize costs. The purchasing manager would order the largest possible quantities in order to maximize the available discounts. The inventory control manager would minimize inventories in order to reduce the funds committed to inventory and the carrying costs of the inventory. Sales managers would maintain large quantities of finished goods inventories on hand to provide the best possible customer service. To the individual manager, each of these strategies would appear to be in the best interests of the firm. Without studied coordination and assessment of the interaction of the various individual plans and strategies, however, it is possible for any one individual strategy to be counterproductive when considered in light of the firm's overall objectives.

Before-the-Fact Control

The communication and coordination which result from the budgeting process introduce an element of continuous before-the-fact control. Every manager knows what is expected of him in terms of performance in a given budgeting period. The manager then supervises his division and its employees to meet the budgeted goals in the most effective and efficient manner.

In developing budgets, managers must establish and justify a need for resources. This formalization of the segment's needs serves as a control factor in the planning function. Using this method, operating and financial constraints of the firm become obvious to each manager.

A Basis for After-the-Fact Control and Performance Evaluation

Because the budgeting process serves as a basis for measuring a manager's performance, each manager knows that he will be judged by his ability to satisfy the goals of his department budget. Any variations from the budget are analyzed after the performance takes place. If the planning and budgeting process does not take place, control after-the-fact is almost non-existent because of the difficulty in determining what performance should have been attained by a given manager.

Identification of Weak Areas of the Firm

Through formal planning, weak segments of the firm can be identified. Potential operating and financial factors such as an unsatisfactory contribution margin in a segment, a production bottleneck, a poor sales mix, excessive inventories or accounts receivable, and insufficient cash flows can be readily identified. Any imbalance between segments of the firm becomes apparent in the planning process.

Motivation for Management

When lower-level management is involved in the budgeting process, these managers become directly involved with the goals, objectives, problems, and policies of the firm. The budgeting process assists in identifying the importance of a manager's job in the overall performance of the firm. Coordinated action of all employees toward achieving the firm's goals becomes a major objective of the individual managers. Because the goals of each segment have been established in conjunction with the overall goals and policies of the firm through the coordinating aspects of budgeting, the manager's own self-interests should be served by acting in the best interest of the firm.

GENERAL COMPREHENSIVE BUDGETING RELATIONSHIPS

The concept of comprehensive budgeting covers the entire area of planning, control and performance evaluation. Illustration 10–1 presents the skeletal relationships of the general types of budgets. This illustration should be viewed as the "tip of an iceberg," in that more specific budgets and special budgets are prepared for management at all levels using the general budgets as guidelines. Budgets should be sufficiently detailed and specialized to provide plans for the day-to-day operations at the lowest level of management.

Illustration 10-1
General Budgeting Relationships for
Major Budget Categories

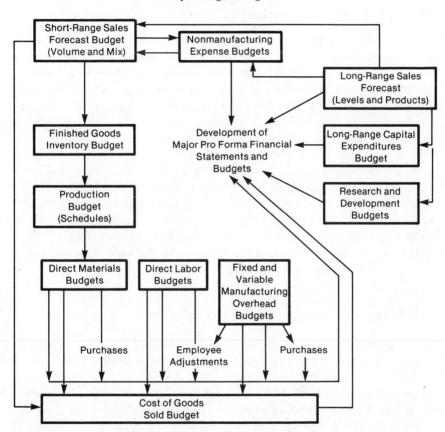

Illustration 10–1 identifies the major budget categories, their interrelationships and their ultimate articulation into pro-forma or projected financial statements. All budgets except those involving long-range sales forecasts, research and development expenditures, and long-range capital expenditures are covered in this chapter. Long-range capital budgeting is discussed in Chapter 14.

The major budgets and pro-forma financial statements developed in this chapter are:

1. Budgeted cost of goods manufactured statement
2. Budgeted cost of goods sold statement

3. Budgeted income statement
4. Cash budget
5. Budgeted stockholders' equity statement
6. Budgeted balance sheet

ROLE OF STANDARD COSTS IN BUDGETING

If established attainable standards are available, these standards can serve as the basis for developing the budget. Attainable standards are useful in budget development because standard costs define a series of relationships among various inputs and outputs of production. Once these relationships are established via the standard cost system, sales and/or production forecasts can be expanded into more detailed budgets through the application of the established relationships between the input and output measures. For example, if the standard labor cost for making one unit of a product is two direct labor hours at $4 per hour, then this input measure of two direct labor hours at $4 is equal to the output measure of one unit of product (in terms of a direct labor input measure.) If 500 units of the product are forecast for production, direct labor costs of $4,000 (500 units $\times$ 2 hours $\times$ $4) can be budgeted for that product. Since the standard cost for direct labor is $8 per unit of product, the budgeted direct labor cost is $4,000.

BUDGETING: A COMPREHENSIVE EXAMPLE

In July of 1980, Sax's president requested that the Power Turbine Shaft Division establish a planning, control and performance evaluation system that could be used in the Division's 1981 operations. The president requested that the variable costing format for measuring income be used for short-range profit planning purposes. The Division's financial staff was given until November 1, 1980 to establish a planning system and until December 1, 1980 to submit the Division's month-by-month plans for the first quarter of 1981.

The finance department analyzed the Power Turbine Shaft Division's operations and established forecasts and management policies for both the operational (or performance) budgets and the financial (or resource) budgets for 1981. Management considered the standard costs for manufacturing attainable and realistic and recommended that these costs be used wherever possible in the budgeting process. The management policies and forecasts are separated into two categories: (1) those policies and forecasts which primarily affect the operating budgets and (2) those policies and forecasts which primarily affect the financial budgets. As the operating and financial budgets are fundamentally related, this segregation of policies and forecasts is not strict.

Eighteen management policies and forecasts established by Sax Company are listed. The first six policies are related to income statement items and therefore primarily affect the operating budget. The policies and forecasts numbered seven through eighteen are concerned with various balance sheet accounts and, as such, primarily affect the financial budget. The projected balance sheet for December 31, 1980 for the Power Turbine Shaft Division is presented in Illustration 10-2. The beginning balances in the permanent accounts are necessary for financial planning for the first quarter of 1981.

Illustration 10-2
Sax Company
Power Turbine Shaft Division
Projected Balance Sheet As Of December 31, 1980

Assets			Liabilities and Stockholders' Equity		
Current Assets:			Current Liabilities:		
Cash	$	40,000	Accounts Payable	$	60,000
Accounts Receivable		424,400	Wages Payable		18,000
Direct Materials Inventories:			Total Current		
Steel Billets @ Standard		96,000	Liabilities	$	78,000
Ball Bearings @ Standard		48,000			
Indirect Materials and					
Supplies		30,000			
Work-In-Process @ Standard					
Variable Cost		300,000			
Finished Goods @ Standard			Long-Term Liabilities:		
Variable Cost		249,600			
Total Current Assets		$1,188,000	Long-Term Debt		1,200,000
			Total Liabilities		$1,278,000
Long-Term Assets:					
Equipment	$ 600,000				
Less: Accumulated					
Depreciation	60,000				
Net: Equipment		$ 540,000			
Plant	$3,000,000		Stockholders' Equity:		
Less: Accumulated					
Depreciation	150,000		Stockholders'		
Net: Plant		2,850,000	Investment		3,300,000
Total Long-Term Assets		$3,390,000	Total Liabilities and Stockholders'		
Total Assets		$4,578,000	Equity		$4,578,000

Federal income taxes are not considered in the budgeting process for the Power Turbine Shaft Division, as all income tax budgeting is handled by corporate headquarters.

Management Policies and Forecasts Affecting the Operating Budget—1981

1. The standard sales price of $50 per power turbine shaft should be maintained during 1981. New competition has not entered the market, and is unlikely to do so during 1981. A projected sales forecast, in units, will be developed by the sales manager of the division.

2. The standard variable production cost of $10.40 from Illustration 8–2 will be used for planning purposes. For convenience, the pertinent standards from Illustration 8–2 are presented again in Illustration 10–3.

Illustration 10-3
Sax Company
Power Turbine Shaft Division

Summary of Standard Variable Manufacturing
Costs Per Unit of Production

Materials @ Standard	
1 Steel Billet	$ 4.00
2 Ball Bearings	2.00
Direct Labor @ Standard ½ Hour @ $6.00 per hour	3.00
Variable Manufacturing Overhead @ Standard *	1.40
	$10.40

* Basis of application to product is standard direct labor hours. Application rate is $2.80 per standard direct labor hour.

3. Variable selling costs were $5 per unit sold in 1980; no change is expected.

4. Fixed manufacturing overhead costs are budgeted at $360,000. These costs are incurred uniformly throughout the year at a rate of $30,000 per month. An individual cost breakdown will be presented in a separate budget. Depreciation is a non-cash expense. (See Policy and Forecast items 13 and 14.)

5. Fixed selling and administrative expenses will be budgeted at $2,004,000 in 1981.

6. Annual interest expense on long-term debt is $132,000, payable in equal monthly payments of $11,000 (See item 17).

Management Policies and Forecasts Affecting the Financial Budget—1981

7. A minimum cash balance of $40,000 is necessary in order to provide sufficient cash to support day-to-day operations. If the Division

needs to borrow cash to maintain the $40,000 balance, it can be borrowed from corporate headquarters. Cash must be borrowed and repaid in $5,000 increments.

8. All sales are made by the sales force on a credit basis. Sax Company provides customers with credit terms of net/30. Customers normally pay within 30 days and bad debts are rare.

9. There should always be sufficient direct (raw) materials on hand to meet the production demands for the next two month period.

10. Indirect materials and supplies inventory should be maintained at a level of $30,000. This inventory account will be replenished monthly to maintain a level of $30,000.

11. The work-in-process inventory should be maintained at a balance of approximately $300,000.

12. The finished goods inventory should be maintained at a level sufficient to meet the next two months' demand for power turbine shafts.

13. The original cost of the equipment in the Power Turbine Shaft Division was $600,000. The equipment has an estimated life of 10 years with no salvage value anticipated. Sax Company uses the straight-line method of depreciation. The equipment was purchased on January 1, 1980. Depreciation expense for equipment will be $5,000 per month in 1981.

14. The original cost of the plant was $3,000,000. The estimated life of the plant is 20 years. No salvage value is anticipated. As is the case with the equipment, straight-line depreciation will be used in depreciating the plant. The plant was purchased on January 1, 1980. Depreciation expense will be $12,500 per month in 1981.

15. Accounts payable represent credit purchases of direct materials on net/30 terms. Accounts payable are paid on time, but never sooner than necessary. Therefore, payments lag behind actual purchases by 30 days.

16. Wages payable are stabilized at approximately $18,000, because Sax's policy is to hold the first two weeks pay earned by each employee. Wages are paid on the fifteenth and on the last business day of each month.

17. A long-term debt of $1,200,000 is outstanding. Interest payments of $11,000 are made monthly. Principal payments of $30,000 per quarter will be made on the loan for 10 years. The initial principal payment will be made on March 31, 1981.

18. Sax Company has an investment of $3,300,000 that is traceable to the Power Turbine Shaft Division. This represents the stockholders' equity (corporate investment) in the Division.

DEVELOPMENT OF THE MAJOR OPERATING AND PERFORMANCE BUDGETS

Sales Budget (Budget #1)

The sales budget is usually the starting point for short-range profit planning. If the sales projections are inaccurate, all subsequent budgets will be unreliable because these budgets are based, either directly or indirectly, on the sales budgets.

Sales forecasting is an art that relies upon both external and internal information gathered by the marketing or the sales department of the firm. External information sources such as industry periodicals, trade journals, analyses of general economic conditions, and marketing surveys can be used to aid in the development of a sales forecast. Information available internally, such as the firm's past performance and salesmen's estimates, can assist in projecting sales. Sales management assimilates and assesses all available information regarding sales projections, and then uses this information and their professional judgment to establish a reliable sales forecast.

The management of Sax Company requires a monthly sales forecast for the first quarter of 1981 and for the months of April and May. Forecasts for April and May are necessary to plan the ending inventories for the first quarter of 1981 in accordance with management's policies. (See items 9-12 in Management Policies and Forecasts.)

The sales manager reviewed the pertinent estimates of industry demand and the Power Turbine Shaft Division's position in the industry. Each salesman developed a sales forecast for his or her territory by key (large) customers and in the aggregate for small customers. The sales manager also examined the sales volume for the last three years and checked trends and monthly fluctuations. With the assistance and approval of the other key managers in the Division, the sales manager prepared the following sales budget.

Budget #1
Sales Budget
(January-May, 1981)

Month	Units	Dollars
January	12,000	$ 600,000
February	12,000	600,000
March	17,000	850,000
Total First Quarter Sales Forecast	41,000	$2,050,000
April	20,000	$1,000,000
May	20,000	1,000,000

Finished Goods Inventory Budget and Production Budget (Budgets #2 and #3)

The production budget is prepared after the sales budget has been finalized. Finished goods inventory serves as the buffer between the level of sales and the level of production. Most firms prefer to maintain a reasonably stable level of production even when faced with fluctuating product demand. Fluctuating production volume causes obvious problems in scheduling and cost control and adversely affects employee morale due to overtime or temporary layoffs.

Most firms maintain some minimum level of finished goods inventory in order to provide satisfactory customer service. There is also a maximum level of inventory that most firms will not exceed because of the cost of carrying inventory, the capital committed to the inventory, and the fear of inventory obsolescence or possible spoilage.

The Power Turbine Shaft Division has a management policy (Item 12 in Management Policies and Forecasts) requiring that the ending finished goods inventory balance be maintained at a level sufficient to meet the next two months' anticipated sales demands. The finished goods inventory balance expected on December 31, 1980 is 24,000 units. (Illustration 10-2 shows finished goods inventory at standard cost of $249,600 or 24,000 units.) This quantity of finished goods inventory is sufficient to meet the forecasted January 1981 sales of 12,000 units and February sales of 12,000 units. At the end of January 1981, the finished goods inventory should be at a level of 29,000 units, which will meet the forecasted sales for February 1981 (12,000 units) and March 1981 (17,000 units). The finished goods inventory budget, Budget #2, for the Power Turbine Shaft Division quantifies management's finished goods inventory policy. The sales budget, Budget #1, is the basis used to establish ending finished goods inventory balances.

Budget #2
Finished Goods Budget
(1st Quarter, 1981)

Date	Units	Dollars at Standard Variable Cost of $10.40
January 1	24,000	$249,600
January 31	29,000	301,600
February 28	37,000	384,800
March 31	40,000	416,000

The production budget is based upon this fundamental accounting inventory relationship: beginning finished goods inventory plus the cost of goods manufactured less the cost of goods sold is equal to the ending inventory of finished goods. After completing the sales budget and the finished goods budget, production requirements (Budget #3) can be calculated to comply with the specified inventory and sales figures.

Budget #3
Production Budget In Units
(1st Quarter, 1981)

	January	February	March	Quarter Total
Sales (Budget #1)	12,000	12,000	17,000	41,000
Desired Ending Finished Goods Inventory (Budget #2)	29,000—	37,000⌐	40,000	40,000
Total	41,000	49,000	57,000	81,000
Less: Beginning Finished Goods Inventory (Budget #2)	24,000 ↦	29,000 ↳	37,000	24,000
Production Requirements	17,000	20,000	20,000	57,000

Direct Materials Requirements and Purchases Budgets (Budgets #4, #5 and #6)

Once the production budget is prepared, the raw materials budget and the raw materials purchases budget can be developed. The amount of raw materials necessary depends upon both the ending raw materials inventory requirements established by management and the production requirements established in the production budget. Item 9 of the Management Policies and Forecasts requires that the Power Turbine Shaft Division maintain a level of raw materials inventories at the end of each month that is sufficient to meet the next two months' production demands. Management decided that the standard usage and costs of one steel billet at $4 and two ball bearings at $1 each (from Illustration 10–3) were realistic and attainable. The December 31, 1980 direct (raw) materials inventory from Illustration 10-2 is 24,000 steel billets ($96,000/$4.00) and 48,000 ball bearings ($48,000/$1.00). The desired ending raw materials inventories for March 31, 1981 are large enough to provide for the budgeted April production of 13,000 units and the budgeted May production of 10,000 units as per Item 9.

The preparation of the direct materials purchases budget (Budget #5) requires converting the estimated monthly unit purchases of raw materials into a budget expressed in terms of dollars. The monthly purchase requirements are developed in Budget #4 in units. The direct material purchases budget (Budget #5) is then prepared in terms of

Budget #4
Direct Materials Requirements Budget (In Units)
(1st Quarter, 1981)

Steel Billets (One per Finished Unit)

	January	February	March	Quarter Total
Production Requirements (Budget #3)	17,000	20,000	20,000	57,000
Desired Ending Direct Materials Inventory	40,000	33,000	23,000	23,000
Total	57,000	53,000	43,000	80,000
Less: Beginning Direct Materials Inventory	24,000	→40,000	→33,000	24,000
Purchase Requirements	33,000	13,000	10,000	56,000

Ball Bearings (Two per Finished Unit)

	January	February	March	Quarter Total
Production Requirements (Budget #3)	34,000	40,000	40,000	114,000
Desired Ending Direct Materials Inventory	80,000	66,000	46,000	46,000
Total	114,000	106,000	86,000	160,000
Less: Beginning Direct Materials Inventory	48,000	>80,000	→66,000	48,000
Purchase Requirements	66,000	26,000	20,000	112,000

dollars. The costs or purchase prices assigned to the purchase requirements in Budget #5 are the standard costs for raw materials found in Illustration 10-3. Management believes that the standard costs are the best estimate of the purchase prices that the Power Turbine Shaft Division will have to pay for direct materials. The standard cost of steel billets is $4 and the standard cost of ball bearings is $1.

The direct materials usage budget (Budget #6) can be prepared at this point, or it can be included as part of the cost of goods manufactured budget (Budget #12). The direct materials usage budget can be prepared using the relationships inherent in the accounting inventory equation: beginning raw materials inventory plus purchases less the amount transferred to work-in-process equals the ending raw materials inventory. An alternative method is to convert the production requirements from the direct materials requirements budget (Budget #4) into dollars. The direct materials usage budget (Budget #5) converts the unit production requirements from Budget #4 into dollars.

Budget #5
Direct Materials Purchases Budget
(1st Quarter, 1981)

Steel Billets

	January	February	March	Quarter Total
Purchase Requirements (Budget #4)	33,000	13,000	10,000	56,000
Standard Cost per Unit (Illustration 10–3)	$ 4.00	$ 4.00	$ 4.00	$ 4.00
Total Billet Purchases	$132,000	$52,000	$40,000	$224,000

Ball Bearings

	January	February	March	Quarter Total
Purchase Requirements (Budget #4)	66,000	26,000	20,000	112,000
Standard Cost per Unit (Illustration 10–3)	$ 1.00	$ 1.00	$ 1.00	$ 1.00
Total Ball Bearing Purchases ..	$ 66,000	$26,000	$20,000	$112,000
Total Direct Material Purchases	$198,000	$78,000	$60,000	$336,000

Budget #6
Direct Materials Usage Budget
(1st Quarter, 1981)

Steel Billets

	January	February	March	Quarter Total
Production Requirements (Budget #4)	17,000	20,000	20,000	57,000
Standard Cost per Unit (Illustration 10–3)	$ 4.00	$ 4.00	$ 4.00	$ 4.00
Total Usage	$68,000	$80,000	$80,000	$228,000

Ball Bearings

	January	February	March	Quarter Total
Production Requirements (Budget #4)	34,000	40,000	40,000	114,000
Standard Cost per Unit (Illustration 10–3)	$ 1.00	$ 1.00	$ 1.00	$ 1.00
Total Usage	$34,000	$40,000	$40,000	$114,000

Direct Labor Budget (Budget #7)

For the direct labor budget, the Power Turbine Shaft Division uses the standard time of one-half hour per power turbine shaft and a standard direct labor cost of $6 per hour (Illustration 10-3). The production schedule, Budget #3, is the basis for developing the direct labor budget (Budget #7).

Budget #7
Direct Labor Budget
(1st Quarter, 1981)

	January	February	March	Quarter Total
Production Requirements—Units (Budget #3)	17,000	20,000	20,000	57,000
Direct Labor per Unit in Hours	.5	.5	.5	.5
Direct Labor Requirements in Hours	8,500	10,000	10,000	28,500
Direct Labor Cost per Hour	$ 6.00	$ 6.00	$ 6.00	$ 6.00
	$51,000	$60,000	$60,000	$171,000

Manufacturing Overhead Budgets (Budgets #8 and #9)

Standard costs for manufacturing overhead, which were computed in Illustration 10–3, are used for planning purposes. The variable manufacturing overhead can be planned on the basis of units of production (Budget #3) or using direct labor hours at standard (Budget #7). The same budgeted cost will result using either basis. Since units of production are used as the basis of activity in the other production related budgets, the activity measure for the variable manufacturing overhead budget (Budget #8) will also be units of production.

The fixed manufacturing overhead costs are budgeted at $360,000 annually (Item 4 in Management Policies and Forecasts). Individual items of the fixed overhead costs for the Division were updated to reflect current changes in costs. Management considers the breakdown of fixed manufacturing overhead costs reflected in Budget #9 to be reasonable approximations of 1981 expenditures for overhead. Because fixed manufacturing overhead costs are linked primarily to the passage of time, management decided that an equal amount should be budgeted for each month of 1981.

Budget #8
Variable Manufacturing Overhead Costs Budget
(1st Quarter, 1981)

	January	February	March	Quarter Total
Production Requirements—Units (Budget #3)	17,000	20,000	20,000	57,000
Variable Manufacturing Overhead per Unit Produced:				
Rework Time . . . . $ .10	$ 1,700	$ 2,000	$ 2,000	$ 5,700
Waiting Time 06	1,020	1,200	1,200	3,420
Setup Time 08	1,360	1,600	1,600	4,560
Indirect Materials and Supplies 60	10,200	12,000	12,000	34,200
Indirect Labor 46	7,820	9,200	9,200	26,220
Electricity 10	1,700	2,000	2,000	5,700
Total $1.40	$23,800	$28,000	$28,000	$79,800

Budget #9
Fixed Manufacturing Overhead Costs Budget
(1st Quarter, 1981)

	January	February	March	Quarter Total
Indirect Materials and Supplies . .	$ 750	$ 750	$ 750	$ 2,250
Indirect Labor	2,200	2,200	2,200	6,600
Electricity	2,000	2,000	2,000	6,000
Heat	800	800	800	2,400
Equipment Depreciation	5,000	5,000	5,000	15,000
Plant Depreciation	12,500	12,500	12,500	37,500
Factory Property Taxes	6,750	6,750	6,750	20,250
	$30,000	$30,000	$30,000	$90,000

Non-Manufacturing Expense Budgets (Budgets #10 and #11)

The budgeted non-manufacturing expenses include variable selling costs of $5 per unit sold, $2,004,000 annually in fixed selling and administrative expenses, and annual interest expense on long-term debt of $132,000. These expenses were discussed in Management Policies and Forecasts, Items 3, 5, and 6, respectively. The activity basis for establishing the variable selling costs budget is the sales budget (Budget #1), because sales volume determines the amount of variable selling costs.

Over half of the fixed selling and administrative expenses budgeted are for monthly salaries. All other fixed selling and administrative expenses are also prorated into equal monthly installments for budgeting purposes, even though actual expenditures may be considerably more erratic.

Budget #10
Variable Selling Costs Budget
(1st Quarter, 1981)

	January	February	March	Quarter Total
Forecast Unit Sales (Budget #1)	12,000	12,000	17,000	41,000
Variable Selling Cost per Unit	$ 5.00	$ 5.00	$ 5.00	$ 5.00
Total Variable Selling Cost	$60,000	$60,000	$85,000	$205,000

Budget #11
Fixed Non-Manufacturing Costs Budget
(1st Quarter, 1981)

	January	February	March	Quarter Total
Selling and Administrative Expenses:				
Salaries	$ 96,000	$ 96,000	$ 96,000	$288,000
Advertising	28,000	28,000	28,000	84,000
Office Supplies	3,000	3,000	3,000	9,000
Travel	8,500	8,500	8,500	25,500
Telephone	5,000	5,000	5,000	15,000
Insurance	1,500	1,500	1,500	4,500
Research and Development	25,000	25,000	25,000	75,000
Total Selling and Administrative Expenses	$167,000	$167,000	$167,000	$501,000
Interest Expense	11,000	11,000	11,000	33,000
Total Non-Manufacturing Expenses	$178,000	$178,000	$178,000	$534,000

DEVELOPMENT OF THE MAJOR OPERATING OR PERFORMANCE BUDGETED FINANCIAL STATEMENTS

The major operating or pro-forma budgeted financial statements can be prepared using the Management Policies and Forecasts, and Budgets #1 through #11. The major operating budgeted financial statements are the cost of goods manufactured statement, the cost of goods sold statement, and the income statement.

Budgeted Cost of Goods Manufactured Statement (Budget #12)

The budgeted cost of goods manufactured statement is a projection and analysis of the changes occurring in the work-in-process account during the budgeted period. The work-in-process account at January 1, 1981, is projected to have a balance of $300,000 (Illustration 10-2). Management expects to maintain this $300,000 balance in work-in-process throughout the year (Item 11 of Management Policies and Forecasts). The variable manufacturing costs which are added to work-in-process each month can be determined from the budgets previously prepared for direct materials, direct labor, and variable manufacturing overhead. The budgeted cost of goods manufactured statement is presented in Budget #12.

✓

Budget #12
Budgeted Cost of Goods Manufactured Statement
For The Quarter Ending March 31, 1981

	January	February	March	Quarter Total
Beginning Work-In-Process . .	$300,000	$300,000	$300,000	$300,000
Add: Manufacturing Costs				
Direct Materials:				
Steel Billets (Budget #6)	68,000	80,000	80,000	228,000
Ball Bearings (Budget #6)	34,000	40,000	40,000	114,000
Direct Labor (Budget #7)	51,000	60,000	60,000	171,000
Variable Manufacturing				
Overhead (Budget #8)	23,800	28,000	28,000	79,800
Total Available	$476,800	$508,000	$508,000	$892,800
Less: Ending				
Work-In-Process	300,000	300,000	300,000	300,000
Cost of Goods Manufactured	$176,800	$208,000	$208,000	$592,800

Budgeted Cost of Goods Sold Statement (Budget #13)

The budgeted cost of goods sold statement is a projection and an analysis of the changes occurring in the finished goods account during the budget period. The beginning finished goods inventory is budgeted for $249,600 (Budget #2 or Illustration 10-2). The additional forecast data are taken from the budgeted cost of goods manufactured statement and the finished goods budget. The budgets are prepared on a variable costing basis; therefore, only variable costs are considered in the cost of goods sold.

Budgeted Income Statement (Budget #14)

Budget #14, the budgeted income statement, is the forecasted results of operations for the budget period using the variable costing format for income determination. Note that Budget #14 shows two contribution margins—one after variable manufacturing costs are deducted from sales

Budget #13
Budgeted Variable Cost of Goods Sold Statement
(1st Quarter, 1981)

	January	February	March	Quarter Total
Beginning Finished Goods Inventory (Budget #2) . .	$249,600	$301,600	$384,800	$249,600
Add: Budgeted Cost of Goods Manufactured (Budget #12)	176,800	208,000	208,000	592,800
Total Available	$426,400	$509,600	$592,800	$842,400
Ending Finished Goods Inventory (Budget #2) . .	301,600	384,800	416,000	416,000
Cost of Goods Sold	$124,800	$124,800	$176,800	$426,400

revenues and one after *all* variable costs are deducted from sales revenues. This refinement of the contribution margin approach reveals the source of the various contribution margins. The contribution margin computed by deducting *all* variable costs is the contribution margin available to cover fixed costs and profits. Therefore, it is the more significant of the two contribution margins. The budgeted income statement is presented on an accrual basis, not on a cash flow basis.

Budget #14
Budgeted Income Statement For The
Quarter Ending March 31, 1981

	January	February	March	Quarter Total
Sales Revenues (Budget #1)	$600,000	$600,000	$850,000	$2,050,000
Less: Variable Cost of Goods Sold (Budget #13) . . .	124,800	124,800	176,800	426,400
Contribution Margin from Manufacturing	$475,200	$475,200	$673,200	$1,623,600
Less: Variable Selling Costs (Budget #10)	60,000	60,000	85,000	205,000
Contribution Margin	$415,200	$415,200	$588,200	$1,418,600
Less:				
Fixed Manufacturing Overhead Costs (Budget #9)	$ 30,000	$ 30,000	$ 30,000	$ 90,000
Fixed Selling and Administrative Costs (Budget #11)	167,000	167,000	167,000	501,000
Interest Expense (Budget #11)	11,000	11,000	11,000	33,000
Total Fixed Expenses	$208,000	$208,000	$208,000	$ 624,000
Budgeted Income Before Taxes	$207,200	$207,200	$380,200	$ 794,600

DEVELOPMENT OF THE MAJOR FINANCIAL OR RESOURCE BUDGETS

Once the operating or performance budgets are prepared, the financial or resource budgets can be prepared. The financial budgets rely mainly on the data included in the beginning balance sheet as presented in Illustration 10–2, the performance budgets and the Management Policies and Forecasts.

All balance sheet accounts are permanent accounts in which the accounting relationship (beginning balance in the account plus additions to the account less withdrawals from the account equals the ending balance) must be maintained. The ending account balances appear on the budgeted balance sheet. A number of ending balances for the permanent accounts have already been established by the performance budgets or by the Management Policies and Forecasts. Each account on the balance sheet is budgeted individually and then combined with other permanent accounts to develop the budgeted balance sheet. The ending cash balance cannot be ascertained until all other March 31, 1981 budgeted account balances have been determined, because data developed in the other budgeted permanent accounts are necessary in order to develop the cash budget. The accounts are considered in their order on the balance sheet.

Accounts Receivable Budget (Budget #15)

Collections of accounts receivable lag one month behind sales. The ending accounts receivable balance on March 31, 1981 is equal to sales of $850,000 which are budgeted for March (Budget #1). The beginning accounts receivable for 1981 is forecasted at $424,400 (Illustration 10-2).

Budget #15
Accounts Receivable Budget
(1st Quarter, 1981)

	January	February	March	Quarter Total
Beginning Accounts Receivable (Illustration 10–2) .	$ 424,400	→$ 600,000	→$ 600,000	$ 424,400
Sales for the Month (Budget #1)	600,000	600,000	850,000	2,050,000
Total	$1,024,400	$1,200,000	$1,450,000	$2,474,400
Ending Accounts Receivable	600,000—	600,000—	850,000	850,000
Collection of Accounts Receivable	$ 424,400	$ 600,000	$ 600,000	$1,624,400

Inventory Budgets (Budgets #16 and #17)

For the most part, inventory budgets are developed from operating budgets, because the ending inventory balance is dictated by management policy. The direct materials inventory budget is developed using the information provided in the direct materials purchases budget (Budget #5) and the budgeted cost of goods manufactured statement (Budget #12).

Budget #16
Direct Materials Budget
(1st Quarter, 1981)

Steel Billets

	January	February	March	Quarter Total
Beginning Inventory (Illustration 10–2)	$ 96,000	→$160,000	→$132,000	$ 96,000
Add: Purchases (Budget #5)	132,000	52,000	40,000	224,000
Total Materials Available	$228,000	$212,000	$172,000	$320,000
Less: Transfers to Work-in-Process (Budget #6)	68,000	80,000	80,000	228,000
Ending Inventory	$160,000	$132,000	$ 92,000	$ 92,000

Ball Bearings

	January	February	March	Quarter Total
Beginning Inventory (Illustration 10–2)	$ 48,000	→$ 80,000	→$ 66,000	$ 48,000
Add: Purchases (Budget #5)	66,000	26,000	20,000	112,000
Total Materials Available	$114,000	$106,000	$ 86,000	$160,000
Less Transfers to Work-in-Process (Budget #6)	34,000	40,000	40,000	114,000
Ending Inventory	$ 80,000	$ 66,000	$ 46,000	$ 46,000

The indirect materials and supplies budget is to be maintained at a level of $30,000 (item 10 in Management Policies and Forecasts). Purchases each month are therefore equal to the amount of indirect materials and supplies used. These data are found in the manufacturing overhead budgets (Budgets #8 and #9).

The work-in-process inventory account is to be maintained at a level of $300,000 in order to insure relatively stable production volume requirements (Item 11 in Management Policies and Forecasts).

The finished goods inventory balances are determined by the sales forecast and the requirement that a quantity of finished goods sufficient to meet demand for two months in advance be on hand (Item 12 in the Management Policies and Forecasts). The monthly ending inventory balances required for finished goods are developed in Budget #2. A budget for finished goods inventory levels is also developed by using the budgeted cost of goods manufactured statement (Budget #12) and the budgeted variable cost of goods sold statement (Budget #13).

Budget #17
Finished Goods Budget
(1st Quarter, 1981)

	January	February	March	Quarter Total
Beginning Inventory of Finished Goods (Illustration 10–2)	$249,600	→$301,600	→$384,800	$249,600
Add: Cost of Goods Manufactured (Budget #12)	176,800	208,000	208,000	592,000
Total Goods Available	$426,400	$509,600	$592,800	$842,400
Less: Cost of Goods Sold (Budget #13)	124,800	124.800	176,800	426,400
Ending Inventory of Finished Goods	$301,600┘	$384,800┘	$416,000	$416,000

Fixed Asset Budgets (Budget #18)

The Power Turbine Shaft Division does not anticipate buying, selling, or trading any fixed assets in 1981. The original cost of the equipment was $600,000. The estimated life of the equipment is 10 years, no salvage value is anticipated and straight-line depreciation is used to depreciate the equipment. Only one year's depreciation (1980) has been recognized on the equipment prior to the preparation of the 1981 budget.

The original cost of the plant was $3,000,000. A 20-year life is anticipated with no salvage value and straight-line depreciation is used as the basis for depreciating the plant. Both the equipment and plant depreciation were included in the fixed manufacturing overhead costs budget (Budget #9). The calculation of net book values is presented in Budget #18.

Budget #18
Fixed Asset Budget
(1st Quarter, 1981)

Equipment

	January	February	March	Quarter Total
Original Cost	$600,000	$600,000	$600,000	$600,000
Less: Beginning Accumulated Depreciation	60,000	65,000	70,000	60,000
Less: Depreciation for the Period (Budget #9)	5,000	5,000	5,000	15,000
Accumulated Depreciation to Date	$ 65,000	$ 70,000	$ 75,000	$ 75,000
Net Book Value	$535,000	$530,000	$525,000	$525,000

Plant

	January	February	March	Quarter Total
Original Cost	$3,000,000	$3,000,000	$3,000,000	$3,000,000
Less: Beginning Accumulated Depreciation	150,000	162,500	175,000	150,000
Less: Depreciation for the Period (Budget #9)	12,500	12,500	12,500	37,500
Accumulated Depreciation to Date	$ 162,500	$ 175,000	$ 187,500	$ 187,500
Net Book Value	$2,837,500	$2,825,000	$2,812,500	$2,812,500

Accounts Payable and Wages Payable Budget (Budget #19)

Accounts payable represent direct material purchases; therefore, the accounts payable budget is based upon the direct material purchases budget (Budget #5). Credit terms in the industry and for the Power Turbine Shaft Division are net/30. The payments of accounts payable lag behind the purchases schedule by 30 days (Item 15 of Management Policies and Forecasts). The beginning accounts payable balance of $60,000 (Illustration 10-2) will be paid in January of 1981. The January, 1981, purchases of $198,000 will be paid in February of 1981.

Wages are paid on the fifteenth and on the last business day of each month. The outstanding wages payable at the end of any month is $18,000; this represents the wages earned by employees for the first two weeks that they are employed (Item 16 in Management Policies and

Forecasts). The budgeted wages paid are the monthly wages determined in the direct labor budget (Budget #7).

Budget #19
Accounts Payable Budget
(1st Quarter, 1981)

	January	February	March	Quarter Total
Beginning Accounts Payable (Illustration 10–2)	$ 60,000	→$198,000	→$ 78,000	$ 60,000
Add: Purchases of Direct Materials (Budget #5) . .	198,000	78,000	60,000	336,000
Total	$258,000	$276,000	$138,000	$396,000
Less: Payments on Accounts Payable	60,000	198,000	78,000	336,000
Ending Accounts Payable . .	$198,000	$ 78,000	$ 60,000	$ 60,000

Long-Term Debt Budget (Budget #20)

The Power Turbine Shaft Division does not foresee any additional borrowing in 1981. A current long-term debt of $1,200,000 is outstanding and requires monthly interest payments of $11,000 and principal payments of $30,000 per quarter beginning March 31, 1981 (Item 17 of Management Policies and Forecasts). The current payment schedule is projected in Budget #20.

Budget #20
Long-Term Debt Budget
(1st Quarter, 1981)

Loan Payments

	January	February	March	Quarter Total
Interest Payments . . .	$ 11,000	$ 11,000	$ 11,000	$ 33,000
Principal Payments . .	–0–	–0–	30,000	30,000
Total	$ 11,000	$ 11,000	$ 41,000	$ 63,000

Balance of Principal

	January	February	March	Quarter Total
Beginning Principal (Illustration 10–2) .	$1,200,000	→$1,200,000	→$1,200,000	$1,200,000
Less: Principal Payments	–0–	–0–	30,000	30,000
Net Principal	$1,200,000	$1,200,000	$1,170,000	$1,170,000

DEVELOPMENT OF THE MAJOR FINANCIAL OR RESOURCE BUDGETED FINANCIAL STATEMENTS

The next step in the budgeting process is the preparation of three major budgeted resource financial statements:

1. A cash budget
2. A stockholders' equity (corporate investment) statement
3. A budgeted balance sheet

Cash Budget (Budget #21)

A cash budget is an analysis of the cash account in terms of cash receipts and disbursements, and as such can facilitate the planning and control of cash flows. One intent of a cash budget is to establish minimum balance requirements so that normal cash needs can be met without borrowing. Determination of a minimum balance also frees surplus cash for investment. Cash budgeting is also necessary in order to anticipate possible cash shortages and thus allow adequate time to arrange borrowing. Cash budgeting is usually planned for very short periods (i.e., weekly or bi-weekly) in order that the budget be as responsive as possible to the cash needs of the company, for there can be drastic financial implications when a firm runs out of cash.

The primary source of cash for the Power Turbine Shaft Division is customer receipts (Budget #15). The cash balance and company borrowing policies (Item 7 of Management Policies and Forecasts) require a minimum cash balance of $40,000 to sustain the operations of the division. Any necessary cash can be borrowed from corporate headquarters, but only in increments of $5,000.

A number of factors affect cash disbursements:

1. The payment schedule for accounts payable for direct material purchases is presented in the accounts payable budget (Budget #19).
2. Wages payable are paid in the month earned and can be determined from the direct labor budget (Budget #7).
3. The long-term debt repayment schedule is found in the long-term debt budget (Budget #20).
4. All variable (Budget #8) and fixed manufacturing overhead costs (Budget #9) are paid in the month incurred except for the semi-annual property taxes in Budget #9. The property taxes are paid on June 30 and December 31. (Remember, depreciation is a non-cash expense and therefore is not considered in the cash budget).
5. All non-manufacturing costs (Budgets #10 and #11) are paid in the month incurred.

Budgets for cash receipts and cash disbursements could be prepared separately. A complete cash budget is then prepared which incorporates both receipts and disbursements and reconciles the beginning and ending cash balances. Budget #21, the cash budget, includes all the budgeted factors which affect the cash position.

Budgeted Stockholders' Equity Statement (Budget #22)

The budgeted stockholders' equity statement, Budget #22, is the projected analysis of the change in Sax Company's investment in the Power Turbine Shaft Division. Corporate headquarters plans no increase or decrease in the investment in the division for the first quarter of 1981.

Budgeted or Pro Forma Balance Sheet (Budget #23)

The budgeted or pro forma balance sheet in Budget #23 is the result of all budgets developed which involved assets, liabilities, or stockholders' equity. Management Policies and Forecasts have an added impact on the budgeted balance sheet. The function of management is to establish guidelines for obtaining and utilizing resources. If management requires certain balances in given accounts in order to attain the goals and objectives of the firm, then the budget should be prepared in light of these policies. For example, the budgeted balances in indirect materials and supplies, work-in-process, and wages payable were established by Management Policies and Forecasts. All other accounts were affected, either directly or indirectly, by management policies designed to utilize the resources of Sax Company in the most efficient and effective manner.

SUMMARY

Most firms employ some form of routine annual budgeting process resulting in segment-by-segment monthly budgets for the coming year. The process normally begins with the development of company objectives and lower management's projection of needs to meet those objectives. The budgeting process culminates in a formal integration of all divisional budgets into a corporate budget. The monthly budgets are updated at given intervals to reflect any new or additional information that may be pertinent.

Short-range planning or budgeting has several general benefits. One primary benefit is that a budget communicates the short-range plans of the firm to each manager and thereby facilitates coordination of the efforts and activities of all segments of the company. The budget process also serves as an element of *before-the-fact* control because each man-

✓Budget #21
Cash Budget
(1st Quarter, 1981)

	January	February	March	Quarter Total
Cash Receipts:				
Collections of Accounts Receivable (Illustration 10–2, Budget #15) . .	$424,400	$600,000	$600,000	$1,624,400
Cash Disbursements:				
Accounts Payable (Illustration 10–2, Budget #19)	$ 60,000	$198,000	$ 78,000	$ 336,000
Payments for Direct Labor (Budget #7)	51,000	60,000	60,000	171,000
Long-Term Debt Principal Repayment (Budget #20)	–0–	–0–	30,000	30,000
Long-Term Debt Interest Payment (Budget #11 or 20)	11,000	11,000	11,000	33,000
Variable Manufacturing Overhead (Budget #8)	23,800	28,000	28,000	79,800
Fixed Manufacturing Overhead (Budget #9)[a]	5,750	5,750	5,750	17,250
Variable Selling Costs (Budget #10)	60,000	60,000	85,000	205,000
Fixed Selling and Administrative Costs (Budget #11)[b]	167,000	167,000	167,000	501,000
Total Disbursements	$378,550	$529,750	$464,750	$1,373,050
Excess (Deficit) of Cash Receipts Over Disbursements	$ 45,850	$ 70,250	$135,250	$ 251,350
Beginning Cash Balance .	40,000	→ 85,850	→ 156,100	40,000
Ending Cash Balance Before Borrowing or Repayment	$ 85,850	$156,100	$291,350	$ 291,350
Borrowing from Corporate Headquarters . . .	–0–	–0–	–0–	–0–
Repayment to Corporate Headquarters . . .	–0–	–0–	–0–	–0–
Ending Cash Balance	$ 85,850	$156,100	$291,350	$ 291,350

[a] Equipment and plant depreciation is not a cash outflow. The monthly cash outflows for fixed manufacturing overhead must be adjusted accordingly. For example, January—[$30,000-$6,750 (property taxes) — $17,500 (depreciation)] = $5,750 net cash outflow.

[b] Interest expense was considered separately in this cash budget. The January through March cash outflows are $178,000 — $11,000 (interest) = $167,000.

Budget #22
Budgeted Stockholders' Equity Statement
(1st Quarter, 1981)

	January	February	March	Quarter Total
Beginning Corporate Investment (Illustration 10–2)	$3,300,000	→ $3,507,200	→ $3,714,400	$3,300,000
Add: Income (Budget #14) . . .	207,200	207,200	380,200	794,600
Less: Withdrawals by Corporate Headquarters	–0–	–0–	–0–	–0–
Ending Corporate Investment . .	$3,507,200 ⌐	$3,714,400 ⌐	$4,094,600	$4,094,600

Budget #23
Budgeted Monthly Balance Sheets
(1st Quarter, 1981)

	January 31	February 28	March 31
ASSETS			
Current Assets:			
Cash (Budget #21)	$ 85,850	$ 156,100	$ 291,350
Accounts Receivable (Budget #15)	600,000	600,000	850,000
Direct Materials Inventories:			
Steel Billets @ Standard (Budget #16)	160,000	132,000	92,000
Ball Bearings @ Standard (Budget #16)	80,000	66,000	46,000
Indirect Materials and Supplies . . .	30,000[a]	30,000[a]	30,000[a]
Work-in-Process @ Standard Variable Cost	300,000[b]	300,000[b]	300,000[b]
Finished Goods @ Standard Variable Cost (Budget #17) . . .	301,600	384,800	416,000
Total Current Assets (Lines 2, 3, & 5–9)	$1,557,450	$1,668,900	$2,025,350
Long-Term Assets:			
Equipment (Budget #18)	$ 600,000	$ 600,000	$ 600,000
Less: Accumulated Depreciation (Budget #18)	65,000	70,000	75,000
Net: Equipment (Budget #18) . .	535,000	530,000	525,000
Plant (Budget #18)	3,000,000	3,000,000	3,000,000
Less: Accumulated Depreciation (Budget #18)	162,500	175,000	187,500
Net: Plant (Budget #18)	2,837,500	2,825,000	2,812,500
Total Long-Term Assets (Lines 14, 17)	3,372,500	3,355,000	3,337,500
Total Assets (Lines 10, 18)	$4,929,950	$5,023,900	$5,362,850

	January 31	February 28	March 31
LIABILITIES AND STOCKHOLDERS' EQUITY			
Current Liabilities:			
Accounts Payable (Budget #19) . .	$ 198,000	$ 78,000	$ 60,000
Wages Payable	18,000c	18,000c	18,000c
Deferred Factory Property Taxes			
(Budget #9)	6,750d	13,500d	20,250d
Total Current Liabilities			
(Lines 20–23)	$ 222,750	$ 109,500	$ 98,250
Long-Term Debt (Budget #20) . . .	1,200,000	1,200,000	1,170,000
Total Liabilities			
(Lines 24 & 25)	$1,422,750	$1,309,500	$1,268,250
Stockholders' Equity			
Corporate Investment			
(Budget #22)	3,507,200	3,714,400	4,094,600
Total Liabilities and Stockholders'			
Equity (Lines 26 & 28)	$4,929,950	$5,023,900	$5,362,850

a Item 10, Management Policies and Forecasts
b Item 11, Management Policies and Forecasts
c Item 16, Management Policies and Forecasts
d Deferred factory property taxes are $6,750 per month. The property taxes are paid on June 30 and December 31.

ager must justify his requests for resources. In addition, the budget serves as a basis for *after-the-fact* control by providing a benchmark against which actual performance can be measured. Formal budgeting can identify weak areas of the firm by pinpointing unsatisfactory contribution margins, production bottlenecks, etc. Finally, by involving various personnel in the budgeting process, the budget becomes an effective motivational tool for employees and management.

The basic end-product of the budgeting process is a set of budgeted or pro-forma financial statements. In developing these statements, a firm generally finds it necessary to produce numerous specialized budgets and schedules. The starting point in the budgeting process is generally a projection of sales in units for the budget period. Estimates are then made to determine the level of finished goods inventory and production requirements necessary to meet this anticipated demand for the product. Information from the production budget is then used to forecast direct material requirements and to prepare the purchases budget. The direct labor and manufacturing overhead budgets are also prepared based on the production budget.

The budgets for non-manufacturing expenses are completed and the major budgeted operating statements are then prepared. These statements include the budgeted cost of goods manufactured statement, the budgeted cost of goods sold statement, and the budgeted income statement. To develop the major financial or resource budgets, the firm must prepare additional budgets and associated schedules for each asset, liability, and owner's equity account. The final result is a budgeted or pro forma balance sheet for the firm.

This chapter introduced the use of budgeting as a basis for performance evaluation. The following two chapters provide additional information regarding the reporting of performance for the segments of a firm.

KEY DEFINITIONS

Budget—formalized plans prepared by management, generally on a segment-by-segment basis, for a specified period in the near future. Budgets may be prepared for a wide range of operating and financial factors such as sales, production and manufacturing expenses. These factors are the basis for the major operating or performance and financial or resource budgeted (pro-forma) financial statements. They may be long or short-term (most firms use both).

Budgeted balance sheet—the projected balance sheet of the firm showing the expected financial position of the firm at a given point in time during or at the conclusion of the budget period.

Budgeted cost of goods manufactured statement—a projection and analysis of the changes occurring in the work-in-process account during the budget period.

Budgeted cost of goods sold statement—a projection and analysis of the changes occurring in the finished goods account during the budget period.

Budgeted income statement—the forecasted results of operations for the budget period.

Budgeted stockholders' equity statement—a projected analysis of investment changes in the firm during the budget period.

Budgeted owner's equity statement—a projected analysis of investment change in the firm during the budget period.

Cash budget—an analysis of the cash account in terms of anticipated cash receipts and disbursements in order to establish cash balances over the budget period for the planning and control of cash.

Comprehensive budgeting—a system encompassing and integrating the areas of planning, control and performance evaluation for the entire company.

Intermediate-range planning—planning to achieve objectives for which the firm is striving in the next three to five years.

Long-range planning—planning for the distant future.

Major financial resource budgeted statements—cash budget, stockholders' equity or corporate investment statement, and budgeted balance sheet.

Major operating budgeted financial statements—cost of goods manufactured statement, the cost of goods sold statement, and the income statement.

Short-range planning—also known as budgeting or profit planning, this planning consists of management's financial expectation for the near future, a period in which the firm faces factors which cannot be altered in the short-term.

QUESTIONS

1. What is the definition of constraining factors and how do they relate to short-range planning?
2. Name two specific ways in which long-range planning differs from short-range planning.
3. Briefly describe the normal procedure for preparing a budget.
4. Is the approved annual budget the end of the planning process and if not, what follows?
5. Two of the benefits of short-range planning are communication and co-ordination. Why are these two factors important to the firm?
6. How can short-range planning act as a motivator for management?
7. How does short-range planning yield a basis for after-the-fact control?
8. At what stage in the short-range budgeting process is the sales budget formulated? What external sources are used to establish a reliable sales forecast?
9. Why do firms maintain a minimum and a maximum level of inventory?
10. What is a cash budget and what is its purpose?
11. What factors do the normal operating cash receipts of a firm depend on?
12. What is the last budget which is usually made in the short-range profit planning procedure and why is it the last?

EXERCISES

10–1 You have been hired by the ABC Company to prepare a raw materials purchasing budget from the following data:

	Units
Predicted sales	25,000
Current finished goods inventory	6,250
Desired ending finished goods inventory	10,000
Currrent raw materials inventory	57,500
Desired ending raw materials inventory	72,500
Units of raw materials per unit of output	15
Current work-in-process inventory	0
Desired ending work-in-process inventory	0

10–2 The VIP Corporation has beginning inventory of 720 units. They predict sales for June to be 960 units.

Required:

a. If VIP Corporation wants an ending inventory of 900 units, how many units should they produce?

b. If the desired ending inventory is 598 units, how many units should they produce?

10–3 The Downhill Ski Company has forecasted sales in February to be 38,500 pairs of skis. The Company has three areas for sales, New

England, Middle West and Rocky Mountains. The New England area captures about 35% of the sales and the price is $90.00. The Middle West and Rocky Mountain areas sell 28% and 37%, respectively. The price is $120.00 in the Middle West and $165.00 in the Rocky Mountains.

Required:

Prepare a sales budget for February showing quantity and dollar sales in each area as well as a total for the company.

10–4   The Foolery Company has requested the construction of an income budget for sales of $7,200, $6,300, and $7,680. The company accountant has estimated that variable costs are 67% of sales and fixed costs are $2,400 per year.

Required:

Prepare the three budgets the Foolery Company has requested.

✓ 10–5   The Nelson Company produces two products, standard and custom. For 1981, the company plans to produce 4,000 units of each product. These products require the raw materials given below:

	Cost/Unit	Standard	Custom
X	2.00	2 units	
Y	2.50	1 unit	1 unit
Z	1.25		3 units

Required:

Prepare a material usage budget for 1981.

10–6   Given below is the beginning inventory and the desired ending inventory of raw materials for Jones, Inc.

		Beginning		Ending
Material	# Units	Cost per Unit	# Units	Cost per Unit
A	400	$.50	300	$.50
B	2000	.40	2000	.40
C	600	.90	750	.90

The company plans to produce 40,000 units of Product X and 37,500 units of Product Z. Product X requires 2 units of A, 1 unit of B, and 1 unit of C. Product Z requires 1 unit of B and 3 units of C.

Required:

Prepare a purchases budget in units and dollars for raw materials.

10–7   You have been asked to prepare a sales budget broken down by month for the first quarter of 1981.

Required:

Prepare the requested sales budget from the information given below. Your answer should show the sales budget in units and dollars.

Sales price, $10 per unit.

Sales for December, 1980, 5,000 units.

Sales are expected to increase by 3% each month.

10-8   Gamma, Inc. plans to produce 25,000 units of Alpha and 29,000 units of Beta. The units go through cutting and finishing processes. Alpha requires 2 hours cutting and ¾ hour in finishing at direct labor rates of $2.00 and $3.50 respectively. Beta requires 1 hour in cutting and 2 hours in finishing at the same rates.

Required:

Prepare a direct labor budget for Gamma, Inc.

10-9   Rite, Inc. manufactures pencils. During 1981, they predict a sales volume of 25,240,000 pencils. At the present time, their finished goods inventory has 1,500,000 pencils. Rite hopes to increase this inventory by 15% at the end of the year. At the present time there is no work-in-process inventory.

Required:

Prepare a production budget by units.

10-10   The Task Company is to begin operations in January. They have budgeted January sales of $34,000, February sales of $40,000, March sales of $42,000 and April sales of $38,000. Prepare a budget of cash receipts from sales for the first five months of the year if 75% of sales are collected the month following sale, 16% the second month, 6% the third month, and the balance is bad debts.

10-11   The sales budget of Wackie Toy Co. projects the following level of sales for the second quarter: April 20,000 units, May 22,000 units and June 19,000 units. The finished goods budget shows desired ending inventories as follows: April 30,000 units, May 35,000 units and June 25,000 units. The ending desired inventory for March was 28,000 units.

Required:

Prepare a production budget in units for the second quarter.

10-12   Vandergelder Inc. produces hockey sticks with a standard cost of material of $1.75 per stick. The raw materials production requirements for the last quarter of 1980 are as follows: October = 27,000 units, November = 35,000 units and December = 40,000 units. It requires ¹⁄₁₀ hours of direct labor per stick at a cost of $3.00 per hour. Rework costs amount to $.05 per unit. Waiting time is zero and set up time is $.02 per unit. Indirect materials and supplies total $.40 per unit. Indirect labor is $.15 per unit and electricity is $.08 per unit.

Required:

Prepare the direct materials usage budget, the direct labor budget, and the variable manufacturing overhead budget for the last quarter.

PROBLEMS SERIES A

10A-1   Lazyman, Inc., a producer of mattresses, has predicted total sales of 190,500 mattresses in 198‰. The company has three outlets for the product, the East Coast, the West Coast, and Southern United States. The mattresses sell for $180, $200 and $215 respectively. The East Coast captures 40% of the market with the other two areas dividing the remainder equally.

In 1980, it took 40 pounds of stuffing at $2.00 per pound and 20 yards of material at $1.50 per yard to make one mattress. Lazyman expects the cost of stuffing to go up 15% and the material to go up 8%. It takes 1½ hours of direct labor, which cost $6.50 per hour in 1980, to make one mattress. Due to a new labor contract, labor costs per hour will rise 20% in 1981. Because of improved machinery, it will only take 1¼ hours to make one mattress in 1981. Variable costs will be applied at a rate of $4.50 per direct labor hour. This is the same rate as was used in 1980. Fixed overhead costs are expected to be $200,000, and administrative costs to be $150,000.

At the end of 1980, the inventory consisted of 620 finished mattresses, no work-in-process, 800 pounds of stuffing, and 600 yards of material. They plan to increase all of their inventories except work-in-process by 30% at the end of 1981. Lazyman uses Fifo and variable costing for inventory costing purposes.

Required:

a. Production budget in units
b. Direct material requirements budget (in units)
c. Direct material purchase budget (in dollars)
d. Direct material usage budget
e. Direct labor budget
f. Variable manufacturing overhead budget
g. Cost of goods manufactured statement
h. Cost of goods sold statement
i. Income statement

10A-2   Barcelana, Inc. produces two products, A and B. The company plans to produce 5,000 units of A and 6,000 units of B. Production requirements for raw material are given below

	Cost/unit	A	B
X	$2.60	3 units	2 units
Y	$4.20	2 units	
Z	$1.80		4 units

It takes 3½ hours of direct labor to produce one unit of A and 3 hours to produce one unit of B. It costs $4.00 for one hour of direct labor. Variable costs are applied at $2.90 per direct labor hour. Assume variable costing and no beginning or ending inventories.

Required:

Determine the cost of goods manufactured for Barcelana, Inc. Prepare the necessary budgets used to arrive at this answer.

10A–3   During December, 1980, the Burns Co. sold 40,000 gallons of charcoal lighter. In the first quarter of 1981, the company expects sales to increase 20% each month. The company normally collects 30% of the sales price in the month of the sale, 50% in the second month, and the remainder in the next month. Sales for November 1980 totaled 35,000 gallons. A gallon of charcoal lighter sold for $.60 in 1980, but the company plans to raise the price to $.68 per gallon in 1981 due to increasing costs.

Required:

You are to prepare a sales budget and an accounts receivable budget for the first quarter of 1981.

10A–4   Jenkins, Inc., makes two products G and X. G sells for $8.00 per unit and X sells for $10.00 per unit.

The company's expected production schedule for the fourth quarter is:

	G	X
October	5,000	6,000
November	6,000	6,500
December	5,200	7,000

Raw materials needed for production are:

	Cost/unit	G	X
A	$ .75	3	3
B	.90	2	1
C	2.00		2

There are 200 units of A, 150 units of B, and 100 units of C in beginning inventory. They plan to increase the ending inventories by 15 units at the end of each month.

Jenkins pays for 60% of their purchases in the month of the purchase and the remainder in the next month. Beginning accounts payable are $23,250.

Required:

You are to prepare a direct material purchases budget and an accounts payable budget for the fourth quarter.

10A–5   The condensed income statement of the Howle Manufacturing Corporation for 1980 is as follows:

1978

Sales (30,000 units)		$450,000
Sales returns, allowances & discounts		13,500
Net sales		$436,500
Cost of goods sold		306,000
Gross profit on sales		$130,500
Selling expenses	$60,000	
Administrative expenses	30,000	90,000
Net profit before income taxes		$ 40,500

The budget committee has estimated the following changes in income and costs for 1981.

30% increase in the number of units sold
20% increase in the material unit cost
15% increase in the direct labor cost per unit
10% increase in the production overhead cost per unit
14% increase in the selling expenses
 7% increase in the administrative expenses

As inventory quantities remain fairly constant, the committee considered that, for budget purposes, any change in inventory valuation can be ignored. The composition of the cost of finished product during 1980 for materials, direct labor and production overhead, respectively, was in the ratio of 3 to 2 to 1. No changes in production methods or credit policies were contemplated for 1981.

Required:

Using the above data, you are to prepare the projected 1981 income statement and compute the unit sales price (rounded to the nearest full cent) at which the Howle Manufacturing Corporation must sell its only product in 1981 in order to earn a budgeted profit (before income taxes) of exactly $60,000.

(CPA, adapted)

10A–6   Below are given the condensed financial statements of the Flophouse Hotel:

Flophouse Hotel
Balance Sheet
December 31, 1980

Cash	$ 10,000	
Accounts receivable (net)	25,000	
Other current assets	5,000	$ 40,000
Fixed assets	$120,000	
Less: Accumulated depreciation	36,000	84,000
Total assets		$124,000
Accrued payables		$ 20,000
Mortgage payable		40,000
Flophouse, capital		64,000
Total Liabilities and Equities		$124,000

Flophouse Hotel
Income Statement
Year 1980

Revenues	$250,000
Expenses	200,000
Income	$ 50,000

Other data:

1. Revenues for 1981 are expected to increase by 20%.
2. Fixed expenses will remain constant at $100,000; the remaining expenses will continue to vary directly and proportionally with revenue.
3. Accounts receivable at December 31, 1981 are expected to be 10% of 1981 revenue.
4. The hotel plans a fixed asset addition on July 1, 1981, costing $50,000. All fixed assets have a useful life of 10 years and no salvage value.
5. Accounts payable at December 31, 1981, are expected to aggregate 10% of total expenses.
6. **The 1981 mortgage principal payment is $2,000.**
7. The owner plans to withdraw $25,000 during the year.

Required:

Prepare the following for the Flophouse Hotel for 1981:

a. Operating budget (budgeted income statement)
b. Cash budget
c. Pro forma balance sheet as of December 31, 1981

10A–7 In 1981, Sammy, Inc., sold 80,500 units of its product for $65 each. Of these sales, 80 percent were for cash. On December 31, 1980, accounts payable totaled $26,870 and accounts receivable totaled $22,560, both of which were paid or received during 1981. Seventy-five percent of direct materials were purchased for cash.

Sammy paid all of its direct labor and overhead in cash. Direct labor costs $4.25 per hour and variable overhead is $2.30 per direct labor hour. It takes 2½ hours to make one unit of the product. Direct materials total $10.65 per unit. There are no beginning or ending work-in-process inventories. Beginning and ending finished goods totaled 670 units and 950 units, respectively. Beginning raw material inventories were $8,524.00 and ending raw material inventories were $9,056.50. Total fixed overhead was $35,960 with depreciation totaling $9,840.

Variable selling costs are $.18 per unit. Fixed selling and administrative expenses are $150,000. The company pays $1,000 per month on long-term debt. The company's beginning cash balance in 1981 was $32,645.

Required:

Prepare a cash budget for 1981.

10A-8   The Lamb Company has asked you to supply them with a budgeted cost of goods manufactured statement covering the first quarter of 1981. Work-in-process inventory on January 1, 1981 was $30,000. It is expected that this inventory will be increased by 2 percent in each of the budgeted months.

There are to be 2,500 units produced in January and this will be increased by 500 units in each of the next two months. It took 3 pounds of raw material at $2 per pound to produce one unit in 1980. In 1981, the price of raw material is expected to increase by $.05 per pound. On January 1, there was no raw material inventory.

It takes 15 minutes to produce one unit and employees are paid $6.00 an hour. Variable manufacturing overhead is applied at $5.50 an hour. Fixed manufacturing overhead is $20,000 per month.

Required:

A budgeted cost of goods manufactured statement for the first quarter of 1981.

10A-9   The Suppy Company intends to expand in the last quarter of the year ended December 31, 1981. In order to accomplish this expansion, they must purchase two new pieces of machinery and a used warehouse. On October 1, they plan to purchase the warehouse at a cost of $45,000. The warehouse will have no salvage value and is to be depreciated on the straight-line basis over a period of 20 years.

On November 1, they will purchase the first ot the two machines at a cost of $27,450. This machine is to be depreciated using the sum-of-the-years' digits over a 7-year life. A $5,000 salvage value is expected at the end of its life.

On December 1, the last machine is to be purchased at a cost of $12,000. This machine is expected to have a $1,500 salvage value at the end of 5 years. It is to be depreciated on the straight-line basis.

Total fixed assets for the Suppy Company on September 30 were $1,500,650. Accumulated depreciation to that date was $800,000. These assets are all depreciated on the straight-line basis over a period of 10 years.

Required:

Prepare a fixed asset budget for the last quarter of 1980. Round to the nearest whole dollar.

Prepare a fixed asset budget for the last quarter of 1981. Round to the nearest whole dollar.

10A-10 The Jafa Corporation uses variable costing for managerial purposes and prepared their December 31, 1980 balance sheet on a direct costing basis as follows:

Jafa Corporation
Balance Sheet
As of December 31, 1980

Current Assets			
Cash		$ 10,000	
Marketable Securities		50,000	
Accounts Receivable		80,000	
Inventories			
Finished Goods	$ 67,500		
Work-in-Process	45,000		
Raw Materials	9,000	$121,500	
Total Current Assets			$ 261,500
Long-Term Assets			
Equipment (factory)	$ 300,000		
Less: Accumulated Depreciation .	72,000	$228,000	
Plant	$1,000,000		
Less: Accumulated Depreciation .	180,000	$820,000	
Property		200,000	
Total Long-Term Assets			$1,248,000
Other Assets			
Intangibles (net)		$ 10,000	
Loan to Officer of Company . . .		10,000	20,000
Total Assets			$1,529,500
Current Liabilities			
Accounts Payable		$ 25,680	
Other Payables		10,000	
Notes Payable (one month note due January 15, 1981)		50,000	
Current Portion of Long-term Debt (due March 31, 1981)		50,000	
Total Current Liabilities			$ 135,680
Long-term Debt (8%, 10 years, interest payable December 31, repayment of principal at rate of $50,000 per year beginning in 1981)			450,000
Total Liabilities			$ 585,680
Owners' Equity			
Common Stock (issued and out- standing, 70,000 shares, $10 per share)		$700,000	
Retained Earnings		243,820	
Total Owners' Equity			$ 943,820
Total Equities			$1,529,500

Some recent and forecast data are:

	Actual		Forecast			
	Nov.	Dec.	Jan.	Feb.	Mar.	Apr.
Cash Sales (units) . . .	1,200	1,200	1,000	1,000	1,000	2,000
Credit Sales (units) . . .	10,000	10,000	8,000	8,000	8,000	20,000
Selling and Administrative Expenses . . .	$20,000	$20,000	$20,000	$20,000	$20,000	$20,000
Fixed Manufacturing Expenses 1 .	15,000	15,000	15,000	15,000	15,000	15,000

1 Excluding depreciation and amortization.

The company manufactures an automobile safety seat for children which it sells directly to a number of automobile dealers in its four state region and to retail customers through its own outlet. The selling price through their own outlet is $30; to the dealers, the price is $20.

Since all sales through its own outlet are on a cash basis, and sales to dealers (all on account) have been long established, bad debts are negligible. Terms of credit sales are net 30; 60% of the credit sales are paid in the month of the sale and the remaining 40% of the credit sales are paid in the month after the sale.

Raw materials cost $5 per unit. All purchases of raw materials are on account. Accounts payable are on terms of net 30 days. 40% are paid in the month of purchase and 60% are paid in the following month. Direct labor and variable manufacturing overhead costs are $10 per unit. Direct labor and variable manufacturing overhead costs are incurred in direct proportion to the percentage of completion and paid in cash when incurred.

At the end of each month, desired inventory levels are as follows:

Raw materials—20% of next month's requirements
Work-in-process—50% of next month's requirements
Finished goods—50% of next month's requirements

Work-in-process is assumed to be 50% completed at the end of the month. Raw materials are added at the beginning of production.

Depreciation on the equipment is $4,000 per month and depreciation on the plant is $5,000 per month. Amortization of intangibles is $500 per month.

Selling and administrative expenses are all fixed and half are paid in the month incurred with the balance paid in the following month.

Fixed manufacturing expenses that require cash payments are paid in the month incurred.

Long-term debt-principal is to be paid each March 31, starting in 1981 at a rate of $50,000 per year.

The loan to the officer was made on December 31, 1980 and is due March 31, 1981 plus interest at 6% per annum.

The firm requires a minimum cash balance of $10,000 at the end of each month. If the balance is less, marketable securities are sold in multiples of $5,000 at the end of the month. If necessary, cash is borrowed in multiples of $1,000 at the end of the month. Marketable securities earn 6% per annum and the interest is collected at the end of each month. The short-term interest rate on notes payable is 12% per annum and is paid at the time the note is repaid.

Taxes are to be ignored.

Required:

Prepare a statement forecasting the cash balance including any necessary cash transactions to achieve company cash management objectives for January, 1981.

Hint: Since the estimated sales for January and February are the same, 9,000 units, there are also no inventory changes from January 1 to February 1.

(CMA, adapted)

10A–11   Presented below is the income statement and balance sheet for the Lane Ax Company.

Lane Ax Co.
Income Statement
For the Year 1980

Revenues	$770,000
Cost of goods sold	(530,000)
Contribution margin	$240,000
Operating expenses (including depreciation)	(40,000)
Fixed expenses	(90,000)
Selling and administrative expense	(40,000)
Net income	$ 70,000

Lane Ax Co.
Balance Sheet
1980

Assets		
Cash		$ 32,000
Accounts receivable		57,500
Other current assets		47,000
Total current assets		$136,500
Property, plant & equipment	$180,000	
Less: Accumulated depreciation	(54,000)	126,000
Total assets		$262,500

Liabilities

Accounts payable . . . . $ 21,000
Long-term liabilities 127,000
Owners' capital 114,500

Total liabilities and owners' capital $262,500

Additional Information:

1. Revenues should increase by 15% in 1981.
2. Cost of goods sold will increase by 12% in 1981 and selling and administrative expenses will increase by 10%.
3. 1981 payment on long-term debt is $30,000.
4. The property, plant & equipment are depreciated over 10 years using the straight-line method and zero salvage value.
5. Ending accounts receivables are expected to be $53,130.
6. Capital will be reduced by $96,000 from withdrawals by the owners.
7. Fixed expenses will increase by 10% in 1981.
8. Ending accounts payable will be $18,000.
9. Operating expenses (other than depreciation) will increase by 15%.

Required:

a. Prepare a projected income statement for 1981.
b. Prepare a projected balance sheet as of December 31, 1981.
c. Prepare a cash budget for 1981.

PROBLEMS SERIES B

10B-1   D. Duck, Inc. produces pillows which sell for $15.50. In 1981, they expect to sell 200,000 pillows.

The pillows consist of material, feathers, zippers, and thread. Standard usage is 2 yards of material, 2 pounds of feathers, 1 zipper, and 6 yards of thread. In 1980 material cost $2.50 per yard, feathers were $.80 per pound, zippers were $.15 each, and thread was $.002 per yard. In 1981, the cost of material is expected to rise 20%, the cost of feathers will rise 15%, zippers will cost $.16, and thread will remain the same.

In 1980, it took ½ hour of direct labor at $5.00 per hour to make one pillow. Direct labor costs per hour will rise 12% in 1981 due to a cost of living increase. Variable costs will be applied at the same rate in 1981 as was used in 1980—$3.00 per direct labor hour. Fixed costs will be $130,000 and administrative and selling costs will be $225,000.

At the end of 1980, inventories consisted of 1,200 pillows in finished goods, 5,000 yards of material, 3,500 pounds of feathers, 900 zippers, and 6,000 yards of thread. They plan to increase each of these inventories by 40% at the end of 1981. D. Duck uses Fifo and variable costing for inventory costing purposes.

Required:

a. Production budget in units.
b. Direct material requirements budget in units.
c. Direct material purchases budget in dollars.
d. Direct material usage budget.
e. Direct labor budget.
f. Variable manufacturing overhead budget.
g. Budgeted cost of goods manufactured statement.
h. Budgeted cost of goods sold statement.
i. Budgeted income statement.

10B-2   Stanfield Manufacturing Co. produces two products, Good and Better. It takes 1½ hours of direct labor to produce one unit of Good and 3 hours to produce one unit of Better. Direct labor costs $5.00 per hour. Variable overhead is applied at a rate of $1.70 per direct labor hour.

In 1981, Stanfield plans to produce 8,000 units of Good and 5,000 units of Better. Requirements for direct materials are as follows:

	Cost/unit	Good	Better
A	$1.00	3	3
B	.95	2	3
C	2.20		2

Required:

Determine the budgeted cost of goods manufactured for Stanfield Manufacturing Co. Prepare the necessary supporting budgets used to arrive at this answer.

10B-3   During February and March, the Farm Fresh Egg Co. sold 110,000 and 90,000 dozen eggs, respectively. The eggs sell for $.49 per dozen for the small eggs, $.56 for medium eggs, $.60 for large eggs, and $.68 for extra large eggs. The ratio of eggs from small to extra large is 1-3-4-2 respectively. Sales for the second quarter are expected to increase 20% each month. Collections on sales are 50% in the month of the sale, 40% the next month, and 10% the third month.

Required:

Your job is to prepare a sales budget for February through June and an accounts receivable budget for April through June.

10B-4   Southern Manufacturing Corporation makes two products. Product One sells for $18.00 and Product Two sells for $25.00. Southern expects sales to equal production for the third quarter. In May the company sold 40,000 units of Product One and 30,000 units of Product

Two. In June they sold 52,000 and 36,000. They expect sales to continue to rise at this same rate in July, August and September.

Raw materials needed for the production of one unit are:

	Cost/Unit	Product One	Product Two
R	$ .50	4	5
S	.95	3	2
F . . . :	1.20	3	5

There are 1,000 units of R, 1,200 units of S and 1,500 units of F in inventory on June 30. Southern wants to decrease these inventories by 5% per month.

Southern pays for 50% of its purchases in the month of the purchase, 40% in the next month, and 10% in the third month. Purchases made in May and June were $650,745 and $814,040, respectively.

Required:

Prepare a direct material purchases budget and an accounts payable budget for the months of July, August, and September.

10B–5   The condensed income statement of the Jones Manufacturing Corporation for 1980 is as follows:

Sales (100,000 units)		$3,000,000
Sales returns, allowances, and discounts		12,000
Net sales		$2,988,000
Cost of goods sold		1,215,000
Gross profit		$1,773,000
Selling expense	$360,000	
Administrative expense	840,000	1,200,000
Net profit before income taxes		$ 573,000

The budget committee has estimated the following changes in income and costs for 1981:

25% increase in the number of units sold
15% increase in the material cost
20% increase in the direct labor cost per unit
10% increase in the production overhead cost per unit
12% increase in selling expenses
14% increase in administrative expense

As inventory quantities remain fairly constant, the committee considered that, for budget purposes, any change in inventory valuation can be ignored. The composition of the cost of finished product during 1980 for materials, direct labor, and production overhead, respectively was in the ratio of 4 to 3 to 2. No changes in production methods or credit policies are contemplated for 1981.

Required:

Using the above data, you are to prepare the projected 1981 income statement and compute the unit sales price (rounded to the nearest full cent) at which the Jones Manufacturing Corporation must sell its only product in 1981 in order to earn a budgeted profit (before income taxes) of $650,000.

(CPA, adapted)

10B–6   Below are given the condensed financial statements of the Stabler Inn:

Stabler Inn
Balance Sheet
December 31, 1980

Cash	$ 30,000	
Accounts receivable (net)	75,000	
Other current assets	15,000	$120,000
Fixed assets	$360,000	
Less: Accumulated depreciation . .	108,000	252,000
Total assets		$372,000
Accounts payable		$ 60,000
Mortgage payable		120,000
Ken Stabler, capital		192,000
Total liabilities and capital		$372,000

Stabler Inn
Income Statement
for the year ending December 31, 1980

Revenues	$750,000
Expenses	600,000
Income	$150,000

Other data:

1. Revenues for 1981 are expected to increase by one-third.
2. Fixed expenses will remain constant at $150,000; the remaining expenses will continue to vary directly and proportionally with revenue.
3. Accounts receivable at December 31, 1981 are expected to be 10% of 1981 revenue.
4. The Inn plans a fixed asset addition on January 1, 1981, costing $150,000. All fixed assets have a useful life of 10 years, are depreciated on a straight-line basis, and have no salvage value.
5. Accounts payable at December 31, 1981, are expected to aggregate 10% of total expenses.

6. The 1981 mortgage payment is $12,000.
7. The owner plans to withdraw $60,000 during the year.
8. Other current assets at December 31, 1981 were the same as at December 31, 1980.

Required:

Prepare the following for the Stabler Inn for 1981:

a. Operating budget (budgeted income statement).
b. Cash budget.
c. Pro forma balance sheet as of December 31, 1981.

10B–7   In 1980, Lincaln, Inc. sold 95,460 units of its product. Each unit sells for $59.00. Seventy-five percent of these sales were for cash; the remainder were not paid by the end of the year.

Beginning finished goods inventory totaled 5,250 units; at the end of the year there were 7,860 units on hand. The company had no beginning or ending work-in-process inventories.

Direct material costs are $14.25 per unit. Ninety percent of the direct material purchases are paid in the year of the purchase. On January 1, 1980, direct materials on hand totaled $14,250. On January 1, 1981 they totaled $12,825.

It takes 3¼ hours of direct labor at $4.00 per hour to produce one unit of the product. Variable overhead is applied at $4.80 per direct labor hour. Fixed overhead is $89,500 per year. Plant depreciation is $19,400 per year, and equipment depreciation is $12,300 per year. All of the direct labor and factory overhead is paid in the year incurred.

Variable selling costs are $.27 per unit sold. Fixed selling and administrative expenses are $160,000 per year. The company has a debt of $200,000 of which 20% is paid per year. Interest of 6% is paid on the total debt outstanding at the beginning of the year. On January 1, 1980, 60% of the debt was still outstanding.

On January 1, 1980, accounts receivable were $53,260 and accounts payable were $84,250, all of which were received or paid during the year. The beginning cash balance was $380,226.

Required:

Prepare a cash budget for 1980.

10B–8   The Jones Company manufactures only one product, trinkets. In the second quarter of 1980, it is expected that 10,000 units will be produced in April, 12,000 in May, and 9,480 in June. The work-in-process inventory on March 31 was valued at $2,500. This inventory is expected to increase or decrease in the same proportion as production. 8,000 trinkets were produced in March.

It took 5 ounces of raw material at $.08 an ounce to produce one trinket in the first quarter of 1980. The price of raw material used is expected to go up $.02 in each month in the second quarter. There is no beginning raw materials inventory.

Employees can make one trinket every 10 minutes and they are paid $2.50 an hour. Variable manufacturing overhead is applied at $1.00 an hour and there is no fixed manufacturing overhead.

Required:

A budgeted cost of goods manufactured statement for the second quarter of 1980.

10B-9   The total fixed assets (at cost) of the Jenkins Company on January 1, 1981 was $2,185,000. Accumulated depreciation to date was $1,265,000. These assets have been depreciated over a period of 20 years on the straight-line basis.

In the first quarter of 1981, they plan to purchase four pieces of equipment. The first is a bulldozer which will be purchased on January 2 at a cost of $18,000. The bulldozer will be depreciated over a life of 9 years with no salvage value.

The next two pieces of equipment are tractors which will be purchased on February 1 at a cost of $6,500 a piece. Both will have salvage values of $1,200 at the end of their 10-year lives and will be depreciated on the straight-line basis.

The fourth purchase will be made on March 1. It will be a small pick-up truck and will cost $4,600. It will be depreciated over a period of 8 years using the sum-of-the-years' digits method. A salvage value of $800 is expected at the end of the eighth year.

Required:

Prepare a fixed asset budget for the first quarter of 1981. Round to the nearest whole dollar.

10B-10   The Barker Corporation manufactures and distributes wooden baseball bats. The unit sales volume for the past two months and the estimate for the next four months is:

October (actual)	70,000	January (estimated) . . .	90,000
November (actual)	50,000	February (estimated) . .	90,000
December (estimated) . .	50,000	March (estimated)	120,000

The bats are sold for $3 each. All sales are made on account. One-half of the accounts are collected in the month of the sale, 40 percent are collected in the month following the sale, and the remaining 10 percent in the second month following the sale. Customers who pay in the month of the sale receive a 2 percent cash discount.

The production schedule for the six-month period beginning with October is:

October (actual)	90,000	January (estimated) . . .	90,000
November (actual)	90,000	February (estimated) . .	100,000
December (estimated) . .	90,000	March (estimated)	100,000

Since wooden blocks from which the bats are made are purchased a year in advance in order to be aged, Barker pays $60,000 a month for raw materials. Workers can produce 7.5 bats per hour. Normal monthly output is 75,000 bats. Employees are paid $4.00 per hour for regular time and time and one-half for overtime. All hours over the normal monthly output of 75,000 bats are overtime hours.

Other manufacturing costs include variable overhead of $0.30 per unit and annual fixed overhead of $280,000. Depreciation charges totaling $40,000 are included among the fixed overhead. Selling expenses include variable costs of $0.20 per unit and annual fixed costs of $60,000. Fixed administrative costs are $120,000 annually. All fixed costs are incurred uniformly throughout the year.

The controller has accumulated the following additional information:

1. The balances of selected accounts as of November 30, 1980, are as follows:

Cash	$ 12,000
Marketable securities (cost and market are the same)	40,000
Accounts receivable	96,000
Prepaid expenses	4,800
Account payable (arising from raw material purchase)	300,000
Accrued vacation pay	9,500
Equipment note payable	102,000
Accrued income taxes payable	50,000

2. Interest to be received from the company's temporary investments is estimated at $500 for December.
3. Prepaid expenses of $3,600 will expire during December, and the balance of the prepaid account is estimated at $4,200 for the end of December.
4. Barker purchased new machinery in 1980 as part of a plant modernization program. The machinery was financed by a 24-month note of $144,000. The terms call for equal principal payments over the next 24 months with interest paid at the rate of one percent per month on the unpaid balance at the first of the month. The first payment was made May 1, 1980.
5. Old equipment, which has a book value of $8,000, is to be sold during December for $7,500.
6. Each month the company accrues $1,700 for vacation pay by charging Vacation Pay Expense and crediting Accrued Vacation Pay. The plant closes for two weeks in June when all plant employees take a vacation.
7. Quarterly dividends of $0.20 per share will be paid on December 15 to stockholders of record. Barker Corporation has authorized 10,000 shares. The company has issued 7,500 shares, and 500 of these are classified as treasury stock.

8. The quarterly income taxes payment of $50,000 is due on December 15, 1980.

Required:

Prepare a schedule which forecasts the cash position at December 31, 1980.

(CMA adapted)

10B-11 The following are the balance sheet and income statement for the Berkley Co. for 1980.

Berkley Co.
Balance Sheet
1980

Assets

Cash		$ 32,000
Accounts receivable		22,250
Other current assets		74,300
Total current assets		$128,550
Property, plant & equipment	$240,000	
Accumulated depreciation	(60,000)	180,000
Total assets		$308,550

Liabilities

Accounts payable	$ 26,000
Mortgage payable	165,000
Owners' equity	117,550
Total liabilities and owners' equity	$308,550

Berkley Co.
Income Statement
for Year Ending December 31, 1980

Revenues	$220,000
Cost of goods sold	63,000
Contribution margin	157,000
Operating expenses (including depreciation)	25,000
Other expenses	102,000
	$ 30,000

Additional information:

1. There is an expected increase in revenues of 20%.
2. Cost of goods sold is also expected to increase 20%.
3. Operating expenses other than depreciation will increase by 15%.
4. Assets are depreciated on a straight-line basis over 20 years.
5. Other expenses will increase by 10%.
6. Owners will add $30,000 to the firm for further investments.

7. Machinery will be purchased for $40,000 on December 15 (ignore any depreciation).
8. Ending accounts payable will be $28,500.
9. Mortgage payment for 1981 is $5,000.
10. Ending accounts receivable are expected to be $26,400.

Required:

a. Pro forma income statement
b. Cash budget
c. Pro forma balance sheet

10B-12 The Patton Corporation has gone through a period of rapid expansion to reach its present size of seven divisions. The expansion program has placed strains on its cash resources. Therefore, the need for better cash planning at the corporate level has become very important.

At the present time each division is responsible for the collection of receivables and the disbursements for all operating expenses and approved capital projects. The corporation does exercise control over division activities and has attempted to coordinate the cash needs of the divisions and the corporation. However, it has not yet developed effective division cash reports from which it can determine the needs and availability of cash in the next budgetary year. As a result of inadequate information, the corporation permitted some divisions to make expenditures for goods and services which need not have been made or which could have been postponed until a later time while other divisions had to delay expenditures which should have had a greater priority.

The 1981 cash receipts and disbursements plan prepared by the Western Division for submission to the corporate office is presented below.

The following additional information was used by the Western Division to develop the cash receipts and disbursements budget.

1. Receipts—Miscellaneous receipts are estimated proceeds from the sales of unneeded equipment.
2. Sales—Travel and entertainment represents the costs required to produce the sales volume projected for the year. The other sales costs consist of $50,000 for training new sales personnel, $25,000 for attendance by sales personnel at association meetings (not sales shows), and $125,000 for sales management salaries.
3. Administration—The personnel costs include $50,000 for salary and department operating costs, $20,000 for training new personnel, and $40,000 for management training courses for current employees. The general management costs include salaries and office costs for the division management, $310,000, plus $10,000 for officials' travel to Patton Corporation meetings and $30,000 for in-

dustry and association conferences.

4. Capital expenditures—Planned expenditures for capital items during 1981 are as follows:

Capital programs approved by the corporation:

Items ordered for delivery in 1981.. $300,000
Items to be ordered in 1981 for
   delivery in 1981................ $700,000
New programs to be submitted to
   corporation during 1981......... $240,000

Western Division
Budgeted Cash Receipts and Disbursements
For the Year Ended December 31, 1981
(000 omitted)

Receipts:	
Collections on account.............	$9,320
Miscellaneous....................	36
	$9,356
Disbursements:	
Production	
Raw materials.................	2,240
Labor and fringe benefits........	2,076
Overhead.....................	2,100
Sales	
Commissions..................	395
Travel & entertainment..........	600
Other........................	200
Administrative	
Accounting....................	80
Personnel....................	110
General management...........	350
Capital expenditures..............	1,240
	$9,391
Excess of receipts over	
(under) disbursements..............	$ (35)

Required:

Present a revised Budgeted Cash Receipts and Disbursement Statement for the Western Division. Design the format of the revised statement to include adequate detail so as to improve the ability of the corporation to judge the urgency of the cash needs. Such a statement would be submitted by all divisions to provide the basis for overall corporation cash planning.

(CMA, adapted)

10B-13   The Melcher Co. produces farm equipment at several plants. The business is seasonal and cyclical in nature. The company has attempted to use budgeting for planning and controlling activities, but the variable nature of the business has caused some company officials to be skeptical about the usefulness of budgeting to the company. The accountant for the Adrian plant has been using a system he calls "flexible budgeting" to help his plant management control operations.

The company President asks him to explain what the term means, how he applies the system at the Adrian plant and how it can be applied to the company as a whole. The accountant presents the following data as part of his explanation.

Budget data for 1981

Normal monthly capacity of the plant in direct labor hours	10,000 hours	
Material costs 6 lbs. @ $1.50	$9.00 per unit	
Labor costs 2 hours @ $3.00	$6.00 per unit	

Overhead estimate at normal monthly capacity

Variable (controllable):	
Indirect labor	$ 6,650
Indirect materials	600
Repairs	750
Total Variable	$ 8,000
Fixed (non-controllable):	
Depreciation	3,250
Supervision	3,000
Total Fixed	$ 6,250
Total Fixed and Variable	$14,250

Planned units for January 1981	4,000
Planned units for February 1981	6,000

Actual data for January 1981

Hours worked	8,400
Units produced	3,800
Costs incurred:	
Material (24,000 lbs.)	$36,000
Direct Labor	25,200
Indirect Labor	6,000
Indirect Materials	600
Repairs	1,800
Depreciation	3,250
Supervision	3,000
Total	$75,850

Required:

a. Prepare a budget for January.
b. Prepare a report for January comparing actual and budgeted costs for the actual activity for the month.

(CMA adapted)

10B-14   Over the past several years, the Programme Corporation has encountered difficulties estimating its cash flows. The result has been a rather strained relationship with its banker.

Programme's controller would like to develop a means by which he can forecast the firm's monthly operating cash flows. The following data was gathered to facilitate the development of such a forecast.

1. Sales have been and are expected to increase at .5% each month.
2. 30% of each month's sales are for cash; the other 70% are on open account.
3. Of the credit sales, 80% are collected in the first month following the sale and the remaining 20% are collected in the second month. There are no bad debts.
4. Gross margin on sales averages 25%.
5. Programme purchases enough inventory each month to cover the following month's sales.
6. All inventory purchases are paid for in the month of purchase at a 2% cash discount.
7. Monthly expenses are: Payroll - $1,500; Rent - $400; Depreciation -$120; Other cash expenses - 1% of that month's sales. There are no accruals.
8. Ignore the effects of corporate income taxes, dividends and equipment acquisitions.

Required:

Using the data above, develop a mathematical model the controller can use for his calculations. Your model should be capable of calculating the monthly operating cash inflows and outflows for any specified month.

(CMA adapted)

10B-15   The Wyoming Division of Reid Corporation produces an intricate component part used in Reid's major product line. The division manager has been concerned recently by a lack of coordination between purchasing and production personnel and believes that a monthly budgeting system would be better than the present system.

Wyoming's division manager has decided to develop budget information for the third quarter of the current year as a trial before the budget system is implemented for an entire fiscal year. In response to the division manager's request for data which could be used to develop budget information, the division controller accumulated the following data.

Sales

Sales through June 30, 1981, the first six months of the current year, are 24,000 units. Actual sales in units for May and June and estimated unit sales for the next four months are detailed as follows:

May (actual)........... 4,000
June (actual)........... 4,000
July (estimated)........ 5,000
August (estimated)..... 6,000
September (estimated).. 7,000
October (estimated).... 7,000

Wyoming Division expects to sell 60,000 units during the year ending December 31, 1981.

Direct Material

Data regarding the materials used in the component are shown in the schedule below. The desired monthly ending inventory for all direct materials is to have sufficient materials on hand to produce the next month's estimated sales.

Direct material	Units of direct materials per finished component	Cost per unit	Inventory level 6/30/81
#101	6	$2.40	35,000 units
#211	4	3.60	30,000 units
#242	2	1.20	14,000 units

Direct labor

Each component must pass through three different processes to be completed. Data regarding the direct labor is presented below.

Process	Direct labor hours per finished component	Cost per direct labor hour
Forming	.80	$8.00
Assembly	2.00	5.50
Finishing	.25	6.00

Factory Overhead

The division produced 27,000 components during this six-month period through June 30, 1981. The actual variable overhead costs incurred during this six-month period are shown below. The division controller believes the variable overhead costs will be incurred at the same rate during the last six months of 1981.

Supplies	$ 59,400
Electricity	27,000
Indirect labor...............	54,000
Other	8,100
Total variable overhead.......	$148,500

The fixed overhead costs incurred during the first six months of 1981 amounted to $93,500. Fixed overhead costs are budgeted for the full year as follows:

Supervision	$ 60,000
Taxes	7,200
Depreciation	86,400
Other	32,400
Total fixed overhead.........	$186,000

Finished Goods Inventory

The desired monthly ending inventory in units of completed components is 80 percent of the next month's estimated sales. There are 5,000 finished units in the inventory on June 30, 1981.

Required:

a. Prepare a production budget in units for the Wyoming Division for the third quarter ending September 30, 1981.

b. Without prejudice to your answer in Requirement a, assume the Wyoming Division plans to produce 18,000 units during the third quarter ending September 30, 1981, and 60,000 units for the year ending December 31, 1981.

    1. Prepare a Direct Materials Purchase Budget in units and dollars for the third quarter ending September 30, 1981.

    2. Prepare a Direct Labor Budget in hours and dollars for the third quarter ending September 30, 1981.

    3. Prepare a Factory Overhead Budget for the six-month period ending December 31, 1981.

c.   Assume Wyoming Division actually produced 38,000 components during the six-month period of July 1 - December 31, 1981, and incurred variable overhead of $203,300 and fixed overhead of $95,000. Evaluate Wyoming Division's performance for the last six months of 1981 with respect to its control of factory overhead costs. Show and explain briefly any supporting calculations used in your evaluation.

(CMA, adapted)

Learning Objectives

Chapter 11 introduces the concept of responsibility accounting and the role it plays in management accounting systems. This chapter also discusses performance reporting for cost centers. Studying this chapter should enable you to:

1. Distinguish between controllable costs and direct costs and explain why this distinction is important to responsibility accounting.
2. Discuss the general types of responsibility centers.
3. Explain how a typical responsibility accounting system functions.
4. Describe a performance report and explain how it is used in a responsibility accounting system.
5. List and evaluate the guidelines which have been developed for assigning controllability.
6. Recognize the problems created by the existence of service department costs.
7. Discuss how the use of a responsibility accounting system might result in suboptimization of organizational goals.

11

Responsibility Accounting and Performance Reporting for Cost Centers

RESPONSIBILITY accounting is an accounting system which emphasizes the human element of the firm and its effect on operations. Responsibility accounting stresses the control or influence that a manager can exert within the segment of the organization which operates under his direction. Ideally, the manager's participation in establishing the budget for his segment and his responsibility for its operations is based on those economic factors that he can control or at least influence. The manager is held responsible for attaining the performance level which was budgeted for his segment.

Responsibility accounting aids in the delegation of authority by permitting the various levels of management within the firm to make decisions regarding those economic factors which they can control. Accounting information is collected and classified on the basis of the responsibility structure of the organization. This information, in part, is the same information which is collected for planning and financial accounting purposes, but is reclassified to meet responsibility accounting needs.

CONTROLLABLE ECONOMIC FACTORS

The controllable economic factors which are found in any firm include revenues, costs, assets, liabilities, and stockholders' equity. Somewhere in the management hierarchy, decisions regarding all of these factors are made. Responsibility accounting identifies the individuals who are making these decisions and aids in holding these individuals accountable for their decisions and actions.

Two classifications or definitions of costs are appropriate for responsibility accounting purposes: controllable costs and noncontrollable costs. These concepts of controllable and noncontrollable may also be applied to revenues, assets, liabilities, and owners' equity as will be explained later in this chapter.

CONTROLLABLE VERSUS NONCONTROLLABLE COSTS

Responsibility accounting requires that costs be classified in terms of the ability of individuals to influence costs in a given time period. The following definition of controllable costs, while more stringent than need be for responsibility accounting, is nonetheless applicable: A controllable cost is a cost which can be traced to a specific responsibility center on a nonarbitrary basis and which can be directly influenced by the manager of that center in a given time period. A noncontrollable cost cannot be directly influenced by the responsibility center manager. Thus it is the managers who influence specific costs who should participate in planning those costs and who should be held accountable for those costs during the operating period. If the entire firm is considered to be a responsibility center, all costs are considered controllable by someone at some level in the organization. Therefore, in assigning costs to a responsiblity center, the controllability of costs by someone in that center is a primary consideration.

There are certain common misconceptions regarding controllable costs, fixed costs, variable costs, direct or traceable costs, and indirect or common costs. It is important to note that the dichotomy of fixed and variable costs has no relationship to controllable and noncontrollable costs. All costs within a given responsibility center can be classified either as direct or indirect costs. Direct costs are those costs that can be traced to a given segment of the organization (in this case, a responsibility center) on a non-arbitrary basis. Theoretically, if a responsibility center was eliminated, the direct cost would also be eliminated. All controllable costs are direct costs, because controllable costs can be traced to a specific cost center. However, all direct costs in a responsibility center may not be controllable by the manager of that center. For example, depreciation on equipment might be traceable to a production foreman's responsibility center, even though the foreman cannot control that particular cost.

Indirect or common costs are those costs which are common to more than one segment of the organization (in this case, the responsibility center). Any cost assignment is based on some arbitrary method of allocation. Therefore, all indirect costs are noncontrollable costs for any specific responsibility center.

At each level within the organization, a manager is held directly responsible for the controllable costs of his operation. In addition, he is also responsible for the controllable costs of those segments which are headed by his subordinates. This structure of responsibility provides for the delegation of authority at the lowest possible level of management and recognition of the chain of command and span of control principles.

FORMS OF RESPONSIBILITY CENTERS

Responsibility centers can be classified based on the financial factors which the manager in charge of the responsibility center can influence. A common method of classification is to consider a responsibility center as either a cost center, a profit center or an investment center. Each of these forms of responsibility centers is discussed below.

Cost Centers

The difference between a cost center and an expense center is related to the concept of period versus product costs. The costs of an expense center are usually period costs, while the costs of a cost center normally relate to product costs which are inventoried until the goods are sold. The terms cost and expense center are often considered to be interchangeable in practice.

In a production department where output can be measured objectively in dollars and a specific output is associated with a given cost level, the term cost center is usually used in describing the segment. The segment manager is then held accountable for a specific dollar output at a given cost level.

Cost centers or expense centers are established when conditions are such that the responsible manager can influence only costs. For a cost to be incurred in a given cost center, that cost center should be required to produce a specified amount of output. Since, in certain cases, output cannot feasibly be measured in terms of dollars, the term expense center may be appropriate. Examples of such cases are the accounting department's and purchasing department's contributions to the firm.

Profit Centers

Profit centers are established in those situations where the responsibility center manager can influence both the expenses and revenues of his center. In practice, all or part of the revenues reported by many profit centers are actually the result of sales to other segments of the firm. The price attached to these "intersegment" sales is called a transfer price and is discussed in Chapter 12. For managerial accounting purposes, a profit center must have measurable outputs if a transfer price is to be used to measure intersegment sales. Of course, for financial accounting purposes, only sales to third parties are considered in determining income. The profit center concept is useful, however, in that it allows the manager to make decisions concerning costs and revenues in attaining the expected profit for his segment.

Investment Centers

The investment center concept places the responsible manager in a situation that is analogous to running his own business. The investment center manager is held responsible for producing a future planned income by utilizing a certain amount of invested capital. In other words, the investment center manager can influence revenues, expenses, and the capital invested in his segment. This manager must utilize all resources available to him in order to acquire the best overall results possible. Most divisions of large corporations are actually investment centers, but the term is not widely used in practice. Instead, investment centers are usually referred to as profit centers.

ORGANIZATION STRUCTURE AND RESPONSIBILITY ACCOUNTING

To be effective, responsibility accounting systems are developed along the decision-making lines of authority. If the organizational structure is developed on the basis of authority and decision-making responsibilities, then planning, control and performance reporting can be developed using the same organizational structure.

The job descriptions for the managers in the various responsibility centers should identify the functions, responsibilities, and authority of the manager with respect to his position. Each manager should be concerned with the controllable economic factors that fall within his sphere of responsibilities. In addition, the integration provided by the planning function should assure that the responsibility centers will all act in the best interests of the entire firm. In other words, the ideal situation is for a manager to act in the best interests of his segment while also simultaneously acting in the best interests of the firm as a whole.

ILLUSTRATION OF RESPONSIBILITY ACCOUNTING COST CENTERS

As was previously stated, the responsibility accounting system should be related to the general lines of accountability and authority found in the company's organization chart, if at all possible. A partial organization chart of Sax Company is presented in Illustration 11-1. Only the segment which is related to the Power Turbine Shaft Division is included in detail.

Illustration 11-1
Segments of Organization Chart Relevant to
the Power Turbine Shaft Division

The budgets found in Chapter 10 (Short-Range Planning) are developed for the entire division on an accrual accounting basis. For responsibility accounting purposes, these budgets have limited usefulness because the format and detail does not permit the assignment of specific managerial responsibility. To be useful for responsibility accounting purposes, the forecast budgets would have to be recast according to the responsibility format, starting at the lowest level of management where controllable factors can be identified and where the decision-making process takes place. Illustration 11-2 is an example of a responsibility forecast budget for the manager of the machining department for the month of February 1981.

The forecast budget, and ultimately, the entire performance report for the machining department is based on those factors subject to the control of the machining department manager. Illustration 11-2 is only one po-

Illustration 11-2
Responsibility Budget
Machining Department

Manager—Machining Department
Month *February*

Forecast Production 20,000
Actual Production

		(1)	(2)	(3)	(4)	(5)	(6)
			Flexible (Control) Budget at Standard			*Variances (Unfavorable)*	
	Per Unit	*Forecast Budget at Standard* a		*Actual This Month*	*Actual Year To Date* b	*This Month*	*Year To Date* c
Controllable Costs:							
Direct Labor	$2.00	$ 40,000			$ 33,500		$500
Direct Materials	4.00	80,000			68,000		–0–
Rework Time	.05	1,000			500		350
Setup Time	.04	800			1,020		(340)
Indirect Materials & Supplies	.30	6,000			4,900		200
Total Controllable Costs .	$6.39	$127,800			$107,920		$710

a Column (1)   refers to the budget for one month only. In this case, it represents the forecast for the month of February.
b This column pertains to January performance only. None of the performance in February is yet included in the actual to date.
c This column is explained in the text.

tential format for such a responsibility budget. A firm generally uses that format which best meets the needs of its management.

The forecast budget (column 1) for the machining department is prepared using established standards for the controllable costs at a level of 20,000 units of production. Last month's (January) production of 17,000 units represents the year-to-date production costs at the beginning of February. The actual controllable costs incurred in producing the 17,000 units are given in column four of Illustration 11–2. The flexible (control) budget for the year-to-date is developed by considering the year-to-date variances (column 6), and the actual controllable costs (column 4). For example, the direct labor cost at standard that should have been used to date is the actual cost of $33,500 plus the favorable variance of $500, for a total cost of $34,000.

During February, the machining department completed 21,000 units of the product. This department had the same dollar amount of work-in-process inventory at the end of the month as it had at the beginning of the month. The forecast budget was developed on the basis of 20,000 units of production, but 21,000 units were actually produced. To prepare a performance report when there are variable controllable costs involved, a flexible budget or a control budget must be prepared after-the-fact, but before any variances can be calculated. The control budget considers the actual activity that took place at the standard cost of producing that activity. Actual costs accumulated in the records are then compared with the standard costs at the same level of activity (21,000 units for February). Illustration 11-3 shows the completed responsibility report for the machining department.

The performance report presented in Illustration 11–3 for the machining department manager includes more detail than is necessary for a variance analysis of the controllable costs. All six columns of Illustration 11–3 should be reviewed in order to understand the use of responsibility accounting for planning, control, and performance evaluation purposes.

The forecast budget (column 1) included in the responsibility report presented in Illustration 11–3 is not needed for variance analysis purposes. The basis of performance reporting for a cost center is the comparison of budgeted costs and actual costs for the output produced. Measures other than cost factors, such as percentage of volume attained, efficiency ratios, and cost ratios are also usually developed. In certain situations, these measures may be more important than cost variances.

The actual collection of costs and related information for responsibility accounting takes place on a regular basis. Actual performance reporting for financial control takes place as frequently as management deems nec-

Illustration 11-3
Responsibility Report
Machining Department

Manager—Machining Department
Month *February*

Forecast Production 20,000
Actual Production 21,000

	Per Unit	(1) *Forecast Budget at Standard* [a]	(2) *Flexible (Control) Budget at Standard* [b]	(3) *Actual This Month* [c]	(4) *Actual Year To Date* [d]	(5) *This Month* [e]	(6) *Year To Date* [f]
						Variances (Unfavorable)	
Controllable Costs:							
Direct Labor	$2.00	$ 40,000	$ 42,000	$ 43,000	$ 76,500	($1,000)	($ 500)
Direct Materials	4.00	80,000	84,000	84,400	152,400	(400)	(400)
Rework Time	.05	1,000	1,050	800	1,300	250	600
Setup Time	.04	800	840	700	1,720	140	(200)
Indirect Materials & Supplies	.30	6,000	6,300	5,500	10,400	800	1,000
Total Controllable Costs	$6.39	$127,800	$134,190	$134,400	$242,320	($ 210)	$ 500

a Column one is the original forecast budget for 20,000 units of production at the standard cost.
b Column two is the flexible or control budget prepared at the end of the reporting period. The basis for this budget is actual activity, 21,000 units, at the standard cost.
c Column three is the actual controllable costs incurred at the actual production level of 21,000 units.
d Column four is actual production costs for the year-to-date (for January and February). When column four from Illustration 11-2 is added to column three from Illustration 11-3, the sum of the two equals the actual year-to-date, column four, in Illustration 11-3.
e The variances from the budgeted amounts for the month of February represents the difference between columns two and three—the control budget costs at 21,000 units and the actual costs at 21,000 units. These variances are presented in column five.
f Column six shows the variances between the control budget and actual costs for the year-to-date. To develop column six in Illustration 11-3, the year-to-date variances on February 1 (from Illustration 11-2) and the variances for February from column five in Illustration 11-3 must be summed.

essary to evaluate a given cost center. The performance report should be viewed as an additional cost control tool for the use of the responsible manager as well as a performance evaluation tool for the use of his superiors.

THE RESPONSIBILITY ACCOUNTING SYSTEM

Performance reports are integrated by responsibility levels. If a subordinate is responsible for a given financial factor, the subordinate's superior is also responsible for that same factor. The organization chart presented in Illustration 11–1 outlines the levels of responsibility in the Power Turbine Shaft Division. Performance reporting, both within the Division and to the President of Sax Company, follows the lines of authority and responsibility established by the organization chart.

The reporting relationships established for responsibility accounting are identified in Illustration 11–4. Each of the reports is condensed at the next level of management by reporting only the "bottom line" of subordinates' performance reports.

The total controllable costs which were included on the performance report of the manager of the machining department become a single line on the report of the production manager. The production manager's performance report also includes the bottom line from the finishing and pressing department manager's report. The production manager is also held responsible for the other costs of production which neither the manager of the machining department nor the manager of the finishing and pressing department can influence. As the production manager can influence only costs, his sphere of responsibility is a cost center.

The bottom line on the production manager's performance report becomes one line of the general manager's performance report. The controllable cost totals of the sales manager and division staff are also a part of the general manager's performance report. All Power Turbine Shaft Division costs which are controllable by the general manager appear on the general manager's performance report. In addition, the general manager has controllable revenues from the sales manager's performance report. Therefore, at a minimum, the general manager's sphere of responsibility may be considered a profit center. If the general manager can also influence capital investment, then his sphere of responsibility is an investment center.

The controllable income for the Power Turbine Shaft Division can be traced to a single line item included on the company president's performance report. The company president is held responsible for all of the subordinates within the firm. His sphere of responsibility is obviously an investment center because the president can control revenues, costs, and capital investments.

Illustration 11-4
Responsibility Accounting Performance Reports
President—Sax Company
Month *February*

	Budget		Variances (Unfavorable)	
	This Month	*Year To Date*	*This Month*	*Year To Date*
Controllable Income:				
→Power Turbine Shaft Division	$119,100	$ 300,700	($6,200)	($2,480)
Other Divisions °	256,000	552,000	2,000	4,500
Total Controllable Income . . .	$375,100	$ 852,700	($4,200)	$2,020
Controllable Costs:				
Other Corporate Costs ° . . .	150,000	300,000	(5,000)	(6,000)
Controllable Income	$225,100	$ 552,700	($9,200)	($3,980)

General Manager—Power Turbine Shaft Division
Month *February*

	Budget		Variances (Unfavorable)	
	This Month	*Year To Date*	*This Month*	*Year To Date*
Controllable Revenues:				
Sales Manager	$575,000	$1,175,000	($5,000)	($3,000)
Controllable Costs:				
Sales Manager	134,000	270,500	500	2,000
→Production Manager	219,250	396,800	(250)	720
Division Staff	73,500	147,000	(1,500)	(1,600)
Other Division Costs °	29,150	60,000	50	(600)
Controllable Income	$119,100	$ 300,700	($6,200)	($2,480)

Production Manager
Month *February*

	Budget		Variances (Unfavorable)	
	This Month	*Year To Date*	*This Month*	*Year To Date*
Controllable Costs:				
→Machining Department	$134,190	$ 242,320	($ 210)	$ 500
Finishing and Pressing Department	71,190	128,820	190	900
Other Costs °	13,870	25,660	(230)	(680)
	$219,250	$ 396,800	($ 250)	$ 720

Manager—Machining Department
Month *February*

Forecast Production This Month   20,000
Actual Production This Month   21,000
Actual Production Year to Date   38,000

	Budget		Variances (Unfavorable)	
	This Month	*Year To Date*	*This Month*	*Year To Date*
Controllable Costs:				
Direct Labor	$ 42,000	$ 76,500	($1,000)	($ 500)
Direct Materials	84,000	152,400	(400)	(400)
Rework Time	1,050	1,300	250	600
Setup Time	840	1,720	140	(200)
Indirect Materials and Supplies	6,300	10,400	800	1,000
Total Controllable Costs	$134,190	$ 242,320	($ 210)	$ 500

° These numbers are condensed. In an actual report, detail would be presented.

MANAGEMENT BY EXCEPTION

After the forecast budgets are developed with the participation of management, it is up to the managers to meet or achieve the plans as stated in their budgets. When actual results are recorded and the performance reports are prepared, management need only consider the significant variances from the budget. The performance report should place major emphasis on variances, because variances should be the focus of management's attention. The reports in Illustration 11–4 contain the minimum information necessary for the month or year-to-date variances. The emphasis on variances assists management in concentrating its attention on the exceptions from the budget. This is called management by exception. In order to increase the emphasis on variances, many firms express variances both in dollars and as percentages of the budget. The budgeted amounts found in the performance reports are dependent on the emphasis of management and on the type of responsibility center producing the report (i.e., cost center, profit center, or investment center).

THE REPORTING CYCLE

The timing of reporting is crucial because reports must meet the needs of management. If the nature of a responsibility center's operations are such that a daily report is necessary for control purposes, then that center should receive the performance report on a daily basis. Remember, responsibility reporting is considered a tool for management use, not a threat. Variances are early warnings to management that something needs attention. The more important the item is to management, the more critical the time factor becomes.

Each manager should receive only those reports he needs. Again, a sensitive area may warrant daily reporting. However, a manager whose operations do not require daily or weekly reports should not be included on the same reporting cycle as a manager of a more sensitive area. Typically, the longest internal reporting cycle is about one month.

Non-current information is of little value in identifying problem areas. Managers need up-to-date information in order to correct current problems. A performance report delivered today which presents an analysis of the operations which is three months old has limited usefulness in correcting current problems or measuring current performance.

IDENTIFYING RESPONSIBILITY

Controllability is not always easy to identify due to the fact that very few cost items fall under the decision-making sphere of a single individual.

Responsibility accounting requires that the individual with the most influence over costs be responsible and be held accountable for those costs. An American Accounting Association Committee identified guidelines that could be used, along with good judgment, in making the controllability decision.[1]

1. If a person has authority over both the acquisition and the use of the service, he should be charged with the cost of such service.
2. If the person can significantly influence the amount of cost through his own action, he may be charged with such cost.
3. Even if the person cannot significantly influence the amount of cost through his own direct action, he may be charged with those elements with which management desires him to be concerned, so that he will help to influence those who are responsible.

The first two guidelines are workable, but implementing the third can cause difficulties. The interrelationships of decisions also pose certain difficult, but solvable, problems in assigning cost responsibility.

For example, production planning may plan the number of units to be produced and the quantity and quality of the raw materials to be purchased. The purchasing department then acquires the raw materials. A number of events can occur that could affect variances from the point of purchase to the warehousing of the finished goods:

1. There may be a variance from the standard price. If this is the case, the purchasing manager will be held responsible for this variance.
2. It is possible that the material price variance would be favorable, but the materials could be of substandard quality. A production foreman requisitions the materials, rejects them due to their low quality, and, as a result, has an idle work force on his hands. If the foreman accepts the materials, with or without knowledge of their low quality, a host of other variances can arise. Because of the low quality of the materials, an unfavorable materials usage variance is probable. The labor usage variance could well be unfavorable due to the difficulty involved in working with low quality materials. Scrap and rework variances will be unfavorable. The obvious solution for the foreman is to reject the materials. However, if the favorable materials price variance were greater than all of the production related unfavorable variances, and if the final product were of the quality desired by the firm, the materials should be used. This would be to the over-all advantage of the firm.
3. Suppose that the materials price variance was unfavorable because

---

[1] "Report of Committee on Cost Concepts and Standards," *The Accounting Review,* April 1956, p. 189.

a higher quality material was purchased. The purchasing manager will show the unfavorable variance on his performance report. The production foreman's performance report will not be affected by the price of the raw materials used, but the high quality raw materials may have a favorable impact on a number of the production variances. The overall favorable or unfavorable impact can only be measured by considering all of the variances produced by using the higher priced, higher quality materials.

Responsibility for Service Department Costs

Service departments also present problems in responsibility accounting. If a maintenance department is responsible for the upkeep of production equipment, maintenance costs are still affected by the degree of care exercised by production personnel. Although maintenance is held responsible for the costs of maintaining equipment, production personnel can certainly influence the total maintenance costs incurred.

An approach to solving this problem of "dual responsibility" is to charge each department a standard price per hour for every hour of maintenance the department uses. This charge appears as an expense on the performance report of the department using the service. If maintenance costs exceed the department's maintenance budget, then the user department's manager will incur an unfavorable cost variance.

The maintenance department is responsible for staffing its work force in order to meet both scheduled maintenance and any emergencies which may arise. Maintenance users are then billed at a standard rate for maintenance services with a separate billing for any costs for materials or parts. Theoretically, the maintenance department could make a "profit" in the sense that its billings could exceed its costs. The attempt of this internal pricing scheme is to reduce excessive requests for services. The services will no longer be viewed as *free* by the user departments. Cost reponsibility is placed with managers who can influence the costs.

Responsibility Accounting and Human Behavior

Decisions are made by managers at all levels of an organization. Top management develops the goals and objectives of the firm and all management should work together to attain these goals and objectives. Individual managers also have their own personal goals which they are striving to attain. Professional goals are generally only one aspect of personal goals. Any aspect of control should result in decisions which are both in the best interest of the firm's goals and objectives and in the best personal interest of the manager.

If responsibility accounting is to be a useful tool in planning, control, and performance evaluation, then the entire system must be designed to eliminate or reduce the potential of a manager making decisions that appear to be in his own best interest, but are not in the best interest of the firm. The responsibility accounting system must be useful and provide performance measures based on controllable factors. Some reward structure must be developed, even if it is only verbal, to provide incentives for management and employees to act in the best interests of the firm.

SUMMARY

Under a responsibility accounting system, a manager participates in establishing the budget for the economic factors over which he has control or influence. He is then held responsible for reaching that budget. The responsibility system is generally integrated into the regular accounting system and includes information regarding controllable economic factors.

Responsibility centers are normally classified according to the economic factors that the manager of the center can influence. In the most common type of responsibility center, the cost or expense center, only costs are considered controllable by the manager of the center. The manager is generally held responsible for a specified amount of output given the costs incurred. Only those costs which are under the control of the manager are considered in evaluating his performance. A cost center typically refers to the control of the manager over product costs whereas an expense center refers to a manager's control over non-manufacturing costs. A profit center exists in those circumstances where the manager can influence both revenues and expenses associated with his segment. In the most comprehensive form of responsibility centers, the investment center, the manager is similar to a sole proprietor in that he has control over capital investments as well as revenues and expenses.

The responsibility accounting system is generally developed along lines of organizational authority. Managers at each level are responsible for their own individual financial factors as well as those of their subordinates. The system typically uses a performance report that emphasizes variances from the budget. These reports are prepared at intervals which permit the timely and effective correction of deviations from the budget.

Since control is often difficult to identify with any given individual, controllability must at times be delegated for responsibility accounting purposes. Guidelines have been established in order to assist in the controllability decision. In addition, service department costs may create problems and require the use of an allocation process, for example the charge of an internal "expense" for each hour of service consumed by a department.

One danger in using a responsibility accounting system is that a manager may take actions or make decisions that optimize his segment's performance but which are not beneficial to the firm as a whole. If possible, the system should be designed to eliminate every possibility of this occurring and should provide incentives for management at all levels to act in the best interests of the firm.

This chapter has introduced the concept of responsibility centers and illustrated the performance reporting for a cost center. The following chapter discusses performance reporting for the remaining types of responsibility centers: profit and investment centers.

KEY DEFINITIONS

Controllable cost—a cost that can be traced to a specific responsibility center on a non-arbitrary basis and is influenced by the manager of that center in a given time period.

Cost center—a type of responsibility center where the manager influences only costs and is held accountable for a specific output at a given cost level.

Direct costs—costs which can be traced to a given segment or responsibility segment of the organization on a non-arbitrary basis. All direct costs may not necessarily be controllable costs of a specific responsibility center.

Indirect costs—costs which are common to more than one segment or responsibility center of the organization. All indirect costs are non-controllable costs for any particular responsibility center.

Investment center—a type of responsibility center where the manager can influence revenues, expenses, and capital invested in his center to attain the best performance possible.

Management by exception—when variances from the budgets are emphasized in reporting procedures so that management concentrates its attention on these variances or exceptions from the budget.

Non-controllable cost—a cost which cannot be directly influenced by the manager of the responsibility center.

Profit center—a type of responsibility center where the manager can influence both revenues and expenses for his center.

Responsibility accounting—an accounting system in which the accountability for costs is assigned to a segment manager of the firm based on the amount of control or influence he possesses over those costs.

Responsibility performance reports—reports concerning the performance of various responsibility centers of the firm with respect to controllable costs. They report variances that result from a comparison of budgeted and actual controllable costs.

QUESTIONS

1. What is responsibility accounting? What additional accounting costs are added by responsibility accounting?
2. What is a controllable cost? How are controllable costs related to direct costs?
3. What is the relationship between indirect costs and noncontrollable costs?
4. When is the term "expense center" the more appropriate description of a responsibility center? When should the term "cost center" be used?
5. What is a profit center and what does it accomplish?
6. Where should management's attention be focused after performance reports have been prepared? What is the term for this?
7. In what two ways is the timing of responsibility reporting crucial?
8. What criteria are used in setting responsibility in a center? Briefly outline the three guidelines identified by the American Accounting Association.
9. In what manner may the problem of dual responsibility among service departments possibly be solved?
10. How can managers be shown that decisions made in the best interest of the firm are also in the best interest of the manager?

EXERCISES

11-1 The manager of Department 1 is responsible for costs incurred by his department. As a manager, he is responsible for the purchase of supplies, maintenance and repair costs, and labor costs. Following are costs identifiable to his department:

Departmental supplies	$1,500
Manager's salary	1,000
Direct labor	5,000
Indirect materials	800
Repairs and maintenance	550
Depreciation of equipment	1,000
Heat, light and power	350

Required:

Identify the costs which are controllable by the manager.

11-2 Determine whether each of the following costs is controllable or noncontrollable by a manufacturing department manager.

a. Depreciation on building and equipment
b. Supplies and indirect materials
c. Rent on building
d. Heat, light and power
e. Maintenance and repair costs
f. Salary of salesmen

g. Direct labor
h. Rework time

11-3 You have been hired by the Par Golf Company to look into its cost system to determine the cause of the increased costs in making golf clubs. In touring the factory you have learned that to make a wood club, certain materials are required. Jack Palmer, the president of Par Golf, had required that some system for standards be established and you have found them to be:

1 head @ $4.00
1 shaft @ $1.00
1 grip @ $2.00

During the past year, you have discovered that 10,000 woods were produced at a total cost of $71,800. Mr. Palmer said that this was an unfavorable variance of $1,800 and he wants to know where to lay the blame. Your investigation shows that Joe Duffer was the purchasing agent for shafts. Since Joe considered all shafts to be equal, he got the cheapest shaft possible at $.90. Unfortunately this required the assembly department to use 12 shafts to successfully complete 10 clubs. Other information showed actual costs of:

10,100 heads at a total cost of $40,000
10,200 grips at a total cost of $21,000

Required:

a. Calculate the total material quantity and price variances.
b. Who should be given the shaft variance?

11-4 The following data are taken from the records of a specific cost center which is controlled by a manager. Furthermore, a plant Vice President supervises the manager.

Raw materials and supplies	$10,000
Depreciation on equipment	500
Repair and maintenance costs	600
Direct labor	15,000
Heat, light and power	1,000
Salary of manager	12,000
Rental for floor space	200
Rework time	500
Salary of Vice President	20,000

Required:

Which of the above costs are controllable by the manager? Which are controllable by the plant Vice President?

11-5 Given below are the controllable costs for the assembly division of the Hays Manufacturing Company for October.

Budgeted production was 4,000 units.
Actual production was 5,000 units.
Standard costs:
  Direct labor—$5 per unit
  Direct material—$3 per unit
  Supplies—$0.75 per unit
  Other—$0.10 per unit
Actual costs for the month were as follows:

Direct labor	$25,850
Direct material	14,600
Supplies	3,500
Other	500

Required:

Prepare a responsibility accounting performance report showing variances for the assembly division for October.

11-6 The Love Tennis Company has been experiencing dissension between its purchasing and manufacturing divisions. The division that has the largest favorable variance has been promised a free tennis lesson with the company pro, Rod Connors. Your job is to determine the material and labor variances and assign them to the competing divisions.

The standard racket is comprised of:

String, 80 ft. @ $.05 per foot	=	$ 4.00
Frame @ $6.00	=	6.00
Grip @ $1.00	=	1.00
Total standard material cost per racket	=	$11.00

The standard time required to construct a racket is 1 hour at $5.00 per hour. The standard string used is a high quality catgut. In an attempt to win the contest for the purchasing division, Billy Riggs, a real hustler, purchased a cheaper nylon string at 4¢ a foot. Unfortunately, 100 feet of string per racket was required and this also increased the direct labor time per racket to 1.1 hours.

During the past month, 5,000 rackets were completed. The following data were available:

5,100 frames used—total cost = $30,400
5,200 grips used—total cost = $ 5,400
direct labor—total cost = $25,000

Required:

a. Calculate material quantity and price variances. Calculate direct labor efficiency and rate variances.
b. Assign the variances previously calculated to the division responsible.

11-7 The ABC Department of the Fox Company budgeted 1,000 units of production for April and allowed 3,000 direct labor hours for this production at a standard rate of $5.00 per hour. During March a mandatory pay raise was established which increased the labor rate to $5.75 per hour. There was no labor efficiency variance.

Required:

a. Compute the variance.
b. If the variance is unfavorable, is it fair to charge the departmental supervisor with the variance? In other words, was this specific situation controllable or noncontrollable by the supervisor?

11-8   The general foreman of Department I is responsible for the purchase of supplies, the hiring of employees and for repairs and maintenance. The following information shows all costs traceable to Department I during November.

a. Direct materials
b. Direct labor
c. Supplies and indirect materials
d. Salary of foreman
e. Salary of production manager
f. Depreciation of equipment
g. Depreciation of building
h. Rental of building
i. Advertising expense
j. Repairs and maintenance

Required:

Prepare a list of all the costs controllable by the foreman.

11-9   The following data indicate various costs traceable to the machinery department of Star Manufacturing Company for April:

	Budgeted	Actual
Direct materials	$12,000	$11,000
Direct labor	15,000	17,500
Salary of department manager	15,000	15,000
Heat, light and power	1,000	850
Repairs and maintenance	1,200	1,500
Supplies	800	600
Depreciation on equipment	500	500

Ken Fargo, the manager, is responsible for various costs incurred by the machinery department except for his own salary, which is established by upper management and for any allocated costs. Both budgeted and actual costs are at 10,000 units of production.

Required:

Prepare a responsibility accounting report for April, showing all costs controllable by Mr. Fargo. Show all variances.

11-10   The organization chart given below shows the lines of responsibility for the Stacy Manufacturing Company:

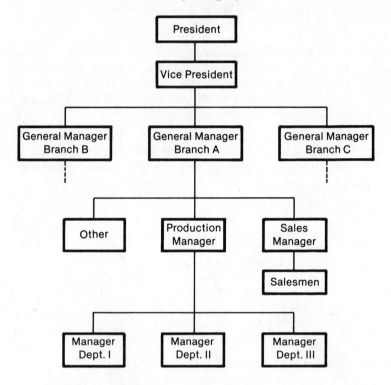

Determine whether the responsibility center for each of the following is most likely a cost, profit or investment center.

a.   Manager, Dept. III
b.   President
c.   Vice President
d.   Production manager
e.   General manager, Branch A
f.   Sales manager
g.   Salesmen on commission and with expense accounts

11-11   The production manager of Department II is responsible for various costs incurred by his department. Production planning determines the quantity and quality of raw materials to be purchased. The Purchasing Department is responsible for acquiring the raw materials ordered by the production manager.

Assume that the standard price per unit of raw material is $5.00. 2,000 units of raw material are to be ordered. Due to an increase in price, the purchasing department acquires the 2,000 units of raw material at $5.50 per unit.

Required:

a. Calculate the variance.

b. Which department should be charged with this variance?

11-12 Bob Smart is general manager of the Production Division of the
Texas Auto Company. One of his responsibilities is the acquisition of
raw materials from the purchasing department which orders them
from an outside supplier.

Assume that the standard price per unit of raw material is $2.50.
1,000 units of raw material are ordered by the purchasing department at a price of $1.50 per unit, but the materials ordered are of
sub-standard quality. If the production division works with the inferior raw material, the following variances are anticipated: a $500
unfavorable material usage variance and a $700 unfavorable labor
usage variance.

Required:

Should the production manager accept or reject the shipment of sub-
standard raw material? Support your answer.

PROBLEMS SERIES A

11A-1 The production manager, Mr. Jones, is responsible for the Production
Division of the Harris Tool Manufacturing Company. He is unable to
influence the amount of raw material used to produce a given number of units. He is also responsible for hiring and firing his employees.
He is authorized to establish the rates at which his employees will be
paid. He is responsible for the purchase of all supplies and indirect
materials and for repairs and maintenance. Mr. Jones is not held responsible for costs allocated to his department.

From the list of costs given below, select those controllable by the
production manager and those noncontrollable by him. Give a list
and total for each type.

Raw materials	$ 5,500
Depreciation on machinery	1,000
Heat, light and power	700
Maintenance and repairs	500
Direct labor	10,000
Rework time	600
Supervision of factory by guards	400
Lease rental on building	1,000
Supplies	500

11A-2 The Marshall Door Corporation is organized on a functional basis
and uses a responsibility accounting system. The production division, one of the five main divisions, is supervised by a general manager. The production division consists of three producing departments and three service departments.

During July, 10,000 units were produced by the production division. Given below are the controllable costs incurred by the six departments and the manager. Also shown in the first column are the budgeted totals.

	Budget Totals	Direct Material	Direct Labor	Manu-facturing Overhead	Total
Producing Departments					
1	$187,000	$25,000	$65,000	$100,000	$190,000
2	122,000	15,000	40,000	65,000	120,000
3	66,500	8,000	22,000	37,000	67,000
Service Departments					
A	10,000	–	–	7,500	7,500
B	8,000	–	–	10,000	10,000
C	4,500	–	–	5,000	5,000
Production manager	13,000	–	–	13,000	13,000

Required:

Prepare a cost responsibility accounting report showing all controllable costs for the production manager of the production division for July. Show all variances.

11A–3   Given below are data for the production department of the Morris Manufacturing Company for the month of September.

Forecast production . . . . 10,000 units
Actual production . . . . 12,000 units
Standards for controllable costs:
    Direct labor . . . . $3.00 per unit
    Direct material . . . . 5.00 per unit
    Rework and set up time . . . . . . 0.10 per unit
    Supplies and indirect materials . . . 0.50 per unit
Actual costs for month:
    Direct labor $37,000
    Direct material 59,500
    Rework time 1,000
    Supplies 5,500

Required:

Prepare a responsibility accounting performance report for the production department for September. Make your report similar to the one in Illustration 11-3. Show forecast and control budgets, actual costs and all variances.

11A–4   The Mitchell-Parks Corporation uses responsibility reporting (performance reports) for its various departments. Given below is a comparison of actual costs with control budgeted costs for Production Department A for May. The department manager is held responsible for various costs incurred by his department such as the purchase of materials, the hiring of employees and the requisition of repairs and maintenance. Although the manager's salary is listed under "production salaries and wages," his salary is not controllable by him. The Vice President of production determines the manager's salary.

Assume that 10,000 units of production were budgeted and 11,000 were actually produced during May. The manager's salary is $1,200 per month.

	Budgeted	Actual
Departmental costs		
Direct materia. ($5 per unit)	$ 50,000	$ 51,000
Production salaries and wages		
($1,200 plus $4 per unit)	41,200	48,000
Repairs and maintenance (fixed)	1,000	850
Indirect materials and supplies (fixed)	15,000	14,700
Depreciation on machinery (fixed)	500	500
Salary of superintendent (fixed)	20,000	20,000
Heat, light, and power ($500 plus		
$.05 per unit)	1,000	1,100
Total costs	$128,700	$136,150

Required:

Prepare a revised reponsibility accounting performance report for Production Department A showing the actual variances from the budget for May. Show only the costs that are controllable by the manager.

11A-5 John Able is the manager of the Finishing and Processing Division at the Houston Plant of the Morgan Company. His responsibility report for March is as follows:

	Flexible Budget	Actual	Variances (unfavorable)
Controllable Costs:			
Direct materials	$10,000	$12,500	($2,500)
Direct labor	5,000	6,900	(1,900)
Supplies	850	600	250
Repairs and maintenance	1,000	1,200	(200)
Total controllable costs	$16,850	$21,200	($4,350)

Additional data:

1. 5,000 pounds of raw material at a price of $2.00 per pound were budgeted for March ($10,000). During March the puchasing department could not obtain the materials at $2.00 per pound. The price increased to $2.50 per pound. Therefore, 5,000 pounds of raw material were obtained at a price of $2.50 per pound ($12,500).

2. When the budget was prepared in January, the labor rate was $5.00 per hour. However, the labor rate was increased to

$6.00 per hour when a union contract was signed in February. Also, 100 hours of overtime were authorized during March even though no amount of overtime had been approved by the budget. Overtime was paid at a rate of 1½ times the regular rate ($9.00 per hour). This overtime was incurred during an emergency in which Mr. Able's department aided another department. The budget allowed 1,000 hours; the actual hours worked conformed to the budgeted hours plus the 100 authorized overtime hours.

Required:

a. Is the given responsibility report for Mr. Able's department a fair one? Mr. Able argues that he should not be charged with the unfavorable variances resulting from direct materials and direct labor. Do you agree with Mr. Able's argument?

b. Prepare a revised responsibility report showing only those costs controllable by Mr. Able and variances chargeable to him.

11A-6   Baker and Carr Enterprises consists of four divisions which are supervised by the manufacturing Vice President; the four divisions are the assembly division, the finishing and processing division, the machining division and the packing division. Each division is supervised by a manager and each division consists of several departments. Each department is supervised by a department head. Responsibility accounting performance reports are prepared monthly for each department head, the division manager and the Vice President.

The finishing and processing division consists of two departments. The following data for the finishing and processing division for December show the controllable costs of the manager:

	Department X		Department Y	
	Budgeted	*Actual*	*Budgeted*	*Actual*
Controllable Costs:				
Direct materials	$12,000	$12,500	$ 9,500	$ 9,400
Direct labor	25,000	27,500	18,000	16,500
Supplies	2,000	1,600	1,200	1,350
Repairs and maintenance .	1,000	950	700	850
Total controllable costs . .	$40,000	$42,550	$29,400	$28,100

Additional data:

Total controllable costs for the other three divisions for December were as follows:

	Budgeted	*Actual*
Assembly division	$135,000	$132,600
Machining division	117,500	120,200
Packing division	175,600	172,050

Required:

a. Prepare a performance report for the division manager of finishing and processing assuming that "Other Costs" for this division are:

Budgeted—$100,000
Actual   —$ 99,000

b. Prepare a performance report for the manufacturing Vice President assuming that "Other Costs" for his segment are:

Budgeted—$ 55,000
Actual   —$ 57,100

11A–7 Following is a simplified organizational chart showing the lines of responsibility for the Carter Company:

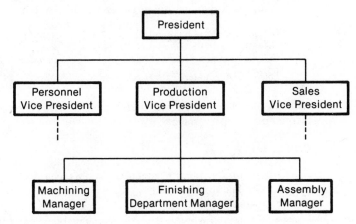

Prepare a chart like the one shown below. Determine whether each given account is a cost controllable by the four officers shown on the chart. Give answers as "Yes" or "No."

Controllable Costs

	By Manager of Machining Department	By Vice President of Production	By Vice President of Sales	By President
Production-direct materials				
Salary of sales Vice President				
Salesmen salaries				
Direct labor—assembly				
Supplies—finishing				
Repairs and maintenance— machining				
Salary of manager				
Depreciation— machinery				

11A–8   The following data indicate the standard material, quantity and cost per unit of the product produced by the manufacturing department:

2 pounds of material X @ $2.00 per pound
2 pounds of material Y @ $1.50 per pound
1 pound of material Z @ $1.00 per pound

Due to an error in the purchasing department, an insufficient amount of material Y was ordered. Therefore, material X was substituted for material Y. Furthermore, the price of material Z increased to $1.25 per pound. The manufacturing department produced 5,000 units of the product at the actual quantities used and the actual costs:

14,000 pounds of material X @ $2.00 per pound = $28,000
6,000 pounds of material Y @ $1.50 per pound =   9,000
5,000 pounds of material Z @ $1.25 per pound =   6,250

Total cost for material for production of 5,000 units $43,250

As a result, the manufacturing department was charged with unfavorable material variances.

Required:

a.   Compute the amount of material variance charged to the department. Separate the material variance into quantity and price variances.
b.   Should the unfavorable material variance be charged to the manufacturing department? If not, who should probably be charged with it?

11A–9   Assuming that this applies to a Production Department, classify each of the following items into: Controllable (C) and Noncontrollable (NC) costs, Direct (D) and Indirect (I) costs.

a.   Advertising expense
b.   Direct materials
c.   Depreciation on equipment
d.   Direct labor
e.   Supplies used
f.   Depreciation on building
g.   Salary of department head
h.   Heat, light, and power
i.   Rental of plant
j.   Indirect materials.

11A–10 The Sutton Company consists of three divisions—the sales division, production division, and personnel division. Each division is supervised by a manager who is held responsible for various costs. The approved budgets (flexible) for each division are as follows:

	Sales Manager	Production Manager	Personnel Manager
Controllable Costs:			
Direct materials	–	$10,000	–
Direct labor	–	25,000	–
Salaries	$50,000	–	$35,000
Supplies	1,000	2,000	1,500
Repairs and maintenance	500	1,500	500
Total	$51,500	$38,500	$37,000

The actual costs incurred by each division are as follows:

	Sales	Production	Personnel
Controllable Costs:			
Direct materials	–	$12,000	–
Direct labor	–	23,800	–
Salaries	$51,000	–	$34,000
Supplies	800	1,700	1,450
Repairs and maintenance	300	1,100	350
Total	$52,100	$38,600	$35,800

Required:

a. Prepare a responsibility accounting performance report for the production division showing budget, actual and variances. (Period is June.)

b. Prepare a performance report for the Vice President who is responsible for all three divisions. In preparing the report, use only "Total Controllable Costs" for each division. It is not necessary to itemize each cost. Also assume that "Other Costs for Vice President" are: Budgeted—$35,000; Actual—$34,400.

PROBLEMS SERIES B

11B-1 Robin Smith is the regional sales manager for International Fragrances, Inc. As such, she is responsible for the management of sales personnel in her area, including the determination of sales salaries. Company policy, however, requires that a minimum salary of $12,000 per year be paid to each sales person.

As a sales manager, Ms. Smith is also responsible for budgeting and arranging for all local and regional advertising and other selling expenses in her area. National advertising is handled by the corporate offices of International Fragrances with total annual costs allocated to each regional area.

Cost information for Ms. Smith's region follows below:

Total sales salaries: (13 sales personnel)	$215,000
Local advertising and promotion	78,000
Regional advertising and promotion	155,000
National advertising	200,000
Display, set-up costs	12,000
Miscellaneous expenses	7,500

Required:

Given the above information, prepare a schedule of controllable and noncontrollable costs for Ms. Smith.

11B–2   The Dura-Battery Manufacturing Company is composed of three main divisions. The sales division is under the supervision of the Vice President in charge of marketing. There are five regional sales offices and a national office in this division.

During September, the company reached their target sales of $700,000 for the month. Given below are the controllable costs incurred by the five regional offices and the national offices. Budgeted totals for the month are shown in the first column.

Regional Offices	Budget Totals	Sales Salaries and Commissions	Promotion & Advertising	Other Selling & Administrative Costs	Totals
1	$10,000	$4,800	$6,500	$750	$12,050
2	10,000	3,300	4,200	900	8,400
3	12,000	6,000	4,500	1,500	12,000
4	12,000	7,150	5,280	888	13,318
5	15,000	8,900	7,000	1,250	17,150
National Office	40,000	–0–	18,050	22,799	40,849

Required:

Prepare a responsibility accounting performance report for the Vice President of marketing for September. Show all variances.

11B–3   The following information is for the production department of the Danish Furniture Manufacturers, Inc. for April.

Forecast production 7,000
Actual production 6,550

Standards for controllable costs:
Direct material . . . . $45.00 per unit
Direct labor . . . . 25.00 per unit
Indirect labor . . . . 7.50 per unit
Indirect materials and supplies . . . . 4.00 per unit
Rework and set-up time . . . . 1.50 per unit
Actual costs for the month:
Direct material $305,000
Direct labor 175,000
Indirect labor 47,500
Indirect materials and supplies 23,500
Rework and set-up time 8,850

Required:

Prepare a responsibility accounting performance report for the production department for April. Show forecast and control budgets, actual costs and all variances (See Illustration 11-3).

11B–4   The Serv-U-Tron Corporation, a manufacturer of home appliances, uses responsibility reporting for all departments. Given below is a schedule of budgeted and actual costs for the finishing department for July. The department manager is responsible for costs incurred by his department except for three items: the purchase of materials which is carried out by a central purchasing department, his own salary which is determined by the General Manager of operations, and depreciation and utility costs which are allocated among the production departments. In addition, all department managers are required to adhere to governmental regulations which stipulate that the minimum wage by law is $2.50 per hour.

During July, 500 units of production were budgeted and actually produced. The finishing department manager's salary per month is $1,350. A total of 25 production workers who each worked 160 hours were employed by the department in July. Because of the high demand for lightweight steel, the department used 350 lbs. of this material during the month at an actual price that was $.02 per lb. greater than the standard price.

Total Departmental Costs	Budgeted	Actual
Direct materials	$ 1,500	$ 2,060
Production salaries and wages	14,400	15,500
Heat, light, and power costs	750	815
Depreciation on equipment	900	900
Repairs and maintenance	450	465
Indirect materials and supplies	200	290
Total costs	$18,200	$20,030

Required:

Prepare a revised responsibility accounting performance report for the finishing department showing only those costs that are controllable by the manager and resulting actual variances from the budget for July.

11B–5 Kathy Sims is the production manager for the Q-T Toy Company. The production department consists of two divisions: assembly and finishing. Her responsibility performance report for October is as follows:

	Flexible Budget	Actual	Variances (unfavorable)
Controllable Costs:			
Direct materials	$ 9,500	$11,560	($2,060)
Direct labor	13,500	17,200	($3,700)
Supplies	600	710	(110)
Repairs and maintenance	300	320	(20)
Total controllable costs	$23,900	$29,790	($5,890)

Additional data

1. Included in the above are costs resulting from production of Christmas toy displays to be used in the company's promotion campaign according to the specifications of the Marketing department. Costs of this project were: direct materials—$750;

direct labor—$425; supplies—$70. This project was not provided for in the production department's budget.

2. During the month Ms. Sims was instructed by the Vice President of Operations to process special rush orders from customers to insure delivery in advance of the Christmas season. This resulted in 250 hours of overtime at an overtime rate of $8.50 per hour, even though this overtime had not been included in the budget.

Required:

a. Does the given responsibility report fairly account for the above costs? Ms. Sims believes that she should not be charged with unfavorable variances totalling $5,890. Do you agree with Ms. Sims? Why?

b. Prepare a revised responsibility report showing only those costs controllable by Ms. Sims and the resulting variances, if any, chargeable to her.

11B–6 The Oil Company of America, Inc. consists of three divisions supervised by the Vice President of Operations: research and development, exploration, and production and refining. Each division is supervised by a general manager and each consists of several departments. Each department has a department manager. Responsibility accounting performance reports are prepared monthly for each department manager, general manager and Vice President.

The production and refining division consists of three departments. The information provided below shows the controllable costs for departments 1, 2 and 3 in the production and refining division for February.

	Dept. 1		Dept. 2		Dept. 3	
	Budgeted	Actual	Budgeted	Actual	Budgeted	Actual
Controllable Costs:						
Direct labor .	$28,000	$26,500	$13,000	$14,800	$30,000	$30,000
Direct materials . .	55,000	57,450	25,000	23,000	60,000	61,190
Repairs and maintenance	6,500	5,980	2,100	2,555	7,500	6,450
Supplies . . .	2,200	2,100	1,500	1,310	800	630
Other indirect costs	3,000	2,550	1,400	1,560	700	820
Total controllable costs	$94,700	$94,580	$43,000	$43,225	$99,000	$99,090

Additional data:

Total controllable costs for the other two divisions for February were as follows:

	Budgeted	Actual
Research and development	$125,000	$139,700
Exploration	75,000	73,800

Required:

a. Prepare a responsibility accounting performance report for Department 1 showing the budgeted costs, actual costs and variances.

b. Prepare a performance report for the general manager of the production and refining division assuming that "Other Costs" for this division are: Budgeted—$80,000; Actual—$76,600.

c. Prepare a performance report for the Vice President of Operations assuming that "Other Costs" for his segment are: Budgeted—$105,000; Actual—$96,000.

11B–7 Given below is the basic organization chart showing the lines of responsibility for the Nature Valley Dairies, Inc.

For each item listed below, determine whether it is a cost controllable by each of the officers shown on the chart. Give answers as "Yes" or "No."

Controllable Costs

	By Sales Mgr.	By Production Dept. Mgr.	By Mktg. Vice Pres.	By Vice Pres. of Operations	By President
Quality Control Inspector salaries				✓	✓
Direct labor-production		✓		✓	✓
Delivery truck expenses				✓	✓
Advertising expense				✓	✓
Direct materials-packaging				✓	✓
Salary of Financial Vice President					✓
Repairs and maintenance-delivery				✓	✓
Salaries of quality control inspectors					
Salesmen salaries	✓		✓	N	✓
Raw materials-production	✓			✓	✓
Depreciation-production machinery				✓	✓
Excessive product spoilage due to electrical blackout					

11B–8   The production department of Mandy Enterprises, Inc. manufactures one product using three groups of workers classified according to their skill level: unskilled, semi-skilled and skilled. The wage rate for each skill level is as follows: $2.20 per hour, $2.90 per hour and $4.50 per hour, respectively. The standard direct labor hours per skill level for each unit of product are as follows:

5.50 hours @ $2.20 per hour
4.00 hours @ $2.90 per hour
2.50 hours @ $4.50 per hour

At the beginning of the month, a new union contract was signed which increased the skilled wage rate by 30% and the semi-skilled wage rate by 10%. Due to an error by the purchasing department, inferior quality raw materials were purchased. This required additional finishing work by the skilled workers. The total of this additional direct labor by skilled workers was 60 hours.

During the month the production department produced 130 units at the actual quantities and actual costs:

700 hours @ ·$2.20 per hour = $1,540.00
555 hours @ $3.19 per hour =   1,770.45
380 hours @ $5.85 per hour =   2,223.00
                              $5,533.45

As a result, the production department was charged with unfavorable labor variances.

Required:

a. Compute the amount of total labor variance charged to the department. Separate the labor variance into labor rate and efficiency variances.

b. Should all of the labor variances be charged to the production department? If not, how much should the department be charged with, and who else should probably be charged with the remainder?

11B-9 Assuming that the following applies to the local sales office of a computer manufacturer, classify each of the following into:

1. Controllable (C) and Noncontrollable (NC) costs.
2. Direct (D) and Indirect (I) costs.

a. Salesmen salaries
b. Local TV advertising
c. Salesmen travel expenses
d. Share of regional advertising budget
e. Salary of sales manager
f. Share of national advertising budget
g. Rental of sales office
h. Office salaries and supplies
i. Share of regional salesmen's convention
j. Promotional display

11B-10 The Cooke Company is composed of three divisions: marketing, production, and administrative services. The approved (flexible) budgets for each division for March are as follows:

	Marketing Manager	Production Manager	Administrative Services Manager
Controllable costs:			
Direct materials	–	$18,000	–
Direct labor	–	32,500	–
Salaries	$55,000	40,000	$75,000
Supplies	3,800	750	9,500
Maintenance	1,200	1,200	1,200
Totals	$60,000	$92,450	$85,700

The actual costs incurred by each division are as follows:

	Marketing	Production	Administrative Service
Controllable costs:			
Direct materials	–	$21,800	–
Direct labor	–	30,050	–
Salaries	$55,600	40,000	$73,000
Supplies	3,650	800	9,250
Maintenance	1,200	1,200	1,200
Totals	$60,450	$93,850	$83,450

Required:

a. Prepare a responsibility accounting performance report for the production division.

b. Prepare a performance report for the Vice President in charge of all three divisions. In preparing the report it is permissible to use only "Total Controllable Costs" for each division. Assume that "Other Costs" for the Vice President are: Budgeted— $25,000; Actual—$25,600.

11B-11 Elwood bank is a large municipal bank with several branch offices. The bank has a computer department which handles all data processing for the bank's operations. In addition, the bank acts as a service bureau by selling its expertise in systems development and excess machine time to several small business firms.

The computer department currently is treated as an expense center of the bank. The manager of the computer department prepares an expense budget annually for approval by senior bank officials. Monthly operating reports compare actual and budgeted expenses. Revenues from the department's service bureau activities are treated as "other income" by the bank and are not reflected on the computer department's operating reports. The costs of serving these clients are included in departmental reports, however.

The manager of the computer department has proposed that the bank management convert the computer department to a profit or investment center.

Required:

a. Describe the characteristics which differentiate (1) an expense center, (2) a profit center, and (3) an investment center from each other.

b. Would the manager of the computer department be likely to conduct the operations of the department differently if the department were classified as a profit center or an investment center rather than as an expense center? Explain your answer.

(CMA adapted)

11B-12 The Noton Company has operated a comprehensive budgeting system for many years. This system is a major component of the company's program to control operations and costs at its widely scattered plants. Periodically the plants' general managers gather to discuss the overall company control system with the top management.

At this year's meeting the budgetary system was severely criticized by one of the most senior plant managers. He said that the system discriminated unfairly against the older, well-run and established plants in favor of the newer plants. The impact was lower year-end bonuses and poor performance ratings. In addition, there were psychological consequences in the form of lower employee morale. In his judgment, revisions in the system were needed to make it more effective. The basic factors of Noton's budget include:

1. Announcement of an annual improvement percentage target established by top management.
2. Plant submission of budgets implementing the annual improvement target.
3. Management review and revision of the proposed budget.
4. Establishment and distribution of the final budget.

To support his argument, he compared the budget revisions and performance results. The older plants were expected to achieve the improvement target but often were unable to meet it. On the other hand, the newer plants were often excused from meeting a portion of this target in their budgets. However, their performance was usually better than the final budget.

He further argued that the company did not recognize the operating differences which made attainment of the annual improvement factor difficult, if not impossible. His plant has been producing essentially the same product for its 20 years of existence. The machinery and equipment, which underwent many modifications in the first five years, have had no major changes in recent years. Because they are old, repair and maintenance costs have increased each year, and the machines are less reliable. The plant management team has been together for the last ten years and works well together. The labor force is mature, with many of the employees having the highest seniority in the company. In his judgment, the significant improvements have been "wrung out" of the plant over the years and that merely keeping even is difficult.

For comparison he noted that one plant opened within the past four years would have an easier time meeting the company's expectations. The plant is new, containing modern equipment that is in some cases still experimental. Major modifications in equipment and operating systems have been made each year as the plant management has obtained a better understanding of the operations. The plant's management, although experienced, has been together only since its opening. The plant is located in a previously nonindustrial area and therefore has a relatively inexperienced work force.

Required:

a. Evaluate the manufacturing manager's views.
b. Equitable application of a budget system requires the ability of corporate management to remove "budgetary slack" in plant budgets. Discuss how each plant could conceal "slack" in its budget.

(CMA, adapted)

Learning Objectives

Chapter 12 discusses performance reporting for both profit centers and investment centers. Studying this chapter should enable you to:

1. Identify those financial factors considered controllable in each type of responsibility center.
2. Explain the concept of decentralization and discuss how decentralization is related to responsibility accounting.
3. Identify the usual types of transfer prices and discuss the advantages and disadvantages of each.
4. Describe the types of variances typically used in the performance evaluation of a profit center.
5. Know and apply the basic return on investment formula.
6. Discuss the problems involved in defining the concept of assets utilized.

12

Performance Reporting for Profit Centers and Investment Centers

RESPONSIBILITY accounting for profit centers and investment centers encompasses many controllable factors in addition to costs. The performance report for a cost center, discussed in Chapter 11, is based on the capability of the manager of that cost center to produce the required output at the specified quality at the standard cost of producing that output. A profit center is evaluated on both its controllable costs and its revenues. A major objective of a manager in a profit center is to realize the budgeted income for the center within the budget period.

An investment center manager is responsible for earning a budgeted return on the assets used by the center. The investment center manager should be able to make those decisions that affect revenues, costs, and invested assets for the responsibility center.

DECENTRALIZATION AND RESPONSIBILITY ACCOUNTING

As a financial tool, responsibility accounting permits a performance evaluation of the manager who makes decisions with regard to the factors under his influence and within the limits established by the top management of the firm. Responsibility accounting permits the decentralization of decision making in that the manager of each responsibility center is charged with making decisions with regard to that operation. The efforts of the individual managers are coordinated by top management, company policy, planning and any other methods for coordination that may be established by the firm.

In effect, decentralization places each profit or investment center manager in a position similar to an independent entrepreneur operating under a minimum set of constraints or policies. This procedure provides incentives for managers because performance, and therefore bonuses, are measured as if an individual manager were a sole proprietor with that segment of the firm as his own business.

The definition of the financial components of income and invested assets for both profit centers and investment centers poses certain problems from an accounting standpoint. Among these problems are: (1) determining the appropriate measure of revenues when intracompany sales are made between segments or divisions of the firm, and (2) defining assets invested in a center for purposes of calculating the return on investment for investment centers.[1]

TRANSFER PRICING FOR INTRACOMPANY SALES

A transfer price is the price that one segment of an organization pays to another segment within the same organization for the output or service of the supplying segment. In determining the performance of each unit, a transfer price is the basis for: (1) interunit sales from the viewpoint of the selling unit, and (2) variable costs to the buying unit. For financial reporting purposes, the firm recognizes a sale only when goods or services are sold to buyers external to the firm and not when one segment or division of a company sells to another. However, for purposes of performance measurement by segments, an internal sale is considered in calculating segment income; otherwise, the responsible manager would be encouraged to make only external sales in order to maximize income. Of course, top management wishes to establish transfer prices which will maximize the objectives of the firm as a whole.

Generally, the manager of a responsibility center attempts to operate his unit in such a manner as to maximize the profits of the center. Establishing a fair transfer price permits segment managers to make decisions that are in the best interest of the segment as well as in the best interests of the entire firm. These transfer prices are usually market-based, cost-based and/or negotiated. In most cases a transfer price is a combination of these bases.

Market-Based Transfer Prices

If a competitive market price is available for a product also sold internally, then the equitable transfer price, from both a theoretical and prac-

---

[1] The problem of common costs discussed in Chapter 11 and the problems involved in the allocation of these costs could have been included in this discussion and should be considered by the reader.

tical viewpoint, is the external competitive market price adjusted for any savings in cost, such as selling expenses. If savings are realized as a result of the ability of a unit to sell its product within the firm, then those savings should be fairly distributed or allocated between the buying and selling units. Examples of factors resulting from intersegment sales which may cause cost savings include improved planning, more efficient production runs or the elimination or reduction of selling and distribution expenses. A market-based transfer price for intersegment sales is the closest approximation to an "arm's length" transaction.

Any shortcomings of a market-based transfer price are usually related to the operations or uncertainties concerning the market place. Few markets are truly competitive in an economic sense and any price may be affected by the presence of a few large buyers or sellers. Market prices are also influenced by such factors as supply and demand, quantity discounts and product quality. All of these factors must be considered when an internal transfer price based on market price is established for internal company use.

Cost-Based Transfer Prices—Full Cost

Transfer prices for intersegment sales based on full cost or full cost-plus are common for the following reasons:

1. Certain products have limited or nonexistent outside markets.
2. The full cost transfer price concept is understandable to both the buyer and the seller.
3. Cost accumulations are made for inventory costing purposes so a "cost figure" is readily available.

If the transfer price is based on the actual costs incurred, then the supplying segment may have little incentive to control its costs because the full cost will be recovered by the transfer price. On the other hand, if a normal or standard cost transfer price is used, then this measure of costs which *should* have been incurred by the supplying segment provides an incentive to control costs. The use of a normal or standard cost is also consistent with the basic concepts of responsibility accounting because any efficiencies or inefficiencies are identified with the responsibility center where the cost is incurred.

Cost-Based Transfer Prices—Variable Cost

A variable cost or variable cost-plus transfer price may be justified on a theoretical basis since this transfer price is consistent with the traditional "short-run" economic decision model of a firm. A "short-run" economic decision model assumes that the manager of the supplying segment cannot influence the fixed costs of the segment in the short-run. Therefore the manager is accountable for only the variable costs of the segment and the interunit sales price should be determined using only variable costs as a base.

Negotiated Transfer Prices

Most transfer pricing approaches are negotiated in practice because an equitable price for both the selling and buying segments must be established if the price is to be meaningful. When transfer prices are based on negotiation, both the supplying and the buying segment managers arrive at a fair transfer price considering any information concerning costs and market conditions available to them. A truly negotiated transfer price assumes that neither manager involved in the negotiations has an unfair bargaining position.

In any negotiated transfer price, some arbitration procedure may be necessary in order to neutralize friction or unreasonable positions assumed by one or both of the managers. For all practical purposes, if the buying segment *must* purchase the goods or services internally or the selling segment *must* sell to the buying segment, an unfair bargaining situation may develop. In these cases, company policy or company transfer price formulas may be used to establish the price.

RETURN ON INVESTMENT AS A MEASURE OF PERFORMANCE

When a manager is able to influence revenues, costs and capital investments in a segment, that manager is said to be responsible for an investment center. Performance measures for an investment center should consider the profit element in relation to the size of the asset base used to earn that profit. A performance measure that attempts to relate income (from the income statement) to the assets utilized (from the balance sheet) is the concept of return on investment. The general formula for return on investment (ROI) is as follows:

$$ROI = \frac{Income}{Assets\ Utilized}$$

The exact definitions for both income and assets utilized may vary from firm to firm. The two elements in the equation, income and assets utilized to earn that income, may be analyzed in terms of their respective components:

ROI = Profit Margin on Sales $\times$ Sales Turnover of Assets

$$= \frac{\text{Income}}{\text{Sales}} \times \frac{\text{Sales}}{\text{Assets Utilized}}$$

The profit margin on sales is a measure of the profitability of a firm while the turnover of assets is an indication of the assets used in relationship to the sales level achieved during the same accounting period. These ratios identify two of the factors that a manager in an investment center should be able to control or influence. The return on investment for a center may be improved by increasing sales, reducing expenses, reducing the level of the assets utilized or by some combination of these three factors. The relationship of the profit margin on sales and the turnover of assets describes the relationship between profit planning and asset (or capital) management. A firm that experiences a two percent profit margin and an asset turnover of ten times in a given accounting period provides the same return on investment as a firm with a ten percent profit margin and an asset turnover of two times per period. In both of these cases, the return on investment is 20 percent.

Firm A   Firm B
ROI = 2% $\times$ 10 = 20%   ROI = 10% $\times$ 2 = 20%

PROBLEMS IN DEFINING ASSETS UTILIZED

In order to effectively use the ROI measure to evaluate the performance of an investment center manager, a consistent definition of assets utilized must be established. Responsibility accounting for investment centers requires that the investment center manager be able to influence the "package" of assets for which he is held responsible. Most managers of an investment center have inherited the majority of the fixed assets of their center from the prior manager. The age and condition of the assets, the depreciation policy in use and the original cost of the assets all play a significant role in the measurement of the appropriate asset base to be used. These factors must be considered in developing a planned or target return on investment. A commonly accepted measure of assets used is total net assets (total original cost of assets less any accumulated depreciation on those assets).

Joint assets pose an additional problem. Many large corporations have established centralized cash, accounts receivable, and long-term debt management; therefore, investment centers in these firms do not have control over cash, accounts receivable or long-term debt. These financial factors are managed by corporate headquarters. In these instances, the centrally-managed financial factors are allocated to the various investment centers involved. An attempt is made to impute the values (including interest expense and interest payable for long-term debt) that would be reported in the financial statements of the investment center if the segment could control these financial factors. This procedure forces the investment center manager to consider and control the factors used as the basis for the allocation of the joint assets if he is to maintain control of ROI for his investment center.

PERFORMANCE EVALUATION OF PROFIT CENTERS

The analysis of variances of a profit center should explain why actual income differed from the forecast budgeted income for the accounting period under consideration. The general types of variances that can be used to analyze and explain the reasons for the difference between the forecasted income and the actual income are: [2]

1. Sales volume variance [2]   3. Price variance
2. Sales mix variance [2]   4. Expense variance

Illustration 12–1 presents the variance worksheet that will be used in preparing the performance report for Mr. Gess, the manager of the Industrial Filter Division of Sax Company.. The division produces and sells over 100 different filters all with different contribution margins.

The controllable revenues and costs of this division are used to illustrate performance evaluation and reporting for a profit center even though Sax Company considers the Industrial Filter Division to be an investment center. In a later section of this chapter, Mr. Gess's controllable assets and income statement information will be considered in an illustration of the performance evaluation of an investment center.

Illustration 12–1 includes only controllable revenues and costs in order to be consistent with the concept of responsibility accounting. Each of the columns included in the variance worksheet should be reviewed prior to the preparation of the profit center performance report.

The forecast budget is based on the anticipated sales volume and mix of filters for the Industrial Filters Division. The selling prices and costs included in the budget are the standard prices and costs for the Division. This budget was prepared prior to the start of the accounting period.

The control budget is prepared after the end of the accounting period. At that point, the actual quantities of filters sold are known. The control budget is a flexible budget prepared after-the-fact using the actual quantity and mix sold at the standard selling prices and costs. Any differences between the individual price or cost factors found on the forecast and

---

[2] There are other methods of calculating sales volume and mix variances in addition to the approaches used in this text. A contribution margin approach is used here to analyze these two variances.

Illustration 12-1
Sax Company
Industrial Filter Division
Variance Worksheet

	Forecast Budget (Forecast volume and mix at standard prices and costs) (1)		Control Budget (or Flexible Budget) (Actual volume and mix at standard prices and costs) (2)		Actual (Actual volume and mix at actual prices and costs) (3)		Variances*	
	Budget	Budget	Budget	Budget	Actual	Actual	Volume/Mix (2-1)	Price/Expense (Cost) (3-2)
Sales Revenue..........	$1,500	100%	$1,400	100.0%	$1,500	100%	($100)	$100
Less: Variable Costs								
Cost of Goods Sold.........	810	54	700	50.0	840	56.0	110	(140)
Salesmen's Commissions.....	150	10	140	10.0	150	10.0	10	(10)
Contribution Margin.........	540	36	$560	40.0	$510	34.0	$20	($50)
Less: Fixed Costs								
Manufacturing Overhead....	$270	18	$270	19.3	$283	18.9	0	($13)
Selling & Administrative....	195	13	195	13.9	122	8.1	0	73
Total Fixed Costs............	$465	31%	$465	33.2%	$405	27.0%	0	$60
Income Before Taxes.........	$75	5%	$95	6.8%	$105	7.0%	$20	$10

*Stated as favorable or (unfavorable) as to the impact on income.

control budgets are caused by changes in the volume or mix of products sold since both budgets use standard prices and costs in their preparation. Therefore this variance can be broken down into two component parts: the sales volume variance and the sales mix variance.

The column on the variance worksheet headed "actual" is taken directly from the accounting records of the Division. Actual costs and prices at actual volume and mix are shown in these accounts. If the actual data are compared with the data in the control budget, variances can be identified as either selling price or expense (cost) variances because the actual volume and mix of products sold are used in preparing the control budget.

The performance report should identify the impact of the variances on income since a profit center manager is held responsible for achieving an established budgeted income figure. Variances are calculated in order to isolate specific impacts on profits when all other factors are held constant. For example, the sales volume variance should provide an explanation of the impact of sales volume on profits. The impact of product mix, sales prices and costs are separated from the sales volume variance.

Sales Volume Variance

If the actual volume of products sold at standard prices differs from the forecasted volume of products sold at standard prices, then the result is a sales volume variance. The formula for calculating the sales volume variance is as follows:

$$\begin{matrix} \text{Sales} \\ \text{Volume} \\ \text{Variance} \end{matrix} = \begin{bmatrix} \text{Forecasted Volume} & \text{Actual Volume} \\ \text{of Sales at} & - \text{ of Sales at} \\ \text{Standard Prices} & \text{Standard Prices} \end{bmatrix} \times \begin{matrix} \text{Forecasted} \\ \text{Contribution} \\ \text{Margin} \\ \text{Percentage} \end{matrix}$$

The forecasted sales volume at the standard price is $1,500. The actual sales volume at the standard price is $1,400. Sales volume at standard prices decreased; therefore, the variance is unfavorable. The forecast contribution margin is 36 percent. If the results for the Industrial Filter Division are substituted in the formula, the sales volume variance is:

$$\text{Sales Volume Variance} = (\$1,500 - \$1,400) \times .36$$
$$= \$36 \text{ unfavorable variance}$$

If all financial factors except sales volume had occurred as forecasted, actual income would have been $36 less than budgeted income as a result of the decline in sales volume.

Sales Mix Variance

If the contribution margin percentage for the forecasted mix and standard prices and costs (forecast budget) differs from the contribution margin percentage for the actual mix and standard prices and costs (control budget), then a sales mix variance results. The forecast budget contribution margin percentage from Illustration 12-1 is 36 percent ($540/$1,500). The contribution margin percentage from the control budget is $560/$1,400 or 40 percent. The formula for calculating the sales mix variance is:

$$\text{Sales Mix Variance} = \begin{bmatrix} \text{Contribution Margin} & \text{Contribution Margin} \\ \text{Percentage from the} & - & \text{Percentage from the} \\ \text{Forecast Budget} & \text{Control Budget} \end{bmatrix} \times$$

$$\begin{array}{c} \text{Sales on the} \\ \text{Control (Flexible) Budget} \end{array}$$

If the contribution margin percentage used in the control budget is greater than the contribution margin percentage in the forecast budget, the resulting sales mix variance is favorable. This is because the actual mix of products sold at the standard prices and costs represents a more profitable mix than was originally forecasted or anticipated. Sales volume does not affect the contribution margin percentage. Even if the forecast budget sales volume had doubled, the control contribution margin percentage would be the same as the forecasted contribution margin so long as the sales mix remained constant.

If the results from the Industrial Filter Division are used in the formula, the sales mix variance is calculated as follows:

$$\begin{aligned} \text{Sales Mix Variance} &= (.36 - .40) \times \$1,400 \\ &= \$56 \text{ favorable variance} \end{aligned}$$

The impact on actual income as compared to forecasted income as a favorable $56 because the actual mix of products sold was a more profitable mix than was originally anticipated and budgeted.

Sales Price Variance

The sales price variance is taken directly from the variance worksheet. This variance is the difference between standard prices at actual volume and mix (control budget) and actual prices at actual volume mix (actual). In the case of the Industrial Filter Division, sales revenue at actual volume and mix and standard price totaled $1,400. Actual sales revenues are $1,500 (from Illustration 12-1). Actual revenues exceeded control budget revenues by $100; therefore, the sales price variance is a favorable $100.

Salesmen's commissions increased by $10 due to an increase in actual prices charged customers over the standard prices. It could be argued that the actual sales price variance was $90 ($100 increase in revenues less $10 increase in commissions) because of the impact of salesmen's commissions.

Expense Variances

The expense variances or cost variances are taken directly from the variance worksheet presented in Illustration 12-1. Variable cost variances represent the traditional approach to variance analysis. Standard costs at actual volume and mix (control budget) are compared with actual costs at actual volume and mix (actual amounts). If actual amounts are less than standard, the variance is favorable. The variable cost expense variances include an unfavorable cost of goods sold variance of $140 and, as indicated above, an unfavorable salesmen's commissions expense of $10. The variance in salesmen's commissions was caused by the favorable sales price variance and, as previously stated, may be considered a reduction in the sales price variance on a performance report.

Fixed cost variances may also be taken directly from the variance worksheet presented in Illustration 12-1. There are no volume or mix variances for fixed costs because the budgeted fixed costs are not affected by volume or mix changes within the relevant range.[3] The fixed cost variances are caused by spending. Manufacturing overhead has exceeded the budgeted amount by $13. The selling and administrative expense variance is a favorable variance of $73. The impact of these expense variances on actual before-tax income is on a one-to-one basis, that is, for every dollar of favorable expense variance, actual income increases by a dollar over budgeted before-tax income.

PERFORMANCE REPORTS FOR PROFIT CENTERS

The performance report for the Industrial Filter Division of Sax Company presented in Illustration 12-2 is based on the worksheet presented in Illustration 12-1. A performance report, such as the one shown in Illustration 12-2, explains the major reasons for achieving $105 in profit instead of the forecasted profit of $75. The format of the performance report for the Industrial Filter Division begins with the forecasted budgeted income and then analyzes the volume and mix variances in

---

[3] Remember that Sax Company uses the variable costing approach for internal planning, control and performance evaluation. Fixed manufacturing costs are treated as period costs

order to arrive at the control budgeted income. The impact of the sales price variances and the expense variances on the control budget income is then computed in order to arrive at the actual income before taxes.

The net effect of the operations of the current period results in an income amount in the Industrial Filter Division that is $30 more than the amount originally budgeted. Illustration 12-2 summarizes the combination of factors that caused the net $30 favorable variance from budgeted income before taxes.

Illustration 12-2
Sax Company
Industrial Filter Division
Performance Report
Manager: Mr. Gess
( ) = Unfavorable

Forecast Budgeted Income Before Taxes	$ 75
Sales Volume Variance ($1,500 — $1,400) X .36 =	(36)

Sales Mix Variance:

Forecast Budget Contribution Margin	$ 540 / $1,500	= .36
Control Budget Contribution Margin	$ 560 / $1,400	= .40
Change in Contribution margin caused by Change in Mix		= .04

Sales Mix Variance $1,400 X .04 =	56
Control Budgeted Income Before Taxes	$95
Sales Price Variances:	
Increased Prices to Customers $1,500 — $1,400 =	100
Less: Increase in Salesmen's Commissions $100 X .10 =	(10)
Cost of Goods Sold Cost Variances	(140)
Fixed Cost Spending Variances:	
Manufacturing Overhead	(13)
Selling and Administrative	73
Actual Income Before Taxes	$105

PERFORMANCE EVALUATION OF INVESTMENT CENTERS

The management of Sax Company views the Industrial Filter Division as an investment center. The balance sheet used to determine the assets or capital employed in this Division is based on the traceable assets, liabilities and corporate investment. In other words, only those balance sheet factors which are directly traceable to the Industrial Filter Division are used to determine the capital utilized in the Division.

Management recognizes that a measure of return-on-investment (ROI) is only one indication of overall performance. Since no single correct means of calculating return on investment exists, all divisions of the firm that are considered investment centers may be held responsible for two different budgeted rates of return: a rate-of-return on total traceable assets and a rate-of-return on traceable corporate investment. In these measures, the budgeted assets or the budgeted corporate investment at the end of the year is used as the basis for the ROI calculation. The use of the budgeted assets utilized provides the division managers with a target asset package or corporate investment.

The rate of return on total traceable assets is important because it provides a measure of how well the responsible manager utilized the resources that were available to him. Return on corporate investment traceable to the division is used to provide a measure of the financial performance of the firm's capital investment in that division. Each division may borrow money externally and, through the use of leverage, increase its return on corporate investment. Cash could also be borrowed internally from corporate headquarters. When cash is borrowed from corporate headquarters, corporate investment in that division is increased. When cash is sent to corporate headquarters, corporate investment is reduced.

Sax Company has established and maintains a monthly reporting system. Rates of return are calculated on a monthly basis to assure the adherence of a division to its budgets and to encourage the responsible manager to attempt to attain the budgeted returns on investment. Illustration 12–3 presents the budgeted and actual balance sheets for the past year for the Industrial Filter Division.

The worksheet analyzing the income statement variance was presented in Illustration 12–1.

BUDGETED ROI VERSUS ACTUAL ROI

The budgeted returns for the year using budgeted end-of-year total assets and corporate investment from Illustration 12-3 and the forecast budgeted income from Illustration 12-1 are as follows:[4]

$$\text{ROI on Total Assets} = \frac{\text{Profit}}{\text{Margin}} \times \frac{\text{Asset}}{\text{Turnover}}$$

$$= \frac{\text{Profit}}{\text{Sales}} \times \frac{\text{Sales}}{\text{Assets Utilized}}$$

$$= \frac{\$75}{\$1,500} \times \frac{\$1,500}{\$600}$$

---

[4] It is common to use average total assets and average corporate investment for the accounting period instead of end-of-year totals. End-of-year totals could be influenced by last minute decisions and could present a distorted perspective when compared to averages.

$$= \quad .05 \text{ X } 2.5$$

$$= \quad .125 \text{ or } 12\tfrac{1}{2}\%$$

ROI on Corporate
Investment $= \dfrac{\text{Profit}}{\text{Sales}} \text{ X } \dfrac{\text{Sales}}{\text{Corporate Investment}}$

$$= \quad \dfrac{\$75}{\$1,500} \text{ X } \dfrac{\$1,500}{\$300}$$

$$= \quad .05 \text{ X } 5$$

$$= \quad .25 \text{ or } 25\%$$

The results for the year using actual end-of-year total assets and corporate investment from Illustration 12-3 and the actual income from Illustration 12-1 are as follows:

ROI on Total Assets $= \dfrac{\$105}{\$1,500} \text{ X } \dfrac{\$1,500}{\$500}$

$$= \quad .07 \text{ X } 3$$

$$= \quad .21 \text{ or } 21\%$$

ROI on Corporate
Investment $= \dfrac{\$105}{\$1,500} \text{ X } \dfrac{\$1,500}{\$200}$

$$= \quad .07 \text{ X } 7.5$$

$$= \quad .525 \text{ or } 52\tfrac{1}{2}\%$$

Mr. Gess, the manager of the investment center, was able to exceed the budgeted return on total assets by increasing both the actual profit margin and asset turnover compared to budget. The budgeted profit margin was 5 percent and the budgeted asset turnover was 2.5 times. The actual profit margin and budgeted asset turnover was 7 percent and 3 times, respectively.

An analysis of the increased profit margin can be made from Illustration 12-2. The sales volume, sales commissions, cost of goods sold and manufacturing overhead variances were all unfavorable, but were less in total than the favorable variances for sales mix, sales prices, and selling and administrative expenses. Thus a net favorable variance resulted in a 2% increase in the profit margin.

Illustration 12-3
Sax Company
Industrial Filter Division
Budgeted and Actual Balance Sheets
Manager: Mr. Gess

	Budget	Actual	Variances
ASSETS			
Current Assets:			
Cash.	$ 20	$ 20	$ 0
Accounts Receivable.	100	60	(40)
Direct Materials Inventories.	50	20	(30)
Indirect Materials and Supplies.	10	5	(5)
Work-in-Process Inventories.	30	30	0
Finished Goods on a Variable			
Costing Basis.	90	65	(25)
Long-Term Assets:			
Equipment (Net of Accumulated			
Depreciation)	100	100	0
Plant (Net of Accumulated			
Depreciation)	200	200	0
Total Assets.	$600	$500	($100)
LIABILITIES AND STOCKHOLDERS' EQUITY			
Current Liabilities:			
Accounts Payable.	$ 75	$ 80	$ 5
Wages Payable.	50	40	(10)
Long-Term Liabilities:			
Long-Term Debt.	175	180	5
Stockholders' Equity:			
Corporate Investment.	300	200	(100)
Total Liabilities and Stockholders'			
Equity	$600	$500	($100)
Return on Total Assets (Income from			
Illustration 12-1).	12½ %	21 %	
Return on Corporate Investment			
(Income from Illustration 12-1).	25 %	52½%	

Budgeted and actual total revenues were the same. To increase asset turnover, Mr. Gess reduced assets by $100. This reduction may, in fact, represent only a short-run improvement in the utilization of resources if the budgeted amounts in Illustration 12-3 are assumed to be the amounts necessary to fund the operations of the Division over a long-run period.

The actual return on corporate investment exceeded the budgeted return by 27.5 percent. Mr. Gess accomplished the increased return by increasing the profit margin by 2 percent and decreasing corporate investment by $100. The decrease in corporate investment was sufficient to increase the turnover of corporate investment from a budgeted 5 times to an actual turnover of 7.5 times.

In addition to the cash transfers made to corporate headquarters (which reduced corporate investment in the Division by $100), Mr. Gess reduced accounts receivable by $40, direct materials inventories by $30, indirect materials and supplies by $5 and finished goods inventory by $25. He increased accounts payable by $5 and long-term debt by $5. Wages payable was reduced by $10. The variances from budget for these balance sheet accounts must be considered in view of the Division's needs before any statements or conclusions may be made regarding Mr. Gess's management approach.

If the performance report presented in Illustration 12-2 and the budgeted and actual balance sheets and other analyses included in Illustration 12-3 are all considered, the following statements can be made concerning Mr. Gess's management of the Industrial Filter Division.

1. The sales volume variance was an unfavorable $36 because budgeted sales were not attained.
2. The sales mix variance was a favorable $56. The actual mix included a greater proportion of the more profitable filters than was originally budgeted.
3. The sales prices charged to some or all customers were higher than standard. This enabled the division to make an additional $100 in gross sales revenues or $90 net after the increased salesman's commissions.
4. The production cost variances charged to the cost of goods sold for the year were unfavorable and thus decreased the division's income by $140.
5. The fixed cost spending variances totaled $60 favorable. This increased the income of the division by $60.
6. The division's actual income before taxes was $105. This was $30 above the forecast budget income.

A selected measure of income is used as the numerator in all return-on-investment equations. The denominator will always be based on a selected measure of resources utilized. By controlling or influencing either the numerator or the denominator (or both) the manager can influence ROI. The denominators as defined by the Sax Company are total traceable assets for the first measure and traceable corporate investment for the second measure.

Mr. Gess increased the numerator, income before taxes, without increasing revenues. The denominator was reduced by decreasing the assets utilized and decreasing corporate investment by the same amount. Total liabilities did not change from budgeted, although individual balances in the accounts were changed.

SUMMARY

Responsibility accounting for profit centers and investment centers is similar to that for cost centers. Additional financial factors, however, must be taken into account. While the cost center is concerned only with controllable costs, the profit center is responsible for controllable revenues and costs. The investment center is responsible for controllable capital investments as well as controllable revenues and costs. Although responsibility accounting for these additional financial factors permits considerable decentralization, it also creates new problems.

One of the problems associated with responsibility accounting for profit centers relates to the measurement of revenues when sales are made between company segments. The primary types of transfer prices used to measure such revenues are: (1) market-based price, (2) cost-based price, and (3) negotiated price. Each of these transfer prices has its advantages and disadvantages and the actual transfer price used by a firm will probably be a combination of these methods.

The procedure for evaluating the performance of profit centers includes a detailed analysis of the variances from budgeted net income. The variances generally included in such an analysis are: (1) sales volume variance, (2) sales mix variance, (3) sales price variance, and (4) cost or expense variance. The first three variances are related to revenues realized by the center and the cost or expense variance is related to costs incurred by the center.

Responsibility accounting for investment centers also requires a method for evaluating performance. One common performance evaluation technique is to relate income to the assets utilized to earn that income. This relationship is determined by calculating the return on investment (ROI). However, the return on investment calculation requires that the amount of assets utilized be known.

The performance evaluation of an investment center may include more than one ROI calculation since "assets utilized" may be defined several ways. For instance, the actual rate of return on total traceable assets may be calculated in addition to the usual calculation of the rate of return on corporate investment. Budgeted ROI and actual ROI are compared and an analysis of any differences between the two is made. In addition, a firm may wish to analyze the various components of the ROI figure to determine if the desired ROI is being met in an acceptable manner.

This chapter concludes the discussion of responsibility accounting systems. Chapter 13 discusses the various accounting approaches to planning special decisions.

KEY DEFINITIONS

Control budget—a flexible budget prepared at the end of an accounting period using the actual quantity and mix sold at the standard selling prices and costs.

Cost-based transfer price—a transfer price which may be based on the actual, standard or variable costs of the supplying segment.

Expense variances—the differences between the standard and actual costs or expenses at the actual volume and mix.

Market-based transfer price—a transfer price based on the external market price less any savings in cost; it is the closest approximation to an arm's length transaction that segments can achieve.

Negotiated transfer price—a transfer price which is established by agreement of both the selling and buying segments of the firm.

Return on investment—measures the ability of a firm, or segment within a firm, to utilize available resources effectively by expressing profit or income as a percentage of invested assets.

Sales mix variance—occurs when the contribution margin percentage at the forecasted mix and standard prices and costs (forecast budget) differs from the contribution margin percentage at actual mix and standard prices (control budget).

Sales price variance—the difference between standard prices at actual volume and mix (control budget) and actual prices at actual volume and mix.

Sales volume variance—occurs when the actual sales volume of products sold at the standard prices (control budget) differs from the forecasted sales volume of products sold at the standard prices (forecast budget).

Transfer price—the price that one segment of a firm pays to another segment of the same firm for the output or service of the supplying segment.

QUESTIONS

1. What does decentralization attempt to do?
2. What is a transfer price and why does it pose certain problems in performance measurement by segments?
3. What are the shortcomings of a market-based transfer price? A cost-based transfer price?
4. The return on investment formula is made up of two components: margin

on sales and turnover of capital. Explain what each of these respective components signify.

5. Name two problems which are encountered in defining capital utilized in an investment center.

6. What is the reason for a sales mix variance? Does volume affect this variance?

7. What is the difference between a sales price and expense variance?

8. What causes a fixed cost variance when the variable costing approach is used? What impact does this variance have on actual income?

9. How can a responsible manager meet his budgeted return on investment if his actual margin on sales is below that budgeted? Give one example.

10. What specific method can a manager use to reduce his current assets in order to increase his actual asset turnover ratio? What is a disadvantage of this method?

EXERCISES

12–1 During 1981, the James Company had sales of $1,000,000 and income of $450,000. It employed capital of $15,000,000.

Required:

Determine the return on investment for 1981.

12–2 In 1980, Sleeper, Inc. forecasted sales of 500,000 mattresses at $150 per mattress. At the end of the year, the company determined that it had sold 498,000 mattresses at an average price of $158 per mattress. The forecasted contribution margin percentage was 42%.

Required:

Determine the sales volume variance and the sales price variance.

12–3 The Rubber Tire Company forecasted that 200,000 tires would be sold at a price of $60 per tire for the year. After checking figures at the end of the year, it was discovered that 210,000 tires were sold at a price of $59. The company had forecasted a contribution margin of 30%.

Required:

Determine the sales volume variance and the sales price variance.

12–4 Variable expenses for Jackson, Inc. are based on direct labor hours. They are $4.80 per direct labor hour. In 1980, 654,860 direct labor hours were worked. The variable costs were $4.83 per hour.

Required:

Determine the variable cost variance.

12–5 The Thomson Company has two divisions. Division 1 normally sells

75% of its output to Division 2 for $10, the same price as it sells to other customers.

Given below are the results for the year:

	Division 1	Division 2
Sales to outsiders	$15,000	$200,000
Sales to Division 2	45,000	–0–
Total	$60,000	$200,000
Transfer costs	–0–	45,000
Other variable costs	15,600	35,000
Contribution margin	$44,400	$120,000
Fixed costs	25,000	80,000
Net income before taxes	$19,400	$ 40,000

Required:

a. Prepare a report consolidating the two divisions.

b. If Division 2 could purchase the product from an outside source for $9.00 by purchasing their total needs from that source, should Division 1 meet this price? Assume that Division 1 can sell no more than 75% of their production to outsiders. (Consider this from the viewpoint of the overall company.)

12–6 Division C of the Glaser Company has the following budget for 1981:

	Forecast Budget
Sales @ $10/unit *	$40,000
Variable costs @ $5/unit *	20,000
Contribution margin	$20,000
Fixed costs	10,000
Net income before taxes	$10,000

* Weighted average based on forecast sales mix.

The weighted average contribution margin on the control budget is $15,000, which is a 48 percent contribution margin. Actual sales in 1981 were $35,000, variable costs were $16,000 and fixed costs were $11,000. Total assets for Division C were budgeted at $30,000 but were actually $35,000.

Required:

Prepare a variance worksheet in good form for 1981 assuming that Division C is a profit center.

12–7 You have been hired by East Money Inc. to work in their cost accounting department. Your first job is to calculate the ROI. Unfortunately, the sales figures for the past year have been lost. Eager to show your technical skill you state that you can still calculate ROI with only the income of $60,000 and the investment of $720,000 being known.

Required:

Calculate the ROI and show how the volume of sales has no effect.

12–8   Department A of the Stonewall Company has been purchasing the rods it uses in concrete slabs from Department B of the same company for $50 per ton. Department A purchases about 90% of the production of B. In the current year, B expects to have sales of about 1,600 tons. The remaining 10% of B's sales are to outside customers for $51 with terms of 2/10, N/30. Approximately 60% of the outside sales are paid within ten days, and about 3% of the outside sales are never paid.

A has been negotiating with several other suppliers for these rods and finds its can purchase them from an outside supplier for $48 per ton. Unless Department B lowers its price, A will use the outside supplier.

After doing some market research, B feels that it can sell 90% of its present capacity to outside customers for $51 @ 2/10, N/30, or 95% for $50 @ 2/10, N/30. Under these two arrangements, Department A will buy all purchases from outsiders.

Variable costs for the rods are $20 per ton and fixed costs are $21,000 per year. Selling expenses are $1.50 per ton if sold to outside customers.

Required:

If Department B does not consider the rest of the firm, what should it do?

12–9   Alcorn, Inc. has 2 divisions, R and S. R sells approximately 80% of its output to S for $15, but charges outside customers $15.50 because Alcorn must pay its salesman 3% of the selling price on sales to outside customers.

Given below are the results for 1981:

	Division R	Division S
Sales to outsiders	$ 9,300	$72,000
Sales to Division S	36,000	–0–
Total	$45,300	$72,000
Transfer costs	–0–	36,000
Variable costs	9,000	9,600
Salesman's commission	279	2,160
Contribution margin	$36,021	$24,240
Fixed costs	23,000	10,000
Net income before taxes	$13,021	$14,240

Required:

a.   Prepare a report consolidating the two divisions.
b.   If Division S could purchase the product for $14.25 from an outside source, should R meet this price? Assume R could sell 90% of their production to outsiders for $15. If R sells to S, it can

still sell 20% of its production to outside customers for $15.50. (Consider this from the viewpoint of the overall company.)

12–10   The following data pertain to the hardware division of Hogan Incorporated. The company has set a 20 percent return on investment as the profit objective of the hardware division.

Sales revenue $200,000
Net income . . . . $ 50,000
Capital used $333,000

Required:

Was the hardware division successful in meeting its profit objective of 20 percent ROI? If the answer is no, give two suggestions for increasing the ROI to the desired number.

12–11   From the information listed below, calculate the sales mix variance for the Mondale Company.

	Forecast Budget	*Control Budget*
Sales revenue	$360,000	$320,000
Variable costs:		
Cost of goods sold	223,200	192,100
Salesmen's commissions	18,000	16,000
Selling expenses	3,600	3,100
Fixed costs:		
Salaries	18,000	18,000
Rent	8,000	8,000

PROBLEMS SERIES A

12A–1   The following data pertain to three investment centers of Alpha Enterprises for the year.

	I	*II*	*III*
Net income before taxes	$100,000	$ 150,000	$ 80,000
Sales revenue	800,000	1,000,000	700,000
Total assets	500,000	625,000	300,000
Corporate investment	300,000	500,000	200,000

Required:

a.   Calculate the margin on sales, turnover of total assets, and the ROI on total assets for the three investment centers.
b.   Calculate the turnover of total corporate investment and the ROI on corporate investment for the three investment centers.
c.   For "A and B" above, rank the three investment centers in order, highest return listed first.

12A–2   The following information relates to the assembly division of the Omega Corporation for the year. The budgeted ROI on total assets was set at 20 percent and the budgeted ROI on corporate investment was set at 25 percent.

```
Net income before taxes . . . . .  $100,000
Sales . . . . . . . . . . . . . . .    800,000
Total assets . . . . . . . . . . .     600,000
Corporate investment . . . . . . .     400,000
```

Required:

a. Compute the actual ROI on total assets and the actual ROI on corporate investments.

b. Name two ways that the ROI on total assets may be improved, and two ways the ROI on corporate investment may be improved if necessary for this situation.

12A–3   You are presently trying to encourage people to invest in your new company that manufactures an automatic dirty diaper washer. Potential investors are constantly asking what ROI can be expected. Unfortunately, you have not been in business long enough to know what the actual ROI is. However, you do expect one-third of all sales to equal income before taxes. The volume of sales is completely dependent on the corporate investment, sales always being one-half of the corporate investment.

Required:

a. Calculate the ROI on corporate investment that is expected.

b. If you are able to get investors to contribute $420,000, what will be the income before tax?

12A–4   The manufacturing division of the Marple Corporation produces two products, Y and Z. The following data refer to the two products:

	Y	Z
Selling price	$6	$10
Variable costs:		
Cost of goods sold	$3	$ 4
Sales commissions	$0.60	$ 1

Total fixed costs were budgeted at $56,000 for the year.
Sales revenue was budgeted (forecast) as follows:

	Amount	Units
Product Y	$ 60,000	10,000
Product Z	$100,000	10,000

Given below is the income statement for the year reflecting the actual data.

```
Sales revenue . . . . . . . . . . . . . . . .         $160,000
Less:  Variable costs
          Cost of goods sold . .  $80,000
          Sales commissions . . .  16,000          96,000
Contribution margin . . . . . . . . . . . .            64,000
```

Less: Fixed costs		48,000
Income before taxes		$ 16,000

Actual units sold . . . . . . 13,000(Y)   7,000(Z)

Required:

a. Prepare a variances worksheet for the manufacturing division. Determine the income before taxes for the forecast budget and the control budget. Determine the volume/mix and price/expense variance.

b. Prepare a performance report for the manager of the manufacturing division in which the forecast budget income is reconciled with the actual income before taxes.

12A–5 The following data refer to the production division of the Gypsy Company which produces two products, C and D.

1. General information:

> Selling price of C and D was $10 per unit
> Standard variable costs were:
>   60% of sales for C
>   40% of sales for D
> Fixed costs were budgeted at $40,000

2. Sales for the year were forecast budgeted as follows:

Product C	$ 40,000	4,000 units
Product D	60,000	6,000 units
	$100,000	

3. The actual income statement is presented below:

Sales revenue:		
Product C (5,000 units)	$50,000	
Product D (5,000 units)	50,000	$100,000
Less: Variable costs		51,000
Contribution margin		49,000
Less: Fixed costs		34,000
Income before taxes		$ 15,000

Required:

Prepare a performance report for the production division in which the forecast budget income is reconciled with the actual income. Show all variances on the report.

12A–6 Mr. Phillips is the manager of the finishing and processing division of the Anderson Company. The finishing and processing division is a profit center. The following data illustrate a partial variance worksheet for the division:

Anderson Company
Finishing and Processing Division
Variance Worksheet

	Forecast Budget	Control Budget	Actual
Sales	$1,000,000	$900,000	$1,000,000
Less: Variable costs	700,000	625,000	750,000
Contribution margin	300,000	275,000	250,000
Less: Fixed costs	200,000	200,000	160,000
Income before taxes	$ 100,000	$ 75,000	$ 90,000

Required:

a. Compute the following variances:
  1. Sales volume
  2. Sales mix
  3. Sales price
  4. Expense
b. Prepare a performance report for the division.

12A–7 Following are the (budget and actual) condensed balance sheets of the Carpet Division of the Jackson Company for the year. The manager of the Carpet Division is Mr. Baker.

	Budget	Actual
Assets		
Current assets	$200,000	$150,000
Long-term assets	300,000	300,000
Total assets	$500,000	$450,000
Liabilities and Corporate Investment:		
Current liabilities	$100,000	$ 75,000
Long-term liabilities	100,000	125,000
Corporate investment	300,000	250,000
Total liabilities and corporate investment . . .	$500,000	$450,000

Additional data:

Budgeted net income = $50,000
Actual net income   = $45,000
Sales (budget)   = $400,000
Sales (actual)   = $450,000

Required:

Calculate the budgeted and actual rates of return on total assets and the budgeted and actual rates of return on corporate investments.

Did Mr. Baker attain the budgeted returns on investments?

12A–8 Following are the forecast budget and actual income statements of a manufacturing company for a year.

	Forecast Budget	Actual
Units sold	10,000 @ $10 per unit	12,000
Sales revenue	$100,000 (100%)	$130,000 (100%)
Less: Variable costs * . . .	70,000	90,000
Contribution margin	30,000 (30%)	40,000 (30.8%)
Less: Fixed costs	20,000	15,000
Income before taxes	$ 10,000	$ 25,000

* Variable costs (standard) are $7.00 per unit.

Required:

Prepare a peformance report for the manufacturing company.

12A–9 Determine the answers for a through h in each of the three independent cases below:

	A	B	C
Sales revenue	$100,000	$500,000	*f*
Net income	*a*	$ 50,000	$ 30,000
Corporate investment used	*b*	$250,000	$150,000
Margin on sales (%)	*c*	*d*	5%
Turnover of corporate investment . .	.5	2	*g*
Return on corporate investment . . .	10%	*e*	*h*

12A–10 The following data pertain to a division of the Oxford Manufacturing Company which produces and sells two products, A and B.

Forecast Budget
  Sales were budgeted as follows:
    Product A—10,000 units @ $5 per unit = $50,000
    Product B—20,000 units @ $10 per unit = $200,000
  The standard variable costs are:
    Product A—$2.00 per unit
    Product B—$6.00 per unit
  The total fixed costs were budgeted at $90,000.

Actual data
  Sales revenue:
    Product A—sold 15,000 units @ $6 = $ 90,000
    Product B—sold 16,000 units @ $12 = 192,000
                                        $282,000
  Variable costs totaled $150,000
  Fixed costs totaled $100,000

Required:

a. Compute the following variances:

    1. Sales volume

    2. Sales mix

    3. Sales price

    4. Expense-variable and fixed

  b. Prepare a performance report for this division of the Oxford Manufacturing Company which reconciles the forecast budget income with the actual income.

12A–11 George Johnson was hired on July 1, 1979 as Assistant General Manager of the Botel Division of Staple, Inc. It was understood that he would be elevated to General Manager of the division on January 1, 1981, when the then current General Manager retired and this was duly done. In addition to becoming acquainted with the division and the General Manager's duties, Mr. Johnson was specifically charged with the responsibility for development of the 1980 and 1981 budgets. As General Manager in 1981, he was, obviously, responsible for the 1982 budget.

    The Staple Company is a multiproduct company which is highly

Botel Division (000 omitted)

	Actual			Budget	
Accounts	1979	1980	1981	1981	1982
Sales......................	$1,000	$1,500	$1,800	$2,000	$2,400
Less division variable costs:					
Material and labor......	250	375	450	500	600
Repairs...............	50	75	50	100	120
Supplies..............	20	30	36	40	48
Less division managed costs:					
Employee training......	30	35	25	40	45
Maintenance..............	50	55	40	60	70
Less division committed costs:					
Depreciation..........	120	160	160	200	200
Rent.................	80	100	110	140	140
Total..............	600	$ 830	$ 871	$1,080	$1,223
Division net contribution.............	$ 400	$ 670	$ 929	$ 920	$1,177
Division investment:					
Accounts receivable.......	$ 100	$ 150	$ 180	$ 200	$ 240
Inventory...............	200	300	270	400	480
Fixed assets.............	1,590	2,565	2,800	3,380	4,000
Less: Accounts and wages payable..........	(150)	(225)	(350)	(300)	(360)
Net investment.............	$1,740	$2,790	$2,900	$3,680	$4,360
Contribution return net investment...........	23%	24%	32%	25%	27%

decentralized. Each division is quite autonomous. The corporation staff approves division prepared operating budgets but seldom makes major changes in them. The corporate staff actively participates in decisions requiring capital investment (for expansion or replacement) and makes the final decisions. The division management is responsible for implementing the capital program. The major method used by the Staple Corporation to measure division performance is Contribution Return on Division Net Investment. The budgets presented below were approved by the corporation. Revision of the 1982 budget is not considered necessary even though 1981 actual departed from the approved 1981 budget.

Required:

a. Identify Mr. Johnson's responsibilities under the management and measurement program described above.
b. Appraise the performance of Mr. Johnson in 1981.
c. Recommend to the President any changes in the responsibilities assigned to managers or in the measurement methods used to evaluate division management based upon your analysis.

(CMA, adapted)

PROBLEMS SERIES B

12B–1   Below is data pertaining to three divisions of the Acorn Company for the year 1980:

	I	II	III
Net income before taxes	$ 150,000	$ 180,000	$ 95,000
Sales revenue	1,200,000	1,140,000	665,000
Total assets	750,000	1,100,000	390,000
Corporate investment	560,000	975,000	340,000

Required:

a. Calculate the profit margin, turnover of total assets, and the return on total assets for each division.
b. Calculate the turnover of total corporate investment and the return on corporate investment for each division.
c. Which of the divisions showed the best performance in 1980 according to your calculations?

12B–2   The budgeted return on total assets for the Barcelona Corporation for 1980 was set at 17% and the budgeted return on corporate investment was set at 22%. Below is information relating to what actually happened in 1980.

Net income before taxes . . . . . . $ 305,000

```
Sales . . . . . . . . . . . . . . . . .   2,592,000
Total assets . . . . . . . . . . . . .   1,965,000
Corporate investment  . . . . . . .   1,540,000
```

Required:

Compute the actual return on total assets and the actual return on corporate investments for 1980. Did the Barcelona Corporation hit their target returns?

12B–3   A study of the past records of the Garden Co. reveals that sales are always 20% of the size of the corporate investment. Corporate investment is presently set at $700,000. The mark-up above total costs of all items is set at 33⅓%. (This amount can be assumed to be profit before tax.)

Sales 140,000

The company desires to make a profit of $50,000 before tax.

Required:

Calculate how much more corporate investment is needed to achieve the desired income. What ROI on corporate investment is this?

12B–4   Kingston Company, a subsidiary of the Queenstar Corporation, produces two products, alpha and beta. The following data refer to the two products:

	Alpha	*Beta*
Selling price	$12	$18
Variable costs:		
Cost of goods sold	$ 8	$13
Selling expenses	$ 0.90	$ 1.20

Total fixed costs were budgeted at $91,900 for the year 1980. Sales revenue for 1980 was budgeted as follows:

	Amount	*Units*
Alpha	$156,000	13,000
Beta	$252,000	14,000

Given below is the income statement for 1980 reflecting the actual data:

```
Sales . . . . . . . . . . . . . . . . . . . . . . . .   $452,922
Less:  Variable costs
         Cost of goods sold   307,107
         Sales  commissions    31,222          338,329
Contribution margin . . . . . . . . . . . . . .     114,593
Less:  Fixed  costs . . . . . . . . . . . . . .      98,600
Income before taxes . . . . . . . . . . . . . .   $ 15,993
```

Actual units sold: 13,900 (Alpha)   15,100 (Beta)

Required:

a. Prepare a variance worksheet for the Kingston Company similar to Illustration 12–1. Determine the income before taxes for the forecast budget and the control budget. Determine the volume/mix and price/expense variances.

b. Prepare a performance report for the chief executive of the Kingston Company similar to Illustration 12–2 in which the forecast budget income is reconciled with the actual income before taxes.

12B–5   The following data refer to the manufacturing division of the City Company which produces two products, King and Kong.

1.   General information:

> Standard variable costs were:
> $12 per unit for King
> $11 per unit for Kong
> Fixed costs were budgeted at $80,000

2.   Sales for 1980 were forecast as follows:

King	$120,000	6,000 units $20
Kong	$100,000	5,000 units $20

3.   The actual income statement is presented below:

Sales revenue:		
King (6,200 units) . . .	$125,240	
Kong (4,900 units) . . .	99,470	$224,710
Less: Variable costs		129,670
Contribution margin		95,040
Less: Fixed costs		78,600
Income before taxes		$ 16,440

Required:

Prepare a performance report for the manufacturing division in which the forecast budget income is reconciled with the actual income. Show all variances on the report.

12B–6   Below is a partial variance worksheet for the production division of the Munroe Corporation:

Munroe Corporation
Production Division
Variance Worksheet

	Forecast Budget	Control Budget	Actual
Sales	$930,000	$925,000	$955,000
Less: Variable costs	604,500	582,750	630,300
Contribution margin	325,500	342,250	324,700
Less: Fixed costs	196,000	196,000	214,000
Income before taxes	$129,500	$146,250	$110,700

Required:

a. Compute the following variances:
   1. Sales volume
   2. Sales mix
   3. Sales price
   4. Expense (variable and fixed)
b. Prepare a performance report for the division as shown in Illustration 12–2.

12B–7   Below are the condensed balance sheets (budget and actual) of the Nomad Division of the Marathon Company for the year. The manager for this division is Mr. Danny Findler.

	Budget	Actual
Assets:		
Current assets	$ 245,000	$254,000
Long-term assets	850,000	710,000
Total assets	$1,095,000	$964,000
Liabilities and Corporate Investment		
Current liabilities	$ 150,000	$135,000
Long-term liabilities	200,000	230,000
Corporate investment	745,000	599,000
Total liabilities and corporate investment	$1,095,000	$964,000

Additional data:

Budget net income = $ 125,000
Actual net income = $ 118,000
Sales (budget)   = $1,125,000
Sales (actual)   = $1,128,000

Required:
Calculate the budgeted and actual rates of return on total assets and

the budgeted and actual rates of return on corporate investments. Did Mr. Findler attain the budgeted returns on investments?

12B–8 Below are the forecast and actual income statements for the Ged Company for the year.

	Forecast Budget	Actual
Revenue	$80,000 (100%)	$87,000 (100%)
Less: Variable costs	50,000	52,200
Contribution margin	30,000 (37.5%)	34,800 (40%)
Less: Fixed assets	15,000	12,800
Income before taxes	$15,000	$22,000
Units sold	8,000	8,700

Required:

Prepare a performance report for the Ged Company.

12B–9 Fill in the blanks in each of the three independent cases below:

	I	II	III
Sales revenue	$250,000	d	$300,000
Net income	a	$10,000	g
Total assets used	b	$50,000	h
Margin on sales (%)	2%	8%	5%
Turnover of total assets	1.6	e	3
Return on total assets (%)	c	f	15%

12B–10 The following data pertain to the manufacturing department of the Grossman Company which produces three products, Alpha, Beta, and Gamma.

Forecast budget
Sales were budgeted as follows:

Alpha	— 5,000 units @ $2 = $ 10,000
Beta	—10,000 units @ $4 = $ 40,000
Gamma	—15,000 units @ $6 = $ 90,000
	$140,000

The standard variable costs are:
Alpha —$1.10 per unit
Beta —$3.20 per unit
Gamma—$4.00 per unit
The total fixed costs were budgeted at $12,000.

Actual data
Sales revenue

Alpha	—sold	4,600	units	@ $2.10	= $	9,660
Beta	—sold	10,300	units	@ $4.30	= $	44,290
Gamma	—sold	15,600	units	@ $5.90	= $	92,040
						$145,990

Variable costs totaled $100,600
Fixed costs totaled $ 15,900

Required:

a. Compute the following variances:
   1. Sales volume
   2. Sales mix
   3. Sales price
   4. Expense-variable and fixed
b. Prepare a performance report for the manufacturing department of the Grossman Company which reconciles the forecast budget income with the actual income.

12B–11   The Argon County Hospital is located in the county seat. Argon county is a well known summer resort area. The county population doubles during the vacation months (May–August) and hospital activity more than doubles during these months. The hospital is organized into several departments. Although it is a relatively small hospital, its pleasant surroundings have attracted a well-trained and competent medical staff.

An administrator was hired a year ago to improve the business activities of the hospital. Among the new ideas he has introduced is responsibility accounting. This program was announced along with quarterly cost reports supplied to department heads. Previously cost data were presented to department heads infrequently. Excerpts from the announcement and the report received by the laundry supervisor are presented below.

The hospital has adopted a "responsibility accounting system." From now on you will receive quarterly reports comparing the costs of operating your department with budgeted costs. The reports will highlight the differences (variations) so you can zero in on the departure from budgeted costs. (This is called "management by exception.") Responsibility accounting means you are accountable for keeping the costs in your department within the budget. The variations from the budget will help you identify what costs are out of line and the size of the variation will indicate which ones are the most important. Your first such report accompanies this announcement

Argon County Hospital
Performance Report—Laundry Department
July - September 1983

	Budget	Actual	(Over) Under Budget	Percent (Over) Under Budget
Patient days	9,500	11,900	(2,400)	(25)
Pounds processed —laundry	125,000	156,000	(31,000)	(25)
Costs				
Laundry labor	$ 9,000	$12,500	$(3,500)	(39)
Supplies	1,100	1,875	(775)	(70)
Water, water heating & softening	1,700	2,500	(800)	(47)
Maintenance	1,400	2,200	(800)	(57)
Supervisor's salary	3,150	3,750	(600)	(19)
Allocated administration costs	4,000	5,000	(1,000)	(25)
Equipment depreciation	1,200	1,250	(50)	(4)
	$21,550	$29,075	$(7,525)	(35)

Administrator's Comments: Costs are significantly above budget for the quarter. Particular attention needs to be paid to labor, supplies and maintenance.

The annual budget for 1983 was constructed by the new administrator. Quarterly budgets were computed as one-fourth of the annual budget. The administrator compiled the budget from analysis of the prior three years' costs. The analysis showed that all costs increased each year with more rapid increases between the second and third year. He considered establishing the budget at an average of the prior three years' costs hoping that the installation of the system would reduce costs to this level. However, in view of the rapidly increasing prices he finally chose 1982 costs less 3 percent for the 1983 budget. The activity level measured by patient days and pounds of laundry processed was set at 1982 volume, which was approximately equal to the volume of each of the past three years.

Required:

a. Comment on the method used to construct the budget.
b. What information should be communicated by variations from budgets?
c. Does the report effectively communicate the level of efficiency of this department? Give reasons for your answer.

(CMA, adapted)

12B-12 The Texon Co. is organized into autonomous divisions along regional market lines. Each division manager is responsible for sales, cost of operations, acquisition and financing of divisional assets and working capital management.

The vice president of general operations for the company will retire in September 1981. A review of the performance, attitudes, and skills of several management employees has been undertaken. Interviews with qualified outside candidates also have been held. The selection committee has narrowed the choice to the managers of Divisions A and F.

Both candidates were appointed division managers in late 1977. The manager of Division A had been the assistant manager of that division for the prior five years. The manager of Division F had served as assistant division manager of Division B before being appointed to his present post. He took over Division F, a division newly formed in 1976, when its first manager left to join a competitor. The financial results of their performance in the past three years are summarized in the tables.

	DIVISION A			DIVISION F		
	1978	1979	1980	1978	1979	1980
			(000 omitted)			
Estimated industry sales -market area........	$10,000	$12,000	$13,000	$5,000	$6,000	$6,500
Division sales..........	$ 1,000	$ 1,100	$ 1,210	$ 450	$ 600	$ 750
Variable costs..........	$ 300	$ 320	$ 345	$ 135	$ 175	$ 210
Managed costs........	400	405	420	170	200	230
Committed costs.......	275	325	350	140	200	250
Total costs........	$ 975	$ 1,050	$ 1,115	$ 445	$ 575	$ 690
Net income........	$ 25	$ 50	$ 95	$ 5	$ 25	$ 60
Assets employed........	$ 330	$ 340	$ 360	$ 170	$ 240	$ 300
Liabilities incurred.....	103	105	115	47	100	130
Net investment........	227	235	245	123	140	170
Return on investment...	11%	21%	39%	04%	18%	35%

Required:

a. Texon Co. measures the performance of the divisions and the division managers on the basis of their return on Investment (ROI). Is this an appropriate measurement for the division managers? Explain.

b. Many believe that a single measure, such as ROI, is inadequate to fully evaluate performance. What additional measure(s) could be used for performance evaluation? Give reasons for each measure listed.

c. On the basis of the information given, which manager would you recommend for vice president of general operations? Present reasons to support you answer.

(CMA, adapted)

12B-13   The Lorax Electric Company manufactures a large variety of systems and individual components for the electronics industry. The firm is organized into several divisions with division managers given the authority to make virtually all operating decisions. Management control over divisional operations is maintained by a system of divisional profit and return on investment measures which are reviewed regularly by top management. The top management of Lorax has been quite pleased with the effectiveness of the system they have been using and believe that it is responsible for the company's improved profitability over the last few years.

The Devices Division manufactures solid-state devices and is operating at capacity. The Systems Division has asked the Devices Division to supply a large quantity of integrated circuit IC378. The Devices Division currently is selling this component to its regular customers at $40 per hundred.

The Systems Division, which is operating at about 60 percent capacity, wants this particular component for a digital clock system. It has an opportunity to supply large quantities of these digital clock systems to Centonic Electric, a major producer of clock radios and other popular electronic home entertainment equipment. This is the first opportunity any of the Lorax divisions have had to do business with Centonic Electric. Centonic Electric has offered to pay $7.50 per clock system.

The Systems Division prepared an analysis of the probable costs to produce the clock systems. The amount that could be paid to the Devices Division for the integrated circuits was determined by working backward from the selling price. The cost estimates employed by the division reflected the highest per unit cost the Systems Division could incur for each cost component and still leave a sufficient margin so that the division's income statement could show reasonable improvement. The cost estimates are summarized below:

Proposed selling price.........		$7.50
Costs excluding required integrated circuits (IC378)		
Components purchased from outside suppliers........	$2.75	
Circuit board etching—labor and variable overhead....	.40	
Assembly, testing, packaging— labor and variable overhead.............	1.35	
Fixed overhead allocations..	1.50	
Profit margin.............	.50	6.50
Amount which can be paid for integrated circuits IC378 (5 @ $20 per hundred).....		$1.00

As a result of this analysis, the Systems Division offered the Devices Division a price of $20 per hundred for the integrated circuit. This bid was refused by the manager of the Devices Division because he felt the Systems Division should at least meet the price of $40 per hundred which regular customers pay. When the Systems Division found that it could not obtain a comparable integrated circuit from outside vendors, the situation was brought to an arbitration committee which had been set up to review such problems.

The arbitration committee prepared an analysis which showed that $.15 would cover variable costs of producing the integrated circuit, $.28 would cover the full cost including fixed overhead, and $.35 would provide a gross margin equal to the average gross margin on all of the products sold by the Devices Division. The manager of the Systems Division reacted by stating, "They could sell us that integrated circuit for $.20 and still earn a positive contribution toward profit. In fact, they should be required to sell at their variable cost—$.15 and not be allowed to take advantage of us."

Lou Belcher, manager of Devices, countered by arguing that, "It doesn't make sense to sell to the Systems Division at $20 per hundred when we can get $40 per hundred outside on all we can produce. In fact, Systems could pay us up to almost $60 per hundred and they would still have a positive contribution profit."

The recommendation of the committee, to set the price at $.35 per unit ($35 per hundred), so that Devices could earn a "fair" gross margin, was rejected by both division managers. Consequently, the problem was brought to the attention of the vice president of operations and his staff.

Required:

a. What is the immediate economic effect on the Lorax Company as a whole if the Devices Division were required to supply IC378 to the Systems Division at $.35 per unit—the price recommended by the arbitration committee. Explain your answer.

b. Discuss the advisability of intervention by top management as a solution to transfer pricing disputes between division managers such as the one experienced by Lorax Electric Company.

c. Suppose that Lorax adopted a policy of requiring that the price to be paid in all internal transfers by the buying division would be equal to the variable costs per unit of the selling division for that product and that the supplying division would be required to sell if the buying division decided to buy the item. Discuss the consequences of adopting such a policy as a way of avoiding the need for the arbitration committee or for intervention by the vice president.

(CMA, adapted)

12B-14   The Ajax division of Gunnco, operating at capacity, has been asked by the Defco division of Gunnco Corporation to supply it with Electrical Fitting Number 1726. Ajax sells this part to its regular customers for $7.50 each. Defco, which is operating at 50% capacity, is willing to pay $5.00 each for the fitting. Defco will put the fitting into a brake unit which it is manufacturing on essentially a cost plus basis for a commercial airplane manufacturer.

Ajax has a variable cost of producing fitting number 1726 of $4.25. The cost of the brake unit as being built by Defco is as follows:

Purchased Parts—Outside vendors........	$22.50
Ajax fitting—1726.....................	5.00
Other variable costs..................	14.00
Fixed overhead and	
administration......................	8.00
	$49.50

Defco believes the price concession is necessary to get the job.

The company uses return on investment and dollar profits in the measurement of division and division manager performance.

Required:

a.   Consider that you are the division controller of Ajax. Would you recommend that Ajax supply fitting 1726 to Defco? (Ignore any income tax issues.) Why or why not?

b.   Would it be to the short-run economic advantage of the Gunnco Corporation for the Ajax division to supply Defco division with fitting 1726 at $5.00 each? (Ignore any income tax issues.) Explain your answer.

c.   Discuss the organizational and manager behavior difficulties, if any, inherent in this situation. As the Gunnco Controller what would you advise the Gunnco Corporation President to do in this situation?

(CMA, adapted)

Learning Objectives

Chapter 13 discusses the cost concepts and accounting approaches which are related to the planning of special decisions. Studying this chapter should enable you to:

1. Provide examples of the types of decisions which are commonly referred to as special decisions.
2. Discuss the concept of relevance as it relates to the planning of special decisions.
3. Describe how the accounting records may provide useful information for the special decision-making process.
4. Identify the two characteristics which are common to all costs used for decision making.
5. Define and give examples of the various classifications of decision-making costs.
6. Discuss and apply the general formats for presenting relevant information for special decision making.
7. Identify those factors that should be considered in pricing a product.

13

Planning Special Decisions: Accounting Approaches

ACCOUNTING records and the accounting information system serve as the basic means for accumulating information on a historical cost basis for financial accounting purposes. Accounting also plays an important role both in the normal and recurring aspects of budgeting and in the control and performance evaluation functions. For financial accounting purposes, the role of record keeping is basically historical in nature. With regard to managerial accounting, record keeping is a combination of both forward looking projections and, on a selected basis, historical accumulations for purposes of comparison. In both of these instances, the accounting system is designed to capture and communicate recurring information.

The focus of this chapter emphasizes the accounting approaches which may be used for accumulating and presenting the information required for use in making decisions that are neither recurring nor routine. Examples of the type of decisions that fall into the non-recurring or special decision category include:

1. Accept or reject decisions for a special customer order.
2. Make or buy decisions for a specific component of the firm's products.
3. Continuance or discontinuance of an operating segment, such as a sales territory or a product line.
4. Pricing decisions.

RELEVANCE: THE KEY TO DECISION MAKING

The key to selecting an alternative in any decision-making process is to focus attention on the relevant information. Relevant information for decision-making purposes is that information which differs among the various alternatives under consideration. For example, if you were considering the purchase of a candy bar from a vending machine and all of the candy bars available cost 25 cents, the decision would not be based on the cost of the candy bar since all bars have the identical price. However, if you decided that you wanted a candy bar with peanuts and only two of the candy bars available met this criterion, then this is relevant information. The decision is now narrowed to only two alternatives, but additional relevant information is necessary in order to make the final choice. Thus, if you were allergic to chocolate and one of the two bars with peanuts contained chocolate, then this fact is also relevant to you in making the decision to select the candy bar that contains peanuts but no chocolate. The concept of relevance in the planning of special decisions is identical to the relevance considered in the candy bar example. The relevant factors analyzed in the candy purchasing decision were those factors that differed among the alternatives.

IMPORTANCE OF BOTH QUALITATIVE AND QUANTITATIVE FACTORS

The desire for a candy bar with peanuts but no chocolate is an example of the use of a qualitative factor in a decision-making process. Qualitative factors are not expressed in either numerical or monetary terms, yet for any particular decision, a qualitative factor may be the most important consideration. In fact, for many management decisions, qualitative factors are of primary significance and concern.

Accounting concepts play an important role in developing the quantitative factors which are considered in special decisions. Quantitative factors are those factors that can be expressed in numbers. In some instances, the quantitative factors are estimates or forecasts based on the subjective judgments of knowledgeable people or on specific studies designed to develop the estimates. The only quantitative factor in the candy bar example was the price of 25 cents, which was irrelevant to the decision since all of the available bars cost 25 cents.

DECISION-MAKING COST CONCEPTS

Decision making is, by definition, a process of selecting among various alternatives. The availability of all relevant information for each possible alternative would greatly facilitate this process. However, the cost of gathering all potentially useful information for each alternative is extreme. Therefore, although the accounting information system is not designed in terms of providing special decision-making information, accounting records often serve as a basis for accumulating the data which must be considered in making a special decision. For example, if a company is considering producing (with its existing equipment) a subassembly that it is presently buying, then accounting records could play a major role in developing the data required for the analysis. The cost of using the existing equipment to produce current products can be determined from the accounting records. This cost is then adjusted to reflect the different specifications required for the subassembly. The adjusted data serves as the basis for estimating the costs of manufacturing the subassembly.

Costs applicable to the decision-making process are classified differently than those costs which were defined for income determination purposes and for purposes of planning, control, and performance evaluation. Analysis of costs which are relevant to the decision-making process need not follow particular rules or special formats. These costs may be either product costs or period costs, fixed costs or variable costs, controllable costs or noncontrollable costs, common costs or traceable costs. However, all costs used for decision making do have two common characteristics:

1.   They are relevant, i.e., the costs will differ under the various alternatives.
2.   They are costs which are anticipated in the future under each of the various alternatives.

The cost definitions and the discussions of these definitions which follow are the basic concepts required in developing the accounting approaches used to analyze special decisions.

Relevant Costs

As previously indicated, relevant costs are those future costs that differ under the various alternatives that the firm is considering. Precision and accuracy are not always primary factors in determining relevance. Many relevant costs must be estimates since the precise cost may be known only after a particular alternative is selected and implemented.

The concepts of relevancy and accuracy are illustrated by the following example. Assume that during the next spring break you intend to visit a resort area. This resort is 1200 miles from your school and you have decided either to drive alone or to fly tourist class. A three hour direct flight is available at a round-trip cost of $400. Driving time is two days each way, thus time spent at the resort will be curtailed if this alternative is chosen. Regardless of whether you fly or drive, 14 nights and 15 days of vacation are available to you. Motel accommodations will cost $20 per day, and you expect to stay at a motel every night, including those nights spent on the road if you choose to drive. Food will cost $9 per day, and your car averages 25 miles per gallon of gasoline at an average cost of $1.50 per gallon. Your best estimate of the other costs such as oil, repairs, etc., total approximately $50. If you do not take your car, you do not anticipate renting a car during your stay at the resort. The resort has a courtesy car available that provides airport transportation at no cost. We will assume that the decision, as far as you are concerned, is strictly one of minimizing your vacation costs.

A summary of the total cost for each alternative follows:

By Car		By Airplane	
Oil, repairs, etc.	$ 50	Air fare	$400
Motel—14 nights @ $20	280	Motel—14 nights @ $20	280
Food—15 days @ $9	135	Food—15 days @ $9	135
Gasoline:			
$\frac{2400 \text{ miles}}{25 \text{ miles per gallon}}$ X $1.50	144		
Total cost by car	$609	Total cost by airplane	$815

As the above analysis indicates, you can save $206 ($815 — $609) by driving instead of flying. Note that in order to make this decision, all the costs do not have to considered. Only those costs that differ between the alternatives should be considered. Motel and food costs are identical under each alternative; therefore, these costs are irrelevant to the decision. If only relevant costs are considered, the cost data can be presented as follows:

By Car		By Airplane	
Oil, repairs, etc.	$ 50	Air fare	$400
Gasoline:			
$\frac{2400 \text{ miles}}{25 \text{ miles per gallon}}$ X $1.50	144		
Relevant cost by car	$194	Relevant cost by airplane	$400

The difference between the two alternatives is still $206—the difference between the relevant costs. Eliminating costs which are common to both alternatives has no bearing on the difference between alternatives.

The degree of accuracy in the accumulation of relevant costs is questionable. Numerous factors, such as accidents or breakdowns of the car, could alter the cost of driving. The price of gasoline could increase or decrease, and the air fare could also change.

This example considered only quantitative decision factors. In addition to these factors, there are numerous qualitative factors to consider:

the additional time that might be spent at the resort, the personal inconvenience of driving 2,400 miles, the countryside that can be seen by driving, and the safety factors of flying versus driving. None of these factors can be easily quantified and used as direct inputs in the decision-making process. Accounting approaches to decision making emphasize the quantitative factors and, at most, can only aid in identifying the qualitative factors.

Opportunity Costs

An opportunity cost is a measure of benefits that could have been derived had an alternative choice been made. For example, an opportunity cost could be the income foregone by not choosing the next best alternative which was under consideration. An opportunity cost may not always be measured with a high degree of certainty.

The concept of opportunity cost is related to every activity an individual or a firm undertakes, because an alternative course of action always exists. An opportunity cost is always associated with the commitment of scarce resources. For example, assume that you could work this evening for three hours and earn a total of $10. Instead, you choose to go out on the town and spend $15. You chose an alternative, and the income foregone or the opportunity cost associated with your decision was $10. The fact that you actually spent $15 does not affect what you gave up by choosing to go out rather than to work.

Another example of opportunity cost is illustrated by the decision to scrap defective products instead of reworking these units and selling them in the usual market. If a company had defective products that could be sold for 25 cents per unit as scrap or which could be reworked at an additional cost of 10 cents per unit and sold for 50 cents, then there is an opportunity cost involved for either alternative selected. The opportunity cost of the reworking alternative is the scrap value of 25 cents per unit. The opportunity cost of scrapping is 40 cents (the selling price of 50 cents less the reworking cost of 10 cents per unit). Note that the original production cost is not mentioned in either case as it is irrelevant in measuring opportunity cost. The production cost resulted from the initial decision to produce the units; it had already been incurred under either alternative.

Incremental or Differential Costs

An incremental or differential cost is the difference between the total costs of the various available alternatives. In practice, the term "incremental cost" is often used to describe the difference in costs incurred by producing at two different levels of activity. To illustrate the concept of incremental cost, assume that you decide to rent a car at a fixed charge of $15 a day plus a mileage charge of 20 cents per mile. The rental agency will reimburse you for any gasoline and similar expenses which you might incur. If you drive the car 800 miles in a four-day period, your rental cost is calculated as follows:

Rental Cost for 4 Days and 800 Miles
Fixed Costs—4 days @ $15.00......................	$ 60
Variable Costs—800 miles @ $.20....................	160
Total Rental Costs................................	$220

Assume that you decide to keep the car an additional day in order to make a 150-mile side trip. The incremental costs of keeping the çar and making this extra trip are calculated as follows:

Rental Costs—4 Days Versus 5 Days

	4 Days and 800 Miles	5 Days and 950 Miles	Incremental Costs
Fixed Costs—$15.00/Day	$ 60	$ 75	$15
Variable Costs—$.20/Mile	160	190	30
Totals	$220	$265	$45

It should be obvious that incremental or differential costs are always relevant costs when making a selection between or among alternatives.

Escapable or Avoidable Costs

As the term implies, escapable or avoidable costs are those costs which are saved or eliminated by making a particular decision or selecting a certain alternative. The concept of escapable costs is useful for decision-making purposes because, in many instances, certain costs may be avoided when one alternative is selected over another. This cost definition is frequently used in discussing the elimination of a division or a segment of a business.

If elimination of a segment of a firm is an alternative under consideration, escapable costs are limited to those costs that are directly traceable to that segment. Any arbitrarily allocated costs will still be incurred even if the segment is eliminated, and the remaining segments of the firm will be required to absorb these costs. An example of this concept is discussed later in this chapter when the elimination of segments is illustrated.

Out-Of-Pocket Costs

Out-of-pocket costs are those costs that require a definite outlay of funds. Relevant out-of-pocket costs are those costs which differ among the various alternatives being considered. Expenses such as depreciation or allocated costs are not considered out-of-pocket costs.

Sunk Costs

Sunk costs are costs which have already been incurred and which cannot be changed regardless of the selected alternative. Sunk costs are irrelevant as far as deciding among alternatives is concerned. An investment in fixed assets is a common example of a sunk cost. Once an asset is acquired, its original cost or net book-value is not considered in making future decisions. A relevant cost is a future cost which differs among the alternatives available. Costs which have already been incurred are neither future expenditures nor do these costs differ under the various alternatives under consideration.

If one alternative calls for the sale of an existing asset, the cash received for that asset and any tax implications of a gain or loss on the sale are relevant to that alternative. The net cash received from the sale of an asset, not the original cost or net book value of the asset, is the relevant information. The cost of retaining an asset is the net selling price of the asset because the cash received could be reinvested. It is impossible to reinvest the original cost or the net book value of a retained asset in another alternative; it is a sunk cost. The original cost is relevant only for purposes of calculating depreciation expense for the income statement, for calculating net book values for the balance sheet, and for determining tax implications regarding a sale.

GENERAL ACCOUNTING FORMATS FOR ARRANGING RELEVANT INFORMATION

Any format used for arranging decision-making information should emphasize those factors that differ among the available alternatives. Two general accounting formats used to arrange relevant information for the use of decision makers include:

1. Incremental cost and/or incremental revenue approach.
2. Contribution margin approach.

Neither of these general formats is applicable to every decision. For example, the contribution margin format requires that both revenues and the related variable costs be known in order for the contribution margin to be computed. In addition, the contribution margin format does not explicitly consider fixed costs; therefore, it is valid only when fixed costs are irrelevant. It should be noted that the contribution margin approach is not a "full" costing approach. Both formats are illustrated in the following special order decision-making process.

SPECIAL ORDERS: AN EXAMPLE

The Karson Company has idle capacity available in its manufacturing operations. A buyer outside Karson's usual marketing area has made an offer to purchase 50 units of a standard product, Edd, at a price of $1 per unit. Edd is normally sold by the Karson Company for $2. The Karson Company does not currently sell this product in the buyer's geographical area nor does the company plan to sell it in that area in the future. This is essentially a one-time purchase by this potential customer. Any freight expense will be paid by the buyer. If Karson Company sells to this buyer, it will have no impact on its current customers.

The *current* budget for Karson Company is as follows:

Karson Company
Budget for Product
Line-Edd

Relevant Range of Production	400-750 Units
Basis for Fixed Overhead Allocation	500 Units
Budgeted Sales 500 Units @ $2.00	$1,000
Variable Costs 500 Units @ $.75	375
Contribution Margin	$ 625
Fixed Production Costs 500 Units @ $.50	250
Fixed Selling and Administrative Costs	300
Budgeted Income Before Taxes	$ 75

Any approach to the decision to produce the special order for sale at $1 per unit which is based on full or absorption costing would result in a recommendation to reject the order since the proposed selling price is less than the full cost. The current full cost of the product (with the fixed overhead allocated over production of 500 units) is $1.25 per unit [($375 + 250)/500]. Even with fixed overhead of $250 allocated over 550 units of production, the full cost of the product on a per unit basis would be in excess of $1.20 [($412.50 + $250)/550].

However, the additional order of 50 units has come at a time when idle capacity is available and when this additional production will not affect the total fixed overhead costs incurred. A production level of 550 units is well within the relevant range of activity for the firm. Quantitatively, both formats for analyzing this special decision will agree, since fixed costs are not relevant to the decision.

Contribution Margin

	Per Unit	Total for 50 Units
Revenues	$1.00	$50.00
Variable Costs	.75	37.50
Contribution Margin	$ .25	$12.50

The above analysis provides the information necessary to make a decision using the contribution margin approach. The additional sales provide a contribution margin of $12.50 or $.25 per unit, which can be applied to the recovery of the unchanged fixed costs. Thus, given the existence of idle capacity, the decision to sell the additional 50 units of Edd appears to be financially sound.

The following analysis presents the information required to make a decision using the incremental income approach:

Incremental Costs and Revenues

	Budget Without the Order	Budget With the Order	Incremental Costs and Revenues
Budgeted Sales:			
500 units @ $2.00	$1,000.00	$1,000.00	–0–
50 units @ $1.00	–0–	50.00	$50.00
Variable Costs:			
500 units @ $.75	375.00	375.00	–0–
50 units @ $.75	–0–	37.50	37.50
Contribution Margin	$ 625.00	$ 637.50	$12.50
Fixed Production Costs	$ 250.00	$ 250.00	–0–
Fixed Selling and Administrative Costs	300.00	300.00	–0–
Budgeted Income Before Taxes	$ 75.00	$ 87.50	$12.50

If the special order is accepted, the incremental budgeted net income before taxes will be $12.50. Given that all other cost factors remain the same, management should accept the order. Remember, there was idle capacity available. Without this idle capacity, the decision may have been to reject the order.

MAKE OR BUY: AN EXAMPLE

In the short-run, for a firm to consider making component parts for products rather than purchasing those parts from vendors, the firm must have available idle capacity and the ability to make the parts. The question is one of using the idle capacity to produce the parts, using the capacity for other purposes, or allowing the capacity to go unused.

If only quantitative factors are considered in the decision to make or buy a part, the current purchase price must be known. The cost to make the part must also be determined. The only relevant costs for this decision are those costs that would be incurred if the part is made. Any arbitrarily allocated costs that could not be avoided if the part were not made are irrelevant. These costs are incurred by the firm under either alternative.

The accounting department made a study and developed the following cost of manufacturing the part. The normal demand for this part is 25 units per year.

Costs to Manufacture a Component Part

	Per Unit	Total at 25 Units
Direct materials	$ .20	$ 5.00
Direct labor	1.10	27.50
Variable overhead	.30	7.50
Avoidable fixed overhead	.40	10.00
Total	$2.00	$50.00

According to the quantitative data, if the purchase price of the part exceeds $2.00, then the firm should make the part itself.

There are also qualitative factors which should be considered in a make or buy decision. Examples of these qualitative factors include the following:

1. What quality is necessary? Can the firm make a better quality part?
2. Will the idle capacity be available? For how long will it be available?
3. Will current vendors of the part be willing to sell to the firm in the future if the supply of raw materials becomes limited?
4. Will future opportunities be lost because of the lack of idle capacity resulting from a decision to make the part?

The make or buy decision may be used in a number of contexts. For example, should a firm use a service bureau for computer work or establish its own facility? Should in-house salesmen be used or should commissioned factory representatives who sell for a number of firms be used? Should employees be used on special jobs or should consultants be employed?

ELIMINATION OF SEGMENTS: AN EXAMPLE

Elimination of a segment of a business such as a product line, division, or sales territory is based on the incremental (or differential) revenues which are lost and the incremental (or differential) costs which are avoided if the segment is dropped. Recall that conventional financial reports are based on full costs which include the arbitrary allocations of common costs.

Assume that a firm has one plant and three products. The firm prepares financial reports on the basis of full costs by product line. The actual performance for the previous year is presented in the following income statement.

Income Statement by Product Lines

	Product Line #1	Product Line #2	Product Line #3	Total
Net Sales	$200	$400	$400	$1,000
Cost of goods sold:				
Direct labor	64	48	48	160
Direct material	60	90	150	300
Variable overhead	20	40	40	100
Fixed overhead:				
Property taxes	8	6	6	20
Property insurance	4	3	3	10
Depreciation	32	24	24	80
Other	8	6	6	20
Total cost of goods sold	$196	$217	$277	$ 690
Gross margin	$ 4	$183	$123	$ 310
Expenses:				
Selling	12	24	24	60
Advertising	24	48	48	120
Interest	12	12	12	36
General and administrative	15	15	15	45
Total expenses	$ 63	$ 99	$ 99	$ 261
Net income (loss) before taxes	($ 59)	$ 84	$ 24	$ 49

It appears that product Line #1 is somewhat undesirable because it is operating at a loss. It might be erroneously inferred that if this line were dropped, the total net income before taxes for the firm would increase. Before any decisions can be made, however, each cost and expense item must be analyzed to determine which costs and expenses would be eliminated if the product line were dropped. The basis of allocation of each cost must also be identified in order to aid in the determination of that portion, if any, of the cost which would be eliminated by dropping the product line. All revenues from product Line #1 would be lost if the line were discontinued.

Analysis of Incremental Factors

	Product Line #1	Bases of Allocation	Incremental Costs and Revenue of Product Line #1
Net Sales	$200	none—directly traceable	$200
Cost of goods sold:			
Direct labor	64	none—directly traceable	64
Direct material	60	none—directly traceable	60
Variable overhead	20	none—directly traceable	20
Fixed overhead:			
Property taxes	8	direct labor hours	–0–
Property insurance	4	direct labor hours	–0–
Depreciation	32	direct labor hours	–0–
Other	8	direct labor hours	–0–
Total cost of goods sold . . .	$196		$144

	Product Line #1	Bases of Allocation	Incremental Costs and Revenue of Product Line #1
Gross margin	$ 4		$ 56
Expenses:			
Selling	12	percentage of sales	3
Advertising	24	percentage of sales	–0–
Interest	12	equal portions	–0–
General and administrative	15	equal portions	5
Total expenses	$ 63		$ 8
Net income (loss) before taxes .	($ 59)		$ 48

If product Line #1 were dropped, product Lines #2 and #3 would then have to absorb $107 (the difference between a $59 loss and $48 before tax income) in common costs which are now allocated to product Line #1. Income before taxes would have been $48 less last year because product Lines #2 and #3 would have had to absorb all of the fixed overhead and all fixed selling and administrative expenses. If a new income statement were prepared for the firm for the prior year, assuming that product Line #1 was dropped, the results would be as follows:

	Total Before Dropping Product Line #1	Incremental Costs and Revenues on Product Line #1	Total Without Product Line #1
Net sales	$1,000	($200)	$800
Cost of goods sold:			
Direct labor	160	(64)	96
Direct materials	300	(60)	240
Variable overhead	100	(20)	80
Fixed overhead:			
Property taxes	20	–0–	20
Property insurance	10	–0–	10
Depreciation	80	–0–	80
Other	20	–0–	20
Total cost of goods sold	$ 690	(144)	$546
Gross margin	$ 310	($ 56)	$254
Expenses:			
Selling	60	(3)	57
Advertising	120	–0–	120
Interest	36	–0–	36
General and administrative . . .	45	(5)	40
Total expenses	$ 261	($ 8)	$253
Net income before taxes	$ 49	($ 48)	$ 1

Without product Line #1, income before taxes is only $1, not $49. If only the incremental revenues and costs are considered, product Line #1 provides a contribution margin of $48 that is available to cover common fixed costs which would not be eliminated if the product line were eliminated.

If a similar analysis were applied to product Lines #2 and #3, it would demonstrate that each of these lines provide substantial funds from operations to cover common costs and contribute toward profits. As long as a segment of the organization provides incremental revenues in excess of incremental costs, the segment is contributing to the recovery of common fixed costs and thus making a contribution toward profit. The firm would reduce its total net income by eliminating such a segment.

PRODUCT PRICING TECHNIQUES

The factors affecting a pricing decision cannot be completely defined as there is neither a consistent theoretical nor practical approach that is appropriate for every situation that a firm might encounter. While the pricing decision is viewed by many firms as a short-run decision, the long-run implications are substantial. In the long-run, the prices charged for the entire line of products sold by a firm must first cover the fixed costs and then provide an acceptable margin of profit. Certain products will never be acceptable on a profit-making basis, but must be carried in order to provide a complete product line. Also, a product in the initial stages of market entry may not generate profits in the short-run.

The factors considered in a pricing decision include the following:

1. The economic considerations of supply and demand at different prices in a given time period.
2. The economic considerations of competition and substitute products.
3. The nature of the product and any competitive advantage which may result from unique capabilities or legal protection such as a patent.
4. Marketing considerations associated with selling and related to factors such as brand name, advertising, promotion, service capabilities, special applications, etc.
5. Legal implications of a given price in a specific market such as those covered under the Robinson-Patman Act which prohibits discriminatory prices that could reduce competition.
6. The investment which is required to produce the volume of product required.
7. The cost of producing the product.

From an accounting standpoint, the emphasis is on the last two items (6 and 7 above). In the short-run, the emphasis in accounting may focus on basic manufacturing costs rather than on the investment required to produce the product. However, it is obvious that the investment required directly affects the cost of producing a product in any given time period.

In some instances, it is possible that the investment should never have been made.

The discussion of pricing in this chapter considers two basic short-run cost approaches to pricing: (1) the contribution margin approach and (2) the cost-volume-profit approach. Chapter 14 discusses the long-range implications of whether or not the investment in assets should be made by the firm.

The Contribution Margin Approach to Product Pricing: An Example

The contribution margin approach is a short-run technique which may be used for product pricing. This method identifies the minimum price that can be charged for a product, assuming fixed costs do not change, without affecting the firm's profit. The minimum cost, and therefore price, is the total of all variable costs incurred in manufacturing and selling the product. Obviously, if the price charged for all products is equal to the variable costs of producing those products, the firm would operate at a loss. The total mix of products must cover all variable and fixed costs, and must provide a profit which allows the firm to obtain a satisfactory return on its investment.

Assume that a firm has developed a product that it wishes to introduce to the greatest potential market. The firm decides that the introductory price should be the lowest possible price that will neither increase nor decrease current profits. Management does not believe that fixed costs have been affected by this product. After reviewing the cost of making the product, the accounting department developed the following cost summary on a contribution margin format for management's use.

Pricing Decision—Using
The Contribution Margin Approach

Direct materials	$ .50
Direct labor	.75
Variable overhead	.30
Distribution costs	.05
Total variable cost	$1.60

If no other costs are involved, the minimum selling price of the product could be set at $1.60. At this price, the current profits from the sale of other products are not eroded. This approach has some merit in bidding situations, where the minimum price based on variable costs can be established and fixed costs do not change. After this absolute minimum is established, management can establish a price that provides a positive contribution margin.

Directly Traceable Costs and the Cost-Profit-Volume
Approach to Product Pricing: An Example

When a pricing approach based on costs is made, and fixed costs of any kind are considered, the question of volume must also be considered because the fixed cost per unit decreases as the volume increases. If the firm discussed in the contribution margin approach to pricing example was required to rent a warehouse for one year at a cost of $260 and anticipated an advertising campaign of $500 in addition to the variable costs already considered, the minimum price calculation to allow cost recovery becomes somewhat more complex. The new cost structure for the product would be as follows:

Pricing Decision—Using the Directly
Traceable Costs and the Cost-Profit-Volume Approach

Variable Costs:
Direct materials . . . . $ .50
Direct labor 75
Variable overhead 30
Distribution costs 05

Variable costs per unit $1.60

Managed Fixed Costs:
Warehousing $260
Advertising 500

Total managed fixed costs $760

The minimum price the firm must charge is greater than $1.60 per unit if the $760 of managed fixed costs are to be recovered. The problem of volume is now introduced. Management must determine an anticipated volume in order to determine the absolute minimum price possible. The minimum price is

$$\$1.60 + \frac{\$760}{\text{anticipated volume}}$$

If the anticipated volume were 1,000 units, the absolute minimum price would be

$$\$1.60 + \frac{\$760}{1,000 \text{ units}} = \$2.36 \text{ per unit}$$

At a price of $2.36, the profits of the firm would neither be increased nor decreased by the sale of this specific product, assuming that other products sold and other costs incurred remain constant.

SUMMARY

The management of a firm is often called upon to make special decisions of a non-recurring nature. Information used for special decisions may include historical data obtained directly from the accounting records as well as future projections based upon this data. In addition, a firm may find it necessary to conduct special studies to generate information which is not generally accumulated in the accounting records but which is required to make a given special decision.

Although both qualitative and quantitative factors are considered in the decision-making process, the accountant is generally concerned with providing only quantitative data; that is, data that can be expressed in numbers. Cost data for special decision making is a primary type of quantitative data provided by accountants.

All costs used for special decision making have two common characteristics. First, they must be relevant costs; that is, the costs must differ among the available alternatives. Second, the costs must be costs that are anticipated or expected in the future if one of the available alternatives is selected.

An opportunity cost measures the benefits that could have been derived had an alternative choice been made. Incremental cost, also referred to as differential cost, is the difference between the total costs of available alternatives. Escapable or avoidable costs are those costs that will be eliminated by selecting a given alternative. Costs that will require a definite outlay of funds, as opposed to depreciation or allocated costs, are often referred to as out-of-pocket costs. Any of the above costs may be relevant costs for special decision-making purposes. Sunk costs, on the other hand, are irrelevant for decision making because they represent past expenditures that cannot be changed regardless of the alternative chosen.

Examples of special decisions include decisions to: (1) accept or reject a special order from a customer, (2) make or buy a component part, (3) continue or eliminate a segment of the business, and (4) determine a price to charge for a product. No single special format exists for presenting information for special decision-making purposes. However, among the formats in general use are the incremental cost and/or revenue approach and the contribution margin approach. Although either format may be used in the analysis of a special decision, the incremental approach is more appropriate in cases where fixed costs are relevant.

This chapter has discussed many of the factors which must be considered in making special decisions. Chapter 14 discusses an additional factor, the investment of the firm's resources used in the long-range operations of the business.

KEY DEFINITIONS

Contribution margin approach—a general format for arranging relevant decision-making information showing additional revenues and related variable costs to be incurred under various alternatives in determining a contribution margin.

Escapable or avoidable costs—costs which may be eliminated by making a particular decision or selecting a certain alternative.

Incremental cost and revenue approach—a general format for arranging relevant decision-making information which considers total costs and revenues to be incurred under various alternatives in determining an incremental net income or loss.

Incremental or differential cost—the difference between the total costs of available alternatives.

Opportunity cost—a measurement of benefits that could have been derived had an alternative choice been made.

Out-of-pocket costs—costs requiring a definite outlay of funds.

Relevant costs—future costs which differ under the alternatives under consideration in a decision-making situation.

Sunk costs—those costs which are irrelevant for future decisions because the expenditure has already been made and cannot be changed regardless of the alternative selected.

QUESTIONS

1. What information should be considered relevant in making a non-recurring or special decision?
2. What is the difference between qualitative and quantitative factors used in making a decision? Which factor(s) do accounting records play an important role in developing?
3. Define opportunity costs and explain when they are most likely to be incurred.
4. What is an incremental cost and when is it relevant in making a decision?
5. What classification of cost might be an escapable cost when one considers eliminating a segment of a firm?
6. Why is depreciation not considered an out-of-pocket cost?
7. For what purposes is the original cost of an asset relevant in making a decision?
8. Give two examples stating decision-making situations in which the contribution margin approach would not be appropriate.
9. When a pricing decision is being made, on what factors is the emphasis placed from an accounting standpoint?
10. How is the contribution margin approach used in setting the minimum price for a product?

EXERCISES

13–1   Company A, a manufacturing firm, wants to know if it should manufacture or purchase part #29.

	Manufacture	Purchase
Direct materials	9,800	–0–
Purchased parts	–0–	20,000
Direct labor	6,300	–0–
Power	2,000	–0–
Other costs	1,500	–0–

13–2   In 1978 and 1979 the Chipper Company overproduced its Product L
because of an increasing demand for this product. In 1980 another
company began to produce an improved model of this product which
made Chipper Company's Product L obsolete. After inventory was
counted in 1980, they found they had $50,604 of Product L. After
considering many alternatives, it was determined that they could
sell the product for scrap for $6,850 or recycle it into another prod-
uct. It will cost $12,500 to rework the product, and it will sell for
$20,500. In addition to the additional cost, salesmen will receive
3 percent of the selling price.

Required:

What should be done with Product L?

13–3   The Squeak-E Tennis Shoe Company sells 20,000 pairs of tennis
shoes annually. They have fixed costs of $38,000 and direct costs of
$6.00 per pair. The shoes sell for $9.00 per pair. Squeak-E has a
capacity of 5,000 in excess of the 20,000 pairs of shoes they sell annually. They have just received an offer from a company outside their
present sales territory to buy 4,500 pairs of tennis shoes for $6.25
per pair.

Required:

a.   Should they accept this order?
b.   If Squeak-E did not have the excess capacity, should they accept the order?

13–4   The Easy Sleep Company is a large manufacturer of waterbeds. Unfortunately, due to the current water shortage, waterbeds have been
forbidden by law. Easy Sleep has a $60,000 inventory of waterbeds
at the present time. Easy Sleep must make a decision to sell the
waterbeds as scrap for a total of $5,000, or modify the beds to be
sold as life rafts. The modification will cost a total of $12,000, which
includes the purchase of a special machine. (This machine will be
sold after the modifications are finished for $3,000.) The total sales
expected from the life rafts are $16,000 less 10% sales commissions.

Required:

Should Easy Sleep modify the beds or sell them as scrap?

13–5 The following income statements were prepared by the accounting department for Russel Company for 1980. Assume all fixed expenses are allocated on an arbitrary basis to each department.

	Department J	Department K	Department L
Sales	$130,000	$200,000	$145,000
Variable cost of goods sold . .	90,000	120,000	70,000
Contribution margin from manufacturing	$ 40,000	$ 80,000	$ 75,000
Operating expenses:			
Fixed expenses	25,000	40,000	35,000
Variable selling expenses . .	5,000	8,000	4,000
Fixed selling expenses . . .	10,000	16,000	12,000
Net income	–0–	$ 16,000	$ 24,000

Required:

The president of Russel Company feels department J should be eliminated. How would you advise her?

13–6 Tipton, Inc. manufactures automobile parts. In 1980 the company had a large turnover in management. The new management decided to take a physical count of inventory. When they were finished, they found they had an excessive supply of parts for 1965 automobiles totaling $95,000. After checking further into the matter, it was decided the parts could be remachined for $25,000 and sold for $37,000, or they could be sold for scrap for $7,000.

Required:

What should Tipton, Inc. do?

13–7 The following information was made available concerning the 4 departments of the Roast Company.

	Dept. A	Dept. B	Dept. C	Dept. D
Sales	$100,000	$20,000	$50,000	$70,000
Variable cost of goods sold	70,000	10,000	30,000	45,000
Contribution margin from manufacturing	$ 30,000	$10,000	$20,000	$25,000
Operating expenses:				
Fixed expenses	20,000	4,000	10,000	15,000
Variable selling expenses .	10,000	3,000	6,000	12,000
Net income (loss)	–0–	$ 3,000	$ 4,000	($ 2,000)

Chuck Roast, the president of the company, has decided that one department must be dropped. Fixed expenses have been arbitrarily assigned according to the sales of each department. No matter which department is dropped the fixed expenses will be reduced one-fourth.

Required:

Which department should be dropped so as to give the greatest benefit to the company? What will be the company's income?

13-8   The Z Company makes saws; last year it sold 30,000 saws at a price of $5.00 and produced them at an average cost of $3.00. The sales manager thinks 40,000 units could be sold at a price of $4.30. The plant manager estimates that 40,000 units could be produced at a cost of $2.80 each.

Required:

What effect will this have on profit?

13-9   Ralph Company sells three products. Product B has yielded a net loss of $10,000 for the past three years, and there is no reason to expect a change in the future. Company officials also feel that the sales of the three products are not interrelated. Fixed expenses are allocated equally among the products in determining product profitability. Company records show:

	Product A	Product B	Product C
Contribution margin per unit	$6.50	$4.00	$7.00
Net income (loss)	$13,000	($10,000)	$16,000
Total annual fixed expenses are:	$42,000		

Required:

Based on the information given, should Product B be dropped?

13-10   Allen Tool Company is making plans for the coming year. Management feels that a target profit of $425,000 before income taxes would represent a satisfactory continuation of their growth pattern of earnings, which has been a steady 7% over the last 6 years. Marketing management has studied the market for the coming year and predicted the following sales possibilities.

	Selling Price	Advertising	Unit Sales
Alternative A	$5.00	No change	1,000,000
Alternative B	5.00	Up $60,000	1,120,000
Alternative C	5.50	No change	700,000
Alternative D	5.50	Up $60,000	810,000

Estimated fixed expenses for next year are $825,000 and estimated variable expenses are $3.75 per unit of product. These expense estimates do not include any changes in advertising. Note: In your answer show any necessary computations.

Required:

a.   What should the marketing strategy be?

b.   Suppose that management decided to change the selling price to $5.25 and raise advertising $45,000. If this will give unit sales of 775,000, will the target profit be achieved?

13-11   The Davis Company has been producing 20,000 units per month but wants to begin producing 25,000 units per month (capacity is 28,000 units per month) because of an increase in demand for their product. Davis has the following cost structure:

> Selling price = $1.60 per unit
> Variable manufacturing costs = $.35 per unit
> Fixed manufacturing costs = $15,400
> Variable selling expense = 5% of selling cost
> Fixed selling expense = $2,000

Required:

a.   Determine the incremental revenues and costs.

b.   Should Davis produce the additional units?

13-12   Russel, Inc. has been purchasing a component part from another company since it began operations five years ago. Russel now has a steady demand for its product and feels it has the capacity to produce the component part itself. Russel purchased 120,000 units at a cost of $1.10 per unit last year and feels it will purchase 10% more this year for the same price. If Russel produces this part, its costs will be:

> Direct materials   = $.45 per unit
> Direct labor   = $.30 per unit
> Variable overhead   = $.20 per unit
> Avoidable fixed overhead = $33,000

Required:

Should Russel Company purchase this part or produce it itself?

PROBLEMS SERIES A

13A-1   The Shelby Company normally produces and sells 50,000 units per year, but has the capacity to produce 75,000 units per year. Last year the company had the following income:

Sales		$450,000
Variable costs:		
Material	$100,000	
Labor	140,000	
Overhead	70,000	
Selling	13,500	
Shipping	25,000	348,500
Contribution margin		$101,500
Fixed overhead		30,000
Fixed selling and administrative expenses		42,000
Net income before taxes		$ 29,500

Shelby Company does not expect these relationships to change this year.

Another company that is not within Shelby's selling area has offered to buy 20,000 units at $6.90 per unit. Since there will be no salesmen involved, Shelby will not have to pay the sales commissions.

Required:

Determine whether Shelby should sell these units at $6.90. Give the incremental profit or loss if the extra units are sold.

13A–2 Woodville, Inc. has been buying one of its component parts for $6.47 per unit. The management of Woodville feels that the company could make this part with an increase in fixed costs of $27,000. They expect to need about 18,000 units per year. Variable costs per unit will be:

Direct materials	$2.00
Direct labor	1.80
Variable overhead	1.28

Required:

Determine whether the company should make the part or continue to purchase the part.

13A–3 The Silsbee Company has three products. Product #2 has incurred a loss for the past two years; therefore, management would like to drop this line. Given an income statement for 1980, you are to determine whether the company should drop this product. All "Fixed Overhead" items are allocated to the products as are all items under "Expenses" except selling expenses. Selling expenses are 2% of sales plus an allocated amount.

	Product Line #1	Product Line #2	Product Line #3	Total
Net sales	$280,000	$220,000	$300,000	$800,000
Cost of goods sold:				
Direct labor	$ 21,000	$ 34,500	$ 20,000	$ 75,500
Direct materials	25,000	24,600	24,000	73,600
Variable overhead	14,000	19,300	15,200	48,500
Fixed overhead				
Property taxes	28,000	22,000	30,000	80,000
Depreciation	56,000	44,000	60,000	160,000
Other	24,500	19,250	26,250	70,000
Total cost of goods sold . . .	$168,500	$163,650	$175,450	$507,600
Gross margin	$111,500	$ 56,350	$124,550	$292,400
Expenses:				
Selling expenses	$ 26,600	$ 20,900	$ 28,500	$ 76,000
Advertising	28,000	22,000	30,000	80,000
General and Admn.				
Expenses	42,000	33,000	45,000	120,000
Total expenses	$ 96,600	$ 75,900	$103,500	$276,000
Net income before taxes . .	$ 14,900	($ 19,550)	$ 21,050	$ 16,400

13A–4 Rick Rock, a well-known criminal, was considering the future revenues he could generate from two possible jobs. Due to risk and capital requirements, Rick can choose only one of the 2 possible alternatives. The breakdown of costs for each job was as follows:

Liquid Liquor Store (Job #1)

1 gun	$ 50
1 get-a-way bicycle	$ 100
1 ski mask	$ 10
1 day's observation	$ 70
1 laundry bag	$ 3
Expected payoff	$ 800

Easy Money Bank (Job #2)

3 guns	$ 240
2 accomplices	$2,000
1 get-a-way car	$1,000
Floor plans	$ 150
1 ski mask	$ 10
1 week's observation	$ 350
1 attache case	$ 60
Expected payoff	$4,400

Both jobs will be charged $150 for plane tickets to get Rick out of the state.

Required:

a. Which alternative is best for Rick assuming risk is the same?
b. Which cost(s) is irrelevant in making this decision?
c. What is the opportunity cost of the best alternative?

13A-5 Samuelson, Inc. is considering making a new product. The company has excess capacity on its machinery with which it can make the product. Since only minor adjustments to the machinery will be necessary in order to make the product, fixed costs will not increase. Variable costs per unit include:

Direct materials = 5 pounds @ $.89 per pound
Direct labor = 1½ hours @ $4.20 per hour
Variable overhead = 1½ hours @ $1.50 per hour
Distribution costs = $.25 per unit
Sales commissions = 2% of selling price

The company wants to introduce this product at the lowest possible price in order to induce customers to use their product rather than the competitor's product.

Required:

Determine the selling price of the product using the contribution margin approach.

13A-6 Harrington, Inc. plans to introduce a new product in 1981. The company would like to make 10% profit on the sales. They feel that they will be able to sell from 9,000 to 12,000 units in 1981. Variable costs per unit associated with the new product are:

Direct materials = 2 pounds of x @ $.32 per pound
3 pounds of z @ $.62 per pound
Direct labor = 1¼ hours @ $5.20 per hour
Variable overhead = 1¼ hours @ $2.60 per hour
Selling and distribution expense = $.35 per unit

In order to make this product, fixed production costs will increase by $34,000 per year. An advertising campaign costing $20,000 will also be initiated to promote the product.

Required:

Determine the range of selling prices for sales from 9,000 to 12,000 units.

13A–7   The Three Musketeer's Company is trying to decide whether they should spend $30,000 on an advertising campaign which will be in effect from May to December 1980. Below are the cost and production data for the first four months of 1980.

Months	Costs	Units Produced
1	$65,000	10,000
2	$70,000	12,000
3	$55,000	8,000
4	$60,000	9,000

The selling price is $7.50 per unit.

If the company maintains their present advertising strategy (no advertising), they expect sales to average 10,000 units a month for the last eight months of 1980. However, if they contract for the $30,000 advertising expenditure, they expect sales per month to increase to an average of 12,000 units for the last eight months of the year.

Required:

Using the method of semi-averages to separate costs into their fixed and variable components, decide whether this $30,000 advertising expenditure should be made.

13A–8   The Phono Company has a rather stringent attitude toward allowing credit to risky customers. The sales manager, however, believes that it would be more profitable to give the credit in the expectation that enough of these "high-risk" customers will pay their bills to allow the company to earn a contribution to fixed costs.

Presently, a decision must be made on this matter. Eight "high-risk" customers have each asked to purchase a television set on credit. The TV's sell for $350 apiece. Experience in the past shows that 75% of all "high-risk" customers will pay and 25% will not. Assume a total loss on any merchandise not paid for. The variable cost per T.V. set is $250.

Required:

Assuming that fixed costs will stay the same regardless of whether the TV's are sold to these eight customers, decide if Phono Company should sell the TV's.

13A-9   The Acre Company is in the business of spraying potato fields for weeds in northern Idaho. It has recently been offered two large jobs, but since they must be performed at the same time, only one of them can be chosen. Below are data relating to both jobs.

Job No. 1

Contract price	$ 9,250
Materials	$ 2,000
Labor	$ 3,600
Maintenance	$ 500
Insurance	$ 350
Depreciation	$ 1,700

Job No. 2

Contract price	$15,350
Materials	$ 3,360
Labor	$ 5,100
Maintenance	$ 750
Insurance	$ 410
Traveling expenses (This job is located 50 miles from the main office.)	$ 150
Depreciation	$ 1,700

Both jobs are charged with the depreciation on two spray-planes which were purchased three years earlier for $100,000.

Required:

a. Which alternative is best?
b. What cost(s) is irrelevant in making this decision?
c. What is the opportunity cost of the best alternative?
d. Identify the sunk costs in this decision.

13A-10   Costello and Costello Company paves driveways for residential homes. The average driveway costs about $5,000 to pave as determined below:

Direct materials	$2,500
Direct labor	1,500
Overhead	1,000
	$5,000

The overhead cost includes both fixed and variable costs and it is always allocated to each job by multiplying two-third's times direct labor. Total overhead for the year is $50,000 of which $40,000 is fixed. The remainder is variable and is directly proportional to direct labor. Mr. Costello has always used a direct markup of 25% on full costs in the past but his wife believes he should change his pricing strategy to the contribution margin approach. He has extra time and capacity to do more jobs than he gets orders for, so he decides to listen to what his wife has to say.

Currently, a customer has offered to pay $4,800 to have his driveway paved. This driveway is what Mr. Costello defines as an "average" driveway and therefore he usually charges $6,250 for the job (25% × $5,000) + $5,000.

Required:

a.   Taking his wife's advice, what is the minimum selling price which could be charged if Mr. Costello used the contribution margin approach to pricing?

b.   Should Mr. Costello pave this customer's driveway for $4,800? (CMA, adapted)

13A-11   The Simpson Shoe Company is a national wholesale firm organized in ten regions. The New England Region is divided into two territories, A and B, with one salesman for each territory. This salesman takes orders directly from retail stores in his territory and these orders are filled through the regional warehouse in Boston.

The results of operations for the New England Region (and territories A and B) for the year ended December 31, 1980 are as follows:

	Territory A	Territory B	Total
Sales	$350,000	$150,000	$500,000
Less expenses:			
Cost of sales	192,500	82,500	275,000
Direct advertising fees	12,500	10,500	23,000
Freight-out	4,500	3,000	7,500
Bad-debt expense	7,000	3,000	10,000
Supplies	7,250	5,250	12,500
Salesmen's salaries and commissions . .	25,500	15,500	41,000
Other salaries and wages	31,000	19,000	50,000
Employee benefits	9,750	6,750	16,500
Warehouse depreciation	15,000	15,000	30,000
Heat, light, and electricity (warehouse)	5,000	5,000	10,000
Territory contribution	$ 40,000	$(15,500)	$ 24,500
Units ordered	35,000	15,000	50,000
Pounds shipped	60,000	40,000	100,000

Explanatory notes:

1.   Freight-out and supplies are allocated on the basis of pounds shipped, except a fixed portion of supplies equal to $2,500 is divided equally.

2.   Bad debt expense is 2% of sales.

3.   Advertising fees are allocated directly to the territory they benefit.

4.   Each salesman receives a 5% commission on sales plus his regular salary.

5. Salaries, wages, and employee benefits at the regional office are
    as follows:

Three wage earners (equally paid and allocated in proportion
  to units ordered) $30,000
Regional warehouse manager (allocated equally to each
  territory) 20,000
Employee benefits (allocated at 25% of total salaries and
  wages paid per territory, excluding commissions) 16,500
                                                        $66,500

6. Warehouse depreciation and operating costs are allocated equally
    between the territories.

Required:

**Decide whether the Simpson Shoe Company should drop Territory B in
the New England Region. Assume that approximately the same results
of operations will result for Territory B in 1981 as resulted in 1980. Also
assume that *no* salesman will be dismissed regardless of what decision is
made, but if the territory is dropped, two wage earners will be put on a
part-time basis.**

(CMA, adapted)

13A–12 The following information summarizes the cost and revenue struc-
tures for Ace Sporting Goods manufacturer. Three products, racketball rackets, golf clubs, and lawn darts, are produced by the Iron
Rod Division.

    The Controller has given you the assignment of determining the
following: (a) minimum pricing policy for short-run and long-run
operations, (b) which product should be increased if there is excess
capacity—assuming no additional fixed costs, and (c) which product,
if any, should be dropped if demand increases 10 percent for racketball rackets, 6 percent for golf clubs, and 50 percent for lawn darts
and the products are sold at their current sales price. Fixed costs are
allocated to each product: (Assume that these fixed costs are directly
related to the products as indicated. Thus, if a product is dropped,
so are its fixed costs.) 26 percent to racketball rackets, 57 percent to
golf clubs, and 17 percent to lawn darts. (Note—the company will
not suffer a loss in plant and equipment if a product is dropped from
the Iron Rod Division.)

	Racketball Rackets	Golf Clubs	Lawn Darts
Demand (in Units)	150,000	225,000	500,000
Current sales price	$15.95	$78.75	$7.95
Variable costs	$7.88	$51.25	$2.25

Fixed Costs:	
Plant and equipment depreciation	$5,750,000
Manufacturing overhead	2,225,000
Selling and administrative	1,780,000
Total	$9,755,000

PROBLEMS SERIES B

13B–1   In 1980, the Bowen Company produced and sold 65,000 units. Bowen
sold each of these units for $11.00. The income statement for 1980 is
given below.

Sales		$715,000
Variable Costs:		
Material	$175,500	
Labor	156,000	
Overhead	91,000	
Selling	32,500	
Shipping	39,000	494,000
Contribution Margin		$221,000
Fixed Overhead		40,000
Fixed Selling and Administrative Expenses		65,000
Net Income before taxes		$116,000

Bowen Company does not expect the variable relationships to change in
1981, nor does it expect the fixed costs to change within a range of
50,000 to 100,000 units.

The company has projected sales of 70,000 units in 1981 at $11.00.
However, another company is negotiating with Bowen for a one time
sale of 20,000 units for $7.20 each. There will be no selling or shipping
costs involved in the sale.

Required:

Determine whether Bowen should sell these units. Give the incremental profit or loss if the extra units are sold.

13B–2   Cleburn, Inc. purchases component parts X and Y from two separate
companies for $10.16 and $8.42, respectively. They purchase 30,000
units of each part in one year. The company has excess capacity available in which it can produce only one of the parts. Fixed costs will
increase by $27,000 for X or $24,000 for Y. Variable costs will be:

	X	Y
Direct materials	$3.75	$2.25
Direct labor	4.00	3.10
Variable overhead	1.30	2.12

Required:

Determine whether the company should produce X or Y. If it can
produce both at a profit, determine which one it should produce.

13B–3   Wilson, Wilson, and Company has three products. Management
would like to drop Product X since it has not shown a profit for the
past three years. Given below is the company's most recent income
statement:

	Product X	Product Y	Product Z	Total
Net sales	$450,000	$450,000	$600,000	$1,500,000
Cost of goods sold:				
Direct labor	$160,000	$ 70,000	$ 50,000	$ 280,000
Direct materials . . .	120,000	45,000	80,000	245,000
Variable overhead .	56,000	50,000	59,000	165,000
Fixed overhead:				
Property taxes . .	30,000	30,000	40,000	100,000
Depreciation . . .	42,000	42,000	56,000	140,000
Other	24,000	24,000	32,000	80,000
Total cost of goods sold	$432,000	$261,000	$317,000	$1,010,000
Gross margin	$ 18,000	$189,000	$283,000	$ 490,000
Expenses:				
Selling expenses . .	$ 25,500	$ 25,500	$ 34,000	$ 85,000
Advertising	36,000	36,000	48,000	120,000
General and administrative				
expenses	48,000	48,000	64,000	160,000
Total expenses	$109,500	$109,500	$146,000	$ 365,000
Net income before taxes	($91,500)	$ 79,500	$137,000	$ 125,000

General and administrative expenses are totally allocated, while selling expenses are 3% of sales plus an allocated amount and advertising expenses are 2% of sales plus an allocated amount.

Required:

You have been asked to determine whether Product X should be dropped.

13B–4   Ira Smart was entering the construction business and was faced with choosing between two possible opportunities; building a $50,000 house or a $70,000 gas station. Ira had already purchased a $10,000 truck that had an expected ten-year life and no salvage value. The breakdown of the costs for each job are as follows:

House

Insurance	$ 600
Workers	15,000
Building Permit	1,000
Materials	10,000
Depreciation	1,000
Contract Price	50,000

Gas Station

Crane	$ 3,000
Insurance	1,500
Materials	14,000
Building Permit	1,000
Workers	20,000
Depreciation	1,000
Contract Price	70,000

Required:

a. Which job is most profitable for Mr. Smart?
b. What is the opportunity cost of the job chosen in "a"?
c. Which costs are irrelevant?
d. Which costs are sunk costs?

13B–5   International Products, Inc. has decided to introduce a new product. The company wants to sell the product at its lowest possible price in order to introduce it to the greatest potential market. Management does not feel this will affect fixed costs. **Variable costs per unit related to the product will be:**

> Direct materials = 3 pounds @ $1.20 per pound 3.60
> Direct labor = 2 hours @ $3.60 per hour 7.20
> Variable overhead = 2 hours @ $.90 per hour 1.80
> Distribution costs = $.20 per unit
> Advertising costs = $.10 per unit
> Sales commissions = 5% of selling price

Required:

Determine the selling price of the product using the contribution margin approach.

13B–6   General Company would like to produce a new product in 1981 but is uncertain whether it can meet the market price of $16.50. If they can meet the price, they feel they can sell 15,000 units in the first year.
  Variable costs per unit for the new product would be:

> Direct materials = 4 pounds @ $1.00 per pound
> Direct labor = 1 hour @ $4.50 per hour
> Variable overhead = 1 hour @ $2.00 per hour
> Selling and distribution expenses = $.25 per unit

Fixed production costs will increase by $60,000 per year. Advertising will increase by $22,500 per year.

Required:

Determine the lowest possible selling price General Company can charge for the product.

13B–7   The Micky Mouse Company is in the process of renewing its advertising contract for the first two quarters of 1981. The president has asked you to give him relevant information on this $50,000 expenditure in order to find out if it is worth the money to renew this contract. Below are the cost and production data for the year ended 1980. The costs do not include the advertising expenditure.

Quarters	Costs	Units Produced
1	$85,000	110,000
2	$86,000	115,000
3	$90,000	123,000
4	$94,000	128,000

The selling price per unit is $.80.

If the company renews the contract, sales are expected to average 33,000 units a month. However, if they don't renew their contract, sales are expected to decline to an average of 27,500 units a month.

Required:

Using the high-low method, separate the total costs into their variable and fixed components, and decide whether the company should renew this contract.

13B–8   The Kogwell Company is in the business of selling stereo equipment in a college town. Since school has started again, ten college students have applied to buy stereo systems on credit. Since these students only have part-time jobs, they are considered "high-risk" customers. Past experience has shown that 40% of this type of customer will take off with the merchandise and never pay for it. A stereo system sells for $500 and variable costs amount to $325 for the merchandise and $10 for delivery expenses. There are no financing charges.

Required:

Decide if the Kogwell Company should sell the stereo systems to these ten college students. Make your decision based on whether selling the merchandise will result in recovery of the costs necessary to sell the merchandise.

13B–9   The Smith and Jones Company does small remodeling jobs for residential homes and commercial office buildings. Recently they have been offered two major remodeling jobs, both requiring six months to complete. The problem is that both of the jobs must be performed at the same time. The data for each job is:

Job No. 1

Contract price	$60,000
Direct materials	$18,900
Direct labor	$ 8,560
Indirect materials	$ 4,500
Supervisor's salary (for 6 months)	$12,500
Warehouse depreciation (for 6 months)	$ 3,245
Depreciation on tools (for 6 months)	$ 2,550

Job No. 2

Contract price	$56,000
Direct materials	$17,600
Direct labor	$ 7,950
Indirect materials	$ 3,450
Supervisor's salary (for 6 months)	$12,500
Warehouse depreciation (for 6 months)	$ 3,245
Depreciation on tools (for 6 months)	$ 2,550

The company has one other alternative. They can contract to do two small jobs a month as has been done in the past. The average contract price of one of these jobs is $5,500; direct materials average 30% of contract price, direct labor 20%, and indirect materials 10%.

Required:

a.   Which of the three alternatives is the most profitable?
b.   Identify which costs are irrelevant to this decision.
c.   What are the opportunity costs associated with choosing the best alternative?

13B-10   E. Berg and Sons build custom-made pleasure boats which range in price from $10,000 to $250,000. For the past 30 years, Mr. Berg, Sr. has determined the selling price of each boat by estimating the costs of materials, labor, a prorated portion of overhead, and adding 20% to these estimated costs.

For example, a recent price quotation was determined as follows:

Direct materials	$ 5,000
Direct labor	8,000
Overhead	2,000
	$15,000
Plus 20%	3,000
Selling price	$18,000

The overhead figure was determined by estimating total overhead costs for the year and allocating them at 25% of direct labor.

If a customer rejected the price and business was slack, Mr. Berg, Sr. would often be willing to reduce his markup to as little as 5% over estimated costs. Thus, average markup for the year is estimated at 15%.

Mr. Ed Berg, Jr. has just completed a course on pricing and believes the firm could use some of the techniques discussed in the course. The course emphasized the contribution margin approach to pricing and Mr. Berg, Jr. feels such an approach would be helpful in determining the selling prices of their custom-made pleasure boats.

Total overhead which includes selling and administrative expenses for the year has been estimated at $150,000 of which $90,000 is fixed and the remainder is variable in direct proportion to direct labor.

Required:

a.   Assume the customer in the example rejected the $18,000 quotation and also rejected a $15,750 quotation (5% markup) during a slack period. The customer countered with a $15,000 offer.
   1.   What is the difference in net income for the year between accepting or rejecting the customer's offer?
   2.   What is the minimum selling price Mr. Berg, Jr. could have quoted without reducing or increasing net income?
b.   What advantages does the contribution margin approach to pricing have over the approach used by Mr. Berg, Sr.?

c. What pitfalls are there, if any, to contribution margin pricing?
(CMA, adapted)

13B–11 The Scent Company sells men's toiletries to retail stores throughout
the United States. For planning and control purposes the Scent Company is organized into twelve geographic regions with two to six
territories within each region. One salesman is assigned to each territory and has exclusive rights to all sales made in that territory. Merchandise is shipped from the manufacturing plant to the twelve
regional warehouses, and the sales in each territory are shipped from
the regional warehouse. National headquarters allocates a specific
amount at the beginning of the year for regional advertising.

The results of operations for the South Atlantic Region for the year
ended September 30, 1980 are presented below:

Scent Company
Statement of Operations for
South Atlantic Region
For the Year Ended September 30, 1980

Net Sales		$900,000
Costs and Expenses:		
Advertising Fees	$ 54,700	
Bad Debt Expense	3,600	
Cost of Sales	460,000	
Freight-Out	22,600	
Insurance	10,000	
Salaries and Employee Benefits	81,600	
Sales Commissions	36,000	
Supplies	12,000	
Travel and Entertainment	14,100	
Wages and Employee Benefits	36,000	
Warehouse Depreciation	8,000	
Warehouse Operating Costs	15,000	
Total Costs and Expenses		753,600
Territory Contribution		$146,400

The South Atlantic Region consists of two territories—Green and
Purple. The salaries and employee benefits consist of the following
items:

Regional vice-president	$24,000
Regional marketing manager	15,000
Regional warehouse manager	13,400
Salesmen (one for each territory with all receiving the same salary base)	15,600
Employee benefits (20 percent)	13,600
	$81,600

The salesmen receive a base salary plus a 4 percent commission
on all items sold in their territory. Bad-debt expense has averaged

.4 percent of net sales in the past. Travel and entertainment costs are incurred by the salesmen calling upon their customers. Freight-out is a function of the quantity of goods shipped and the distance shipped. Thirty percent of the insurance is expended for protection of the inventory while it is in the regional warehouse, and the remainder is incurred for the protection of the warehouse. Supplies are used in the warehouse for packing the merchandise that is shipped. Wages relate to the hourly paid employees who fill orders in the warehouse. The warehouse operating costs account contains such costs as heat, light, and maintenance.

The following cost analyses and statistics by territory for the current year are representative of past experience and are representative of expected future operations.

	Green	Purple	Total
Sales	$300,000	$600,000	$900,000
Cost of sales	$184,000	$276,000	$460,000
Advertising fees	$ 21,800	$ 32,000	$ 54,700
Travel and entertainment	$ 6,300	$ 7,800	$ 14,100
Freight-out	$ 9,000	$ 13,600	$ 22,600
Units sold	150,000	350,000	500,000
Pounds shipped	210,000	390,000	600,000
Salesmen miles traveled	21,600	38,400	60,000

The top management of Scent Company wants the regional vice-presidents to present their operating data in a more meaningful manner. Therefore, management has requested the regions to separate their operating costs into the fixed and variable components of order-getting (for example, sales commissions), order-filling (for example, freight-out), and administration. The data are to be presented in the following format:

	Territory Costs		Regional	Total
	Green	Purple	Costs	Costs
Order-getting				
Order-filling				
Administration				

Required:

a.   Using management's suggested format, prepare a schedule which presents the costs for the region by territory with the costs separated into variable and fixed categories by order-getting, order-filling, and administrative functions. [Hint: Allocate supplies, wages and employment benefits when necessary on the basis of pounds shipped; and allocate insurance (on inventory) on the basis of cost of goods sold dollars.]

b.   Suppose the top management of Scent Company is considering splitting the Purple Territory into two separate territories (Red and Blue). From the data that has been presented, identify what data would be relevant to this decision (either for or against) and indicate what other data you would collect to aid top management in its decision.

(CMA, adapted)

13B–12   The Feel Better While You Live Company produces a high protein drink and vitamins A, C, and E. With changing market conditions, the company has hired you to evaluate the current pricing strategy for these products. The following information is available.

	High Protein Drink	A	Vitamins C	E
Demand (in packages) . .	1,000,000	1,250,000	2,500,000	750,000
Current sales price				
(per package)	$7.98	$2.95	$1.95	$3.95
Variable costs				
(per package)	$2.45	$ .51	$ .65	$ .74

Fixed Costs	
Plant and equipment depreciation	$ 2,450,000
Manufacturing overhead	3,950,000
Selling and administrative	3,780,000
Total	$10,180,000

Note—Fixed costs are distributed as follows: 56 percent to protein drink, 12 percent to Vitamin A, 15 percent to Vitamin C and 17 percent to Vitamin E. (Assume that these fixed costs are directly related to the products as indicated. Thus, if a product is dropped, so are its fixed costs.)

Required:

a. What would be the minimum price for short-run and long-run operations?

b. Which product, if any, should be dropped if demand increases 30 percent for the high protein drink and 12 percent for each of the vitamins? (Assume there is no loss in disposing of fixed assets.)

c. What is your evaluation of the current pricing strategy, given the available information?

d. Given the current pricing policy, how much profit will this company make?

13B-13   George Jackson operates a small machine shop. He manufactures one standard product available from many other similar businesses and he also manufactures products to customer order. His accountant prepared the annual income statement shown below:

	Custom Sales	Standard Sales	Total
Sales	$50,000	$25,000	$75,000
Material	$10,000	$ 8,000	$18,000
Labor	20,000	9,000	29,000
Depreciation	6,300	3,600	9,900
Power	700	400	1,100
Rent	6,000	1,000	7,000
Heat and light...........	600	100	700
Other	400	900	1,300
	$44,000	$23,000	$67,000
	$ 6,000	$ 2,000	$ 8,000

The depreciation charges are for machines used in the respective product lines. The power charge is apportioned on the estimate of power consumed. The rent is for the building space which has been leased for 10 years at $7,000 per year. The rent, and heat and light are apportioned to the product lines based on amount of floor space occupied. All other costs are current expenses identified with the product line causing them.

A valued custom parts customer has asked Mr. Jackson if he would manufacture 5,000 units for him. Mr. Jackson is working at capacity and would have to give up some other business in order to take this business. He can't renege on custom orders already agreed to but he could reduce the output of his standard product by about one-half for one year while producing the specially requested custom part. The customer is willing to pay $7.00 for each part. The material cost will be about $2.00 per unit and the labor will be $3.60 per unit. Mr. Jackson will have to spend $2,000 for a special device which will be discarded when the job is done.

Required:

a.   Calculate and present the following costs related to the 5,000 unit custom order:
1.   The incremental cost of the order;
2.   The full cost of the order;
3.   The opportunity cost of taking the order;
4.   The sunk costs related to the order.
b.   Should Mr. Jackson take the order? Explain your answer.
(CMA, adapted)

13B-14 Anchor Company manufactures several different styles of jewelry cases. Management estimates that during the third quarter of 1981 the company will be operating at 80 percent of normal capacity. Because the company desires a higher utilization of plant capacity, the company will consider a special order.

Anchor has received special order inquiries from two companies. The first order is from JCP Inc., which would like to market a jewelry case similar to one of Anchor's cases. The JCP jewelry case would be marketed under JCP's own label. JCP Inc. has offered Anchor $5.75 per jewelry case for 20,000 cases to be shipped by October 1, 1981. The cost data for the Anchor jewelry case which would be similar to the specifications of the JCP special order are as follows:

Regular selling price per unit..........	$9.00
Cost per unit	
Raw materials...................	$2.50
Direct labor .5 hrs. @ $6.00........	3.00
Overhead .25 machine hrs. @ $4.00..	1.00
Total costs......................	$6.50

According to the specifications provided by JCP Inc., the special order case requires less expensive raw materials. Consequently, the raw materials will only cost $2.25 per case. Management has estimated that the remaining costs, labor time, and machine time will be the same as the Anchor jewely case.

The second special order was submitted by the Krage Co. for 7,500 jewelry cases at $7.50 per case. These jewelry cases, as with the JCP cases, would be marketed under the Krage label and have to be shipped by October 1, 1981. However, the Krage jewelry case is different from any jewelry case in the Anchor line. The estimated per unit costs of this case are as follows:

Raw materials...................	$3.25
Direct labor .5 hrs. @ $6.00........	3.00
Overhead .5 machine hrs. @ $4.00...	2.00
Total costs......................	$8.25

In addition, Anchor will incur $1,500 in additional set-up costs and will have to purchase a $2,500 special device to manufacture these cases; this device will be discarded once the special order is completed.

The Anchor manufacturing capabilities are limited to the total machine hours available. The plant capacity under normal operations is 90,000 machine hours per year or 7,500 machine hours per month. The budgeted fixed overhead for 1981 amounts to $216,000. All manufacturing overhead costs are applied to production on the basis of machine hours at $4.00 per hour.

Anchor will have the entire third quarter to work on the special orders. Management does not expect any repeat sales to be generated from either special order. Company practice precludes Anchor from subcontracting any portion of an order when special orders are not expected to generate repeat sales.

Required:

Should Anchor Company accept either special order? Justify your answer and show your calculations.

(CMA, adapted)

13B-15   The Justa Corporation produces and sells three products. The three products, A, B, and C, are sold in a local market and in a regional market. At the end of the first quarter of the current year, the following income statement has been prepared:

	Total	*Local*	*Regional*
Sales....................	$1,300,000	$1,000,000	$300,000
Cost of Goods Sold.......	1,010,000	775,000	235,000
Gross Margin...........	$ 290,000	$ 225,000	$ 65,000
Selling Expenses.........	$ 105,000	$ 60,000	$ 45,000
Administrative			
Expenses	52,000	40,000	12,000
	$ 157,000	$ 100,000	$ 57,000
Net Income.............	$ 133,000	$ 125,000	$ 8,000

Management has expressed special concern with the regional market because of the extremely poor return on sales. This market was entered a year ago because of excess capacity. It was originally believed that the return on sales would improve with time, but after a year no noticeable improvement can be seen from the results as reported in the above quarterly statement.

In attempting to decide whether to eliminate the regional market, the following information has been gathered:

		Products	
	A	*B*	*C*
Sales....................	$ 500,000	$ 400,000	$400,000
Variable Manufacturing			
Expenses as a			
Percentage of Sales...	60%	70%	60%

Variable Selling Expenses as a Percentage of Sales...	3%	2%	2%

Product	Sales by Markets Local	Regional
A	$400,000	$100,000
B	300,000	100,000
C	300,000	100,000

All administrative expenses and fixed manufacturing expenses are common to the three products and the two markets and are fixed for the period. Remaining selling expenses are fixed for the period and separable by market. All fixed expenses are based upon a prorated yearly amount.

Required:

a. Prepare the quarterly income statement showing contribution margins by markets.

b. Assuming there are no alternative uses for the Justa Corporation's present capacity, would you recommend dropping the regional market? Why or why not?

c. Prepare the quarterly income statement showing contribution margins by products.

d. It is believed that a new product can be ready for sale next year if the Justa Corporation decides to go ahead with continued research. The new product can be produced by simply converting equipment presently used in producing Product C. This conversion will increase fixed costs by $10,000 per quarter. What must be the minimum contribution margin per quarter for the new product to make the changeover financially feasible?
(CMA, adapted)

13B-16 The Vernom Corporation, which produces and sells to wholesalers a highly successful line of summer lotions and insect repellents, has decided to diversify in order to stabilize sales throughout the year. A natural area for the company to consider is the production of winter lotions and creams to prevent dry and chapped skin.

After considerable research, a winter products line has been developed. However, because of the conservative nature of the company management, Vernom's president has decided to introduce only one of the new products for this coming winter. If the product is a success, further expansion in future years will be initiated.

The product selected (called Chap-off) is a lip balm that will be sold in a lipstick type tube. The product will be sold to wholesalers in boxes of 24 tubes for $8.00 per box. Because of available capacity, no additional fixed charges will be incurred to produce the product. However, a $100,000 fixed charge will be absorbed by the product to allocate a fair share of the company's present fixed costs to the new product.

Using the estimated sales and production of 100,000 boxes of Chap-off as the standard volume, the accounting department has developed the following costs:

Direct Labor............	$2.00/box
Direct Materials.........	$3.00/box
Total Overhead.........	$1.50/box
Total	$6.50/box

Vernom has approached a cosmetics manufacturer to discuss the possibility of purchasing the tubes for Chap-off. The purchase price of the empty tubes from the cosmetics manufacturer would be $.90 per 24 tubes. If the Vernom Corporation accepts the purchase proposal, it is estimated that direct labor and variable overhead costs would be reduced by 10 percent and direct material costs would be reduced by 20 percent.

Required:

a. Should the Vernom Corporation make or buy the tubes? Show calculations to support your answer.

b. What would be the maximum purchase price acceptable to the Vernom Corporation for the tubes? Support your answer with an appropriate explanation.

c. Instead of sales of 100,000 boxes, revised estimates show sales volume at 125,000 boxes. At this new volume additional equipment, at an annual rental of $10,000, must be acquired to manufacture the tubes. However, this incremental cost would be the only additional fixed cost required even if sales increased to 300,000 boxes. (The 300,000 level is the goal for the third year of production.) Under these circumstances should the Vernom Corporation make or buy the tubes? Show calculations to support your answer.

d. The company has the option of making and buying at the same time. What would be your answer to part c if this alternative was considered? Show calculations to support your answer.

e. What nonquantifiable factors should the Vernom Corporation consider in determining whether they should make or buy the lipstick tubes?

(CMA, adapted)

13B-17 The management of Bay Company is considering a proposal to install a third production department within its existing factory building. With the company's present production setup, raw material is passed through Department I to produce materials A and B in equal proportions. Material A is then passed through Department II to yield product C. Material B is presently being sold "as is" at a price of $20.25 per pound. Product C has a selling price of $100 per pound.

The per pound standard costs currently being used by the Bay Company are as follows:

	Department I (Materials A&B)	Department II (Product C)	(Material B)
Prior Department Costs.	$ 0	$53.03	$13.47
Direct Material........	20.00	0	0
Direct Labor..........	7.00	12.00	0
Variable Overhead.....	3.00	5.00	0
Fixed Overhead:			
Attributable.........	2.25	2.25	0
Allocated:			
(2/3, 1/3).........	1.00	1.00	0
	$33.25	$73.28	$13.47

These standard costs were developed by using an estimated production volume of 200,000 pounds of raw material as the standard volume. The company assigns Department I costs to materials A and B in proportion to their net sales values at the point of separation, computed by deducting subsequent standard production costs from sales prices. The $300,000 of common fixed overhead costs are allocated to the two producing departments on the basis of the space used by the departments.

The proposed Department III would be used to process material B into product D. It is expected that any quantity of product D can be sold for $30.00 per pound. Standard costs per pound under this proposal were developed by using 200,000 pounds of raw material as the standard volume and are as follows:

	Department I (Materials A&B)	Department II (Product C)	Department III (Product D)
Prior Department Costs.	$ 0	$52.80	$13.20
Direct Material........	20.00	0	0
Direct Labor..........	7.00	12.00	5.50
Variable Overhead.....	3.00	5.00	2.00
Fixed Overhead:			
Attributable.........	2.25	2.25	1.75
Allocated			
(1/2, 1/4, 1/4)........	.75	.75	.75
	$33.00	$72.80	$23.20

Required:

a. If (1) sales and production levels are expected to remain constant in the foreseeable future, and (2) there are no foreseeable alternative uses for the available factory space, should the Bay Company install Department III and thereby produce product D? Show calculations to support your answer.

b. Instead of constant sales and production levels, suppose that under the present production setup $1,000,000 additions to the factory building must be made every 10 years to accommodate growth. Suppose also that proper maintenance gives these factory additions an infinite life and that all such maintenance costs are included in the standard costs which are set forth in the text of the problem. How would the analysis that you performed in part a be changed if the installation of Department III shortened the interval at which the $1,000,000 factory additions are made from 10 years to 6 years? Be as specific as possible in your answer.

(CMA, adapted)

Learning Objectives

Chapter 14 discusses the basic steps of the capital budgeting process, with special emphasis on evaluating and choosing among alternative long-term investments. Studying this chapter should enable you to:

1. Identify constraints affecting a firm's use of capital.
2. Discuss the principal types of data used to make capital budgeting decisions.
3. Explain how income tax considerations may affect the capital budgeting decision.
4. Describe the basic steps in developing a capital budget on a project-by-project basis.
5. Apply the various techniques of evaluating and/or ranking alternative investment possibilities.

14

Long-Range Planning: Capital Budgeting

In The previous chapter, the emphasis was on making a choice from among two or more alternatives when only revenues, cost savings, and costs are relevant to the decision. In that context the commitment of resources was not a relevant financial factor. In this chapter, however, the long-term investment of the firm's resources is a major consideration in the decision-making process.

Long-range investments imply a use of capital by the firm. Suppliers of capital demand an acceptable return on this resource. Management must balance the firm's demand for capital necessitated by new investments with the available supply of capital. The process of managing the supply and demand of capital and making decisions with regard to the use of available capital is referred to as capital budgeting. The capital budget is a list and analysis of all the long-range investments in which the firm is considering investing its available supply of capital. Acceptable capital investments must be consistent with the goals and objectives of the firm.

A capital budget may be regarded as both short and long-term. The capital budgeting decision considers both the firm's financial ability to provide acceptable returns on current and future capital and the degree to which the investment meshes with the firm's other short and long-range goals.

Once management has committed the firm's capital to specific long-term investments, the firm may have limited its potential investment alternatives for some time into the future. Once a capital investment is made, it is normally difficult to modify at a later date without incurring considerable losses. Usually, the original outlay for any investment can only be recovered through the use of the asset involved.

TYPES OF ACCOUNTING INFORMATION NECESSARY FOR CAPITAL BUDGETING DECISIONS

Accounting information which may prove useful in capital budgeting decisions includes both accrual and cash flow data. Accrual accounting information is based on generally accepted accounting principles which normally have a tendency to average the various financial factors involved in determining revenues, costs, and investments. Therefore, analysis based on accrual accounting information will reflect this averaging approach.

Generally accepted accounting principles are not considered in estimating cash inflows and outflows. Thus, the cash flows from an investment proposal will not necessarily coincide with either the income or the accrual accounting cost savings from an investment. For example, an investment in an asset usually requires an immediate cash outlay for the acquisition cost of the asset. From an accrual accounting standpoint, this cost is allocated to the appropriate time periods over the asset's projected life through the process of depreciation.

INCOME TAX IMPLICATIONS FOR CAPITAL BUDGETING DECISIONS

There are numerous income tax implications that should be considered in the capital budgeting decision. Certain tax considerations are beyond the scope of this text. However, the basic impact of income taxes and the investment tax credit should be considered in a capital budgeting analysis.

In order to stimulate the nation's capital investment, certain types of investments are given favorable federal income tax treatment in the United States. One means of stimulating investment in selected assets is the investment tax credit, which at this writing is a maximum of ten percent of the cost of the asset. If a firm purchases an asset eligible for the investment tax credit and if the asset is depreciated over a period of at least three years, the firm is entitled to deduct a percentage of that asset's cost from its federal income tax liability in the year in which the asset is acquired.[1] Thus, the investment tax credit actually reduces the firm's

---

[1] A carryback of three years and carryforward of seven years is allowed when the firm is unable to utilize the credit in the year the asset is acquired. The specified

net cash outflow for the asset by the amount of the investment tax credit allowed. In addition to this tax credit, which is a direct reduction of the amount of federal income tax liability (*not* the cost of the asset), the firm realizes further tax savings in that it can depreciate the total cost of the asset (less its salvage value) over the useful life of the asset ignoring the investment tax credit claimed. (The importance of the investment tax credit is obvious, but in the interest of simplicity it is ignored in the examples used in this chapter.)

Income tax implications with regard to any revenues, cost savings, or expenses associated with a capital investment must be considered. Assuming a 40 percent income tax rate, revenues or cost savings represent an after tax inflow of 60 percent of their gross amount (100 percent—40 percent). In other words, revenues (or cost savings in excess of expenses) associated with the proposed capital investment are taxed at 40 percent; 60 percent of the gross amount accrues to the firm. Likewise, expenses requiring a cash outlay have an after tax cost of only 60 percent of their stated amount.

Another income tax factor that should be considered in capital budgeting decisions is the effect of the depreciation taken on long-term investments upon taxable income and cash flows. Although it is a non-cash expense, depreciation is an allowable deduction for income tax purposes and as such causes a lower taxable net income and, consequently, lower taxes. The depreciation allowance indirectly reduces cash outflows by lowering the income tax liability. For example, assume a firm purchases an asset at a cost of $10,000 and depreciates this asset using the straight-line method, assuming a useful life of ten years with no salvage value. The firm will recognize depreciation expense of $1,000 a year ($10,000/10 years). If the firm's effective tax rate is 40 percent, that firm will realize a $400 tax savings ($1,000 X .40) in each of the 10 years the asset is depreciated.

THE CAPITAL BUDGET

Proposals for capital expenditures may be initiated by any group within the organization. Employees may propose an idea via suggestions to man-

---

portion allowed is based on the estimated useful life of the asset. If the asset has a useful life of at least seven years, the full 10 percent credit is allowed. If the life is less than seven, but at least five years, only two-thirds of the credit is allowed. If the life is at least three, but less than five years, only one-third of the credit is allowed. A recapture provision exists if the asset is disposed of prior to the end of its estimated useful life, thus causing the asset to be classified in a shorter life category. This would occur if an asset were purchased which has an estimated useful life of eight years (thereby qualifying for the full credit) but was disposed of after six years. In this case, one-third of the investment credit would be recaptured (i.e., one-third of the credit taken previously would be added to increase the tax liability in the year the asset was sold.)

agement; the research and development department may develop new products or alter current products so as to require capital outlays; technological change may introduce new methods; product demand may necessitate additional plant, equipment, warehouses, offices or other assets; or assets may simply wear out and necessitate replacement.

The process of developing the capital budget on a project-by-project basis may be divided into five steps: [2]

1. Initiating the idea and specifications.
2. Reviewing the request.
3. Making a decision regarding the request.
4. Controlling the project's progress and funds.
5. Conducting a post-audit of the results of the decision.

The five steps are presented here in order to structure the coverage and discussion of long-range capital investments. In practice, the distinction among these steps may not be as apparent or clear-cut as the above listing would lead one to believe.

INITIATION OF THE IDEA AND SPECIFICATIONS

In firms where numerous capital expenditure requests must be considered, the format of the request and the channels through which the request must be routed or directed are normally identified in the firm's policy manual. The sponsor of the request usually develops the basic idea with the aid of the appropriate supporting personnel from accounting, management, industrial engineering, the legal department, etc. If a specific department has the responsibility for developing the specifications and the capital expenditure request form for projects, the input of the original sponsor may be limited to developing the idea and basic estimates of the benefits and costs. An example of a request for a capital expenditure is presented in Illustration 14-1.

REVIEW OF THE REQUEST

If a firm is large and has numerous capital budgeting proposals, the request is normally reviewed by the sponsor's supervisor. The decision to accept or reject the proposal may be made at a lower level of management provided that the request is within the manager's capital budget limit. For example, department heads may have the authority to approve projects with a cost of up to $4,000 on an individual basis, with a maximum total of $15,000 in expenditures established for a given year. A divi-

---

[2] Six steps might be more appropriate if the firm wishes to consider the available alternative financing techniques.

Illustration 14-1
Capital Expenditure Request

Sax Company
Capital Expenditure Request

Project Title _____   Date _____

Project No. _____

Proposal Overview (Attach Detail)

Direct Capital Required _____   Depreciation Technique _____

Working Capital Required _____

Project Life _____

Average Revenues or Cost Savings _____

Average Period Expenses _____

Net Added Profits Before Taxes _____

Net Added Profits After Taxes _____

Average Annual Cash Flow _____

Justification:

Cash Payback _____   Present Value Index _____

Accounting Rate of Return _____   Internal Rate of Return _____

Net Present Value _____

Comments:

(Division)	Approval Date	(Corporate)	Approval Date
Project Sponsor _____		_____	
General Manager _____		_____	
Division Controller _____		_____	

sion manager may be able to approve expenditures of up to $30,000 with an aggregate limit of $150,000 in any given year. The president may be authorized to approve expenditures of up to $500,000 with an annual aggregate of $5,000,000. Normal procedures indicate that major capital expenditures should be approved by the board of directors.

The basis for establishing the various limits on expenditures at different levels within the organization is developed at the annual budget review session with top management. At this session, current proposals and related estimates are reviewed, combined and coordinated with ongoing projects from prior years and with projects in other segments or divisions of the organization. As might be expected, the forms and procedures for capital budgeting decisions in smaller firms are usually not as clearly developed or as formal as they are in larger firms.

MAKING A DECISION REGARDING THE REQUEST

There are numerous tools or techniques available to aid management in making capital budgeting decisions. Each of these techniques has strengths and weaknesses. Management normally employs several of these techniques. The most difficult part of the capital budgeting decision may well be obtaining quantifiable input data, i.e., the information and forecasts surrounding the project. After the initial proposal is prepared, making additional calculations to develop an unbiased perspective regarding a decision does not usually require significant effort or cost. If the firm has a computer facility or access to a computer service bureau, a program is usually available which will handle the basic techniques discussed in this chapter.

The techniques used to analyze proposed capital budgeting decisions may be classified into two general categories: (1) those techniques that ignore the time value of money and (2) those techniques that consider the time value of money.

Techniques That Ignore Time Value

There are several project evaluation techniques which do not consider the time value of money. While none of these methods should be used exclusively, they do have the advantages of being simple and easy to compute. They provide management with a quick method to facilitate a review of project feasibility. However, if the project involves large cash flow streams, the unadjusted evaluation techniques should generally be used as additional information to supplement a time value adjusted technique. Four project evaluation techniques which ignore the time value of money are discussed in the following section of this chapter.

No Choice or Urgency—Making the Decision

The distinguishing characteristic of the no choice or urgency technique is the real or implied need to make a decision immediately because of the particular circumstances at hand. This approach is the least desirable of the various capital budgeting techniques because, due to the urgency of the situation, profitability considerations are not analyzed, but rather are left to chance.

Urgency implies quick remedial action rather than deliberative action undertaken after a careful analysis of the available alternatives. If the potential resources involved are not great, the urgency criterion is probably justified. An effective planning scheme and a limitation on the amount of investment involved reduces the probability of large expenditures being made using the no choice or urgency plea as the basis for the decision.

Qualitative Reasons—Making the Decision

A second capital budgeting technique which does not consider the time value of money is based on qualitative rather than quantitative reasoning. In every capital budgeting decision, there are certain qualitative aspects that must be considered in addition to the available quantitative information. However, a capital budgeting decision based solely on qualitative criteria should be made only when the qualitative statements can be made with some degree of accuracy and when there is no quantifiable information available.

Qualitative reasoning is considered in many decisions made in areas such as organizational behavior or social commitment of resources. For example, if a firm chooses to install a lunchroom for its employees, this decision cannot be evaluated solely on its monetary returns. The lunchroom may have positive social value for the company which in and of itself justifies the investment. Although an investment in an employee lunchroom may produce quantifiable benefits for the firm in the form of increased revenues, decreased costs, increased productivity, lower employee turnover, or more satisfied employees, these benefits can only be measured indirectly in relation to the capital investment.

Qualitative reasons involved in capital budgeting decisions range from such factors as employee incentive plans to community relations activities for profit-oriented companies. In these decisions, it is frequently difficult to specify and quantify the benefits attributable to the investment except by comparing some aspect of the firm or its activities before and after the decision to see if a change appears to have taken place.

Payback Period—Making the Decision

The payback period is the amount of time required to produce net cash flows sufficient to recover the initial investment outlay. The payback technique does not consider the timing of the receipt of money, but is based totally on an analysis of cash flows. Moreover, the payback method does not measure the profitability of a project. This method is a simple calculation which determines the amount of time required to recover, in cash flows, the initial net investment in an asset.

The payback technique is widely used for a rough analysis of small investments that do not justify or warrant in-depth study or analysis. Despite its simplicity, the approach does have merit in the following situations:

1. If a company-wide policy requires payback within a stated time period for all capital investments below a selected dollar limit, the payback technique can effectively and efficiently screen small investment proposals before a formal request for expenditure is prepared.
2. If there is an element of uncertainty with regard to the estimates of future cash inflows or cost savings, the payback calculation provides a measure of how soon the firm can expect to recover its initial investment.
3. If cash flow is a major problem for a firm, timing of the cash returns from an investment may be considered crucial; thus the payback technique may provide relevant information.

The payback approach may be applied in several ways. The general formula is as follows:

$$\text{Payback period} = \frac{\text{Net Original Investment}}{\text{Annual Cash Inflows or Cost Savings}}$$

As long as the annual cash inflows are equal in amount, this general formula is applicable. If unequal cash inflows are expected, average cash inflows may be used or the projected unequal cash inflows for each year may be reviewed in order to determine the payback period.

To illustrate the use of the payback technique, assume that Sax Company is considering a labor-saving device that costs $1,000 and provides the following cash flow savings:

Year	Cash Flow Savings	Cumulative Cash Flow	Cumulative Cash Flow Net of Investment
1	$ 400	$ 400	($600)
2	300	700	(300)
3	300	1,000	0
4	300	1,300	300
5	200	1,500	500
Total	$1,500		

The average cash savings is $300 ($1500/5 years). Using this average cash savings, the payback period is calculated as follows:

$$\text{Payback} = \frac{\$1,000}{\$300} = 3\frac{1}{3} \text{ years}$$

If the cash savings are reviewed by specific years, the payback period is three years because $1,000 is recovered in the first three years.

The major weakness of the payback method is the disregard for the timing of the receipts and therefore the time value of money. A managerial decision which demonstrates the problem caused by a disregard for the time value of money is shown below:

	Investment A	Investment B
Cash Outflow	$1,000	$1,000
Cash Inflows		
Year 1	$ 200	$ 700
Year 2	300	200
Year 3	500	100
Payback Period	3 Years	3 Years

Alternative Investments A and B have the same investment outlays, same payback periods and are equally important to the firm. However, because capital available for investment is limited, only one investment can be selected. Since the payback period is the same for both Investment A and Investment B either alternative is equally desirable if the payback method is used as the sole criterion in choosing between these investments. An analysis of the timing of the cash flows expected under Investment B, however, points out that this investment provides a greater cash flow in the first year than does Investment A. Because there is a time value associated with future cash receipts (that is, a dollar today is of greater value to the firm than a dollar to be received next year), investment B is the better choice. The payback technique ignores the time value of money and thus is not an effective gauge of an investment's worth. The payback calculation is useful as a ranking technique in that it provides an index of the cash recovery period for an investment being contemplated. Payback should not be considered a comprehensive criterion in a capital budgeting analysis.

Accountant's Rate of Return—Making the Decision

The accountant's rate of return (ARR, also referred to as the unadjusted rate of return or accounting rate of return) also fails to consider the time value of money. Accrual accounting income is used as the basis for benefit measurement. Since income is considered in the formula, the technique does give some recognition to profitability.

The formula used for the accountant's rate of return is:

$$\frac{\text{Average Incremental Increase in Annual Net Income}}{\text{Net Original Investment Outlay}}$$

The accountant's rate of return may also be computed using the average investment outlay as the denominator. The formula then becomes:

$$\frac{\text{Average Incremental Increase in Annual Net Income}}{\dfrac{(\text{Original Investment} + \text{Salvage Value})}{2}}$$

The payback example can be used to illustrate the use of the accountant's rate of return, if certain additional assumptions are made. The labor-saving device considered in the payback example will be depreciated using the straight-line method over an expected life of five years. The salvage value of the asset at the end of five years is estimated to be $100. Sax Company wishes to make the analysis on a before-tax basis using both the original investment and the average investment.

$$\text{ARR Using Original Investment} = \frac{(\$1,500/5 \text{ years}) - \$180 \text{ Depreciation}}{\$1,000} =$$

$$\frac{\$300 - \$180}{\$1,000} = 12\%$$

$$\text{ARR Using Average Investment} = \frac{(\$1,500/5 \text{ years}) - \$180 \text{ Depreciation}}{\dfrac{(\$1,000 + 100 \text{ Salvage})}{2}} =$$

$$\frac{\$300 - \$180}{\$550} = 21.8\%$$

The accounting rate of return, like the payback technique, is a ranking technique. Alternative investments may be ranked in the order of their profitability to provide another measure to be used in making the capital budgeting decision.

TIME VALUE OF MONEY TECHNIQUES

Capital budgeting techniques which consider the time value of money are referred to as discounted cash-flow methods. A dollar today has a greater value than does a dollar one year from now; moreover, a dollar to be received one year from now has a greater value to a firm today than a dollar to be received five years from now. Money has value over time because it can be invested and a return on the investment can be realized.

The emphasis of capital budgeting techniques that consider the time value of money is on the timing and magnitude of cash flows. Two general discounted cash flow techniques available to assist in making capital budgeting decisions are the net present value method and the internal rate of return method. These two techniques and a variation of the net present value technique, the present value index, are considered in this chapter.

The concept of present value is discussed in the Appendix to this chapter. One must understand the Appendix and must be able to use Tables 14A–1 and 14A–2 prior to considering the net present value and the internal rate of return techniques. If you are unfamiliar with this concept you should go to the Appendix before continuing with the chapter material.

The techniques that employ the concept of the time value of money usually consider the impact of income taxes on cash flows utilized in the analysis. If income tax implications are not considered, the analysis of cash flows is incomplete and inaccurate. Two similar pre-tax investment alternatives may produce entirely different results on an after-tax basis. For this reason, after-tax cash flows should be used in an analysis in which income taxes are a relevant factor.

Net Present Value—Making the Decision

The net present value technique requires that the management of a firm specify the minimum desired rate of return on an after-tax basis which must be earned on capital investments in order to make them acceptable to the firm. This minimum acceptable rate is usually referred to as the cost of capital. In essence, the net present value technique discounts all projected outflows and inflows of cash back to the present period using the cost of capital as the discount rate. If the present value of anticipated cash inflows exceeds the present value of anticipated cash outflows, the project is acceptable because the investment is earning an after-tax return which is greater than the cost of capital. If the present value of projected cash inflows is equal to the present value of projected cash outflows then the net present value of the project is zero, and the project is earning exactly the cost of capital. If the net present value is negative, the project is earning less than the cost of capital because the present value of anticipated cash outflows is greater than the present value of anticipated cash inflows.

More than one of the alternatives under consideration may be capable of earning a return greater than the minimum return acceptable to management. When more than one alternative is acceptable using the net present value criterion, management will further compare the acceptable alternatives and then make its decision. The following example illustrates the use of the net present value technique and the alternative means of approaching an investment decision.

Northern Printing Company is considering the purchase of a new off-set printing press at a cost of $16,000. This press has an estimated useful life of five years and will result in a savings in operating costs of $5,000 per year over its useful life. The straight-line method of depreciation will be used and the estimated salvage value of the equipment is $1,000 at the end of year five. The equipment will require an overhaul costing $2,500 (considered a maintenance expense) at the end of the third year. Northern has alternative investment possibilities for the $16,000 that will yield a return of 16 percent after taxes. Because this alternative exists, the management of Northern has decided to use a rate of 16 percent as the cost of capital in evaluating the possible purchase of the printing press. In the past, Northern has averaged a 40 percent tax rate on its earned income. Management anticipates that a similar tax rate will be incurred in the future. If the offset printing press does not earn a projected return of 16 percent after taxes, Northern Printing Company does not wish to invest its resources in this project.

Part A of Illustration 14–2 identifies the cash flow impacts of the printing press on an annual basis. The discounting factors used are taken from Table 14A–1, Present Value of $1.00. Part B of Illustration 14–2 uses the annuity table, Table 14A–2, Present Value of Annuity of $1.00 per Period. For purposes of illustration, assume that all inflows or outflows of cash, with the exception of the initial investment, take place at the end of the year.

In part A of Illustration 14–2, the present value of the initial outlay of $16,000 is $16,000, because the money is paid out immediately. The cost savings realized each year are discounted to reflect their current dollar value if the rate of return on the funds is 16 percent. The cost savings are also multiplied by 60 percent (100 percent minus the income tax rate of 40 percent) to reflect the related income tax implications. If the printing press is purchased, the reductions in costs cause income to rise by $5,000 per year. At a 40 percent income tax rate, an additional $2,000 in income taxes is incurred annually. Therefore, the $5,000 reduction in costs is worth only $3,000 to Northern Printing after taxes.

The depreciation on the asset represents a tax shelter amounting to $3,000 per year. No cash is paid or received for depreciation, but it is a tax deductible expense used in arriving at taxable income for the period. Net income before taxes is reduced by the annual depreciation charge of $3,000, and income taxes are reduced by 40 percent of $3,000. The tax savings resulting from depreciation expense reduces the outflow of cash required to pay income taxes. Therefore, it is considered a cash inflow just as a cost savings is considered an inflow.

The overhaul expense at the end of the third year will not increase the life of the asset. This expense represents a cash outlay that will be incurred and which will be deductible at the end of year three for income tax purposes. With a 40 percent tax rate, the effective cost of the overhaul is 60 percent of the cash outlay of $2,500, or $1,500. Without this overhaul, the net income before taxes for the period would be $2,500 higher and additional taxes of $1,000 (.40 × $2,500) would have to be paid. Thus the net cost of the overhaul is $1,500.

Illustration 14-2
Net Present Value Technique

Part A: Year by Year Discounting

Outflows Year	Description	Before Tax	After Tax	Present Value Factor- 16%	Present Value
0	Printing Press Investment	$16,000	$16,000	1.000	$16,000.00
3	Overhaul Expense	2,500	1,500a	.641	961.50
			Total Outflows		$16,961.50

Inflows					
1	Operating Savings	$ 5,000	$ 3,000a	.862	$ 2,586.00
1	Depreciation	3,000	1,200b	.862	1,034.40
2	Operating Savings	5,000	3,000	.743	2,229.00
2	Depreciation	3,000	1,200	.743	891.60
3	Operating Savings	5,000	3,000	.641	1,923.00
3	Depreciation	3,000	1,200	.641	769.20
4	Operating Savings	5,000	3,000	.552	1,656.00
4	Depreciation	3,000	1,200	.552	662.40
5	Operating Savings	5,000	3,000	.476	1,428.00
5	Depreciation	3,000	1,200	.476	571.20
5	Salvage Value	1,000	1,000	.476	476.00
			Total Inflows		$14,226.80
			Net Present Value		($ 2,734.70)

Part B: Using the Annuity Table for the Same Inflows and Outflows Occurring in Multiple Years

Outflows					
0	Printing Press	$16,000	$16,000	1.000	$16,000.00
3	Overhaul Expense	2,500	1,500	.641	961.50
			Total Outflows		$16,961.50

Inflows					
1–5	Operating Savings	5,000	3,000	3.274	$ 9,822.00
1–5	Depreciation	3,000	1,200	3.274	3,928.80
5	Salvage Value	1,000	1,000	.476	476.00
			Total Inflows		$14,226.80
			Net Present Value		($ 2,734.70)

a Savings or Operating expenses are multiplied by 1 — the tax rate (in this example: 1 — .40 = .60).
b Depreciation expenses are multiplied by the tax rate.

Note the difference between the treatment of depreciation, a tax deductible item, and the overhaul which is also a deductible item for tax purposes. If no cash is paid for a tax deductible item, the amount of the effective cost savings is the tax rate multiplied by the amount of the tax deduction. If cash is paid for a tax deductible item, the effective cost (not the cost savings) of the item is 100 percent minus the tax rate. As shown in Illustration 14-2, the depreciation tax savings is considered an inflow and the overhaul cost is considered an outflow in the analysis.

The salvage value of $1,000 at the end of year five represents an inflow that has no tax implications, because Northern Printing Company is assuming no gain or loss on the disposal of the equipment. If a gain or loss on disposal were anticipated, then the income tax effects of this gain or loss would have to be considered. However, since the gain or loss may fall under special tax rates for capital gains, the 40 percent income tax rate may not be applicable.

The same principles underlying the calculations in Part A of Illustration 14–2 are also applicable to Part B. By using the annuity table to calculate the present values of the inflows and outflows for the two annuities (cost savings and depreciation tax savings), the time required to perform the calculations on a year by year basis has been reduced.

The net present value of the offset printing press is a negative $2,734.70. The present value of the outflows exceeds the present value of the inflows by that amount. Therefore, this potential investment is not expected to earn the required 16 percent after-tax return. Rather, the investment will earn something less than 16 percent. Had the net present value of the inflows exceeded the net present value of the outflows, then this investment could be expected to earn a rate of return in excess of 16 percent and would, therefore, have been an acceptable project for the company.

The net present value technique is the theoretically correct capital budgeting decision guide. It is not a ranking technique nor does it provide an answer that specifies the magnitude of the projected effective return on an investment.

Present Value Index—Making the Decision

The present value or profitability index converts the present value of the inflows and outflows as determined by the net present value method into an index. To derive this index, the present value of the inflows is divided by the present value of the outflows. The higher the ratio, the higher the rate of return per dollar invested in the proposed project. A ratio of less than one indicates that a proposed project is expected to earn a return less than the cost of capital. A proposed project with a present value index of one will earn exactly the cost of capital, while a present value index greater than one indicates a return in excess of the cost of capital.

The previously discussed net present value technique provides an answer stated in terms of current dollars. If only net present values are considered in selecting alternative projects, large dollar projects will normally have a net present value greater than that for small projects, even though the large projects may not be earning a rate of return as great as that earned by the small projects. The usefulness of the present value index is that different projects or investments can be ranked in terms of their relative profitability. The absolute dollar values for all projects can be converted to a relative measure of the profitability through the present value index. The present value index of the offset printing press in Illustration 14–2 is:

$$\text{Present Value Index} = \frac{\text{Present Value of Inflows}}{\text{Present Value of Outflows}}$$

$$= \frac{\$14,226.80}{\$16,961.50} = .839$$

An index of .839 indicates that the project will not earn the 16 percent rate of return or stated cost of capital.

Internal Rate of Return with Equal Cash Flows— Making the Decision

In the net present value technique discussed above, the required rate of return (cost of capital) is specified and the results indicate if the project will earn that rate, a greater rate or a smaller rate but the actual rate the project will earn is not determined. The internal rate of return or the time adjusted rate of return method determines the effective rate of return that a proposed project *will* earn over its expected life. The internal rate of return for the proposed project is then compared to the required rate of return to determine whether to accept or reject the project. The internal rate of return is that interest rate that equates the present value of the inflows with the present value of the outflows for the investment. The following example will illustrate the calculation of an approximation of the internal rate of return when the expected cash flows from a project are equal each period and therefore approximate an annuity.

Harry's Garage is considering purchasing a wheel alignment machine costing $10,000. Harry estimates that this machine will generate $10,000 annually in additional revenues and will cost $6,000 to operate on an annual basis. The machine has an estimated life of ten years with no salvage value anticipated. The straight-line method is used to depreciate the machine. Harry is currently taxed in the 50 percent tax bracket. He would like to know the effective annual rate of return on this machine on an after-tax basis.

To find the internal rate of return for Harry, the initial step is to determine the net annual after-tax cash flows generated by the wheel alignment machine.

Sales Revenue (cash).........................		$10,000
Less: Expenses		
Operating Costs (cash)......	$6,000	
Depreciation (non-cash).....	1,000	7,000
Net Income Before Taxes....................		$ 3,000
Income Taxes (cash)........................		1,500
Net Income After Taxes.....................		$ 1,500
Add Back: Depreciation (non-cash).........		1,000
Net Annual Cash Flow.......................		$ 2,500

If the potential investment has a minimal salvage value and if the payback on the investment is less than one-half the life of the asset, the payback method can be used in conjunction with the Present Value of an Annuity of $1.00 per Period shown in Table 14A–2 to approximate the internal rate of return.

$$\text{Payback Period} = \frac{\$10,000}{\$\ 2,500} = 4 \text{ years}$$

The payback period on the wheel alignment machine is four years, less than one-half the estimated life of the machine. Next, go to Table 14A–2 and scan horizontally the ten time period row (the life of the machine) to find the table value that approximates the payback period of four years. A table factor of exactly four does not exist, but if it did, it would fall somewhere between 4.192 and 3.923, the amounts for the 20 and 22 percent columns. The actual rate of return on the wheel alignment machine is between 20 and 22 percent. Precision may be increased by interpolation between the two rates, but given the measure of uncertainty in the initial estimates, the range of the two rates is probably adequate.

A proof of the solution for the internal rate of return for the wheel alignment machine is as follows:

Discounted at 22 percent	Inflow	Outflow
Initial Costs		$10,000.00
Sales Revenues ($10,000 × 3.923 × .5)	$19,615.00	
Operating Costs ($6,000 × 3.923 × .5)		11,769.00
Depreciation Tax Savings ($1,000 × 3.923 × .5)	1,961.50	
Present Values	$21,576.50	$21,769.00
Net Present Value		($192.50)

Discounted at 20 percent	Inflow	Outflow
Initial Costs		$10,000.00
Sales Revenue ($10,000 × 4.192 × .5)	$20,960.00	
Operating Costs ($6,000 × 4.192 × .5)		12,576.00
Depreciation Tax Savings ($1,000 × 4.192 × .5)	2,096.00	
Present Values	$23,056.00	$22,576.00
Net Present Value	$480.00	

If the cash inflows and outflows are discounted at a rate of 22 percent, then it can be seen that the investment has a net present value of a negative $192.50 and therefore earns an internal rate of return of less than 22 percent. If the investment is discounted at 20 percent, the net present value is a positive $480.00. The discount factor which would make the present values of the inflows and outflows equal lies at some point between those two rates.

Internal Rate of Return with Unequal Cash Flows— Making the Decision

Significantly unequal annual cash flows preclude the use of the payback period and the present value of an annuity table to approximate the internal rate of return, except as an initial starting point. To illustrate the calculation of the internal rate of return with unequal cash flows, the Northern Printing Company example from Illustration 14-2 is used. For convenience, the basic data are reproduced in the following example:

> Initial Cost—$16,000
> 5 Year Life
> Salvage Value—$1,000
> Straight-Line Depreciation—$3,000 per year
>
> Overhaul at the End of 3 Years—$2,500
>
> Annual Operating Cost Savings—$5,000
> Tax Rate = 40%

The initial step is to approximate the area of the Present Value of Annuity of $1.00 per Period table (Table 14A–2) that will be utilized.[3] Once again, an estimate of the payback period can be used to isolate the appropriate present value of an annuity factor.

---

[3] An alternative approach, which will not be covered, would entail solving the formula for the discount (interest) rate that would produce a zero net present value. That specific discount rate would be the internal rate of return.

Year	Calculations of After-Tax Cash Flows		Cumulative Cash Flow
0	Initial Cost	= ($16,000)	($16,000)
1	($5,000 × .6) + ($3,000 × .4)	= 4,200	(11,800)
2	($5,000 × .6) + ($3,000 × .4)	= 4,200	(7,600)
3	($2,500 × .6) + ($3,000 × .4)	= 2,700	(4,900)
4	($5,000 × .6) + ($3,000 × .4)	= 4,200	(700)
5	($5,000 × .6) + ($3,000 × .4) + $1,000 =	5,200	4,500

Payback period = approximately 4 years.

In the five time period row, the table factor of 4 years falls between 4.1002 and 3.9927, the amounts for the 7 and 8 percent columns of the Present Value of an Annuity Table—shown in Table 14A-2. Discounting of the cash outflows and inflows at 7 and 8 percent for this investment is shown as follows:

Discounted at 7%

	Year	Description	Before Tax	After Tax	Present Value Factor	Present Value
Inflows	1-5	Operating Savings	$ 5,000	$ 3,000	4.1002	$12,300.60
	1-5	Depreciation	3,000	1,200	4.1002	4,920.24
	5	Salvage Value	1,000	1,000	.7130	713.00
				Total Inflows		$17,933.84
Outflows	0	Printing Press	$16,000	$16,000	1.0000	$16,000.00
	3	Overhaul Expense	2,500	1,500	.8163	1,224.45
				Total Outflows		$17,224.45
				Net Present Value		$ 709.39

Discounted at 8%

	Year	Description	Before Tax	After Tax	Present Value Factor	Present Value
Inflows	1-5	Operating Savings	$ 5,000	$ 3,000	3.9927	$11,978.10
	1-5	Depreciation	3,000	1,200	3.9927	4,791.24
	5	Salvage Value	1,000	1,000	.6806	680.60
				Total Inflows		$17,449.94
Outflows	0	Printing Press	$16,000	$16,000	1.0000	$16,000.00
	3	Overhaul Expense	2,500	1,500	.7938	1,190.70
				Total Outflows		$17,190.70
				Net Present Value		$ 259.24

At 7 percent the net present value of the investment is a positive $709.39, while using the 8 percent discount rate produces a net present value of $259.24. Since the use of an 8 percent discount rate produces a positive net present value, the actual internal rate of return for the printing press is somewhat greater than 8 percent. If a 10% discount rate is used, the net present value will be negative. Therefore, the internal rate of return must be between 8% and 10%. Unequal cash flows require calculating with different trial discount rates until the two adjacent rates are found that identify the crossover point of the net present value. That is, one rate produces a positive net present value and the adjacent rate produces a negative net present value. The "true" internal rate of return could be found by interpolation after finding the crossover point.

Time Value of Money and Accelerated Depreciation Techniques

The straight-line method of depreciation has been used in each of the previous illustrations. If an accelerated depreciation method which is acceptable for income tax purposes is used, the pattern of the tax savings will, of course, change.[4] Using an accelerated rather than a straight-line method of depreciation will result in greater tax savings in the early life of an investment which, in turn, causes a change in the present value of the depreciation tax savings. If income taxes are relevant to the decision, accelerated depreciation will always provide a greater present value for the after-tax savings than that provided by the straight-line method of depreciation.

To illustrate this point, we will review the offset printing press example from Illustration 14–2. Recall that the printing press had a cost of $16,000, a five-year life, and an estimated salvage value of $1,000. Northern Printing Company had a cost of capital of 16 percent and was in the 40 percent tax bracket. The present value of the straight-line depreciation tax savings in Part B of Illustration 14–2 was found to be $3,928.80. If the sum-of-the-years' digits method of depreciation were used instead of the straight-line method, the tax savings from depreciation would be:

Sum-of-the-Years' Digits Depreciation

	Depreciation	Tax Rate	Present Value Factor 16%	Present Value
Year 1 $15,000 × 5/15 =	$5,000 ×	.4 ×	0.862 =	$1,724.00
Year 2 15,000 × 4/15 =	4,000 ×	.4 ×	0.743 =	1,188.80
Year 3 15,000 × 3/15 =	3,000 ×	.4 ×	0.641 =	769.20
Year 4 15,000 × 2/15 =	2,000 ×	.4 ×	0.552 =	441.60
Year 5 15,000 × 1/15 =	1,000 ×	.4 ×	0.476 =	190.40
Present Value				$4,314.00

Note that the present value of the tax savings increases from $3,928.80 to $4,314 when the sum-of-the-years' digits depreciation method is used rather than the straight-line method.

---

[4] As a general statement, the depreciation methods that are permissable for tax purposes are: straight-line, double-declining balance, and sum-of-the-years' digits.

CONTROLLING THE PROJECT'S PROGRESS AND FUNDS

Once a capital investment decision has been made by management, the next step in the capital budgeting process becomes important. Control must be established over the resources committed to the project and over the progress of the project. A budget and cost record is established for each project of the firm. The budget and actual costs must agree if a budget overrun is to be avoided. The original capital expenditure proposal is based on the best information available at the time the proposal is initiated. Therefore, variances are to be expected, but the variances should be explainable. As a rule of thumb, large capital expenditures should have smaller variances on a percentage basis, because they justify more in-depth planning.

The progress of the project must also be closely monitored. Many capital expenditure projects are closely related to the activities of other segments of the organization. When this interrelationship exists, a delay in the completion of one project could cause problems in other segments of the organization. Project delays usually mean increased costs. Illustration 14-3 is an example of a format which may be used for a capital expenditure budget for a firm.

Illustration 14-3
Capital Expenditure Budget

Sax Company Capital Expenditure Budget for 1981							
Project Origination	Total Budgeted	Budgeted For This Year	Actual For This Year	Under (Over) For This Year	Under (Over) to Date	Estimated Under (Over) For Total Project	Comment
Corporate:							
Project No. 9457							
Project No. 9459							
Power Turbine Shaft:							
Project No. 9425							
Project No. 9426							
Filters:							
Project No. 8567							
Project No. 8973							
Project No. 9367							
Tanks:							
Project No. 9410							
Project No. 9411							
Total ($)							

When a project is significantly off budget in terms of either dollars or time, an investigation should be undertaken. It may be necessary to revise the appropriation or the date of completion in order to coordinate expenditures for the entire firm.

A review of all on-going projects should be made on a regular basis. However, it is possible that a change in circumstances, technology, or economic conditions might warrant abandoning a capital investment project before its completion. The immediate losses resulting from abandonment may be less than the anticipated losses if the project is completed.

POST-AUDIT OF THE RESULTS OF THE DECISION

A post-audit of all major capital expenditures and a sample of the smaller expenditures should be made after completion of the projects in order to determine if the benefits expected from the projects did in fact accrue to the firm. There are certain problems associated with post-audits. Many expenditures are not independent of other operations, and the benefits derived from such expenditures are often neither easily nor objectively measurable. In addition, it may be necessary to convert the accounting records from an accrual basis to a cash flow basis if the original decision to make the expenditure was based on cash flows.

Post-audits can assist in identifying past mistakes made in planning capital expenditures, and can, hopefully, improve future inputs into this type of decision. In addition, the individuals responsible for preparing the estimates will probably be more cautious in their treatment of the capital expenditure decision when they are aware that their estimates will be reviewed upon the completion of the project and the subsequent start of operations.

SUMMARY

The process of managing the demand for capital and planning the use of available capital is referred to as capital budgeting. Capital budgeting includes analyzing and selecting alternative long-range investments which insure that the firm will meet both current and future profitability demands. Information required in the capital budgeting process is based on both accrual accounting and cash flow data. In addition, a firm must consider the income tax implications of any investment under consideration, especially if the investment tax credit is a factor.

The process of developing a capital budget on a project-by-project basis is divided into five basic steps: (1) initiating the idea and specifications; (2) reviewing the request; (3) making a decision regarding the request; (4) controlling the project progress and funds; and (5) conducting a post-audit of the results of the decision.

In making the decision regarding a particular capital investment request, a firm may choose to use various financial analysis techniques. The payback technique is a simple calculation which determines the amount of time required to recover, in cash, the initial net investment in an asset. The accountant's rate of return or unadjusted rate of return method is a measure of profitability, but does not consider the time value of money. Both the payback method and accountant's rate of return are tools that can be used to rank the relative desirability of alternative investments and are useful tools when employed along with other methods of analysis.

Capital budgeting techniques which consider the time value of money are referred to as discounted cash flow approaches. Among these techniques are the net present value technique, present value index and the internal rate of return technique. These approaches place emphasis on the timing and magnitude of cash flows.

APPENDIX: PRESENT VALUES

The Present Value Concept

When resources, usually cash, are invested there is an opportunity cost involved. An opportunity cost is defined as the income foregone by not choosing the next best alternative investment. When projects which require the use of resources are short-term, the opportunity cost is usually not substantial because the investment is only committed for a short period of time and will soon be converted back to cash and made available for possible reinvestment. When such projects have a long life, however, the cash inflows and outflows will occur over a long time period. The value of the cash flows over a long time period are not equal in terms of the value of a cash flow today (the present value).

The present value of $1 received today is $1 because it can be invested in assets with a value of $1 or deposited in a savings account to accumulate interest. The present value of $1 to be received one year from now is less than $1 because the opportunity to invest it and earn a return is lost for one year. The rational economic person would not give up $1 today to receive $1 a year from now because he could invest or save the $1 today and receive more than a $1 a year from now.

Calculating the Present Value of a Future Single Sum

The amount that would have to be invested today in order to receive $1 a year from now can be determined by using the following formula:

$$\text{Present Value} = \frac{\text{Future Value}}{(1 + \text{Interest Rate})^N}$$

(Where N = to the number of time periods to receipt or payment.)

If an interest rate of 10 percent and an annual interest compounding period* are assumed, the numerical formula for the present value of $1 to be received one year from now is:

$$\text{Present Value} = \frac{\$1}{(1 + .10)^1}$$

$$= \frac{\$1}{1.10}$$

$$= \$.90909$$

The present value of $1 one year from now with annual compounding is $.90909. If a 10 percent return on investment could be earned, the rational economic person would consider receiving $.90909 today the same as receiving $1 one year from today, given all other factors are equal. The sum of $.90909 will equal $1 one year from now at a 10 percent annual compounding as can be seen from the following calculation.

$$\text{Future Value} = \text{Present Value X } (1 + \text{Interest Rate})^N$$
$$= \$.90909 \ (1 + .10)^1$$
$$= \$.90909 \text{ X } 1.10$$
$$= \$1.00 \ (\text{Rounded})$$

To illustrate the calculation of the present value of a lump sum payment occurring more than one interest period in the future, assume that an investor could earn 10 percent compounded annually on his investment. The investor needs to plan his investment so that at the end of 3 years, he will have accumulated enough funds to pay a debt of $1 due the third year. To determine what sum must be invested today in order to meet the debt of $1 three years from now, the present value formula can be solved as follows:

$$\text{Present Value} = \frac{\$1}{(1 + .10)^3}$$

$$\text{Present Value} = \frac{\$1}{1.331}$$

$$\text{Present Value} = \$.7513$$

---

* An interest compounding period is that period over which interest will be calculated. If the compounding period is one year on bank savings accounts and interest is stated at 4%, the interest on $1 for a year would be $1 × .04 = $.04. If interest is to be compounded semi-annually, the interest on one dollar for a year would be $1 × .02 = $.02 plus $1.02 × .02 = $.0204. The total interest would be $.0404 under semi-annual compounding. The additional $.0004 in interest with semi-annual compounding is the interest on the $.02 interest from the first-half of the year.

The sum of $.7513 must be deposited at 10 percent interest compounded annually in order to produce one dollar at the end of three years. The calculation of interest per year and the total interest to date is presented in the following table.

Year	(1) Beginning of Year Principal and Accumulated Interest	×	Interest Rate	=	(3) Interest For This Year	(1) + (3) End of Year Principle and Accumulated Interest	Interest to Date
1	$.75130	×	.10	=	$.07513	$ .82643	$.07513
2	.82643	×	.10	=	.08264	.90907	.15777
3	.90907	×	.10	=	.09097	1.00000	.24874

Fortunately, the calculations of present values do not have to be computed manually for each individual receipt or disbursement. Tables have been developed from the formulas that provide a present value factor for $1 for any time period and at any interest rate. Table 14A–1, Present Value of $1.00, is presented at the end of this Appendix. This table provides the present value factors for computing the present value of a lump sum amount to be received in some future number of periods discounted at a given interest rate.

To illustrate the use of Table 14A-1, assume that the present value of $1 is to be calculated at a 10 percent discount rate compounded annually for a three-year period. Go to Table 14A-1 in the 10 percent column and look down the row to the present value factor for three periods. The present value factor is 0.7513; therefore, the present value of $1 to be received three interest periods from today discounted at a rate of 10 percent is $1 X .7513 = $.7513.

Calculating the Present Value of an Annuity

An annuity is a series of equal payments or receipts of cash to be paid or received over a number of equal time periods. An ordinary annuity will have equal payments or receipts at the end of each equal time period. The present value of any stream of payments or receipts can be calculated using the present value formula for a single sum or Table 14A-1 and computing the present value for each amount for each time period. Alternatively, the present value of an annuity table (Table 14A-2) may be used to find the present value of the cash stream.

Assume that $1 is to be received at the end of each year for the next three years and interest is to be calculated at 10 percent compounded annually. There are several ways that the present value of this cash flow can be computed. Two ways to compute the present value were discussed in the prior section of this Appendix when the present value of a single sum was calculated.

Alternative One:

The present value of the total stream can be calculated by using the present value formula.

$$\text{Present Value} = \frac{\$1}{(1 + .10)^1} + \frac{\$1}{(1 + .10)^2} + \frac{\$1}{(1 + .10)^3}$$

$$\text{Present Value} = \frac{\$1}{1.10} + \frac{\$1}{1.21} + \frac{\$1}{1.331}$$

$$\text{Present Value} = \$.9091 + \$.8264 + \$.7513$$

$$\text{Present Value} = \$2.4868$$

Alternative Two:

The present value can be calculated using Table 14A–1.

Inflows	×	Present Value Factors	=	Present Value
$1	×	.9091	=	$ .9091
$1	×	.8264	=	.8264
$1	×	.7513	=	.7513
$1	×	2.4868	=	$2.4868

The third alternative is to use Table 14A–2, Present Value of Annuity of $1.00 per Period, at the end of this Appendix. Table 14A–2 is a summation of Table 14A–1. To understand this look at the present value factors for 10 percent for one time period on both Tables. They are both .9091. Now look at the present value factors for two time periods at 10 percent. In Table 14A–1, the present value factor is 0.8264. In Table 14A–2, the present value factor is 1.7355; the sum of the first time period factor of 0.9091 plus the second time period factor of 0.8264 from Table 14A–1.

If the present value of a $1 annuity at the end of each year for three years is to be calculated using Table 14A–2, look at the 10 percent column and the row for the three periods to find the present value factor of 2.4869. *One* annuity payment or receipt is multiplied by the present value factor to compute the present value of the annuity, in this case $1 × 2.4869 = $2.4869. There is a slight rounding difference (at the fourth decimal point) between alternatives one and two as compared to alternative three.

KEY DEFINITIONS

Accountant's rate of return—a measure of the profitability of various capital

Table 14A-1
Present Value of $1.00

Periods (n)	1%	1½%	2%	2½%	3%	3½%	4%	4½%	5%	6%	7%	8%	10%
1......	0.9901	0.9852	0.9804	0.9756	0.9709	0.9662	0.9615	0.9569	0.9524	0.9434	0.9346	0.9259	0.9091
2......	0.9803	0.9707	0.9612	0.9518	0.9426	0.9335	0.9246	0.9157	0.9070	0.8900	0.8734	0.8573	0.8264
3......	0.9706	0.9563	0.9423	0.9286	0.9151	0.9019	0.8890	0.8763	0.8638	0.8396	0.8163	0.7938	0.7513
4......	0.9610	0.9422	0.9238	0.9060	0.8885	0.8714	0.8548	0.8386	0.8227	0.7921	0.7629	0.7350	0.6830
5......	0.9515	0.9283	0.9057	0.8839	0.8626	0.8420	0.8219	0.8025	0.7835	0.7473	0.7130	0.6806	0.6209
6......	0.9420	0.9145	0.8880	0.8623	0.8375	0.8135	0.7903	0.7679	0.7462	0.7050	0.6663	0.6302	0.5645
7......	0.9327	0.9010	0.8706	0.8413	0.8131	0.7860	0.7599	0.7348	0.7107	0.6651	0.6227	0.5835	0.5132
8......	0.9235	0.8877	0.8535	0.8207	0.7894	0.7594	0.7307	0.7032	0.6768	0.6274	0.5820	0.5403	0.4665
9......	0.9143	0.8746	0.8368	0.8007	0.7664	0.7337	0.7026	0.6729	0.6446	0.5919	0.5439	0.5002	0.4241
10......	0.9053	0.8617	0.8203	0.7812	0.7441	0.7089	0.6756	0.6439	0.6139	0.5584	0.5083	0.4632	0.3855
11......	0.8963	0.8489	0.8043	0.7621	0.7224	0.6849	0.6496	0.6162	0.5847	0.5268	0.4751	0.4289	0.3505
12......	0.8874	0.8364	0.7885	0.7436	0.7014	0.6618	0.6246	0.5897	0.5568	0.4970	0.4440	0.3971	0.3186
13......	0.8787	0.8240	0.7730	0.7254	0.6810	0.6394	0.6006	0.5643	0.5303	0.4688	0.4150	0.3677	0.2897
14......	0.8700	0.8118	0.7579	0.7077	0.6611	0.6178	0.5775	0.5400	0.5051	0.4423	0.3878	0.3405	0.2633
15......	0.8613	0.7999	0.7430	0.6905	0.6419	0.5969	0.5553	0.5167	0.4810	0.4173	0.3624	0.3153	0.2394
16......	0.8528	0.7880	0.7284	0.6736	0.6232	0.5767	0.5339	0.4945	0.4581	0.3936	0.3387	0.2919	0.2176
17......	0.8444	0.7764	0.7142	0.6572	0.6050	0.5572	0.5134	0.4732	0.4363	0.3714	0.3166	0.2703	0.1978
18......	0.8360	0.7649	0.7002	0.6412	0.5874	0.5384	0.4936	0.4528	0.4155	0.3503	0.2959	0.2502	0.1799
19......	0.8277	0.7536	0.6864	0.6255	0.5703	0.5202	0.4746	0.4333	0.3957	0.3305	0.2765	0.2317	0.1635
20......	0.8195	0.7425	0.6730	0.6103	0.5537	0.5026	0.4564	0.4146	0.3769	0.3118	0.2584	0.2145	0.1486
21......	0.8114	0.7315	0.6598	0.5954	0.5375	0.4856	0.4388	0.3968	0.3589	0.2942	0.2415	0.1987	0.1351
22......	0.8034	0.7207	0.6468	0.5809	0.5219	0.4692	0.4220	0.3797	0.3418	0.2775	0.2257	0.1839	0.1228
23......	0.7954	0.7100	0.6342	0.5667	0.5067	0.4533	0.4057	0.3634	0.3256	0.2618	0.2109	0.1703	0.1117
24......	0.7876	0.6995	0.6217	0.5529	0.4919	0.4380	0.3901	0.3477	0.3101	0.2470	0.1971	0.1577	0.1015
25......	0.7798	0.6892	0.6095	0.5394	0.4776	0.4231	0.3751	0.3327	0.2953	0.2330	0.1842	0.1460	0.0923
26......	0.7720	0.6790	0.5976	0.5262	0.4637	0.4088	0.3607	0.3184	0.2812	0.2198	0.1722	0.1352	0.0839
27......	0.7644	0.6690	0.5859	0.5134	0.4502	0.3950	0.3468	0.3047	0.2678	0.2074	0.1609	0.1252	0.0763
28......	0.7568	0.6591	0.5744	0.5009	0.4371	0.3817	0.3335	0.2916	0.2551	0.1956	0.1504	0.1159	0.0693
29......	0.7493	0.6494	0.5631	0.4887	0.4243	0.3687	0.3207	0.2790	0.2429	0.1846	0.1406	0.1073	0.0630
30......	0.7419	0.6398	0.5521	0.4767	0.4120	0.3563	0.3083	0.2670	0.2314	0.1741	0.1314	0.0994	0.0573
40......	0.6717	0.5513	0.4529	0.3724	0.3066	0.2526	0.2083	0.1719	0.1420	0.0972	0.0668	0.0460	0.0221
50......	0.6080	0.4750	0.3715	0.2909	0.2281	0.1791	0.1407	0.1107	0.0872	0.0543	0.0339	0.0213	0.0085

Table 14A-1 (Continued)
Present Value of $1.00

12%	14%	15%	16%	18%	20%	22%	24%	25%	26%	28%	30%	40%	50%
0.893	0.877	0.870	0.862	0.847	0.833	0.820	0.806	0.800	0.794	0.781	0.769	0.714	0.667
0.797	0.769	0.756	0.743	0.718	0.694	0.672	0.650	0.640	0.630	0.610	0.592	0.510	0.444
0.712	0.675	0.658	0.641	0.609	0.579	0.551	0.524	0.512	0.500	0.477	0.455	0.364	0.296
0.636	0.592	0.572	0.552	0.516	0.482	0.451	0.423	0.410	0.397	0.373	0.350	0.260	0.198
0.567	0.519	0.497	0.476	0.437	0.402	0.370	0.341	0.328	0.315	0.291	0.269	0.186	0.132
0.507	0.456	0.432	0.410	0.370	0.335	0.303	0.275	0.262	0.250	0.227	0.207	0.133	0.088
0.452	0.400	0.376	0.354	0.314	0.279	0.249	0.222	0.210	0.198	0.178	0.159	0.095	0.059
0.404	0.351	0.327	0.305	0.266	0.233	0.204	0.179	0.168	0.157	0.139	0.123	0.068	0.039
0.361	0.308	0.284	0.263	0.225	0.194	0.167	0.144	0.134	0.125	0.108	0.094	0.048	0.026
0.322	0.270	0.247	0.227	0.191	0.162	0.137	0.116	0.107	0.099	0.085	0.073	0.035	0.017
0.287	0.237	0.215	0.195	0.162	0.135	0.112	0.094	0.086	0.079	0.066	0.056	0.025	0.012
0.257	0.208	0.187	0.168	0.137	0.112	0.092	0.076	0.069	0.062	0.052	0.043	0.018	0.008
0.229	0.182	0.163	0.145	0.116	0.093	0.075	0.061	0.055	0.050	0.040	0.033	0.013	0.005
0.205	0.160	0.141	0.125	0.099	0.078	0.062	0.049	0.044	0.039	0.032	0.025	0.009	0.003
0.183	0.140	0.123	0.108	0.084	0.065	0.051	0.040	0.035	0.031	0.025	0.020	0.006	0.002
0.163	0.123	0.107	0.093	0.071	0.054	0.042	0.032	0.028	0.025	0.019	0.015	0.005	0.002
0.146	0.108	0.093	0.080	0.060	0.045	0.034	0.026	0.023	0.020	0.015	0.012	0.003	0.001
0.130	0.095	0.081	0.069	0.051	0.038	0.028	0.021	0.018	0.016	0.012	0.009	0.002	0.001
0.116	0.083	0.070	0.060	0.043	0.031	0.023	0.017	0.014	0.012	0.009	0.007	0.002	
0.104	0.073	0.061	0.051	0.037	0.026	0.019	0.014	0.012	0.010	0.007	0.005	0.001	
0.093	0.064	0.053	0.044	0.031	0.022	0.015	0.011	0.009	0.008	0.006	0.004	0.001	
0.083	0.056	0.046	0.038	0.026	0.018	0.013	0.009	0.007	0.006	0.004	0.003	0.001	
0.074	0.049	0.040	0.033	0.022	0.015	0.010	0.007	0.006	0.005	0.003	0.002		
0.066	0.043	0.035	0.028	0.019	0.013	0.008	0.006	0.005	0.004	0.003	0.002		
0.059	0.038	0.030	0.024	0.016	0.010	0.007	0.005	0.004	0.003	0.002	0.001		
0.053	0.033	0.026	0.021	0.014	0.009	0.006	0.004	0.003	0.002	0.002	0.001		
0.047	0.029	0.023	0.018	0.011	0.007	0.005	0.003	0.002	0.002	0.001	0.001		
0.042	0.026	0.020	0.016	0.010	0.006	0.004	0.002	0.002	0.002	0.001	0.001		
0.037	0.022	0.017	0.014	0.008	0.005	0.003	0.002	0.002	0.001	0.001	0.001		
0.033	0.020	0.015	0.012	0.007	0.004	0.003	0.002	0.001	0.001	0.001			
0.011	0.005	0.004	0.003	0.001	0.001								
0.003	0.001	0.001	0.001										

Table 14A-2
Present Value of Annuity of $1.00 Per Period

Periods (n)	1%	1½%	2%	2½%	3%	3½%	4%	4½%	5%	6%	7%
1....	0.9901	0.9852	0.9804	0.9756	0.9709	0.9662	0.9615	0.9569	0.9524	0.9434	0.9346
2....	1.9704	1.9559	1.9416	1.9274	1.9135	1.8997	1.8861	1.8727	1.8594	1.8334	1.8080
3....	2.9410	2.9122	2.8839	2.8560	2.8286	2.8016	2.7751	2.7490	2.7232	2.6730	2.6243
4....	3.9020	3.8544	3.8077	3.7620	3.7171	3.6731	3.6299	3.5875	3.5460	3.4651	3.3872
5....	4.8534	4.7826	4.7135	4.6458	4.5797	4.5151	4.4518	4.3900	4.3295	4.2124	4.1002
6....	5.7955	5.6972	5.6014	5.5081	5.4172	5.3286	5.2421	5.1579	5.0757	4.9173	4.7665
7....	6.7282	6.5982	6.4720	6.3494	6.2303	6.1145	6.0021	5.8927	5.7864	5.5824	5.3893
8....	7.6517	7.4859	7.3255	7.1701	7.0197	6.8740	6.7327	6.5959	6.4632	6.2098	5.9713
9....	8.5660	8.3605	8.1622	7.9709	7.7861	7.6077	7.4353	7.2688	7.1078	6.8017	6.5152
10....	9.4713	9.2222	8.9826	8.7521	8.5302	8.3166	8.1109	7.9127	7.7217	7.3601	7.0236
11....	10.3676	10.0711	9.7868	9.5142	9.2526	9.0016	8.7605	8.5289	8.3064	7.8869	7.4987
12....	11.2551	10.9075	10.5753	10.2578	9.9540	9.6633	9.3851	9.1186	8.8633	8.3838	7.9427
13....	12.1337	11.7315	11.3484	10.9832	10.6350	10.3027	9.9856	9.6829	9.3936	8.8527	8.3577
14....	13.0037	12.5434	12.1062	11.6909	11.2961	10.9205	10.5631	10.2228	9.8986	9.2950	8.7455
15....	13.8651	13.3432	12.8493	12.3814	11.9379	11.5174	11.1184	10.7395	10.3797	9.7122	9.1079
16....	14.7179	14.1313	13.5777	13.0550	12.5611	12.0941	11.6523	11.2340	10.8378	10.1059	9.4466
17....	15.5623	14.9076	14.2919	13.7122	13.1661	12.6513	12.1657	11.7072	11.2741	10.4773	9.7632
18....	16.3983	15.6726	14.9920	14.3534	13.7535	13.1897	12.6593	12.1600	11.6896	10.8276	10.0591
19....	17.2260	16.4262	15.6785	14.9789	14.3238	13.7098	13.1339	12.5933	12.0853	11.1581	10.3356
20....	18.0456	17.1686	16.3514	15.5892	14.8775	14.2124	13.5903	13.0079	12.4622	11.4699	10.5940
21....	18.8570	17.9001	17.0112	16.1845	15.4150	14.6980	14.0292	13.4047	12.8212	11.7640	10.8355
22....	19.6604	18.6208	17.6580	16.7654	15.9369	15.1671	14.4511	13.7844	13.1630	12.0416	11.0612
23....	20.4558	19.3309	18.2922	17.3321	16.4436	15.6204	14.8568	14.1478	13.4886	12.3034	11.2722
24....	21.2434	20.0304	18.9139	17.8850	16.9355	16.0584	15.2470	14.4955	13.7986	12.5504	11.4693
25....	22.0232	20.7196	19.5235	18.4244	17.4131	16.4815	15.6221	14.8282	14.0939	12.7834	11.6536
26....	22.7952	21.3986	20.1210	18.9506	17.8768	16.8904	15.9828	15.1466	14.3752	13.0032	11.8258
27....	23.5596	22.0676	20.7069	19.4640	18.3270	17.2854	16.3296	15.4513	14.6430	13.2105	11.9867
28....	24.3164	22.7267	21.2813	19.9649	18.7641	17.6670	16.6631	15.7429	14.8981	13.4062	12.1371
29....	25.0658	23.3761	21.8444	20.4535	19.1885	18.0358	16.9837	16.0219	15.1411	13.5907	12.2777
30....	25.8077	24.0158	22.3965	20.9303	19.6004	18.3920	17.2920	16.2889	15.3725	13.7648	12.4090
40....	32.8347	29.9158	27.3555	25.1028	23.1148	21.3551	19.7928	18.4016	17.1591	15.0463	13.3317
50....	39.1961	34.9997	31.4236	28.3623	25.7298	23.4556	21.4822	19.7620	18.2559	15.7619	13.8007

Table 14A-2 (Continued)
Present Value of Annuity of $1.00 Per Period

8%	10%	12%	14%	15%	16%	18%	20%	22%	24%	25%	26%	28%	30%	40%	50%
0.9259	0.9091	0.893	0.877	0.870	0.862	0.847	0.833	0.820	0.806	0.800	0.794	0.781	0.769	0.714	0.667
1.7833	1.7355	1.690	1.647	1.626	1.605	1.566	1.528	1.492	1.457	1.440	1.424	1.392	1.361	1.224	1.111
2.5771	2.4869	2.402	2.322	2.283	2.246	2.174	2.106	2.042	1.981	1.952	1.923	1.868	1.816	1.589	1.407
3.3121	3.1699	3.037	2.914	2.855	2.798	2.690	2.589	2.494	2.404	2.362	2.320	2.241	2.166	1.849	1.605
3.9927	3.7908	3.605	3.433	3.352	3.274	3.127	2.991	2.864	2.745	2.689	2.635	2.532	2.436	2.035	1.737
4.6229	4.3553	4.111	3.889	3.784	3.685	3.498	3.326	3.167	3.020	2.951	2.885	2.759	2.643	2.168	1.824
5.2064	4.8684	4.564	4.288	4.160	4.039	3.812	3.605	3.416	3.242	3.161	3.083	2.937	2.802	2.263	1.883
5.7466	5.3349	4.968	4.639	4.487	4.344	4.078	3.837	3.619	3.421	3.329	3.241	3.076	2.925	2.331	1.922
6.2469	5.7590	5.328	4.946	4.772	4.607	4.303	4.031	3.786	3.566	3.463	3.366	3.184	3.019	2.379	1.948
6.7101	6.1446	5.650	5.216	5.019	4.833	4.494	4.192	3.923	3.682	3.571	3.465	3.269	3.092	2.414	1.965
7.1390	6.4951	5.988	5.453	5.234	5.029	4.656	4.327	4.035	3.776	3.656	3.544	3.335	3.147	2.438	1.977
7.5361	6.8137	6.194	5.660	5.421	5.197	4.793	4.439	4.127	3.851	3.725	3.606	3.387	3.190	2.456	1.985
7.9038	7.1034	6.424	5.842	5.583	5.342	4.910	4.533	4.203	3.912	3.780	3.656	3.427	3.223	2.468	1.990
8.2442	7.3667	6.628	6.002	5.724	5.468	5.008	4.611	4.265	3.962	3.824	3.695	3.459	3.249	2.477	1.993
8.5595	7.6061	6.811	6.142	5.847	5.575	5.092	4.675	4.315	4.001	3.859	3.726	3.483	3.268	2.484	1.995
8.8514	7.8237	6.974	6.265	5.954	5.669	5.162	4.730	4.357	4.033	3.887	3.751	3.503	3.283	2.489	1.997
9.1216	8.0216	7.120	6.373	6.047	5.749	5.222	4.775	4.391	4.059	3.910	3.771	3.518	3.295	2.492	1.998
9.3719	8.2014	7.250	6.467	6.128	5.818	5.273	4.812	4.419	4.080	3.928	3.786	3.529	3.304	2.494	1.999
9.6036	8.3649	7.366	6.550	6.198	5.877	5.316	4.844	4.442	4.097	3.942	3.799	3.539	3.311	2.496	1.999
9.8181	8.5136	7.469	6.623	6.259	5.929	5.353	4.870	4.460	4.110	3.954	3.808	3.546	3.316	2.497	1.999
10.0168	8.6487	7.562	6.687	6.312	5.973	5.384	4.891	4.476	4.121	3.963	3.816	3.551	3.320	2.498	2.000
10.2007	8.7715	7.645	6.743	6.359	6.011	5.410	4.909	4.488	4.130	3.970	3.822	3.556	3.323	2.498	2.000
10.3711	8.8832	7.718	6.792	6.399	6.044	5.432	4.925	4.499	4.137	3.976	3.827	3.559	3.325	2.499	2.000
10.5288	8.9847	7.784	6.835	6.434	6.073	5.451	4.937	4.507	4.143	3.981	3.831	3.562	3.327	2.499	2.000
10.6748	9.0770	7.843	6.873	6.464	6.097	5.467	4.948	4.514	4.147	3.985	3.834	3.564	3.329	2.499	2.000
10.8100	9.1609	7.896	6.906	6.491	6.118	5.480	4.956	4.520	4.151	3.988	3.837	3.566	3.330	2.500	2.000
10.9352	9.2372	7.943	6.935	6.514	6.136	5.492	4.964	4.524	4.154	3.990	3.839	3.567	3.331	2.500	2.000
11.0511	9.3066	7.984	6.961	6.534	6.152	5.502	4.970	4.528	4.157	3.992	3.840	3.568	3.331	2.500	2.000
11.1584	9.3696	8.022	6.983	6.551	6.166	5.510	4.975	4.531	4.159	3.994	3.841	3.569	3.332	2.500	2.000
11.2578	9.4269	8.055	7.003	6.566	6.177	5.517	4.979	4.534	4.160	3.995	3.842	3.569	3.332	2.500	2.000
11.9246	9.7791	8.244	7.105	6.642	6.234	5.548	4.997	4.544	4.166	3.999	3.846	3.571	3.333	2.500	2.000
12.2335	9.9148	8.304	7.133	6.661	6.246	5.554	4.999	4.545	4.167	4.000	3.846	3.571	3.333	2.500	2.000

expenditures which expresses the related incremental increases in income as a percentage of the net original or average investment outlay.

Capital budgeting—a process of planning and managing the investment of the firm's capital on a long-term basis. A capital budget includes a listing and analysis of all investment alternatives in which the firm is considering investing its supply of capital.

Cost of capital—the minimum acceptable rate of return (usually on an after-tax basis) required by the management of a firm to be earned by a capital expenditure.

Internal rate of return—that interest rate which, when used to discount the cash flows, will make the present value of the inflows exactly equal to the present value of the outflows of the investment.

Net present value method—technique that discounts all projected cash outflows and inflows related to a capital project back to the present period using the cost of capital as the discount rate.

Payback method—a technique used to consider alternative capital expenditures which does not measure profitability but merely calculates the amount of time required to recover the initial net investment in an asset.

Post-audit—a review of major capital expenditures made after the completion of a project in order to determine if benefits actually accrued to the firm as planned.

Present value index—a relative measure of profitability for ranking capital investment projects which is computed by dividing the present value of inflows by the present value of outflows.

QUESTIONS

1. Define capital budgeting. Is it used for short or long-term planning? Explain.

2. How is the investment tax credit treated on the federal income tax return? Why did the federal government place into tax law this type of credit?

3. Name three ways in which the initiation of a capital expenditure may come about. Who or what governs the format and channels of a capital budget request in a large firm?

4. Who normally makes the ultimate decision on a major capital expenditure? If the expenditure is not a major one, who may make the ultimate decision instead?

5. When is the "no choice" or urgency technique for making a decision justified? Why is this technique considered the least favorable of the capital budgeting techniques?

6. What is the primary purpose of using the payback technique in making a capital budgeting decision?

7. What are two similarities between the payback technique and the accountant's rate of return when used to make a decision?

8. Using the net present value technique, how does one decide whether the project is acceptable or not?

9. Using the present value index as a decision-making technique, what must the index be in order to accept the project on the basis that it earns the proposed cost of capital?

10. What are the purposes of a post-audit of the results of a decision?

EXERCISES

14–1 Compute the net present value of these three individual cases at a rate of 10%.

	Outlay	Future Period Inflows			
	0	1	2	3	4
A	($2,000)	$1,150		$1,150	
B	($2,000)	$1,150			$1,150
C	($2,000)		$1,150	$1,150	

Required:

a. Which of these three investments is the most desirable?

b. Which is more desirable using 6% interest?

14–2 Compute the internal rate of return for each of the following independent investments.

	Outlay	Future Period Inflows		
	0	1	2	3
A	($3,000)	$1,575		$1,735
B	($3,000)	$1,500	$1,780	
C	($3,000)		$1,700	$1,690

Required:

If the investments are mutually exclusive, which one would you choose?

14–3 Compute the payback period for each of these independent cases.

	Cost of Investment	Cash Proceeds per Year
A	$20,000	$5,000
B	$15,000	$3,000
C	$24,000	$8,000

Required:

Based on this information, which of these investments is the best?

14-4 The James Company purchased a machine several years ago for $20,000. Its book value is $8,000. The company is considering purchasing a new machine for $22,500. The salvage value of the old machine at this time is $3,275. Ignoring taxes, what is the net cash outlay for the new asset?

14–5 Weido, Inc. is considering the purchase of a new machine for $2,200.

The machine has a life of 5 years and a salvage value of $200. It will be depreciated on a straight-line basis. Cash inflows will be:

Year	Inflows
1	$ 600
2	800
3	500
4	750
5	650
Total	$3,300

Required:

Determine the accountant's rate of return using:

a.   the original investment
b.   the average investment

14–6   A nonprofit organization is considering the purchase of a certain depreciable capital asset. The asset costs $10,000.

It is expected that the asset will bring an incremental increase in annual net income of $3,500 for each year of its five-year life. The desired discount rate is 10%. Since it is a nonprofit organization, income taxes and depreciation are ignored.

Required:

a.   What is the payback period?
b.   What is the accountant's rate of return on original investment?
c.   What is the net present value of the investment?
d.   What is the present value index?

14–7   You are considering an outlay of X dollars which will produce an annual benefit of Y dollars per year for Z years. Your cost of capital is 10%.

Use the following alternative choices to answer *a* to *c* below:

1.   0%
2.   exactly 10%
3.   equal to or greater than 10%
4.   equal to or less than 10%
5.   greater than 10%
6.   less than 10%
7.   none of the above
8.   cannot determine from the data given

a.   If the present value of the Y dollars per year for Z years is X dollars, the return from the investment is _____.
b.   If the present value of the Y dollars per year for Z years is

X + 1 dollars, the return from the investment is _____.

c.   If the present value of the Y dollars per year for Z years is X—1 dollars, the return from the investment is _____.

14-8   Jess, Inc. is considering purchasing a new machine for $18,000. It will have a useful life of 10 years, a salvage value of $3,000, and be depreciated on a straight-line basis.

The old machine, which cost $15,000, has been depreciated for 5 of its 15-year useful life. It is not expected to have any salvage value at the end of 15 years. It is being depreciated using straight-line. At the present time, the machine can be sold for $9,000. Any gain or loss on the sale can be considered ordinary income.

The company's cost of capital is 12%. The tax rate is 40%. The new machine will save the company $2,500 per year.

Required:

Using the net present value method, decide whether the company should purchase the new machine.

14-9   A firm is considering the purchase of a new piece of equipment. Below are the basic data relevant to this purchase.

Initial cost—$24,000
8-year life
Salvage value—$2,000
Straight-line depreciation
Overhaul at the end of year four—$6,000
Operating cost savings—$7,000 per year
Tax Rate—50%

Required:

Determine this equipment's internal rate of return. Round to the nearest dollar.

14-10   A company is considering purchasing a new machine for $12,000. The new machine will have a useful life of 10 years and a salvage value of $2,000. It will be depreciated on a straight-line basis.

The old machine, which cost $10,000, also has a useful life of 10 more years but has been fully depreciated for tax purposes. It can be sold for $500 at the present time.

The company's cost of capital is 6%, and the tax rate is 50 percent. The new machine will save the company $2,000 per year.

Required:

Using the net present value method, decide whether the company should purchase the new machine.

14-11   The Fattening Donuts Company was deciding what size fryer to purchase. Machine A is capable of producing 120 donuts per minute while machine B can produce 180 donuts per minute. It has been calculated that Machine A will produce a cash flow savings of $400 each year for 5 years, while machine B will produce a cash flow savings of $100 the first year and that amount will double each year through the fifth year. Machine A can be purchased for $1,400 while the cost of machine B is $1,800.

Required:

a.   Calculate the payback period of both machines using the average cash inflows.

b.   Given the results of "*a*" above, which machine should be purchased?

14-12   Bob, the barber, was considering purchasing a new machine that would be used to stimulate the scalp and speed hair growth. Faster hair growth would mean more hair cuts and increased revenues. The machine costs $1,700 and has a useful life of 4 years with a salvage value of $100. The expected cash inflows that will be generated are:

Year	Inflows
1	$ 600
2	$ 700
3	$ 600
4	$ 500
	$2,400

Required:

Determine the accountant's rate of return using:

a.   the original investment

b.   the average investment.

14-13   Determine the present value of $1,000 due in five years at each of the following interest rates:

a.   6 percent

b.   8 percent

c.   10 percent

14-14   An investor wishes to have $5,000 available at the end of five years. State the amount of money that must be invested at the present time if the interest rate is:

a.   6 percent

b.   8 percent

c.   12 percent

14-15   Determine the present value of an annuity for a period of five years with annual payments of $2,000, assuming that the interest rate is:

a. 7 percent
b. 10 percent
c. 12 percent

14–16 What is the maximum amount you would be willing to pay at the present time in order to receive 10 annual payments of $1,000 beginning one year from now? The current interest rate is 10 percent.

PROBLEM SERIES A

14A-1 The Acme Company is currently using a machine which was purchased on January 1, 1978 at a cost of $8,600. It was assigned a useful life of 8 years and a salvage value of $600. The straight-line method of depreciation is used. The company is considering replacing this machine on January 1, 1981 with a new machine which would cost $9,000. The new machine would have a useful life of 5 years and a salvage value of $1,000. The straight-line method of depreciation would be used.

With the new machine, expected direct labor savings would be $1,250 per year for the 5 years. The old machine can be sold immediately for $3,500. Assume that the tax impact from the sale of the old machine occurs immediately when the sale is made.

The tax rate is 40%. The cost of capital (or rate of discount) is 16%.

Required:

Determine the following as they relate to the purchase of the new machine.

a. Net cash flow per year
b. Present value of the net outlay
c. Pay back period
d. Advantage (or disadvantage) of the new machine (in present value)

14A–2 Rental, Inc. is considering the purchase of six garden tillers to add to its rental fleet. The following estimates have been made:

Cost of six tillers	$15,000
Rental Receipts (annual)	12,000
Expenses:	
Maintenance	3,000
Advertising	800
Depreciation (5 year life)	3,000
Salvage value at end of 5 years	–0–

Assume that advertising is not a deductible expense for tax purposes and that a 40% tax rate applies to all other revenue and expense items.

Required:

a.   Determine the after-tax cash flow per year.

b.   Find the net present value of the investment (assume a 14% cost of capital).

c.   Find the internal rate of return of the investment.

14A-3   The Dizzy Company is considering a new mixing machine. They have narrowed the decision down to two choices but are unsure how to arrive at a final decision. It is your job to analyze the two machines so that the management of Dizzy can make their final decision. Assume a 40% tax rate, sum-of-the-years digit depreciation, and a 10% cost of capital.

	Machine A	Machine B
Cost	$47,000	$60,000
Useful life	5 years	5 years
Salvage value	$ 2,000	–0–
Annual before-tax cost savings	$14,500	$18,000

14A-4   The Concerned Company is considering purchasing a replacement machine on January 1, 1981. The present machine was acquired on January 1, 1980 at a cost of $12,000 and was assigned a useful life of 6 years, no salvage value and depreciated on a straight-line basis. If it is replaced, it can be sold immediately for $9,000. You may assume that any gain or loss on the sale is treated as ordinary income or expense for tax purposes and the tax impact from the sale of the present machine occurs immediately when the sale is made.

The list price of the replacement machine is $16,000. Shipping charges are $300 and installation is $200. Double-declining balance depreciation will be used on the new machine. The new equipment will have a useful life of 5 years and a salvage value of $1,500.

Estimated cash savings before taxes and depreciation will be $2,500. The income tax rate is 40% and all savings are assumed to take place at the end of each year.

The firm's cost of capital is 12%.

All calculations should be in dollars only (round cents).

Required:

Decide whether the company should replace the present equipment using both the payback method and the net present value method.

14A-5   The Aggie Corporation of Snook, Texas is considering construction of a new motel containing 180 rooms.

The motel will cost $3,250,600 which will be paid to the contractor on the day the motel opens for business.

Additional information:

1.   Assume a 360 day operating year.

2. Half of the rooms are single rooms and half are double rooms (i.e., one and two person rooms only).
3. The daily rate is $13.00 for a single room and $24.00 for a double room.
4. The motel will operate at full capacity for all 360 days.
5. Cash operating expenses are expected to be $675,000 per year, assumed payable at the *end* of each year.
6. Assume all room rentals will be collected at end of each year.
7. Assume no income taxes, i.e., ignore taxes.
8. Assume a cost of capital of 10%.
9. Owner plans to keep the motel for 7 years and then sell it for $500,000.

Required:

You are to decide whether this is a good investment using the net present value method and the present value index.

14A–6 Taylor, Inc. has hired you for all of their capital budgeting decisions. Mr. Taylor, president of Taylor, Inc. feels that payback is the best method to use. You, however, feel that net present value analysis will yield more information and allow you to make a wiser decision. The company wants to purchase some new machinery. Given the information below, you are to use both methods of analysis and make a decision on investing. Taylor, Inc. requires a ten year maximum payback. Discuss your decision.

	Old Machine	New Machine
Cost	$10,000	$20,000
Useful life remaining	15 years	15 years
Depreciation method	Straight-line	Straight-line
Accumulated depreciation	$10,000	$ –0–
Scrap value at present	$ 400	N/A
Scrap value in 15 years	$ –0–	$ 500
Direct labor saving/year		$ 3,000
Additional electricity costs per year		$ 500
Tax rate—40%		
Time value of money—8%		

14A–7 Fritz Company is considering an investment in a new machine to improve the production of one of their products. The old machine requires a great deal of maintenance because of its age, so the company feels it will save about $10,000 per year in maintenance costs if it purchases the new machine. The power bill will increase by $.06 per unit but the company will also be saving $.48 per unit in labor costs. The machine will cost $375,000 and has a useful life of 10 years with no salvage value at that time. It will be depreciated on the straight-line basis. Production will equal sales in all years. In years 1 through 5 production will be 90,000 units but it will increase by 20,000 units in each of the remaining years. The old machine is fully depreciated and will be abandoned in a field behind the factory.

Required:

If the company's minimum rate of return is 12% and a tax rate of 40%, should the investment be undertaken? Find the internal rate of return for the investment. (Round to the nearest cent.)

14A–8   Franco, Inc. has been using the payback method as the sole criterion for capital budgeting decisions. You are the newest member of the Franco staff, having just graduated from college. You realize from courses you have taken that payback is not the best criterion. You feel that the net present value method is better, but so far have been unable to convince management of this.

Management is preparing to purchase a new machine for their new product. The machine appears very good using payback but, again, you are not certain they are making the right decision. There are three machines to choose from; Machine 1 is the one management wants to purchase. From the information given below, prepare an analysis using both the payback method and the net present value method. Use specific cash flows for payback, not the average cash flows. Make your recommendations to management. (Round cents to dollars.)

	Machine 1	Machine 2	Machine 3
Cost	$25,000	$30,000	$28,000
Useful life	6 years	6 years	6 years
Depreciation method	Straight-line	Straight-line	Straight-line
Scrap value in 6 years	$ 400	$ 600	$ 1,000
Before-tax cash flow per year:			
Year 1	$10,000	$ 6,000	$11,000
Year 2	9,000	7,000	10,000
Year 3	8,000	7,500	8,800
Year 4	4,000	8,000	7,500
Year 5	3,000	6,000	7,000
Year 6	2,000	4,000	6,000

Tax rate = 40%
Cost of capital = 10%
Maximum payback period 4 years

14A–9   Beta Corporation recently learned of a patent on the production of a semi-automatic paper collator that can be obtained at a cost of $60,000 cash. The semi-automatic model is vastly superior to the manual model that the corporation now produces. At a cost of $40,000, present equipment could be modified to accommodate the production of the new semi-automatic model. Such modifications would not affect the remaining useful life of 4 years or the salvage value of $10,000 that the equipment now has. Variable costs, however, would increase by one dollar per unit. Fixed costs, other than relevant amortization charges, would not be affected. If the equipment is modified, the manual model cannot be produced.

The current income statement relative to the manual collator appears as follows:

```
Sales (100,000 units @ $4) . . . . . . . . . . . . . $400,000
Variable costs . . . . . . . . . . . $180,000
Fixed Costs * . . . . . . . . . . .   120,000
Total Costs . . . . . . . . . . . . . . . . . . . . . $300,000
   Net Income before income taxes . . . . . . . . $100,000
   Income taxes (40%) . . . . . . . . . . . . . . . .   40,000
   Net Income after income taxes . . . . . . . . $ 60,000
```

> * All fixed costs are directly allocable to the production of the manual collator and include depreciation on equipment of $20,000, calculated on the straight-line basis with a useful life of 10 years.

Market research has disclosed three important findings relative to the new semi-automatic model. First, a particular competitor will certainly purchase the patent if Beta Corporation does not. If this were to happen, Beta Corporation's sales of the manual collator would fall to 70,000 units per year. Second, if no increase in the selling price is made, Beta Corporation could sell approximately 190,000 units per year of the semi-automatic model. Third, because of the advances being made in this area, the patent will be completely worthless at the end of 4 years.

Required:

Prepare a schedule which shows the after-tax cash flows for the two alternatives. Assume that the corporation will use the sum-of-the-years' digits method for depreciating the costs of modifying the equipment.

Also, by using the net present value method, decide whether Beta Corporation should manufacture the semi-automatic collator. Assume the cost of capital is 18% and all operating revenues and expenses occur at the end of the year.

(CMA, adapted)

14A–10   James Company is trying to decide whether to handle a new automotive product which has an expected life of eight years. Using the data below, determine whether this venture will be profitable. (Round cents to the nearest dollar.) Use the net present value method.

1. The new product will require new factory equipment costing $1,200,000. The useful life of the equipment is eight years, with no salvage value at the end of that time. The depreciation schedule is:

Year	Depreciation
1	$ 266,667
2	233,333
3	200,000
4	166,667
5	133,333
6	100,000
7	66,667
8	33,333
	$1,200,000

2. The new product will be produced in an old plant the company already owns which is not in use. The old plant has a book value of $50,000 and is being depreciated on a straight-line basis at $5,000 annually. The estimated sales value of the building is $40,000; this price should remain stable over the next eight years. The plant is likely to be depreciated for at least ten more years and would have no salvage value.

3. The company's tax rate is 40%. Its cost of capital is 12%.

4. Net cash inflows from operations before depreciation and income taxes will be $450,000 in years 1, 2, and 3, $670,000 in years 4, 5, and 6, and $160,000 in years 7 and 8.

5. An initial sales promotion in year 1 will amount to a cost of $400,000. $25,000 will be spent on promotion in all other years. The entire amount is deductible for income tax purposes in the year of the expenditure.

14A-11   A. J. Voit was considering replacing his coal truck with a newer model that would lower his expenses, therefore providing increased savings. Voit's old truck had a book value of $27,500, a remaining life of 10 years and a market value of $5,000. Should the old truck be retained, its salvage value at the end of ten years would be $5,000. The new truck had a list price of $55,000 and a useful life of 10 years with a $5,000 scrap value. The cost savings generated by the new truck will be $3,000 yearly for repair costs. The new model will also run more efficiently and create a savings of $.20 per mile. Assume that the tax impact from the sale of the old truck occurs immediately when the sale is made. The truck is driven 10,000 miles annually.

The tax rate is 40%. The cost of capital is 10%. Assume straight-line depreciation is used for the trucks.

Required:

Determine whether Voit should invest in the new truck. Use the net present value method.

PROBLEMS SERIES B

14B-1   On January 1, 1981 Acrome, Inc. is considering the replacement of equipment presently in use. The equipment was acquired on January 1, 1977, at a cost of $11,000, and was assigned a useful life of 10 years and $1,000 salvage value. It was depreciated on a straight-line basis. If it is replaced, it can be sold immediately for $9,000. You may assume that any gain or loss on the sale will be treated as ordinary income or expense for tax purposes.

The installed cost of the replacement machine is $15,000. Sum-of-the-years' digits depreciation will be used on the new equipment. The machine will have a useful life of six (6) years with a salvage value of zero (0).

Estimated before-tax, before-depreciation cash savings as a result of the use of the new machine will be $4,000. The income tax rate is 35%.

The company has a cost of capital of 10%.

Required:

Complete the following information:

a.   The present value of the outlay (net) for the new machine.
b.   The net cash savings for each year.
c.   The present value of the cash savings each year.
d.   The advantage (or disadvantage) of buying the new machine.

14B-2   The shop manager has approached you with a proposal to purchase some loading equipment in your factory. The delivered price of this equipment is $22,000. You estimate that this would reduce your labor costs by $8,000 a year, but it would increase your maintenance charges and other indirect costs by $1,600. The estimated life of the equipment is nine years and will have no salvage value.

Your company's policy is to accept no capital expenditure proposal unless it promises to provide a return on investment in excess of 20 percent before taxes.

Required:

a.   Determine the cash flow per year before taxes.
b.   Find the net present value of the investment before taxes.
c.   Find the internal rate of return of the investment before taxes.

14B-3   The Grahm Company is considering three mutually exclusive proposals, all of which would require an initial cash outlay of $90,000. The company has estimated that the net cash proceeds from each proposal would be:

	Proposal A	Proposal B	Proposal C
End of Year 1	$50,000	$30,000	$30,000
2	40,000	30,000	30,000
3	30,000	30,000	60,000
4	20,000	30,000	20,000
5	20,000	30,000	20,000
6	20,000	30,000	20,000

Since only one of the three proposals can be accepted, the president of the company has argued that the decision should be made on the basis of a present value analysis. However, the treasurer of the company believes that the decision should be made on the basis of a payback analysis.

Required:

Rank the three proposals as to their desirability by: (a) the present value method (cost of capital is 12%), and (b) payback method. (Note: Do not consider taxes.)

14B–4   The Konkel Company has the opportunity to purchase a new machine on January 1, 1981 for $31,000. The machine which is now being used was purchased on January 1, 1976 at a cost of $20,000. The machine was given a useful life of 10 years with a salvage value of $2,000. It is being depreciated on a straight-line basis. If the machine is replaced, it can be sold for $11,500. You may assume that any gain or loss on the sale is ordinary income.

The new equipment is expected to have a useful life of 5 years and no salvage value. It will be depreciated on the sum-of-the-years' digits method. Shipping charges on the new machine are $300 and installation charges are $700. It is estimated that power costs will increase by $50 per month, but maintenance costs should decrease by $700 per year. Other cash savings should be $8,000 in 1981 and $6,900 per year thereafter.

The income tax rate of the firm is 40%. Management of Konkel will not accept an investment unless the return on capital is at least 15%.

Required:

Decide whether the company should replace the present equipment, using both the payback method and the net present value method. (Round cents to the nearest dollar.)

14B–5   Sam Jones is considering opening a service station in his home town. The station will be leased for 3 years at $75,000 per year. The total lease will be paid on the day he opens the station. At the station, he will sell gasoline, oil, and a small variety of common car parts. Additional information:

1. Assume a 350 day operating year.
2. On the average, 180 customers using an average of 15 gallons each will be served daily.

3. Ten percent of the customers will need 2 quarts of oil each, and five percent will need one of the other items.
4. The company's contribution margin will be $.15 per gallon of gas, $.25 per quart of oil, and $.43 per average purchase of other items.
5. Other costs will be $24,000 per year.
6. Assume all collections and payments other than the lease payment are made at the end of the year.
7. Sam wants to make 25% before taxes.

Required:

You are to decide whether this is a good investment using the net present value method and the present value index. (Round cents to the nearest dollar.)

14B–6 Vivian, Inc. has hired you for all of their capital budgeting decisions. Ms. Vivian, president of Vivian, Inc., feels that payback is the best method to use. You, however, feel that net present value analysis will yield more information and allow you to make a wiser decision. The company wants to purchase some new machinery. Given the following information, you are to use both methods of analysis and make a decision. Discuss your answer.

	Old Machine	New Machine
Cost..........................	$8,000	$13,900
Estimated useful life...........	8 years	6 years
Salvage value.................	-0-	$ 1,300
Depreciation method..........	Straight-line	Straight-line
Scrap value at present.........	$2,000	N/A
Before-tax, before-depreciation savings....................	-0-	$3,500
Book value..................	$6,000	N/A
Tax rate = 50%		
Cost of capital = 10%		

14B–7 University, Inc., wants to purchase a new machine to replace the one presently in use. Maintenance costs will be lowered by $2,000 per year if the machine is purchased. Power costs will increase by $.02 per unit, but labor costs will decrease by $.62 per unit. The old machine is fully depreciated but could be sold for $300. The new machine will cost $220,000 plus $1,600 shipping and installation. The new machine will have a useful life of 8 years and a salvage value of $20,000; it will be depreciated using the straight-line method. In years one through three, production will be 120,000 units. It will increase by 30,000 units per year in each of the remaining years.

Required:

Determine whether the investment should be undertaken if the company's cost of capital is 10% and the tax rate is 40%. Find the internal rate of return for the investment. (Round to the nearest cent.)

14B–8   Gardner, Inc. has been using the payback method as the sole criterion for capital budgeting decisions. You would like to compare payback to the net present value method in order to see if the results are consistent. Since management is considering purchasing a new machine to replace a worn out one, you feel this would be a good time to begin the comparison. The old machine is fully depreciated.

From the information given below, prepare an analysis using payback and net present value. Make recommendations to management. (Round cents to the nearest dollar).

	Old Machine	Machine 1	Machine 2
Cost	$18,000	$28,000	$28,000
Useful life	0 years	5 years	8 years
Depreciation method	N/A	Straight-line	Straight-line
Scrap value at present	$ 500	N/A	N/A
Scrap value in 5 years	N/A	$ 600	$ 800
Before-tax cash savings	–0–	$ 7,500	$ 6,000
Tax rate = 35%			
Cost of capital = 10%			

14B–9   The Edwards Corporation is considering adding a new stapler to one of its product lines. More equipment will be required to produce the new stapler. There are three alternative ways to acquire the needed equipment: (1) purchase general-purpose equipment, (2) lease general-purpose equipment, (3) build special-purpose equipment. A fourth alternative, purchase of the special-purpose equipment, has been ruled out because it would be prohibitively expensive.

The general-purpose equipment can be purchased for $125,000. The equipment has an estimated salvage of $15,000 at the end of its useful life of ten years. At the end of five years the equipment can be used elsewhere in the plant or be sold for $40,000.

Alternatively, the general-purpose equipment can be acquired by a five-year lease for $40,000 annual rent. The lessor will assume all responsibility for taxes, insurance, and maintenance.

Special-purpose equipment can be constructed by the Contract Equipment Department of the Edwards Corporation. While the department is operating at a level which is normal for the time of year, it is below full capacity. The department could produce the equipment without interfering with its regular revenue-producing activities.

The estimated departmental costs for the construction of the special-purpose equipment are:

Materials and parts	$ 75,000
Direct Labor (DL)	60,000
Variable overhead (50% of DL$)	30,000
	$165,000

However, the cost of the equipment for depreciation purposes is $180,000, a full cost basis. This full cost includes $15,000 of fixed overhead which would be incurred regardless of whether or not the equipment was constructed.

Engineering and management studies provide the following revenue and cost estimates (excluding lease payments and depreciation) for producing the new stapler depending upon the equipment used:

| | General-Purpose Equip. | | Self-Constructed Equipment |
	Leased	Purchased	
Unit selling price	$5.00	$5.00	$5.00
Unit production costs:			
Materials	$1.80	$1.80	$1.70
Conversion costs	1.65	1.65	1.40
Total unit production costs . . .	$3.45	$3.45	$3.10
Unit contribution margin	$1.55	$1.55	$1.90
Estimated unit volume	40,000	40,000	40,000
Estimated total contribution margin	$62,000	$62,000	$76,000
Other costs:			
Supervision	$16,000	$16,000	$18,000
Taxes and insurance	–0–	3,000	5,000
Maintenance	–0–	3,000	2,000
Total	$16,000	$22,000	$25,000

The company will depreciate the general-purpose machine over ten years on the sum-of-the-years' digits (S-Y-D) method. At the end of five years the accumulated depreciation will total $80,000. (The present value of this amount for the first five years is $62,100.) The special-purpose machine will be depreciated over five years on the S-Y-D method. Its salvage value at the end of that time is estimated to be $30,000.

The company uses an after-tax cost of capital of 10 percent. Its marginal tax rate is 40 percent.

Required:

Calculate which of the three options would be the best using the net present value method.

(CMA, adapted)

14B–10 Davis, Inc. is considering purchasing a new machine which has an expected life of 10 years. Using the data below, determine whether this venture will be profitable. (Round cents to the nearest dollar.)

1. The new machine, which will cost $40,000, will have a useful life of 6 years. At the end of that time, it is expected to have a salvage value of $1,000. The depreciation schedule is:

Year	Depreciation
1	$11,143
2	9,286
3	7,429
4	5,571
5	3,714
6	1,857
	$39,000

2. The new machine will not be replacing an old machine. It will be used to handle an increase in demand for the company's product.

3. Net cash inflows from operations before depreciation and taxes will be $9,500 in years 1 through 3, $12,000 in years 4 and 5, and $8,000 in year 6.

4. The company's tax rate is 40% with a cost of capital of 10%.

14B-11 Divided Airline is purchasing another plane to fly between Slippery Rock and New York. The plane has a list price of $1,000,000, an expected life of 10 years with no salvage value. The new plane will replace an older plane that had cost $600,000 and is to be sold for $50,000. The present book value of the older plane is $80,000. The cost savings generated each year by the new plane are anticipated to be $90,000 for repairs and maintenance. Due to improved efficiency, a $1 savings is also anticipated for each passenger. The company uses straight-line depreciation.

The tax rate is 40% and the cost of capital is 8%.

Required:

Determine the following as they relate to the purchase of the new plane.

a. The net cash outlay required to buy the new plane.
b. Number of passengers that must be flown each year for there to be no advantage or disadvantage in the present value of the new plane. (Assume the same number of miles are flown each year.)

Index

557